Real Estate and Property Law for Paralegals

ASPEN COLLEGE SERIES

Real Estate and Property Law for Paralegals

Third Edition

NEAL R. BEVANS, J.D.

Western Piedmont Community College

Wolters Kluwer
Law & Business

Copyright © 2012 CCH Incorporated.

Published by Wolters Kluwer Law & Business in New York.

Wolters Kluwer Law & Business serves customers worldwide with CCH, Aspen Publishers, and Kluwer Law International products. (www.wolterskluwerlb.com)

To contact Customer Service, e-mail customer.service@wolterskluwer.com, call 1-800-234-1660, fax 1-800-901-9075, or mail correspondence to:

Wolters Kluwer Law & Business
Attn: Order Department
PO Box 990
Frederick, MD 21705

Printed in the United States of America.

1 2 3 4 5 6 7 8 9 0

ISBN 978-0-7355-0783-8

Library of Congress Cataloging-in-Publication Data
Bevans, Neal R., 1961-
   Real estate and property law for paralegals / Neal R. Bevans. — 3rd ed.
      p. cm. — (Aspen college series)
   Includes index.
   ISBN 978-0-7355-0783-8 — ISBN 0-7355-0783-X
1. Real property — United States.   2. Conveyancing — United States.   3. Vendors and purchasers — United States.   4. Legal assistants — United States.
   I. Title.
   KF570.B48 2012
   346.7304'3 — dc23

                                                                              2012014585

About Wolters Kluwer Law & Business

Wolters Kluwer Law & Business is a leading global provider of intelligent information and digital solutions for legal and business professionals in key specialty areas, and respected educational resources for professors and law students. Wolters Kluwer Law & Business connects legal and business professionals as well as those in the education market with timely, specialized authoritative content and information-enabled solutions to support success through productivity, accuracy and mobility.

Serving customers worldwide, Wolters Kluwer Law & Business products include those under the Aspen Publishers, CCH, Kluwer Law International, Loislaw, Best Case, ftwilliam.com and MediRegs family of products.

CCH products have been a trusted resource since 1913, and are highly regarded resources for legal, securities, antitrust and trade regulation, government contracting, banking, pension, payroll, employment and labor, and healthcare reimbursement and compliance professionals.

Aspen Publishers products provide essential information to attorneys, business professionals and law students. Written by preeminent authorities, the product line offers analytical and practical information in a range of specialty practice areas from securities law and intellectual property to mergers and acquisitions and pension/benefits. Aspen's trusted legal education resources provide professors and students with high-quality, up-to-date and effective resources for successful instruction and study in all areas of the law.

Kluwer Law International products provide the global business community with reliable international legal information in English. Legal practitioners, corporate counsel and business executives around the world rely on Kluwer Law journals, looseleafs, books, and electronic products for comprehensive information in many areas of international legal practice.

Loislaw is a comprehensive online legal research product providing legal content to law firm practitioners of various specializations. Loislaw provides attorneys with the ability to quickly and efficiently find the necessary legal information they need, when and where they need it, by facilitating access to primary law as well as state-specific law, records, forms and treatises.

Best Case Solutions is the leading bankruptcy software product to the bankruptcy industry. It provides software and workflow tools to flawlessly streamline petition preparation and the electronic filing process, while timely incorporating ever-changing court requirements.

ftwilliam.com offers employee benefits professionals the highest quality plan documents (retirement, welfare and non-qualified) and government forms (5500/PBGC, 1099 and IRS) software at highly competitive prices.

MediRegs products provide integrated health care compliance content and software solutions for professionals in healthcare, higher education and life sciences, including professionals in accounting, law and consulting.

Wolters Kluwer Law & Business, a division of Wolters Kluwer, is headquartered in New York. Wolters Kluwer is a market-leading global information services company focused on professionals.

For my parents, Patricia and Robert Bevans

Summary
of Contents

Contents		*xi*
Preface		*xxxv*
Acknowledgments		*xli*

Chapter 1	An Introduction to Real Estate	1
Chapter 2	Estates in Real Property	27
Chapter 3	Property Descriptions and Determining Property Boundaries	49
Chapter 4	Transferring Title to Real Estate	75
Chapter 5	Rights Associated with Real Estate	107
Chapter 6	Real Estate Contracts	133
Chapter 7	Landlord and Tenant Law	157
Chapter 8	Real Estate Deeds	189
Chapter 9	Mortgages and Financing the Purchase of Real Estate	217
Chapter 10	Public and Private Restrictions on the Use of Land	261
Chapter 11	Real Estate Professions	291
Chapter 12	Title Insurance and Title Examinations	323
Chapter 13	The Closing	355
Chapter 14	Taxation Issues in Real Property	391

Glossary		*413*
Appendix		*417*
Index		*463*

Contents

PREFACE   xxxv
ACKNOWLEDGMENTS   xli

 AN INTRODUCTION TO REAL ESTATE

> ### Focus of This Chapter
>
> This chapter introduces the basic concepts of real and personal property,
> introduces the rich and complex world of real property, and explains the various
> categories of real property.

I. INTRODUCTION   **1**

II. REAL PROPERTY VERSUS PERSONAL PROPERTY   **1**

     A. What Makes Real Property So Unique?   3
     B. Physical Characteristics of Land   4
     C. Economic Characteristics of Land   4

Tech Topic: Fannie Mae and the Mortgage Meltdown   6

III. THE REAL ESTATE MARKET   **7**

IV. CLASSIFYING PROPERTY BY USE   **8**

     A. Unimproved Land   8
     B. Residential Property   9
         1. Single-Family Homes   9
         2. Apartments   9
         3. Condominiums and Townhouses   9
             a. Condominiums   9
             b. Townhouses   10
         4. Cooperatives   10
         5. Mobile Homes   10
         6. Manufactured Housing and "Kit" Homes   12

C. Commercial Property   12
    1. Retail/Wholesale   12
    2. Shopping Centers and Malls   13
D. Industrial Property   13
    1. Industrial Parks   13
    2. Light Industry/ Heavy Industry   13
E. Farm and Rural Property   13
F. Recreational Property   14
G. Government-Owned Land   14

● **ANNOTATED DOCUMENT**
  REAL ESTATE SALES LISTING   **14**

Ethics: An Introduction   *14*
Case Excerpt: Jenning v. Bindseil   *15*
Skills You Need in the Real World   *21*
Online Research   *21*
Chapter Summary   *23*
Review Questions   *24*
Practical Applications   *24*
Web Sites   *24*
Terms and Phrases   *25*
Significant Cases   *25*

 ESTATES IN REAL PROPERTY

> ## Focus of This Chapter
>
> This chapter provides an in-depth explanation of the rights, duties, and responsibilities that derive from estates, as well as the implications of various types of estates on the rights and abilities of the owners.

I. INTRODUCTION   **27**

II. REAL PROPERTY ESTATES   **27**

III. FEE SIMPLE ESTATE   **28**

A. Rights of Fee Simple Owners   29
B. Conditional Fee Simple Estates   29
    1. Fee Simple Determinable   31
    2. Fee Simple on a Condition Subsequent   31

Tech Topic: Online Access to Real Estate Records   *32*

IV. LIFE ESTATES **32**

   A. Historical Basis of Life Estates   33
      1. Dower and Curtesy   33
   B. Remaindermen   33
   C. Waste   34
   D. Court Doctrines That Affect Life Estates   34
   E. Life Estate Pur Autre Vie   35

V. CONCURRENT OWNERSHIP IN REAL ESTATE **35**

   A. Tenants in Common   35
   B. Joint Tenancy   36
      1. Right of Survivorship   37
   C. Tenancy by Entirety   38
      1. Tenancy by Entirety and Civil Unions   38
   D. Tenancy in Partnership   39
   E. The Right to Partition   39

● **ANNOTATED DOCUMENT**
   CREATING A LIFE ESTATE   40

Ethics: Drafting Deeds   *40*
Case Excerpt: In re Estate of Payne   *40*
Skills You Need in the Real World   *45*
Chapter Summary   *46*
Review Questions   *46*
Discussion Questions   *47*
Practical Applications   *47*
Web Sites   *48*
Terms and Phrases   *48*
Significant Cases   *48*

3 PROPERTY DESCRIPTIONS AND DETERMINING PROPERTY BOUNDARIES

Focus of This Chapter

This chapter explores the many different methods used across the nation to describe property. Because metes and bounds descriptions are an essential part of property descriptions in nearly half the country, we explore this topic in depth and go through the process of drawing out a description based on the wording of the description. The chapter also explores other property description techniques and provides a basic description of surveying.

I. INTRODUCTION   **49**

II. THE HISTORY OF PROPERTY BOUNDARIES   **50**

III. PROPERTY DESCRIPTIONS IN DEEDS   **51**

A. The Elements of a Valid Property Description   51
B. Legal Requirements for Property Descriptions in Deeds   51
C. Referring to Other Documents to Prove Property Boundaries   52
D. Litigating Property Boundaries   53
   1. Ambiguous Property Descriptions   53
     a. Patent Ambiguities   54
     b. Parol Evidence and Property Descriptions   54
   2. Latently Ambiguous Property Descriptions   55

IV. METES AND BOUNDS DESCRIPTIONS   **55**

A. Drafting Metes and Bounds Descriptions   57

Tech Topic: Real Estate Marketing Technology   *58*
B. Using Technology to Help with Metes and Bounds Drawings   59

V. OTHER METHODS TO DESCRIBE PROPERTY: GOVERNMENT SURVEY SYSTEM   **59**

A. Tract Indexing   60
B. Plats   60
C. Torrens Registration   60

VI. WATER RIGHTS   **61**

A. The Right to Use Water   61
   1. Court Doctrines That Affect Water Rights   62
B. Natural Forces That Affect Property Boundaries   62
   1. Accretion   62
   2. Erosion   62
   3. Avulsion   62
   4. Reliction   63
C. Water and Property Boundaries   63
   1. Navigable Waters   63
     a. Boundary Lines Along Navigable Bodies of Water   63
   2. Non-Navigable Waters   63

● **ANNOTATED DOCUMENT**
METES AND BOUNDS DESCRIPTION   64

Ethics: Confidentiality and Real Estate Practice   *64*
Case Excerpt: Panetta v. Equity One, Inc.   *65*
Skills You Need in the Real World   *70*
Drawing Property Descriptions   *70*
Chapter Summary   *71*
Review Questions   *71*
Discussion Questions   *72*

Practical Applications   72
Web Sites   72
Terms and Phrases   73
Significant Cases   73

4   TRANSFERRING TITLE TO REAL ESTATE

Focus of This Chapter

This chapter addresses the numerous ways that title to real estate can be transferred, through both voluntary and involuntary means. The chapter emphasizes the practical concerns for paralegals in many of these transfers.

I.   INTRODUCTION   **75**

II. VOLUNTARY TRANSFERS OF TITLE   **76**

  A. Sale   76
    1. The Basic Requirements of Sale of Real Property   78
      a. Mutual Assent   78
      b. Consideration   78
      c. Capacity   79
        i. Infants   79
        ii. Intoxicated Persons   79
        iii. Mentally Incompetent Persons   79
      d. Property Description   80

Tech Topic: Robo-Signing   80
  B. Will (Probate)   82
    1. The Minimum Requirements of a Will   82
      a. The Will Must Be in Writing   82
      b. The Will Must Be Witnessed   82
      c. The Will Must Be Signed by the Testator   83
        i. Nuncupative Wills   83
        ii. Holographic Wills   83
      d. The Will Must Clearly Express the Testator's State
        of Mind   84
      e. The Will Must Clearly Devise Property to a Specific
        Beneficiary   84
    2. Wills Versus Sales   85
      a. Distinguishing Between Wills and Sales   85
    3. Different Methods Used to Transfer Title Through Wills   86
      a. Intestate Succession   86
      b. Testate Succession   86

C. Gift   86
D. Dedication   86
E. Homesteading   87

III. INVOLUNTARY TRANSFERS OF TITLE   87

A. Foreclosure   87
    1. Power of Sale Foreclosure   88
        a. The Right to Foreclose   88
        b. Default   89
        c. Notice to the Borrower   89
        d. Steps in Foreclosure   90
        e. The Foreclosure Auction   90
        f. The Right of Redemption   91
        g. Purchasing Property at a Foreclosure Sale   92
        h. Terminating the Rights of Other Creditors   92
        i. Mortgages and Deeds of Trust   93
B. Condemnation (Eminent Domain)   93
    1. The Process of Eminent Domain: Condemnation   93
        a. Inverse Condemnation   94
C. Partition   94
D. Escheat   94
E. Civil Judgment   94
F. Adverse Possession   95
    1. Why Does the Doctrine of Adverse Possession Exist?   95
    2. The Elements of Adverse Possession   96
        a. Open, Continuous, Notorious, and Hostile Possession   96
        b. Color of Title   97
    3. Specified Time Periods for Adverse Possession   97
G. Tax Auctions   98

● ANNOTATED DOCUMENT
NOTICE OF FORECLOSURE   98

Ethics: Fraudulent Transfers   99
Case Excerpt: Thompson v. Central of Georgia R.R.   99
Skills You Need in the Real World   102
Chapter Summary   102
Review Questions   103
Discussion Questions   104
Practical Applications   104
Web Sites   104
Terms and Phrases   105
Significant Cases   105

5 RIGHTS ASSOCIATED WITH REAL ESTATE

> ### Focus of This Chapter
> The chapter begins with a description of fixtures, explores the relationship of fixtures to real estate, and then describes how the law of trade fixtures differs significantly from the general rule of fixtures. From there, the chapter explores the role of liens, easements, and other rights associated with real property.

I.	**INTRODUCTION**	**107**
II.	**FIXTURES**	**108**
	A. Determining When Personal Property Becomes a Fixture	109
	1. Intent Test	109
	2. Manner of Attachment Test	109
	3. Use Test	110
	4. Damage Test	110
	B. Trade Fixtures	110
III.	**EASEMENTS**	**111**
	A. Appurtenant Easements	112
	B. In Gross Easements	112
Tech Topic: Cellphone Tower Easements		*113*
	C. Easements Run with the Land	113
	D. Creating Easements	113
	1. Agreement	113
	2. Deed Reservation	114
	3. Implication	114
	4. Necessity	114
	5. Prescription	115
	6. Eminent Domain	115
	E. Terminating Easements	116
	1. The Easement Is No Longer Needed	116
	2. The Properties Have Merged	116
	3. The Parties Enter into an Agreement	116
	4. The Easement Is Abandoned	117
IV.	**LICENSES**	**117**
V.	**PROFIT À PRENDRE**	**117**
VI.	**LIENS**	**118**

VII. ASSESSMENTS   **119**

VIII. AIR RIGHTS   **120**

IX. WATER RIGHTS   **121**

    A. The Right to Draw Water   121
    B. Subterranean Water   121
    C. Terminology for Water Rights   122

X. MINERAL RIGHTS   **122**

● **ANNOTATED DOCUMENT**
  LIEN   **123**

Ethics: Unauthorized Practice of Law   *124*
Case Excerpt: Kelo v. City of New London, Conn.   *124*
Skills You Need in the Real World   *128*
Chapter Summary   *128*
Review Questions   *129*
Discussion Questions   *130*
Practical Applications   *130*
Web Sites   *130*
Terms and Phrases   *131*
Significant Cases   *131*

REAL ESTATE CONTRACTS

> ### Focus of This Chapter
> The law of contracts and real estate has a long and rich history. This chapter first introduces the general law of contracts and then explains how contract law principles apply to specific real estate transactions.

I. INTRODUCTION   **133**

    A. What Is a Contract?   134
      1. Offer   134
        a. Offers Do Not Require Specific Language   135

Tech Topic: Communicating Offers Via Email, Text, or Twitter   *135*
        b. The Reasonable Person Standard and Offers   136
      2. Acceptance   136
        a. Rejecting an Offer   136
        b. Communicating the Acceptance to the Offeror   137

c. The Mailbox Rule 138
d. Counteroffers 138
3. Mutual Assent 139
4. Consideration 139
5. Legality 139
6. Capacity 139

II. THE STATUTE OF FRAUDS 140

III. FORMATION ISSUES IN CONTRACT LAW 141

A. Guidelines That Courts Use to Interpret Contracts 142
B. Mistake 142
1. Effect of a Ruling of Mistake 142
C. Fraud 142

IV. REAL ESTATE CONTRACTS 143

A. Listing Agreement 143
1. Open Listing 143
2. Exclusive Listing 143
3. Multiple Listing 144
B. Offer of Purchase and Contract 144
1. Property Description 144
2. Purchase of Personal Property 144
3. Purchase Price Details 145
4. Conditions 145
5. Evidence of Title 145
6. Property Disclosures 145
7. Risk of Loss Provisions 145
8. Closing Provisions 145
9. Signature Provisions 148
C. Options 148

V. CONTRACT CLAUSES 148

A. Time Is of the Essence 148
B. Title 149
C. Escrow 149
D. Insurance (Risk of Loss) 149

VI. BREACH OF CONTRACT 149

A. Remedies for Breach 150
1. Remedies for the Seller 150
2. Remedies for the Buyer 150
3. Remedies for the Broker 150

● **ANNOTATED DOCUMENT**
  OFFER OF PURCHASE FOR REAL ESTATE   150

Ethics: Legal Research   *151*
Case Excerpt: Donald Yoo Corp. v. Laszlo N. Tauber, M.D.
and Associates   *151*
Skills You Need in the Real World   *153*
Chapter Summary   *154*
Review Questions   *154*
Discussion Questions   *155*
Practical Applications   *155*
Web Sites   *156*
Terms and Phrases   *156*
Significant Cases   *156*

7   LANDLORD AND TENANT LAW

Focus of This Chapter

The law of leasehold estates is explored in depth in this chapter. The chapter examines the rights and duties of landlords and tenants, and addresses issues such as eviction and the various types of landlord-tenant relationships.

I. INTRODUCTION   **157**

II. CREATING A LANDLORD-TENANT RELATIONSHIP   **158**

   A. Historical Background on Landlord-Tenant Law   158
   B. Modern Changes to the Landlord-Tenant Relationship   158

Tech Topic: Using Wi-Fi to Lure Tenants   *159*

III. LEASES   **159**

   A. Fixed Rent Leases   160
   B. Percentage Leases   160
   C. Net Leases   160
   D. Rent-to-Own Leases   160
   E. Ground Leases   161
   F. Timber Leases   161
   G. Mineral Leases   161
      1. Distinguishing Between Leases and Licenses   162
   H. Oil and Gas Leases   162

    I. Common Lease Provisions   162
        1. Rent   162
        2. Late Payments and Fees   163
        3. Pet and Security Deposits   163
        4. Renewal Provisions   163
        5. Persons Permitted on the Leased Premises   163
        6. Acceptance of Leased Premises   164
        7. Modifying or Altering the Premises   164
        8. Subletting   164
        9. Notice   164
    J. Commercial Leases   165
    K. Trade Fixtures   165
    L. Public Policy Concerns in Leases   166
    M. Federal Law Requirements   166
    N. Statute of Frauds Considerations   167

 IV. **DUTIES CREATED BY THE LANDLORD-TENANT
     RELATIONSHIP**   **167**

    A. Uniform Residential Landlord and Tenant Act   167
    B. Landlord's Rights   168
        1. Right to Re-Enter Premises   169
        2. Duty to Repair   169
        3. Landlord's Duties to Third Parties   170
        4. Landlords and Discriminatory Practices   170
    C. Tenant's Rights   171
        1. Use and Enjoyment by Tenant   171
    D. Legal Doctrines That Arise in the Landlord-Tenant Relationship   172
        1. Warranty of Habitability   172
        2. Quiet Enjoyment   172
    E. Tenant's Duties to Landlord   172
        1. Tenant's Responsibility for Damages to Leased Premises   173
            a. Ordinary Wear and Tear   173
            b. Damage Deposits   174
            c. Pet Deposits   174
    F. Remedies for Breach of Duty   174
        1. Tenant's Remedies Against Landlord   174
            a. Damages That Can Be Awarded to the Tenant   174
                i. Equitable Relief   174
                ii. Compensatory Damages   175
                iii. Punitive Damages   175
            b. Constructive Eviction   176
            c. Actions for Wrongful Eviction   176
        2. Landlord's Remedies Against Tenant   177
            a. Eviction   177
                i. Procedures to Evict   177
                ii. Self-Help Eviction   178
                iii. Retaliatory Eviction   178

**V. CLASSIFYING LANDLORD-TENANT
     RELATIONSHIPS**   **179**

   A. Tenancy for Years   179
      1. Creating a Tenancy for Years   179
      2. Terminating a Tenancy for Years   180
   B. Tenancy from Year to Year   180
      1. Creating a Tenancy from Year to Year   180
      2. Terminating a Tenancy from Year to Year   180
   C. Tenancy at Will   180
      1. Creating a Tenancy at Will   181
      2. Terminating a Tenancy at Will   181
   D. Tenancy at Sufferance   181
      1. Creating a Tenancy at Sufferance   181
      2. Terminating a Tenancy at Sufferance   181

● **ANNOTATED DOCUMENT**
   APARTMENT LEASE   **182**

   Ethics: Landlords Who Violate State Law   *182*
   Case Excerpt: Copeland v. Lincoln   *182*
   Skills You Need in the Real World   *185*
   Chapter Summary   *186*
   Review Questions   *186*
   Discussion Questions   *187*
   Practical Applications   *187*
   Web Sites   *187*
   Terms and Phrases   *188*
   Significant Cases   *188*

 REAL ESTATE DEEDS

Focus of This Chapter

This chapter addresses the construction of deeds, beginning with a general description of the role of deeds in real estate transactions, and then describing the specifics of various types of deeds, from general warranty deeds to quitclaim deeds.

I. INTRODUCTION   **189**

   A. A Brief History of Deeds   189

II. ELEMENTS OF DEEDS   **190**

   A. Minimum Requirements of a Deed   191

1. Deeds Must Be in Writing   191
2. Deeds Must Identify the Grantor and Grantee   192
3. The Grantor Must Sign the Deed   193
4. The Parties Must Have Legal Capacity   195
5. The Property Conveyed Must Be Adequately Described   195
   a. Court Interpretations of Ambiguous Property Descriptions   196
6. The Deed Must Contain Language Indicating an Intention
   to Convey Property Rights   197
7. The Deed Must Be Delivered by the Grantor and Accepted
   by the Grantee   197
   a. Proving Delivery   199

Tech Topic: Electronic Recording   *199*
   b. Delivery in Escrow   200
8. The Deed Must Be Attested and Acknowledged   200
   a. Attestation   200
   b. Acknowledgment   200
9. Other Deed Provisions   200
   a. Seals   200
   b. Consideration   201
   c. Exceptions and Exclusions   201
10. Nonessential Deed Provisions   201
   a. Witnesses   202
   b. Date   202

III. TYPES OF DEEDS   **202**

A. General Warranty Deeds   202
   1. Seizin   203
   2. Quiet Enjoyment   203
   3. Against Encumbrances   203
   4. Further Assurance   203
   5. Warranty Forever   203
B. Special Warranty Deeds   203
C. Deeds of Trust/Mortgages   204
D. Quitclaim Deed   205

IV. RECORDING STATUTES   **206**

A. Notice Recording Statutes   206
B. Race-Notice Recording Statutes   206
C. Race Recording Statutes   207

● **ANNOTATED DOCUMENT**
GENERAL WARRANTY DEED   207

Ethics: Use of Forms   *208*
Case Excerpt: Estate of Dykes v. Estate of Williams   *209*
Skills You Need in the Real World   *213*

Chapter Summary   *214*
Review Questions   *214*
Discussion Questions   *215*
Practical Applications   *215*
Web Sites   *215*
Terms and Phrases   *216*
Significant Cases   *216*

⑨ **MORTGAGES AND FINANCING THE PURCHASE OF REAL ESTATE**

Focus of This Chapter

Mortgages are the lifeblood of real estate sales. This chapter examines mortgages (deeds of trust) in great detail, concentrating not only on the basic legal requirements of a mortgage, but also on the clauses commonly found in mortgages.

I. INTRODUCTION   **217**

II. MORTGAGE MARKETS   **219**

A. Primary Mortgage Market   219

Tech Topic: Social Media Monitoring   *220*
B. Secondary Mortgage Market   220
   1. Federal Agencies in the Secondary Mortgage Market   221
     a. Fannie Mae   222
     b. Ginnie Mae   223
     c. Freddie Mac   223
     d. HUD   223
     e. The Role of the Federal Reserve Board   223
     f. Troubled Asset Relief Program   224
   2. Important Federal Legislation That Governs Real
     Estate Financing   225
     a. Federal Truth in Lending Laws   225
     b. Real Estate Settlement Procedures Act   225

III. THE LEGAL REQUIREMENTS OF A MORTGAGE/ DEED OF TRUST   **228**

A. Mortgages vs. Deeds of Trust   229
   1. Deeds of Trust   229
B. The Elements of a Mortgage   229
   1. Mortgages Must Be in Writing   230
   2. The Parties Must Be Identified   230
   3. Specific Clauses in Mortgages   231

a. Property as Collateral 231
b. Promissory Note 231
c. Granting Clause 231
d. Description of the Debt 231
e. Power of Sale Provision 232
f. Taxes and Insurance 232
g. Estoppel Certificate 232
h. Acceleration Clause 232
i. Due on Sale Clause 232
j. Interest Escalation Clause 233
k. Prepayment Clause 233
l. Attorney's Fees 233
C. Recording Mortgages 233
1. Priority of Mortgages 233
a. Subordination Agreement 233

IV. TYPES OF MORTGAGES **234**

A. Fixed-Rate Mortgages 235
1. Amortization 235
B. Adjustable-Rate Mortgages 235
1. Rate Caps 236
C. Other Types of Mortgages 236
1. Balloon Mortgages 237
2. Purchase-Money Mortgages 237
3. Wraparound Mortgages 237
4. Second Mortgages 238
5. Equity Lines of Credit 238

V. QUALIFYING FOR A MORTGAGE **239**

A. Underwriting 239
1. Risk Assessment 239
2. Borrower's Credit History 239
a. Consumer Reporting Agencies 239
b. The Fair Credit Reporting Act 240
3. Points 240
B. Appraisal 240
C. The Rise of Internet Lenders 245

VI. DISCHARGING A MORTGAGE **246**

VII. FORECLOSURE **246**

A. Judicial Foreclosure 246
B. Power of Sale Foreclosure 247
1. The Foreclosure Auction 247
2. Rising Foreclosure Rates 247

● **ANNOTATED DOCUMENT**
RESIDENTIAL MORTGAGE   **248**

Ethics: Predatory Lending   *252*
Case Excerpt: Bayview Loan Servicing, LLC v. Simmons   *253*
Skills You Need in the Real World   *257*
Chapter Summary   *257*
Review Questions   *258*
Discussion Questions   *259*
Practical Applications   *259*
Web Sites   *259*
Terms and Phrases   *260*
Significant Cases   *260*

10 PUBLIC AND PRIVATE RESTRICTIONS ON THE USE OF LAND

Focus of This Chapter

This chapter explores both public and private restrictions on the use of real estate by landowners. Public restrictions, such as zoning, are explained. Private restrictions, such as restrictive covenants, are examined in detail. Special emphasis is placed on the role of the paralegal in researching, preparing, and locating various public and private land use restrictions.

I. INTRODUCTION   **261**

II. PUBLIC RESTRICTIONS ON PRIVATE LAND   **262**

A. Zoning   262
  1. Aesthetic Zoning   263
  2. Enforcing Zoning Regulations   263
  3. Types of Zoning Categories   264
    a. Residential   264
    b. Commercial   264
    c. Industrial   264
  4. Exceptions to Zoning Classifications   266
    a. Nonconforming Use   266
    b. Conditional Use Permit   266
    c. Variance   266
    d. Unconstitutional or Illegal Zoning Regulations   267
      i. "Spot" Zoning   268

Tech Topic: Virtual Planning   *269*
B. Building Codes   269
C. Planning Boards   269

    D. Historical Districts   269
    E. Urban Planning   270
    F. Interstate Land Sales Full Disclosure Act   271
    G. Environmental Issues   271
       1. The Superfund   272

III. PRIVATE RESTRICTIONS ON LAND USE   **272**

    A. Restrictive Covenants   272
       1. Creating Covenants   273
       2. Restrictive Covenants "Touch and Concern"   273
       3. Typical Covenants   274
       4. Illegal or Unconstitutional Covenants   274
       5. Enforcing Covenants   276
       6. Terminating Restrictive Covenants   276
          a. Stated Time Period   276
          b. Abandonment   276
          c. Changed Conditions   276
          d. Merger   277
    B. Subdivision Rules and Regulations   277
    C. Nuisance Actions   277
       1. Public Nuisance   278
       2. Private Nuisance   278

● **ANNOTATED DOCUMENT**
   RESTRICTIVE COVENANTS   **279**

Ethics: Discriminatory Restrictive Covenants   *280*
Case Excerpt: Hawkins View Architectural Control Committee v. Cooper   *281*
Skills You Need in the Real World   *286*
Chapter Summary   *286*
Review Questions   *287*
Discussion Questions   *288*
Practical Applications   *288*
Web Sites   *288*
Terms and Phrases   *288*
Significant Cases   *289*

 REAL ESTATE PROFESSIONS

Focus of This Chapter

Various real estate professions are profiled in this chapter, from real estate brokers to law firms that specialize in real estate issues. The chapter also addresses the day-to-day activities of real estate paralegals.

I. INTRODUCTION   **291**

II. THE LAW OF AGENCY   **292**

    A. Creating an Agency Relationship   292
      1. Agent's Duty to the Principal   292
        a. Obedience   293
        b. Care   293
        c. Loyalty   293
        d. Accounting   294
      2. Agent's Duty to Third Parties   294
        a. The Duty of Honesty and Fair Dealing 294
        b. Duty Not to Commit Fraud   295
          i. Material Facts   295
          ii. Sales Tactics   295
        c. Duty to Avoid Negligent Misrepresentation 296
      3. Principal's Duty to Agent   296
        a. Duty to Compensate the Agent   296
        b. Duty to Cooperate   297
        c. Duty Not to Unfairly Injure the Agent's Reputation 298
    B. Independent Contractors   298

III. APPLYING AGENCY LAW TO REAL ESTATE TRANSACTIONS   **298**

    A. A Real Estate Agent's Duty of Care   299
    B. An Agent's Responsibility to Disclose Information   299
    C. Classifications of Real Estate Agents   300
      1. Real Estate Brokers and Real Estate Agents   300
      2. Becoming a Real Estate Broker or Agent   301
      3. Regulations That Govern Real Estate Agents   302
      4. Services Provided by Real Estate Agents and Brokers 303
        a. Multiple Listing Service   303
        b. Locating and Prequalifying Buyers   303

    Tech Topic: Advertising Real Estate   *304*

IV. OTHER REAL ESTATE PROFESSIONS   **304**

    A. Real Estate Investments   305
      1. Advantages of Real Estate Investments   305
        a. Appreciation in Value   305
        b. Impact on Credit Rating   305
        c. Potential Source of Funds   305
        d. Tax Advantages   306
      2. Disadvantages of Real Estate Investments   306
        a. Poor Liquidity   306
        b. Property Taxes   306

c. Maintenance Costs	306
d. Financing and Down Payment Costs	307
3. Real Estate Investment Trusts	307
4. Small Investors and "Do It Yourselfers"	307
B. Loan Officers	308
1. Online Loan Applications	308
2. Internet Mortgage Lenders	308
C. Appraisers	308
1. The Importance of Real Estate Valuation	309
a. Comparative Market Analysis	309
D. Surveyors	310
E. The Legal Team	310
1. Real Estate Attorneys	310
2. Real Estate Paralegals	310
3. Real Estate Title Searchers	310
a. The Role of Technology in the Real Estate Law Office	312
F. Contractors	312
G. Property Managers	312
H. Inspectors	312
1. Conducting a Real Estate Inspection	313

● **ANNOTATED DOCUMENT**
REAL ESTATE APPRAISAL   **314**

Ethics: Real Estate Professionals' Codes of Ethics	*315*
Case Excerpt: Wheat v. Lindsley	*315*
Skills You Need in the Real World	*319*
Chapter Summary	*320*
Review Questions	*321*
Discussion Questions	*321*
Practical Applications	*321*
Web Sites	*322*
Terms and Phrases	*322*
Significant Cases	*322*

 TITLE INSURANCE AND TITLE EXAMINATIONS

Focus of This Chapter

Title examinations are treated as a separate chapter because states have radically different approaches to this issue. Regional differences in the method (and even the role) of title examinations in real property transactions are examined closely. This chapter emphasizes the role of the legal team in general and the paralegal in particular in carrying out the various steps of a real estate title examination. The chapter also provides basis forms for title examinations.

I. INTRODUCTION   **323**

II. TITLE INSURANCE   **324**

    A. What Title Insurance Does   324
    B. Obtaining Title Insurance   324
       1. Title Insurance Policy   325
       2. Title Insurance Premium   326
       3. Terminating the Policy   326

III. TITLE EXAMINATIONS   **326**

    A. What Is a Title Examination?   326
    B. Beginning a Title Search   327
       1. Names of the Current Owners   329
          a. Grantor-Grantee Index   329
          b. Tract Index   329
       2. Description of the Property to Be Conveyed   329
       3. Time Period   329
       4. Tax ID Number   330
       5. Deed Book and Page Number   330
       6. Surveys and Plats   330

IV. STEPS IN A TITLE SEARCH   **331**

    A. Creating a Client File   331
    B. Step 1: Creating the Chain of Title   332
       1. The Tax Office   332
       2. Creating the Links in the Chain of Ownership   333
       3. Technological Innovations in Land Records   333

Tech Topic: Online Title Searches   *335*
    C. Step 2: Establishing the Out or Adverse Conveyances   335
       1. Reviewing Title Documents   336
          a. Mortgage or Deed of Trust Issues in Title Examinations   336
       2. Liens   337
       3. UCC Listings   337
       4. Marriage, Birth, and Death Records   337
       5. Probate Records   339
       6. Judgments   339
          a. The Clerk of Court's Office   339
    D. Step 3: Compiling the Information   339
       1. Title Abstracts   340
    E. Preliminary and Final Title Certificates   340
       1. Legal Malpractice and Title Examinations   340
          a. Tacking   342
    F. The Paralegal's Role in Title Searches   343

V.   COMMON PROBLEMS IN TITLE SEARCHES   **344**

    A. Sub-divided Properties   344
    B. Holes or Breaks in the Chain of Title   344

● **THE ANNOTATED DOCUMENT**
   CHAIN OF TITLE   **345**

Ethics: Tacking and Other Shortcuts   347
Case Excerpt: Estate of Fleming v. Nicholson   347
Skills You Need in the Real World   350
Chapter Summary   351
Review Questions   351
Discussion Questions   352
Practical Applications   352
Web Sites   352
Terms and Phrases   353
Significant Cases   353

13   THE CLOSING

Focus of This Chapter

This chapter provides a general introduction to closing/settlement procedures nationwide and then examines the specifics of this process in various locales across the country to provide specific examples of how the process is actually carried out. The paralegal's role in the closing is examined in detail.

I.   INTRODUCTION   **355**

    A. What Is a Closing?   356

II. BASIC PREPARATIONS TO CONDUCT A CLOSING   **356**

    A. Mortgages   356
    B. Attorney Representation   357
    C. Establishing the Date for the Closing   357
       1. Time Is of the Essence   358
    D. Gathering Documents and Information for the Closing   358
       1. Title Search   359
          a. Title Defects   359
          b. Attorney Certifications   359
       2. Legal Description of the Property   359
       3. Loan Payoff Amounts   360
          a. Seller's Information   360
       4. Tax Information   360

      5. Termite and Other Inspections   360
   E. Loan-Closing Software   361

III. THE PROCEDURE AT THE CLOSING   361

   A. Preparing the Loan Package   362
   B. Verifying Hazard Insurance   362
   C. Documents Exchanged at the Closing   362
      1. General Warranty Deed   363
        a. Preparing the Deed   363
      2. Mortgage   363
        a. Promissory Note   363
        b. Subordination Agreements   363
      3. IRS Forms   364
        a. IRS Form 4506   364
        b. W-9 Form   364
      4. Lien Waiver Affidavits   364
      5. HUD-1 Settlement Form   364
      6. Bill of Sale for Personal Property   365
      7. Compliance Agreement   365
      8. Credit Insurance or Protection Plan Addendum   365
      9. Loan Application   365
     10. USA Patriot Act Requirements   365
     11. PMI Disclosure   366
     12. Trust Disbursement Records   366
     13. Truth in Lending Documentation   366
     14. Termite Inspection Letter   369
     15. Survey   369
        a. Seller's Affidavit   369

IV. CONDUCTING THE CLOSING   369

   A. People Normally Present at a Closing   371
      1. Closing Professional   371
        a. Attorney   371
        b. Paralegal   371
      2. Buyers   372
      3. Sellers   372
      4. Real Estate Agent   372
   B. Disbursing the Funds   372
      1. Lender's Fees   373
        a. Escrow Accounts for Insurance and Taxes   373
      2. Attorney's Fees   373
      3. Recording Fees   373
      4. Seller's Profit on the Transaction   373
      5. Certified Funds from the Buyer   373
      6. Real Estate Agent's Commission   374
      7. Tax Payments   374

	a. Proration	374
	i. Actual Days Method of Proration	375
	ii. 30-Day Month Method of Proration	375
	iii. Prorating Other Bills	375

V. OTHER CLOSING ISSUES   **375**

A. "Escrow" Closings   375
    1. The Doctrine of Relation Back   376
B. Dual Representation   376

VI. AFTER THE CLOSING   **377**

A. Filing and Priority   377

● **THE ANNOTATED DOCUMENT**
SETTLEMENT STATEMENT   **378**

Ethics: Delegating the Closing to the Paralegal   *380*
Case Excerpt: Countrywide Home Loans, Inc. v. Kentucky Bar Ass'n   *380*
Skills You Need in the Real World   *387*
Chapter Summary   *387*
Review Questions   *388*
Discussion Questions   *389*
Practical Applications   *389*
Web Sites   *390*
Terms and Phrases   *390*
Significant Cases   *390*

 14   **TAXATION ISSUES IN REAL PROPERTY**

Focus of This Chapter

This chapter focuses not only on the important issue of how real estate taxes are assessed and collected, but also on the extensive information available through various tax records.

I. INTRODUCTION   **391**

II. REAL PROPERTY TAXES   **391**

A. Ad Valorem Taxation   392
    1. The Power to Levy Taxes   392
B. What Can Be Taxed?   392
    1. Tax Exemptions   393
       a. Homestead Exemption   393

b. Charitable Exemption 393
c. Nonprofit Exemption 394
d. Government Exemption 394
    i. Enterprise Zones 394
C. How Tax Values Are Determined 395
    1. Tax Assessment 395
    a. Challenging an Assessment 396
    2. Calculating the Tax Rate 396
    a. Reassessment 397
D. Paying Taxes 397
    1. Enforcing Tax Regulations 397
    a. Tax Liens 397
        i. Setting Priorities in Tax Liens 398
    b. Foreclosing a Tax Lien 398

Tech Topic: Real Estate and Taxation 399

III. ASSESSMENTS **399**

● ANNOTATED DOCUMENT
COUNTY TAX RECORD **401**

Ethics: Tax Dodges 402
Case Excerpt: Metropolitan Gov't of Nashville and Davidson
County v. Delinquent Taxpayers 402
Skills You Need in the Real World 410
Chapter Summary 410
Review Questions 410
Discussion Questions 411
Practical Applications 411
Web Sites 412
Terms and Phrases 412
Significant Cases 412

GLOSSARY 413
APPENDIX 417
INDEX 463

Preface

INTRODUCTION

The third edition of this book is a major revision on the first two editions. As anyone knows who has watched the news or been involved in any aspect of real estate, the world of real estate has undergone some dramatic changes in recent years. This text addresses many of those changes, while continuing to stick to the original concept of balancing theory and practice. In addition to all of the original elements of the text, I have also expanded some materials, as well as added brand new sections, such as "Tech Topics," that discuss technological innovations in real estate practice. I have updated the materials as much as possible, while continuing to lay a proper foundation in real estate law that covers topics as diverse as the basics of fee simple ownership, landlord-tenant law, restrictive covenants, closing procedures, and taxation, to name just a few.

As in previous editions, the day-to-day practice of law is never far from consideration of the material presented. The text continues to place a strong emphasis on practical applications of real estate law. Graphs, exhibits, and other visual aids have also been revamped and new learning features placed at the end of the chapters will further engage students. Ethical issues continue to be a paramount concern, especially in the wake of some of the questionable, if not illegal, practices engaged in by some attorneys, lending institutions, and others that may have caused in whole or in part the recent economic downturn in the United States and many other countries. The text continues to provide information for paralegals about practical issues, such as how to research deeds, decipher mortgage clauses, and even conduct a full-blown title examination, with special emphasis on the impact that software and the Internet have had on all of these endeavors.

FEATURES

The book was designed with the reader in mind. The text presents the material in a variety of methods to tap into different learning styles. Many examples of actual documents are provided as figures throughout each chapter. In addition, various features lend a strong visual element to the text. The features found in the text include the following:

■ **Chapter Objectives**

Each chapter begins with clearly stated learning objectives to guide readers in their studies.

■ **Issue at a Glance**

Scattered throughout each chapter are small synopses of issues discussed in the chapter. These synopses are positioned adjacent to the material under discussion, not only as a way of helping the reader synthesize important issues, but also as a visual marker for later study.

■ **Tech Topics**

This newest edition contains a brand new feature not found in previous editions: "Tech Topics." Each chapter presents an examination of technological innovations that affect the practice of real estate law, from online lenders to "robo-signing," among many others.

■ **Definitions**

As each new term is introduced, it is also defined for the student. These on-the-spot definitions provide a handy reference.

■ **Examples**

Each chapter contains not only discussions of the theoretical underpinnings of law, but also practical examples to assist the student in building the reasoning skills needed to succeed in the legal field.

■ **Annotated Documents**

In addition to the documents provided as figures throughout the text, each chapter contains one relevant annotated document to highlight the practical application of issues discussed in the chapter.

■ **Ethics**

Ethics is a vital component of any legal text, so the ethical implications of a real estate practice are emphasized in each chapter. In order to emphasize the important role that ethics plays in law, each chapter contains a separate ethical discussion.

■ **Skills You Need in the Real World**

The text places strong emphasis on balancing theoretical discussion with practical examples. This is readily apparent in the "Skills" section found at the conclusion of each chapter. Here, the author addresses how the student can build an entire skill set, from researching public records to drafting property descriptions.

■ **Case Excerpts**

Each chapter contains a case excerpt designed to emphasize some of the points raised in that chapter and to provide material for classroom discussions. These cases have been updated to reflect recent changes in the law since the publication of the first edition.

■ **Case Questions**

At the conclusion of each case are questions relevant to that case that spur classroom discussion and ask the student to relate the case to the material brought out in each chapter.

■ **Chapter Summary**

Each chapter contains a concise summary of the major issues discussed. This feature helps readers focus on the important points raised in the chapter.

■ **Review Questions**

Extensive review questions test the student's comprehension of the issues under discussion. These review questions, coupled with the Discussion Questions, provide rich material for classroom discussions.

■ **Practical Applications**

The Practical Applications section, found at the conclusion of each chapter, emphasizes the practical aspects of law and building important skills. Where the review and discussion questions encourage dialogue about the topics in each chapter, the Practical Applications allow the student to put this theoretical knowledge to practical use and to make a stronger connection with the material.

■ **Web Sites**

The Internet is becoming an increasingly vital link for students, and a list of web sites is included at the end of each chapter to assist students in gathering more information about the chapter topics. Web sites in each chapter focus on important real estate concepts or provide direct access to the amazing amount of detail currently provided about real estate topics, including access to public documents.

■ **Key Terms and Phrases**

A list of key terms and phrases used in each chapter assists the student in mastering the concepts presented.

■ **Crosswords and Word Mazes**

Additional student activities are included in this latest edition, including crosswords and word mazes that help students master the terms and phrases presented.

■ **Significant Cases**

In order to assist both students and instructors, the author has included a new section in the second edition that provides cites to noteworthy or other significant cases relevant to the topics discussed in the chapter.

■ **Non-Gender Specific Language**

In recognition of the impact of gender-specific language, the author has adopted the following convention in the text: Even-numbered chapters use "he" in general discussions and examples, while the odd-numbered chapters use "she" for the same purposes.

PEDAGOGY

The following features are included in the text to take advantage of different student learning styles:

- Learning objectives stated at the beginning of each chapter
- Terms and legal vocabulary in bold and defined immediately for the student; also listed in the Glossary for later reference
- Many different forms of visual aids that illustrate crucial points
- Professional profiles to help the student make a personal connection with the material
- Lesson plans in the instructor's manual that provide alternative presentations of the material
- End-of-chapter questions, activities, and assignments to hone the student's understanding
- End-of-chapter ethical discussion
- Web sites for further research and/or discussion

INSTRUCTOR'S MANUAL

The author has developed an extensive instructor's manual to accompany the text. This instructor's manual provides a wealth of resources for the instructor. The instructor's manual and other ancillary materials are available to download at the companion website to accompany the text, at www.aspenlawschool.com/bevans_realestate3

■ **Suggested Syllabi**

Suggested syllabi are provided for various versions of an Introduction to Law course, including alternate syllabi for instructors who emphasize theoretical over practical, or practical over theoretical.

■ **Lesson Plans**

The author provides several different lesson plans to help instructors who must present introductory courses in 6-, 8-, 10-, 12-, or 16-week formats.

- **Chapter Lecture Outline and Discussion**

  Each chapter is outlined for the instructor and annotations are provided throughout the outline to provide additional discussion and classroom material for the instructor.

- **Additional Web Resources**

  The instructor's manual also contains additional web sites to provide other resources for classroom discussion and assignments.

- **Additional Assignments**

  In addition to the chapter review questions and discussion questions, the author also provides more assignments in the instructor's manual.

- **Answers to Review Questions and Discussion Questions**

  The end-of-chapter review questions are answered in detail. The author also provides suggested answers for the discussion questions.

- **Test Bank**

  The test bank includes a variety of test questions, including:

  Essay Questions (five per chapter)
  Short Answer (ten per chapter)
  Multiple Choice (25 per chapter)
  True-False (ten per chapter)

- **Additional Instructor's Materials**

  1 Power Point Slides

  The author has prepared a PowerPoint® presentation for each chapter of the text.

  2 Additional Cases

  Additional cases are provided for classroom discussion. These can be used in a variety of ways, including as lecture handouts and additional assignments.

Acknowledgments

The author would like to thank the following for their help in creating this book: Betsy Kenny, Carol McGeehan, Richard Mixter, David Herzig, Troy Froebe, Renee Cote, Sylvia Rebert, Jacqueline Landis and Lisa Burnett.

Real Estate and Property Law for Paralegals

An Introduction
to Real Estate

Focus of This Chapter

This chapter introduces the basic concepts of real and personal property, introduces the rich and complex world of real property, and explains the various categories of real property.

Chapter Learning Objectives

After completing this chapter, you should be able to:

■ Explain the differences between real and personal property
■ Explain the economic characteristics of real property
■ Describe the real estate market
■ List and explain the various classifications of real property
■ Explain the differences between residential, commercial, and industrial property

INTRODUCTION

In this chapter we examine the basic concepts of real property. We first examine how real property differs from personal property, and then dig deeper into the issues by showing how the unique qualities of real property are revealed in a wide variety of ways, from how land is classified to how title to real property is conveyed from a seller to a buyer.

REAL PROPERTY VERSUS PERSONAL PROPERTY

All property can be divided into two classifications: real property or personal property. Although the original meanings of these terms had special relevance in regard to how a case was brought — and the court in which the action could be brought — these days the differences have more to do with the way that ownership interests are transferred, as well as other differences. In the modern era real property refers to land — and anything permanently attached to land. Personal property refers to all other types of property. As such, real property refers to the land, houses, trees, and any other permanent structures. Personal property refers to non–real estate items, including everything from apples to automobiles.

ISSUE AT A GLANCE

"Real property" refers to land and anything permanently attached to land.

The reason that the law makes a distinction between these two types of property is that the classification affects many of the rights and legal remedies available to the owners. For one thing, the way that ownership is transferred in real estate is different from the way it is transferred in personal property. We will see time and again that there is a great deal of symbolism in real estate transactions. In Chapter 2, we will see that the modern real estate transaction still holds many of the same features used in the Middle Ages and earlier. That is particularly true when it comes to transferring title to real property. For personal property, possession often equates to ownership. Bills of sale, receipts, and other indicia of title are helpful in proving ownership of personal property, but possession is the best way. In fact, the old common law rule that "possession is nine-tenths of the law" is a maxim that applies to personal property, not real property. "Possession" in the context of real property obviously means something different than the ability to carry the property around with you.

ISSUE AT A GLANCE

Real property ownership interests are transferred in a different way than ownership interests in personal property.

Statute of Frauds
Originally enacted in England and later adopted in all American states, this statute requires certain types of contracts to be in writing before they can be enforced. Typical contracts covered by the Statute of Frauds include contracts to answer for the debt of another and transactions involving real estate.

Real property ownership interests are transferred by deed. The deed is the evidence of ownership. Delivery and acceptance of the deed are the physical acts that transfer ownership from one person to another. Another difference between real property and personal property is taxation. Taxes are assessed differently on personal property and real property. Taxes on personal property usually are assessed by sale price, while taxes on real property are based on the assessed value. We explore these and many other differences in later chapters.

The transfer of ownership interest in real estate is required to be in writing under the **Statute of Frauds**. However, most transfers of personal property are not required to be in writing. We explore the Statute of Frauds in greater detail in Chapter 8.

PERSONAL PROPERTY	REAL PROPERTY	FIGURE 1-1
Usually refers to mobile items	Always refers to land	Differences Between Real Property and Personal Property
Often taxed on sale price	Often taxed on assessed value	
Ownership is evidenced by possession	Ownershop is evidence by deed	
Statue of Frauds usually does not apply	Statute of Frauds applies to almost all transations	

Knowing how to classify property as real or personal also has a practical consideration: In a real estate transaction, there is no need to refer to the specific items of real property that are being sold. The house, trees, soil, and attached garage are never mentioned in the deed. The seller may remove personal property items, such as furniture, beds, and unattached appliances, unless the parties have specifically negotiated the sale of these items of personal property. The sale of real property involves the sale of all items that are permanently attached to the land, which is why there is no need to list them. Personal property, on the other hand, must be specifically listed as to all items for which title is changing hands.

In the past, the difference in classification between real and personal property also had an effect on probate law. Real property interests were transferred to heirs in different ways than personal property. Although many of those probate rules have changed, there are still important differences that arise in transferring title through an estate proceeding.

A. WHAT MAKES REAL PROPERTY SO UNIQUE?

Real property is a unique and specialized area of law for several reasons. As we will see throughout this chapter, real property has its own set of rules for selling, buying, mortgaging, and investing. Real property also has unique physical attributes. For one thing, real estate occupies a fixed point on the globe. Rivers may change course, houses may be torn down, but the underlying land remains where it is. Land that is submerged under a lake is still there, if inaccessible.

Real property has its own set of laws, statutes, cases, and judicial interpretations that make it an entirely separate branch of law. Many attorneys devote their careers to this one area of law. It is as specialized as criminal defense, trademark, and labor law. Attorneys and paralegals can spend decades in the practice of real property law and still not learn all its aspects. During the course of this book, we discuss many of the legal implications that arise from real property, from easements to encroachments, from mortgages to metes and bounds descriptions, while learning a great deal about property law in all its rich diversity.

Real property is also unique because of the financial arrangements used to purchase it. Later, we examine the issue of deeds of trust and mortgages and the legal impact of these financing instruments on real estate ownership.

Sidebar

Most states have their own statewide real estate treatise. Usually written by a noted scholar or attorney, a real estate treatise is a great source of information about real property law in a particular state. It provides not only legal background but also practical applications. You should locate and acquire your own copy of the real property treatise for your state.

B. PHYSICAL CHARACTERISTICS OF LAND

Real property has several distinctive characteristics that separate it from personal property. As mentioned above, land occupies a specific point on the globe. Unlike personal property, land is fixed and immovable; it cannot be relocated. For this reason, it is the perfect vehicle for assessing taxes. (In Chapter 14, we explore how real estate taxes are assessed.) Another physical characteristic of real estate is that no two pieces of land are identical. Each one is unique, with its own special characteristics and chain of ownership. Also, because land is located within different jurisdictions, the rules governing real estate transactions vary considerably. Land falls under the law of whatever state it happens to be located in. A single individual can own land in any number of different states and each parcel falls under different rules and statutes. An owner cannot claim that simply because he is the owner of all the tracts that they should all fall under one set of rules.

In rem jurisdiction
A court's power to render decisions based on the location of the land within the court's geographic boundaries.

Personal jurisdiction
A court's power to render decisions based on an individual's personal connections and interactions within the court's geographic boundaries.

This fact controls some of the rules regarding lawsuits involving real estate. There is a specific term for this type of jurisdiction — **in rem jurisdiction**. This is a court's power to enter decisions and rulings simply because the land involved happens to be within the court's geographic limits. In most lawsuits, the court's jurisdiction is based on **personal jurisdiction**, that is, power over the people involved in the suit. However, in some lawsuits, a court acquires jurisdictional power simply because a tract of land lies within its geographic boundaries. We explore many of these jurisdictional questions in Chapter 4.

C. ECONOMIC CHARACTERISTICS OF LAND

In addition to the unique physical characteristics, land also has some interesting economic characteristics. For one thing, land has traditionally been an excellent investment. In the past, a person's wealth was measured by the extent of his real estate holdings. Land ownership continues to be an important source of investment income for many individuals.

Land also offers some economic benefits to persons who are not wealthy. In fact, one of the best economic benefits of land ownership is the tax consequences of home ownership. In Chapter 4, we explore how a homeowner earns a substantial tax benefit from being able to deduct mortgage interest payments from his yearly income tax return.

Another interesting aspect of real estate is that unlike almost all other purchases, it generally appreciates in value. Because there is a fixed supply of land, and an ever-growing population, the realities of supply and demand put upward pressure on real estate prices. In many areas of the country, the value of a person's

Sidebar

There is at least one major movie star who earns more money every year from his real estate investments than the millions he makes on making action films.

FIGURE 1-2

Physical Characteristics of Land

Land is
- Permanently fixed and immovable
- Unique; no two pieces of land are exactly the same

- Used by local governments for assessing taxes

Year	Homeownership Rates[a] (Seasonally Adjusted)			
	First Quarter	Second Quarter	Third Quarter ↓	Fourth Quarter
2011	66.4	66.0	66.1	
2010	67.2	67.0	66.7	66.6
2009	67.4	67.4	67.4	67.3
2008	67.9	68.1	67.7	67.5
2007	68.5	68.3	68.0	67.8
2006	68.6	68.8	68.9	68.8
2005	69.2	68.8	68.7	68.9
2004	68.7	69.4	68.9	69.0
2003	68.1	68.2	68.3	68.5
2002[b]	67.9	67.8	67.9	68.2
2001	67.6	67.9	67.9	67.9
2000	67.1	67.3	67.5	67.5
1999	66.7	66.7	66.8	66.9
1998	66.0	66.1	66.6	66.5
1997	65.5	65.7	65.8	65.8
1996	65.3	65.4	65.4	65.4
1995	64.4	64.7	64.8	65.1

FIGURE 1-3

Homeownership Rates for the United States: 1995–2011. Housing Characteristics: 2010. 2010 Census Briefs. U.S. Census Bureau

[a] Standard errors for quarterly home ownership rates for the United States generally are 0.3 percent.
[b] Revised in 2002 to incorporate information collected in Census 2000.

home and land increases about 6 percent a year. This makes land an attractive investment even for those of a moderate income. However, like any other item, land can also decrease in value. In recent years the value of real estate, especially residential real estate, has either failed to rise or has actually dropped. Still the price fluctuations of land are relatively minor, especially when you compare the long-term prices of real estate to other commodities.

In recent years, falling interest rates have also encouraged people to refinance their homes. This has the advantage of allowing an owner to receive some of the **equity** value in a home as cash that can be spent on home improvement, or used to finance college tuition, vacations, or any number of projects.

Equity
A homeowner's value in property once the amount owed on the property is subtracted from its current fair market value.

EXAMPLE 1-1

Juan purchased his home 15 years ago and has been making regular monthly mortgage payments on it. His original loan amount was for $150,000. In the past 15 years, he has lowered the balance of the loan to $85,000. However, because Juan's house has steadily been appreciating in value over the years, the house is now worth $220,000. How much equity does Juan have?

Answer: Juan has $135,000 in equity. How do we arrive at this amount? Subtract the amount that Juan owes on the house from the current value ($220,000 − $85,000 = $135,000).

Tech Topic
FANNIE MAE AND THE MORTGAGE MELTDOWN

Did technology play a part in the epic mortgage meltdown of 2008?

There were many contributing factors, but Fannie Mae's (the Federal National Mortgage Association) use of underwriting software might have helped initiate the slide.

As a government-sponsored entity, Fannie Mae buys loans from banks, which in theory frees up the banks' cash to make more loans. The goal of the company is to help middle- and lower-income homebuyers be able to purchase houses.

Fannie Mae was prohibited by law from buying subprime loans, the root of the great meltdown. However, at the height of the real estate boom, company officials realized that they were losing market share because of government restrictions and took steps to stretch the boundaries of creditworthiness as far as they could.

Fannie Mae had been using automated underwriting software for years to expedite loan applications. But to increase their loan portfolios, they introduced "documentation relief" into their software, which made it easier for questionable homebuyers to qualify.

Lenders using this software weren't obligated to use human judgment in verifying the worthiness of a loan application. Added to this lack of oversight was the fact that many borrowers were including false information on their applications. The result was that the underwriting software approved questionable loans that resulted in tens of thousands of subsequent foreclosures.

Did Fannie Mae's software directly cause the mortgage meltdown? Probably not. But the company used the technology to push the limits of government regulation in qualifying homebuyers, which most certainly added to an already burgeoning crisis.

Equity itself is another aspect of the economic characteristics of land ownership. When we say that a person has equity in his home, what we are actually saying is that there is a difference between what the person owes on the home and what the home (and land) are actually worth.

Although this appears to be a simple paper gain, Juan can actually borrow against his equity. He can apply for a second mortgage and borrow against this "paper value" for real money.

EXAMPLE 1-2

Now, let's take the same numbers and show how Juan can end up in a situation that is all too common today. His home value is "underwater," meaning that his house is worth less than what he owes on it.

Juan's original loan amount, 15 years ago, was $150,000. However, three years ago, he took out a second mortgage on his home for the amount of $40,000. He used the money to fix up the home. Using the same numbers as the first example, Juan had paid down his original loan to $85,000, but because the real estate market has crumbled, Juan's house is worth $100,000. Juan owes $125,000 ($85,000 + $40,000). Juan now owes $25,000 more than the house is actually worth.

THE REAL ESTATE MARKET

There is a market for land, just as there is a market for commodities or goods. The real estate market has its own rules and regulations. It also has participants, such as brokers, agents, loan correspondents, and attorneys and paralegals, to name just a few. We explore the role played by these participants as we develop the concepts of real estate in later chapters.

We begin our discussion of the real estate market with a straightforward example.

EXAMPLE 1-3

Maria and Vern Seller have outgrown their house and want to put it up for sale. They contact Good & Better Real Estate Agency to discuss their options. Alvin Agent tells them that if they sign a listing agreement with the agency, Good & Better will advertise their house for sale, put a sign in their yard, list the home in the Multiple Listing Service, and make every effort to give the house the best chance of being sold.

Maria and Vern decide to put their house up for sale and they list it with Good & Better. Bill Buyer sees the house listed and decides that he wants to purchase the home. He contacts Good & Better and gets the price particulars. Then he goes to a bank, meets with a loan officer, and arranges financing to purchase the home. Finally, he buys the home from the Sellers.

Although we have oversimplified the typical real estate transaction in Example 1-3, it gives us a starting point to discuss how the real estate market functions.

In any market there must be buyers and sellers. Maria and Vern are sellers and Bill is a buyer. Good & Better is acting for Maria and Vern to list the house for sale. In exchange for this service, Good & Better will receive a percentage of the total sale price (called a commission). The Sellers could have put their house up for sale on their own. For instance, they could have paid for an ad in the local newspaper, put a sign in their yard, and printed brochures to distribute to various places around the city, but they have decided that they would prefer to leave the job of marketing their home to professionals. Later, we will see that listing a home with a real estate agent brings certain advantages that are almost impossible for a single home seller to match.

When Bill Buyer decides to purchase the Sellers' home, he goes to a bank to borrow money. Most people who buy homes must obtain a mortgage because few people have that much ready cash on hand. The real estate market also includes banks and other lending institutions. The banks in turn rely on others to review a borrower's application, assess the possible risk of the transaction, and establish the actual value of the home.

Throughout this book, we examine not only the theoretical basis of real property, but also the day-to-day activities of real estate professionals. We will also see that, in many ways, the health of the real estate market is an indicator of the strength of the overall economy. The recent economic downturn in the U.S. and across the world has been precipitated, at least in part, by a severe contraction in housing sales, rising foreclosure rates, and an unwieldy credit market. Before we can delve into these topics, we must have a firm understanding of the various ways that real estate is classified.

CLASSIFYING PROPERTY BY USE

One of the oldest and most easily understood methods of classifying property is by the use to which it is put. There are several different categories of property, including residential property, condominiums, mobile homes, manufactured housing, commercial property, and industrial and farm property.

However, before we set out these classifications, we first examine exactly how the term *land* is defined. For our purposes, we define land as including the grass, soil, trees, and anything else permanently affixed to the ground, including the soil underneath and the structures above. This includes the owner's air rights in the space above the property. With this working definition of land, we now examine specific subcategories of land.

A. UNIMPROVED LAND

Improvements
Buildings, fences, barns, and other structures that add value to raw land.

Unimproved land
Raw land that contains no structures.

When land contains **improvements**, it means that it contains structures. **Unimproved land** has no buildings or other structures on it, so it is often referred to as raw land. Such property can be developed into any number of uses: homes, businesses, farms, or parks. Once land has been improved, it can be reclassified into residential, farm, commercial, industrial, or recreational. The categories are all based on the way in which the land is used.

FIGURE 1-4

Owner-Occupied Units as a Percentage of All Occupied Housing Units: 1890–2010.

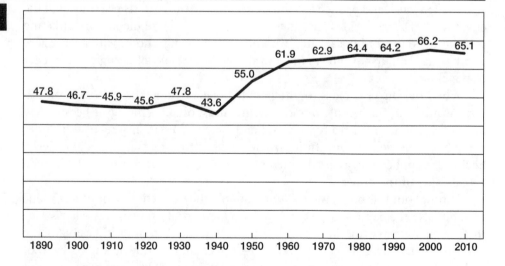

Source: U.S. Census Bureau, Census of Population and Housing, decennial volumes, and 2010 *Census Summary File 1.*

ISSUE AT
A GLANCE

B. RESIDENTIAL PROPERTY

Property categorized as residential refers to land that has a structure designed to be used for personal living, such as a home. There are numerous subcategories of residential properties, including single- and multi-family units, apartments, condominiums, mobile homes, and manufactured homes.

1. SINGLE-FAMILY HOMES

The category of single-family homes includes residential houses, duplexes (two-family units sharing a single roof), triplexes (three-family units), and four-family homes (four-family units). When more than four family units share a single roof, the law characterizes that arrangement as an apartment.

2. APARTMENTS

The technical definition of an **apartment** is a type of residential real estate consisting of five or more living units per building. However, we all use the term to describe a wide range of landlord-tenant relationships. In many large urban areas, there may be hundreds of apartments in any given complex. Apartments are popular because the residents have far less responsibility for maintaining the building, they generally have no responsibility for keeping up the grounds, and they do not require a large initial investment to move in. On the other hand, while apartment buildings can be a great financial investment for the owners, they provide few, if any, financial advantages for the residents. Apartment residents, or tenants, pay rent to the apartment owners in exchange for the use of the premises. We examine landlord-tenant law in greater detail in Chapter 7.

Apartment
A leased residence containing more than five living units sharing a single roof or foundation.

3. CONDOMINIUMS AND TOWNHOUSES

Condominiums and townhouses share many characteristics, but there are important differences that a legal professional should know.

a. Condominiums

A **condominium** resembles an apartment, but is actually more like a hybrid between a home and an apartment. The tenant in an apartment does not have any ownership interests in the dwelling. He must seek permission from the owner before making changes to the interior, and is not allowed to make any changes to the exterior. A condominium gives the resident an ownership interest in the interior of the dwelling, but no rights to the exterior. Regarding the interior, the resident has the

Condominium
A form of real property in which the owner has full title to the interior, but not the exterior, of the structure.

same legal rights as a homeowner. Condominiums can be sold just like homes, but the only thing that is being sold is what is inside the four walls. No actual land is transferred in the sale of a condominium. The owner of a condominium receives the same favorable tax treatment as a homeowner, but does not have the responsibility of exterior upkeep and maintenance. Condominium owners must pay yearly fees to homeowners' associations that contract with maintenance firms to take care of yard work and to maintain the various facilities. Condominiums often have pool and gym facilities and are very attractive to people who do not want the burden of home maintenance, yet wish to receive the financial benefits of home ownership.

Condominiums typically have common areas that are owned and maintained by a homeowners' association. These common areas consist of the sidewalks connecting the various units and the amenities, such as swimming pools, tennis courts, and walking trails. A condominium owner usually pays mandatory annual dues to the homeowners' association to defray the cost of maintaining these public areas.

b. Townhouses

Townhouse
A form of real property in which the owner has title to both the interior and exterior of a structure that resembles an apartment instead of a traditional residence.

While condominium owners have legal rights only to the inside of their individual units, **townhouse** residents own the entire unit, both the interior and exterior walls. They also own the land that the townhouse is situated on. In many states, there are no specific statutes that govern the creation of townhouses. Instead, in most states, the same rules and statutes that govern single-family homes control townhouses.

4. COOPERATIVES

Cooperatives, unlike condominiums and townhouses, are often large tracts of land, or working farms in which several persons have an ownership interest. Unlike condominiums, both interior and exterior portions of the property are owned jointly by all the members of the cooperative. These may also include large buildings owned by members.

5. MOBILE HOMES

Mobile homes are usually considered to be personal property and not real property. This classification carries with it some important consequences. The owner of a mobile home does not receive the same kind of favorable tax treatment as does a homeowner. The mobile home owners cannot, for instance, "write off" their mortgage interest payments for the year on their annual income tax return. Mobile homes can be reclassified as real property, but usually only after removing the wheels of the unit and permanently affixing it to the ground. Because houses are by their very nature permanently attached to the real estate — thus becoming reclassified as real estate — anything that a mobile home owner can do to duplicate this process will push the mobile home away from a personal property classification toward a real property classification.

When a mobile home is considered to be personal property, it usually falls under the jurisdiction of the Uniform Commercial Code, not state real property

Area	Total housing units in 2000	Housing units in 2010				Percent change, 2000 to 2010				
		Total	Percent vacant	Occupied	Percent owner-occupied	All housing units	Vacant units	Occupied units		
								Total	Owner	Renter
United States ...	**115,904,641**	**131,704,730**	**11.4**	**116,716,292**	**65.1**	**13.6**	**43.8**	**10.7**	**8.8**	**14.2**
REGION										
Northeast	22,180,440	23,647,636	10.3	21,215,415	62.2	6.6	28.4	4.6	4.4	5.0
Midwest	26,963,635	29,483,646	11.1	26,215,951	69.2	9.3	46.6	6.0	4.5	9.6
South	42,382,546	49,980,829	12.7	43,609,929	66.7	17.9	45.9	14.7	12.0	20.6
West...................	24,378,020	28,592,619	10.2	25,674,997	60.5	17.3	50.9	14.4	12.6	17.3
STATE										
Alabama	1,963,711	2,171,853	13.3	1,883,791	69.7	10.6	27.1	8.4	4.3	19.4
Alaska	260,978	306,967	15.9	258,058	63.1	17.6	24.2	16.5	17.5	14.7
Arizona	2,189,189	2,844,526	16.3	2,380,990	66.0	29.9	61.0	25.2	21.5	33.2
Arkansas	1,173,043	1,316,299	12.9	1,147,084	67.0	12.2	29.8	10.0	6.2	18.7
California	12,214,549	13,680,081	8.1	12,577,498	55.9	12.0	54.9	9.3	7.5	11.8
Colorado	1,808,037	2,212,898	10.8	1,972,868	65.5	22.4	60.2	19.0	15.9	25.4
Connecticut	1,385,975	1,487,891	7.9	1,371,087	67.5	7.4	38.5	5.3	6.4	3.2
Delaware	343,072	405,885	15.7	342,297	72.1	18.3	43.4	14.6	14.2	15.6
District of Columbia	274,845	296,719	10.1	266,707	42.0	8.0	13.2	7.4	10.7	5.1
Florida	7,302,947	8,989,580	17.5	7,420,802	67.4	23.1	62.6	17.1	12.5	27.7
Georgia...............	3,281,737	4,088,801	12.3	3,585,584	65.7	24.6	82.7	19.3	16.0	26.0
Hawaii	460,542	519,508	12.4	455,338	57.7	12.8	12.0	12.9	15.3	9.9
Idaho	527,824	667,796	13.2	579,408	69.9	26.5	51.9	23.4	19.1	34.6
Illinois	4,885,615	5,296,715	8.7	4,836,972	67.5	8.4	56.5	5.3	5.7	4.7
Indiana	2,532,319	2,795,541	10.5	2,502,154	69.9	10.4	49.7	7.1	4.7	13.0
Iowa	1,232,511	1,336,417	8.6	1,221,576	72.1	8.4	38.0	6.3	5.9	7.3
Kansas	1,131,200	1,233,215	9.8	1,112,096	67.8	9.0	29.8	7.1	4.8	12.3
Kentucky	1,750,927	1,927,164	10.8	1,719,965	68.7	10.1	29.3	8.1	5.0	15.8
Louisiana	1,847,181	1,964,981	12.0	1,728,360	67.2	6.4	23.8	4.4	3.3	6.6
Maine	651,901	721,830	22.8	557,219	71.3	10.7	23.1	7.5	7.1	8.5
Maryland	2,145,283	2,378,814	9.3	2,156,411	67.5	10.9	35.3	8.9	8.5	9.6
Massachusetts	2,621,989	2,808,254	9.3	2,547,075	62.3	7.1	46.4	4.2	5.2	2.6
Michigan	4,234,279	4,532,233	14.6	3,872,508	72.1	7.0	47.1	2.3	–	8.7
Minnesota	2,065,946	2,347,201	11.1	2,087,227	73.0	13.6	52.2	10.1	7.9	16.8
Mississippi...........	1,161,953	1,274,719	12.5	1,115,768	69.6	9.7	37.6	6.6	2.7	17.0
Missouri	2,442,017	2,712,729	12.4	2,375,611	68.8	11.1	36.3	8.2	5.9	13.7
Montana..............	412,633	482,825	15.2	409,607	68.0	17.0	35.7	14.2	12.4	18.2
Nebraska	722,668	796,193	9.5	721,130	67.2	10.3	34.0	8.2	7.9	9.0
Nevada	827,457	1,173,814	14.3	1,006,250	58.8	41.9	119.6	34.0	29.4	41.1
New Hampshire ...	547,024	614,754	15.6	518,973	71.0	12.4	32.3	9.3	11.4	4.7
New Jersey	3,310,275	3,553,562	9.5	3,214,360	65.4	7.3	38.1	4.9	4.5	5.6
New Mexico	780,579	901,388	12.2	791,395	68.5	15.5	7.2	16.7	14.3	22.5
NewYork	7,679,307	8,108,103	9.7	7,317,755	53.3	5.6	27.0	3.7	4.2	3.1
North Carolina......	3,523,944	4,327,528	13.5	3,745,155	66.7	22.8	48.6	19.6	15.0	30.0
North Dakota	289,677	317,498	11.4	281,192	65.4	9.6	11.6	9.3	7.4	13.3
Ohio....................	4,783,051	5,127,508	10.2	4,603,435	67.6	7.2	55.4	3.5	1.3	8.7
Oklahoma	1,514,400	1,664,378	12.3	1,460,450	67.2	9.9	18.5	8.8	6.9	12.9
Oregon	1,452,709	1,675,562	9.3	1,518,938	62.2	15.3	31.6	13.9	10.2	20.5
Pennsylvania	5,249,750	5,567,315	9.9	5,018,904	69.6	6.0	16.0	5.1	2.5	11.4
Rhode Island	439,837	463,388	10.7	413,600	60.7	5.4	58.5	1.3	2.4	–0.4
South Carolina	1,753,670	2,137,683	15.7	1,801,181	69.3	21.9	53.1	17.4	12.7	29.6
South Dakota	323,208	363,438	11.3	322,282	68.1	12.4	24.9	11.0	10.9	11.3
Tennessee	2,439,443	2,812,133	11.3	2,493,552	68.2	15.3	54.2	11.7	8.9	18.1
Texas	8,157,575	9,977,436	10.6	8,922,933	63.7	22.3	38.0	20.7	20.5	21.0
Utah	768,594	979,709	10.4	877,692	70.4	27.5	51.6	25.2	23.2	30.0
Vermont	294,382	322,539	20.5	256,442	70.7	9.6	23.0	6.6	6.8	5.9
Virginia................	2,904,192	3,364,939	9.2	3,056,058	67.2	15.9	50.7	13.2	11.8	16.2
Washington	2,451,075	2,885,677	9.2	2,620,076	63.9	17.7	47.8	15.4	14.1	17.6
West Virginia........	844,623	881,917	13.4	763,831	73.4	4.4	9.2	3.7	1.3	11.0
Wisconsin	2,321,144	2,624,358	13.1	2,279,768	68.1	13.1	45.6	9.4	8.8	10.6
Wyoming	223,854	261,868	13.4	226,879	69.2	17.0	15.7	17.2	15.9	20.2
Puerto Rico	**1,418,476**	**1,636,946**	**15.9**	**1,376,531**	**71.6**	**15.4**	**65.7**	**9.1**	**7.2**	**14.3**

– Percentage founds to 0.0   Sources: U.S. Census Bureau, *Census 2000 Summary File 1 and 2010 Census Summary File 1.*

FIGURE 1-5

General Housing Characteristics for the United States, Regions, States, and Puerto Rico: 2000–2010 laws. The Uniform Commercial Code governs transactions in personal property, and has very specific rules about the transfer of ownership, shipment of goods, and other issues. These rules differ from real property rules in significant ways. Some state decisions actually hold that a mobile home is a form of motor vehicle, not real estate.[1] In order for a mobile home to change from a classification of personal property to real property, several actions must take place. Among them are:

- The homeowner establishes the mobile home on the land with an obvious intent to make it permanent.
- The homeowner clearly intends to treat the mobile home as real property.
- The homeowner pays taxes on the mobile home as though it were a house.

6. MANUFACTURED HOUSING AND "KIT" HOMES

In recent years there has been a huge upswing in the construction of manufactured housing. Manufactured homes are homes in which all or some of the fabrication occurs away from the actual home site. In prior decades, manufactured housing fell into the same category as mobile homes. However, because these newer houses are actually permanently affixed to the real estate, and are never intended to be movable, most states have abolished the distinction between manufactured homes and traditional homes that are constructed entirely on the site.

C. COMMERCIAL PROPERTY

Commercial property consists of lots and buildings specifically designed for businesses. These properties range from doctors' offices to malls. They all share some common features, however. First, they are not designed as living spaces. People do not reside in commercial properties; they work in them. Second, commercial properties have design features not commonly seen in residential properties — parking lots, elevators, and trade and customer entrances. They must abide by specific federal and state regulations, such as the Americans with Disabilities Act, which dictates design features such as handicapped parking and ramps for wheelchair access.

1. RETAIL/WHOLESALE

Retail and wholesale properties are designed for what most of us would term normal business purposes. Retail properties include stores and shops of an almost infinite variety. Wholesale properties comprise warehouses and supply depots where the merchandise is stored. Wholesale establishments are also where business owners go to order the merchandise that they will later sell on a retail basis to members of the public.

---

[1] *Hughes v. Young*, 115 N. C. App. 325, 328, 444 S.E.2d 248, 260 (1994).

2. SHOPPING CENTERS AND MALLS

Malls and shopping centers have become increasingly important to the U.S. economy in the past several decades. Some shopping malls occupy hundreds of square acres and function much like small cities. There are numerous legal issues involved in the selection, construction, and maintenance of such a huge facility. The same concerns are found, to a lesser extent, in shopping centers and other areas specifically devoted to the business of providing merchandise to the public.

D. INDUSTRIAL PROPERTY

Another classification of property is industrial property. This consists of factories, research facilities, and other production facilities. Loud noises, noxious fumes, and dangerous manufacturing practices are often associated with these structures. Because of these drawbacks, industrial properties are usually located away from residential areas, where their offensive qualities can be contained, at least to an extent.

1. INDUSTRIAL PARKS

In recognition of the important role of industry, some towns and cities have created industrial parks. These parks are designed to group numerous industries in a central location, often close to major highways, electrical grids, and other infrastructure that assists the businesses in their operations. They are often landscaped and quite attractive.

2. LIGHT INDUSTRY/HEAVY INDUSTRY

Industrial property can be further broken down into two subcategories: light industry and heavy industry. Light industry includes any manufacturing plant or factory that does not emit excessive odors or machinery noises. Heavy industry, on the other hand, involves noxious odors, heavy traffic in and out of the plant, and/or excessive noise. Heavy industry is usually located as far from residential properties as possible, not only due to these factors, but also because some factories emit pollution and use dangerous chemicals in their manufacturing processes.

E. FARM AND RURAL PROPERTY

Farm and rural property is a designation for those areas reserved for agriculture. These areas are devoted to the cultivation of crops or livestock. They may also consist of vast tracts of land that are usually not zoned and are often taxed at a low rate.

F. RECREATIONAL PROPERTY

Recreational property consists of federal, state, county, or city-owned parks. These areas have been set aside specifically for the use of citizens and residents. They are usually located near wooded areas, lakes, or rivers, where people can congregate to enjoy the outdoors.

G. GOVERNMENT-OWNED LAND

The final classification of real estate is the vast acreage in the United States that is owned by federal or state governments. If you consider the size of military bases, prisons, governmental facilities, state-owned schools, and the numerous other government-owned properties, you will not be surprised to learn the government owns nearly one-third of the land in the continental United States.

 **ANNOTATED DOCUMENT**   REAL ESTATE SALES LISTING

Sales listings put a lot of information into a very small space

The owner indicates that the sale price is non-negotiable

Springfield subdivision; three-bedroom two-bath, garage, finished basement, central air and heat, $125,000 firm. Enjoy spacious living in this contemporary home that has all the amenities. Fireplace, luxurious master bath and state-of-the-art security system.

 **ETHICS**   AN INTRODUCTION

Ethical rules are important for all legal professionals. The state bar maintains strict rules about a wide range of activities associated with real estate practice, especially in the area of trust accounts. Later, we will see that clients routinely deposit large sums of money into attorney trust accounts prior to a real estate closing. This money, including the interest drawn on it, must be monitored with scrupulous care. Real estate ethical standards are strict in regard to attorney-client privilege and self-dealing. Other real estate professionals, including real estate brokers and agents, also have ethical standards. We explore the ethical concerns facing all these professionals in later chapters of this book.

JENNINGS v. BINDSEIL

JENNINGS v. BINDSEIL
258 S.W.3d 190, 192 -198, 258 S.W.3d 190 (Tex.App.–Austin, 2008)

OPINION

DIANE HENSON, Justice.

Johnie Jennings appeals from a summary judgment granted in favor of a coalition of landowners on Bindseil Lane in Comal County, Texas. The Bindseil Landowners brought suit against Jennings under the Texas Declaratory Judgment Act (TDJA) and the Texas Property Code, seeking a declaratory judgment that a certain structure placed by Jennings on his property violated a deed restriction prohibiting mobile homes on the property. The Bindseil Landowners further sought a declaratory judgment that Jennings had proper notice that his act of placing the structure on his property would violate the deed restriction. The trial court granted the Bindseil Landowners' motion for summary judgment on their requests for declaratory relief. The trial court also granted the Bindseil Landowners' request for a permanent injunction, preventing Jennings from maintaining the structure on his property and requiring that he remove the structure and all associated equipment. Because we hold that a question of fact exists regarding whether the deed restriction prohibits the type of structure Jennings placed on his property, we reverse the trial court's order and remand the case for trial.

BACKGROUND

In 1999, Jennings purchased 2.25 acres in rural Comal County from Allen and Betty Knodel. In 2004, Jennings purchased a modular home, also referred to as industrialized housing, for assembly on the property.[2] When Jennings's home was delivered to his property on December 22, 2004, a neighboring landowner objected to the delivery, claiming that the structure violated a deed restriction against mobile homes that was applicable to Jennings's property.

Industrialized housing is governed by chapter 1202 of the Texas Occupations Code, while manufactured housing is governed by chapter 1201. "Industrialized housing" is defined as:

A residential structure that is:

---

[2] Because this case revolves around the applicability of certain terminology to describe various types of housing, we will use the terms "modular home" and "industrialized housing" interchangeably to refer to the type of structure defined in § 1202.002(a) of the Texas Occupations Code. We will use the term "manufactured housing" to refer to the type of structure defined in § 1201.003(9) of the Texas Occupations Code.

(1) designed for the occupancy of one or more families;

(2) constructed in one or more modules or constructed using one or more modular components built at a location other than the permanent site; and

(3) designed to be used as a permanent residential structure when the module or the modular component is transported to the permanent site and erected or installed on a permanent foundation system. Tex. Occ.Code Ann. § 1202.002(a) (West 2004).

"Manufactured housing" is defined as "a HUD-code manufactured home or a mobile home." Tex. Occ.Code Ann. § 1201.003(15) (West 2004 & Supp.2007). According to § 1201.003(9) of the Texas Occupations Code:

"HUD-code manufactured home":

(A) means a structure:

(i) constructed on or after June 15, 1976, according to the rules of the United States Department of Housing and Urban Development;

(ii) built on a permanent chassis;

(iii) designed for use as a dwelling with or without a permanent foundation when the structure is connected to the required utilities;

(iv) transportable in one or more sections; and

(v) in the traveling mode, at least eight body feet in width or at least 40 body feet in length or, when erected on site, at least 320 square feet;

(B) includes the plumbing, heating, air conditioning, and electrical systems of the home; and

(C) does not include a recreational vehicle as defined by 24 C.F.R. Section 3282.8(g).Tex. Occ.Code Ann. § 1201.003(9) (West 2004 & Supp.2007).

The statutory definition of "mobile home" is essentially identical to that of a "HUD-code manufactured home" except that a mobile home is a structure constructed before June 15, 1976 and is not required to meet HUD requirements. See Tex. Occ.Code Ann. § 1201.003(17) (West 2004 & Supp.2007).

The deed restriction at issue was written by Dan Bindseil in 1978 and states:

No mobile home or homes or temporary houses or residences shall be placed upon or remain upon the property conveyed hereby, nor shall such property be used for the purposes of a tourist park, trailer court, mobile home park or community, nor for an overnight camping or trailer facility.

Jennings concedes that the deed restriction applies to his property and that he had notice of the restriction when he purchased the property. However, Jennings argues that after researching modular homes and contacting the state agency responsible for regulating modular homes, he came to the conclusion that a modular home would not violate the deed restriction against mobile homes.

Jennings's home was delivered in the form of two factory-constructed modular units mounted on a flat-bed truck and driven onto the property. The units were then connected on site and attached to the property on a permanent concrete foundation. The home required extensive on-site finish work, including completion of the roof and installation of dormers. The house plans for the home call for front and back porches and a carport to be installed, but the porches and carport were not completed, due to the injunction resulting from this litigation, which prohibited any further work on the home.

On February 14, 2005, the Bindseil Landowners filed suit against Jennings to enforce the deed restriction against mobile homes. Jennings counter-claimed, requesting a declaratory judgment that his home was not subject to the restriction. The parties filed cross motions for summary judgment, and the trial court granted the Bindseil Landowners' motion, declaring that the deed restriction prohibits modular homes, that Jennings's home was in violation of the deed restriction, and that Jennings was on notice that his acts were in violation of the restriction. The court also granted a permanent injunction, prohibiting Jennings from maintaining the home and requiring him to remove it from the property within 30 days. The trial court denied the Bindseil Landowners' request to impose statutory penalties, but granted their request for attorney's fees. Jennings's traditional and no-evidence motions for summary judgment were denied.

Jennings argues on appeal that the deed restriction does not apply to his modular home. In the alternative, he argues that the deed restriction is ambiguous and that fact questions exist regarding whether the deed restriction applies to his home and whether he was on notice that his home violated the deed restriction. He further argues that the Bindseil Landowners are not entitled to injunctive relief because they failed to conclusively establish that they would be harmed by the presence of a modular home on his property.

We review a trial court's grant of injunctive relief for an abuse of discretion. Operation Rescue–Nat'l v. Planned Parenthood, 975 S.W.2d 546, 560 (Tex.1998). An abuse of discretion occurs when a trial court acts in an unreasonable or arbitrary manner, or without reference to guiding rules or principles. Holubec v. Brandenberger, 214 S.W.3d 650, 657 (Tex.App.-Austin 2006, no pet.).

DISCUSSION

Deed Restrictions

Covenants restricting the free use of land are not favored by the courts, but will be enforced if they are clearly worded and confined to a lawful purpose. Wilmoth v. Wilcox, 734 S.W.2d 656, 657 (Tex.1987). When the language of a restrictive covenant is unambiguous, the Texas Property Code requires that the restrictive covenant be liberally construed to give effect to its purpose and intent. Tex. Prop.Code Ann. § 202.003(a) (West 2007). However, if the language is found to be ambiguous, the restrictive covenant is construed strictly against the party seeking to enforce the restriction, and all doubts must be resolved in favor of the free and unrestricted use of the property. Wilmoth, 734 S.W.2d at 657. The words and phrases in the restriction must be given their commonly accepted meaning as of the date the restriction was written and must not be enlarged, extended, changed, or stretched by construction. Id. at 657–58.

Restrictive covenants are subject to the general rules of contract construction. Pilarcik v. Emmons, 966 S.W.2d 474, 478 (Tex.1998). If a restrictive covenant is subject to more than one reasonable interpretation so that the intention of the parties cannot be determined, the restriction is ambiguous. See Columbia Gas Transmission Corp. v. New Ulm Gas, Ltd., 940 S.W.2d 587, 589 (Tex.1996). Whether a restrictive covenant is ambiguous is a question of law that must be decided by examining the covenant as a whole in light of the circumstances present when it was drafted. See id.

The deed restriction on Jennings's property prohibits "mobile homes." To determine if ambiguity exists, we must look to the common and ordinary meaning of the term "mobile home" as of the date the restriction was drafted to determine if the prohibition on mobile homes is susceptible to two or more meanings. See Dempsey v. Apache Shores Prop. Owners Assoc., Inc., 737 S.W.2d 589, 592 (Tex.App.-Austin 1987, no writ).

"Mobile home" is a term generally used to describe factory-built residential structures. The terminology used to describe these structures has evolved over the years to keep pace with innovations in technology and design. The original term generally associated with such housing was "house trailer." As the Texas Supreme Court observed in Wilmoth, 734 S.W.2d at 658, "in the late 1960's the term 'mobile home' began to replace the term 'house trailer.' In the late 1970's the industry applied the term 'manufactured homes' to the products, replacing the name 'mobile home.' " As the industry began to make design improvements and use different names to avoid negative connotations associated with original types of factory-built housing, legislative changes were made to reflect the new terminology. See Dempsey, 737 S.W.2d at 592 ("At the time the restricted covenants were drafted between 1968 and 1972, there was statutorily only the 'mobile home.' When the need became apparent, legislation was enacted to protect consumers and the terms 'manufactured homes,' 'modular homes,' and later 'industrialized housing' were employed. . . .").

As the terms used to describe various forms of factory-built housing have evolved, the regulation of such structures has also become highly specialized. Currently, manufactured housing is regulated by the Texas Department of Housing and Community Affairs (TDHCA), while modular homes are regulated by the Texas Department of Licensing and Regulation (TDLR). However, this Court has recognized that, while a statutory scheme has evolved that differentiates manufactured homes from modular homes, "the differences between the two are technical and minor." Id.

Jennings argues that the current regulatory, statutory, and other distinctions between his home and other types of factory-built housing are sufficient to exclude his home from the language of the deed restriction. According to a letter from TDLR sent to Jennings on February 22, 2005:

The primary difference between an industrialized (modular) home and a manufactured (HUD) home are:

a. The codes to which the homes are built. Modular housing in the State of Texas is constructed to the same codes as site- built housing. Manufactured housing is constructed to Federal HUD code standards;
b. Modular homes must be installed on a permanent foundation system;
c. Titles are not issued for modular homes. Once installed the home becomes part of the real property; and
d. A municipality may not discriminate against modular homes built under the IHB program from being placed inside city limits or restrict these buildings to areas zoned for "manufactured" housing. (Please reference § 1202.251(b) of the Occupations Code).

Jennings emphasizes the fact that municipalities may not discriminate against modular homes in zoning decisions or adopt regulations that are more restrictive for modular homes than for site-built homes, including restricting the location of modular homes to areas zoned for manufactured housing. Significantly, however, while a municipality may not adopt a regulation "that is more restrictive for industrialized housing than that required" for site-built housing, the statute further states, "This section does not . . . affect deed restrictions." Tex. Occ.Code Ann. § 1202.253(e), (f)(2) (West 2004 & Supp.2007). This language makes it clear that the legislature recognized the existence of deed restrictions prohibiting factory-built housing and indicated a clear intention that such restrictions were to remain unaffected by subsequent regulatory and statutory distinctions.

The deed restriction at issue here was written in 1978, before the terms "manufactured housing," "modular housing," or "industrialized housing" were commonly used. Because we must "look to the common and ordinary meaning of the term 'mobile home' as of the date the covenant was drafted," Dempsey, 737 S.W.2d at 592, the current distinctions between modular homes and manufactured homes are not dispositive. As we noted in Dempsey, "the covenant drafters had no way to predict these subsequent technical statutory distinctions, and the language they chose should be viewed in that light." Id. at 593.

Because the covenant drafters did not have the benefit of subsequent technical statutory distinctions at the time the deed restriction on "mobile homes" was written, we hold that the covenant is unambiguous in its prohibition of mobile homes and any generic successors, regardless of minor changes in construction technology, design, or regulation. To hold otherwise would essentially require drafters of restrictive covenants to foresee an infinite array of technological advances that might take place in the future and to draft a restriction prohibiting structures described by terminology that does not yet exist. Furthermore, "restrictive covenants would be rendered meaningless if they could be implicitly subverted by legislatively changing the name of that which is prohibited." Id. at 593. Therefore, we hold that the restrictive covenant prohibiting mobile homes is unambiguous as written and must be liberally construed to give effect to its purpose and intent, which was to prohibit mobile homes and their generic successors. See Tex. Prop.Code Ann. § 202.003(a). Thus, the question at hand is whether Jennings's home constitutes a mobile home or a generic successor, notwithstanding the label used by statute or regulatory authorities to describe such a structure in 2008.

However, when we held that the deed restriction against mobile homes in Dempsey was unambiguous, a jury had already made a factual finding that the structure at issue — a double-wide manufactured home — actually qualified as a mobile home. See id. at 593 ("Double-wides were considered 'mobile homes' at the time the covenants were drafted and the jury found, based on considerable evidence, that despite improvements in quality and appearance, they are still 'mobile homes' today. We cannot say that finding is legally or factually erroneous.").

In the present case, we do not have the benefit of a jury determination regarding whether the structure Jennings placed on his property constitutes a mobile home or a generic successor as prohibited by the deed restriction.[3] As a result, summary judgment is improper because a fact question exists regarding whether Jennings's home qualifies as

---

[3] Due to the differences between manufactured homes and modular homes, we acknowledge that the issue of whether Jennings's home constitutes a "mobile home" or a generic successor may be a closer question than the determination made in Dempsey, 737 S.W.2d at 591, and Wilmoth, 734 S.W.2d at 657, that a double-wide manufactured home is a "mobile home." While Jennings's home may not have differed significantly in appearance from two double-wide manufactured homes labeled as "modular units" and connected on site, such a determination is necessarily a fact issue for the jury to decide.

the type of structure that the deed restriction prohibits. Therefore, we reverse the trial court's judgment declaring that Jennings's home violates the deed restriction against mobile homes and remand the cause for a determination of whether Jennings's home constitutes a mobile home or a generic successor of a mobile home as prohibited by the deed restriction, giving effect to the liberal construction required for unambiguous deed restrictions. See Tex. Prop.Code Ann. § 202.003(a).

NOTICE

A purchaser is bound only by those restrictive covenants of which he has actual or constructive notice. Davis v. Huey, 620 S.W.2d 561, 565–66 (Tex.1981). Jennings concedes that he had notice of the deed restriction prohibiting mobile homes, but argues that because of his independent research and the information he received from government agencies, he was acting on a good-faith belief that his *198 home did not violate the restriction. Jennings's good-faith belief, however, is irrelevant. A purchaser is bound by restrictive covenants of which he has notice, regardless of whether he believed that his actions violated the restriction. See Pheasant Run Homeowners Assoc., Inc. v. Kastor, 47 S.W.3d 747, 753–54 (Tex.App.-Houston [14th Dist.] 2001, pet. denied) (holding that property owners who are aware of deed restrictions and accompanying guidelines are considered to be on notice of such restrictions despite believing that guidelines are unclear and inapplicable); Tien Tao Assoc., Inc. v. Kingsbridge Park Cmty. Assoc., Inc., 953 S.W.2d 525, 528 (Tex.App.-Houston, 1st Dist. 1997, no pet.) (holding that property owner could not argue it had no notice of deed restrictions simply because guidelines were unclear when owner acknowledged having copy of such restrictions).

However, because we have determined that a fact issue exists regarding whether Jennings's home is prohibited by the deed restriction, we also reverse and remand the issue of whether Jennings had notice that his actions in placing such a structure on his property violated the deed restriction. We cannot conclude that Jennings was on notice that his actions violated the restriction when there has been no final determination regarding whether a violation actually occurred. As a result, the trial court's declaratory judgment that Jennings had notice that his actions violated the restriction is also reversed and remanded.

THE PERMANENT INJUNCTION

Jennings argues that the Bindseil Landowners have not established that they will suffer an actual and substantial injury because of the presence of a modular home on Jennings's property. While the general rule is that one seeking injunctive relief must establish an actual and substantial injury, "there is a well-settled exception to the general rule in restrictive covenant cases." Gigowski v. Russell, 718 S.W.2d 16, 21 (Tex.App.-Tyler 1986, no writ.). A covenant restricting the use of land may be enforced by injunction without a showing of any particular amount of damages, provided there is a distinct or substantial breach of the restrictive covenant. Id. However, because we have determined that the Bindseil Landowners failed to conclusively establish through summary-judgment evidence that Jennings committed a distinct or substantial breach of the deed restriction against mobile homes, we also reverse the trial court's judgment issuing a permanent injunction.

ATTORNEY'S FEES

In its order granting summary judgment in favor of the Bindseil Landowners, the trial court granted the Bindseil Landowners' request for attorney's fees. Because we have reversed and remanded this case for a factual determination regarding whether the structure placed on Jennings's property was in violation of the deed restriction against mobile homes, we also remand the issue of attorney's fees for the trial court's reconsideration pending the outcome of the necessary factual determination.

CONCLUSION

Because a genuine issue of material fact exists regarding whether the structure Jennings placed on his property constitutes a mobile home or a generic successor as prohibited by the deed restriction applicable to his property, we reverse the trial court's judgment and remand this case for further proceedings consistent with this opinion.

CASE QUESTIONS

1   What was the nature of the action brought by the Bindseil Landowners?
2   According to the Texas Occupations Code, how is a residential structure defined?
3   What does the court say about deed restrictions and covenants?
4   Explain the court's reasoning concerning "generic successors" in restrictive covenants and the impact that it has on the court's decision.

SKILLS YOU NEED IN THE REAL WORLD

HOW A PARALEGAL CAN DO SOME BASIC INVESTIGATIVE WORK

Most paralegals are not trained to carry out investigations. Many would be surprised to learn that knowing basic investigative techniques could be a real asset in the marketplace. When a firm needs basic information about a case, the most common method of obtaining it is for the attorney to investigate the basic details and then rely on discovery to ferret out additional details. However, there are times when this process is not efficient. Some cases do not have the financial resources to justify an attorney's time. In such a situation, the other alternative — a private detective — may also be too costly. Not all clients can afford the added expense of a private investigator. However, a paralegal who knows some basic investigative techniques can learn a great deal about a case, with less of a cost investment, and that paralegal will become even more indispensable to the firm in the process.

WHAT FACTS DO YOU NEED?

Before a paralegal can begin to investigate a claim, she must first decide what facts are the most important to discover. For a plaintiff's firm, the most important facts are those that support the cause of action. Without that support, there can be no valid claim.

USING PUBLIC RECORDS TO GATHER INFORMATION

Suppose your firm is investigating the defendant (or the person who will be the defendant if the lawsuit is actually filed). What public records can help a paralegal learn more information about this person? The best place to start is the local courthouse.

THE COURTHOUSE

The local courthouse is a gold mine of information, if you know where to look. Consider the following resources:

- **Clerk's Office** The local clerk's office maintains records about all civil and criminal cases in the county. Using the computer databases, a paralegal can learn whether someone has been sued, divorced, or convicted of a crime.
- **Deed Room or Registrar's Office** Sometimes called the registrar's office, or the land office, the deed room is where all records of real estate transactions are stored. In this office, a paralegal can find out what real estate a defendant owns (useful in evaluating the likelihood of enforcing a judgment against him).
- **Tax Office** The tax office is required to keep extensive records about real estate and other items. In some tax offices, you can even see a digital photo of the house. In larger counties, such as metropolitan areas, this information is available at public access terminals. A picture of the house and all of the details are just a mouse click away.

INTERNET

The Internet also offers some valuable research tools. There are numerous sites that allow you to search out a person's address, telephone number, email address, and other information. However, there are also questionable sites that claim to provide you with a complete background on a person for a nominal fee. Unless the site is one that you recognize as a reputable company, you should avoid such sites. There is a great deal of free information available about persons, but if you plan on paying for research, the best bet is still a private detective.

Keep these sources in mind if you are ever called upon to do some basic investigative work in a case.

ONLINE RESEARCH

Each chapter of this text includes a section called "Skills You Need in the Real World." Its purpose is to provide you with practical, hands-on information that you can put to immediate use in real estate practice. We cover topics as varied as reviewing probate records, researching liens, and preparing HUD settlement statements.

In this introductory chapter, one of the most important skills you can acquire as a real estate professional is the ability to quickly and efficiently research real property questions. In the past, paralegals and attorneys relied on printed materials, but modern practice relies a great deal on the Internet. Not only can you find excellent free and pay legal research sites on the Internet, but you can also locate a wealth of real estate information ranging from online real estate transactions to Google Earth and aerial photographs to sites that will give you directions from your current location to the property itself. You should review each of these chapters for the specific web sites given, but also develop your own helpful web sites and keep them handy. More and more public records and other information will be available online so that your problem as a paralegal will not be whether you can find something, but how to find the most reliable information in a sea of data.

CHAPTER SUMMARY

Property can be divided into two broad categories: real property and personal property. Personal property consists of moveable items that are not permanently attached to real estate. Real property, on the other hand, consists of land and anything permanently affixed to land. Real estate has specific and unique characteristics. Among its physical characteristics: Land occupies a fixed point on the globe. No two parcels of real estate are identical. Land is immovable and permanent. Among its economic characteristics: Land generally appreciates in value over time. It also makes an excellent investment. There is a market for real estate, just as there are markets for other products. The real estate market consists of buyers and sellers, as well as professionals involved in facilitating the sale, funding the sale, and making sure that the legalities of the sale are observed. One way of classifying real estate is by the way that it is used. Unimproved land is vacant land that has no structures placed upon it. Land can be further categorized into residential property, which is reserved for living space; commercial property, which is designed for businesses; and industrial property, which is reserved for manufacturing and warehousing products.

REVIEW QUESTIONS

1   What is the definition of real property?
2   What is the Statute of Frauds?
3   What are some of the primary differences between real and personal property?
4   What are some of the aspects of real property law that make it unique?
5   List and explain some of the physical characteristics of land.
6   Describe the economic characteristics of real property.
7   What makes real estate such an attractive investment?
8   Explain equity.
9   What is the real estate market?
10 What is unimproved land?
11 List and explain the various classifications of real property.
12 What are the elements that make a residence qualify as an apartment?
13 What is the difference between a condominium and a townhouse?
14 When does a mobile home or manufactured home qualify as real property?
15 What is the difference between residential and commercial property?
16 How much land in the United States is government-owned?
17 Why are ethical rules important for real estate practitioners?
18 Explain how Fannie Mae's software may have contributed to the mortgage meltdown in the U.S.

PRACTICAL APPLICATIONS

1   Go online and find a local house for sale. What can you learn about the home from the Internet listing? What is the sale price? How many square feet is the house? Are the sellers offering any incentives to prospective buyers? Does the home come with a warranty?
2   Locate web sites that explain how and why the real estate market in the U.S. and other countries has suffered so severely in recent years.

WEB SITES

Real Property Law: Legal Research Institute
http://www.law.cornell.edu/wex/real_property

Nolo's Plain English Dictionary—Real Estate
http://www.nolo.com/dictionary/real-estate-term.html

New York State Bar — Real Property Law
http://www.nysba.org

Search string: Real Property Law section
Real Estate Law (HG.org)
http://www.hg.org/realest.html

Real property vs. personal property
http://www.realestateabc.com/insights/property.htm

TERMS AND PHRASES

Apartment	Improvements	Statute of Frauds
Condominium	In rem jurisdiction	Townhouse
Equity	Personal jurisdiction	Unimproved land

SIGNIFICANT CASES

Barber v. Dixon, 62 N.C. App. 455, 302 S.E.2d 915 (1983)
Owens v. Ousey, 241 S.W.3d 124 (Tex. App.-Austin, 2007)
John Skotzke Concrete Const., Inc. v. Kowalczyk, 736 N.W.2d 543 (Wis. App., 2007)
Finger v. Daskam, 301 Wis. 2d 751, 731 N.W.2d 385 (Wis. App., 2007)
Greentree Servicing, LLC v. Decanio, 948 So.2d 1033 (Fla. App. 5 Dist., 2007)

Estates in Real Property

Focus of This Chapter

This chapter provides an in-depth explanation of the rights, duties, and responsibilities that derive from estates, as well as the implications of various types of estates on the rights and abilities of the owners.

Chapter Learning Objectives

After completing this chapter, you should be able to:

- Explain the rights created by fee simple absolute estates
- Define the differences between conditional fee estates, such as fee simple determinable and fee simple on a condition subsequent
- Describe how a life estate is created
- Explain the types of estates available to two or more owners of a single parcel of real estate
- Define the rights and obligations of joint owners

INTRODUCTION

In this chapter, we explore the various types of ownership of real property. These property rights, or estates, range from complete ownership in fee simple to estates with fewer rights, such as life estates. We also examine the rights and responsibilities of two or more individuals who own property together.

REAL PROPERTY ESTATES

An estate is a bundle of rights that accompany title to property. Different estates have different rights. There are numerous types of estates, from fee simple

Estate
A right to use or enjoy real property.

absolute to life estates and several different forms of concurrent ownership estates. **Estates** can be either present estates or future estates. A present estate confers an immediate benefit on the owner. A future estate, on the other hand, will only confer a right at some point in the future. For example, a testator can write a will that states that her parcel of real estate will go to a specific heir on the testator's death. The heir does not have an immediate right. The heir cannot, for example, mortgage the property, sell it, or take any action on it until the testator dies. The heir has a potential future interest. In the first part of this chapter, we focus on present estates, but future estates figure prominently in our discussion of life estates.

When there is a dispute about the type of estate involved, or when the estate was created, courts follow a general rule that what the parties intended is generally controlling. If the parties said that they intended a specific type of estate, such as fee simple, the courts will work to interpret the language so that such an estate is recognized. If there is a dispute about when the estate is created, courts opt for a test that provides that an estate was created as early as possible. These rules give some guidance and a measure of predictability to court actions on estate questions.

We define an estate in land as the quality of title that an owner possesses to use and enjoy the property, and the extent of that ownership.

FEE SIMPLE ESTATE

Fee simple absolute
The real property estate in which an owner has the right to give, sell, mortgage, and lease the property, among other rights.

A person who has **fee simple** ownership in property has the most complete set of rights that it is possible to have in a parcel of real estate. She can give, sell, mortgage, use, and possess the property. Fee simple owners possess all of the following rights:

- The right to make a gift of the property to another
- The right to put the property up for sale
- The right to raise crops on the property and to sell those crops
- The right to use and possess the property
- The right to mortgage the property
- The right to lease the property to others

Fee simple rights are often described as an assorted "bundle" of rights. When a person acquires title in fee simple to a parcel, this bundle of rights is conveyed along with title. Imagining fee simple rights as a bundle has the added advantage of being able to describe the owner's ability to convey some of the rights to others, while retaining other rights. The classic example is a landlord-tenant relationship. A landlord conveys some of her fee simple rights to a tenant. The tenant receives the right to use, possess, and enjoy the property, while the landlord retains all the other rights. Because the landlord retains the right to sell and mortgage the property, the tenant cannot do so. On the other hand, the landlord no longer has the right to possess the property and cannot, for instance, move onto the premises after creating a lease arrangement with the tenant. The landlord no longer has that right and will not get it back until the rental agreement terminates. We explore landlord-tenant relationships in greater detail in Chapter 7.

The word "fee" originated under English law and referred to a grant from the king to an individual landowner. The fee was the emblem of the owner's obligation to provide military or tax support to the monarch. In Chapter 8, when we discuss the details of a typical real estate transaction, we will see that much of the ceremony that accompanied a real estate transaction still exists in one form or another in modern real estate practice.

Under the modern approach to real estate law, a fee simple absolute estate not only confers specific rights on the owner, but also guarantees that the parcel itself is free from encumbrances. A fee simple title is one that has no liens or other impediments that would prevent the owner from freely transferring it to another.

Fee simple absolute title is the highest set of rights that a person can possess in real property.

ISSUE AT A GLANCE

A. RIGHTS OF FEE SIMPLE OWNERS

An owner in fee simple has the highest and best form of title in real property, but that does not mean that the owner can do anything with the property. All owners have limitations on their rights, whether imposed by law or practice. Fee simple owners also assume certain obligations when they take title to property. For instance, we will see in Chapter 10 that real estate owners are limited by public laws and private acts. Laws can prevent an owner from carrying out specific actions on her property, such as operating a business in a residential area. Private acts, such as restrictive covenants, can go even further and prevent the homeowner from putting specific structures on the property or even building a home with an unapproved architectural style.

In addition to these restrictions on fee simple titles, there are legal conditions that may have a significant impact on the owner's use of the property. These legal restraints that can be placed on fee simple absolute titles come in two forms: fee simple determinable and fee simple on a condition subsequent estates.

B. CONDITIONAL FEE SIMPLE ESTATES

Although we have said that fee simple absolute ownership is the highest and best form of real estate title, there are provisions that can limit even this estate.

When a seller (grantor) places conditions on fee simple ownership, this can be referred to as fee simple defeasible estates. Fee simple defeasible estates fall into one of two categories:

1 Fee simple determinable
2 Fee simple subject to a condition subsequent

When either of these categories exists, an owner who believes she has taken unconditional title to property actually has a limitation. Because of the legal difficulties that these two conditional fee simple estates have created over the decades, most practitioners no longer use either estate to limit the way that property can be used. These estates are too cumbersome and fraught with legal problems. However, they do remain in existence.

FIGURE 2-1

Ten States with the Highest Percentage of Seasonal, Recreational, or Occasional Use Homes: 2010.

Area	Total housing units	For seasonal, recreational, or occasional use	Percent
United States....................	131,704,730	4,649,298	3.5
Maine.................................	721,830	118,310	16.4
Vermont..............................	322,539	50,198	15.6
New Hampshire	614,754	63,910	10.4
Alaska	306,967	27,901	9.1
Delaware	405,885	35,939	8.9
Montana..............................	482,825	38,510	8.0
Wisconsin	2,624,358	193,046	7.4
Florida	8,989,580	657,070	7.3
Arizona	2,844,526	184,327	6.5
Idaho..................................	667,796	41,660	6.2

Source: U.S. Census Bureau, *2010 Census Summary File 1.*

Before we discuss the particulars of either of these limiting conditions on a fee simple title, we first address a more fundamental question: Why would anyone impose a condition on fee simple absolute title? The answer is simple: The seller has specific wishes for the property and wants a legal method to enforce these wishes. Consider Example 2-1.

EXAMPLE 2-1

Ramon wants to buy Carla's property, but Carla is reluctant. She has always wanted to deed her property to the state so that it will be used as a park or nature preserve. Ramon suggests deeding it to him, but inserting a condition that will satisfy this desire. Carla can deed the property to him as fee simple, but insert a condition that the property can only be used as a park or nature preserve. Ramon will have complete ownership in the property, but if he ever violates the condition, either the title will revert to Carla or Carla can sue him for damages.

These days, there are other methods Carla can use to enforce her wishes for the property's use, but in the past Carla did not have such options. The only way for her to be sure about how the property would be used was to create a fee simple with a condition. The only difference between the two conditional fee simple estates is what happens when the condition is violated.

1. FEE SIMPLE DETERMINABLE

A fee simple determinable estate is created when a person transfers property to another with a stipulation that the property be used in a certain way, outlined in Example 2-1. Carla conveys her property to Ramon, but inserts a stipulation that the property should always be used as a park or nature preserve. If Carla includes language in the deed that automatically conveys title to the property back to her or her heirs, the condition is described as fee simple determinable. Under this classification, when Ramon, or anyone else who later owns the property, violates the condition, the title will automatically revert to someone else. Obviously, this is a drastic measure and one that might cause future buyers to hesitate to buy the property. After all, who wants to spend a great deal of money to buy a parcel of real estate only to learn that title to it might automatically shift to someone else if she violates a condition? The other problem with fee simple determinable estates is that once they are imposed on property, they remain with the title as it passes from owner to owner. Although the original arrangement in Example 2-1 was between Ramon and Carla, it binds future owners as well.

Because of these problems, modern real estate practitioners do not use fee simple determinable estates. Courts have also been extremely wary of these conditions and have routinely struck down deed clauses where the language creating a fee simple determinable estate is ambiguous or poorly worded. However, fee simple determinable estates are still legal and a person can create one if she desires to do so. Modern court decisions require the seller to insert language in the deed that specifically provides that upon the happening of a particular event, title to the property will vest in another. Without that specificity, courts are inclined to ignore the condition and treat the title as a normal fee simple absolute.

2. FEE SIMPLE ON A CONDITION SUBSEQUENT

A fee simple on a condition subsequent closely resembles, and is often confused with, fee simple determinable. The distinguishing feature between them is that while the fee simple determinable automatically transfers title on the happening of a specific event, a fee simple on a condition subsequent gives the grantor (or grantor's heirs) the right to challenge title. When a deed contains a fee simple on a condition subsequent and a future owner stops using the property in the way prescribed by the original owner, the owner's heirs can file suit to have title awarded to them. They will not, however, automatically receive title to the property.

Both fee simple determinable and fee simple on a condition subsequent estates raise a host of potential problems when they are used. The language used to create them is often strictly interpreted by the courts, rendering them ineffective if they do not follow the exact letter of the law. The other problem with both estates is that they frequently do not achieve their purpose. Because courts scrutinize both so closely, a person who wished to limit the way that land can be used in the future would be better served using some other method, such as restrictive covenants, covered in detail in Chapter 10.

Tech Topic
ONLINE ACCESS TO REAL ESTATE RECORDS

As recently as a couple of decades ago, the only way to research real estate records was to trudge down to the county courthouse and sift through reels of microfilm indexes. Researching efforts improved vastly when property indexes were computerized, but a trip to the courthouse was still necessary.

Then came the Internet, and most localities were quick to make their records available for purchase online. Armed with only a property owner's name or a parcel number, you can locate real estate records from your home computer, including deeds, mortgages, liens, reconveyances, and releases. In most cases, you will be able to view only the essential elements, such as the name of the property holder and the type of record. To see the details, you will usually have to order the complete document and pay a fee for it. Once you have paid the fee, the documents are either viewable immediately as a PDF file or mailed to you within a few days.

To find property records online, visit your county government's web site. Look for a link to recorded deeds, real estate records, or something similar. Chances are you will find a searchable database to help track down what you are seeking.

LIFE ESTATES

In the last section, we saw that fee simple determinable and fee simple on a condition subsequent estates are rarely used. However, that is not true of life estates. They are extremely common.

Life estate
An estate granted to a specific person, allowing that person to use, possess, enjoy, and take profits from the real estate, but only as long as the person lives. On the possessor's death, title vests in a remainderman.

A **life estate** is created when an owner leaves her property to another person, but only as long as the person lives. When the person dies, the title to the property automatically vests in someone else. The typical formula used to create a life estate is as simple as: To *A*, for her life, then to *B*.

An owner might include this provision in a deed or a will. As you can see, life estates are relatively easy to create. Unlike fee simple determinable estates, they are not closely scrutinized. The reason that they are not given the same level of review is that, unlike fee simple estates, they are simple and straightforward devices that provide for an orderly conveyance of property. In the example above, there are very few complications that can arise. Under the life estate, *A* will receive the property from the owner and hold it for *A*'s life. When *A* dies, the title to the property automatically vests in *B*. Of course, there are always complications, but the basic system works very well.

The person who receives the benefit of a life estate is often referred to as a life tenant, or the holder of a life estate. We will use the term *life tenant* to describe this person's estate. A life tenant has almost all of the rights to the property that the original owner enjoyed. A life tenant can possess, use, and grow crops on the real estate. A life tenant can even sell the property, but the person who purchases it has an important limitation. The new purchaser can only possess the property as long as *A* is alive. When *A* dies, title to the property will automatically transfer to *B*. It is unlikely that anyone would be willing to buy the property under this limitation, but it does point out the broad extent of a life tenant's rights to the property. Thus, a life tenant could be described as possessing fee simple rights with a time limit.

A. HISTORICAL BASIS OF LIFE ESTATES

The reason that life estates were created in the first place was to provide a mechanism to allow a surviving spouse to retain rights in the marital property after the death of the other spouse. This was particularly true in the past when wives did not enjoy the same rights as husbands. A surviving husband was free to take any action with the marital property, but a surviving wife faced many legal hurdles. To ensure that wives could retain the marital home after the husband's death, states created the concepts of "dower" and "curtesy."

1. DOWER AND CURTESY

Under the ancient concepts of **dower and curtesy**, a surviving spouse had a legal right to a priority claim on a fraction of the marital property. This fraction could be from one-third to one-half of the property acquired by the couple during their marriage. The terms actually mean the same thing, but dower refers to the amount that a surviving wife could claim, while curtesy refers to the claim raised by a surviving husband. Under old state laws, the amount that could be claimed varied depending on the sex of the surviving partner. However, those laws have been ruled unconstitutional because they are based on sex discrimination. As a result, most states have abolished dower and curtesy and replaced it with **forced share** or **statutory share**. Under either concept, a surviving spouse is automatically granted a life estate in the marital residence and has other rights to checking and deposit accounts, retirement accounts, and other issues that arise under estate proceedings.

Dower and curtesy
A provision of common law that provided that a set portion of the marital property would automatically vest in a surviving spouse. Dower refers to the portion allotted to a surviving wife, while curtesy referred to the portion allotted to a surviving husband.

Forced share
The statutory claim that a surviving spouse has in the marital estate.

Statutory share
Synonymous with forced share.

B. REMAINDERMEN

In the example set out above, *A* receives a life estate and upon *A*'s death the title to the property automatically vests in *B*. In this example, *B* is referred to as a remainderman. A **remainderman** is someone who has future interest in real estate, but no present interest. (In some states, this future interest is referred to as a reversionary interest.) This division between present interests and future interests is important

Remainderman
A person with a future interest in property, but no present rights.

and merits further discussion. A person with a present interest has the immediate right to the property. This person can make changes to the property, sell it, give it away, and carry out any of the actions that we normally associate with fee simple absolute title. However, a person with a future interest has severe limitations. Her interest in the property will not vest until a future date. In a life estate, the remainderman will not receive the property until the life tenant dies. Until that time, the remainderman has few legal rights. The remainderman cannot, for example, enter the premises and make changes to the property. A remainderman has no present right to use or enjoy the property. However, the remainderman does have some rights. Because the property will eventually vest in the remainderman, if the remainderman observes that the life tenant is destroying the property, she can bring suit to stop the life tenant. The life tenant's action is referred to as engaging in **waste.**

Waste
An action by a life tenant that adversely affects the nature or quality of the remainderman's future interest in real property.

C. WASTE

When we use the term *waste* in the context of a life estate, we are talking about any action by the life tenant that adversely affects the quality of the estate that will eventually transfer to the remainderman. In this context, waste takes on a very specific and limited meaning. A remainderman cannot sue for any action that could potentially cause a diminution in value of her future interest. Instead, the remainderman must allege specific actions taken by the life tenant that could result in a total loss of value. Examples of waste include destruction of fields where crops would be raised, failure to maintain the premises, failure to pay property taxes, and any other action that affects the value of the property. A remainderman can, for instance, bring suit to prevent the seizure of the property for back taxes or to satisfy a civil judgment against the life tenant.

A life estate can have important consequences in taxation. For instance, a life estate created by one spouse for the other can qualify under the federal marital deduction rule, meaning that the surviving spouse may be able to postpone estate taxes until he or she also dies. However, if the life tenant and remainderman agree to sell the property and extinguish the life estate, the tax situation will change dramatically and may be classified as a taxable gift.

D. COURT DOCTRINES THAT AFFECT LIFE ESTATES

There are several court doctrines that can affect a life estate. One such doctrine is merger. Under the merger doctrine, the same person is designated as the remainderman and the life tenant. When that occurs, there is no longer a life estate. Instead, the title merges in one person and the life estate is eliminated. How would such a situation arise? Consider Example 2-2.

EXAMPLE 2-2

Raul writes a provision in his will leaving his property to Amy as a life estate, and on Amy's death, to his heirs. When Raul dies, Amy is Raul's only heir. The life estate and the future estate merge and Amy is the owner in fee simple absolute.

E. LIFE ESTATE PUR AUTRE VIE

In addition to the normal configuration of a life estate, in which *A* receives the property for her life and then it goes to *B*, there are other options. For instance, there is a provision to allow the life estate to be measured by the life of another. Under a life estate **pur autre vie**, an owner in fee simple conveys a life estate to one person that terminates on the death of another person. The language used to create it is "to *A* for the life of *B*." One might wonder why anyone would create such a situation. There are several reasons to create a life estate measured by the life of someone other than the individual who is actually in possession of the premises. The owner might wish to convey the property to an individual, but measure it by the lifespan of a much older person. This would effectively provide the individual with a few years to enjoy the premises before it would transfer to others. It would provide temporary shelter for a family member, but not provide him with lifelong accommodations.

Pur autre vie
(French) "For another's life."

CONCURRENT OWNERSHIP IN REAL ESTATE

Our discussions so far have assumed that there is a single owner of the real property. However, as you know, many parcels of real estate are held in the names of two or more individuals. In this section, we explore how property rights are apportioned between concurrent owners. Before we can proceed with that discussion, however, we should outline the terminology. When there are multiple owners for a single piece of property, they are referred to as co-tenants. There are several different types of co-tenant arrangements, including tenants in common, joint tenancy, and tenants by entirety, to name just a few. See Figure 2-2.

- Tenants in common can have separate, unequal interests.
- Each tenant has the right to possess and use the property.

- There is no right of survivorship.
- Each tenant may transfer ownership interest to others.

FIGURE 2-2

Features of Tenancy in Common

A. TENANTS IN COMMON

A **tenancy in common** is created when real property is conveyed to two or more persons and there is no clear indication about the type of co-tenancy involved. When there is no distinction between the parties as to the nature of their relationship, most states will assume that a tenancy in common arrangement was intended. Under a tenancy in common, the right of each co-tenant to the real estate transfers to her heirs on death. Each co-tenant has equal right to use and possess the property, but

Tenancy in common
A type of concurrent ownership in which two or more people own property together without the right of survivorship.

may own the property in unequal shares. For instance, one co-tenant might possess 20 percent of the property while the other possesses 80 percent of the property.

A tenancy in common can be created in a variety of ways. An owner might convey title interest to two or more individuals with nothing being said about the nature of the relationship between the co-tenants. In such a situation, most courts would assume that a tenancy in common was intended. A tenancy in common can also be created by gift or by probate proceeding. No matter how the relationship is created, the basic features remain the same. The co-tenants can own unequal shares on the property and they are free to transfer their interest in the property to anyone else.

B. JOINT TENANCY

Joint tenancy
A type of concurrent ownership in which two or more individuals own property together, with equal ownership rights and the right of survivorship.

A **joint tenancy** is a different form of concurrent ownership. Similar to a tenancy in common, joint tenancy has one important difference. Joint tenants enjoy the right of survivorship. The right of survivorship provides that in the event that one of the co-tenants dies, her right to the property automatically transfers to the surviving co-tenant. This arrangement effectively precludes the co-tenant's heirs from receiving any of the property interest. Because this arrangement avoids probate proceedings, courts give it close scrutiny and require the parties to specifically state their intention of creating a joint tenancy. See Example 2-3.

EXAMPLE 2-3	Joint tenancy or tenancy in common? The following provision appears on the deed. Is it a joint tenancy or tenancy in common?

    To Amy and Raul as co-owners.

    Answer: Because this sentence does not contain any specific provision creating a joint tenancy, it must be a tenancy in common.

FIGURE 2-3	Except as otherwise provided herein, in all estates, real or personal, held in joint tenancy, the part or share of any tenant dying shall not descend or go to the surviving tenant, but shall descend or be vested in the heirs, executors, or administrators, respectively, of the tenant so dying, in the same manner as estates held by tenancy in common. . . . Nothing in this section prevents the creation of a joint tenancy with right of survivorship in real or personal property if the instrument creating the joint tenancy expressly provides for a right of survivorship, and no other document shall be necessary to establish said right of survivorship.

Defining the Right of Survivorship

In order to create a joint tenancy, the law requires the parties to specifically state their intention of creating the right of survivorship between the co-tenants.

Without this clearly stated provision, most courts will interpret language conveying title interest to two or more people as a tenancy in common.[1]

1. RIGHT OF SURVIVORSHIP

Joint tenancies create the **right of survivorship** among the co-tenants.
What, exactly, is the right of survivorship? Stated simply, it is the right of one
co-tenant to assume full ownership of the property on the death of the other co-
tenant. However, this simple statement belies a complex area of law. See Figure 2-3.
Because the right of survivorship precludes a co-tenant's heirs from receiving
property interests through probate proceedings, courts give close scrutiny to
any arrangement that purports to create a joint tenancy. This is not to say that
the law does not favor the creation of joint tenancies, but it does require the parties
to be specific about their intentions. For example, if two or more owners wish to
create a joint tenancy they must employ words such as: To *A* and *B*, as joint tenants,
not as tenants in common, and with the right of survivorship.

Right of survivorship
The right of a co-tenant to take
fee simple title to property on
the death of the other
co-tenant.

EXAMPLE 2-4

Michael executes a deed containing the following language: to Conrad and his girlfriend,
out of love and respect for all his help, I leave my property on Main Street, Los Angeles,
California, to him.
     Does this create a right of survivorship?
     Answer: No. In order to take advantage of the law of joint tenancy, the parties must
use the proper terms and make the necessary legal indications before it is created. When
courts take a strict view of how and when a joint tenancy is created, this deed will fail the
test. It does not use the words "right of survivorship," but more importantly there is no
specificity as to who Conrad's "girlfriend" is or, even worse, which property on Main
Street, Los Angeles, Michael is referring to. There is no reference to what type of tenancy
is created. Therefore, most courts would rule, assuming that the court found the language sufficient to transfer any rights, to be a tenancy in common, not a joint tenancy.

Courts require that degree of specificity in the language creating a joint tenancy
to demonstrate that the parties clearly intended to preclude their heirs from receiving any interest in the property. Most states have standing rules declaring that a
joint tenancy will never be presumed. If the parties do not clearly state their
intentions, the arrangement is usually considered to be a tenancy in common
instead of a joint tenancy.

The right of survivorship provides that on the death of the last
co-tenant, the remaining owner acquires the property in fee simple
absolute.

 ISSUE AT
A GLANCE

---

[1] N.C. Gen. Stat. § 41-2.

C. TENANCY BY ENTIRETY

Tenancy by entirety
A joint tenancy with the right of survivorship that is only available to lawfully married couples.

Tenancy by entirety is a joint tenancy that is reserved for married couples. Although not all states refer to this arrangement as a tenancy by entirety, all states confer special privileges to married couples that are not enjoyed by domestic partners or live-in lovers. Under this arrangement, when one spouse dies, the other receives full title to the property, pending any other estate proceeding such as forced share or statutory share.

With recent decisions by several state supreme courts legalizing homosexual marriage, it is an open question as to whether the rights of joint tenancy apply in these situations. There is no question that at some point the United States Supreme Court will weigh in on the issue and help establish whether gay married couples can also be tenants by entirety. The growing confusion in this area of law arises not only from the decision by the Massachusetts Supreme Judicial Court legalizing homosexual marriage, but also from federal acts such as the Defense of Marriage Act[2] that specifically defines marriage as the union of one man and one woman.

Tenancy by entirety is a co-tenancy that is reserved for married couples; it creates the right of survivorship.

FIGURE 2-4

Tenancy in Common Compared to Joint Tenancy

Tenants in Common

1. Co-tenants can have unequal interests in the property
2. Co-tenants do not have right of survivorship
3. When the arrangement is unclear, tenancy in common is assumed
4. The interest of the co-tenant is conveyed to her heirs through probate proceeding

Joint Tenant

1. All co-tenants have equal, undivided interests
2. Co-tenants have right of survivorship
3. Joint tenancy must be specifically stated by the parties
4. Co-tenants' heirs are precluded from receiving an interest in the property; surviving co-tenants automatically receive full title to property

1. TENANCY BY ENTIRETY AND CIVIL UNIONS

In states that have enacted civil unions that permit couples of the same sex to marry one another, there is a debate concerning whether in addition to

---

[2] 1 U.S.C.A. § 7.

receiving insurance benefits and other entitlements traditionally reserved to married couples, those who join together under civil unions should also receive the benefit of legally recognized tenancy by entirety in their real estate. The question has been answered in different ways across the country. In some states, the consensus seems to be that if a civil union is recognized and awarded all of the same rights as a marriage, then a civil union will also create a tenancy by entirety relationship. However, there are also states that take an opposite view that no such legally recognized estate is created. In those situations, a couple joined under a civil union might be required to convey property to one another as joint tenants in order to remove any potential confusion about the rights of each.

D. TENANCY IN PARTNERSHIP

Among the other types of concurrent ownership acknowledged under the law is **tenancy in partnership** A relatively recent phenomenon, tenancy in partnership recognizes a legal relationship between business partners. Under the rules of tenancy in partnership, business partners enjoy the right of survivorship to all business-related property. To qualify for this tenancy, the partners must have a partnership agreement and actually be in business together. Under a tenancy in partnership, no partner can sell, transfer, or mortgage partnership property without the consent of the other partners. The advantage of a tenancy in partnership is that an individual partner's creditors are not permitted to attach business property to satisfy a personal debt. Similar to a joint tenancy, the business assets automatically vest in the surviving partners in the event of the death of any partner.

Tenancy in partnership
A type of concurrent ownership among business partners, with the right of survivorship.

E. THE RIGHT TO PARTITION

Regardless of the type of tenancy arrangement, most co-tenants enjoy the right of **partition**. A partition is the division of the property along the ownership lines. In a tenancy in common, for example, where one co-tenant owns 80 percent and the other owns 20 percent, a partition proceeding might divide up the land according to the percentage. However, it isn't always practical or even possible to physically divide up parcels of real estate by the percentage of ownership. Instead, the property will be sold and the proceeds of the sale divided according to the percentage of ownership rights. Obviously the right to partition is not universal in all concurrent ownership estates. For instance, in a tenancy by entirety, a married couple would not have the right to partition the marital property. Instead, they must first go through a divorce proceeding terminating the marriage. Only then would they have the right to partition marital property. Partitions are most commonly seen in the dissolution of tenancies in common and joint tenancies.

Partition
The right of co-tenants to divide property according to their ownership interests.

CREATING A LIFE ESTATE

Life estates are usually
created in a will

John Doe owns the
property

Mary Doe is the life tenant

John Jr. and Tammy are the
remaindermen

Last Will and Testament for
John Doe

I hereby leave all of my real
property to my wife, Mary Doe, for
her life and then, on her death, to our
children John Jr. and Tammy.

DRAFTING DEEDS

Unauthorized practice of law is a crime in all states. Paralegals and legal assistants
come close to crossing the line into unauthorized practice of law when they assist
others in preparing deeds and other documents related to fee simple absolute and
life estates. What might seem like a simple assignment to help another prepare a
deed might be construed as practicing law without a license when that deed
involves creating a life estate appropriate to the person's probate situation.

CASE EXCERPT — IN RE ESTATE OF PAYNE

IN RE ESTATE OF PAYNE
186 N.J. 324, 895 A.2d 428 (N.J., 2006)

JUSTICE WALLACE delivered the opinion of the Court.

In this will contest, decedent had executed a will with a specific provision for his estate to
pay to the joint tenant of a property he owned in Maine an amount equivalent to the
mortgage debts on that property. Other than the "payment of all my just debts" clause,
the will did not have a provision for the estate to pay the mortgage debts on decedent's
home in New Jersey. Decedent bequeathed his New Jersey property to his partner, who
lived with him in that residence. The trial court concluded that decedent's partner and not
the estate was responsible for payment of the mortgage debts on the New Jersey property.
The Appellate Division affirmed. We conclude that application of the doctrine of
probable intent demonstrates that decedent intended to bequeath the New Jersey property to his partner debt-free. We reverse.

Decedent Ted Payne met Don Burton in 1997. Both men were suffering from AIDS. By May 1997, they began living together at Payne's residence in Morristown. At that time, Payne was a Managing Director of Finance at Metropolitan Life, and Burton was disabled.

Payne had previously acquired a vacation home in Harpswell, Maine. He purchased the property jointly with Frederick "Rick" Wohlfarth with the right of survivorship. Payne and Wohlfarth previously had lived together as partners but at the time they purchased the property their relationship had ended. They remained friends and agreed that the first to die would satisfy the balance of the mortgages on the property and that each would provide for that in his will.

Payne and Wohlfarth exchanged drafts of their wills to ensure the language concerning the payment of the mortgage debts on the Maine property would be similar. In his March 13, 1998, will, Payne bequeathed to Wohlfarth his half interest in the Maine property and a sum equal to the amount necessary to pay off the mortgage debts on the Maine property reduced by the proceeds of any life insurance policy on Payne's life payable to Wohlfarth. Payne also bequeathed the personal property located in Morristown to Wohlfarth and divided the residue among nieces, nephews, godchildren, charities, and educational institutions. The March 13, 1998, will made no provision for Burton.

In July 1998, Payne sold the Morristown residence and purchased a home in Harding Township, New Jersey. Burton resided in the home with Payne. According to Burton, while traveling to Maine in the summer of 1999 or 2000, he and Payne discussed the care of Payne's two dogs upon Payne's death. Burton expressed concern about his ability to provide a home for himself and the dogs on his limited income. He claimed that Payne told him not to worry because he would leave the house to him and that his life insurance proceeds would pay off the mortgage on the house. Burton also maintained that a similar conversation took place on another trip to Maine during the summer of 2000. At that time, Payne allegedly again stated that Burton would inherit the New Jersey property debt-free.

At some point, Payne contacted his attorney, Jack Wolff, to change his 1998 will. On August 15, 2000, Wolff mailed to Payne a revised draft. The primary change in the will provided for the gift to Burton of Payne's personal property located in the New Jersey home.

Payne reviewed the draft of the will and on November 16, 2000, wrote to Wolff outlining several other changes. Payne specified that there was a second mortgage on the Maine property and that his estate should pay that mortgage. In addition, he noted that the address of the New Jersey real estate should be listed as Harding Township and not Morristown. Wolff made the corrections in the will and forwarded another draft to Payne on November 21, 2000.

Payne's deteriorating health forced him to leave his position with Metropolitan Life in September 2001. It became necessary for Burton to assist Payne with his hygiene needs, the preparation of meals, transportation to and from his medical appointments, and the care of his dogs.

Payne still had not executed his revised will. On October 1, 2001, he wrote to Wolff explaining that the will appeared to give only the contents of the house to Burton, but his intent was to give the house and the contents to Burton. Payne also inquired whether he should retain the reference to the Maine property in the will because a friend informed him that it would pass automatically to the surviving owner and that inclusion in the will might cause adverse tax consequences.

Wolff made the changes and on October 15, 2001, forwarded a revised draft to Payne. The draft deleted the reference to a gift of the Maine property to Wohlfarth. Wolff also expressed his desire to review the deed to the Maine property to confirm that title was taken jointly with the right of survivorship. He also noted the possibility of federal estate tax consequences even though the Maine property would pass outside of the will.

Payne reviewed the latest draft of the will with Burton, who expressed several concerns. Burton believed the description of him as a "friend" failed to accurately describe their relationship. They agreed that the will should refer to Burton as Payne's "partner." Burton also questioned why the will provided for the payment of the mortgage on the Maine property but lacked similar language concerning the New Jersey property. Payne responded that it was necessary to provide expressly for payment of the mortgage debts on the Maine property because it was jointly owned property, and that the clause in his will directing payment of all his just debts provided for the debt on the New Jersey property.

Following that discussion, Payne wrote Wolff on November 11, 2001, instructing him to refer to Burton as his "partner" instead of as his "friend." He enclosed a copy of the Maine deed to verify that the property was held as joint tenants with the right of survivorship with Wohlfarth. Payne requested that Wolff prepare a Power of Attorney and Medical Directive in favor of Burton and asked for guidance concerning the tax and financial aspects of planning his estate due to its complexity. The crucial language in the November 11, 2001, letter provided that

> [a]s may be evident from my will, I want the debt encumbering my real estate liquidated by whatever means so that it passes to the beneficiaries free and clear and I don't want it to be necessary for the properties to be sold in order to satisfy the debt, which, I assume, would come due upon my death. Providing for the mortgage financing on the house in Maine has been a prominent issue with Oakey Point, which Mr. Wohlfarth and I may resolve by using credit life insurance in a refinancing which we are presently contemplating.
>
> At present, the major source of cash to the estate would come from life insurance proceeds of about $1 million and I have viewed this cash as available to be directed to pay off the mortgage balances which may exist at the time. However, this might not be true if estate taxes are assessed on the gross value of the real estate, which is currently worth between $1.7 million and $2.2 million, and there is a big tax liability to satisfy ahead of addressing the mortgages. There is another $300,000–$400,000 (assuming the stock market is bottoming out) of investments which would be available to the estate to pay taxes and debt.
>
> It has been suggested that I structure the life insurance proceeds to be paid into a trust outside of the estate where the trust would be directed to use the proceeds to repay the real estate debt. I am not inclined to create another level of complexity such as this unless it is necessary.
>
> Maybe we can sort through some of these issues when I come in to sign the will and other documents.

After receiving that letter, the sole change Wolff made in the will was to designate Burton as "partner." On March 4, 2002, Wolff wrote to Payne enclosing the revised will, power of attorney, and living will.

Wolff arranged to have Payne execute the documents in his office on March 14, 2002. Unfortunately, Payne was hospitalized on March 13, 2002. The following day Burton telephoned Wolff, informed him of Payne's hospitalization, and requested that Wolff deliver the original documents to the hospital for Payne to execute. Wolff went to the hospital and spoke to Payne in the Intensive Care Unit. After asking Payne several questions, Wolff was satisfied that Payne was lucid and wanted to execute the will and related documents. Payne then signed the will, power of attorney and living will.

The next day Payne lapsed into a coma and remained in that condition until his death on April 21, 2002. Daulton Lewis was named executor of the will. Lewis informed Burton that he was responsible for paying the outstanding debt on the New Jersey property. Burton replied that Payne wanted any mortgages on the house satisfied from his estate and intended that the property would pass to him debt-free.

At the time of Payne's death, the approximate value of his real estate was $900,000 for the New Jersey property and $375,000 for his one-half interest in the Maine property. The New Jersey property was encumbered by a mortgage in the amount of $347,190 and a line of credit of $92,458, and the Maine property was encumbered by a mortgage of $302,450 and a second mortgage of $106,092. The estate ultimately received life insurance proceeds totaling $1,053,425. Payne's estate satisfied the obligations on the Maine property but refused to pay the debt on the New Jersey property because it was bequeathed to a named beneficiary.

Burton filed a complaint against the estate. He alleged that at the time of Payne's death, he had been living with Payne as his partner for approximately four years, that Payne informed him that he would inherit the New Jersey property debt-free, and that the November 11, 2001, letter from Payne to Wolff expressed that intent. Answers were filed by the executor and various other beneficiaries. At the bench trial, Burton testified that his relationship with Payne was like a marriage in every way. He outlined three conversations he had with Payne in which Payne expressed his desire to give Burton the New Jersey property debt-free.

Wolff, who had drafted the will, testified that Payne instructed him to provide for the estate to pay the balance of the mortgages on the Maine property but had not instructed him to do the same for the mortgage debts on the New Jersey property. Wolff acknowledged that he had neither discussed with Payne the difference in treatment of the two properties nor estate tax issues. When he received the November 11, 2001, letter, Wolff did not interpret the letter to mean that Payne wanted the mortgage debts on the New Jersey property satisfied out of his estate. It was Wolff's belief that except for changing the description of Burton from "friend" to "partner," the will was satisfactory to Payne. On cross-examination, Wolff explained that despite the reference in the November 11, 2001, letter that Payne wanted the mortgage debts encumbering the real estate paid off so "it passes to my beneficiaries free and clear," he believed Payne was only referring to the Maine property. Wolff admitted that following the November 11, 2001, letter, he never met with Payne to sort through some of the issues raised in the letter and never discussed with Payne whether his use of the word "properties" was a mistake.

Lewis, the executor of the estate, testified that he was a long-time friend of Payne, and that Payne was the godfather to his daughter. He said that his daughter was one of numerous beneficiaries under the residuary clause of Payne's will. It was not until after Payne's death that he became aware that Payne had named him executor. Lewis, who was a lawyer, said that Wohlfarth was one of his clients. Lewis recalled a conversation with Payne and Wohlfarth wherein they discussed a testamentary plan in which the first to die would pay off the mortgage debts on the Maine property.

Wohlfarth testified that he had both a personal and a business relationship with Payne. Even after their close personal relationship ended, he said they continued to maintain a business relationship. In 1997, the two of them purchased the Maine property jointly, each contributing to the purchase price and being obligated on the mortgage. Wohlfarth stated that Lewis was his attorney and had drafted his will. Following a discussion with Lewis, it was Wohlfarth's understanding that "at some point the money in the estate would be disbursed to pay off the various mortgages." He had agreed with Payne that the first to die would pay off the mortgage debts on the Maine property either through the estate or with life insurance proceeds. He and Payne had exchanged wills and both had a similar clause about paying off the mortgage debts on the Maine property.

The trial court found that the November 11, 2001, letter was evidence of Payne's desire to find a way that Burton would be protected from the mortgage payments. However, the court concluded that Payne was looking in other directions for that help and never expressed an intent that other beneficiaries be saddled with the expense of having the estate satisfy the mortgage. The court rejected the "all my just debts" clause of the will as evidencing Payne's intention to cover the mortgage debts on the real estate because he "had a detailed disposition with respect to the [Maine] property owned by decedent and Wohlfarth." The court reasoned that it would not be necessary to specifically provide for the debt on the Maine property if "the all my debts clause could just have easily covered the same item with respect to the Maine property." Additionally, the court held that Payne's alleged intention to have the "all my just debts" clause apply to the mortgage debts for both properties was inconsistent with Wolff's testimony that Payne was detail oriented in their dealings. The court concluded that Burton failed to meet the burden of establishing that Payne intended to give him the New Jersey property debt-free.

The reasoning that persuades us to find in favor of Burton on the New Jersey property and to interpret the "just debts clause" to require the estate to pay off the mortgage debts on the New Jersey property also supports our conclusion that Payne's probable intent was to pay off the mortgage debts on the Maine property first and then to pay off the mortgage debts on the New Jersey property. In his November 11, 2001, letter, Payne reinforced that position by stating that payment of the mortgage debts on the Maine property "has been a prominent issue." Further, Payne provided for the payment of the mortgages on the Maine property in his March 13, 1998, will, and he never wavered in that regard. At all times, Payne expressed his intent to pay off the mortgage debts on the Maine property by a specific bequest to Wohlfarth.

We conclude that if Payne were faced with the question of priority as between payment of the mortgage debts on the Maine property and the mortgage debts on the New Jersey property, his probable intent would be to pay the Maine debts first. See N.J.S.A. 3B:23-14 ("[s]hares of the distributees abate as may be found necessary to give effect to the intention of the testator.")

The judgment of the Appellate Division is reversed, and the case is remanded to the trial court for further proceedings consistent with this opinion.

Justice RIVERA-SOTO, dissenting.

In this case, the testator held ownership interests in two homes in different states. More importantly, the nature of testator's ownership in those two properties was different: he owned his vacation home in Maine in joint ownership with another, which joint ownership had a right of survivorship, while he alone owned his primary New Jersey home. The testator's will reflected this dichotomy: although it specifically provided that, as part of his estate, the mortgages on the Maine home were to be satisfied out of his estate, there was no parallel provision made for any mortgages that may have encumbered his New Jersey home.

In the face of clearly dissimilar treatment by the testator of his two separate real property holdings, the majority holds that both the trial court and the Appellate Division erred in determining this testator's probable intent and that, instead, the "application of the doctrine of probable intent demonstrates that decedent intended to bequeath the New Jersey property to his partner debt-free." Ante, 186 N.J. at 327, 895 A.2d at 429-30 (2006). I cannot agree.

The only credible proofs tendered that the testator's will did not represent fairly the testator's intent consisted of extrinsic evidence in the form of a letter from the testator to his counsel that preceded the testator's execution of the will by several months. Unlike the majority's expansive application of extrinsic evidence in order to divine the testator's probable intent, caution mandates that we hew closely to the limits we have placed on the use of extrinsic evidence as a barometer of a testator's probable intent. As we made clear in Wilson v. Flowers, 58 N.J. 250, 263, 277 A.2d 199 (1971):

Held side-by-side, there is no ambiguity in the explicit terms of the will generated by that letter. The testator simply does not state in that letter what the majority holds here, that it was the testator's intent that his New Jersey home pass unencumbered to his devisee. On the contrary, it is the letter that is ambiguous while the will itself is patently clear: the mortgages on the Maine vacation home were to be satisfied from the estate, while no such provision was made in respect of the New Jersey home.

I respectfully dissent.

CASE QUESTIONS:

1 Explain the arrangement between Payne and Wohlfarth for the residence in Maine.
2 What statements did Payne purportedly make to Burton?
3 What critical section does the court refer to in the letter dated November 11, 2001, and what effect does that have on the court's decision?
4 Why did Payne's estate satisfy the mortgage on the Maine property, but not the New Jersey property?
5 Explain the reasoning set out in the dissent.

SKILLS YOU NEED IN THE REAL WORLD

IDENTIFYING ESTATES

As a real estate professional, it is important for you to be able to identify the different types of real property estates recognized in your state. For instance, does your state recognize fee simple determinable estates? What language is necessary to create such an estate? Similarly, are there limitations on life estates in your jurisdiction? For example, there is an old common law rule, referred to as the rule in Shelley's case, that specifically barred an owner from leaving a life estate to a person who might also be a remainderman. Under that old rule, the property would pass as fee simple title instead of establishing a life estate. Does that rule still apply in your state? In addition to these legal questions, it is also important for you to stay current on real property issues in state and federal appellate decisions that might concern real estate. As we have seen in this chapter, a ruling from the United States Supreme Court on homosexual marriage will have profound implications on concurrent ownership of real property.

CHAPTER SUMMARY

Ownership in real estate brings with it a wide assortment of rights. When a person owns property in fee simple absolute, she has the highest and best form of real property ownership. Among the rights invested in a fee simple absolute owner are the right to sell, give away, mortgage, and otherwise encumber the property. Traditionally, there have been two sub-classifications of fee simple absolute title. They include fee simple determinable and fee simple on a condition subsequent. These two limitations on fee simple absolute title are based on a limitation on how the property can be used. In modern real estate practice, they are rarely seen. A person may also receive a life estate in real property. A person who has a life estate has the authority to use and enjoy the property, but only as long as she is alive. Upon the life tenant's death, the property title transfers automatically to a predetermined person, referred to as a remainderman. A remainderman has a future interest in the property held in a life estate, but has no present interest. A remainderman can bring an action for the life tenant's waste or destruction in value of the property, but can do very little else until the life estate terminates. When property is held by two or more people, it is referred to as concurrent ownership. Concurrent ownership comes in a variety of different tenancies. A tenancy in common involves the ownership of the real estate parcel by two or more individuals with unequal shares in the property. Joint tenancy, on the other hand, is a form of concurrent ownership that allows the right of survivorship. When one of the joint tenants dies, the title automatically vests in the surviving tenants, bypassing the estate process. Tenancy by entirety is a concurrent ownership estate reserved for legally married couples. Tenancy in partnership is a legal doctrine that allows business partners to own property together. Partition is the right of co-tenants to bring an action to physically divide property along ownership lines or to sell the property and divide the profit based on percentage of ownership.

REVIEW QUESTIONS

1. What is a real property estate?
2. What is the difference between a present estate and a future estate?

3 What are the rights that an owner in fee simple absolute enjoys?

4 What limitations are placed on the rights of a fee simple absolute owner?

5 What is a fee simple determinable estate and how does it compare to a fee simplé absolute estate?

6 What is a fee simple on a condition subsequent estate and how does it compare to a fee simple determinable and a fee simple absolute estate?

7 Why have fee simple determinable estates fallen into disuse?

8 Draft a deed provision that contains a fee simple determinable clause.

9 What is a life estate?

10 What limitations does a life tenant have on her ability to use the property subject to a life estate?

11 Provide an example of a clause that would create a life estate.

12 What is a remainderman?

13 What is dower and curtesy?

14 What is the historical basis for the creation of life estates?

15 What is waste as that term applies to life estates?

16 What is a life estate pur autre vie?

17 Compare and contrast tenancies in common with joint tenancies.

18 What is the right of survivorship?

19 What is a tenancy by entirety?

20 What is a tenancy in partnership?

21 What is partition?

22 Explain why the government lost in this chapter's case excerpt.

DISCUSSION QUESTIONS

Should tenancy by entirety be extended to gay couples, whether in civil unions or in some form of legally sanctioned homosexual marriage?

PRACTICAL APPLICATIONS

 Draft a clause that would create each of the following estates:

1 Fee simple on a condition subsequent

2 Life estate

3 Joint tenancy

4 Tenancy in common

WEB SITES

Life Estate Pur Autre Vie — Legal Information Institute
http://www.law.cornell.edu/wex/life_estate_pur_autre_vie

Joint Tenancy — South Dakota State Bar
http://www.sdbar.org/pamphlets/joint_tenancy.shtm

What Joint Tenancy Means
http://www.mtgprofessor.com/A%20-%20Bob%20Bruss/
Joint_Tenancy.htm

A Guide to Property Titles — New York Times
http://www.nytimes.com/2007/02/04/realestate/04Home.html

Tenancy by Entirety in Bankruptcy
http://www.ilnb.uscourts.gov/opinions/JudgeWedoff/TBEoutline.pdf

TERMS AND PHRASES

Dower and curtesy	Life estate	Statutory share
Estate	Partition	Tenancy by entirety
Fee simple absolute	Pur autre vie	Tenants in common
Forced share	Remainderman	Tenancy in partnership
Joint tenancy	Right of survivorship	Waste

SIGNIFICANT CASES

Breezy Point Holiday Harbor Lodge-Beechside Apt. Owners' Ass'n v. B.P. Partnership, 531 N.W.2d 917 (Minn. Ct. App. 1995)
Wright v. Bloom, 69 Ohio St.3d 596, 635 N.E.2d 31 (1994)
Nunn v. Keith, 289 Ala. 518, 268 So.2d 792 (1972)
In re LaGarce's Estate, 487 S.W.2d 493 (Mo., 1972)
Vetter v. Hampton, 54 Ohio St.2d 227, 375 N.E.2d 804 (Ohio, 1978)
Chambers v. Cardinal, 177 Md. App. 418, 935 A.2d 502 (Md. App., 2007)
People v. Rosenfeld, 17 Misc. 3d 253, 844 N.Y.S.2d 587 (N.Y. Sup., 2007)

Property Descriptions and Determining Property Boundaries

Focus of This Chapter

This chapter explores the many different methods used across the nation to describe property. Because metes and bounds descriptions are an essential part of property descriptions in much of the country, we explore this topic in depth and go through the process of drawing out a description based on the wording of the description. The chapter also explores other property description techniques and provides a basic description of surveying.

Chapter Learning Objectives

After completing this chapter, you should be able to:

■ Draw a metes and bounds description
■ Explain the water rights available to landowners
■ Define the role of property descriptions in accurately describing particular real estate tracts
■ Describe how property boundaries change when they are bordered by water

INTRODUCTION

In the first chapter, we described real estate as the land and anything permanently attached to the land. However, that description does not help when it comes time to properly describe a parcel of real estate that is being sold. Real estate must be accurately described not only to ensure that the correct parcel is changing hands, but also because of the peculiar nature of land itself. In this chapter, we examine how to create accurate property descriptions and then describe how natural processes can affect those boundaries. We also explore the vitally important issue of water rights.

Before we can discuss how real estate property descriptions are compiled, we must first address a basic question: Why is an accurate property description so important?

When any item is sold, it is important that both parties know exactly what they are buying and are able to identify the specific item that is the subject of the sale. With automobiles, this identification might be in the form of the vehicle identification number. For other items, there are serial numbers and other identifying marks. But this process doesn't work for land. For one thing, land is fixed; it cannot be transported. For another, one parcel of land looks very much like another. Imagine yourself walking through the woods, breathing in the country air and generally enjoying the quiet. As you walk, you pay little attention to the fact that you are crossing over the boundaries of various tracts. In fact, without fences or signs to warn you, there is no way for you to determine exactly whose property you are on. Now, consider this same situation from a buyer's perspective. Just as you could not tell where one piece of property began and another ended, the buyer also does not know the exact parameters of his property. With items of personal property, that question is always easy: You own the object. But land is not an object and the unique nature of real estate raises two interesting and vitally important points:

- What are the boundaries of the property?
- What identifies this parcel from every other parcel?

Because neither one of these questions can be answered from the land itself, buyers and sellers are forced to rely on other sources for answers. This is not a new problem, which explains why surveying and describing tracts of land has an ancient history.

 ## THE HISTORY OF PROPERTY BOUNDARIES

From the moment that societies began dividing up property for use by its members, it became a paramount concern to pinpoint exactly where one person's plot ended and another's began.

Ancient Egyptians used surveying techniques to divide up parcels and as a way to redetermine property boundaries after the yearly floods they suffered. Before the construction of the Aswan Dam in the 1960s, the Nile flooded every year. This flooding submerged the lands along the river and often destroyed fences and other structures used to identify property boundaries. Egyptians used surveying techniques to quickly and efficiently identify property boundaries after the flood waters receded. These surveying techniques were so accurate that they were also employed to build the great Egyptian monuments, such as the Pyramid of Giza and Luxor Temple.

PROPERTY DESCRIPTIONS IN DEEDS

Because the description of the parcel's boundaries is so important for both buyers and sellers, it has always been necessary to have a system in place to identify land boundaries. However, there are other reasons why adequate property descriptions are important. We have already referred to the Statute of Frauds discussed in greater detail in Chapter 6. That statute requires many aspects of a real estate transaction to be reduced to writing. Therefore, the actual boundaries for each parcel must be written down in order to create a legally valid transaction.

A. THE ELEMENTS OF A VALID PROPERTY DESCRIPTION

There are two critical elements pertaining to a property description.

1 The property description must sufficiently *describe* the property in the deed.
2 The property description can also *make reference to other documents* that sufficiently describe the property.

Let's start with one method of property description that we are all familiar with: street address. If we accept that identifying a particular parcel is important, why can't we simply rely on street addresses in all our documents? Although this appears to be a fairly reasonable approach, there are some practical limitations with this method. For one thing, what if there are two streets in the town with the same name? Visitors to Atlanta, Georgia, are often confused by the sheer number of streets with "Peachtree" in the name. If you are selling the lot known as 1001 Peachtree Street, which lot are you selling? A property description must provide a specific method for identifying one tract from all others. Street address doesn't meet that standard.

A property description is sufficient in itself when it:

■ **Clearly identifies a unique parcel of real estate**
■ **Makes specific references to property lines/roadways/other landmarks**

ISSUE AT
A GLANCE

B. LEGAL REQUIREMENTS FOR PROPERTY DESCRIPTIONS IN DEEDS

As we have seen, street address is not sufficient to properly identify the real estate in question. Add to this the fact that each state has statutes that mandate particular types of property descriptions and you begin to see the need for precise property descriptions that not only adequately pinpoint the property in question, but also meet the legal standards. Statutes require a property description that is adequate at the time that the deed is recorded. The property description cannot be added later. The description must stand on its own, giving specific reference points for the boundary lines and making reference to other natural or artificial boundaries and landmarks. In states that use a tract indexing method to record deeds discussed in greater detail in Chapter 8, the tract must be specific and refer to the correct parcel. In states that follow a metes and bounds system to describe land (discussed in this chapter), the description must show how the parcel is unique compared to all others. The final description must provide enough information so that anyone could properly identify the property.

C. REFERRING TO OTHER DOCUMENTS TO PROVE PROPERTY BOUNDARIES

The property description can refer to another document not included in the deed, but that other document must make the property description complete. The category of "other documents" includes plats, surveys, and other information provided in the public records. We examine the function of plats and surveys later in this chapter. When a property description refers to other documents, those documents become a legally binding aspect of the property description. Consider Example 3-1.

EXAMPLE 3-1

Katie has recently conveyed a one-acre tract to Lisa. In the section of the deed where the property description is provided, Katie has written: "the one-acre lot shown on Plat 45-672, land records of Anywhere County." Is this a sufficient property description?

Answer: Yes. Because Katie has specified a public document that adequately identifies the parcel, the property description is legally valid.

When a property description refers to a plat, survey, or other public record, that document becomes a part of the deed. Both documents are now intertwined and someone who wished to know the exact boundaries of the property would be forced to refer to both the deed and the plat. Many states have laws that make the document as much a part of the deed as if it were actually written down and included with the deed.

EXAMPLE 3-2

Is this property description sufficient?

"That one-acre lot that we visited yesterday and that is known as the old Smith place." Answer: No.

The problem with a description like this is that there are too many unknowns to make this parcel identifiable. The parties may understand what they are talking about, but the law requires more. The property description must be sufficient so that anyone could understand it. This description fails that test.

D. LITIGATING PROPERTY BOUNDARIES

When a question arises about exactly where the property boundaries are, the parties often find themselves in court, presenting their case to a judge and a jury. If there is some confusion about exactly where the boundaries are, how do the parties prove their case?

At a minimum, the parties must prove the following to satisfy the court regarding the boundaries of a particular parcel:

- The description details the boundaries of the parcel;
- The description conforms to the physical features of the parcel;
- The description is accurate; and
- The description refers to natural boundaries and other features that specify a unique parcel of land.

If a party is unable to prove these elements, the court is likely to rule against him. The practical result of ruling against one party is a ruling in favor of the other. When a property boundary is under dispute, the court will side with one owner or the other. Consider Example 3-3.

EXAMPLE 3-3

Lisa owns 1.3 acres. She lives there with her husband and children and has done so for years. The area is rural and most of the surrounding tracts have never been developed. One day, Lisa gets a letter in the mail from Missy. Missy has purchased the adjoining lot and has noticed that Lisa's fence and shed have been constructed across Missy's property line. Missy demands that Lisa remove both immediately. Lisa reviews her original title documents and finds that her deed makes reference to a large oak tree as forming the corner of her lot with the adjacent lot. It also provides that her property line runs from the old oak tree to a stump that is only a few feet from the road. Walking that straight line clearly places the fence and the shed on her side of the property. Missy has a deed that states that she owns 1.5 acres and describes the boundary line in question as "running along the property adjacent in a north-westerly direction until it reaches Choctaw Road."

If this case goes to litigation, who will win?

Answer: Lisa. Why? Her deed provides some information that could give a third party a clear indication of where the property line is. Although referring to an old oak tree isn't the best description, if there is only one oak tree and one stump, it provides a better description than Missy's deed.

---

1. AMBIGUOUS PROPERTY DESCRIPTIONS

What happens when a property boundary, such as the one in Example 3-3, is ambiguous or open to interpretation? How do the courts resolve ambiguities in property descriptions? There are actually two different classifications of ambiguous property descriptions: patent ambiguities and latent ambiguities. The classification of a particular property description as patently ambiguous or latently ambiguous has enormous consequences when courts address property descriptions.

a. Patent Ambiguities

Patently ambiguous
A description that is invalid on its face.

A **patently ambiguous** property description is so vague that the property cannot be identified. Such a designation has a dramatic effect on the proceedings. Courts will rule that patently ambiguous property descriptions do not convey property and therefore the sale is voided. The court will rule that the deed is invalid and cancel the entire transaction. The standard that most states use to define patently ambiguous property descriptions is any description that leaves the land to be conveyed in a state of absolute uncertainty. Patently ambiguous descriptions do not, by their very terms, offer any assistance to help clear up the confusion. In the face of a void description, is there some way that the parties can provide additional information? For instance, is it possible to present testimony from the people involved in the transaction to help identify the exact parcel?

b. Parol Evidence and Property Descriptions

Parol evidence
Oral testimony offered to explain or interpret the provisions of a written document, such as the property description in a deed.

Parol evidence is oral testimony offered to prove an element in a written document. Is such testimony permissible to help clear up a patently ambiguous property description? No. The rule about parol evidence is simple: Oral testimony cannot rectify a poorly drafted document. The reasons behind the parol evidence rule stretch back for centuries, but are based squarely on common sense. A written document must stand on its own. While it can clear up discrepancies, it cannot be proven by oral testimony. Why? The temptation would be too great on the parties to spin their testimony to help support their position. Permitting a party to interpret the language in a deed also attacks the fundamental reason to have documents in writing in the first place: to establish the basic terms of the transaction. The parol evidence rule applies not only to deeds but also to many other written documents.

What happens when a property description appears to be patently ambiguous, but it references another document that exactly pinpoints the property's location? In that situation, the description is classified as latently ambiguous.

ISSUE AT A GLANCE

Under the parol evidence rule, a property description must stand on its own; courts will not consider evidence or testimony that seeks to explain or expand on a patently ambiguous property description.

EXAMPLE 3-4

Rod conveys a half-acre tract to Katie. The property description reads:

"All that tract or acreage containing .5 acres and described as 100 feet on each side, forming a perfect square, with one point of the square pointing directly at the winter sun's rising point."

As you can tell from reading this description, any tract that is 100 feet on each side does not equal to one half acre. In fact, a 100 foot square parcel is considerably less than

> The plot to be purchased is + or – 25 acres to be determined by a survey for property behind Mr. Fox's property, to run to the first field by the road. This being the same as the plot shown in tax map 21, Lot 23, in Pearson county.*

FIGURE 3-1

Example of a Latently Ambiguous Property Description

a half acre. The other problem with this deed is that the "point" of this square cannot be determined. Where exactly is the winter sun's rising point? The sun rises at different points on the horizon throughout the year and this description fails to provide sufficient explanation of both the size and the orientation of the property.

2. LATENTLY AMBIGUOUS PROPERTY DESCRIPTIONS

Latently ambiguous property descriptions are insufficient when viewed by themselves, but become valid when they refer to some other document through which a more precise identification can be made. Consider the following description: "I hereby sell to Ben all of my land in Burke County." Such a description would be patently ambiguous. However, if this same wording includes a reference to "as set out in deed book, 432, page 15," this patently ambiguous description becomes a latently ambiguous description. Although the original description does not specify a unique and identifiable property, the reference to the deed book makes it a legally valid description. In order for a latently ambiguous description to be legal, it must refer to some public document or an entry in the public records. Unlike patently ambiguous descriptions, parol evidence can be used to explain or interpret the provisions.

Latently ambiguous
A description that appears to be invalid, but refers to a document through which the property can be adequately described.

Latently ambiguous descriptions appear to be inadequate, but refer to other documents that prove the parcel is specific and unique.

 ISSUE AT A GLANCE

 METES AND BOUNDS DESCRIPTIONS

The original colonies of the Americas, and the future 13 states of the United States, adopted metes and bounds property descriptions primarily because it was the English system and the original states adopted English law as the model for the nation. This method of property description continues to be used in these states, and a few others, even though many other states have adopted tract indexing and other methods. Because there is such a diversity of methods used to describe property, we examine metes and bounds descriptions thoroughly in this chapter, and then discuss other states' methods in later chapters.

---

* Adapted from *Wolfe v. Villines*, 610 S.E.2d 754 (N.C. App. 2005).

Most of the states along the Eastern seaboard of the United States use the metes and bounds system to describe land. A metes and bounds description sets out the distance and direction of the property's boundaries. Metes (distance) and bounds (direction) follow the course of the property lines from a point of beginning (P.O.B.) in a clockwise description, from border to border until returning to the P.O.B. In many ways, a metes and bounds description is similar to the way treasure maps describe the location of the prize. However, instead of "twelve paces west to an old stump, then twenty paces east to the mouth of a cave" and thus to the buried treasure, a metes and bounds description is actually a step-by-step tour of the entire property line. Instead of treasure, the end of a metes and bounds description brings you back to where you started. Along the way, it describes every twist and turn of the property so that there can be no doubt about the exact location of boundary lines.

> Starting from the northwestern most point of lot 9 Plat Book 28 page 30 thence N. 85 degrees 07' 20" W. 37.40 feet to the point and place of beginning; thence N. 85 degrees 07' 20" W. 102.46 feet; thence N. 11 degrees 18' 10" W. 36.37 feet to a point which is the northeastern most point of the Smith property thence S. 70 degrees 38' 18" E. 139.66 feet to the point and place of beginning (P.O.B.).

Metes and bounds descriptions are very precise. Distances are given to 1/100 of a foot and directions are given not only in degrees, but also in finer gradations of minutes and seconds. The degrees refer to the hash marks on a typical drawing compass. For instance, "N. 85 degrees 07' 20" W. 37.40 feet," directs the reader directly North, and then 7 degrees to the West. The designation 20" W is so tiny that it is almost impossible to see on a typical compass. A surveyor would have instruments delicate enough to discern this gradation, but most real estate practitioners would not. If you were drawing this line, and you designated North as the direction toward the top edge of the page, your line would be at a slight angle toward the upper left corner. We draw out metes and bounds descriptions in the next section of this chapter.

Metes and bounds descriptions can present problems for legal professionals. For instance, a parcel with an unusual shape could have a description that goes on for dozens of lines. Recopying that description to another document always runs the risk of leaving out a line and thus rendering the entire description invalid. Metes and bounds descriptions must be word perfect from deed to deed.

Another problem for legal professionals involves older metes and bounds descriptions. For one thing, they do not use the same terminology or units of measure. Consider the following example:

> BEING Grant No. 97 by the State to Juan Amigo, dated April 13, 1870, recorded in Book L — 2 page 644, Brunswick County Registry, and more particularly described by metes and bounds as follows: BEGINNING at a stake in the southwest corner of the new survey in your old line; running thence south 72 degrees east 150 poles to your corner on the Sea Banks; thence along the sea shore South 18 degrees West 384 poles to a stake at the end of the bank near a small inlet; thence across the sound South 72

FIGURE 3-2

Conversion Chart for Old
Metes and Bounds Descriptors

1 chain = 66 feet

1 rod = 16.5 feet

1 pole = 16.5 feet

1 perch = 16.5 feet

1 link = 7.92 inches

1 acre = 43,560 square feet, or

Square acre = 208.71 feet on each side

1 mile = 5,280 feet

degrees west 115 poles to your old line; thence along said line to the place and point of BEGINNING; containing three hundred acres, more or less.[1]

This description does not describe the directions in finer gradations of degrees; instead it simply provides "South 72 degrees west." However, that is not the real problem presented by this property description. How long is a "pole"?

In deeds from the 1960s and earlier, units of measure are given in unfamiliar terms, such as "poles," "rods," and "chains." These are all units of distance, in the same way that miles and yards are units of distance. When deciphering these older property descriptions, you must first convert poles and chains into feet and then draw the description based on the conversion. See Figure 3-2 for a conversion chart.

A. DRAFTING METES AND BOUNDS DESCRIPTIONS

It is important for any legal professional to know how to draft metes and bounds descriptions, if that is the system used in your state. Being able to draw metes and bounds descriptions helps you visualize the property descriptions in a way that simply reading distances and directions never can. Drawing out the description also allows you to compare your drawing with other, known drawings of the same property. You can compare your drawing to plats, tax maps, and other drawings of the parcel. A drawing will help you immediately identify when the property description is in error (or is actually the description for an entirely different parcel).

To draw metes and bounds descriptions, you will need a circular land measure compass, or a semi-circular protractor. Land measure compasses can be obtained from many sources; for example they are given out as a promotional item from title insurance or surveying companies. You will also need a regular straight ruler.

To begin, get a blank piece of paper and then locate a point on the paper to serve as your point of beginning (P.O.B.). One way of deciding where your P.O.B. will be is by reading through the entire description and locating the longest boundary line. If the longest described line is on the North-South axis, then your P.O.B. should be

---

[1] *Resort Development Co. v. Phillips*, 278 N.C. 69, 178 S.E.2d 813 (1971).

toward the bottom of your blank page. If the longest line is on the East-West axis, your P.O.B. should be closer to the left-hand margin of your page. The reason we specify the left-hand margin of the blank page is that metes and bounds descriptions are written in a clockwise fashion, meaning that they usually start on the left-hand side of the page and progress in a clockwise manner from there.

Here is a relatively basic example.

EXAMPLE 3-5   From P.O.B., N 30 degrees E, 100 feet, then S 30 degrees E, 100 feet, then S 30 degrees West, 100 feet, then N 30 degrees W, 100 feet to P.O.B.

You can start to draw this description by first locating a spot toward the lower left-hand corner of your blank page. Draw a dot there. Place the center of your compass on this point, with North on the compass pointing directly toward the top of the page. A direction such as "N 30 degrees E," means "North 30 degrees towards the East." Locate North, and then go 30 degrees toward the East. In this situation, you will go right, down the curve of your compass or protractor until you locate 30 degrees. Mark that point and then remove your compass. You should now have two points: your original P.O.B. and the mark indicating North 30 degrees East from that point. You can now draw a line connecting these lines, but before you do, there is one other matter. How long should this line be?

The description states that the line is "N 30 degrees E, 100 feet." Obviously, we must scale down 100 feet to some distance that will fit on a sheet of paper. One way

---

Tech Topic
REAL ESTATE MARKETING TECHNOLOGY

It should be no surprise that technology has made massive inroads into marketing methods for both residential and commercial real estate. In residential real estate alone, the increase in use of mobile devices has produced a concurrent avalanche of marketing tools. Homebuyers have access to web sites with profuse details about properties for sale. Smartphone apps can retrieve property information according to GPS coordinates. Furthermore, users can elect to receive alerts about certain types of properties so that when they travel near those properties, an automatic notification is sent to their mobile phone.

Additionally, many Realtors are now using Quick Response, or QR, codes (which look like a block of code about an inch square) in their print ads. A prospective buyer uses a smartphone app to take a picture of the QR code, which then reveals details about the property or leads the buyer to the property's web site.

Commercial real estate brokers have likewise adopted technology tools in their marketing. In recent years, the

industry has embraced online listings that widened their access to prospective investors. Email marketing has allowed commercial real estate firms to simultaneously market directly to their databases of owners and brokers. Firms have even used social media such as LinkedIn, Facebook, and Twitter to generate leads. Another marketing avenue has been through the use of specialized software that provides a targeted approach to generating, tracking, and nurturing leads.

One of the commercial real estate industry's newer approaches is online auctions. Particularly in a down market, these platforms help push through the bottleneck of unsold commercial property by better meeting price expectations and creating a sense of urgency and excitement.

As technology continues to evolve, it is certain that new real estate marketing tools will continue to emerge.

of doing this is to create a scale in which 1 inch = 100 feet. Most attorneys use a scale closer to 1 inch = 200 feet, to be sure that the drawing actually fits on the page. We will use the 1 inch = 100 feet scale just to keep things simple. Using that scale, the line connecting the P.O.B. along N 30 degrees East mark would measure 1 inch. Place your ruler along the axis of these two lines and measure 1 inch from the P.O.B. You may find that the line doesn't reach your new mark. No problem. That mark was just there to give you a direction. In fact, as soon as you draw your 1-inch line, you should probably erase that N 30 degrees East mark so that it won't cause any later confusion.

You now have a 1-inch line that starts at the left-hand bottom corner of your blank sheet and aims roughly at the upper right corner of the page. Now what? Move your compass to the end of this new line and dial in your new direction. According to our sample, this new direction is "S 30 degrees E, 100 feet." Following the same process that we outlined above, your line will point in the general direction of the lower-right corner of your page and will be 1 inch long. You should end up with a square, with one corner of the square pointing toward the top of your page.

Sometimes a metes and bounds description will give you a direction such as "directly North," or "due North" or simply N 100 feet. In this case, the description simply means directly North, with no angling off to either side.

If you are ready to attempt to draw a real metes and bounds description, complete the Practical Application found at the end of this chapter.

B. USING TECHNOLOGY TO HELP WITH METES AND BOUNDS DRAWINGS

In the era of the Internet and computer-assisted drawing, it should come as no surprise that many companies have developed software to help title searchers and others to draw metes and bounds descriptions. Programs such as MapDraw (*www.informatik.com/mapdraw.html*), Version Tracker (*www.versiontracker.com/dyn/moreinfo/macosx/22791*), and Metes and Bounds Online (*www.metesandboundsonline.com/home.html*) allow users to plug in the various directions and distances and produce a line drawing that can be compared with the plat for the property. Each of these programs can complete the drawing with an ease that would have astonished a title searcher from even a few years ago.

 V   OTHER METHODS TO DESCRIBE PROPERTY: GOVERNMENT SURVEY SYSTEM

In the Public Land Act of 1785, the federal government created a system for surveying vast tracts of land that it planned to give away to new homesteaders. Most of these tracts were located in the new territories of the middle and far west of the Eastern Seaboard. The original colony states continue to use the old metes and bounds descriptions. However, if you are involved in real property practice in midwestern and western states, you may find that your state uses an entirely different system.

A. TRACT INDEXING

In Chapter 12, when we discuss the process involved in carrying out a title search, we will see that there are essentially two systems used to record land transactions. One involves a listing of grantors (sellers) and grantees (buyers). The other system is a tract index. We mention tract indexes in this chapter because they are also used to describe property. In states that use the tract-indexing system, the local government will assign a permanent parcel identification number to each parcel of real estate. This number is usually cross-referenced with the county tax or assessor's office. Any action involving the property is then recorded according to this number. In some areas, all transactions involving the property are actually recorded on a series of cards for a particular parcel. Although this system has the benefit of putting all records for a parcel in one place, the system is not used everywhere. In fact, most states continue to use a variation of the grantor-grantee index (discussed in detail in Chapter 12) along with metes and bounds, plat, or tract reference.

B. PLATS

Plats are drawings of property that are prepared by surveyors. A plat can be recorded in the registrar of deeds or land office and often contains all the same information provided in a metes and bounds or government tract survey property description. Most states give plats the status of official, recorded documents, provided that they meet certain requirements. Once recorded, a plat can be one of the documents referred to in a legally valid property description. See Figure 3-3.

C. TORRENS REGISTRATION

Sir Robert Torrens developed a land registration system in the 1850s for use in tracking land sales in Australia. The Torrens method greatly simplified the rules

---

FIGURE 3-3

Effect of Reference to Plat in Conveyance, Mortgage, or Other Instrument

When any deed, mortgage, or other instrument conveying an interest in or creating a lien on real property refers to the boundaries, metes, courses, or distances of the real estate delineated or shown on any plat of the property or on any blueprint, tracing, photostatic copy, or other copy of the plat which has been recorded as authorized in Code Section 44-2-26 and when the deed, mortgage, or other instrument states the office, book, and page of recordation of the plat or of the blueprint, tracing, photostatic copy, or other copy of the plat, the reference shall be equivalent to setting forth in the deed, mortgage, or other instrument the boundaries, metes, courses, or distances of the real estate as may be delineated or shown on the plat or on the blueprint, tracing, photostatic copy, or other copy thereof.*

---

* O.C.G.A. § 44-2-28.

regarding registration of English deeds by gathering together all information about a particular parcel into a single document. The appealing aspect of the Torrens registration scheme is that when a person wishes to know whether an encumbrance, such as a lien, has been filed against the property, he can simply pull the registration card and read what has been printed there. In many ways the modern tract-index system used in some states is a direct offshoot of the Torrens system. The Torrens system almost completely eliminates the need for a title search and greatly simplifies other aspects of real property titles.

Torrens registration schemes were adopted by most of the original colony states as a way to deal with some of the problems inherent in metes and bounds descriptions—not the least of which is the confusion that they can cause. Although the Torrens system provided an easy and logical organization scheme for real estate records, it was never popular. Many of the states that enacted it have repealed it and even in those states where it is still a legal form of registration, attorneys do not use it. These days, a property that is registered in Torrens is considered to have legal problems and real estate attorneys will take action to have the property removed from the registry.

When property is recorded under a Torrens system, any encumbrance, lien, or judgment against the property is actually written on the Torrens card corresponding to the unique parcel of land in question.

ISSUE AT A GLANCE

VI WATER RIGHTS

The subject of water rights could easily fill an entire volume. Broadly known as **riparian rights**, an owner's right to water is a critical factor. Without water, land is essentially worthless. Riparian rights can be broken into two broad categories: the right to use water and the effect that water has on property boundaries. We address the right to use water first.

Riparian rights
The right to use and draw water for the benefit of real property.

A. THE RIGHT TO USE WATER

What rights do real estate owners have to surface water? The rule in most states is simple: When an owner's land is in contact with water, he has the right to make reasonable use of it. Under ordinary circumstances, all owners whose land borders on a body of water, including rivers and streams, have the right to take water from the source. Obviously, this right is limited to the extent that the owner cannot use so much of the water that it prevents others from doing so. Other limitations on owners include the prohibition against altering the course of a river or polluting it to such an extent that the water becomes unusable for other owners who also border the river.

1. COURT DOCTRINES THAT AFFECT WATER RIGHTS

Many states have adopted the "reasonable use" test to determine when an owner's use of water is excessive or injurious to others. Under this rule, the owner may use the water to an extent considered reasonable under the circumstances. The factors that determine reasonableness will vary from case to case. Among the factors that the court will consider are the individual owners' needs for water. Are they drawing water for drinking and bathing, or to run a business? Are they drawing water simply to use it for decorative purposes, such as fountains and displays? The owners who draw water for personal use will have a much stronger case for water access than the second group who simply use the water for display. Whether a particular owner's water use is reasonable is a question to be determined by a jury.

B. NATURAL FORCES THAT AFFECT PROPERTY BOUNDARIES

When one or more boundary lines of a parcel border on water, the question often becomes, where exactly does one draw the property line? Water levels tend to rise and lower not only through the course of a year, but sometimes during the course of a single day. Property boundaries can be affected not only by tides, but also by the more gradual natural actions that affect boundary lines. Among these natural forces are:

- Accretion
- Erosion
- Avulsion
- Reliction

1. ACCRETION

Accretion is the gradual deposit of soil on an owner's property that expands the total size of the parcel. In this situation, the boundary line shifts to reflect the new expansion of dry land. When accretion occurs by natural forces, it gives the landowner a windfall. Without paying for any additional property, he has gradually acquired more land.

2. EROSION

Erosion is the opposite of accretion. When the action of water slowly takes away soil from a parcel, the owner's overall lot size gradually decreases. The owner is not permitted to adjust his boundaries to reflect the slow loss of acreage.

3. AVULSION

Avulsion is a lesser-known process where dry land is suddenly added or lost by the action of water. Rivers can sometimes shift their courses dramatically, and when this shift results in a change in a property's boundaries, the process is accurately described as avulsion, not accretion or erosion.

4. RELICTION

Reliction is the gradual exposure of dry land by receding waters. Although this process is not common, it can affect a property's boundaries, or even an entire parcel.

C. WATER AND PROPERTY BOUNDARIES

Although government surveys, metes and bounds descriptions, and plat book references are all excellent ways to describe property, there are some situations in which they prove to be inadequate. For instance, none of these written descriptions helps a real estate professional to determine the air rights above the property, or the mineral rights under the surface. Property descriptions also run into practical difficulties. When one line of the property is bordered by a river, lake, or stream, where exactly should the property line be located? If the water level varies, as it usually does, doesn't this mean that the property line also varies, sometimes several times a day? Courts follow a two-prong approach to this issue. The first prong is to determine the classification of the body of water in question. That classification will then determine the rules applicable to boundary lines and watercourses. The first question that must be asked when dealing with water is whether the water is navigable.

1. NAVIGABLE WATERS

A "navigable" body of water is one that is capable of supporting commercial navigation. This means, in essence, a river, lake, or other body of water that a boat could cross. Here a "boat" includes pleasure craft. Under the public trust doctrine that is a feature of most state's policies regarding water, when rivers or lakes are navigable and thus capable of use for commercial purposes, these bodies are the property of the state, not individual landowners. The state retains title to these bodies of water as a way of furthering commerce.

a. Boundary Lines Along Navigable Bodies of Water

When property borders on a navigable body of water, the boundary line is the bank, or the mid-distance between low and high water marks (if the property borders the ocean). This arbitrarily chosen midpoint becomes the owner's boundary line, while the water itself is public (or government) property.

2. NON-NAVIGABLE WATERS

When water is classified as non-navigable, the rules about boundaries change. When a property is bordered by a non-navigable body of water, such as a stream, the owner's property line runs to the middle of the stream. The opposite owner's boundary line also runs to the middle, effectively dividing the stream in half. If the course of the stream changes, the property boundaries will change with it. Obviously, these rules are not a factor when the stream passes through the middle of a parcel. In that case, the only concern for the property owner is the reasonable use of the water itself.

METES AND BOUNDS DESCRIPTION

This deed, made this the 21st day of June, 1991, by and between Elizabeth Wilson, widow, the grantor, and Gary Brown, the grantee, of 1001 Maple Street, anywhere.

That the grantor, for valuable consideration paid by the grantee, the receipt of which is hereby acknowledged, has and by these presents does grant, bargain, sell and convey on to the grantee in fee simple, all that certain lot or parcel of land situated in Anywhere Township, State of Placid, and more particularly described as follows:

Adjoining the lands of Eric Siegel, Ernest Bovine and Edward White, and beginning at an iron stake in the west side of a Street, said stake being located 249.91 feet south 1° five minutes west from the iron stake at the Ernest Bovine corner in the edge of said street and running north 76° 32 minutes west for 595.11 feet along the line on the Ernest Bovine property to an iron stake in Eric Siegel's line; thence South 8° 42 minutes west for 150 feet along the Eric Siegel line to an iron stake; thence South 77° 15 minutes east for 361 feet to a post; thence South 80° East for 252.5 feet to a stake in the edge of said street; thence north 1° five minutes east for 130 feet to the beginning, and containing 1.96 acres, more or less.

Metes and bounds descriptions always provide a point of beginning

Property boundaries are described by distance and direction

Metes and bounds descriptions usually provide total acreage

CONFIDENTIALITY AND REAL ESTATE PRACTICE

A thorough understanding of ethical rules is important no matter what area of law you specialize in. However, there is sometimes a temptation to think that real estate practice does not raise many ethical considerations. Nothing could be further from the truth. Attorneys owe their clients confidentiality. That means that a client can expect private conversations with his or her attorney will not be repeated to others. Confidentiality is one of the core ethical concerns for any legal practitioner, but is confidentiality really all that important in a real estate transaction? Absolutely. Suppose you have a client who is planning to buy several large tracts of land to construct a shopping center. If news of this project leaks out of the law office, the client's plans could be jeopardized. Local owners may unrealistically increase their sale prices, causing the entire project to fail. You should always keep client communications secret.

This means not discussing client business with anyone outside the firm, not other paralegals, not the friendly people at the land office, not even family members. Confidentiality is not only required by both paralegal and attorney ethical codes, but a violation of confidential communications might also result in a legal malpractice action against the firm.

PANETTA v. EQUITY ONE, INC.

 CASE EXCERPT

PANETTA v. EQUITY ONE, INC.
190 N.J. 307, 920 A.2d 638 (N.J., 2007)

Justice LONG delivered the opinion of the Court.

The primary issue in this appeal is whether a conveyance of real property that makes no mention of an abutting riparian grant can be construed under N.J.S.A. 46:3-16 to include that grant as an appurtenance. Unlike a riparian right, which is a license or privilege, a riparian grant is a conveyance in fee simple of real property. As such, without specific mention in the deed or other evidence that the parties intended its inclusion, a riparian grant will not pass as appurtenant to another distinct parcel.

I.

Beginning in 1943, several generations of the Francis family owned the property located at 633 Point Avenue, Brick Township, which consisted of an upland lot designated as Block 934, Lot 23.01 and a riparian grant separately designated as Block 934, Lot 23.03 on the municipal tax map. The riparian grant was created in 1928 and was recorded in Deed Book 781, page 481, in the Ocean County Clerk's Office.

As of 1992, the property was owned by Rowina Schoener Francis and her son George Francis. On April 6th of that year, Rowina and George deeded the property to themselves and to George's wife Carolyn Francis. That deed specifically included and described the upland lot and the riparian grant as tract one and tract two, respectively.

Several years later, in 1995, George was operating a business that was struggling financially. As a result, he applied for a loan from Equity One, Inc. (Equity One), using the property as security. During the application process, George, Carolyn, and Rowina deeded their interest in the upland property to George and Carolyn. That deed, dated March 22, 1995, did not mention the adjacent riparian grant (Lot 23.03) but only described the property as Lot 23.01, Block 934 on the tax map and also contained a metes and bounds description of only the upland lot as provided by the title company.

On March 23, 1995, Equity One agreed to lend George $220,000. As security for the loan, George and Carolyn executed a mortgage in favor of Equity One on property that was described exactly as it had been in the 1995 deed — as Lot 23.01, Block 934 on the tax map and also as 633 Point Avenue. Although the mortgage documents included the language "TOGETHER WITH all the improvements now or hereafter erected on the property, and all easements, appurtenances, and fixtures now or hereafter a part of the property," no mention of the riparian grant (Lot 23.03) was contained therein.

George thereafter defaulted on the loan. Equity One foreclosed on the mortgage, and a sheriff's sale occurred on June 24, 1997. The sheriff's deed contained the same description of the encumbered property as the 1995 deed, including a metes and bounds description of the upland lot only. Equity One was the successful bidder and thus acquired title to the mortgaged property.

Subsequently, Equity One received separate offers to purchase the property from Joseph Panetta, Dennis and Dorothy McKenna, and Anne Covey. Panetta offered to buy the property for $220,000 and Equity One made a counteroffer of $235,000. Panetta agreed to the increased purchase price, and on July 16, 1997, the attorney for Equity One prepared a contract to that effect. Panetta signed the contract and forwarded a $10,000 deposit. However, the contract was never signed by a corporate representative of Equity One.

In the interim, Dennis and Dorothy McKenna offered to purchase the property for $265,000 with the assistance of their real estate agent. The agent forwarded a contract signed by the McKennas, as well as an executed Right-to-Sell Listing Agreement and Dual Agency Consent Agreement. An officer of Equity One signed the contract, but the attorney for Equity One canceled it within the attorney review period. On July 23, 1997, Michael Morris, on behalf of Anne Covey, faxed an offer of $240,000 to Equity One.

On July 25, 1997, Equity One rejected all previous offers and initiated a closed bidding process limited to the three prior bidders — Panetta, McKenna, and Covey. The bid letter communicated Equity One's offer, as "the owner of 633 Point Avenue," to sell the property to the highest bidder subject to a few terms, which included that "no realtor commissions would be paid by seller." Panetta submitted a bid of $255,000 with no other conditions or terms. McKenna submitted a bid of $287,000, describing the property as including both the upland lot and the riparian grant, and conditioned on the realtor's commission being subtracted from the bid offer. Covey submitted a bid of $280,000 with a statement that "said property according to the deed recorded in Ocean County lists a riparian grant which is incorporated in this bid as sale of both the property and the riparian grant."

On July 29, 1997, Equity One informed Covey that her bid was the highest. She promptly forwarded a ten-percent deposit and a contract, inclusive of the riparian grant. The contract was never signed by Equity One. Rather, the following day, the attorney for Equity One, believing a mistake had been made regarding the real estate commission, advised all parties that Equity One would reopen the process on an open competitive basis.

Covey immediately filed suit against Equity One for specific performance; breach of contract; breach of implied covenant of good faith and fair dealing; consumer fraud; fraud; and malicious misrepresentation. Panetta and the McKennas filed separate complaints and the McKennas' realtor successfully moved to intervene. The complaints were consolidated into a single action in the Chancery Division in which the parties stipulated to the facts and agreed that the judge's findings could be based solely on the deposition testimony and documents that had been submitted.

In his June 11, 2004, decision, Judge Clyne determined, as a matter of fact, that George Francis intentionally excluded the riparian grant in securing the mortgage and that Equity One was, in fact, unaware of the grant. Had the situation been otherwise, the judge concluded, Equity One would have required the grant to be included in the mortgage. The judge further held that neither N.J.S.A. 46:3-16 nor any other statute or case requires that a riparian grant follow the upland property as a matter of law. Therefore, he again awarded specific performance to Panetta on the ground that Panetta, whose bid was limited to the upland lot, had submitted the only conforming bid and that an enforceable contract resulted. The judge also dismissed Covey's fraud claim against Equity One and entered final judgment. Covey again appealed.

In a published opinion, the Appellate Division affirmed the dismissal of Covey's fraud and misrepresentation claims but reversed the judgment of specific performance in favor of Panetta. Panetta v. Equity One, 378 N.J. Super. 298, 320, 875 A.2d 991 (App. Div. 2005). Noting that N.J.S.A. 46:3-16 requires that deeds should be construed broadly to include all appurtenances unless expressly excepted, the panel held that, although not mentioned or described, the riparian grant was included in the 1995 conveyance. Id. at 315-17, 875 A.2d 991.

In ruling, the panel declared the intent underlying N.J.S.A. 46:3-16 to be the provision of "certainty and stability in land ownership" and "to prevent fraud by precluding a grantor from attempting to secretly retain, through ambiguous drafting, some part of or interest in land." Id. at 311-12, 875 A.2d 991. Accordingly, the panel determined that "all property interests that may arguably be contained within or deemed appended to a parcel of real property" fall within the statute's "all-encompassing scope" and that a riparian grant is appurtenant to the land to which it is adjacent as a matter of law. Id. at 312-13, 875 A.2d 991. Thus, "the riparian rights were conveyed notwithstanding the absence of any express mention of those rights in the 1995 deed, and notwithstanding the grantors' actual intentions." Id. at 317, 875 A.2d 991.

II.

Panetta argues that the riparian grant was not conveyed with the upland property and that the Appellate Division erred in construing N.J.S.A. 46:3-16 to that effect; that the tax map designation is the critical point that obviates the possibility of the riparian grant being considered an appurtenance; that all property in foreclosure must be clearly identified and the riparian grant was not; and, finally, that he was the highest conforming bidder and should be awarded the property.

Covey argues that she is entitled to the property as a result of her bid in the without-reserve auction; that, as a matter of law, the riparian grant was included with the upland property under N.J.S.A. 46:3-13 and -16; that Equity One is a sophisticated commercial entity and, thus, the Appellate Division's invalidation of her bid based on "confusion" was improper; that the Appellate Division's decision undermines confidence in public auctions; and that Equity One's attempt to redo the auction violated the Consumer Fraud Act, N.J.S.A. 56:8-1 to -20.

Equity One does not take a position on the question of whether the riparian grant was conveyed with the upland property by operation of law but argues that the Appellate Division correctly ordered a rebid based on confusion.

The New Jersey Land Title Association submits that the Appellate Division's decision could adversely affect the stability of titles to real property throughout New Jersey; that the panel confused riparian rights and riparian grants in interpreting N.J.S.A. 46:3-16; and that the intent of the parties governs what property is transferred with a deed.

III.

At the heart of this case is the 1995 deed. Covey argues that that deed transferred the riparian grant as a matter of law and that, when George and Carolyn secured the mortgage, the riparian grant was therefore also included. If Covey is correct, only the contract issues remain to be resolved. If Covey is incorrect and the riparian grant did not pass as a matter of law under the 1995 deed, George and Carolyn only secured the mortgage with the upland lot, and that is all Equity One could have acquired at the sheriff's sale. Under that scenario, only Panetta's bid was conforming. We turn, then, to the applicable legal principles.

A.

Under New Jersey law, deeds are "construed to include all the grantor's estate, right, title, interest, use, possession, property, claim and demand" unless the grantor expressly limits the conveyance. N.J.S.A. 46:3-13. Moreover, N.J.S.A. 46:3-16 provides as follows:

> Every deed conveying land shall, unless an exception shall be made therein, be construed to include all and singular the buildings, improvements, ways, woods, waters, watercourses, rights, liberties, privileges, hereditaments and appurtenances to the same belonging or in anywise appertaining; and the reversion and reversions, remainder and remainders, rents, issues and profits thereof, and of every part and parcel thereof.

The Appellate Division broadly interpreted that statute to sweep in "all property interests that may arguably be contained within or deemed appended to a parcel of real property, whether tangible or intangible." Panetta, supra, 378 N.J. Super. at 312, 875 A.2d 991. In particular, the panel declared that the riparian grant was appurtenant to the upland lot under N.J.S.A. 46:3-16 and that it passed with the deed to the upland lot because that deed did not explicitly exclude it. Id. at 315, 875 A.2d 991.

In ruling as it did, the Appellate Division failed to distinguish between a riparian right and a riparian grant. A riparian right is the right of a riparian landowner to make reasonable use of adjacent water and is facially included in N.J.S.A. 46:3-16. A riparian grant is a separate estate in land. Contrary to the Appellate Division's view, riparian rights and grants are not identical and are not similarly governed by N.J.S.A. 46:3-16. This case centers on a riparian grant of real property identified on the tax map as distinct from the upland lot. That separate designation, which the Appellate Division viewed as inconsequential, is in fact critical.

B.

Riparian means "of, relating to, or located on the banks of a river or stream (or occasionally another body of water, such as a lake)." Black's Law Dictionary 1352 (8th ed. 2004); 6 Waters and Water Rights 1290 (Robert E. Beck, ed., 1991, repl. vol. 2005). Riparian doctrine declares that

> Owners of lands along the banks of a stream or water body have the right to reasonable use of the waters and a correlative right protecting against unreasonable use by others that substantially diminishes the quantity or quality of water. The right

is viewed as a property interest or as appurtenant to the land and does not depend on prior use.

In essence, a riparian right is a license or privilege to access and make reasonable use of water.

Riparian lands are lands lying along the banks of a stream or water body. "The State owns in fee simple all lands that are flowed by the tide up to the high-water line or mark." A riparian grant, in turn, is the method by which the State conveys riparian lands to its citizens. Like other conveyances, a riparian grant is not limited to an upland owner but may, after being offered by the State to the upland owner, be granted to persons who are unconnected to the upland property. N.J.S.A. 12:3-23.

In short, a riparian grant is the conveyance of real property divided from the uplands by a fixed boundary, no different from any other conveyance of land.

Covey's argument to the contrary is simply not correct. She contends that a riparian grant is not like other conveyances. In support, she cites the following language from the original 1928 deed to the Metedeconk Company, the predecessor in title to the Francis family:

> And Also Provided, that if the said The Metedeconk Company is not the owner of the land adjoining the land under water hereby granted, then and in that event this instrument and conveyance, so far as the same binds the State, and all covenants herein on the part of the State, shall be void as affecting any part or parts of said land which joins land not owned by the said The Metedeconk Company.

Covey argues that the deed language shows that a riparian grant is a lesser interest in property because, if separated from the uplands, it reverts to the State. Covey misapprehends the import of that language. Its purpose is not to proscribe severance of the riparian lands from the uplands, but to condition the grant on compliance with the statutory requirement that when riparian lands are sold by the State they must first be offered to the upland owner. See N.J.S.A. 12:3-23. The clauses are placed into the deeds to cause reverters to the State in the event that the initial claim of upland ownership turns out to be false.

Given the description of the riparian grant as an estate in land and "not a mere franchise or incorporeal hereditament," the notion that it is, as a matter of law, appurtenant to the upland property is simply unavailing. An appurtenance "belongs or is attached to something else" and is generally of an incorporeal nature.

Put another way, a riparian right and a riparian grant are conceptually distinct, and that distinction is pivotal in an appurtenance analysis. A riparian right not expressly mentioned in a deed can be appurtenant, but a riparian grant cannot. A contrary conclusion would allow a party to claim an ownership interest in a stranger's riparian lands as "appurtenant" to his own and would place in jeopardy the stability of titles to real property throughout the State.

Generally, if property is not expressly included in the instrument's description, it will not be covered by the mortgage. Here the mortgage did not reference the riparian grant either expressly or obliquely.

Moreover, we note that prior to a foreclosure sale, a sheriff must give signed notice of the time and the place of the sale by public advertisement and that the notice must include an actual description of the property including "either a diagram of the premises or a concise statement indicating the municipality, the tax lot and block and where appropriate, the street and street number, and the dimensions of the premises, as well as the number of feet to the nearest cross street." N.J.S.A. 2A:61-1. Here, the only description of the property in the sheriff's sale notice was what was contained in the 1995 deed — the upland lot. Thus, more could not have been included in the sale.

The judgment of the Appellate Division is reversed. The trial judge's order of specific performance to Panetta is reinstated.

For reversal and reinstatement — Chief Justice ZAZZALI and Justices LONG, LAVECCHIA, ALBIN, WALLACE, RIVERA-SOTO and HOENS — 7.

Opposed — None.

CASE QUESTIONS

1 What is the primary question in this case?
2 How did George Francis become involved with Equity One?
3 What determination did Judge Clyne make in this case?
4 According to the appellate court, what is the "heart" of this case?
5 Under New Jersey law, what rights are conveyed with a deed?
6 How does the New Jersey Supreme Court define "riparian rights"?

 SKILLS YOU NEED IN THE REAL WORLD

DRAWING PROPERTY DESCRIPTIONS

In this chapter, we have discussed in detail the various methods used to adequately describe property. We have seen, for instance, that adequate property descriptions are not only a good way of confirming which tract is actually being sold, but also are required by state law. This brings us to the issue of learning how to actually prepare written drawings of metes and bounds and other property descriptions. Why would a paralegal need this skill? There will be times, it is true, when you can simply locate a plat or other pre-existing drawing and compare it to the written description for accuracy. However, there are many lots that have never been surveyed and for which there are no maps. In those situations, the only way to be sure that the property boundary makes sense — and that there are no gaps in the description — is to actually draw it out yourself. Once you have acquired the skill, you will find that it comes in handy in many other situations as well. For instance, if you can hand draw a property description, you can actually make your own drawing and compare it to questionable surveys. Learning how to draw property descriptions is an important skill for any paralegal who specializes in real estate law.

CHAPTER SUMMARY

One of the most important aspects of real property is the ability to identify a particular parcel that is being transferred. Property descriptions are a way to show how a tract of real property is specific and unique. In this chapter, we have seen that there are several methods used in the United States to describe real property. This chapter specifically examined the use of metes and bounds descriptions to describe property boundaries. A metes and bounds description is the distance and direction of each of the boundary lines such that any described parcel may be drawn precisely.

There are many rights that arise directly from ownership of real estate. Among these rights are riparian, or water, rights. Water rights not only include the ability to draw water for use, but also define how a property's boundaries may change over time by the natural forces that water exerts on the land. Through erosion or accretion, a landowner's property boundaries may change. Accretion is the process of adding additional area to the parcel, while erosion is the process of slowly removing area from the parcel.

REVIEW QUESTIONS

1   Why is it important to have an accurate property description for a real estate transaction?
2   Explain the difference between identifying real property and identifying personal property in a sale.
3   Describe the history of surveying real estate property boundaries.
4   What are the two critical elements of a property description?
5   Why is street address not sufficient to describe a parcel of real estate?
6   Explain the legal requirements for property descriptions in a deed.
7   What types of documents can a legal description refer to in creating a valid legal description?
8   What are patently ambiguous property descriptions?
9   What is the parol evidence rule and how does it apply to patently ambiguous and latently ambiguous property descriptions?
10   What are latently ambiguous property descriptions?
11   What is a metes and bounds description?
12   How long is a "rod"? How long is a "chain"?
13   What equipment do you need to draw a metes and bounds description?
14   What is a tract-indexing system?
15   What is a plat?
16   What is the Torrens registration system?
17   What are riparian rights?
18   Describe the natural forces that can affect property boundaries.
19   Compare and contrast accretion with erosion.
20   Explain the significance of this chapter's case excerpt.

DISCUSSION QUESTIONS

Based on what you have learned about the various methods used to describe real property, should all states be required to follow the same system? If so, which system would you advocate?

PRACTICAL APPLICATIONS

Draw the following metes and bounds descriptions:

For the following exercises, you will need a circular land measure compass. You will also need a regular straight ruler. Place the compass center point over the point of beginning, with North always facing the top of the page. Turn the dial to the desired direction and mark that point with a pencil. Using your straight ruler, measure the corresponding inches from the P.O.B along the direction indicated. Remember, for purposes of this exercise, our conversion is 1 inch = 100 ft.

1   Beginning at a point on the southwest corner of the lot, then proceeding due North 400 feet to a point, then due East 90 degrees 400 feet to a point, then due South 400 feet to a point, then due West 400 feet to the P.O.B.

2   Beginning at a point on the southwest corner of the lot, then North 60 degrees East 200 feet to a point, then South 85 degrees East 300 feet to a point, then South 25 degrees East 300 feet to a point, then South 60 degrees West 200 feet to a point, then North 50 degrees West 550 feet to the P.O.B.

3   Beginning at a point on the North side of the property, South 52 degrees East 250 feet to a point, then South 30 degrees West 250 feet, then South 68 degrees West 300 feet, then North 90 degrees 40 feet to a point, then North 65 degrees East 200 feet to a point, then North 9 degrees West 150 feet to a point, then North 52 degrees West 100 feet to a point, then North 41 degrees East 200 feet to the P.O.B.

WEB SITES

Property Descriptions Summary
http://www.csc.noaa.gov/mbwg/_pdf/products/property_descriptions.PDF

Patently ambiguous descriptions — U.S. Supreme Court Case
http://www.law.cornell.edu/supremecourt/text/355/554

Parol Evidence Rule — Santa Clara Law School
**http://law.scu.edu/FacWebPage/Neustadter/contractsebook/main/com-
mentary/Parolevidence.html**

Metes and Bounds Descriptions — Texas A&M University
**http://agecon2.tamu.edu/people/faculty/lard-curtis/432/PDFs/
MetesAndBounds.pdf**

Metes and Bounds Descriptions Video — Youtube.com
http://www.youtube.com/watch?v=kjCdSUOPWs4

U.S. Public Land Survey System
http://www.dot.ca.gov/hq/row/landsurveys/LSITWorkbook/12.pdf

Real Estate Plats
Search any local land office online

California Division of Water Rights
http://www.swrcb.ca.gov/waterrights/

Accretion, Reliction & Quiet Title Action
http://dnr.alaska.gov/mlw/factsht/accretion.pdf

TERMS AND PHRASES

Latently ambiguous	Riparian rights	Parol evidence
Patently ambiguous		

SIGNIFICANT CASES

Commonwealth Elec. Co. v. MacCardell, 450 Mass. 48, 876 N.E.2d 405 (Mass., 2007)
Stephens v. Dortch, 148 N.C.App. 509, 558 S.E.2d 889 (N.C. App., 2002)
Sila v. Saunders, 274 Neb. 809, 743 N.W.2d 641 (Neb., 2008)
Garner v. Holley, 968 So.2d 234 (La. App. 2 Cir., 2007)
Nebraska v. Iowa, 406 U.S. 117, 92 S. Ct. 1379 (1972)
Strohschein v. Crager, 258 S.W.3d 25, (Ky. App., 2007)

Transferring Title to Real Estate

4

Focus of This Chapter

This chapter addresses the numerous ways that title to real estate can be transferred, through both voluntary and involuntary means. The chapter emphasizes the practical concerns for paralegals in many of these transfers.

Chapter Learning Objectives

After completing this chapter, you should be able to:

■ Distinguish between voluntary transfers and involuntary transfers of title in real estate
■ Explain the basic requirements of a will
■ Compare and contrast dedication and homesteading as a means to transfer real estate title
■ Explain foreclosure
■ List and explain the elements of adverse possession

INTRODUCTION

In this chapter, we examine the various ways that title to property can be transferred, both voluntarily and involuntarily. Under the category of voluntary transfers, there are sales, testate proceedings, gifts, and other means. Involuntary transfers include foreclosure of property rights by a mortgage lender, seizure of property by governmental action through eminent domain, partition of the property, and loss of property rights through adverse possession.

VOLUNTARY TRANSFERS OF TITLE

In this section, we examine the various ways that a property owner can use to voluntarily transfer property rights to others. The methods are listed from the most frequently to least frequently used. Sale of property is by far the most common way of voluntarily transferring title.

A. SALE

When a property owner has title to property, she is entitled to sell that title to anyone else. Sale of real property is similar to the sale of personal property. The current owner surrenders title in exchange for something of value, usually money. The purchaser acquires title in exchange for surrendering the purchase price to the previous owner. It is tempting to think that the sale of real property resembles the sale of personal property in other ways, but that approach would be incorrect. There are important and fundamental differences between real and personal property, as becomes evident when we consider how title to each is transferred.

 **Sale is the most common form of voluntary title transfer in real estate.**

In personal property, one of the best indicators of ownership is possession. The old rule, which we have all heard in one context or another, that "possession is nine-tenths of the law" applies only to personal property, not real property. This rule, an old common law principle, guided courts in determining the ownership of diverse types of personal property, especially property that could not readily be identified. However, ownership of real property has always been characterized differently. The reason for the different approach to ownership — and the transfer of ownership rights — in real property probably stems from several critical factors. For one thing, land has often been a source of wealth. It certainly was the basis of the early English system of patronage between king and subjects. But the significance of land title has survived the societies that created it. Land continues to be an important source of revenue and obligation in modern society. For most people, purchase of the family home is still their largest financial undertaking.

Historically, the procedures involved in transferring title to land also followed different, more rigid controls than those used to transfer title to personal property. Although this is not a history lesson on the development of real property issues, it is interesting to note that there is an entire body of both English and American law concerning the procedures used to transfer real estate title, including "seizin," "fee," and other terms that we return to in Chapter 8 when we address the concept of real estate deeds.

The issue of the many important differences between real property and personal property transactions comes up again and again in issues as diverse as the creation of real estate deeds (Chapter 8), financing real estate purchases (Chapter 9), and the public and private limitations on the way that real property can be used (Chapter 10). However, having said this, it is interesting to note that the preliminary requirements for sale of real property are straightforward.

The original colony states, such as Massachusetts, New York, Georgia, and the Carolinas, were all conveyed by the government of England to one or more individuals. The usual form of this conveyance was by royal charter. These charters gave the residents specific rights to use and to convey the property to others, subject to certain conditions, such as regular tax payments to the king. The Declaration of Independence and the subsequent Revolutionary War severed all ties with England. This raised an interesting question: If the original authority to hold land in the colony states arose from the king's permission, what was the source of authority after the Revolution? The colonies generally adopted an approach that simply substituted the state for the king and made property ownership subject to the power of the new American governments.[1] For states that came into existence after the Revolution, a different system of property authority developed. In many areas, it was the federal government, not individual state governments that had original ownership of the land. This ownership may have derived from purchase from foreign governments, negotiation with Indian tribes, or simple assertion of claim to vast tracts of land.

> ## Sidebar
>
> *Land in the United States originated from many sources, including purchases from England, France, Holland, Mexico, and Spain. In other situations, the federal government purchased land claimed by individual states or held by Native American nations.[2]*

FIGURE 4-1

Home Prices. U.S. Housing Market Conditions, 3rd Quarter 2011. U.S. Department of Housing and Urban Development, Office of Policy Development and Research.

	Latest Quarter ($)	Previous Quarter ($)	Same Quarter Previous Year ($)	% Change from Previous Quarter	% Change from Last Year
New Homes					
Median	219,000	228,100	224,100	−4**	−2**
Average	257,600	267,600	266,000	−4**	−3**
Constant-Quality House[1]	276,200	280,700	279,800	−2**	−1**
Existing Homes					
Median	169,300	168,700	176,900	−	−4
Average	217,500	217,900	225,200	−	−3

** This change is not statistically significant.

[1] Effective with the December 2007 New Residential Sales release in January 2008, the Census Bureau began publishing the Constant Quality (Laspeyres) Price Index with 2005 as the base year. (The previous base year was 1996.) "Constant-Quality House" data are no longer published as a series but are computed for this table from price indexes published by the Census Bureau.

---

[1] *United States v. King*, 44 U.S. (3 How.) 773, 11 L. Ed. 824 (1845).
[2] *Johnson v. M'Intosh*, 21 U.S. (8 Wheat.) 543, 5 L. Ed. 681 (1823).

A question often arises when discussing the sales of real estate: Why should we be concerned about the original source of title for a particular parcel? The original source of title is important because of an ancient principle in real estate law. A person can only receive the quality of title that the previous owner possessed. In other areas of law, a purchaser may actually improve the quality of her title when the purchaser can show that the property was acquired under certain circumstances. However, that is not the case with real property. The quality of title of the new owner derives from the previous owner, and so on, until the original grant of title. If that title had defects, those defects haunt the transactions of every subsequent purchaser.

1. THE BASIC REQUIREMENTS OF SALE OF REAL PROPERTY

The basic requirements of a sale of real property are the same requirements that we might see in any contractual obligation. The parties to the transactions must have:

- Mutual assent
- Consideration
- Capacity
- Property description

Sidebar

Some of the methods used by state and federal governments to obtain land from Native Americans were questionable, at best. Some were outright theft.[3]

ISSUE AT A GLANCE

A sale is a contract between buyers and sellers and must therefore meet all legal requirements of a contract.

a. Mutual Assent

Mutual assent is a contract law element that requires that both parties to the contract know and understand the material features of the contract. For instance, both the buyer and the seller must be in agreement about the property that is the subject of the transaction. Each must understand that she is undertaking a legal obligation.

b. Consideration

Consideration is a requirement for most types of contracts, including the sale of real property. Consideration is often referred to as "bargained-for exchange." This is a legal requirement that both parties to the transaction have a stake in the outcome. Seller *A* is surrendering something of value in exchange for receiving something else of value. In a typical real estate transaction, Seller *A* is surrendering title to the property in exchange for money. Buyer *B* is surrendering

---

[3] *Indian Land Rights: An International Approach to Just Compensation,* 2 Transnatl. L. & Contemp. Probs. 301 (Spring 1992).

money in exchange for title to the property. This exchange would seem to be a given in any contract, so why do all jurisdictions require consideration as an element to a contract, including real estate transactions? Consideration has more to do with enforcing the contract than proving that one existed. If one party to the contract neither gives up nor receives anything of value, how can she truly be said to be bound? Exchange is the core issue in any contract and if one party does not give or receive, how would the contract be enforced? What recourse would the court have in ordering the party to conform to the details of the agreement if the party has no obligations? We return to the topic of consideration in several other contexts throughout this book, both in drafting real estate contracts (Chapter 6) and the importance of consideration in deeds (Chapter 8).

c. Capacity

Another requirement of any contractual agreement is that all parties to the transaction have legal capacity to enter into a transaction. Capacity refers to the party's ability to know and understand the consequences of entering into a legal contract. Persons who lack capacity cannot become parties to a binding contract. Examples of persons who lack capacity include:

- Infants
- Intoxicated persons
- Mentally incompetent persons

i. Infants

At law, an infant is anyone under the age of 18. Contracts cannot be enforced against children. When a party to a contract is revealed to be underage, the court is authorized to void the contract and return the parties to the positions they were in before the contract was ever created.

ii. Intoxicated Persons

If a person can show that she was under the influence of alcohol or some other drug at the time that a contract was created, the court is authorized to void the contract in much the same way that the court can when a party is underage. Here, intoxication refers to a state in which a person is so under the influence that she could not understand the consequences of the obligation. Intoxication does not simply mean that a person had had something to drink. Instead, a person must be intoxicated to the point that she could not form the mental state necessary to enter into a contract.

iii. Mentally Incompetent Persons

A person who suffers from a mental or physical condition that makes it impossible for her to understand the legal obligations imposed by a contract cannot be a party to a contract. In some cases, a court may have declared that a specific person is mentally incompetent and appointed a guardian to handle all of this person's affairs. In other situations, the person may be deemed mentally incompetent after the contract has been created. In such a case, a court would be authorized to void the contract and refuse to enforce it against the mentally incompetent person.

EXAMPLE 4-1

Cory writes out the following document and hands it to Raul:

"I hereby sell to you that parcel of land known as my house, Anytown, USA. The price for this sale is your continued friendship."

Signed: Cory, age 12

Signed: Raul, age 12

Is this a valid real estate transaction?

Answer: No. We can attack this transaction on several grounds. First, there is no consideration for the sale. "Continued friendship" sounds very nice, but most courts would not recognize it as a legal finding of consideration. Even if the court were tempted to rule that consideration exists, there is another problem. The description is hopelessly vague. Added to that, there is the issue of capacity. Both the "buyer" and the "seller" are under the legal age to carry out such a transaction. What changes to the details would result in a valid transaction?

d. Property Description

The previous three requirements of a binding real estate contract have all focused on the capacity of the parties. However, this last element is unique to real property: adequate property description. As we saw in the previous chapter, adequate property description is something more than mere street address. Whether a particular state uses metes and bounds descriptions, plats, tracts, or surveys, it is absolutely essential that the contract set out a specific, unique, and identifiable parcel of real estate as the subject of the real estate contract.

Tech Topic
ROBO-SIGNING

As the mortgage crisis of 2008 began producing massive numbers of foreclosures, questions arose regarding the propriety of banks vigorously foreclosing on tens of thousands of loans. Many foreclosures were determined to be in error; in some cases, banks even foreclosed on the wrong homes. The most disturbing trend during the early tidal wave of foreclosures was that banks would provide fraudulent documentation to the courts.

Bank executives and employees used the practice of robo-signing to produce volumes of erroneous and forged foreclosure documents, most of which were signed with the signatory having no knowledge of the facts within the documents. Bank employees who signed such documents never took the time to verify the information contained therein. Some reports showed that one bank employee robo-signed nearly 10,000 fraudulent foreclosure documents in a single month. In other cases, a low-level bank employee repeatedly forged an executive's signature.

The term robo-signing arose from the robotic act of signing one's name, over and over, without any knowledge of the accuracy of the facts therein. For all the attention paid to the documents' accuracy, they might as well have been computer-generated with an electronic signature.

Although robo-signing is illegal — and most major banks suspended foreclosures while trying to address the problem — it persists today. The legal issues are especially troubling. A homebuyer trying to obtain title insurance, for example, might be delayed or denied if robo-signed documents turn up in the property's history. Forged signatures cast doubt upon who owns the mortgages and the properties they are attached to.

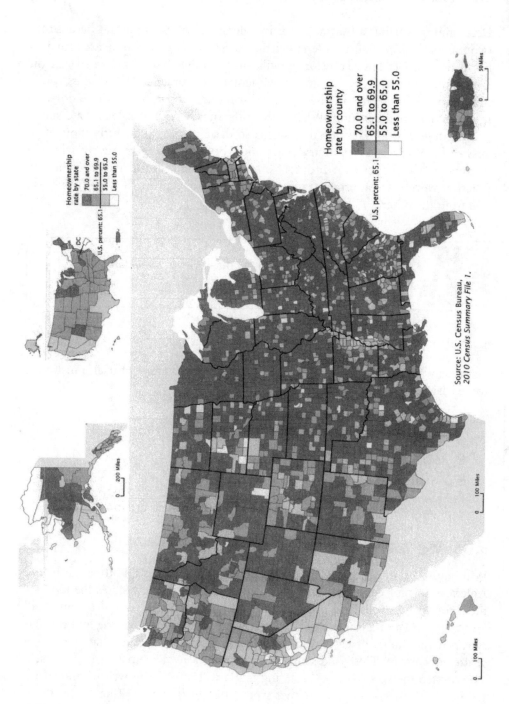

FIGURE 4-2

Homeownership Rates: 2010. Housing Characteristics: 2010. 2010 Census Briefs. U.S. Census Bureau.

Homeownership rate by county

70.0 and over
65.1 to 69.9
55.0 to 65.0
Less than 55.0

U.S. percent: 65.1

Homeownership rate by state

70.0 and over
65.1 to 69.9
55.0 to 65.0
Less than 55.0

U.S. percent: 65.1

Source: U.S. Census Bureau, 2010 Census Summary File 1.

B. WILL (PROBATE)

Determining whether a transaction is by sale or by will is important because the two transactions have such different elements. Sales, as we have seen, are primarily based on contract law. Transfer by will, on the other hand, must meet all the minimum requirements of any testamentary document. We discuss those minimum requirements in the next few sections, but we must first address a more fundamental question: What is the difference between a sale and a disposition through a will? The question seems so basic as to require little thought to answer it. A sale is a voluntary transaction between living parties; a will is a document that disposes of property after the owner's death. However, in the practical world of real estate transactions, it isn't always so easy to distinguish one from the other.

 The ability to leave property to one's heirs is considered an important right for all citizens.

1. THE MINIMUM REQUIREMENTS OF A WILL

Before any property can be passed through a will, the document itself must meet some basic requirements. For instance, it must:

Traditionally, sales were classified as inter vivos (Latin for "between the living") as a way of distinguishing these transactions from testamentary transactions, which only take effect after the property owner dies.

- Be in writing
- Be witnessed
- Be signed by the testator
- Clearly express the testator's state of mind
- Clearly devise property to a specific beneficiary

a. The Will Must Be in Writing

Wills must be in writing. This has been a requirement of both English and American law for centuries. The Statute of Frauds specifically states the requirement for written wills and provides that an unwritten will cannot be enforced. However, the statute is not specific about what constitutes a writing and this has spawned thousands of cases addressing exactly what is — and what is not — a written document. This is a discussion that could easily take up a chapter in itself. We sidestep the issue by simply stating that a will must be in writing and that a writing refers to ink on paper, either typewritten or in handwriting.

b. The Will Must Be Witnessed

When the testator creates a will, her signature and acknowledgment of the will must be witnessed. Under probate law, the testator must sign the will. All states require that the will must also be witnessed, although there is a split about whether the witnesses must actually see the testator sign the document, or even that they know that the document they are witnessing is actually a will. The function of witnesses is obvious. They can testify about the testator's state of mind at the precise moment that the testator signed the will. If the testator was not mentally competent, witnesses could testify to this fact. In some states, the testator must specifically announce that the document is her "last will and testament." This is referred to as **publication** of the will.

Publication
The announcement by a testator to witnesses that she has created a will and wishes to have it witnessed.

c. The Will Must Be Signed by the Testator

The testator's signature on a will has been a staple of American law for centuries. The original English Statute of Frauds required wills to be in writing and that statute was later adopted by the American colonies and later by all states in the Union. The signature requirement remains the law of the land today. However, there are some interesting features under the law about what actually constitutes a signature. For instance, many states still allow a person to sign a will with a mark, instead of a handwritten signature.[4] Some allow a fingerprint instead of a written name. Many states also have provisions that allow another person to sign for the testator, such as when the testator is too ill to sign for himself. In those situations, the person must be acting under the direction of the testator. The signing must be done in the testator's presence.[5]

i. Nuncupative Wills

Although we have said that wills must be in writing, there is a narrow exception that allows oral wills to be probated. A **nuncupative will** is an oral declaration by a testator, usually made shortly before death, before witnesses, about the disposition of her property. Such wills were drastically limited under the Statute of Frauds and usually have strict requirements, such as that three witnesses heard the testator's oral declaration and that the declaration was made when the testator knew death was imminent. Some states also impose a third requirement: that the statement was made inside the testator's home.[6] As a result of these strict requirements, nuncupative wills are rarely presented for probate.

Nuncupative will
An oral will, usually only permitted when the testator is in the last stages of life and is unable to draft a written will.

ii. Holographic Wills

In some situations, the witness requirement for a will can be waived. One such instance is a **holographic will**. A holographic will is one that the testator writes out in her own handwriting and signs. Such a will can be considered valid, even if it is not witnessed.

Holographic will
A will written entirely in the testator's handwriting.

---

[4] *Ahnert v. Ahnert*, 98 Kan. 201 (1916).
[5] *In re Will of Cox*, 139 Me. 261, 29 A.2d 281 (1942).
[6] *Christiansen v. Rumsey*, 91 Idaho 684, 429 P.2d 416 (1967).

ISSUE AT A GLANCE

There are many different types of wills and their legal require-ments differ greatly from those required in a contract for sale of real property.

EXAMPLE 4-2

Anthony has been diagnosed with inoperable cancer and has only a few months to live. He makes an audio recording at home one night, when he is all alone, that states his clear intention to leave all his property, both real and personal, to his brother Michael. On the tape, he acknowledges that he is making the transaction because he knows that he is dying. He seals the tape in an envelope that bears the typed message: "Open in the event of my death."

Is this a valid will?

Answer: If the minimum requirements of a will are the stated intention of the dece-dent, witnessed by others, this audio tape does not meet that standard. Anthony's state-ment made in the presence of others shortly before his death would qualify as a nuncupative will, but that is not the case here. Anthony's recording was not made in front of others and it was not made shortly before his death. The writing on the outside of the envelope also does not help the situation. Those words were typed and there is no signature. The audio tape is not a will.

d. The Will Must Clearly Express the Testator's State of Mind

In addition to being written, signed, and witnessed, a will must also express the testator's mental status. If a person is suffering from some form of mental or physical impairment that renders her incapable of understanding the significance of creating a will, the resulting document is void. Courts will not enforce a will drafted by a person who is mentally incompetent — or drafted by someone else under the testator's direction. This is one reason for the famous phrase found in wills, "I, _____ , being of sound mind." Although this statement is not dispositive of the issue of mental competence, it does point out the significance of the testa-tor's state of mind when the will is executed.

e. The Will Must Clearly Devise Property to a Specific Beneficiary

Devise
To transfer property in a will.

Beneficiary
A person named in a will that the testator intends to receive an interest in property.

Devisee
Another term for beneficiary.

When a will awards property to a specific person, this is usually referred to as a **devise** The person who receives the property in a will is the **beneficiary** or **devisee**. Although there are many technical rules surrounding who may receive (and in what amount) under a will, the general rules are simple: The beneficiary must be someone who is clearly identifiable. The beneficiary must be someone who can be located. There is no requirement that the testator actually identify the beneficiary by name, although this is obviously the best practice. A testator could, for instance, leave property to "my sister's children." Under this clause, any children of the testator's sister alive at the time that the testator dies would be entitled to receive a portion of the estate. However, problems occur in devising the property if it turns out that the testator has more than one sister, or if her sister has no children. This is one reason why it is so important to draft a will carefully. Attention to detail in specifying beneficiaries can forestall many problems later on.

2. WILLS VERSUS SALES

Although the differences between wills and sales seem obvious, it is important to summarize these differences. First of all, the differences may not be as obvious as you might think. The most common differences focus on the nature of the rights conferred on others. Deeds transfer immediate rights; wills transfer future interests. Consider the situation in Example 4-3.

EXAMPLE 4-3

Francesca owns a house that sits on three acres. She agrees to sell her property to her son, Darrell, for $10,000. She writes out a deed with the following provisions: "To my son, Darrell. To take effect on my death."

Is this a sale or transfer through testate proceeding?

If this is a sale, what present right has Darrell received? He does not have the immediate right to take possession of the property. In fact, his right is not triggered until his mother's death. However, if this is a will, it fails to meet the basic legal requirements for such a document.

Some states address the issue of the difference between a sale and a will as one that centers on "present interests." A deed transfers a present interest; a will does not. A present interest is a party's right to enter the land immediately and begin using the land. Wills, by their very nature, cannot transfer present interests. Instead, they transfer future interests. In a will, the beneficiary does not receive any immediate right to property. The beneficiary has a future right to property that will only become a present interest when a specific condition occurs, namely the death of the owner.[7] Prior to the testator's death, no interest passes.

a. Distinguishing Between Wills and Sales

When faced with the difficulties inherent in such transactions, courts have come up with some basic guidelines. For instance, when there is any ambiguity about what kind of transaction is involved, the courts will opt for an interpretation that the document is a deed instead of a will. The simple reason for this guideline is that it is easier to meet the minimum requirements of a deed than of a will. The other reason for this interpretation is that most such cases arise with documents that the parties themselves consider to be deeds, not wills.[8]

---

[7] *Sappingford v. King*, 49 Or. 102, 89 P.142, 90 P.150 (1907).
[8] *Nelson v. Parker*, 687 N.E.2d 187 (Ind. Ct. App. 1996); *Quickel v. Quickel*, 261 N.C. 696, 136 S.E.2d 52 (1964).

3. DIFFERENT METHODS USED TO TRANSFER TITLE THROUGH WILLS

Testators may transfer rights to property in many ways. Because this book does not address the complexity of probate issues, we focus on only two of the most common methods: intestate transfer and testate transfer.

a. Intestate Succession

Intestate
The term for a person who dies without a will.

In situations in which the owner dies without a will, she is said to have died intestate. Persons who die **intestate** do not leave any instructions about how their property should be divided among their heirs. In this situation, the probate court will appoint an administrator who disperses the property based on intestacy statutes. These statutes provide that the decedent's closest heirs, such as her spouse and children, should receive the estate. In situations in which the decedent has no close relatives, the statutes also dictate the share that the decedent's heirs should receive in the estate.

 **A person who dies with a will is said to have died testate; a person who dies without a will is said to have died intestate.**

b. Testate Succession

Testate
The term for a person who drafts a valid will before dying.

When a person dies after having created a will, and that will is judged to be legally sufficient, she is said to have died **testate**. In such a situation, courts will work to carry out the testator's intentions in regard to the transfer of her property.

C. GIFT

A property owner is always free to give property away, assuming that there is no outstanding mortgage or other indebtedness on the property. If there is such an indebtedness, a court may void the transaction, especially if it appears that the transaction was specifically designed to avoid claims raised by creditors. In situations in which a valid gift of real property has occurred, the receiver may also have tax issues to consider. The value of the property may be considered as a gain for purposes of calculating yearly income tax.

D. DEDICATION

When land is dedicated, it means that the owner has given the land over to the government for a specific use. One of the most common uses of dedicated land is for public parks, playgrounds, or recreation areas.[9] **Dedication** is a term that is reserved for a donation of land to the government, not transfers made to religious groups or charities. In those situations, the transfer is normally seen as a gift. Dedication is a process used to provide land for public use, not for private individuals, societies, or institutions.

Dedication
A grant of private land to the government.

E. HOMESTEADING

In some areas of the country where there is an abundance of land, but relatively few people, some states still use a system of awarding land rights to homesteaders. Under this system, which became popular in the late 1800s and early 1900s, a family could claim up to 160 acres of land by simply taking possession, residing there, and working the land as a farm. Most states have done away with this system, but it still exists in the less populous states. A homesteader must claim her 160 acres from government-owned land. Homesteading is not a means for one person to usurp property rights held by another.

 **INVOLUNTARY TRANSFERS OF TITLE**

So far, our discussion has focused on voluntary transfers of title interests in real property. However, there are many transactions in which a person's rights to property may be taken away involuntarily. These methods include:

- Foreclosure
- Eminent domain
- Partition
- Escheat
- Civil judgment
- Adverse possession
- Tax auctions

A. FORECLOSURE

Although we discuss financing real estate purchases in Chapter 9, it is important to note the process of **foreclosure** here. When a person buys real estate and finances that purchase, the lender will insist on a provision in the loan agreement that allows the lender to auction off the property in the event that the borrower fails to make regular payments on the loan. Foreclosure is an action brought by a lending institution or some other party who has received property interest as part of the financial arrangements to purchase real property. Foreclosure is usually the last resort of a lender who is no longer receiving monthly mortgage payments. Part of

Foreclosure
The right of a lender (mortgagee) to initiate an action to auction off property for outstanding indebtedness in a mortgage or deed of trust.

---

[9] *Biglin v. Town of West Orange,* 46 N.J. 367, 217 A.2d 135 (1966).

the paperwork involved in obtaining a mortgage involves transferring a right from the owner to a lending institution to foreclose as a means of protecting its interest in the property.

 **Foreclosure is a legal remedy available to lenders to enforce the obligations in a mortgage.**

The legal theories underlying foreclosure vary from state to state. In some states, for example, when a borrower defaults on the loan, legal title to the property passes to the lender. In other states, the foreclosure action is similar to a lien on the property that can only be foreclosed after judicial action. In still other states, where deeds of trust are common, the financial arrangement is more like a trust whereby a trustee has the right to foreclose on behalf of the lender.

There are generally two types of foreclosure proceedings used in the United States: **judicial foreclosure** and **power of sale foreclosure**.[10] Judicial foreclosure is similar to any other legal action. In a judicial foreclosure, a party requests that a court enter an order divesting the borrower's rights to the property. Because many states have ruled that a judicial foreclosure that fails to abide by each statutory requirement is a void action, most lenders opt for power of sale foreclosure.

Judicial foreclosure
Foreclosure based on state statutes.

Power of sale foreclosure
Foreclosure brought pursuant to a mortgage agreement.

1. POWER OF SALE FORECLOSURE

Under power of sale foreclosure, a lender inserts a contract provision in the mortgage agreement that allows the lender to institute foreclosure actions when the borrower defaults on the loan. This procedure has the benefit of less judicial involvement and gives the lender more latitude in deciding when to bring the foreclosure action. In the next sections, we examine the steps involved in bringing a power of sale foreclosure. The first step is to determine whether the lender has the right to foreclose.

a. The Right to Foreclose

The right to foreclose only becomes available when a borrower fails to meet one of the stipulations in the mortgage agreement. The most common stipulations in mortgage financing are that the borrower:

- Make regular monthly payments on the loan
- Insure the property
- Pay real estate taxes on the property
- Maintain the premises

---

[10] *National Tailoring Co. v. Scott*, 65 Wyo. 64, 196 P.2d 387 (1948).

Failure to meet one of these conditions is referred to as default, and it triggers the foreclosure procedure.

b. Default

When a borrower fails to live up to the agreements in the mortgage, such as failing to make regular monthly payments on the loan, the borrower is considered to be in **default** on the loan. Default has a specific, legal connotation. When a borrower defaults, the lender has the right to initiate foreclosure action. In many ways, a borrower's default on a mortgage is similar to a party's failure to fulfill a contract provision. The lender has the right to cancel the mortgage in the same way that a contract party may sue to terminate a contract.

Default
Violation of a contractual duty.

Mortgage agreements contain specific provisions detailing what actions constitute a default. Although failure to make payments on the loan is the most common type of default, there are situations that technically might qualify as a default. In the previous section, for example, there were listed four general promises or stipulations that a borrower makes to the lender in the mortgage agreement.

A violation of any of these stipulations could result in a foreclosure action. For instance, if the borrower failed to obtain insurance on the property, or failed to pay real estate taxes, the lender could initiate foreclosure proceedings. However, in the hardheaded world of residential mortgage lending, there are other, less drastic methods of dealing with these problems. The lender might take out an insurance policy on the residence and then bill the borrower for the premiums. The lender might also pay real estate taxes to keep the property from being auctioned off for back taxes and then pass these charges on to the borrower.

The most common reason for a foreclosure is the failure to make payments on the loan. Banks often will attempt to work out some type of arrangement short of foreclosure. Foreclosure can be a costly proposition and most lenders opt for it only as a last resort. As we will see in Chapter 9, a foreclosure is often seen as an error on the lender's part. Proper background checks and underwriting should have revealed the possibility that the borrower would go into foreclosure.

c. Notice to the Borrower

Once the lender has decided that foreclosure is the only option, the first step in bringing the action is to notify the borrowers that they are in default and that a foreclosure action is about to commence. The purpose of notifying the borrower is to satisfy the elements of the mortgage that require the lender to accelerate the loan provisions. On default, the lender has the right to notify the borrower that the entire balance of the loan is now due. This is part of the acceleration clause found in most mortgages. Of course, if a borrower is having trouble making monthly mortgage payments, it is highly unlikely that she would be able to pay the entire loan balance. The notice to the borrower usually contains a specific date by which the borrower must pay the entire loan balance or foreclosure actions will begin.

d. Steps in Foreclosure

In states where a foreclosure action must be brought as a form of civil action, the lender must present the case to a judge. In order to bring a foreclosure action, the lender must prove the following elements:

- That the property owner owes a debt to the lender
- That the property owner has failed to make payments on that debt
- That the lender has the right to foreclose on the property

Once the lender has proven these three elements, the lender is entitled to a judicial order forcing foreclosure of the property. Although borrowers are usually permitted to attend this judicial hearing, there is very little room for the borrower to argue against foreclosure. When the judge makes a finding that the borrower is in default, the judge has no option except to order foreclosure of the property pursuant to the mortgage agreement.

The power of sale provision is authorized by statute and must be strictly complied with. These requirements vary from state to state but all have some basic requirements, including:

- Notice provisions to the borrower
- Acceleration of the balance of the loan
- Posting the power of sale provision in the paper for a specific period of time
- Conducting an auction at the time and place stated in the posting

The first step in bringing a foreclosure action is for the lender to post the power of sale provision. This notice, a sample of which appears at the end of the chapter, is usually posted at the local courthouse and in the legal section of the local newspaper. Most states have provisions that require that the power of sale provision be published at least four weeks in a row before the foreclosure auction can be held.

e. The Foreclosure Auction

Once the preliminary steps in a foreclosure action have been completed, including publishing of the power of sale provision, the lender is authorized to auction off the property for the balance due on the loan. The actual auction process varies considerably from state to state. In some states, for example, foreclosure auctions can only be held on a specific day of the month, such as the first Tuesday. In other states, foreclosure auctions can occur on any regular business day. Because auctions have been subject to fraud in the past, many states limit their foreclosure auction procedures to specific times during regular business hours at specific locations. Common limitations on foreclosure actions include provisions that the lender must place the property for auction at the time stated in the advertised notice and at the location given in that notice. In many states, foreclosure auctions do not occur at the property location; they are held at the local courthouse.

f. The Right of Redemption

Because a typical foreclosure action is a form of contract proceedings, many states recognize that the borrower has a right of redemption. The right of redemption is the power of the borrower to purchase the property at the foreclosure auction or to pay off the loan balance prior to the auction to prevent foreclosure in the first place. In some states, the borrower's right to redeem the property is conclusively terminated when the property is sold to another at the foreclosure auction. Other states allow a redemption period that follows the sale. This redemption period, which can be as long as ten business days, allows the borrower the right to redeem the property from the auction purchaser.

Courts have not always recognized the right of a borrower to redeem the property. Historically, default on a mortgage loan was enough to authorize foreclosure and immediate seizure of the property.

Another way of defining foreclosure is to say that the foreclosure action terminates the borrower's right to redeem the property.[11]

	Latest Quarter	Previous Quarter	Same Quarter Previous Year	% Change from Prerious Quarter	% Change from Last Year
Total Past Due (%)					
All Loans	8.44	8.32	9.85	+1	−14
Conventional Subprime Loans	24.33	24.01	27.02	+1	−10
Conventional Subprime ARMs	27.18	26.31	29.50	+3	−8
90 Days Past Due (%)					
All Loans	3.61	3.62	4.82	−	−25
Conventional Subprime Loans	11.84	11.86	14.7	−	−19
Conventional Subprime ARMs	15.36	15.43	18.29	−	−16
Foreclosures Started(%)					
All Loans	0.96	1.08	1.11	−11	−14
Conventional Subprime Loans	2.84	3.08	2.83	−8	−
Conventional Subprime ARMs	3.62	3.67	3.39	−1	+7

Source: National Delinquency Survey, Mortgage Bankers Association

FIGURE 4-3

Delinquencies and Foreclosures. U.S. Housing Market Conditions, 3rd Quarter 2011. U.S. Department of Housing and Urban Development, Office of Policy Development and Research.

---

[11] Coote on Mortgages 1026 (9th ed. 2004).

g. Purchasing Property at a Foreclosure Sale

The process of purchasing property at a foreclosure sale is another area that varies considerably from state to state. However, there are some common elements found in all foreclosure auctions. The procedure involved in beginning the auction is usually straightforward: The lender or lender's representative reads the power of sale provision aloud and then opens bidding on the property. The lender has a standing bid for the balance owed on the mortgage. If no one appears to bid for the property at the foreclosure sale, the lender automatically becomes the winning bidder and receives title to the property. Lenders do not wish for this to happen. Taking over title to a property means that the lender now has responsibility to maintain the premises, to pay taxes on it, and also to arrange for the sale of the property. In many respects, it is easier for the lender when someone appears at the auction and bids on the property.

When a person bids on property at a foreclosure sale, her bid must be higher than the standing bid that the lender has on the property. Suppose that a particular piece of property has an $80,000 mortgage outstanding and is now up for auction. However, the property is actually worth $90,000. If a person bids at the foreclosure auction in excess of the lender's outstanding claim on the property, she is entitled to receive full title to the property, regardless of the fact that she did not pay the full market price of the property. The possibility of acquiring property at less than market rate is one of the most attractive features of a foreclosure auction. Unlike other types of auctions, such as law-enforcement asset seizures, there is no requirement that the bidder pay fair market value on the property. Obviously, the higher the value of the property and the lower the amount of the outstanding mortgage, the greater the chance that there will be competitors in the bid process.

Some states allow a successful bidder several days to come up with the full amount of the bid. In those states, the successful bidder usually must post a percentage of the total bid price that the bidder will forfeit if she fails to come up with the full bid amount. Other states allow bidders to present letters of credit from banks or other lending institutions that specify that the bidder's credit is good up to a specific amount.

h. Terminating the Rights of Other Creditors

When property is foreclosed, all junior lienholders' claims on the property are extinguished. A junior lienholder is someone who has a claim against the property that was filed at some point in time after the mortgage was created. If there is a lien or claim against the property that was filed before the mortgage, which is unlikely, that right would not be terminated by a foreclosure action. However, as we will see in Chapter 9, most banks insist that their first mortgage have priority over all other types of claims; therefore, if the lender brings a foreclosure action, all other claims against the property are extinguished. This means that the successful bidder at a foreclosure auction can usually take possession of the property without having to pay other claims. However, this general rule is subject to some specific exceptions. For instance, tax liens and other government assessments automatically take priority over all other claims, including first mortgages.

i. Mortgages and Deeds of Trust

So far, our discussion about foreclosure has made certain assumptions. One of these assumptions is that mortgages, which are the most popular form of financing of real estate in the United States, and deeds of trust, which are an older form of mortgage financing, proceed along the same lines in a foreclosure action. This is not true; a deed of trust is similar to mortgage only in superficial ways. In a typical foreclosure action, a mortgage lender proceeds against the borrower to auction off the property. Deeds of trust follow a different procedure. When a person obtains a deed of trust, a three-way arrangement is created. The borrower transfers the right of foreclosure to a trustee who acts as a middleman between the lender and the borrower. If the borrower defaults on the loan, the bank notifies the trustee to bring foreclosure proceedings. Because the borrower has already transferred certain rights to the trustee, foreclosing on the deed of trust is a much simpler process than foreclosing on a mortgage. The trustee must notify the borrower that she is in default, and then is allowed to post a power of sale provision in a local newspaper and begin foreclosure proceedings. Deed of trust foreclosures involve much less judicial interaction and therefore can proceed much more quickly. We discuss deeds of trust in greater detail in Chapter 9.

B. CONDEMNATION (EMINENT DOMAIN)

Although foreclosure is the most common way to involuntarily transfer title to real estate, it is not the only method. Another common process is eminent domain. Federal and state governments have the right to seize property, even property held by private individuals, for public use. The power of eminent domain is considered to be one of the inherent powers of government. Without it, governments could not build roads, set aside state parks, or create the infrastructure that we all rely upon.

> **Eminent domain is the power of the government to seize property for governmental purposes.**

ISSUE AT A GLANCE

1. THE PROCESS OF EMINENT DOMAIN: CONDEMNATION

Eminent domain refers to the power of the government to seize property; condemnation is the process of seizure. When the federal or state government decides that a certain parcel of land should be seized, it condemns the property for public use. The landowner cannot challenge the government's right to seize property. As long as the property is used for governmental purposes, a condemnation action will proceed. The only issue in a condemnation action is the amount of the landowner's compensation. The U.S. Constitution provides that landowners must be compensated for any land seized by the government. The amount of compensation is fair market value for the parcel that has been condemned. Fair market value refers to the actual value of the property that a willing buyer would pay to acquire the land.

The determination of fair market value for the seized property often results in a battle of experts, one set hired by the government and the other hired by the landowner. The government's experts may testify that the fair market value of a particular piece of property is $10,000, while a landowner's expert may testify that the actual fair market value of the property is $20,000. The ultimate determination of the amount falls to a judge or jury.

a. Inverse Condemnation

Occasionally, landowners will complain that government action has resulted in a diminution in value of their property. A landowner might claim, for example, that the installation of a sewage treatment plant next to her property has essentially rendered her property valueless. In such a situation, the landowner might bring an inverse condemnation action, alleging that although the government did not directly condemn her property and seize it, government action has resulted in an indirect seizure of the property because the landowner is now unable to sell it to anyone else. When a landowner brings an inverse condemnation action, a judge must determine whether the government's actions have actually resulted in a diminution or total destruction of the landowner's rights and enjoyment in the property.

C. PARTITION

When two or more individuals own property together, each owner has the right to bring a partition action against the other owners. A partition action does exactly what its name suggests: It divides the property by the percentage of ownership in each individual owner. We discussed partition in Chapter 2.

D. ESCHEAT

Escheat
Transfer of title to property to local government when a person dies without heirs.

When a property owner dies and leaves no heirs, title to the property transfers to state or local government. The process of transferring title under these circumstances is referred to as **escheat**. Before the government can claim ownership in the property, it must demonstrate reasonable efforts to locate anyone who would qualify as the decedent's heir. Receiving property through escheat often causes government officials many problems. For instance, there is the issue of upkeep and maintenance. Most governments would prefer not to receive property this way and work diligently to locate individuals who qualify as heirs of the decedent so that they may receive the property instead. Escheat is governed by state statute and must be strictly complied with before title passes to the government.

E. CIVIL JUDGMENT

A person may also lose title to property through the enforcement of a civil judgment. When a person is sued and loses that suit, the winning party has the right to seek payment of the judgment. The winning party may petition the court for an order allowing that party to seize personal assets or real estate owned by the losing party in a civil suit. If the judge authorizes such an action, the losing party's real property may be auctioned off to satisfy the monetary judgment.

F. ADVERSE POSSESSION

One of the more unusual ways for a person to involuntarily lose title to property is the process known as **adverse possession**. Under the doctrine of adverse possession, when a person can show that she has claimed the property owned by another, held that property openly and notoriously, under color of title, and held that property for a specific period of time, that person may petition the court to be awarded fee simple absolute title in the property.

1. WHY DOES THE DOCTRINE OF ADVERSE POSSESSION EXIST?

Why would courts and legislatures create a rule such as adverse possession? There is a simple and practical reason. Because land has been, and continues to be, an important source of wealth, any action that tends to cloud title on real property, or result in a vacuum in ownership rights, is actively discouraged. The law frowns upon freezing title in land in such a way that no one can make use of it. Adverse possession is one way of keeping land usable.

Adverse possession
An action that can be brought by a person who possesses land owned by another, holds that land openly and against the claims of others, and continues in possession for a minimum period of time, such as seven years.

Adverse possession is a legal theory that allows a person to claim lands owned by another after a period of time.

ISSUE AT A GLANCE

Another theory underlying adverse possession is one found in all areas of law. In civil law, there is a doctrine known as laches. Under the **doctrine of laches**, when an individual has the right to challenge an action and fails to do so, she eventually loses that right. In criminal law, when a prosecutor fails to charge an individual with a crime within a specified time period, the statute of limitations bars that prosecution forever. One could easily argue that all branches of law are built on the premise that when an individual has a right and fails to exercise it, the right will be lost. Our legal system is based on the belief that it is always better to know when a particular action is barred forever. Such knowledge helps individuals by allowing them to go on with their lives. It also prevents courts from litigating cases that are decades old, when witness memories, physical evidence, and other relevant information has faded away.

Adverse possession, then, is built on two premises: (1) Real estate is a vital part of our economy and parcels should remain in the stream of commerce, and (2) Parties who have rights and fail to exercise them will often lose them forever.

Doctrine of laches
The legal principle that states that a person who fails to assert a legal right loses it.

Sidebar

Some commentators have said that the statutes authorizing adverse possession arise out of a societal need for the settlement of title issues.

2. THE ELEMENTS OF ADVERSE POSSESSION

Before a person can be awarded title to property through adverse possession, she must satisfy each and every element of the doctrine. Those elements include:

- Open continuous, notorious, and hostile possession
- Under color of title
- For a specified period of time

When a party proves all the elements of adverse possession, the court is authorized to award that party full title in fee simple, based on the finding that the original owner neglected the property and failed to assert her rights.[12,13]

a. Open, Continuous, Notorious, and Hostile Possession

One of the key elements of adverse possession is the requirement that the party actually possess the property. It is not enough for a person to claim title to the land. She must physically move on to the property and demonstrate possession for all to see.[14] In addition to openly possessing the property, the claimant must assert her claim so that it is hostile to the original owner's. This means that the claimant must act as though the property is hers, and prevent others from entering the property, using the property, or taking possession of it. This "hostile" use is the manifestation of the claimant's intent to bring an adverse possession claim at some point in the future.

If the claimant fails to maintain possession in an open, notorious, and hostile fashion, the claimant cannot show the central element of an adverse possession claim: actual possession. Without proof of possession, the claimant will fail.

The claimant must also possess the property continuously during the statutory period. Intermittent possession will not satisfy this element of adverse possession. Instead, the claimant must show that during the mandatory period (which can be as long as 21 years in some states), she had continuous possession of the property and did not permit others to take possession.

In some situations, a previous possessor's use of the property can be tacked onto a new possessor's use. Tacking is the process of adding time periods together to reach the statutory minimum time period, and it can be used in adverse possession. Tacking is a principle we return to in later chapters when we discuss issues such as encroachment and other time-sensitive concerns in real property.

EXAMPLE 4-4

Perry records a deed granting him property that he technically has no right to use. After recording the deed, he does not move on to the property, but he does pay real estate taxes on the land for 21 years. Will Perry be awarded the property through adverse possession?

---

[12] *Republic Nat. Bank of Dallas v. Stetson,* 390 S.W.2d 257 (Tex. 1965).
[13] *Prestwood v. Hunt,* 285 Ala. 525, 234 So. 2d 545 (1970).
[14] *Bailey v. Shanks,* 199 Neb. 29, 255 N.W.2d 866 (1977).

Answer: No. In order to prove a claim of adverse possession, all the elements must be met, especially the first: possession. Merely paying taxes on another's property does not meet all the elements of adverse possession and Perry will not be awarded title to the disputed property.[15]

b. Color of Title

Most states require not only that a claimant possess the property for a specific time period, but also that the claimant originally enter onto the property under "color of title." This phrase means that the claimant's original claim is based, at least in some way, on a legal, viable claim to the property. The claim may not be perfect, but it should at least create an arguable right to the property. Examples of color of title are tax deeds. In this case, a person attends a tax auction, bids on the property, and receives a deed from a local official. This deed may not grant fee simple title, but it is at least color of title that should satisfy the courts. Color of title is required in many states to prevent persons who have no rights or claims to a property from simply trespassing and then claiming ownership. Color of title also helps establish the time period in which the claimant took open and hostile possession of the property. Without some independent evidence of when the claimant took possession, claimants might be tempted to exaggerate the amount of time that they have been in possession in order to hurry the process along.

FIGURE 4-4

Seizure of Property for Unpaid Taxes

Whenever any supplier is delinquent in the payment of the tax, the Controller or his or her authorized representative may forthwith collect the tax due in the following manner: The Controller shall seize any property, real or personal, of the supplier, and thereafter sell the property, or a sufficient part of it, at public auction to pay the tax due together with any penalties, interest and any costs incurred on account of the seizure and sale.*

3. SPECIFIED TIME PERIODS FOR ADVERSE POSSESSION

All states have specific time periods that must elapse before a claimant can be awarded title through adverse possession. In some states, especially when a person claims color of title through a tax deed, that time may be as short as five years,[16] while in others, it could be as long as 20 years.[17]

---

[15] *Perry v. Alford*, 225 N.C. 146, 32 S.E.2d 665 (1945).
* West's Ann. Cal. Rev. & Tax Code § 7891.
[16] O.C.G.A. § 23-3-62.
[17] Gen. Stat. N.C. § 41-40.

G. TAX AUCTIONS

All states have provisions in their laws that allow governments to enforce the payment of property taxes through the use of tax auctions. Without such power, landowners might be inclined to neglect the payment of taxes. The assessment and collection of real estate taxes is one of the primary sources of revenue for local governments. Most state statutes that authorize auction of property for unpaid taxes are similar to the California statute shown in Figure 4-4. Several states permit a successful bidder at a tax auction the right to claim the property under full fee simple title, while others require that the successful bidder file a separate action and request that a court award fee simple title.

ANNOTATED DOCUMENT   NOTICE OF FORECLOSURE

NOTICE OF FORECLOSURE UNDER POWER OF SALE

NOTICE IS HEREBY PUBLISHED of the following default on conditions of the following described mortgage, to wit:

DATE OF MORTGAGE: August 22, 2001

MORTGAGOR(S): Dale J. Doe and John M. Doe, Wife and Husband.

MORTGAGEE: Borrowers' Mortgage, Inc.

DATE AND PLACE OF RECORDING: Recorded August 22, 2001, Town of Anywhere, State of Placid, Document No. 000123445.

COUNTY IN WHICH PROPERTY IS LOCATED: Barnes County

ORIGINAL PRINCIPAL AMOUNT OF MORTGAGE: $153,000.00

AMOUNT DUE AND CLAIMED TO BE DUE AS OF DATE OF NOTICE, INCLUDING TAXES, IF ANY, PAID BY MORTGAGEE: $143,234.56

That prior to the commencement of this mortgage foreclosure proceeding Mortgagee/Assignee of Mortgagee complied with all notice requirements as required by statute;

That no action or proceeding has been instituted at law or otherwise to recover the debt secured by said mortgage, or any part thereof;

PURSUANT to the power of sale contained in said mortgage, the above described property will be sold by the Sheriff of said county as follows:

DATE AND TIME OF SALE: January 11, 2005 at 10:00 A.M.

Notice of default

Names of borrowers

PLACE OF SALE: Barnes County Courthouse, PL, to pay the debt then secured by said Mortgage, and taxes, if any, on said premises, and the costs and disbursements, including attorneys' fees allowed by law subject to redemption within six (6) months from the date of said sale by the mortgagor(s), their personal representatives or assigns.

REDEMPTION: Pursuant to the laws of the state of Placid, the mortgagee has the right to redeem the property within ten (10) business days of the auction and sale by posting the AMOUNT DUE with the Clerk of Superior Court of Barnes County, State of Placid.

Notice Date: November 4, 2004
CLARENCE D. ARROW
BAUGH & ARROW, PLLC
Attorney for Mortgagee

FRAUDULENT TRANSFERS

There are times when clients approach legal professionals with requests to carry out questionable transfers. Individuals who are facing divorce actions or tax audits often wish to transfer title to property to close friends or family members with the understanding that when the legal difficulties are over, they will receive title back. Such a transfer is fraudulent and legal professionals should not become involved in them. Signs that a transfer is designed to defraud creditors include:

The sale price is well below market value.

The client wishes to disguise features of the sale or wishes to wait before recording the deed.

The client asks for advice on ways to shield the transaction from the public records.

The property is given as a gift under circumstances that are unusual.

THOMPSON v. CENTRAL OF GEORGIA R.R.

THOMPSON v. CENTRAL OF GEORGIA R.R.
282 Ga. 264, 646 S.E.2d 669 (Ga., 2007)

BENHAM, Justice.

In 2006, appellee Central of Georgia Railroad ("Railroad") filed a petition to quiet title against all the world with regard to a 13.8-acre tract of land approximately 250 feet deep and 2,500 feet long, lying along one side of a railway in Land Lots 57 and 58 of the Seventh District in Jones County. See OCGA § 23-3-60 et seq. Appellant Ellistine Newton Thompson was the lone respondent to the Railroad's petition, and she claimed ownership of a 780 feet-long × 250 feet-wide portion of the tract claimed by the Railroad. The Railroad also sought removal from the Jones County property records of affidavits of possession filed in 2003 by appellant Thompson concerning the portion of which she claimed ownership. The special master appointed by the superior court held an evidentiary hearing and, following an inspection of the site, entered a report in which he recommended the issuance of a declaration that title to the disputed property was vested in the Railroad free of any claims of Ms. Thompson and that Thompson's 2003 affidavits of possession be stricken from the deed records. In a summary order entered October 11, 2006, the superior court adopted the special master's recommendations.

The chains of title of both the railroad and Ms. Thompson are traceable to common grantors, James Van Buren and Mary Quackenbush. In 1889, the grantors conveyed to the railroad's predecessor-in-title a tract described as being in Land Lot 58 and extending along the railway's right of way for 2,500 feet and a depth of 249 feet. Attached to the deed and referred to therein was a hand-drawn diagram depicting the property conveyed. The deed was recorded in 1889.

In 1906, Van Buren and Quackenbush conveyed 100 acres to Patterson by a recorded deed that described the property conveyed as being in Land Lot 59 and bounded "on the North by the Central of Georgia Railway Company; on the West by land owned by Mariah Cole; and on the South and East by lands owned by the grantors." When Patterson's heirs conveyed 34 acres to Moore in 1938, the recorded deed described the property as being bounded, in pertinent part, "on the North by the Central of Ga. Railroad Company main line; on the West by the Central of Ga. Ry. Co. being the Athens branch of said road. . . ." Moore conveyed the 34 acres to Newton, the mother of appellant Thompson, in 1945 and the recorded deed described the property as being bounded "on the North by the Macon & Athens Railroad, Branch Line of the Central of Georgia Railway Company, and on the East by the Macon & Savannah Railroad Mainline of the Central of Georgia Railway Company. . . ." When Newton quitclaimed 27 acres to her daughter, Thompson, in 2002, the quitclaim deed described the pertinent property boundaries as had the 1945 Moore-Newton deed.

1. Asserting that the deeds which designated the railroad as the boundary conveyed fee title to the centerline of the railroad (see Descendants of Bulloch, Bussey & Co. v. Fowler, 267 Ga. 79, 475 S.E.2d 587 (1996) (involving claims to an abandoned railroad right-of-way)), that a 1973 survey showed the disputed property as belonging to Thompson and her predecessor-in-title, and that Thompson and her predecessor-in-title have continuously owned and exclusively used and occupied their property, included the disputed parcel, since 1945, thereby acquiring title to the disputed parcel by adverse possession under claim of right (OCGA § 44-5-161(a)) and by prescription under color of title (OCGA § 44-5-164), appellant Thompson contends the trial court erred when it did not decree that she holds fee simple title to the disputed parcel.

None of the facts upon which appellant relies was undisputed. The Railroad presented evidence that the 1973 survey upon which appellant relied lacked a requirement for recordation, the surveyor's signature on his seal, the absence of which indicated it was a preliminary "work in progress." Although appellant testified her mother had permitted hunting, gardening, car storage, and a large storage tank on the property, the registered, licensed land surveyor who prepared a survey for the Railroad and who was accepted as an expert in land surveying, testified he had visited the property three times since 2001 and the disputed parcel showed no signs of having been disturbed by any of these activities. In addition, remarks made by appellant to the special master during the on-site inspection and recorded by the court reporter could be interpreted as supportive of the Railroad's position that activities authorized by appellant and her mother took place on land other than the disputed parcel. Appellant testified to ownership of approximately 34 acres which included the disputed parcel, and the Railroad presented evidence she and her predecessor-in-title had owned approximately 32.52 acres that did not include the disputed parcel. The tax commissioner of Jones County testified that the Railroad had paid taxes through the utilities division of the Georgia Department of Revenue on the 13.89 acres the Railroad claimed, and appellant had paid taxes on four parcels totaling 32.52 acres adjacent to the Railroad's property.

In the absence of a timely request for jury trial in a quiet title action submitted to a special master, the special master "is the arbiter of law and fact and decides all issues in the case unless the master 'on his own initiative . . . (requires) a trial by a jury of any question of fact.' Thornton v. REB Properties, 237 Ga. 59, 226 S.E.2d 741 (1976). Neither the special master to whom the petition was submitted nor the trial court which issued the judgment set forth findings of fact which led to the conclusion that title to the disputed parcel was vested in the Railroad, and no party requested that findings of fact be made. Accordingly, the special master's recommendation is analogous to a jury verdict returned on a general verdict form, and the trial court approved that verdict by entering judgment thereon. In such a case, the appellate court affirms the judgment if there is any evidence to support it and construes the evidence with every inference and presumption in favor of upholding the verdict and judgment. Cf. Dailey v. Echols, 265 Ga. App. 459, 460, 594 S.E.2d 658 (2004). In so doing, we conclude there was evidence to support the determination of the special master and the trial court that appellant did not establish prescriptive title to the disputed parcel and affirm the trial court's judgment in favor of the Railroad.

2. Noting that the Railroad did not assert ownership of the disputed parcel between 1899 and 2001, appellant asserts the trial court erred when it did not rule that the Railroad's petition to quiet title was barred by the equitable doctrine of laches. In 2001, after appellant's brother cut timber on the disputed parcel, the Railroad promptly advised appellant's predecessor-in-title that it viewed the act as one of trespass which it would not permit; in 2006, three years after appellant filed affidavits of possession which constituted a cloud upon the Railroad's title, the Railroad filed its petition to quiet title.

"Courts of equity may interpose an equitable bar whenever, from the lapse of time and laches of the complainant, it would be inequitable to allow a party to enforce his legal rights." OCGA § 9-3-3. Laches bars an equitable claim "when the truth cannot be established fairly due to a long delay and the death of essential witnesses." Stone v. Williams, 265 Ga. 480, 458 S.E.2d 343 (1995). "Laches is not merely a question of time, but principally a matter of inequity in permitting the claim to be enforced." Swanson v. Swanson, 269 Ga. 674, 676(2), 501 S.E.2d 491 (1998). Without any evidence regarding when the Railroad became aware of the appellant's affidavits of possession, the reason for the Railroad's delay in filing its petition to quiet title and whether it could have acted sooner than it did, and whether any evidence was lost due to the delay, we cannot say the trial court erred when it did not bar the claim based on laches. Compare id. (laches barred equitable claim made 11 years after complainant knew of defendant's adverse claim); Stone v. Williams, supra (laches barred equitable claim brought 35 years after it allegedly came into being and after death of alleged grantor).

Judgment affirmed.

All the Justices concur.

CASE QUESTIONS

1   Why did the Railroad file an action to quiet title for the tract described in this case?

2   What was the basis of Thompson's adverse possession claim?

3   What did the Railroad claim about the survey and how it was legally ineffective?

4   What is the importance of the Special Master's findings in this case?

 SKILLS YOU NEED IN THE REAL WORLD

REVIEWING PROBATE RECORDS

During the course of your work as a real estate professional, it is vitally important for you to know and understand the types of records that are stored at the local courthouse. Although most of your work may center on the land office or deed room, it also is important for you to be able to locate probate records.

When a person dies with a will, the will is probated and made a matter of public record. There is often a special index listing all people who have received real property through the provisions of a will or by intestate proceeding. When you are trying to locate these records, be aware that they are not always kept in or near the deed room. In some states there is a separate probate court that maintains all records of probate proceedings. In other states, probate records are stored in the clerk of court's office. Wherever they are kept, you should be able to locate them in order to determine if real property has been transferred through a probate proceeding.

CHAPTER SUMMARY

In this chapter, we explored both the voluntary and involuntary transfers of title to real property. Voluntary real property transactions involve sales, gifts, and transfer through probate proceedings. Sale of real property is the most common way that title is transferred. A sale must meet certain minimum requirements, including contractual elements such as capacity and mutual assent. When property is transferred through a probate proceeding, it can be done in one of two ways. When a person dies with a will, she is said to have died testate, and courts will attempt to carry out the decedent's wishes. When a person dies without a will, referred to as dying intestate, the court must determine what the decedent's intentions likely were. Courts are guided by intestate succession statutes that dictate which of the decedents should be given priority in receiving title to property.

Involuntary transfers of title to property can also occur through a borrower's failure to make mortgage payments. Lenders are authorized to institute foreclosure actions in such situations and auction off the real estate for the amount of the outstanding mortgage. Governments may bring condemnation proceedings through their power of eminent domain, which allows them to seize real property from private individuals. When governments seize property, they must compensate the owners by paying fair market value for the property. Co-owners may bring partition actions to divide the ownership of the property. Property may also be lost through escheat, whereby a person dies without heirs and the government takes title to the property. Real estate may also be auctioned off to satisfy civil judgments or back taxes. Finally, title to property may be lost through the process of adverse possession, whereby a person claims property owned by another, takes possession of the property for a specified time, and holds it openly and adversely to other claims. Eventually, the claimant may bring a legal action to have the title awarded to her.

REVIEW QUESTIONS

1   What are some examples of voluntary transfer of real estate title?
2   Why is the question of origin of title so important?
3   What are the minimum requirements of a legal sale?
4   What basic elements must a will have before it is considered legally valid?
5   What are the differences between a will and a sale?
6   What is dedication as that term applies to real estate?
7   How can a person acquire title to real estate through homesteading?
8   When and under what circumstances does foreclosure occur?
9   Explain the basic steps involved in a foreclosure proceeding.
10 What is the right of redemption as that term applies to foreclosures?
11 What is eminent domain?
12 What is condemnation and how does it apply to eminent domain?
13 Explain partition.
14 Describe escheat.
15 How may a person lose title to property through the enforcement of a civil judgment?
16 What is adverse possession? List and explain the basic elements of adverse possession.
17 What is color of title as that term applies to adverse possession?

18   What effect does a tax auction have on the original property owner's rights?
19   Why is it important to be able to locate probate records?
20   Explain the information that can be found in a notice of foreclosure.

DISCUSSION QUESTIONS

1   Is the doctrine of adverse possession a good thing or a bad thing for society? Explain your answer.
2   Should the requirements for transfer of title by sale and transfer of title by will be the same? Why or why not?

PRACTICAL APPLICATIONS

1   Go through real estate brochures to locate houses that are for sale. What inducements do the sellers offer to potential buyers to encourage them to purchase a home?
2   Visit your local courthouse and review a will that has been probated. Probated wills are part of the public record and are freely accessible. Locate an estate in which real estate was conveyed to beneficiaries. How many beneficiaries received a share of the property? What findings did the court make in order to determine that the will was valid?

WEB SITES

Mutual Assent — Legal Research Institute
http://www.law.cornell.edu/wex/mutual_assent

Consideration — Duhaime.org
http://www.duhaime.org/LegalDictionary/C/Consideration.aspx

Requirements of a Will — 'Lectric Law Library
http://www.lectlaw.com/filesh/qfl06.htm

Intestate Succession — Findlaw.com
http://estate.findlaw.com/estate-planning/estate-planning-overview/estate-planning-overview-intestate.html

Eminent Domain — Being Abused? CBS News
http://www.cbsnews.com/stories/2003/09/26/60minutes/main575343.shtml

Eminent Domain — Findlaw.com
http://library.findlaw.com/1999/May/25/130971.html

Power of sale foreclosure — Legal Dictionary Online
http://legal-dictionary.thefreedictionary.com/Power+of+Sale

Escheated Property — Minnesota Management & Budget
http://www.mmb.state.mn.us/escheated-property

Adverse Possession — Legal Information Institute
http://www.law.cornell.edu/wex/adverse_possession

California Adverse Possession
http://www.dot.ca.gov/hq/row/landsurveys/Study_material/California-
Adverse-Possession.pdf

Florida Law of Adverse Possession
http://edis.ifas.ufl.edu/fe678

TERMS AND PHRASES

Adverse possession	Escheat	Power of sale foreclosure
Dedication	Foreclosure	Publication
Default	Holographic will	Testate
Devise	Intestate	Devisee
Judicial foreclosure	Nuncupative will	
Doctrine of laches	Beneficiary	

SIGNIFICANT CASES

Buckner v. Hosch, 987 So. 2d 1149 (Ala. Civ. App., 2007.)
Bustillos v. Murphy, 117 Cal. Rptr. 2d 895 (2002)
Johnson v. Jones, 977 S.W.2d 903 (1998)
Carolina Bank v. Chatham Station, Inc., 651 S.E.2d 386 (2007)
Phil Mechanic Const. Co., Inc. v. Haywood, 325 S.E.2d 1 (N.C. App., 1985)
Dunham v. Hackney Airpark, Inc., 990 P.2d 1224 (1999)

Rights Associated with Real Estate

Focus of This Chapter

The chapter begins with a description of fixtures, explores the relationship of fixtures to real estate, and then describes how the law of trade fixtures differs significantly from the general rule of fixtures. From there, the chapter explores the role of liens, easements, and other rights associated with real property.

Chapter Learning Objectives

After completing this chapter, you should be able to:

- Explain how courts determine what qualifies as a fixture
- Describe how easements are created
- Define the air and mineral rights that real property owners possess
- Explain the purpose of liens
- Describe the importance of water rights

INTRODUCTION

In this chapter, we explore the many different rights associated with real property ownership. From fixtures to licenses, we will see that ownership of real property carries with it numerous rights and obligations. We begin our discussion by examining the legal consequences of attaching personal property to real property—the subject of fixtures.

FIXTURES

Our discussion of the rights associated with real property ownership begins with the interplay of real and personal property. We have seen that personal property consists of items as disparate as apples and airplanes, but what happens when personal property becomes permanently affixed to real property? What effect does this union have on personal property? Does it retain its separate identity? This is more than a theoretical question. There are practical concerns here as well. For example, when title to real property is exchanged, there is no need to list all the individual components that make up the real estate parcel. As we will see in the discussion of deeds (Chapter 8), the only item described in a real estate transaction is the property. Everything permanently attached to the property is transferred with the deed. This explains why structures such as houses are never listed on a real property deed. Because they are permanently attached to the land, they are transferred along with the underlying ground.

ISSUE AT A GLANCE

A fixture is personal property that has become permanently attached to real property.

Fixture
Personal property that has become permanently attached to real property.

The same thing happens when personal property becomes permanently attached to real estate. The term for these items is fixtures. A **fixture** is an item that was formerly classified as personal property, but has become real property by virtue of becoming attached to the real estate. When this attachment (sometimes called annexation) occurs, the personal property is reclassified as real property and will continue to be considered real property. An example of a fixture is found in Example 5-1.

EXAMPLE 5-1

Tonya has placed her house for sale and a young couple has agreed to buy it. On the day of the sale, just before Tonya leaves the house forever, she unbolts a crystal chandelier from the ceiling of the dining room and loads it into her car. When the new owners arrive at the house, they immediately notice that the chandelier is gone. They want to sue Tonya. How is the judge likely to rule?

Answer: The judge will rule that the chandelier, once an item of personal property, has now become a fixture and must remain with the house when it is sold. Unlike other items of personal property such as furniture, books, and table lamps, the chandelier is permanently attached to the real property and must remain with the house when it is sold. The judge will order Tonya to return the chandelier.

ISSUE AT A GLANCE

Fixtures belong to the persons who own the real estate.

A. DETERMINING WHEN PERSONAL PROPERTY BECOMES A FIXTURE

Because the determination of when personal property becomes a fixture is so important, and can have such dire effects, courts have created several tests to help determine when something has crossed the boundary between personal property and real property. Although different states have different standards — and tests — for determining what constitutes a fixture, there are some general guidelines. For instance, courts could use any or all of the following tests:

- Intent
- Manner of attachment
- Use
- Damage resulting from removal

1. INTENT TEST

Courts always look to the intent of the party who placed the item to see whether the personal property was placed there with the idea that it would become part of the real property.[1] In the previous example involving Tonya and the chandelier, one could certainly argue that by bolting the chandelier to the dining room ceiling, Tonya had clearly intended that it should remain there permanently. Contrast this with a table lamp, the placement of which is clearly designed to be temporary. Under the intent test, the chandelier would qualify as a fixture.

Although the courts have ruled that the parties' intentions are controlling when it comes to the issue of determining a fixture, there are times when it is difficult, if not impossible, to determine the parties' intentions. The original parties may no longer be available or they may have made conflicting statements about their intentions. In those situations, the courts would opt for the manner of attachment test.

2. MANNER OF ATTACHMENT TEST

Another method used to determine whether an item qualifies as a fixture is the manner of attachment test. Under this test, the more permanent an attachment, the more likely the item would be classified as a fixture. Consider Example 5-2.

EXAMPLE 5-2

Once the new owners have moved into Tonya's old house, they also notice that, in addition to the missing chandelier, a painting that they liked very much has also been removed. Tonya took the painting down on the same day that she removed the chandelier. The new owners are now requesting that in addition to returning the chandelier, Tonya also return the painting. Does the painting qualify as a fixture?

Here is an example in which the intent test might not provide an answer to this question. However, the manner of attachment test does. Under the manner of attachment

---

[1] *Kaplan v. I. Kaplan, Inc.*, 422 Pa. Super. 215, 619 A.2d 322 (1993).

test, a painting that hangs on the wall by a nail and wire is obviously not intended to remain there permanently. Under the manner of attachment test, the painting would not qualify as a fixture and therefore the new owners cannot compel Tonya to return it.

3. USE TEST

In situations in which intent and manner of attachment do not help to resolve the question of whether an item is a fixture, the use test provides another mechanism. Under the use test, personal property is considered to be a fixture when the item is essential to the use of the real property. Consider Example 5-3.

EXAMPLE 5-3	Carlos has come to our firm with the following problem: He is being transferred out of state and must put his house up for sale. He has also recently installed a heat pump. Carlos wants to know if the heat pump must remain when he sells the house or if he can take it with him. Put another way: Is a heat pump a fixture?

Answer: Under the intent and manner of attachment tests to determine fixture status, there is no equivocation on the question. However, is a heat pump necessary to the use of the real property? The new owners will need to heat and cool their home, so it is obvious that the heating mechanism is necessary for the use of the property. The heat pump is a fixture.[2]

4. DAMAGE TEST

The final test used to determine whether a specific item qualifies as a fixture is to determine how much damage it would cause to remove it. Under this test, if removal of an item would cause extensive damage to the site, courts are more likely to rule that the item is a fixture. Examples of items that would fit under this category would be built-in wall units or furniture constructed on site that would require opening up an exterior wall to remove it. Under the damage test, these items would be classified as fixtures.

If an item satisfies any of the court-created tests, it is classified as a fixture and must remain with the land when the property is sold.

B. TRADE FIXTURES

Trade fixture
A fixture that is necessary to the operation of a business.

The rules about fixtures change when an item is classified as a **trade fixture**. A trade fixture is equipment that is necessary to run a commercial enterprise. Even though this equipment may be permanently attached to the real estate, such as heavy machinery that is bolted to the floor, the person who owns the equipment is

---

[2] *Household Finance Corp. v. BancOhio*, 62 Ohio App. 3d 691, 577 N.E.2d 405 (1989).

allowed to remove it when he sells or otherwise leaves the real property. The rules about trade fixtures are different because trade fixtures are necessary to run a business and it would not make much sense, financial or otherwise, to require someone who had invested thousands of dollars in equipment to leave it behind when the real property was sold. As far as the law is concerned, trade fixtures always remain personal property and can be removed.[3]

So far, our discussion has centered on the rights that owners have to use, or remove, items from real property. In the next section we discuss rights that others have to use a portion of another's property.

A trade fixture may be removed when the business vacates the premises, even though it may have been permanently attached to the real estate.

ISSUE AT A GLANCE

 EASEMENTS

An **easement** is a right held by someone other than the real property owner. When someone has an easement, it means that he has the right to use part of another parcel of land, even though he has no ownership interests in it. Easements are very common. If you consider the layout of a typical neighborhood, you will discover easements existing on almost every parcel. Consider Example 5-4.

Easement
The right of a person other than the landowner to use a portion of the owner's land, for example, a driveway or a right of way.

EXAMPLE 5-4

Juan has recently purchased a new home in a nice subdivision. One day as he is out walking the boundary lines of his property, he realizes that his next-door neighbor's driveway actually cuts across his boundary line. Juan has come to our firm to find out if there is anything that he can do to have the driveway moved.

Our firm investigates the situation and learns that there is an easement on record, granting the next-door neighbor the use of that portion of Juan's property. Barring an agreement by the neighbor to surrender the easement, there is nothing that Juan can do to stop his next-door neighbor from using the driveway, even though it crosses over onto Juan's property.

Easements give non-owners the right to use a small portion of the owner's property.

ISSUE AT A GLANCE

Easements give a non-owner the right to use the owner's property. The reason that easements exist is to provide the maximum possible access from one parcel to

---

[3] *Harris v. Lamar Co.*, 150 N.C. App. 437, 563 S.E.2d 642 (2002).

another. Allowing a person to cross over another person's property to get access to the public streets is seen as a small price to pay to ensure that all property has access.

Easements are broken down into two categories: appurtenant easements and in gross easements. Driveways are examples of appurtenant easements. Technically, this easement allows the use of one parcel for the benefit of another parcel. The law of easements involves two estates, or two parcels of land. One is classified as the dominant estate and the other, the servient. See Figure 5-1. In this example, we see that the servient estate is the one that has the driveway placed for the benefit of the other, dominant, estate. Fortunately, many courts are moving away from this terminology and are focusing more on the parcels that receive the benefit of the easement and the other that must bear the burden of the easement.

FIGURE 5-1 Terminology Used in Easements	A dominant estate is the land for which the easement is used. When A passes over a portion of B's property to access his property, the driveway benefits A's property. A's property is the dominant estate. A servient estate is the land on which the easement is found. When A passes over a portion of B's property, he is using the servient parcel.

A. APPURTENANT EASEMENTS

Appurtenant easement
An easement created for an adjoining dominant estate.

An **appurtenant easement** is the right of an adjoining landowner to use a portion of another parcel for his own benefit. Appurtenant easements always involve two tracts of land and two different owners.

Appurtenant easements involve two tracts of land.

B. IN GROSS EASEMENTS

In gross easement
An easement that allows someone to enter onto the land; there are no dominant or servient estates with in gross easements.

An **in gross easement** is the right of another to enter onto a specific parcel. There is only one parcel involved in an in gross easement. An example of an in gross easement is the right given to local utilities to enter onto property to service telephone poles or underground lines. A person or company that has an in gross easement is not required to seek permission to enter onto the premises.

In gross easements involve only one tract of land.

Tech Topic
CELLPHONE TOWER EASEMENTS

Now that more than 80 percent of the world's population owns a cellphone, the placement of cellphone towers has added a new wrinkle to the world of real estate. Cellphone towers are an essential factor in wireless communication, and they have to be erected somewhere. Wireless carriers spend a great deal of money designing systems around specific radio frequency engineering standards, and they often target specific geographic locations.

Many jurisdictions have zoning ordinances that either allow or prohibit cellphone towers. If a property is an industrial parcel surrounded by residential property, the likelihood that a wireless carrier could use it is high. On the other hand, if a residential property is surrounded by industrial property, the likelihood decreases. Thus, wireless carriers not only have to find a desirable property, they also have to make sure zoning ordinances allow for a tower to be built in that location.

Once a wireless carrier identifies a suitable location, it then must negotiate a lease with the property's owner. In exchange for monetary consideration, either in the form of a monthly lease payment or a lump sum payment, the carrier gains an exclusive easement over the property. The easement includes the transmission and reception of all wireless communication signals and the construction and operation of towers, antennas, and related facilities.

C. EASEMENTS RUN WITH THE LAND

When an owner grants an easement to another, this right is said to **run with the land**. Put another way, this right, once granted, automatically transfers when the property is transferred. New owners are not required to renegotiate terms. The easement remains and if a new owner interferes with the other's use of the easement, the new owner can be sued and enjoined from taking any action to prevent access.

Run with the land
A right that transfers with the title to the property.

D. CREATING EASEMENTS

Now that we have seen how important easements are, we examine how they are created. Easements can be created in any number of ways, but the most common methods are:

- Agreement
- Deed reservation
- Implication
- Necessity
- Prescription
- Eminent domain

1. AGREEMENT

The easiest and most direct way to create an easement is by the agreement of the parties. For instance, a property owner might sell a portion of a much larger tract and then enter into an agreement with the new owner that the new owner will have an easement over a portion of the larger tract. This easement could be recorded and made part of the public record, but it might just as easily remain an informal agreement between the parties that eventually ripens into an important legal right for future owners.

In order for such an easement to be a legally effective agreement, the Statute of Frauds dictates that it must be in writing. The Statute of Frauds is a state-based statute that requires certain types of agreements to be in writing before they will be enforced. We discuss the Statute of Frauds in greater detail in Chapter 6.

When the parties enter into an agreement establishing an easement, they should not only put the agreement in writing, but should also specify the exact location of the easement so that there will not be a question for future owners.

2. DEED RESERVATION

Another method used to create an easement is by simply reserving one in the deed between seller and buyer. The seller can insert a provision in the deed specifying that an easement be created on the recently sold property. This is commonly referred to as deed reservation and is just as binding as an agreement between the parties.

3. IMPLICATION

Another method to create an easement is to assume that the parties intended to create one in their transaction but failed to list it in the deed. Here, courts will rule that the parties must have intended to create an easement but simply forgot to do so. To rule otherwise might create a situation in which a person who buys property cannot access it. After all, when a person crosses another person's property without permission, he is committing trespass. Rather than rule that every time a person who is trying to gain access to his own property is committing a fresh trespass, the courts will rule that the original parties obviously intended to create an easement and neglected to list it in the deed or other documents.

4. NECESSITY

In addition to the voluntary actions of the parties, courts can also take an active role in determining easements. Creating an easement by necessity is based on the commonsense notion that no one would purchase property to which he could not gain access. When a dispute arises about access and the existence of an easement, courts often find that an easement existed simply because one is required to give an owner access to his own land. This does not mean that the landowner gets to pick the best or most advantageous easement. It simply means that every landowner is entitled to physical access to property, not necessarily convenient access. When courts create easements by necessity, they try to place the easement so that it gives an owner access to public roadways, but they are not required to create an easement that is aesthetically pleasing, or even the shortest and most convenient route to those public roads. Consider Example 5-5.

EXAMPLE 5-5

Earl purchased a lot last month, and when he tried to drive onto his property, the adjoining landowner, Carl, refused to let Earl cross his property to gain access. There are no easements recorded for the property and Carl has consistently refused to agree to an easement. Earl brings suit, asking the local court to create an easement by necessity. The judge rules in Earl's favor, but creates a winding, circuitous route across the back edge of Carl's property. Earl wants an easement that is shorter and more direct. Will he get it?

Answer: No. Earl is entitled access to his property, and the court can create an easement across Carl's property to give Earl that access, but the court does not have to place the easement where Earl wants it. Access is access.

5. PRESCRIPTION

When a party acquires an easement by prescription, he is using a method similar to adverse possession, discussed in the previous chapter. As we saw in adverse possession, all states have rules that permit a person who exercises open, notorious, and hostile possession against an original owner may eventually receive full title to the lot. A similar theory will result in the creation of an easement.

In easement by prescription, an adjoining landowner simply begins using a portion of another person's property as a driveway. After a period of time, which varies from state to state, the use will ripen into an easement. The theory underlying easement by prescription is that when the property owner has the right to stop another from using a portion of his property for access and fails to do so, he eventually waives the right to bring any action opposing the use. To satisfy the elements of easement by prescription, the original use must be without permission. Additionally, the party seeking to have an easement declared must also establish the following elements:

- That the easement was established adversely to the rights of the landowner
- That the use has been open and notorious and obvious to all
- That the use has been uninterrupted and continuous for a period of time (as long as 21 years in some states)[4]

6. EMINENT DOMAIN

The final method used to create easements is by the power of the government to seize property. We saw in the last chapter that all governments, local, state, and federal, have the power of eminent domain — the power to seize a private individual's property to use for a government-related project. Of course, the owner must be reimbursed for the value of his property. Eminent domain actions can also apply to easements. Governments can just as easily seize a portion of a lot to use for a new roadway or to widen an existing roadway.

If you think that the rules are stacked in favor of creating an easement on property, you are correct. Courts in all states have ruled that it is important for individuals, and society as a whole, that real property be freely exchanged.

---

[4] *Mitchell v. Golden*, 107 N.C. App. 413, 420 S.E.2d 482 (1992).

Anything, such as prohibiting a person from accessing his own property, that would make certain parcels off limits for real estate transactions is considered an undesirable result. As a consequence, many of the real estate rules that we address throughout this book have, as their underlying principle, the idea that real estate should be made as freely transferable as possible and anything that prevents that freedom of transfer should be eliminated.

If the rules about easements seem to make the creation of easements simpler, the opposite can be said about terminating them.

E. TERMINATING EASEMENTS

When one owner decides that he does not want his next-door neighbor to continue to use a driveway across his property, is there an action that he can take to terminate the easement? Can an owner place a fence or some other obstruction across the easement and declare the easement terminated? The answer is no. One party cannot, unilaterally, cancel an easement. In fact, there are only a few ways that an easement can be extinguished. They include:

- The easement is no longer needed
- The properties have merged
- The parties enter into an agreement
- The easement is abandoned

1. THE EASEMENT IS NO LONGER NEEDED

One way of terminating an easement is to eliminate the need for it. Suppose that Jorge has an easement that gives him access to a public highway. The county builds a new road that runs along a different side of Jorge's property and closes the other highway. Jorge no longer needs an easement to the first highway, because it no longer exists and he has ready access to the new highway. In this situation, the court would rule that the easement has been extinguished through loss of purpose.

2. THE PROPERTIES HAVE MERGED

The basic premise behind an appurtenant easement is that there are two tracts: one that has an easement across it to allow access to another. However, suppose that the same owner buys both parcels. In that situation the easement would disappear. Both parcels have merged and there is no longer a need for an easement. On a more fundamental level, there is no longer a dominant and a servient estate, only a single parcel. A person cannot grant an easement to himself, so the easement terminates through **merger**.

Merger
The combination of two formerly separate tracts into a single unit.

3. THE PARTIES ENTER INTO AN AGREEMENT

The individual parties are always free to enter into an agreement extinguishing the easement. In such a situation, the person who has the easement can simply release his rights to the easement, surrendering the right to the original landowner. In this situation, the agreement rescinds the easement and the other landowner would no longer be required to allow access across his property. Just as with creating an easement, the Statute of Frauds requires a release of easement to be in writing.

4. THE EASEMENT IS ABANDONED

Abandoning an easement is the opposite of creating one by prescription. In **abandonment**, the party who has the easement stops using it, or the other landowner blocks off the easement and the easement holder fails to object. Just as with easements by prescription, when a party has a right and fails to use it, the right will be lost. In this case, the easement holder will eventually lose his right to the easement by failing to object to the other landowner's actions.

Abandonment
Giving up or surrendering all legal rights.

 IV # LICENSES

A **license** is a right granted to a specific individual to come on to someone else's property for a specific purpose. An example of a license is allowing certain people onto the property to hunt or fish. Both private and governmental owners are permitted to license the use of the property. It is very common for governmental agencies to license the use of public lands for logging or hunting, and to require payment from individuals who seek these licenses. A license is different from an easement in that the party who comes onto the land with a license does so for a specific purpose. Licenses do not run with the land as easements do. Instead, a license is more like a contract between the landowner and the person who wishes to enter onto the property.

License
Permission to do a specific act.

A license gives a specific person the right to enter onto the land to do a specific action.

ISSUE AT A GLANCE

 V # PROFIT À PRENDRE

Real property owners have the right to transfer a portion of their rights to others. We have seen this with easements and licenses. However, the owner can transfer other rights as well. For instance, an owner can grant **profit à prendre** to another person. Profit à prendre, or profits, involves taking products generated on the parcel. Examples include harvesting crops from the land, removing timber, or mining the soil. In this situation, a person or company who had been granted a profit could enter the land, remove the specified items, and then resell them. Obviously the landowner and the person taking the products have negotiated this right. Consider Example 5-6.

Profit à prendre
(French) The right of a person to enter onto the land owned by another and remove an item or items previously agreed upon, for example, crops.

EXAMPLE 5-6   Juan owns 16 acres of mountain land that is not suitable for growing crops and is too far away from town to develop as home sites. However, the land is perfect for growing Christmas trees. Juan plants hundreds of trees and then negotiates a contract with Trees 'R Us, granting the company the right to enter onto the land and harvest the trees every year before the Christmas season. Juan has created a profit à prendre arrangement with Trees 'R Us.

How do profits compare with easements? When a person or company has a profit, they can enter onto the land and remove items. Easement holders are allowed to pass over the land, but are certainly not permitted to remove items. Profit holders are also different from license holders, because persons with licenses enter the property for a specific activity, such as hunting or fishing, not harvesting the products of the land itself.

Examples of profit à prendre include allowing someone to come onto the land to:

- Graze cattle[5]
- Remove sand from a beach
- Harvest timber
- Harvest crops

 The right to profits from the land means that someone other than the owner has the right to enter onto the land and remove items, such as crops, minerals, trees, etc.

 LIENS

Lien
A monetary claim against property brought by a creditor that may ripen into a judgment.

So far, our discussion about the rights associated with real property ownership has focused on the privileges that ownership brings. However, there is a downside to real property ownership. For instance, creditors are permitted to file actions against the property to force a landowner to pay a debt. This action usually comes in the form of a **lien**.

A lien is an action filed by a creditor that prevents the sale of the property until the debt is satisfied. This is a very powerful tool to put in the hands of a creditor, so courts and statutes have given it only to specific types of creditors. There are two classes of creditors who can file a lien against property:

1 Materialmen
2 Mechanics

---

[5] *Burlingame v. Marjerrison*, 665 P.2d 1136, 204 Mont. 464 (1983).

These terms are somewhat archaic, but there are important differences between **materialmen** and **mechanics**. When a person is classified as a materialman, it means that he has provided supplies to a landowner. These supplies might be building materials, livestock feed, or even fuel. A mechanic, on the other hand, is a person who provides a service to the landowner. The service might be helping to harvest crops, build a barn, or providing any other service to the landowner. In either situation, the creditor has the right to file a lien against the property when he is not paid.

Although the terms "materialman" and "mechanic" continue to be used, most states have stopped making a distinction between them. Because they both have the right to file a lien, it no longer matters if they provided a service or supplies.

We began this section by saying that a lien acts to prevent the sale of real property, but the issue actually is more complicated than that. In most situations, a lien may prevent the sale, but in other situations, the lien may simply attach to the real property title, eventually ripening into a judgment that a court will insist must be paid. Whether a lien immediately prevents the sale of property, or will eventually become a judgment against the property, depends on applicable state law. However, most banks and lending institutions will not allow a prospective buyer to borrow funds to purchase a home that has a lien placed against it. In practical terms, then, the type of lien is unimportant. Because a lender won't provide funds to purchase a property that has a lien against it, the practical result is that all liens prevent the sale of the property. Before the title can change hands, the lien must be cleared up, at least to the lender's satisfaction. We will see, in later chapters, the effect that lending institutions have had on the field of real property law, often indirectly exerting power to correct issues such as liens and other encumbrances against real property.

When a general contractor builds a home, for example, he will often obtain a lien waiver from subcontractors in exchange for their payment. This waiver prevents the subcontractors from filing a lien against the property to satisfy an outstanding bill owed by the general contractor. When a creditor files a lien, and the homeowner pays the bill, the homeowner should insist on a signed lien waiver from the creditor. See Figure 5-2 for an example of California's lien waiver form.

Materialman
A creditor who has provided supplies for the benefit of a real property owner.

Mechanic
A creditor who has provided a service for the benefit of a real property owner.

 ASSESSMENTS

No discussion of the rights and obligations of landowners would be complete without mentioning **assessments**. An assessment is a bill by a governmental agency for improvement in or near the property. An example of assessments would be putting in sidewalks in subdivisions and then billing the residents for the costs associated with creating the sidewalks. Assessments can come in a wide variety of forms, but most of them focus on improvements created by the government that directly benefit specific parcels of land.

Assessment
A payment made above and beyond normal taxes owed for real property.

FIGURE 5-2

California Conditional Waiver
and Release upon Progress
Payment Form

CONDITIONAL WAIVER AND RELEASE UPON PROGRESS PAYMENT

Civil Code Section 3262(d)(1)

Upon receipt by the undersigned of a check from _____
                                                                   MAKER OF CHECK

in the sum of $ _____ payable to _____
                  AMOUNT OF CHECK   PAYEE OR PAYEES OF CHECK

and when the check has been properly endorsed and has been paid by the bank upon which it is

drawn, this document shall become effective to release any mechanic's lien, stop notice, or bond

right the undersigned has on the job of _____
                                                                 OWNER

located at _____ to the following extent.
                                        JOB DESCRIPTION

This release covers a progress payment for labor, services, equipment, or material furnished to

_____ through _____
              YOUR CUSTOMER   DATE

only and does not cover any retentions retained before or after the release date; extras furnished before
the release date for which payment has not been received; extras or items furnished after the release
date. Rights based upon work performed or items furnished under a written change order which has been
fully executed by the parties prior to the release date are covered by this release unless specifically
reserved by the claimant in this release. This release of any mechanic's lien, stop notice, or bond right
shall not otherwise affect the contract rights, including rights between parties to the contract based upon a
rescission, abandonment, or breach of the contract, or the right of the undersigned to recover
compensation for furnished labor, services, equipment, or material covered by this release if that
furnished labor, services, equipment, or material was not compensated by the progress payment.

Before any recipient of this document relies on it, said party should verify evidence of payment to the
undersigned.

Dated:_____   _____
                                                                    COMPANY NAME

                                       By:_____
                                                                         TITLE

AIR RIGHTS

Before the invention of the airplane, the issue of air rights did not rank very high on
the roster of real property issues. Legal commentators simply assumed that a landowner's rights to the air above his property extended as far into the sky as he
wished. The old common law maxim stated air rights very succinctly: "The rights
of the owner extend all the way to heaven and all the way to hell."[6]

However, the issue changed dramatically when air travel became a new means
of transportation. Suddenly those clearly defined rights were causing legal problems. After all, when a plane crosses over the boundaries of someone's property,
even at 20,000 feet, this is technically a trespass. Even a short plane ride would

---

[6] *Jones v. Loan Association*, 252 N.C. 626, 637, 114 S.E.2d 638, 646 (1960).

result in hundreds, if not thousands, of trespass cases. On a more practical level, courts began dealing with cases involving the construction of buildings so high that they effectively shut out light for other landowners. Given these problems, the issue of air rights was reexamined.

The current state of the law is that a landowner possesses rights in the air above his property to a reasonable height. Determining this reasonable distance depends on several factors. For instance, a farmer might go as high as 100 feet to construct a windmill to draw water or to generate power, while the owners of a high-rise building would need a much greater height to complete a building. One landowner's use of air space also depends on the effect that this use will have on adjoining landowners. The greater the impact on the neighbors, the more likely the court will rule that the use is unreasonable and must be discontinued.

 WATER RIGHTS

The right to use water is one of the most important rights a landowner has. In cities, where water systems are connected to city water lines, homeowners may give little thought to water. But in the countryside, where homeowners draw their water from pumps and wells, the absence of water can mean the difference between a thriving community and a desert. There are entire books written exclusively about this important right. Although our discussion of water rights is not that detailed, it is important for anyone learning about real property law to understand the unique features of water rights.

A. THE RIGHT TO DRAW WATER

The right to draw water is considered one of the most essential and necessary rights that a real property owner possesses. Many states, especially those in the western United States, have crafted statutes specifying exactly how water can be used. For an in-depth analysis of the importance of the right to draw water, read this chapter's case excerpt.

When property borders a river, stream, or lake, the property owner has the right to use some of that water for his own use. In most states, the owner is restricted to "reasonable" use of water. Although the definition of reasonable varies from state to state, most courts define reasonable as use that is commensurate with need and that does not deprive other owners of water for their own purposes.[7]

B. SUBTERRANEAN WATER

If a property owner has rights to surface waters, what about underground waters? Most people who depend on water get it, in one form or another, from underground sources. However, the issues here can become very complicated. When we are

---

[7] *Pine Knoll Association, Inc. v. Cardon*, 126 N.C. App. 155, 484 S.E.2d 446 (1997).

discussing surface waters, the owner's right to the water derives from the simple fact that the property borders on the water. That gives the owner the right to draw the water and to use it. However, can the same be said of subterranean water? For instance, what is the source of a landowner's rights to this water? By its very nature, it cannot be seen and the actual location of the water may be difficult, if not impossible, to establish. There is no way to establish that the property borders on a large underground lake. What gives a property owner the right to use this water?

Most legal authorities point to the deed and the owner's title to the property as the source for the owner's additional right to draw water. This right to draw and use water applies not only to surface waters, but also to subterranean waters.[8] Under this theory, the right to draw water is identical to the rights that property owners have to harvest crops grown on the property, to mine for minerals, or to use the air space above the property. However, that analogy does not hold up under close scrutiny. For one thing, all of those other features are stationary and held within the boundaries of the property. Water, on the other hand, is free flowing. It moves from place to place.

Another theory about underground waters is that they are analogous to surface waters. As we have already seen, when a river or stream bounds a parcel, the landowner has the right to draw a reasonable amount of that water for his use. Many states apply this same rationale to underground waters.

C. TERMINOLOGY FOR WATER RIGHTS

There is some important terminology related to both surface and underground waters. For instance, water that soaks through the soil and pools at some point below the surface is referred to as "percolating" water. On the other hand, water that flows in an underground river is commonly referred to as a "watercourse." These terms are important not only because they distinguish between different types of water, but also because the rights associated with them vary according to their classification. An underground river, for instance, is usually controlled by the same statute that controls aboveground streams. However, percolating water is treated differently.[9]

 MINERAL RIGHTS

The final category of rights associated with real property is mineral rights. One of the rights that come with property ownership is the ability to take useful items from the soil. Property owners can mine for gold, silver, or other useful materials, assuming that such activities do not violate zoning or other ordinances. In many cases, previous owners may have already transferred mineral rights to another party. In the late 1800s and early 1900s, for example, it was not uncommon for mining companies to purchase mineral rights to huge swaths of countryside. Because those rights have already been conveyed away, current owners no longer possess them and therefore have no right to sink mines in their own properties.

---

[8] *State of Nevada ex rel. Shamberger v. United States*, 165 F. Supp. 600 (D. Nev. 1958).
[9] *Bull v. Siegrist*, 169 Or. 180, 126 P.2d 832 (1942).

LIEN

Form 9

Notice of Other Lien Filling

Name and Telephone Number of Contact at Filer (optional)

Return copy to: (Name and Mailing Address)

John Doe
123 Maple Drive
Anywhere, PL 00030

→ Creditor filing lien

Check one:
- ☑ Notice of filing of lien.
- ☐ Notice of full release or discharge of lien.
- ☐ Notice of change of lien

1. Debtor Name: Insert only one debtor in 1a. or 1b.   For Secretary of State Use Only

1a. Entity's Name	1b. Individual's Last Name:	First:	Middle:	Suffix:
MARY ROE, INC.	*ROE*	*MARY*	*R.*	

1c. Mailing Address	City	State	Country	Postal Code
1001 BURKE DR.	*ANYWHERE*	*PL CA.*		*00030*

Landowner who owes debt

2. Additional Debtor Name: Insert only one debtor in 2a. or 2b.

2a. Entity's Name	2b. Individual's Last Name:	First:	Middle:	Suffix:
N/A				

2c. Mailing Address	City	State	Country	Postal Code

3. Lienor's Name: Insert only one lienor name in 3a. or 3b.

3a. Entity's Name	3b. Individual's Last Name:	First:	Middle:	Suffix:
SAME AS ABOVE				

3c. Mailing Address	City	State	Country	Postal Code

4. Type of lien/statutory authority
- ☐ Federal tax lien ☐ State Tax lien ☐ Town tax lien on manufactured housing ☐ Aircraft registration lien
- ☐ Child support lien ☐ Housing Finance Authority lien ☐ Hazardous Waste lien ☐ Employment Security lien
- ☐ Writ of attachment ☐ Road Toll lien ☑ Creditors bill lien ☐ State Food Security Act lien

5. Complete if filing is a release, discharge or change.

Filing Location of initial lien: _____ *N/A* _____

Filing Date of initial lien: _____

File Number: assigned to initial lien: _____   other lien form 9, version 1.1

UNAUTHORIZED PRACTICE OF LAW

Paralegals should always be keenly aware of the dangers posed by answering questions and offering advice to others about legal matters. All states have some variation of the following law: "It shall be unlawful for any person except members of the State Bar who are admitted and licensed to practice in this state, to appear as attorney or counselor at law in any action or proceeding before any judicial body, except in his own behalf as a party thereto; or, by word, sign, letter or advertisement, to hold himself, or themselves, as competent or qualified to give legal advice or counsel, or to prepare legal documents." N.C. Gen. Stat. § 84-4.

As you can see, a paralegal might be guilty of the crime of unauthorized practice of law for giving legal advice or carrying out other actions normally reserved for attorneys. The safest course to take to avoid an allegation of unauthorized practice of law is to review your own state's statutes and also make sure that you identify yourself as a paralegal. Many nonlawyers preface their remarks with the statement, "I cannot give you legal advice," or "You understand that I cannot act as a lawyer, since I'm not a member of the bar." Such statements, and strict compliance with state law, will help you avoid an allegation of unauthorized practice of law.

KELO v. CITY OF NEW LONDON, CONN.

KELO v. CITY OF NEW LONDON, CONN.
545 U.S. 469, 125 S.Ct. 2655 (U.S. Conn., 2005)

Justice STEVENS delivered the opinion of the Court.

In 2000, the city of New London approved a development plan that, in the words of the Supreme Court of Connecticut, was "projected to create in excess of 1,000 jobs, to increase tax and other revenues, and to revitalize an economically distressed city, including its downtown and waterfront areas." 268 Conn. 1, 5, 843 A.2d 500, 507 (2004). In assembling the land needed for this project, the city's development agent has purchased property from willing sellers and proposes to use the power of eminent domain to acquire the remainder of the property from unwilling owners in exchange for just compensation. The question presented is whether the city's proposed disposition of this property qualifies as a "public use" within the meaning of the Takings Clause of the Fifth Amendment to the Constitution.

I

The city of New London (hereinafter City) sits at the junction of the Thames River and the Long Island Sound in southeastern Connecticut. Decades of economic decline led a state agency in 1990 to designate the City a "distressed municipality." In 1996, the Federal Government closed the Naval Undersea Warfare Center, which had been located in the Fort Trumbull area of the City and had employed over 1,500 people. In 1998, the City's unemployment rate was nearly double that of the State, and its population of just under 24,000 residents was at its lowest since 1920.

These conditions prompted state and local officials to target New London, and particularly its Fort Trumbull area, for economic revitalization. To this end, respondent New London Development Corporation (NLDC), a private nonprofit entity established some years earlier to assist the City in planning economic development, was reactivated. In January 1998, the State authorized a $5.35 million bond issue to support the NLDC's planning activities and a $10 million bond issue toward the creation of a Fort Trumbull State Park. In February, the pharmaceutical company Pfizer Inc. announced that it would build a $300 million research facility on a site immediately adjacent to Fort Trumbull; local planners hoped that Pfizer would draw new business to the area, thereby serving as a catalyst to the area's rejuvenation. After receiving initial approval from the city council, the NLDC continued its planning activities and held a series of neighborhood meetings to educate the public about the process. In May, the city council authorized the NLDC to formally submit its plans to the relevant state agencies for review. Upon obtaining state-level approval, the NLDC finalized an integrated development plan focused on 90 acres of the Fort Trumbull area.

The NLDC intended the development plan to capitalize on the arrival of the Pfizer facility and the new commerce it was expected to attract. In addition to creating jobs, generating tax revenue, and helping to "build momentum for the revitalization of downtown New London," id., at 92, the plan was also designed to make the City more attractive and to create leisure and recreational opportunities on the waterfront and in the park.

The city council approved the plan in January 2000, and designated the NLDC as its development agent in charge of implementation. The city council also authorized the NLDC to purchase property or to acquire property by exercising eminent domain in the City's name. § 8-193. The NLDC successfully negotiated the purchase of most of the real estate in the 90-acre area, but its negotiations with petitioners failed. As a consequence, in November 2000, the NLDC initiated the condemnation proceedings that gave rise to this case.

II

Petitioner Susette Kelo has lived in the Fort Trumbull area since 1997. She has made extensive improvements to her house, which she prizes for its water view. Petitioner Wilhelmina Dery was born in her Fort Trumbull house in 1918 and has lived there her entire life. Her husband Charles (also a petitioner) has lived in the house since they married some 60 years ago. In all, the nine petitioners own 15 properties in Fort Trumbull-4 in parcel 3 of the development plan and 11 in parcel 4A. Ten of the parcels are occupied by the owner or a family member; the other five are held as investment properties. There is no allegation that any of these properties is blighted or otherwise in poor condition; rather, they were condemned only because they happen to be located in the development area.

In December 2000, petitioners brought this action in the New London Superior Court. They claimed, among other things, that the taking of their properties would violate the "public use" restriction in the Fifth Amendment. After a 7-day bench trial, the Superior Court granted a permanent restraining order prohibiting the taking of the properties located in parcel 4A (park or marina support).

After the Superior Court ruled, both sides took appeals to the Supreme Court of Connecticut. That court held, over a dissent, that all of the City's proposed takings were valid. It began by upholding the lower court's determination that the takings were authorized by chapter 132, the State's municipal development statute. That statute expresses a legislative determination that the taking of land, even developed land, as part of an economic development project is a "public use" and in the "public interest." Next, the court held that such economic development qualified as a valid public use under both the Federal and State Constitutions.

We granted certiorari to determine whether a city's decision to take property for the purpose of economic development satisfies the "public use" requirement of the Fifth Amendment.

III

Two polar propositions are perfectly clear. On the one hand, it has long been accepted that the sovereign may not take the property of A for the sole purpose of transferring it to another private party B, even though A is paid just compensation. On the other hand, it is equally clear that a State may transfer property from one private party to another if future "use by the public" is the purpose of the taking; the condemnation of land for a railroad with common-carrier duties is a familiar example. Neither of these propositions, however, determines the disposition of this case.

As for the first proposition, the City would no doubt be forbidden from taking petitioners' land for the purpose of conferring a private benefit on a particular private party. Nor would the City be allowed to take property under the mere pretext of a public purpose, when its actual purpose was to bestow a private benefit. The takings before us, however, would be executed pursuant to a "carefully considered" development plan. The trial judge and all the members of the Supreme Court of Connecticut agreed that there was no evidence of an illegitimate purpose in this case. Therefore, as was true of the statute challenged in Midkiff, 467 U.S., at 245, 104 S.Ct. 2321, the City's development plan was not adopted "to benefit a particular class of identifiable individuals."

On the other hand, this is not a case in which the City is planning to open the condemned land-at least not in its entirety-to use by the general public. Nor will the private lessees of the land in any sense be required to operate like common carriers, making their services available to all comers. But although such a projected use would be sufficient to satisfy the public use requirement, this "Court long ago rejected any literal requirement that condemned property be put into use for the general public." Indeed, while many state courts in the mid-19th century endorsed "use by the public" as the proper definition of public use, that narrow view steadily eroded over time. Not only was the "use by the public" test difficult to administer (e.g., what proportion of the public need have access to the property? at what price?), but it proved to be impractical given the diverse and always evolving needs of society. Accordingly, when this Court began applying the Fifth Amendment to the States at the close of the 19th century, it embraced the broader and more natural interpretation of public use as "public purpose." Thus, in a case upholding a mining company's use of an aerial bucket line to transport ore over property it did not own, Justice Holmes' opinion for the Court stressed "the inadequacy of use by the general public as a universal test." We have repeatedly and consistently rejected that narrow test ever since.

The disposition of this case therefore turns on the question whether the City's development plan serves a "public purpose." Without exception, our cases have defined that concept broadly, reflecting our longstanding policy of deference to legislative judgments in this field.

In Berman v. Parker, 348 U.S. 26, 75 S.Ct. 98, 99 L. Ed. 27 (1954), this Court upheld a redevelopment plan targeting a blighted area of Washington, D.C., in which most of the housing for the area's 5,000 inhabitants was beyond repair. Under the plan, the area would be condemned and part of it utilized for the construction of streets, schools, and other public facilities. The remainder of the land would be leased or sold to private parties for the purpose of redevelopment, including the construction of low-cost housing.

The owner of a department store located in the area challenged the condemnation, pointing out that his store was not itself blighted and arguing that the creation of a "better balanced, more attractive community" was not a valid public use. Writing for a unanimous Court, Justice Douglas refused to evaluate this claim in isolation, deferring instead to the legislative and agency judgment that the area "must be planned as a whole" for the plan to be successful. The Court explained that "community redevelopment programs need not, by force of the Constitution, be on a piecemeal basis-lot by lot, building by building." The public use underlying the taking was unequivocally affirmed:

> "We do not sit to determine whether a particular housing project is or is not desirable. The concept of the public welfare is broad and inclusive. . . . The values it represents are spiritual as well as physical, aesthetic as well as monetary. It is within the power of the legislature to determine that the community should be beautiful as well as healthy, spacious as well as clean, well-balanced as well as carefully patrolled. In the present case, the Congress and its authorized agencies have made determinations that take into account a wide variety of values. It is not for us to reappraise them. If those who govern the District of Columbia decide that the Nation's Capital should be beautiful as well as sanitary, there is nothing in the Fifth Amendment that stands in the way."

Viewed as a whole, our jurisprudence has recognized that the needs of society have varied between different parts of the Nation, just as they have evolved over time in response to changed circumstances. Our earliest cases in particular embodied a strong theme of federalism, emphasizing the "great respect" that we owe to state legislatures and state courts in discerning local public needs. For more than a century, our public use jurisprudence has wisely eschewed rigid formulas and intrusive scrutiny in favor of affording legislatures broad latitude in determining what public needs justify the use of the takings power.

The judgment of the Supreme Court of Connecticut is affirmed.

It is so ordered.

CASE QUESTIONS

1 What was the stated purpose of the actions of the city of New London?
2 How did the city carry out condemning property through its power of eminent domain?
3 Was there ever an allegation that the houses that were seized were somehow defective?
4 What grounds did the Court cite for granting cert in this case?
5 Why are the takings in this case different from taking to benefit a private individual or as a mere pretext of public purpose?

 SKILLS YOU NEED IN THE REAL WORLD

RESEARCHING LIENS AND OTHER ASSESSMENTS

We have seen that liens and other types of assessments against property can result in any of a number of potential problems for homeowners. Many of these problems do not surface until the homeowner has put the house up for sale. Then there is little time to correct some of these legal problems. To check the status of real estate for any liens or assessments, you must learn your state's system for recording these items. In some states, for example, liens are filed in the clerk of court's office. They are sometimes cross-referenced with the deed office or land office, but that isn't always the case. You can learn how to search for liens and other assessments by visiting the local government agencies that track them. Learn what office inside the local courthouse or land office is responsible for tracking liens and practice locating liens before you actually need this skill. The time that you spend in this preparation is a wise investment toward building a skill set that will help you throughout your career.

CHAPTER SUMMARY

Fixtures are items of personal property that have become permanently attached to real property. At the moment of attachment, personal property is reclassified as real property. This reclassification has both philosophical and practical consequences. When something becomes permanently attached to real property, it remains with the property when the parcel is sold and there is no requirement to list it separately on the deed.

Easements are the rights of non-owners to use a portion of a real estate parcel. Easements come in two forms: appurtenant easements and in gross easements. An appurtenant easement gives a non-owner the right to use a portion of the owner's property. The most common example of an appurtenant easement is a driveway. An adjoining landowner has the right to use a portion of property that does not belong to him in order to access his own parcel. An in gross easement gives a non-owner the right to enter on the owner's property, usually for the purpose of maintaining utilities.

There are many other rights and obligations associated with real property ownership. Real property owners can be charged for governmental improvements on or near the property. Real property owners can give licenses to others to use their property for specific purposes, such as hunting and fishing. Owners also have specific rights arising from ownership of a real property parcel. For instance, owners have air rights, which give them the right to use the air above their property to a reasonable distance. Owners also have rights in the soil, referred to as mineral rights. These rights give the owner the ability to mine the soil for metals and other useful materials. Finally, an owner can transfer certain rights to others while retaining full ownership. An owner might, for example, transfer the right to harvest crops or the right to mine for minerals to another person.

REVIEW QUESTIONS

1 What is a fixture?
2 What are some of the tests that courts have used to determine when something qualifies as a fixture?
3 What is the difference between a fixture and a trade fixture?
4 What is an easement?
5 What are the two different types of easements?
6 List and explain the ways that easements can be created.
7 List and explain the ways that easements can be terminated.
8 What are assessments?
9 How are licenses and easements different?
10 Explain "profits" from the land.
11 Compare and contrast profits, licenses, and easements.
12 What is the difference between materialmen's liens and mechanics' liens?
13 What are air rights?
14 How would a real property owner's air rights in the eighteenth century compare to those same rights today?
15 How did the development of air travel affect property owners' air rights?
16 Why are water rights important?
17 What rights does an owner of real property have to subterranean water?
18 What are "percolating waters"?
19 Explain mineral rights.
20 Explain the decision in this chapter's case excerpt.

DISCUSSION QUESTIONS

1 Do statutes and court rules favor the creation of easements? Explain your answer.

2 Why is water such an important component of property rights? Explain your answer.

PRACTICAL APPLICATIONS

Visit your local real estate or land office and locate a copy of an easement, lien, or assessment that has been filed against a particular title. What are the details provided on this filing?

WEB SITES

Fixtures – 'Lectric Law
http://www.lectlaw.com/def/f047.htm

Trade Fixtures – Duhaime.org
http://www.duhaime.org/LegalDictionary/T/TradeFixtures.aspx

Easements by implication – Pennsylvania Legislator's Municipal Deskbook
http://www.lgc.state.pa.us/deskbook06/
Issues_Private_Property_Issues_02_Landlocked_Property.pdf

When to Use a Lease, License, Easement – University of California
http://www.ucop.edu/facil/resg/leasing/documents/leaselicense.pdf

Profit a Prendre – Legal Information Institute
http://www.law.cornell.edu/wex/profit_%C3%A0_prendre

Mineral Rights – Michigan Department of Environmental Quality
http://www.michigan.gov/documents/deq/ogs-oilandgas-mineral-
rights_257977_7.pdf

TERMS AND PHRASES

Abandonment	In gross easement	Merger
Appurtenant easement	License	Profit à prendre
Assessment	Lien	Run with the land
Easement	Materialman	Trade fixture
Fixture	Mechanic	

SIGNIFICANT CASES

Kazi v. State Farm Fire and Cas. Co., 15 P.3d 223 (Cal., 2001)

Union County Improvement Authority v. Artaki, LLC, 920 A.2d 125 (N.J. Super. App., 2007)

Stardust Mobile Estates v. City of San Buenaventura, 55 Cal. Rptr. 3d 218 (Cal. App. 2. Dist., 2007)

Freeman v. Barrs, 237 S.W.3d 285 (Mo. App. S. Dist., 2007)

In re Village of Port Chester, 839 N.Y.S.2d 218 (N.Y. App. Div. 2. Dept., 2007)

Green Tree Servicing, LLC v. Random Antics, LLC, 869 N.E.2d 464 (Ind. App., 2007)

Real Estate Contracts

Focus of This Chapter

The law of contracts and real estate has a long and rich history. This chapter first introduces the general law of contracts and then explains how contract law principles apply to specific real estate transactions.

Chapter Learning Objectives

After completing this chapter, you should be able to:

- Define the basic components of any legally binding contract
- Explain the minimum requirements of a valid offer
- Define when and under what circumstances a valid acceptance is made
- Explain the importance of the Statute of Frauds to real estate transactions
- List and describe the various types of clauses that are routinely inserted into real estate contracts

INTRODUCTION

In this chapter, we explore the topic of contract law as it applies to real property transactions. There has always been a close relationship between real estate law and contract law. The two topics are closely interwoven, and it is difficult, if not impossible, to understand one without understanding the other. Real estate practice is rife with examples of contracts, from the lease between a landlord and a tenant, to the offer of purchase between a prospective buyer and seller, to the real estate agent's commission with the seller. Contracts appear at nearly every phase of a real estate transaction.

We explore the relationship between contract and real property law by first addressing the basic components of a contract. We then proceed to specific examples of contracts in real estate practice and the common provisions found in real estate contracts.

But first we must answer the question: What is a contract?

A. WHAT IS A CONTRACT?

Contract
A legally recognized agreement that gives both parties the right to enforce the obligation through legal means.

A **contract** is an agreement between two or more parties. These parties agree to exchange something of value. The value may be in the form of a service for which a person will be paid. It could also be the exchange of title for a particular item, such as a car or a house. The important point to make about contracts is that when one is created, it gives both parties certain rights. Among these rights is the option of using the court system to enforce the contract provisions in the event that one party fails to live up to her agreements.

We concentrate on real estate contracts in this chapter, but the introductory material here applies to all types of contracts. When a contract is created, it gives the parties specific rights and obligations. If a party breaches the terms of the contract, the other party has the right to sue for damages or seek equitable relief.

No matter what the subject of the contract, all contracts have some basic elements. There must be:

- An offer
- An acceptance of that offer
- Mutual assent
- Consideration
- Legality
- Capacity

1. OFFER

An offer is one party's indication of her willingness to enter into a contract. Offers are specific; they invite another person to enter into a legally binding agreement. The details that must be present in an offer include the following:

- Who will be bound by the contract?
- What (services, property, title) will be exchanged?
- What are the terms?
- What is the manner of performance?

If an offer sets out these terms, it will be valid, even if it is vague on some points. For instance, there is no requirement that the offer anticipate all possible issues, or even define specific items such as manner and time of payment. An offer must specify what is being offered and to whom the offer is being made. It must be specific about terms, such as price and how a person can accept the offer. Beyond that, an offer can be silent on other issues.[1]

If the questions in Figure 6-1 can be answered, the offer will be considered legally valid. Consider the question in Example 6-1.

---

[1] *Scott v. Foppe*, 247 N.C. 67, 100 S.E.2d 238 (1957).

- ■ Who can accept?
- ■ What is being offered?
- ■ What will be exchanged?
- ■ What are the terms?
- ■ How can a party indicate acceptance of the offer?

EXAMPLE 6-1

Simon puts a for sale sign on his front yard. Is Simon's sign a valid, legal offer?

Answer: No. Simon's for sale sign cannot be considered an offer because it lacks sufficient information. It does not, for example, specify who can accept, what the sale price is, what the terms are, or what exactly Simon is offering for sale. After all, based on the sign's location, he might just as easily be selling the sod in his front yard. Barring any further developments, courts will not consider Simon's sign to be a valid offer.

a. Offers Do Not Require Specific Language

There is no requirement for offers to contain legal-sounding phrases, such as "party of the first part," or other "legalese." A valid offer can be couched in everyday language and the words used will be given their ordinary meaning. Another test that we can apply to an offer is even more basic. Does the offer create something that another person could accept?

> **Sidebar**
>
> *If Simon's sign is not an offer, does it have any legal significance? Many legal commentators would refer to Simon's sign as an "invitation for offers." Simon is effectively stating to the world his intention of receiving an offer on his home.*

Tech Topic
COMMUNICATING OFFERS VIA EMAIL, TEXT, OR TWITTER

State law varies on the enforceability of unsigned or oral contracts, although most states affirm that if an oral contract is partially performed, the contract is then binding. However, real estate law generally states that an offer on a property must be signed by the buyer, show an acceptance by the seller, and have a written contract by both parties. But with the proliferation of communication by way of email, text message, and Twitter, could electronic offers be enforceable?

In general, the answer is no. The key element of a legitimate offer is the signature. A signed offer can certainly be scanned and faxed or attached to an email, but a simple electronic communication absent the signature will not suffice. Electronic and digitally encrypted signatures are becoming more commonplace and might possibly be an acceptable alternative to the live signature one day. But the underlying technology required to create such signatures would be cumbersome in the fast-paced exchange of offers and counteroffers.

There are provisions that allow for electronic signatures and, where those laws have been enacted, such an offer might be considered legally valid. The best practice is to refer to your state's laws about electronic or digital signatures.

b. The Reasonable Person Standard and Offers

An offer is judged by the reasonable person standard. Under this standard, a particular statement will be construed to be an offer when a reasonable person would have interpreted it that way. Under the reasonable person test, the subjective intent of the parties is not the central issue. Instead, the courts will look to the surrounding circumstances and ask the question, "Under these facts, would a reasonable person have believed that an offer had been made?" Consider Example 6-2.

2. ACCEPTANCE

When a valid offer has been made, the party — referred to as the offeree — has one of several possible options. The offeree can simply ignore the offer and her failure to act will be construed as a rejection of the offer. The offeree can actively reject the offer by stating that she has no intention of accepting. Finally, the offeree can make a counteroffer. We examine each of these possible scenarios.

EXAMPLE 6-2

Jan is jogging through her neighborhood when a man accosts her. The man is obviously intoxicated. He points at the house on the corner and says to Jan, "You're going to buy that house for $100,000 or you'll regret it."

When Jan later refuses to purchase, the man sues. What is the result?

Answer: There is no contract. Leaving aside the issue of the man's obvious intoxication, which would affect his capacity, there is the issue of the reasonable person standard. No one would interpret the man's actions as an offer. Besides that, Jan has not indicated an acceptance.

a. Rejecting an Offer

When a person rejects an offer, there is no possibility of contract. A rejected offer cancels the basic prerequisite of a contract. Once an offer has been rejected, the offeree no longer has any power to accept. In fact, courts often term this phase of the negotiations as placing the **power of acceptance** in another person. If a person has the power of acceptance, it means that she can accept an offer and create a contract. Rejecting an offer cancels the power of acceptance. It is as if the offer has died and cannot be revived.

Power of Acceptance
The legally recognized capacity of a party to accept an offer and create a binding, enforceable contract.

Once rejected, the only way to resurrect a contract is by making a new offer. The original party might restate the offer, at which point the offeree could accept. However, barring this event, there is no offer pending and therefore no possibility of accepting it.

EXAMPLE 6-3

Simon puts up a sign in his front yard that reads, "For sale: 3br/2bath/living room/fireplace/full basement, 2200 sq. ft. $120,000, o.b.o."

Sara sees this sign and correctly interprets it to mean: for sale, house with three bedrooms, two bathrooms, living room, fireplace, full basement, 2,200 square feet at $120,000, or best offer.

Sara goes to Simon's door and says, "Okay."

Has a contract been formed?

Answer: It certainly appears that Simon's sign meets many of the requirements of an offer. It has specific details about what is being offered and for how much. But what about the issue of who can accept? Under Simon's terms, is there anything to indicate that Sara can accept? Put another way, has Simon's sign given anyone who comes by his house the power to accept?

If the answer is no, the sign is not an offer. Just as we saw in an earlier example, Simon's sign is still an invitation to others to make an offer — and to incorporate some of the terms that Simon has laid out.

A contract is the product of a valid offer that has been accepted by another.

ISSUE AT
A GLANCE

Maria has seen Simon's sign and drafts an offer to him containing the following provisions:

EXAMPLE 6-4

- Offer: $115,000, cash at closing
- Fee simple absolute title
- Contingent on financing from a lender at 5% interest for 30 years
- Contingent on the home passing an inspection
- Offer is revoked if not accepted within ten days

Is this a statement that a reasonable person would consider to be a valid offer?

Answer: It is specific about terms and to whom the offer is made. It is also specific about how and when the offer will expire. If Simon were to accept this offer, a binding contract would result. Simon has the power of acceptance, and therefore this is a legally valid offer.

b. Communicating the Acceptance to the Offeror

When an offer is accepted, the acceptance must be communicated to the offeror. If the offeree fails to communicate her intention to accept, there is no binding agreement. Unless the offer specifically limits the method used to communicate the acceptance, it can be sent through any means. An oral offer can be accepted by written correspondence, and vice versa.[2] Later, we will see that the Statute of Frauds, which requires certain contracts to be in writing, usually dictates that offers and acceptances involving real property must be made in writing. However, for most other purposes, as long as the offeror does not limit the manner of acceptance, it can be communicated in any way. However, when an acceptance is made through the mail, special rules apply.

---

[2] *Dudley A. Tyng & Co. v. Converse*, 180 Mich. 195, 146 N.W. 629 (1914).

c. The Mailbox Rule

The so-called mailbox rule sates that an acceptance is legally effective when it is deposited in the U.S. postal system. All states have some version of the mailbox rule.[3] The reason for the rule is simple: Without it, any offer accepted by mail would not be effective until received. We all know that it takes a posted letter from one to three days to reach its intended destination. In the fast-paced world of negotiations, 72 hours is a lifetime. Without a rule that states that an acceptance is effective the moment that it is posted, accepting contracts by letter would be nearly impossible.

Under the mailbox rule, an acceptance is legally effective when it is posted.

d. Counteroffers

A counteroffer technically rejects the original offer and replaces it with a new offer. Although most people don't phrase it this way, a counteroffer actually states the following: "I hereby reject your original offer and instead substitute it with my own offer."

EXAMPLE 6-5

Simon likes Maria's offer, except for the term regarding price. He decides to raise it to $118,000. What is the significance of his change in the price?

Answer: This is a counteroffer.

Who has the power of acceptance now?

Answer: Maria does. She can accept the counteroffer and create a contract; if she rejects, it there will be no contract.

People make counteroffers in negotiations all the time without being aware of the legal consequences. A counteroffer rejects the original offer. In the example above, let's see if we can diagram what has happened.

Maria made the original offer. At that point, Simon had the power of acceptance. Had he accepted, a binding contract would have been created. However, Simon made a counteroffer, which flipped the transaction. At that point, Maria had the power of acceptance. When she accepted Simon's counteroffer, Simon and Maria became parties to a valid contract.

So far, our discussion about contracts has focused on the offer and acceptance. But there are other equally important components of a contract, including mutual assent, capacity, and legality.

---

[3] *Woody v. State, ex rel. Dept. of Corrections,* 83 P.2d 257 (Okla. 1992).

3. MUTUAL ASSENT

Mutual assent is the consequence of a valid offer and acceptance. Otherwise known as a "meeting of the minds," mutual assent is the requirement that the parties know and understand the basic features of the contract. Both parties should be in agreement about what is being sold and for how much. When the parties have a basic misunderstanding about these core issues, the contract may be invalidated on the basis of a mistake. (We discuss mistake later in this chapter.) At its simplest, mutual assent is the requirement that the parties understand the basic agreement in the contract. They must be in agreement about what is being sold and for what amount.

Mutual assent
"Meeting of the minds;" the requirement that the parties to the contract have the same understanding about the contract.

4. CONSIDERATION

Another requirement for a valid contract is **consideration**. Consideration is the requirement that both parties give up something of value in exchange for receiving something else of value. Essentially, consideration is an element of contracts that ensures that both parties are bound to the contract's terms. A contract that binds only one person is no contract at all. Consideration is sometimes referred to as "bargained-for exchange," and that is an accurate description of this requirement. Both parties to a contract must negotiate away a right, service, or object in order to receive some other right, service, or object. In a common example, when homeowners sell their property to others, they are giving up title to the land in exchange for something of value, that is, money. The buyers, on the other hand, are giving up cash in exchange for the title. Consideration usually is not a question in most contracts, where the terms make clear that value is being exchanged. This is especially true in real estate transactions.

Consideration
The contractual requirement that both parties incur some form of legal detriment in exchange for receiving something of value; consideration ensures that both parties are bound to the contract.

> **Consideration ensures that both parties to a contract are giving up something of value in exchange for something else of value; it is also called "bargained for exchange."**

 ISSUE AT A GLANCE

5. LEGALITY

Legality is one of the most understated of contractual requirements. It almost goes without saying that before a contract can be enforced, it must contemplate a legal action. Contracts to carry out crimes are not contracts at all; at least they are not contracts that can be enforced. Without the provision of enforcement, one could easily argue that the agreement does not qualify as a valid contract.

Although it would appear that legality would not be a question in a typical real estate transaction, there are times when legality becomes an issue. For instance, if a lender is charging a mortgage rate higher than that permitted by law, the courts could void the mortgage agreement.

Legality
The requirement that a contract must have a legal subject or action as its subject.

6. CAPACITY

While legality may not be a common concern in contracts, a party's **capacity** frequently is. The requirement of capacity goes directly to each party's state of

Capacity
The requirement that all parties to agreements know and understand the consequences of entering a legally binding contract.

mind at the time that the contract was created. A person is considered to be incompetent to enter into a contract when she lacks the ability to understand the nature and consequences of the agreement.[4] Certain classes of persons are presumed to lack capacity, and any contract entered into by them will be considered void. See Figure 6-2 for a list of classes of persons who lack capacity.

FIGURE 6-2

Persons Who Lack Capacity

- Minors (under the age of 18)
- Persons declared to be mentally incompetent

- Persons who have had their civil rights suspended (prisoners)
- Intoxicated persons

In some circumstances, the court may rule that a contract with a person who lacks capacity is voidable, that is, capable of being cancelled by either of the parties at their option. Examples of voidable contracts include those made with minors or persons who are intoxicated. When the legal impediment disappears, the parties can affirm the contract and create a perfectly legal agreement.

THE STATUTE OF FRAUDS

The Statute of Frauds was developed in England in the 1600s. Originally given the more descriptive name of "The Statute to Prevent Frauds," the statute was an early legislative attempt to protect consumers by requiring certain types of contracts to be in writing before they could be enforceable through the court system. Examples of contracts that fall under the jurisdiction of the Statute of Frauds include:

- Wills
- Contracts to answer for the debt of another
- Contracts in anticipation of marriage (prenuptial/antenuptial agreements)
- Contracts for the sale of land
- Contracts that cannot be performed within one year of the date of their creation
- Contracts for the sale of goods exceeding $500 in value
- Contracts for the sale of securities (stocks, bonds)

Although these classes of contracts are important for different legal areas, for the purposes of real property only two are important: contracts for the sale of land and contracts that cannot be performed within one year of their creation. We address the first of these classifications in this chapter and the second when we

---

[4] *Brown v. United Missouri Bank, N.A.*, 78 F.3d 382 8th Cir. (1996).

discuss landlord-tenant law in Chapter 7. Most states have a version of the Statute of Frauds that is similar to the one provided in Figure 6-3.

All contracts to sell or convey any lands, tenements or hereditaments, or any interest in or concerning them, and all leases and contracts for leasing land for the purpose of digging for gold or other minerals, or for mining generally, of whatever duration; and all other leases and contracts for leasing lands exceeding in duration three years from the making thereof, shall be void unless said contract, or some memorandum or note thereof, be put in writing and signed by the party to be charged therewith, or by some other person by him thereto lawfully authorized.[5]

FIGURE 6-3

Statute of Frauds

The Statute of Frauds applies not only to contracts for the sale of real property, but also to any transaction involving a property right, from mineral leases to option contracts.

The practical effect of the Statute of Frauds is to require that all contracts involving the transfer of real property interests be in writing. If they are not, they are unenforceable. Anyone who brings suit over an oral purchase contract for a real estate parcel will have the case dismissed before it reaches a discussion of its merits.

The question of what constitutes a "writing" often comes up in the context of discussing the Statute of Frauds. There is no requirement, for instance, that specific types of forms, or even particular formulations of words, must be used before a contract satisfies the statute. In fact, the statute is vague about what constitutes a written contract. In most contexts, even the most cursory of documents will satisfy the writing requirement of the Statute of Frauds.

The Statute of Frauds has been enacted in one form or another across the U.S. It requires that specific types of contracts must be in writing before they will be legally enforceable.

ISSUE AT A GLANCE

 FORMATION ISSUES IN CONTRACT LAW

Contract disputes are some of the most common types of lawsuits in the United States. Because of this, courts frequently must interpret contracts and rule on the legality of particular provisions. This puts the courts in an unusual situation: They must decipher the intent of parties who are now hotly contesting those specific issues. Fortunately, over the years, courts have developed general guidelines to assist them in interpreting ambiguous or confusing contract provisions.

---

[5] N. C. Gen. Stat. § 22-2, Contract for sale of land; leases.

A. GUIDELINES THAT COURTS USE TO INTERPRET CONTRACTS

In situations in which the contract has plain and unambiguous language, the courts must interpret the provisions exactly as they are set out in the contract. In cases where the language is ambiguous or difficult to interpret, the court will attempt to resolve the dispute in such a way that a valid contract results. If that is impossible, the court will attempt to resolve the issue in the way that offers the most justice to all parties.

In some situations, the court may find that no contract was ever formed. Such a conclusion would be justified when the parties can prove mistake.

B. MISTAKE

Mistake
A misunderstanding or confusion about a material fact in a contract that is shared by both parties.

When we use the term **mistake** in the context of contract law, we are talking about a very specific factual determination. In normal parlance, mistake refers to a misunderstanding. This is not the definition of mistake in a contract setting. Under that definition, a contract can only be voided when both parties share a misunderstanding about a critical point in the contract. Mistake is a mutual act. If one party claims that she failed to understand a particular provision, this is not mistake and will not result in a determination that the contract is void. Mistake only applies to material facts found in a contract. A material fact could be any of the following:

- The person(s) who will be bound by the contract
- The type of contract entered into
- The subject matter of the contract[6]

1. EFFECT OF A RULING OF MISTAKE

If the court finds that an actual mistake has occurred, the court is empowered to rescind the contract.[7] In such a situation, the court will attempt to put the parties back into the situation that they were in before the contract was ever created. This may mean refunding money, or reimbursing a party for out-of-pocket expenses related to the contract.

C. FRAUD

If a party can show that a contract was obtained under fraudulent circumstances, a court would be authorized to rescind or void the contract. However, it isn't easy to prove fraud. For one thing, the party attempting to void the contract must show that the other party made an intentional, deliberate false statement about a

---

[6] *Yeazell v. Copins*, 98 Ariz. 109, 402 P.2d 541 (1965).
[7] *Lancaster v. Lancaster*, 138 N.C. App. 459, 530 S.E.2d 82 (2000).

material fact. We have already seen that material facts are the key points in question in forming a contract. A false or misleading statement about a non-material fact will not rise to the level of fraud. When a party proves fraud, the court has the power to cancel the contract and enter an order that requires the parties to return any money or property exchanged during the agreement.

REAL ESTATE CONTRACTS

Contracts are the lifeblood of real estate practice and affect nearly every phase of a real property transaction, from listing the house for sale to the closing. Among the important real estate contracts we discuss in this chapter are:

- Listing agreements
- Offer of purchase and contracts
- Options

A. LISTING AGREEMENT

A listing agreement is the contract between a real estate broker and a seller. In the listing agreement, the seller agrees to pay the real estate broker a commission when the broker produces a buyer who is ready, willing, and able to meet the purchase price. The contract is referred to as a "listing contract" because it sets the stage for the manner in which the property will be advertised by the real estate agency. The listing refers not only to how the property will be advertised for sale, but also to how the commission will ultimately be shared. There are three general types of listings:

1 Open listing
2 Exclusive listing
3 Multiple listing

1. OPEN LISTING

An open listing allows the property to be sold through any broker. The seller would be obligated to pay a commission to any broker who produces a buyer capable of purchasing the property. If the seller locates a buyer herself, she does not have to pay a commission. Open listings are not very common.

2. EXCLUSIVE LISTING

Under an exclusive listing agreement, the seller employs only one individual who has legal authority to close the sale. No broker other than the one with whom the seller has a contract will receive a commission for producing a buyer. Because of the limited nature of this arrangement, exclusive listings are also not common.

3. MULTIPLE LISTING

Multiple listings are the most common type of real estate listing because they offer several advantages over open listings and exclusive listings. Under a multiple listing, the listing agent shares a commission with any broker who produces a buyer. This gives all brokers in the area a vested interest in working to sell any property listed in the Multiple Listing Service. The various brokers will share the commission between them. Under a multiple listing, a seller theoretically has every broker in the area working for her.

A listing agreement is the contract between a seller and the real estate broker to list the house for sale and for the broker to produce a buyer who is ready, willing, and able to purchase the home.

B. OFFER OF PURCHASE AND CONTRACT

An offer of purchase and contract is a written document that presents the details of the buyer's offer to the seller to purchase real estate. This contract reflects the negotiations between the buyer and seller and the final terms of their agreement. Among the specifics set out in an offer of purchase and contract are:

- A description of the real estate involved
- A provision for the purchase of any personal property located on the premises
- Purchase price details, including earnest money deposit
- Conditions, including the buyer's financing condition and loan commitment letter
- Evidence of title
- Property disclosures
- Risk of loss provisions
- Closing provisions
- Signature provisions

1. PROPERTY DESCRIPTION

The property in question should be adequately described. An adequate description must be something beyond the street address. Most states have forms that have been preapproved by the state bar or state real estate commission that provide blanks not only for street address of the property, but also for city and town location, as well as legal description.

2. PURCHASE OF PERSONAL PROPERTY

The buyer and seller may, in addition to purchasing real property, also negotiate the purchase of certain items of personal property located on the premises. Because personal property is a separate and distinct class from real property, any personal property items that are purchased along with the real estate must be listed separately.

3. PURCHASE PRICE DETAILS

The offer of purchase and contract will not only include the purchase price, but will also make provision for an earnest money deposit. Earnest money is the money put down by the buyer early in the negotiation process as proof of good faith of the buyer's intention to enter into a contract. This money must be accounted for later on in the sale process.

4. CONDITIONS

The buyer will usually make her offer contingent upon certain events, particularly financing. The buyer's offer usually contains a condition revoking the offer in the event that the buyer is unable to obtain suitable financing. Other conditions may include the buyer's express condition of sale of her current home prior to concluding the purchase of the new home.

5. EVIDENCE OF TITLE

The evidence of title provision in the offer to purchase and contract is the seller's promise to use her best efforts, including hiring attorneys and conducting title searches on the property, to ensure that the buyer receives marketable title to the property in question.

6. PROPERTY DISCLOSURES

Most states require that the buyer receive a copy of the real property residential property disclosures prior to the signing of the offer to purchase and contract. This provision also allows the buyer to conduct a property inspection within a specific time period after signing the contract.

7. RISK OF LOSS PROVISIONS

The offer of purchase and contract provides that the risk of loss, specifically whose insurance company will pay for any damages to the property, rests squarely on the seller prior to closing. After the closing, however, risk of loss shifts to the new owner and her insurance company.

8. CLOSING PROVISIONS

The offer of purchase and contract will also contain provisions concerning the actual closing. In some cases, the buyer may elect to include a "time is of the essence" contract clause provision. This is a clause that requires the closing to occur at a specific date; otherwise, the contract will be considered null and void. We discuss this and other common contract provisions later in this chapter.

FIGURE 6-4

Offer of Purchase and Contract of Sale

THIS OFFER OF PURCHASE AND CONTRACT OF SALE, dated _____ the day of _____ 20 ___ between _____ and _____ (collectively referred to herein as the "Seller") whose address is _____ and _____ and _____ (collectively referred to herein as the "Buyer") whose address is _____ .

1. The Property. The Seller agrees to sell to the Buyer, and the Buyer agrees to purchase from the Seller the fee simple real property located in _____, real property, whose legal description is as follows:

_____

Included in the property hereby sold are all permanently attached fixtures, and the following items, if any, now on the property: kitchen stove and oven, refrigerator, alarm systems, water filters, carpet, fire place screens, draperies, shades, screens, storm doors and windows, venetian blinds, curtain rods, awnings, shrubbery, light fixtures, television aerial, dishwasher, garbage disposal, clothes washer, clothes dryer, window air conditioning units and _____

_____

_____ .

2. Purchase Price. The purchase price for the property is _____ Dollars ($), of which the Buyer has paid _____ Dollars ($) as Earnest Money. The balance of the purchase price shall be paid by the Buyer to the Seller in cash at settlement.

3. Time and Place of Settlement. Unless the parties agree otherwise, settlement shall take place at _____ a.m./p.m., at _____ .

4. Financing Contingency. The Buyer's obligation to purchase the property is contingent upon the Buyer obtaining, from a lending institution, a commitment for a mortgage loan, secured by the property, in the principal amount of not less than _____ Dollars ($), at an interest rate not to exceed _____ percent (____%) per annum, repayable in equal monthly installments of principal and interest over a period of not less than thirty (30) years, and requiring the payment of _____ of points/fees of not more than _____ (____%) percent of the total loan amount. The Buyer shall apply for and receive a commitment of financing from a suitable lending institution within (ten) 10 days of the date of this contract.

5. Termite Infestation or Damage. The Buyer shall have the right to have the dwelling on the property inspected by a licensed pest control operator within ten (10) days of the date of this contract. The fees for this inspection will be borne exclusively by the Buyer. If the inspecting company should report an infestation by termites or other wood-boring insects, the Buyer shall notify the Seller of this fact, in writing, including a written report prepared by the inspecting company. The seller shall have _____

days to correct, repair, or take other suitable action to repair the damage and shall certify this action to the Buyer, in writing.

6. Home Inspection. The Buyer shall have the right at the Buyer's expense to have the dwelling on the property inspected by a home inspection service or engineer within ten (10) days of the date of this contract. This inspection will involve a visual inspection of the mechanical, electrical, plumbing, and structural elements of the premises. Neither the Buyer nor the inspector shall damage the property during the inspection process. The Buyer shall provide the Seller with a copy of the inspector's written report, within a reasonable period of time after the inspection. The failure of the Seller to provide the Buyer or the Buyer's inspector access to said premises will be deemed a violation of this contract and in that event, the Seller shall return the Buyer's earnest money deposit.

7. Evidence of Title. At the closing or settlement of this contract, upon the Buyer's complete payment of all outstanding purchase monies, the Seller shall provide the Buyer evidence of title through a general warranty deed, in fee simple absolute, detailing the Seller's title to the property, free and clear from any encumbrances. The Seller will convey title to the Buyer at the closing. The Seller is responsible for paying any transfer taxes, conveyance fees, or other sales taxes based on this transaction.

8. Risk of Loss. The property shall be held at the risk of the Seller until the settlement occurs. Upon receipt of all closing documents, risk of loss shall vest in the Buyer.

9. Default by the Buyer. In the event of the Buyer's default under this contract, the Seller shall have the right to retain all deposits and earnest money paid by the Buyer as liquidated damages under this contract. The Seller reserves the right to seek additional damages and equitable remedies against the Buyer for a willful breach of this contract.

10. Real Estate Commission. The Seller agrees, at the time and place of closing, to pay a commission of 6 percent to the real estate brokers who have produced a buyer who is ready, willing, and able to conclude the transaction.

11. Entire Agreement. This contract contains the entire agreement of the parties. This contract will not be modified by any parole evidence or other communications not contained herein.

12. Contract Addendum. Time is of the essence in this contract. The closing date for this transaction is the 15th day of May 2005.

The laws of the State of Placid shall govern this contract.
WITNESS the hands and seals of the parties.

_____   _____

Seller   Buyer

_____   _____

Date   Date

9. SIGNATURE PROVISIONS

In Chapter 8, we will see that for a deed to be legally effective, the grantor must sign it. The grantor, or seller, is the only person required to sign the deed, but that is not the case with an offer of purchase and contract. This contract has signature provisions for all parties concerned and must be signed. Without the signatures, the contract is legally insufficient and cannot be enforced.

C. OPTIONS

Option
A contract between a seller and buyer, whereby the seller agrees not to sell the property to another person for a stated period of time.

An **option** is a contract between a seller and a prospective buyer, whereby the seller agrees that he will not sell the property to some other person, but only for a stated period of time. A prospective buyer might seek an option on the property instead of simply buying the property when she is attempting to negotiate contracts with other vendors and is not sure about the ultimate prospects of success. Negotiating an option with a potential seller involves only a small fraction of the money that it would take to actually purchase the property. In this case, the terms of the contract are simply that the seller will not sell or, if she does decide to sell, she will offer the property to the option holder first. If the option holder does not close the transaction within the prescribed period, or the time expires, the contract is cancelled and the seller is free to sell the property to anyone else she chooses.

V   CONTRACT CLAUSES

As you can see from the sample Offer of Purchase and Contract provided in this chapter, there are numerous clauses and provisions contained in this contract. We now examine the more important ones and discuss their significance to the transaction. The important provisions in this contract include:

- Time is of the essence
- Title
- Escrow
- Insurance (Risk of loss)

A. TIME IS OF THE ESSENCE

When a contract contains a "time is of the essence" provision, it means that the closing must occur on the date specified or the contract will be void. This provision is often included in time-sensitive transactions, when a closing must occur at a certain date in order to free up funds for another transaction. For instance, if *A* is buying a new home, *A* needs the funds from the sale of her previous home in order to complete the transaction. Therefore, the closing on the sale of *A*'s home must occur prior to the purchase of her new home. In such a situation, a "time is of the essence" provision puts all parties on alert that the contract has strict time limitations. These provisions have a way of galvanizing the people involved in the transaction to ensure that the closing occurs on or before the date listed in the contract.

B. TITLE

A title clause in a contract (numbered paragraph 7 in the example provided in this chapter) is a provision that spells out exactly what type of title the buyer is expecting to receive at the closing. For instance, in the sample offer of purchase and contract, the buyer is expecting to receive the highest and best type of title: fee simple absolute. We discuss the ramifications of the various types of titles in Chapter 8.

C. ESCROW

When a contract contains a provision for escrow, it means that the parties have agreed to take advantage of an unusual feature of real estate law in order to conclude the closing. As we will see in Chapter 13, an escrow closing allows the parties to sign the documentation for a closing at different times and still complete the closing as though all parties were actually present. To take advantage of this provision, the parties must first agree to it in the offer of purchase and contract.

D. INSURANCE (RISK OF LOSS)

An insurance, or risk of loss, provision in an offer of purchase and contract simply details which party bears the risk of loss during the transaction, and when the risk of loss for any damage or destruction of the premises transfers from the buyer to the seller. In the sample Offer of Purchase and Contract, this provision is found in numbered paragraph 8. The provision provides, in part, "The property shall be held at the risk of the Seller until the settlement occurs." This clause places the burden of property loss or destruction on the seller until the settlement, or closing, occurs. When the closing is complete, the risk of loss then shifts to the buyer, who is now the new owner. The risk of loss provision is important because it dictates which party's insurance company will be liable for damage to the property and when this liability is triggered.

 **BREACH OF CONTRACT**

When one party refuses to live up to her obligations under the contract, the other party is relieved of any further obligation in the contract and may sue for breach of contract. Contract law provides several different remedies and damages for the non-breaching party. The remedy sought often depends on which party is seeking the damages. Sellers might seek a different remedy for a breach than buyers would.

A. REMEDIES FOR BREACH

Breach of contract gives the non-breaching party the right to sue for damages or **equitable remedies**. A court can exercise its equity power to order an injunction, **specific performance,** or other action that is separate and distinct from the court's power to award monetary damages.

Equitable remedies
The power of a trial court to order a party to undertake specific actions, or to refrain from taking specific actions, such as injunctions and specific performance.

Specific performance
A court's order compelling a party to abide by the terms of a contract to which that party was previously in agreement.

1. REMEDIES FOR THE SELLER

When the buyer breaches the contract, the seller might retain the earnest money deposit, which was originally offered to evidence the buyer's good faith and on the condition that it would be forfeited on the buyer's failure to conclude the contract. However, the seller might well seek other remedies. For instance, the seller might decide to sue for monetary damages. Suppose that the seller sold the house to another buyer later on, but at a lower price. The seller would be authorized to sue the breaching buyer for the difference between the original contract price and the reduced price she later obtained.

2. REMEDIES FOR THE BUYER

Although a buyer might also be authorized to sue for monetary damages from a breaching seller, the buyer's main concern is probably concluding the contract. In this situation, the buyer might sue under the equitable remedy of specific performance. Under this doctrine, a court would be authorized to force the seller to comply with the terms of the original contract and sell the house to the buyer.

3. REMEDIES FOR THE BROKER

When a seller refuses to go through with a sale and the broker has completed all of her contractual duties, the broker has a cause of action against the seller for the real estate commission. This commission becomes due when the broker produces a buyer who is ready, willing, and able to conclude the transaction and the sale fails to occur because of the seller's actions. In this situation, the broker would be entitled to the commission even though the sale did not occur.

 **ANNOTATED DOCUMENT**   OFFER OF PURCHASE FOR REAL ESTATE

Offers always identify the parties

This offer, dated the 23rd day of May, 2006, between Marvin Meaty and Melba Meaty, hereafter known as "Seller", and Beula Buyer, hereafter known as "Buyer", sets out

Offer provides the street address of the property, but that is not enough

the details of an offer to purchase real estate located at 123 Maple Drive, Anywhere, Placid, 00030.

1. The seller agrees to sell to the Buyer, and the Buyer agrees to purchase from the Seller the real property located at 123 Maple Drive, Anywhere, Placid, 00030, more fully described as Burke County Tax Map 12400564 As shown in Plat Book 41-1546

> Property description also references tax maps and plats

2. Seller agrees to provide Buyer title in fee simple absolute, free of any encumbrances and in marketable condition.

> Buyer obviously wishes to receive the best type of title: fee simple

LEGAL RESEARCH  ETHICS

It might seem odd to refer to ethical requirements in performing legal research, but it is one of the most overlooked and potentially dangerous areas for any legal professional. Performing adequate legal research is an ethical requirement for attorneys. As a result, it behooves paralegals to understand the importance of legal research. Staying current and up to date on legal issues is one of the most basic parts of the service that legal professionals provide to clients. It also prevents embarrassing situations, such as relying on statutes that have been ruled unconstitutional, or cases that have been reversed by higher courts. In addition to avoiding general embarrassment, shoddy legal research can also leave the attorney open to a claim of legal malpractice.

DONALD YOO CORP. v. LASZLO N. TAUBER, M.D. AND ASSOCIATES  CASE EXCERPT

DONALD YOO CORP. v. LASZLO N. TAUBER, M.D. AND ASSOCIATES
281 A.D.2d 171, 722 N.Y.S.2d 5 (2001)

This is an action to recover a real estate brokerage commission. In 1997, plaintiff approached defendants concerning a client's interest in purchasing commercial property owned by defendants in Manhattan. Plaintiff presented its buyer's offer, along with a claim for a 3% brokerage commission to be paid out of the proceeds of the closing. Negotiations reduced an initial gap of $15 million to a meeting of the minds at $35,720,000. Plaintiff continually reminded defendants that a 3% brokerage commission would be expected out of the closing proceeds. On February 6, 1998, plaintiff conveyed its client's acceptance to defendants, along with a letter prepared for the latter's signature, formalizing the obligation to pay a brokerage commission of $1,070,000 out of the proceeds of the closing. A week later, on February 13, defendants confirmed in writing the purchase price and the commission ("which leaves us $34,650,000 net receipt"). However, this letter added some conditions that had to be satisfied, including the resolution of defendants' effort to remove the property from an existing real estate investment trust portfolio. As the buyer's due-diligence study and inspection of the property continued apace, defendants sought additional extensions of time until expiration of the letter of intent they had signed with a REIT. At first, defendants anticipated this matter would be cleared up by the end of February, then by mid-April, and ultimately, on April 13, the individual defendant asked for the buyer's indulgence when he realized that the REIT letter of intent would not expire until April 23. . . . Fifteen days later, as the news of such an extensive delay was evidently sinking in with the buyer, the individual defendant hit plaintiff with an even bigger surprise — that a new letter of intent had just been signed with a new purchaser who had been introduced to him by a different broker. Plaintiff immediately charged that this "violated our agreement that you promised to sell the property to our customer when the prior REIT's letter of intent expired." Defendants responded, through counsel, that they had never gone beyond the "conditional and indefinite" proposal advanced in their letter of February 13, which constituted "merely a statement of preliminary negotiation."

The motion court, at Commercial Part, found material questions of fact as to whether defendants' letter of February 13 was so conditional as to allow it to escape from the obligation to sell, and whether defendants had actually done anything affirmatively to prevent fulfillment of the condition. Even though this action was not brought by the prospective buyer, the court noted that a disappointed broker may nonetheless recover his commission where the vendor has prevented consummation of the transaction.

A brokerage commission may be legally conditioned upon a closing of title. In Graff v. Billet, 64 N.Y.2d 899, 487 N.Y.S.2d 733, 477 N.E.2d 212, affg. 101 A.D.2d 355, 475 N.Y.S.2d 122, the seminal case on this point, the court reviewed the standard brokerage agreement utilized in New York, which provides that a commission becomes due upon passage of title, except where there is "willful default" on the part of the seller. Plaintiff offers no case where such an exception has been determinative. The case before us does not even present the standard brokerage language in any of the correspondence between the parties. The seller's only acknowledgment of an obligation to pay a commission was clearly conditioned, in its letter of February 13, on the accomplishment of certain pre-contract events. In the absence of a contract, there is no "Graff exception" that would amount to a seller's "willful default" here.

The obligation to pay a broker's commission upon consummation of sale requires a formal act of closing. On at least three occasions in early 1998, plaintiff advised defendants that its commission was, upon consummation of the sale, to be drawn from "the proceeds of the closing" or "payable on closing," to which defendants confirmed, on February 13, that it would be paid from the sales price "at the time of settlement." Clearly, such an agreement could only have been consummated upon an actual closing.

In the absence of a closing, or even of a contract representing a formal agreement on all matters under negotiation, plaintiff has failed to earn its commission, and the complaint should have been dismissed.

CASE QUESTIONS

1 How much in actual dollars did the plaintiff-broker expect to realize from the sale in this case?
2 What was the defendant's response to the plaintiff's allegation that the defendant had entered into a binding contract with the buyer and the broker?
3 According to the court, did the defendants ever enter into an unconditional contract?
4 According to the court, when does the obligation to pay a broker's commission become due?

SKILLS YOU NEED IN THE REAL WORLD

DECIPHERING REAL ESTATE CONTRACTS

One skill that you will need to master is the ability to decipher the various types of contracts that are the meat of real estate practice. Whether they are listing agreements, brokerage agreements, offer of purchase, or any of the other contracts that are involved in real estate transactions, you should learn how to take such contracts apart.

Real estate contracts often appear to be very intimidating when you first read them. Usually they are very long, and have small print and confusing terms. Here are some guidelines to help you decipher real estate contracts.

START WITH WHO

The first and most important aspect of any contract is the identity of the parties. Who is actually bound by this contract? Identifying the parties goes a long way toward discovering the intent of the contract and pinpointing the issues. For instance, if the contract is a listing agreement, then the parties are the seller and the real estate agent. Chances are that the issues between these two parties will revolve around attempts to sell the house and whether the real estate agent earned her commission. Simply identifying the parties helps you understand the potential issues that arise in the contract.

WHAT IS INVOLVED?

What rights, duties, or obligations are put forth in the contract? Put another way, who has the obligation to act and what are they obligated to do? When you pinpoint these parts of the contract, you begin building a solid understanding of what the contract is about.

WHAT ARE THE PENALTIES?

Contracts often list the potential penalties for nonperformance. Does the contract detail what rights a party has when the other party defaults? Has one party contractually agreed to a limitation of possible penalties? Is there a provision calling for the use of a particular state's law to determine breach of contract duty? If you can detail these basic elements of a contract, you will have gone a long way toward understanding even the most complex real estate contract.

CHAPTER SUMMARY

A contract is a legally binding agreement between two or more parties. A contract is a result of negotiations between these parties that consists of an offer, which is one party's stated intention to enter into a binding contract, and the acceptance by the other party of all the terms stated in the offer. When an offer has been accepted, a contract is created. In addition to a valid offer and acceptance, there are some additional contract law requirements. For instance, both parties to the contract must have legal capacity. Legal capacity refers to a party's competence to know and understand the consequences of entering into a contractual obligation. Some parties lack capacity because of mental or physical defects or because of other reasons, such as being underage. Consideration is another contractual element that requires a bargained-for exchange between the parties. This is a contract requirement that necessitates both parties surrender something of value in exchange for something else of value before an enforceable contract will be found under the law.

Contract law is of vital importance in real estate transactions because so many real estate conveyances involve contract principles. In this chapter, we explored offers of purchase, which consist of the binding contract between the seller and buyer, as well as many other types of contracts. We also explored various contract clauses, including the "time is of the essence" clause. This contract clause requires that the closing must occur at a specific date; otherwise the contract will be null and void.

REVIEW QUESTIONS

1   What are the elements of a legally enforceable offer?
2   How does real property law define the "power of acceptance"?
3   What is mutual assent?
4   What is consideration and why is it a necessary component for contract?
5   Explain how a contract may be unenforceable when it does not have a legal subject.

6   What is legal capacity to contract? Provide some examples of individuals who lack such capacity.

7   What is the Statute of Frauds and why is it important in real estate contracts?

8   How is contractual mistake defined in real property?

9   What are the basic elements of an offer of purchase contract?

10 List and explain at least three important provisions of an offer to purchase and contract.

11 Why does the law require both the seller and the buyers sign the offer to purchase and contract?

12 What is an option?

13 How is an offer to purchase and contract different from an option?

14 Explain the significance of a "time is of the essence" contract clause.

15 What are some of the penalties that a seller can seek against a buyer for the buyer's wrongful refusal to perform under the offer to purchase and contract?

16 What are some of the buyer's remedies against a seller who wrongfully refuses to perform under a contract of sale?

17 What types of damages is a seller entitled to against a buyer who refuses to fulfill the obligations of an offer to purchase and contract?

18 Explain why it is so important to understand contract clauses.

19 Describe how you would begin to draft an offer of purchase and contract.

20 What is specific performance?

DISCUSSION QUESTIONS

The Statute of Frauds was created in a time when most people could not read and write. Requiring a contract to be put in writing necessitated the help of someone who could read and write. Is the Statute of Frauds still relevant when the vast majority of people in this country are literate?

PRACTICAL APPLICATIONS

Using the contract of sale form provided in this chapter, create a new contract of sale based on the following facts:

Date of contract: January 11, 2005. Sal Seller and Bill Buyer. Sal's address is 10 Sol St. Bill's address is 12 Third Ave. The property address is 21 Robin Lane, Morgan, State of Placid.

Included in the sale are some built-in tool storage cabinets in the basement.

The purchase price is $121,000. Bill put down $1,000 earnest money. No additional money will be paid prior to closing. The closing is to take place on May 11, 2005, at 3 p.m. in the offices of Al Attorney, 100 Shyster Blvd., Burnett City, State of Placid.

Bill's offer is based on being able to obtain financing at 9% or lower, in the amount of $115,000, for a 30-year loan. He doesn't want to pay more than 2 points.

Sal wants Bill to apply for financing as soon as possible, at least within 10 days of the contract being signed. Bill wants a termite inspection within 10 days of signing the contract.

If termites are found, Sal wants at least 30 days to fix whatever is wrong.

Bill wants to inspect the home within 10 days of signing the contract.

The real estate agent's name is Ron Realtor.

WEB SITES

National Association of Realtors
http://www.realtor.org/rocms.nsf

Women's Council of Realtors
http://www.wcr.org

Real Estate Contract Law (Legal Information Institute)
http://www.law.cornell.edu/topics/real_estate.html

TERMS AND PHRASES

Capacity	Legality	Power of acceptance
Consideration	Mistake	Specific performance
Contract	Mutual assent	
Equitable remedies	Option	

SIGNIFICANT CASES

Baltic v. Rossi, 735 N.Y.S.2d 148 (N.Y.A.D. 2 Dept., 2001)
Bryan v. Moore, 863 A.2d 258 (Del. Ch. 2004)
Ledig v. Duke Energy Corp., 193 S.W.3d 167 (2006)
Nitro Distributing, Inc. v. Dunn, 194 S.W.3d 339 (Mo., 2006)
RegScan, Inc. v. Con-Way Transp. Services, Inc., 875 A.2d 332 (Pa. Super., 2005)
Geodyne Energy Income Production Partnership I-E v. Newton Corp., 161 S.W.3d 482 (Tex., 2005)

Landlord and Tenant Law

Focus of This Chapter

The law of leasehold estates is explored in depth in this chapter. The chapter examines the rights and duties of landlords and tenants, and addresses issues such as eviction and the various types of landlord-tenant relationships.

Chapter Learning Objectives

After completing this chapter, you should be able to:

- Explain the origin of the obligations between landlords and their tenants
- Define the basic features of leasehold estates
- Describe the impact of contract and property law on leasehold estates
- Explain how the law of landlord and tenant relations has changed over time
- Explain how various tenancies are created, administered, and terminated

INTRODUCTION

This chapter is devoted to a discussion of the relationship between landlords and tenants. We have already seen that ownership in fee simple brings with it a host of rights. Many of those rights can be transferred piecemeal. In a life estate, for example, a fee simple owner may transfer most of the rights inherent in real property ownership, but for a limited period. We face a similar situation when discussing **leasehold estate**.

A leasehold estate is one that gives the possessor many of the obvious rights associated with real property, but only conveys these rights for a short period. When the lease term is over, these rights revert to the fee simple owner. The parties to a leasehold arrangement are the **landlord** and the **tenant**. The landlord is usually the owner in fee simple who conveys some of those interests to the tenant. When these rights are conveyed, it means that the landlord no longer possesses:

Leasehold estate
The body of rights conveyed to a tenant from the landlord.

Landlord
The owner of the premises. The landlord retains all the rights normally associated with ownership except use, possession, and enjoyment.

Tenant
The possessor of certain rights transferred away from the landlord; these rights include use, possession, and enjoyment.

- The right to use the property
- The right to occupy the property
- The right to possess the property

Just as important as the rights that are conveyed to tenants are the rights that are not conveyed. For instance, a tenant does not have the right to sell the property. That right remains vested in the landlord. Similarly, the tenant has no right to mortgage the property and also bears no responsibility for paying real estate taxes. The tenant's rights are usually limited to the use and possession of the property.

In this chapter, we examine how the landlord-tenant relationship is created, the rights and obligations that this relationship creates, and how the relationship is terminated.

CREATING A LANDLORD-TENANT RELATIONSHIP

A leasehold arrangement can be created in a number of ways. Once created, the relationship carries with it certain obligations for both parties. However, the historical basis of the relationship was not always so mutually interdependent.

A. HISTORICAL BACKGROUND ON LANDLORD-TENANT LAW

The history of landlord-tenant law stretches back thousands of years. Some of the most prominent members of ancient Roman aristocracy were landlords. Unfortunately, that history is fraught with examples of the one-sided nature of the relationship. Under English and early American common law, landlords had few obligations and were able to evict tenants for any of a number of reasons. Eviction could be a violent process, with landlords engaging in "self-help" eviction, which consisted of physically dragging tenants out of the premises and throwing their belongings onto the street. Until the twentieth century, landlords had few obligations to their tenants beyond providing a dwelling. It wasn't until the 1900s that American law began changing its view of the landlord-tenant relationship. States gradually began changing their laws by imposing more requirements on landlords, such as maintaining structures, with the recognition that legal doctrines such as the warranty of habitability applied to landlords.

B. MODERN CHANGES TO THE LANDLORD-TENANT RELATIONSHIP

Every state has modified, to a greater or lesser extent, its landlord-tenant law. Some of these changes have been brought about by judicial decisions that placed greater responsibilities on landlords; some of the changes were required by changes in the statutes governing landlord-tenant relationships.

Tech Topic
USING WI-FI TO LURE TENANTS

In a down rental market, landlords go to extremes to entice renters, including the promise of free wireless Internet service. On the surface it is a tempting perk, but it comes with some underlying dangers.

Many Wi-Fi users are not aware that when they connect to Wi-Fi through hotspots (such as those at a coffee house), a hotel, or even a place of business, their online activity can be monitored and intercepted—including account numbers and passwords. Similarly, a landlord who provides free Wi-Fi to tenants becomes the de facto Internet service provider. If the landlord is technologically savvy, he can monitor the traffic on the network he is providing. So can the neighbors.

There are steps that tenants can take to protect their data while at the same time enjoying the benefit of free Wi-Fi. One is to be sure to use only secure, encrypted connections while making online transactions. Websites whose URL begins with HTTPS (instead of HTTP) are secured, and although the landlord might be able to see the site that is being visited, he cannot see any of the data sent to it or displayed on it.

Another solution is to use a VPN, or Virtual Private Network, service. A VPN supports remote—and protected—access to the network over the Internet. Originally designed for people who travel frequently or those who often work away from the office, a VPN provides an extra layer of protection from prying eyes.

Under the modern definition of landlord-tenant relationships, landlords have specific duties to their tenants. Among these duties are:

- Keeping the premises in good repair
- Maintaining the premises in a fit and habitable condition
- Keeping all common areas in a safe condition
- Ensuring that the electrical, plumbing, heating, and ventilating systems are all in working order

Landlord-tenant law refers to that large body of cases, statutes, rules, and regulations that govern the creation and termination of residential and commercial property leases.

ISSUE AT A GLANCE

 LEASES

Leases raise a host of issues because of their dual nature. A lease is the embodiment of the contractual agreement between landlords and tenants. It must contain all the basic contractual elements. However, a lease is not only a contractual agreement. It must also contain some additional elements that arise because the agreement

Lease
The contractual arrangement between a landlord and tenant.

involves a real estate transaction. We discuss all these elements later in this chapter. But first we must address the various lease categories, including:

- Fixed-rent leases
- Percentage leases
- Net leases
- Rent-to-own leases
- Ground leases
- Timber leases
- Mineral leases
- Oil and gas leases

A. FIXED RENT LEASES

A fixed-rent lease assesses a flat fee that must be paid periodically. The most common example of a fixed rent lease is a residential lease. In this arrangement, the tenant agrees to pay a specific amount in rent every month. The amount of the rent does not vary from month to month and the tenant is not responsible for paying out additional sums for expenses.

B. PERCENTAGE LEASES

Unlike fixed-rent leases, percentage lease rents change over time. Because they are based in whole or in part on the tenant's income, the amount of the rent may vary from month to month. Percentage leases are used in commercial settings, where the tenant is a business. The landlord receives a report of the tenant's total income for the month and assesses a percentage of the proceeds as the monthly rent. Percentage leases come in many different forms and may be based on gross or net sales or even a combination of percentage of income plus a flat fee.

C. NET LEASES

Net leases make the tenant responsible not only for paying rent, but also for paying all costs associated with the premises, including electricity, water, sewage, and any other costs.

D. RENT-TO-OWN LEASES

Rent-to-own leases are often popular when the economy is in a downturn. Under the most common provisions of a rent-to-own lease, the landlord applies some portion of each month's rent toward a down payment on the purchase of the home. These leases are sometimes referred to as a lease with option to purchase, but whatever the terminology, the basic arrangement is the same: The tenant gets credit for some portion of the rent paid over a period of time and has the right to apply that amount toward the purchase of the premises.

EXAMPLE 7-1

Tony has been renting a house for over five years now. The original arrangement between Tony and the landlord was simple: 10% of Tony's monthly rent would be applied towards a down payment on the purchase of the house. When the amount reached $10,000, Tony would then have the option of purchasing the home. However, the amount was non-refundable because it was part of Tony's rent. The agreement also provided that no modifications of the original agreement were permissible. Tony has found an apartment he likes better than the house and wants to sue the landlord for the amount that has been slowly building up as credit towards his down payment. That amount is $2800. Will Tony win his suit?

Answer: No. Because the agreement provided that the down payment would be based on a percentage of the rent that he actually paid (as opposed to an additional amount paid by Tony every month), Tony is not entitled to a return of any of the money he has paid for rent.[1]

E. GROUND LEASES

Ground leases are arrangements between landlords and tenants where the tenant rents vacant land, often for the purpose of farming or for constructing some building on the lot.

F. TIMBER LEASES

A timber lease allows the tenant to enter onto the landlord's land for the purpose of harvesting trees. The landlord will be paid for the timber that is removed and the tenant, usually a mill or paper company, often has the additional duty of replanting new trees after removing the old ones.

G. MINERAL LEASES

Mineral leases give the tenant the right to enter onto the property, test for the presence of various ores, sink mines, and carry out other actions to extract minerals and other materials from the soil. Most states have provisions that require mineral leases to be in writing before they are considered to be legally enforceable. Mineral leases often raise interesting legal questions. For instance, a mining company might possess a license, but not a lease.

---

[1] *Corbray v. Stevenson,* 98 Wash. 2d 410, 656 P.2d 473 (1982).

1. DISTINGUISHING BETWEEN LEASES AND LICENSES

License
The right to the products of the land, but not the land itself. A licensee might have the right to enter the premises to harvest, but no right to any other use of the property.

When discussing leases, especially mineral or gas leases, there is often an important point about terminology. In some cases, for example, a company might have the right to enter onto a person's property for the purpose of harvesting soil or crops, but have no right to actually possess the property or to make other use of it. The company that holds a **license**, for example, has the right to specific products of the land, but no rights in the real estate. Only leases convey real property interests. Licenses, on the other hand, convey only personal property rights.

ISSUE AT A GLANCE

A license grants the owner the right to enter onto the land for a specific purpose. A leaseholder, on the other hand, has all the rights normally associated with possession.

Licenses fall into the category of "profits à prendre," or the right to take soil, minerals, stones, or other materials from the property, but no right to any other use of the property. (See Chapter 5 for additional discussion of profits à prendre.)

H. OIL AND GAS LEASES

Just as the names suggest, oil and gas leases give the tenant the right to explore for oil and natural gas and to remove these products. This category of leases can become quite complicated, given the speculative nature of drilling for oil, and these leases often involve additional clauses and provisions that provide for new arrangements between the parties if oil or gas is discovered on the property.

I. COMMON LEASE PROVISIONS

Although there is a wide variety of leases available, some common clauses and provisions are often found in the actual, written lease. We examine the contract clauses of a typical residential lease in order to better understand lease provisions. (For a complete residential lease form, see the Appendix.)

1. RENT

One of the most obvious, and most important, provisions of any lease is the issue of rent. Landlords go into the business of renting property for the income that it will generate. Without rent, there is no revenue. All leases have provisions that specify not only the amount of the rent, but also when it should be paid. Most leases also have provisions detailing the consequences of late rental payments.

2. LATE PAYMENTS AND FEES

Many states have provisions that limit how much residential landlords can charge delinquent renters. For instance, a lease may contain a provision that specifies a late fee of $15 or $20 in addition to the outstanding rent. Other states limit late charges to a percentage of the total rent. For instance, state law may allow a late fee of up to 5 percent of the total monthly rent.

3. PET AND SECURITY DEPOSITS

In addition to rent, a lease may contain provisions for a wide variety of other activities. Landlords are permitted to charge deposits to renters with pets, as well as security deposits. The reasoning behind such deposits is that they may help to pay for any damages to the premises by the renter or the renter's pet. However, as we will see later in this chapter, landlords are not permitted to assess tenants for charges for ordinary wear and tear.

(a) Upon termination of the tenancy, property or money held by the landlord as security must be returned less amounts withheld by the landlord for accrued rent and damages which the landlord has suffered by reason of the tenant's noncompliance. Any deduction from the security/rental deposit must be itemized by the landlord in a written notice to the tenant together with the amount due, if any, within thirty days after termination of the tenancy and delivery of possession and demand by the tenant, whichever is later.[2]

FIGURE 7-1

Statutory Limitations on Security Deposits

4. RENEWAL PROVISIONS

It is common for leases to contain clauses specifying how or even if the lease can be renewed. For instance, a lease might provide that the leasehold arrangement automatically renews every year unless the tenant indicates a desire to terminate the relationship. On the other hand, a lease might provide that the lease is terminable at the will of either party after giving specified notice.

5. PERSONS PERMITTED ON THE LEASED PREMISES

Landlords are permitted to restrict the number of persons permitted to be on the leased premises. The lease might contain a provision specifying exactly who is permitted to reside at the rental unit. This provision not only protects the landlord from the additional damage that other individuals might do to the premises, but may also be required by fire codes or other statutes designed to limit the number of individuals residing at one location.

---

[2] S.C. Code Ann. § 27-40-410.

6. ACCEPTANCE OF LEASED PREMISES

Residential leases often contain a provision whereby the tenant explicitly accepts the premises as they appear. This provision demonstrates that at a specific point in time, the tenant was aware of the conditions of the rental unit and found them acceptable.

7. MODIFYING OR ALTERING THE PREMISES

Another provision that is very common in residential leases is a clause that specifically prohibits the tenant from making alterations or modifications to the structure. This does not prevent the tenant from decorating or hanging pictures on the walls. Instead, this provision prevents the tenant from tearing down walls or making other substantial changes to the floors, walls, or ceilings.

8. SUBLETTING

Sublet
One tenant rents the leased premises to another tenant.

The general rule is that a tenant is free to **sublet** the rented premises to another tenant unless the lease provides otherwise. There are many reasons why a tenant would wish to sublet an apartment. The tenant may suddenly need to relocate to another town, and renting the apartment to someone else may be a more cost-effective remedy than paying the balance on the lease. There are also rental units in areas where rent is strictly controlled by the local government. In places such as New York City, a person might be very happy to sublet an apartment where rent control keeps the rent at or below a specific amount. The reasons why a person might want to sublet are the same reasons why a landlord would be eager to deny such access. With a new tenant, one free from a preexisting lease, the landlord is free to charge a higher rent or impose other favorable conditions. Many residential leases outside of rent-controlled areas contain provisions that specifically bar the current tenant from subletting to others. Another variation on the theme prevents subletting unless it is with the landlord's prior approval.

9. NOTICE

Notice provisions in leases cover a wide assortment of activities. Leases may contain notice provisions that specify when a tenant must notify the landlord if the tenant intends to move out at the end of the lease term. Other notice provisions might include changes to the list of persons permitted on the premises. Notice provision requirements imposed in the lease may also pertain to the landlord. For instance, the landlord might be required to give so many days notice to a tenant when he seeks to evict the tenant for nonpayment of rent.

Eviction
The legal process of removing a tenant from the leased premises.

Although we discuss **eviction** in much greater detail later in this chapter, we note here that many residential leases have clauses that detail how and when the eviction process may begin. The most common reason to evict a tenant is for nonpayment of rent, but leases also usually contain provisions that allow landlords to initiate eviction procedures when the tenant is unruly, causing public nuisance, or violating the law.

J. COMMERCIAL LEASES

So far, our discussion has focused on residential leases. Commercial leases involve very different issues. Commercial leases are generally for retail, wholesale, or warehouse businesses, so many of the issues we have discussed, such as pet deposits and persons permitted on the premises, do not apply. However, other concerns will be reflected in a commercial lease. It is not unusual, for instance, for a commercial landlord to require accounting statements, business plans, or other documentation before entering into a lease with a business.

Commercial leases often contain provisions allowing the landlord to forcibly enter the premises and seize inventory or other items to secure rent. The landlord also has the right to bar access to the premises of a tenant who has defaulted on the rental agreement. Obviously such tactics could not be used with residential leases. The rules are different in commercial leases, and that is even more evident regarding fixtures.

K. TRADE FIXTURES

In Chapter 5, we saw that a **fixture** is some item of personal property that becomes permanently attached to real estate. When this attachment occurs, the nature of the item changes. It is reclassified as real property and this reclassification has several important practical consequences. For instance, when an item is a fixture, it means that it remains with the real property when the parcel is sold. The law of fixtures has important consequences when we discuss leases, as well. If an item is classified as a fixture, it means that the tenant is prohibited from removing it when the tenant gives up the lease. Consider Example 7-2.

Fixture
Personal property that has become permanently attached to real property.

EXAMPLE 7-2

Alton has just started college and has moved into his first apartment. He likes the place very much, but it is missing something that Alton considers very important. Because he wants to be an actor, he wants a stage in his living room. He buys lumber, screws supports into the floor and walls, and creates a stage that is three feet high and runs the length of the back wall in his living room. He lives in the apartment for four years, and upon graduation, he notifies the landlord that he will be dismantling the stage and taking it with him. The landlord tells Alton that the stage must remain. Alton wants to sue for the right to remove the stage. Will he win?

Answer: No. Because of the way that the stage was constructed, it is a fixture and will remain with the property (at the option of the landlord).

However, the rules about fixtures change when the lease involves commercial property. **Trade fixtures** are items of personal property that qualify as a fixture, but are used for the tenant's business. Because of their commercial use, the rules about these fixtures are different. When tenants give up their commercial leasehold, they are permitted to remove these fixtures, even when they are fully attached to real property. Tenants are permitted to remove these fixtures even when they must cause some damage to do so. See Example 7-3.

Trade fixture
Personal property that has become permanently attached to real estate but which a merchant requires in order to run his or her business.

EXAMPLE 7-3 Haley runs a bagel store downtown. Her lease has expired and she is going to move her business to another location. She needs to take her big dough mixer. It stands six feet tall, weighs 400 pounds, and is bolted to the floor. The landlord is refusing to allow her to remove it, saying that she would leave two bolt holes in the floor and would have to take off one of the doors in order to get it out. Will she be permitted to remove the mixer?

Answer: Yes. Because the mixer qualifies as a trade fixture, Haley will be allowed to remove it, even though it is bolted to the floor and she will have to take off a door to get it out.

L. PUBLIC POLICY CONCERNS IN LEASES

As we will see later in this chapter, there are both state and federal laws that govern the creation of leases. One of the most important is the Uniform Residential Landlord and Tenant Act (URLTA). All states, whether they have adopted URLTA or not, have provisions in their laws that prevent landlords from requiring tenants to negotiate away legal rights as a condition of obtaining the premises. Such a lease provision would be considered a violation of public policy or unconscionable and would not be enforced. Figure 7-2 provides an example of state law on this issue.

FIGURE 7-2

Violation of Public Policy in Leases

(2) if any provision of a rental agreement was unconscionable when made, the court may enforce the remainder of the agreement without the unconscionable provision or limit the application of any unconscionable provision to avoid an unconscionable result; or

(3) if a settlement in which a party waives or agrees to forego a claim or right under this chapter or under a rental agreement was unconscionable when made, the court may refuse to enforce the settlement, enforce the remainder of the settlement without the unconscionable provision, or limit the application of any unconscionable provision to avoid an unconscionable result.[3]

M. FEDERAL LAW REQUIREMENTS

In addition to some of the state-based legislation that governs rental properties, there are also some federal laws that regulate residential real estate. The Federal Residential Lead Based Hazard Reduction Act of 1992[4] requires landlords who own and lease houses built prior to 1978 to make certain disclosures to potential tenants. These disclosures require the landlord to give the tenant a lead hazard information pamphlet, to disclose the existence of lead-based paint known to be on the premises, and to give the tenant ten days to conduct his own risk assessment or to inspect the premises for lead-based paint.

---

[3] S.C. Code Ann. § 27-40-230.
[4] 42 U.S.C. § 4851.

N. STATUTE OF FRAUDS CONSIDERATIONS

Each state has its own version of the Statute of Frauds. That statute, originally created in England in the 1600s and imported to the American colonies, required certain types of contracts to be in writing before they would be enforceable. Examples of contracts that fall under the modern Statute of Frauds include prenuptial agreements, contracts to answer for the debts of another, and any agreement that cannot be performed within a year. The last category of agreements creates Statute of Frauds concerns in leases. When a rental agreement is for a period longer than twelve months, the Statute of Frauds requires it to be in writing. Without a writing, neither the landlord nor the tenant can enforce the provisions of the lease.

IV DUTIES CREATED BY THE LANDLORD-TENANT RELATIONSHIP

Although landlords had very few duties under the common law, modern statutes have substantially changed the landlord's role in the landlord-tenant relationship. The idea that landlords had few if any obligations to their tenants slowly gave way to new statutory obligations and civil liability. These days, landlords have numerous legal requirements and obligations that they owe to their tenants.

A. UNIFORM RESIDENTIAL LANDLORD AND TENANT ACT

The Uniform Residential Landlord and Tenant Act (URLTA) has been adopted by numerous states. The act provides a basic framework for the many issues that arise in landlord-tenant relationships, from creating the lease to establishing the reasons and procedures to evict a tenant.

(b) Underlying purposes and policies of this chapter are:
(1) to simplify, clarify, modernize, and revise the law governing rental of dwelling units and the rights and obligations of landlords and tenants;
(2) to encourage landlords and tenants to maintain and improve the quality of housing.[5]

FIGURE 7-3

URLTA: Purpose

The Uniform Residential Landlord and Tenant Act provides many other rules, including guidelines for written leases. If the lease is never signed, or properly delivered, URLTA creates a landlord-tenant relationship as soon as the tenant accepts the leased premises. See Figure 7-4.

---

[5] S.C. Code Ann. § 27-40-20.

FIGURE 7-4

URLTA Provisions Concerning Unsigned Leases

Effect of unsigned or undelivered rental agreement.

(a) If the landlord does not sign and deliver a written rental agreement which has been signed and delivered to the landlord by the tenant, acceptance of rent without reservation by the landlord gives the rental agreement the same effect as if it had been signed and delivered by the landlord.[6]

FIGURE 7-5

Landlord's Obligations to the Tenant

- Ensure that the premises are safe and habitable
- Comply with building and housing codes
- Make all repairs required to keep the premises safe
- Remove garbage and trash from common areas

FIGURE 7-6

Landlord's Obligation to Maintain Premises

(1) The landlord at all times during the tenancy shall:

(a) Comply with the requirements of applicable building, housing, and health codes; or

(b) Where there are no applicable building, housing, or health codes, maintain the roofs, windows, screens, doors, floors, steps, porches, exterior walls, foundations, and all other structural components in good repair and capable of resisting normal forces and loads and the plumbing in reasonable working condition. However, the landlord shall not be required to maintain a mobile home or other structure owned by the tenant.[7]

FIGURE 7-7

Excerpt from the Uniform Residential Landlord and Tenant Act

When a tenant breaks a lease, the landlord has three possibilities:

- Refuse to retake possession and continue to collect the rent
- Give notice to tenant, retake possession, and rent the premises to another tenant
- Re-enter the premises, take possession, and cancel the lease[8]

B. LANDLORD'S RIGHTS

Landlords have the right to enter the premises for inspection and to demand payment for rent. Of course, the landlord has the right to re-enter the premises when the tenant vacates, even if the tenant leaves before the lease term expires.

[6] S.C. Code Ann. § 27-40-320.
[7] Fla. Stat. Ann. (West's) § 83.51.
[8] *Wilfred Laboratories, Inc. v. Fifty-Second Street Hotel Associates,* 133 App. Div. 2d 320, 519 N.Y.S.2d 220 (1987).

1. RIGHT TO RE-ENTER PREMISES

Because the landlord surrenders possession of the premises to the tenant as part of the lease arrangement, the landlord has no right to re-enter the premises as he wishes. Although the law does permit a landlord to re-enter the premises to make reasonable repairs and inspections, the landlord has no additional rights to use and possess the premises. The tenant has the absolute right to the use and enjoyment of the premises; the landlord does not. Consider Example 7-4.

EXAMPLE 7-4

Meredith has recently rented an apartment from a landlord named Andy. Meredith has become concerned lately because she has found Andy in her bedroom when she comes home from work. She isn't sure about her rights and needs advice about how to proceed. Andy has told her that because he is the landlord, he can come and go as he pleases. What can she do?

   Answer: Meredith would be within her rights to bring a civil action against Andy for trespass or invasion of privacy. Although Andy has the right to re-enter the premises for the limited purpose of making reasonable repairs, the key word here is "reasonable." Andy does not have the right to visit Meredith's apartment whenever he wishes and he certainly has no right to be in Meredith's bedroom without some express purpose.

2. DUTY TO REPAIR

Although the common law imposed no duty on the landlord to make repairs, that obligation has changed over time.[9] Under the modern view of landlord-tenant relationships, the landlord has the obligation to keep the premises in good condition. This imposes on the landlord the duty to make repairs to ensure the tenants' safety. Failure to do so is considered a breach of the lease and is also a violation of other statutory obligations now imposed on landlords. However, before a landlord becomes liable to make repairs the tenant must report the condition, especially if it is not immediately apparent to the landlord. Consider Example 7-5.

EXAMPLE 7-5

Griffin has rented an upstairs apartment and in the last few weeks he has noticed that when he comes downstairs to go to his car, the two top steps seem a little loose. Two weeks ago, he called the landlord and reported the loose step. Last night, as he was leaving for work, one of the steps snapped under his weight and he was injured. He wants to sue the landlord. Does he have a case?

   Answer: Yes. Because he gave notice to the landlord of the defective steps, and because the landlord failed to take any action to repair them, Griffin has a solid case against the landlord.

   Some state statutes, such as Rhode Island's Landlord-Tenant Act, permit the landlord to shift some repair duties to the tenant. Routine repairs can fall to the

---

[9] *Conley v. Emerald Isle Realty, Inc.,* 350 N.C. 293, 513 S.E.2d 556 (1999).

tenant, but anything requiring the premises to meet state or building codes remains the responsibility of the landlord.[10] Landlords are not permitted to negotiate away their obligations in a lease, even in exchange for lower than average rent. Landlords continue to bear the burden of making major repairs and cannot pass this burden on to tenants.[11] When the landlord fails to meet this responsibility, the tenant is permitted to sue for damages, including the cost incurred by the tenant to make the repair.[12]

FIGURE 7-8

Duty to Make Repairs under URLTA

- Comply with all applicable building, safety, and housing codes
- Make all necessary repairs to keep the premises in a fit and habitable condition
- Keep all common areas clean, safe, and free of garbage
- Maintain and keep in good working order all appliances provided with the leased premises
- Provide running water and hot water
- Provide heat[13]

3. LANDLORD'S DUTIES TO THIRD PARTIES

In addition to the duties that landlords owe their tenants, they also have some duties to third parties. For instance, all states require landlords to keep both residential and commercial rental units free from dangerous conditions. Landlords have a duty to warn about unsafe conditions. Some states go further and impose duties on the landlord to actively protect tenant guests and customers.

4. LANDLORDS AND DISCRIMINATORY PRACTICES

Landlords are barred from engaging in specific types of discriminatory practices. The federal Fair Housing Act and Fair Housing Amendments Act[14] prohibits landlords from engaging in practices such as refusing to rent to individuals on the basis of:

- Race
- Religion
- National origin
- Sex
- Marital status
- Mental or physical disability

---

[10] R.I. Gen. Laws (1956) § 34-18-22(c); *State Water Resources Bd. v. Howard,* 729 A.2d 712 (R.I. 1999).
[11] URLTA § 1.404.
[12] 40 A.L.R. 3d 1369.
[13] URLTA § 2.104.
[14] 42 U.S.C. § § 3601-3619, 3631.

Some states extend this list to include the categories of age or sexual orientation. However, these statutes do permit certain types of discrimination. For instance, a landlord can refuse to rent to a person or business that does not meet specific financial criteria or that has negative references from previous landlords. As long as these rules apply to all renters, the landlord is permitted to refuse to rent to individuals or businesses that do not meet the established criteria.

In addition to these overt tactics, the Fair Housing Act also prohibits more subtle forms of discrimination, such as:

■ Failing to accommodate individuals with disabilities
■ Establishing different terms and conditions for different tenants
■ Using inconsistent policies for some tenants on issues such as pets and late payments

---

FIGURE 7-9

All citizens of the United States shall have the same right, in every State and Territory, as is enjoyed by white citizens thereof to inherit, purchase, lease, sell, hold, and convey real and personal property.[15]

42 U.S.C. § 1982. Property Rights of Citizens

C. TENANT'S RIGHTS

The landlord-tenant relationship confers specific rights on the tenant. For instance, the tenant has the absolute right to use, possess, and enjoy the leased premises. In essence, the landlord has divested these rights and has only a reversionary interest in the premises. When the lease terminates, the property rights automatically revert to the landlord.

1. USE AND ENJOYMENT BY TENANT

The tenant has the right to use and enjoy the premises. Use and enjoyment includes many of the rights normally associated with fee simple title, including full access to all amenities, and the right to redecorate the interior, hang pictures, lay carpets, and bring in furniture. The tenant is free to decorate in a variety of ways, as long as the tenant does not make any structural changes or cause damage to the building.

Sidebar

Renters who are the victims of discrimination can contact the Department of Housing and Urban Development to file a complaint. They may also bring actions under state law.

---

[15] 42 U.S. C. § 1982 Ch. 21.

D. LEGAL DOCTRINES THAT ARISE IN THE LANDLORD-TENANT RELATIONSHIP

Throughout this chapter, we have alluded to the obligations now placed on landlords that were not a feature of the historical landlord-tenant relationship. There are several legal doctrines that apply in this context, including (1) the warranty of habitability, and (2) quiet enjoyment.

1. WARRANTY OF HABITABILITY

Warranty of habitability
A legal doctrine that imposes on landlords the implied duty to provide leased premises that are fit for human habitation.

Historically, tenants had no common law right to habitable premises. Under this rule, the landlord could provide a dwelling in nearly any condition. However, all jurisdictions have modified this original rule. Most have adopted the warranty of habitability. This legal doctrine requires that landlords must provide premises that are fit for human habitation. Modern landlord-tenant law implies a **warranty of habitability** in all residential leases. This requires the landlord to provide a living environment that meets basic standards of cleanliness, safety, and livability. It also imposes a duty on the landlord to maintain the premises in this condition. In many ways, this doctrine is similar to the warranties that courts have implied in other commercial settings. When consumers buy products, courts will often imply warranties covering the fitness of the product for its advertised purpose. The warranty of habitability is a court doctrine that creates a legal relationship between the landlord and the tenant. The landlord provides habitable and safe premises in exchange for the rent paid by the tenant. In this relationship, the obligation of one is premised on the action of the other. The warranty of habitability applies to residential properties, not commercial leases.

2. QUIET ENJOYMENT

Quiet enjoyment
The right of a tenant to use the leased premises unmolested.

The tenant has the right of **quiet enjoyment** in the leased premises. This means that the tenant has the absolute legal right to live in or use the premises free from interference by others. The tenant has the right to order other individuals off the property and to institute trespass actions for people who refuse to leave. Rented apartments and houses can be the subject of burglary actions under the theory that although someone else actually owns the property, the tenant is the person in possession and has the right to quiet enjoyment of the property.

E. TENANT'S DUTIES TO LANDLORD

The landlord-tenant relationship creates duties not only for landlords, but also for tenants. The most obvious tenant obligation is to pay rent, but there are several other important responsibilities that the tenant assumes when entering into a lease. See Figure 7-10.

FIGURE 7-10

Duties Tenants Owe to Their
Landlords

- They must pay rent

- They must keep the premises clean

- They must dispose of garbage

- They must keep plumbing
  fixtures clean

- They are prohibited from destroying,
  altering, or defacing the leased
  premises

- They are obligated to pay for any
  damages above normal wear and tear

Landlords and tenants can enter into agreements to restrict the nature of the relationship, as long as this agreement does not violate state statutes or public policy. For instance, a lease can contain a provision that the premises will be used for limited purposes. Commercial leases often have clauses that limit the manner of use. Such a lease might contain a provision that limits use to a retail business, but prohibits it for use as a residence.

1. TENANT'S RESPONSIBILITY FOR DAMAGES TO LEASED PREMISES

Although the tenant duties outlined in Figure 7-10 are self-explanatory, one category merits further discussion. When a tenant causes damage to the property, the tenant is responsible for paying for the repairs. The question always becomes: What is the extent of the tenant's responsibility for damages? What constitutes "damage" in this context? Damage refers to any destruction or defacing of property that is beyond ordinary wear and tear.

The tenant is responsible for keeping the premises clean; the landlord is responsible for all major repairs and upkeep.

ISSUE AT A GLANCE

a. Ordinary Wear and Tear

Although the tenant is responsible for any damages to the premises that qualify as structural, the landlord cannot insist that the tenant pay for **ordinary wear and tear**. "Wear and tear" is a phrase that covers all the normal dents and scrapes that occur through daily use. Examples of ordinary wear and tear include:

Ordinary wear and tear
The normal dents and scrapes that occur through daily use.

- Light scratches on walls and doors
- Wear on carpeting and floors
- Accumulated dirt and grime
- Nail holes in walls

b. Damage Deposits

As we have already seen, landlords are authorized to assess damage deposits as part of the rental process. These deposits can help defer the costs of repairing any damages that the tenant does to the leased premises. Damage deposits are usually a percentage of one month's rent and can be returned to the tenant if there is no major damage at the end of the lease term.

c. Pet Deposits

As with damage deposits, landlords can also require a pet deposit to defer the costs for stains or torn carpeting that are often associated with pet ownership.

F. REMEDIES FOR BREACH OF DUTY

Because the landlord-tenant relationship creates mutual obligations, both parties have actions against the other when these obligations are breached.

1. TENANT'S REMEDIES AGAINST LANDLORD

When a tenant believes that a landlord has infringed on the tenant's rights, the tenant is free to bring suit. The civil action could be based on contract principles. Under this theory, the tenant alleges that the lease was a contract entered into between the two parties and the landlord has breached this contract by interfering with the tenant's quiet enjoyment or violating the warranty of habitability. But tenants also can bring suits under an entirely different legal theory, for example, they can sue under tort law.

When a tenant sues under tort law, the tenant alleges that the landlord had a duty to the tenant and failed to meet that duty. The tenant might allege, for instance, that because the landlord had a duty to keep the premises safe, when the landlord failed to repair a hole in the sidewalk, he was responsible for the tenant's injuries when the tenant fell into this hole. The issue of tort law involves an entirely different set of concerns that could easily justify its own textbook.

a. Damages That Can Be Awarded to the Tenant

If the tenant can prove a case against the landlord, the tenant, like any successful plaintiff, is entitled to damages. There are many different types of damages, which we summarize here. They include:

- Equitable relief
- Compensatory damages
- Punitive damages

i. Equitable Relief

A tenant can ask a court to exercise its powers of equity in dealing with the issues pending in a landlord-tenant suit. Equity powers refer to a court's authority to order individuals to carry out specific actions, or, in some cases, to stop carrying out actions. The most common type of equitable relief is an injunction. An injunction is a court order demanding that an individual cease carrying out specific actions. In a landlord-tenant case, for example, a court could use its equity powers to order a landlord to stop discriminating against renters, to reinstate a dispossessed tenant, or even to make specific repairs.

ii. Compensatory Damages

In addition to ordering specific forms of equitable relief, a court can also award monetary damages. If a tenant proves financial losses directly tied to the landlord's actions, the court may order the landlord to reimburse the tenant for those losses. Of course, the opposite situation also holds true. A tenant who wrongfully terminates a lease may be ordered to pay damages to a landlord.

In such cases, the question often becomes: How does the court determine the actual amount of damages? Usually, the court calculates damages by the difference in the rent that landlord could have received compared to the rent that the landlord actually received. Consider Example 7-6.

EXAMPLE 7-6

Tonya Tenant abandoned her leased property six months prior to the lease termination. Monthly rent was $600. The premises were vacant for two months before the landlord rented it to another tenant. However, the landlord had to reduce the rent by $100 per month to attract a new tenant. The landlord requests damages in the amount of $3,600, which is what he would have received if Tonya had remained on the premises for the remainder of her lease. When the landlord sues Tonya, what are the landlord's damages?

Answer: Although the landlord would have received $3,600 if Tonya had remained on the premises, he did find a new tenant who leased the premises for the remaining four months of Tonya's lease. The court determines that the landlord is entitled to $1,600 in damages. How did it arrive at this figure?

The court calculated that the total damages that the landlord would have been entitled to receive were $3,600. However, the landlord mitigated his damages by renting the unit to another tenant. This tenant paid $500 per month, meaning that the landlord lost $100 per month for four months, or $400. The premises were also vacant for two months, for a total of $1,200. Adding these two amounts together, the court awards $1,600 in damages.

A court can also calculate compensatory damages for the tenant by calculating the fair market rental of a unit. In cases where the premises have become unfit for habitation, the court will calculate the difference between the rental value of the premises as they should have been and compare that with the rental value of the premises as they are. The difference is the amount of damages that a court can award to a tenant. The tenant is also entitled to compensation for out-of-pocket expenses directly related to the landlord's failure to maintain the premises.

iii. Punitive Damages

In some cases, a tenant may be entitled to an award of punitive damages. Punitive damages are designed to do exactly what the name suggests: They punish the landlord by assessing monetary damages against him that are in excess of the tenant's out-of-pocket and other expenses.

b. Constructive Eviction

Constructive eviction
A legal doctrine that holds that leased premises that are unfit for human habitation effectively prevent the tenant from continuing to live there.

One ground that a tenant can allege in a suit against the landlord is **constructive eviction.** An action for constructive eviction states that the landlord allowed conditions at the rental to deteriorate to such an extent that it was no longer fit for human habitation. Under common law, a tenant could sue a landlord for wrongful eviction when the landlord used physical force to evict the tenant. However, all jurisdictions now recognize the theory of constructive eviction.

Under constructive eviction, the tenant must show that the landlord, or someone working for the landlord, created conditions that effectively made the premises uninhabitable. One of the elements that the tenant must show is that the tenant had to abandon the premises. If the tenant continues to live in the rental unit, the tenant cannot allege constructive eviction.

To qualify as constructive eviction, the tenant must show something beyond a simple desire to leave. The tenant must show that the conditions interfered with the quiet enjoyment of the premises and that the tenant left under protest. Some authorities hold that the landlord's acts must amount to something "grave and permanent" and must clearly indicate the landlord's intention to deprive the tenant of the enjoyment of the leased premises. Consider Examples 7-7 and 7-8.

EXAMPLE 7-7

Larry Landlord has decided that he wants to get out of the landlord business. He has only one remaining tenant, Teresa. He can't find a legal reason to evict her. One day, when Teresa is at work, he boards up all her windows and padlocks her door. Does Teresa have an action for constructive eviction?

Answer: Yes. Many states recognize a cause of action for constructive eviction when the landlord blocks access to the premises. Teresa will most likely win her suit.

EXAMPLE 7-8

Keisha owns a dog and rents an apartment. One day, the landlord stops by and when he sees Keisha's dog, he revs his car engine and threatens to run the dog over. Does Keisha have grounds for constructive eviction?

Answer: No. An action for constructive eviction alleges that the landlord has taken some action to make the premises unfit. Threatening the tenant's dog does not qualify.[16]

c. Actions for Wrongful Eviction

Because eviction is now governed by state statute, landlords who violate the law in evicting tenants are subject to several different sanctions. For instance, the court may allow the tenant to recover possession of the leased premises and is also

---

[16] *Honce v. Vigil,* 1 F.3d 1085 (10th Cir. 1993).

authorized to assess the landlord for monetary damages. If the tenant brings an action for wrongful eviction and proves the case, the tenant would be entitled to:

- Recover possession of the leased premises
- Terminate the lease
- Recover monetary damages against the landlord for various costs incurred by the tenant

2. LANDLORD'S REMEDIES AGAINST TENANT

So far our discussion has focused on the remedies that the tenant has against the landlord. Landlords also have several possible actions against a tenant who defaults on a lease. The most obvious of these is eviction.

a. Eviction

Eviction is the most common, and perhaps most effective, form of sanction that a landlord can bring against a tenant. A landlord is permitted to bring an eviction against a tenant for any of number of reasons, but the most common is for failure to pay rent. Under modern eviction statutes, a landlord must bring a civil action and request a judicial ruling that the tenant is in violation of the lease and can be evicted from the premises.

i. Procedures to Evict

An eviction action often falls under the jurisdiction of small claims court or another specifically designated court. To bring an eviction action, the landlord must prove several elements. These include notifying the tenant that he is in

---

FIGURE 7-11

Notice Required in an Eviction Procedure (Ohio)

A party desiring to commence an action under this chapter shall notify the adverse party to leave the premises, for the possession of which the action is about to be brought, three or more days before beginning the action, by certified mail, return receipt requested, or by handing a written copy of the notice to the defendant in person, or by leaving it at his usual place of abode or at the premises from which the defendant is sought to be evicted. Every notice given under this section by a landlord to recover residential premises shall contain the following language printed or written in a conspicuous manner: "You are being asked to leave the premises. If you do not leave, an eviction action may be initiated against you. If you are in doubt regarding your legal rights and obligations as a tenant, it is recommended that you seek legal assistance."[17]

Under the old common law, a landlord could simply go to the premises and forcibly eject the tenant. This is referred to as self-help eviction.

---

[17] Ohio Rev. Code Ann. § 1923.04.

default, usually by certified mail or by personal service. Once proper notice is given, the landlord may bring an action in the appropriate court, stating that the tenant failed to pay the rent and that proper notice was given, and requesting that the court order the tenant to vacate the premises. The landlord may also request payment for outstanding rent.

ii. Self-Help Eviction

Although the common law allowed landlords to forcibly evict residential tenants, this remedy is no longer available. Such actions are fraught with potential dangers, including the possibility of violence erupting from angry tenants. In almost all jurisdictions in the United States, **self-help eviction** is not an option, at least in residential leasing. Instead, landlords must follow state statutes that create specific steps that must be followed to evict a tenant who has not paid his rent.

> **Self-help eviction**
> The landlord acts without legal process to evict a tenant and instead relies on physical force; no longer permitted in most states, at least for residential leases.

When landlords violate the rules against self-help eviction, they can be civilly liable to the tenant. The tenant is permitted to sue for the landlord's actions, including actions such as intentional infliction of emotional distress.[18] The landlord may also be required to pay for any damage to the tenant's possessions and the costs associated with the tenant's relocation. The court may also reinstate the tenant on the leased premises and invoke the provisions of the previous lease. In some circumstances, the tenant may be entitled to punitive damages, especially when the landlord has acted without legal authority. Commercial tenants may be entitled to damages that include future lost income.

ISSUE AT A GLANCE

Fair rental value is often determined by the amount of the rent paid by the new tenant.

iii. Retaliatory Eviction

Landlords are not permitted to use the eviction process as a way to get rid of tenants who complain about conditions on the premises or tenants who report the landlord's deficiencies to local government officials. Tenants are allowed to raise the defense of retaliatory eviction when the landlord terminates their lease in response to their complaints. Under the Uniform Residential Landlord and Tenant Act, a landlord is prevented from evicting a tenant when:

- The tenant has complained to a governmental agency with jurisdiction over housing and building codes
- The tenant has complained to the landlord about the failure to maintain to the premises
- The tenant has organized or joined a tenants' union

---

[18] *Williams v. Guzzardi*, 875 F.2d 46 (3d Cir.1989).

Allowing a landlord to evict tenants when they complain about the landlord's actions is a violation of public policy.[19] The courts are allowed to presume that the landlord has committed retaliatory eviction when the tenant does any of the above activities and is then evicted. However, courts are not allowed to reach this conclusion when the tenant bases a complaint on any of the actions set out above after the tenant is evicted. If the tenant proves a claim for retaliatory eviction, a court is permitted to reinstate the lease and is also permitted to assess other damages against the landlord. Courts are allowed to apply the statutes prohibiting retaliatory eviction in a liberal way.[20]

V CLASSIFYING LANDLORD-TENANT RELATIONSHIPS

Landlord-tenant relationships come in several different forms, including:  *Test Q.*

- Tenancy for years
- Tenancy from year to year
- Tenancy at will
- Tenancy at sufferance

Each of these tenancies has unique features, including when and how they are created, the duties imposed on the parties, and the ways that each is terminated.

A. TENANCY FOR YEARS

A tenancy for years is any lease arrangement that will terminate on a specific date. Many of these tenancies run for set periods, such as one month or one year. Because of the terminology inherent in calling something a tenancy for years that could actually expire in less time, many legal commentators have suggested that a more appropriate name for this tenancy would be an estate for a stated period. This term is a more accurate description of the process. However, even though the latter name might make more sense, most states still refer to these arrangements as tenancies for years.

1. CREATING A TENANCY FOR YEARS

Tenancies for years are created by the express terms of the lease. The parties specify when the lease begins and when it ends.

---

[19] *Morford v. Lensey Corp.*, 110 Ill. App. 3d 792, 66 Ill. Dec. 372, 442 N.E.2d 933 (1982).
[20] *Kriz v. Taylor*, 92 Cal. App. 3d 302, 154 Cal. Rptr. 824 (1979).

2. TERMINATING A TENANCY FOR YEARS

A tenancy for years expires by its own terms. The parties are not required to give notice to one another of their intention to terminate the lease. Instead, if they wish to continue the arrangement, they must express their intention to renew the lease prior to the termination point or the lease will automatically expire.

ISSUE AT A GLANCE

The notice required to cancel different types of tenancies depends on their legal status. For instance, in a tenancy from year to year, notice to cancel must be received at least one month prior to the stated term of the lease for the notice to be legally effective.

B. TENANCY FROM YEAR TO YEAR

The deceptively named tenancy from year to year is a lease arrangement that usually does not run for a year. Instead, it runs for a series of specific intervals. The most common example is a month-to-month lease. There is also a push to change the name for this tenancy to an estate from period to period. By whatever name, this tenancy automatically renews at the end of the agreed upon term unless the parties agree to terminate.

1. CREATING A TENANCY FROM YEAR TO YEAR

Tenancies from year to year are often created when a tenant has a tenancy for years arrangement and then remains on the premises past the expiration date of that original lease. Most states have provisions that convert an expired tenancy for years into a tenancy from year to year. The significance of this reclassification is found in the method used to terminate the arrangement.

2. TERMINATING A TENANCY FROM YEAR TO YEAR

Tenancies from year to year do not terminate automatically. Instead, the parties must give notice to cancel the lease. The question in such cases often concerns the amount of notice required. By its very nature, there are few details provided in a tenancy from year to year, so the courts cannot refer to a lease for guidance about notice. What courts have done instead is to fashion a notice period based on the lease period. If the tenancy runs for a year, the parties must give at least one month's notice to terminate. If the lease runs from month to month, they must give at least seven days' notice. Without proper notice, the tenancy will automatically renew.

C. TENANCY AT WILL

Tenancies at will have no set terms. This is a lease arrangement where the landlord and the tenant have an informal agreement to lease the premises, "for as long as the

FIGURE 7-12

URLTA: Rental Payment
Determines Tenancy

(d) Unless the rental agreement fixes a definite term, the tenancy is week to week in case of a roomer who pays weekly rent and in all other cases month to month.[21]

tenant desires," or under some similar formula. The lack of specificity about the arrangement means that the tenancy can be created at any time.

1. CREATING A TENANCY AT WILL

The parties create a tenancy at will when they fail to specify the lease terms, in regard to length, notice, renewal, or any other material terms usually found in a landlord-tenant relationship.

2. TERMINATING A TENANCY AT WILL

Either the landlord or the tenant can terminate a tenancy at will at any time. The only requirement is that one give "reasonable notice" to the other of the intention to terminate. What constitutes reasonable notice is determined on a case-by-case basis. The requirement for reasonable notice is to give the tenant enough time to remove personal items from the leased premises.

D. TENANCY AT SUFFERANCE

A tenancy at sufferance is not really a tenancy at all. In the three previous examples, there was an agreement between the landlord and the tenant. However, in tenancy at sufferance, there is no agreement at all. Instead, the tenant remains on the premises without permission. This situation often arises when a tenant remains on the premises after a lease has expired and refuses to leave after being given notice to do so. A tenancy at sufferance relationship often arises while an eviction action is pending.

1. CREATING A TENANCY AT SUFFERANCE

The parties do not create a tenancy at sufferance. Instead, this tenancy comes into existence when the tenant is on the leased premises without permission.

2. TERMINATING A TENANCY AT SUFFERANCE

Because this tenancy is not a voluntary arrangement, there is no notice requirement to terminate it. Instead, the court may authorize the ejection of a tenant at sufferance when the court rules in the landlord's favor in an eviction action.

---

[21] S.C. Code Ann. § 27-40-310.

ANNOTATED DOCUMENT — APARTMENT LEASE

Identifies the landlord

The address of the rental unit

The term of the lease

Termination of the lease clause

IN CONSIDERATION of the rent to be paid. Calvin Cash as landlord (the "Landlord") does hereby lease and rent to Sid Savage as tenant (the "Tenant") and the Tenant does hereby lease and rent from the Landlord the apartment unit known as Apartment Number 24, Building C of the apartment complex known as Qualls Roost located at 324 Queen Street, Apt C24, Morganton, North Carolina 28655 (the "apartment") in accordance with the following terms and condition.

　　1. Term: The terms of this lease shall be for 12 months commencing October 10, 1998 and expiring October 9, 1999 (the "initial Term") Either Landlord or Tenant may terminate the tenancy at the expiration of the initial Term by giving written notice to the other at least thirty (30) days prior to the expiration date of the Initial Term.

ETHICS — LANDLORDS WHO VIOLATE STATE LAW

The legal professional should always be on the lookout for recent cases that illustrate a landlord's responsibility to tenants. As this chapter's case excerpt clearly shows, landlords have numerous obligations to tenants and the failure to meet these obligations can have severe monetary consequences. As case law develops on this point, it behooves legal professionals to keep track of recent decisions by the state appellate courts that modify these obligations or expand on them. Landlord clients should be informed of recent changes in the law in order to keep them on the right side of the law.

CASE EXCERPT — COPELAND v. LINCOLN

COPELAND v. LINCOLN
166 P.3d 245 (Colo. App., 2007)

Opinion by Judge GRAHAM.

In this landlord-tenant action, defendant, Stephen R. Lincoln (Landlord), appeals the trial court's judgment in favor of plaintiffs, Alan and Nicole Copeland (Tenants), finding that they had been constructively evicted. We affirm.

Tenants entered into a lease for a house with Landlord's predecessor in interest. Landlord bought the property in 2004 subject to the lease. During the tenancy, Tenants raised a number of issues regarding the condition of the property. The adequacy of Landlord's response to these issues, as well as the response of the prior owner, was disputed.

On Friday, March 4, 2005, the furnace was inspected by a heating company after Tenants had concerns regarding the amount of propane use and an alarm for a carbon monoxide detector installed by Tenants had gone off. The heating company determined that the furnace had a cracked heat exchanger and that the furnace was unsafe. Landlord was informed late that afternoon by the heating company that the furnace would need to be replaced. A copy of the inspection report was subsequently faxed to Landlord. The adequacy of Landlord's response to the notification that a new furnace was needed was disputed by the parties.

Landlord testified that he told Tenants that he would replace the furnace immediately, and the record shows that Landlord obtained a bid from the heating company, but found another vendor who would install the furnace for less money. Landlord testified that he had set up the delivery and installation of the new furnace for the following Wednesday.

Tenants testified that although Landlord told them he was going to install a new furnace, he did not tell them a specific date when the furnace would be installed. They also testified that the area was experiencing a record "cold snap" and that the temperatures in the house ranged between 45 and 55 degrees. Tenants testified that their family, which included two children, ages three and six, were forced to huddle near a small gas fireplace located in the living room. Tenants also testified that their request for assistance for temporary housing was rebuffed by Landlord. Consequently, Tenants testified that they contacted an attorney who advised them to move out of the house. By Tuesday, March 8, 2005, Tenants had substantially moved out of the house but had not removed all of their possessions by that time.

On Wednesday, when the furnace was set to be installed, Landlord discovered that Tenants had vacated the house. Landlord subsequently changed the locks on the house and retained possession of the items left by Tenants.

Landlord requested that Tenants pay the rent remaining under the lease as a consequence of breaking the lease and as a condition to obtain the return of their possessions. Tenants claimed, among other things, that they were constructively evicted from the house and that Landlord had converted their personal property. Landlord responded that he validly retained possession of Tenants' property and that they failed to give him the required notice pursuant to § 38-12-104, C.R.S.2006, which he argued set forth their only remedy.

Trial was held to the court. Following a hearing, the trial court took the matter under advisement and issued a written order finding that Tenants had been constructively evicted. The court found Landlord's testimony that he told Tenants that he would immediately replace the furnace was not credible. In addition, the court found that based on the hostility between the parties at that time, Tenants were unlikely to believe that Landlord would act quickly to replace the furnace.

The court also rejected Landlord's argument that § 38-12-104 provided the exclusive remedy available to Tenants. Accordingly, the court determined that Tenants' failure to provide written notice under this statute was not fatal to their constructive eviction claim. Thus, the court found that Tenants did not breach the lease by moving out and failing to pay further rent. The court also ordered the return of Tenants' security deposit and awarded them damages in the amount of $2180 for the items retained by Landlord that were not returned or were returned damaged or broken. Landlord then brought this appeal.

I.

Landlord contends that the trial court erred in not finding that § 38-12-104 was the exclusive remedy available to Tenants when a hazardous condition of a gas appliance was reported. We disagree.

As pertinent here, § 38-12-104 provides:

(1) Anytime service personnel from any organization providing gas service to a residential building become aware of any hazardous condition of a gas appliance, piping, or other gas equipment, such personnel shall inform the customer of record at the affected address in writing of the hazardous condition and take any further action provided for by the policies of such personnel's employer. Such written notification shall state the potential nature of the hazard as a fire hazard or a hazard to life, health, property, or public welfare and shall explain the possible cause of the hazard.

(2) If the resident of the residential building is a tenant, such tenant shall immediately inform the landlord of the property or the landlord's agent in writing of the existence of the hazard.

(3) The landlord shall then have seventy-two hours excluding a Saturday, Sunday, or a legal holiday after the actual receipt of the written notice of the hazardous condition to have the hazardous condition repaired by a professional.

(4) If the landlord does not have the repairs made within seventy-two hours excluding a Saturday, Sunday, or a legal holiday, and the condition of the building remains hazardous, the tenant may opt to vacate the premises. After the tenant vacates the premises, the lease or other rental agreement between the landlord and tenant becomes null and void, all rights and future obligations between the landlord and tenant pursuant to the lease or other rental agreement terminate, and the tenant may demand the immediate return of all or any portion of the security deposit held by the landlord to which the tenant is entitled.

Initially, we note that, except with regard to whether § 38-12-104 provided the exclusive remedy available to Tenants, Landlord does not specifically challenge the trial court's finding of constructive eviction. Thus, the question is whether § 38-12-104 abrogates the common law remedy of constructive eviction under the circumstances presented here. We conclude that it does not.

Generally, "any disturbance of a lessee's possession by his lessor which renders the premises unfit for occupancy for the purposes for which they were leased, or which deprives the lessee of the beneficial enjoyment of the premises" constitutes a constructive eviction, provided the lessee quits the premises within a reasonable time. Radinsky v. Weaver, 170 Colo. 169, 174, 460 P.2d 218, 220 (1969). Here, it is not contested that Tenants were constructively evicted for a combination of circumstances. Nor does Landlord claim protection under safe harbor provisions of § 38-12-104. Thus, we are only concerned with Landlord's argument that the statute somehow relegates Tenants to a single remedy and therefore abrogates the common law remedy of constructive eviction.

The supreme court has stated, "Where the interaction of common law and statutory law is at issue, we acknowledge and respect the General Assembly's authority to modify or abrogate common law, but can only recognize such changes when they are clearly expressed." Vigil v. Franklin, 103 P.3d 322, 327 (Colo. 2004). Statutes in derogation of the common law must be strictly construed, so that if the legislature wishes to abrogate rights that would otherwise be available under the common law, it must manifest its intent either expressly or by clear implication. Van Waters & Rogers, Inc. v. Keelan, 840 P.2d 1070 (Colo. 1992). However, under either circumstance, the abrogation must be more than an "imagined connection." Argus Real Estate, Inc. v. E-470 Pub. Highway Auth., 109 P.3d 604, 611 (Colo. 2005).

The plain language of § 38-12-104 does not demonstrate a clear intent by the General Assembly to modify or abrogate the common law. Rather, the statute sets forth special procedures that are applicable when there is a hazardous condition caused by an unsafe gas appliance. It requires that the tenant be notified by the service personnel, that the landlord correct the problem within a specified time, and if the landlord does not so act, that the lease becomes null and void and the tenant is entitled to a refund of the security deposit. Thus, although this statute is applicable to the circumstances presented here, there is no indication that it was intended to replace, rather than supplement, any available common law remedies. Additionally, a review of the scope of § 38-12-104 does not compel a conclusion that the availability of this statutory remedy precludes a common law claim for constructive eviction. See Argus Real Estate, Inc. v. E-470 Pub. Highway Auth., supra, 109 P.3d at 610 (because court found no clear intent by the General Assembly to abrogate the common law doctrine of claim preclusion, it concluded that there was no exception to that doctrine in § 15-11-1106(2), C.R.S.2006).

Therefore, in summary, we conclude that the trial court properly found that § 38-12-104 did not abrogate Tenants' constructive eviction claim.

The judgment is affirmed.

CASE QUESTIONS

1 What were the conditions at the leased premises that led to an allegation of constructive eviction against the landlord?
2 When the landlord found the house practically empty, what actions did he take?
3 What were the trial courts' findings?
4 Did the tenants waive their constructive eviction claim by failing to file a written notice of their claim?
5 How does the court define constructive eviction?

SKILLS YOU NEED IN THE REAL WORLD

RESEARCHING LANDLORD-TENANT LAW

Because the area of landlord-tenant law is rich with case law decisions and statutes, be aware that this area of law changes constantly. Most states have statutes that specifically govern residential leases and it is not uncommon for these laws to change every few years. Similarly, there is a large body of case law, not only from state appellate courts, but also from federal courts that constantly refines and expands on this topic. After all, there are always disgruntled tenants suing landlords, and exasperated landlords seeking to evict nonpaying tenants. You should also be aware that the standards in these cases have slowly changed over time. Fifty years ago, there were virtually no court decisions dictating that landlords must provide air conditioning or even hot water to their tenants as a basic requirement for habitation. As society's standards have slowly risen, so have the court's expectations of landlords.

CHAPTER SUMMARY

The topic of landlord-tenant law has many legal implications. The basics of the arrangement are established when a landlord conveys some of his rights to the tenant. These rights include the right to occupy, use, and enjoy the property. The landlord retains all other rights. The lease sets out the terms of the rental agreements. During the time that a tenant is in possession of the property, referred to as a tenancy, the tenant has both rights and obligations that arise from the relationship. Similarly, the landlord owes duties to the tenant. There are four different classifications of tenancy relationships. A tenancy for years has a specific termination date, after which the landlord-tenant relationship automatically terminates. A tenancy from year to year runs for a specific period of time. This term could be as short as one week or as long as a year. A tenancy at will is created when the parties do not specify the terms of the lease arrangement. A tenancy at sufferance arises when the tenant wrongfully remains on the premises after the lease has expired.

REVIEW QUESTIONS

1 What rights does a landlord transfer to the tenant in a typical lease arrangement?
2 List the landlord's duties to the tenant.
3 Explain the difference between a fixed rent lease and a percentage lease.
4 What is a ground lease?
5 What is a mineral lease?
6 What are the rules that govern pet and security deposits?
7 What is subletting?
8 Give an example of an action that would be permissible under a commercial lease but not a residential lease.
9 How does the Statute of Frauds affect leases?
10 What is the Uniform Residential Landlord and Tenant Act?

11 Name at least three different statutes that are important in residential leasing and explain why they are important.
12 What discriminatory practices are prohibited under federal and state law?
13 What is "ordinary wear and tear"? Briefly describe the two legal doctrines that have evolved in modern landlord-tenant law.
14 What is "self-help" eviction?
15 What are the characteristics of a tenancy for years?
16 What are the characteristics of a tenancy from year to year?
17 How is a tenancy at will created?
18 What is a tenancy at sufferance?
19 Create a table showing the different ways that the four tenancies discussed in this chapter can be terminated.
20 Summarize the chapter's case excerpt.

DISCUSSION QUESTIONS

Has the law of constructive eviction unfairly shifted the legal burden in the landlord-tenant relationship to the landlord? Is constructive eviction too vague? Does it allow tenants to escape their obligations under the lease?

PRACTICAL APPLICATIONS

Using the form provided in the Appendix, create a residential lease for Tonya Tenant and her cat, Missy. They will live in Apartment 301 of Kensington Arms Apartments. The lease will begin on January 1 of next year and run through December 31. The rent is $750 per month. The landlord will charge 5 percent of the first month's rent as a damage deposit and another 5 percent as a pet deposit.

WEB SITES

New York State Rent Administration
http://www.dhcr.state.ny.us/ora/ora.htm

Georgia Superior Court Cooperative Authority
http://www.gsccca.org/search

Census Information on Real Estate and Rental Statistics
http://factfinder.census.gov/servlet/SAFFHousing?_sse=on

Constructive Eviction (Wikipedia)
http://en.wikipedia.org/wiki/Constructive_eviction

Just Cause for Eviction — California
http://www.ci.glendale.ca.us/pdf/justCauseEviction_GenInfoBulletin.pdf

TERMS AND PHRASES

Constructive eviction	License	Tenant
Eviction	Ordinary wear and tear	Trade fixture
Leasehold estate	Quiet enjoyment	Warranty of habitability
Landlord	Sublet	
Lease	Self-help eviction	

SIGNIFICANT CASES

R & J Rhodes, LLC v. Finney, 231 S.W.3d 183 (Mo. App. W. Dist., 2007)
Keenan Packaging Supply, Inc. v. McDermott, 700 N.W.2d 645 (Neb. App., 2005)
Herbert Paul, CPA, PC v. 370 Lex, L.L.C., 794 N.Y.S.2d 869 (N.Y. Sup., 2005)
Staley v. Bouril, 718 A.2d 283 (Pa., 1998)
Dargis v. Paradise Park, Inc., 819 N.E.2d 1220 (Ill. App. 2. Dist., 2004)
Rieman v. Swope, 79 P.3d 399 (Or. App., 2003)
Small v. Durango Partners, LLC, 930 A.2d 297 (Me., 2007)
Housing Authority of Town of Enfield v. Russotto, 41 Conn. L. Rptr. 56 (Conn. Super., 2006)

Real Estate Deeds

INTRODUCTION

In this chapter, we examine the many aspects of deeds. A **deed** is an unusual document in that it embodies both contract and real property law. On one hand, a deed is a contract, setting out basic rights and obligations between the parties. On the other hand, it is the written expression of the transfer of legal rights in real property from one party to another. Deeds have a unique and interesting history that continues to have significance in daily real estate practice.

Deed
The written instrument that conveys real property interests.

A. A BRIEF HISTORY OF DEEDS

In ancient times, a real estate transaction was a symbolic ceremony in which a grantor transferred property and title to a grantee. We saw in Chapter 1 that there are important differences between real property and personal property. This distinction becomes readily apparent when we examine the laws surrounding transfer of title between these two different types of property. In personal property, title changes hands when the actual item is transferred from one owner to another. Let's consider how someone would sell something like a book or an antique desk. After the buyer and seller negotiate a price agreeable to both, the seller accepts money for the item. Here, physical possession is the best indicator of ownership. Although the sale may be accompanied by a bill of sale or some other written expression of the transfer of ownership, possession is the best way to establish the buyer's rights. This is the basis of one of the oldest maxims in common law, "possession is nine-tenths of the law." This approach works well for most types of personal property, but it presents practical difficulties when dealing with real property. First of all, land is immobile and therefore cannot simply be transferred in the same way that personal property can be. An owner cannot always be in physical possession of land in the same way that she could be of a personal item such as a book. Owners routinely leave their real property to conduct other business and to go to work. Because owners cannot always be in physical possession of their land, there had to be some other way to prove ownership. There are other practical problems presented by real property ownership. If you cannot simply take the land with you, how do you prove that you actually own it? How, for instance, do you pass this title on to others? How do your heirs prove that you held interest in land? The deed was created as a way of solving many of these problems.

ISSUE AT A GLANCE

Deeds must meet the requirements of both contract law and real property law.

ELEMENTS OF DEEDS

Real estate deeds are unique because they serve two different functions at the same time. They embody the contractual agreement between the parties and also serve to declare that real property interests have transferred from one party to another. As a result, they must meet the elements of any contract as well as statutory requirements. The end result is a document that is a hybrid: It is both a contract and a declaration.

Before we can go any further into our discussion of deeds, it is important to clarify some of the terminology. Deeds do not list buyers and sellers. Instead, they refer to grantors and grantees. A **grantor** is the person who transfers the property and the **grantee** is the person who receives the property interest. Grantors and sellers are often, but not always, synonymous. The reason for this distinction is that a person could transfer some, but not all, rights in real estate to another. In this scenario, the person who transfers rights is referred to as a grantor (one who grants rights to another) and the person who receives them is the grantee (one who receives rights). See Example 8-1.

Grantor
One who conveys a real property interest.

Grantee
One who receives a real property interest.

Uncle Joe has always had a soft spot in his heart for his niece, Linda. One day, he decides to give Linda a life estate in a house that sits on several acres just outside of town. When it comes time to write up the deed, who is listed as grantor and who is listed as grantee?

EXAMPLE 8-1

Answer: Uncle Joe is listed as grantor and Linda is listed as grantee. Uncle Joe is conveying his interests, so he is listed as the grantor; Linda is receiving rights, so she is listed as grantee.

A. MINIMUM REQUIREMENTS OF A DEED

All states have minimum requirements that deeds must satisfy before they are considered to have any legal significance. These minimum requirements include:

- Deeds must be in writing
- Deeds must identify the grantor and the grantee
- The grantor must sign the deed
- Both parties must have legal capacity
- The property conveyed must be adequately described
- The deed must contain language clearly showing the intent to convey property interests
- The deed must be delivered by the grantor and accepted by the grantee
- The deed must be attested and acknowledged

1. DEEDS MUST BE IN WRITING

One of the most obvious requirements for any deed is the requirement that it be in writing. Oral deeds are unenforceable. The reason that a deed must be in writing is that it falls into that small category of contracts governed by the Statute of Frauds.

The Statute of Frauds was originally created in England as a way to prevent fraud. In those days very few people could read and requiring important contracts to be in writing was a safeguard against unscrupulous practices. The Statute of Frauds was enacted in all states and continues to exist, in one form or another, across the country. The statute covers several different categories of writings, including:

- Promises to answer for the debts of another person
- Prenuptial agreements
- Contracts involving the purchase of goods worth more than $500
- The transfer of real estate interests

See Figure 8-1 for a typical Statute of Frauds.

Although state statutes require deeds to be in writing, there has never been a requirement that particular forms must be used. The parties are free to create their own, handwritten deeds. However, in the age of the Internet and the availability of forms that have passed muster with state bar associations, it makes a great deal of sense to use preprinted forms.

Sidebar

In the past, when real estate transactions took on a more literal meaning, property owners would actually transfer some physical representation of the land to the new buyer. The handover of this "fee" would symbolize the transfer of property rights from the seller to the buyer. Deeds now take the place of that physical transfer. This accounts for many of the features found in deeds that seem odd or out of place.

FIGURE 8-1

Statute of Frauds (Texas)

A conveyance of an estate of inheritance, a freehold, or an estate for more than one year, in land and tenements, must be in writing and must be subscribed and delivered by the conveyor or by the conveyor's agent authorized in writing[1]

ISSUE AT A GLANCE

The Statute of Frauds requires that all deeds must be in writing.

---

2. DEEDS MUST IDENTIFY THE GRANTOR AND GRANTEE

In addition to the requirement that a deed be in writing, deeds must also identify the grantor and the grantee. Here we encounter some unusual provisions of deed law. The grantor must always be identified by name, but there is authority for transferring property to an unnamed grantee. Although the grantee can be unnamed, she must be identifiable. In a situation in which a grantor deeds property to an unnamed individual, the description must be specific and unique enough to identify a specific grantee. Consider Example 8-2.

EXAMPLE 8-2

Uncle Harry has always been a little bit eccentric. Last week, he wrote up and signed a deed for 100 acres of prime farmland. In the grantee line, he wrote: "That redheaded girl who walks by my house everyday at 3 o'clock." Uncle Harry's family members have decided to challenge this deed on the grounds that he is obviously mentally unstable. Is this description of the grantee sufficient to meet the legal requirements for a deed?

Answer: It depends. If there is only one redheaded girl who walks by Uncle Harry's house everyday at 3 o'clock (presumably after school lets out), then the transaction may be valid. However, if there is more than one redheaded girl, or even girls whose hair may be various shades of red to auburn, the transaction will be void for vagueness.

Sidebar

Although the grantor must have legal capacity when the deed is signed, there is no corresponding requirement for the grantee. The person receiving title can be mentally incompetent, a child, or under the influence of alcohol or other drugs at the time of the transaction. The only limitation is that a deed cannot pass title to a deceased grantee.[2]

Although there is flexibility in the method used to identify the grantee, the same does not hold true for the grantor. The grantor must be clearly identified, by name. There is some flexibility when it comes to the grantor's full, legal name and the way that the grantor signs her name. For example, a deed showing the grantor as "William A. Cortez" and signed "Bill Cortez" would be acceptable in any court. "Bill" is a common nickname for "William," and barring any other complications, such as the fact that there is more than one William Cortez in the family, the deed would be sufficient to pass title. The grantor's signature indicates her intention to pass title to the grantee. Interestingly enough, there is usually no requirement for the grantee to sign a deed.

---

[1] Tex. Code Ann. Prop. § 5.021.
[2] *Campbell v. Everhart*, 139 N.C. 503, 52 S.E. 201 (1905).

FIGURE 8-2

Grantor's Name Excerpt from a
General Warranty Deed

```
WILSON  COUNTY

    THIS  DEED, made this 30th day of August, 1999, by and between JOHN  M.
BARNES  and  wife, AMY C. BARNES, GRANTORS, and AMY C. BARNES,  GRANTEE.  3400
Teal Drive, Wilson,
```

Another common problem that directly relates to the names of grantors and grantees is the problem of misnomer. This occurs when the grantor incorrectly identifies the grantee in the deed. When presented with this problem, courts will attempt to resolve the question by trying to identify the person that the grantor actually intended. When that is impossible, the deed will be ruled a nullity and no title interest will pass. Misnomer applies not only to incorrectly named individuals, but also to incorrectly named corporations.

EXAMPLE 8-3

Our firm is looking into a deed that contains a contradiction. In the main part of the deed, the grantor is identified as Samuel S. Johnson, conveying ten acres to Thomas S. Johnson. However, in the body of the deed, there is a reference to ten acres owned in fee simple by "Samuel S. Jones." Samuel S. Johnson signs the deed and that signature is notarized. Is this a valid deed?

Answer: Because the deed refers to the grantor by his correct name at every other point in the transaction except one, and because the grantor signed and notarized his signature as Samuel S. Johnson, the deed is acceptable.[3]

3. THE GRANTOR MUST SIGN THE DEED

In addition to correctly identifying the grantor and the grantee, the deed must also bear the grantor's signature. The signing of the deed indicates the grantor's desire to transfer the interest to the property and that this transfer is done willingly. Many states require the grantor's signature before the deed is considered legally effective.[4] There is, however, no requirement that the grantee must sign the deed. Later we will see that the important action from the grantee's viewpoint is not signing the deed but whether the grantee accepted the deed.

The grantor's signature on the deed indicates her knowing and voluntary transfer of property interests to the grantee.

ISSUE AT
A GLANCE

Why should there be a rule that requires only the grantor to sign the deed? At this point in the transaction, the courts focus on the grantor. After all, it is the grantor who is transferring real property interests. To show a valid transaction, the

---

[3] *Jenkins v. Jenkins*, 148 Pa. 216, 23 A. 985 (Pa.1892).
[4] *Matter of Mills*, 68 N.C. App. 694, 315 S.E.2d 716 (1984).

parties must show that the grantor had the mental ability to transfer real property interests; that she did so voluntarily; and that she was not subject to any force, threat, or intimidation. Many of the requirements to finalize a deed, such as acknowledgment and notarization, help establish these elements.

FIGURE 8-3

Signature Provision from a Deed

BOOK 1785 PAGE 113

THIS INSTRUMENT PREPARED BY JULIE T. WILLIAMS, ATTORNEY
NO TITLE SEARCH PERFORMED - NO OPINION ON TITLE RENDERED

2193

NORTH CAROLINA

WILSON COUNTY

    THIS DEED, made this 30th day of August, 1999, by and between JOHN M. BARNES and wife, AMY C. BARNES, GRANTORS, and AMY C. BARNES, GRANTEE, 3400 Teal Drive, Wilson, NC 27893.

W I T N E S S E T H :

    That said GRANTORS, in consideration of Ten Dollars ($10.00) and other good and valuable considerations in hand paid, the receipt of which is hereby acknowledged, have bargained and sold and by this deed do hereby bargain, sell and convey unto said GRANTEE, her heirs and assigns, in fee simple, that certain lot or parcel of land lying and being situate in the City of Wilson, Wilson County, North Carolina, and more particularly described as follows:

    BEING all of Lot 70 as shown on that map of section One, Millbrook Subdivision as recorded in Plat Book 14, page 260, Wilson County Registry. For reference, see deed recorded in Book 1492, page 169, Wilson County Registry. And being the identical property conveyed in deed dated February 28, 1996 from Charles M. Carter and wife, Margaret S. Carter, recorded in Book 1580, Page 633, Wilson County Registry.

    TO HAVE AND TO HOLD the above described lot or parcel of land with all privileges and appurtenances thereunto belonging or in anywise appertaining unto them, the said GRANTEE, her heirs and assigns in fee simple forever.

    Pursuant to N.C.G.S. Section 39-13.3(c) and any other applicable statutes, the tenancy by the entirety ownership formerly held by GRANTORS is hereby dissolved and ownership is now solely held by the GRANTEE.

    AND the said GRANTORS do hereby covenant that they are seized of said premises in fee and have the right to convey the same in fee simple; that the same is free and clear of all encumbrances, and that they hereby warrant and will forever defend the title to the same against the lawful claims of all persons whomsoever.

    IN TESTIMONY WHEREOF, the GRANTORS have hereunto set their hands and seals the day and year first above written.

WILSON COUNTY NC   10/31/2000

$14.00

STATE OF
NORTH
CAROLINA

Real Estate
Excise Tax

John M. Barnes   (SEAL)
JOHN M. BARNES

Amy C. Barnes   (SEAL)
AMY C. BARNES

Mail: Grantee

4. THE PARTIES MUST HAVE LEGAL CAPACITY

At the time of the signing, delivery, and acceptance of the deed, the grantor must have the mental capacity to carry out the transaction. A grantor who lacks the capacity to enter into a contract is similarly barred from divesting real property rights through a deed. To ensure that the transaction is legally effective, the parties must be able to demonstrate that at the time of the transaction the grantor was free of any mental disease or defect that affected her ability to know and understand the consequences of the transaction.

Because there is a close affinity between contract law and real property law on the question of capacity, it is helpful to point out certain conditions that give rise to a presumption that a person lacks capacity. For instance, a person lacks capacity when she:

- Is under the legal age of majority (18 years old, in most states)
- Is under the influence of alcohol or some other drug
- Has been declared mentally incompetent

If it can be proven that at the time of transaction the grantor lacked legal capacity, the court is empowered to negate the entire transaction and return the property interests to the grantor. The court may also appoint a guardian to oversee the grantor's business affairs in order to avoid similar situations in the future.

5. THE PROPERTY CONVEYED MUST BE ADEQUATELY DESCRIBED

The deed between the grantor and the grantee must contain a description of the property conveyed. This description must be sufficient to show how this particular parcel is separate and unique from all other parcels. As a result of this requirement, street address or mailing address is not sufficient to adequately describe property in a deed, unless the town is laid out in a municipal grid or the deed refers to some other government-imposed survey system. Most states require specific descriptions, such as metes and bounds, tract index, or reference to a government survey. Without this type of specific description, the deed may fail because it is impossible to identify with precision the parcel of land to be transferred between the parties. Incorrect property descriptions are one of the most common problems in modern real estate practice. (See Chapter 3.)

■ Metes and bounds description	■ Government survey
■ Tract index	■ Subdivision and lot number

FIGURE 8-4

Different Methods Used to Describe Real Estate

FIGURE 8-5

Metes and Bounds Description from a General Warranty Deed

Beginning at an iron pin in the northern margin of S. R. 1233 (Leeward Circle), said iron pin marking the southeast corner of Lot 2 in Block "B" of Leeward Point Subdivision as shown on a plat referred to hereinafter, and proceeding thence with the eastern line of Lot 2 North 13° 22' 28" East 136.33 feet to an iron pin, a new corner; thence a new line South 77° 41' 43" East 240.15 feet to an iron pin in the margin of S. R. 1233; thence with the margin of S. R. 1233 South 26° 39' 43" East 50.10 feet to an iron pin, South 66° 23' 42" West 109.37 feet to an iron pin, South 76° 40' 13" West 75.00 feet to an iron pin, and North 78° 03' 47" West 118.00 feet to the Beginning, containing approximately 0.680 acre, according to a survey by David S. Clark, R.L.S., dated February 7, 2000, and being the southern portion of Lot 3 in Block "B" of Leeward Point Subdivision as shown on a plat recorded in Plat Book 2 at Page 157, Alexander County Registry.

Also conveyed hereby is a 1/17th undivided interest in Access Lot 19A in Block "A" of Leeward Point as shown on the aforesaid plat.

EXAMPLE 8-4

Uncle Theo writes out the following deed: "I hereby leave all of my property to my nephew, Theo, Jr." Is this a sufficient description of the land involved?

Answer: Although the description fails to give specifics, if Uncle Theo owns only one tract of land, this description may just be enough to effectively pass title to his nephew.[5]

a. Court Interpretations of Ambiguous Property Descriptions

In cases in which the description in a deed is ambiguous or unclear, a court may be called upon to interpret the language in the deed. Generally, courts try to give effect to the parties' intentions and will attempt to discern the actual location referred to in the deed. When the language is not helpful, the courts may fall back on other evidence, such as the public record, recorded plats, natural landmarks referred to in the deed, surveys of other adjoining properties, total acreage, and distance and directions given in the deed that indicate which parcel is being sold. Only when these methods fail will the court void the deed for vagueness.

FIGURE 8-6

Vagueness of Description Not to Invalidate

No deed or other writing purporting to convey land or an interest in land shall be declared void for vagueness in the description of the thing intended to be granted by reason of the use of the word "adjoining" instead of the words "bounded by," or for the reason that the boundaries given do not go entirely around the land described: Provided, it can be made to appear to the satisfaction of the jury that the grantor owned at the time of the execution of such deed or paper-writing no other land which at all corresponded to the description contained in such deed or paper-writing.[6]

---

[5] *Snyder v. Bridewell*, 267 S.W. 561 (Ark. 1924).
[6] N.C. Gen. Stat. 39-2.

FIGURE 8-7

Habendum Clause

TO HAVE AND TO HOLD the aforesaid tract or parcel of land, and all of the privileges and appurtenances thereto belonging, to the said party of the second part, its successors and assigns in fee simple absolute.

FIGURE 8-7

Habendum Clause

6. THE DEED MUST CONTAIN LANGUAGE INDICATING AN INTENTION TO CONVEY PROPERTY RIGHTS

It is not enough for the parties simply to indicate that they wish to transfer interests in real estate. The deed must also contain unambiguous language clearly showing the intent of the grantor to transfer all of her interest to the grantee. The two most important deed clauses that convey this intention are the **habendum** and **granting clauses**

The purpose of these two clauses is to show the grantor's present intent to transfer her property interests to the grantee. The habendum clause describes the nature of the title that is being transferred. In most situations, the habendum clause would include provisions showing that the grantee is receiving fee simple absolute title. As we have seen in prior chapters, fee simple title gives the grantee all possible rights to property. The granting clause, on the other hand, is the clause that declares the grantor's intention to actually transfer the land to the grantee. Some courts have held that without both clauses, there can be no legal transfer.

Habendum clause
A deed clause that conveys specified rights to the grantee.

Granting clause
A deed clause that demonstrates the grantor's willingness to engage in the transaction.

Habendum clauses discuss the quality or type of title interests conveyed to the grantee; granting clauses show the grantor's intent to transfer.

 ISSUE AT A GLANCE

This is not to say that the law requires a specific formula of words to create a legally valid deed. Both the habendum and granting clauses will be interpreted from the language used by the parties. If, for instance, a party uses the word "grant" or "convey," these words will be considered sufficient to satisfy the granting clause. Similarly, if the grantor mentions the quality of the title passed to the grantee, this will often satisfy the requirements of the habendum clause. Courts generally are liberal in their interpretations of the language used in deeds. The language used can be as simple as "I do hereby grant and convey to you fee simple title to this land."

7. THE DEED MUST BE DELIVERED BY THE GRANTOR AND ACCEPTED BY THE GRANTEE

The requirement of delivery and acceptance of a deed goes back to the ancient history of real estate transactions. So far, our discussion about deeds has focused on their qualities as a contract between the grantor and the grantee. However, when it comes to the issues of delivery and acceptance, we diverge from contract law into other aspects of real estate law. The deed transfer now takes the place of the transfer of a piece of earth as a symbol of the land itself. When the grantor signs the deed and delivers the deed to the grantee, this physical act symbolizes the transfer of the grantor's interest in the property. In order for the transaction to be complete, the grantee must accept the deed offered by the grantor. When this delivery and acceptance is complete, title to the land has changed hands.[7] If anything occurs that interrupts the process of delivery and acceptance, the real estate transaction is not complete. If, for some reason, the grantor signs the deed but fails to deliver, there is no completed transaction. On the other hand, if the grantor signs and delivers the deed but the grantee refuses to accept it, we reach the same result. Consider Example 8-5.

FIGURE 8-8

Signature Provision from a Deed

TO HAVE AND TO HOLD said lands and premises unto the parties of the second part, their heirs and assigns, in fee simple, together with all privileges and appurtenances thereunto belonging.

And the parties of the first part covenant with the parties of the second part that they are seized in fee simple of the land above described and have good right and title to convey the same; that the same is free and clear of all liens and encumbrances, except 1997 ad valorem taxes, and that they will forever warrant and defend the title to the same against all lawful claims and demands of all persons whomsoever.

IN WITNESS WHEREOF, the parties of the first part have hereunto set their hands and affixed their seals, this the day and year first above written.

Bobby Gene Weathington (SEAL)
BOBBY GENE WEATHINGTON

Janice Carol Weathton (SEAL)
JANICE CAROL WEATHINGTON

EXAMPLE 8-5

Gerald Grantor has signed a deed and is about to deliver it to Al Grantee. However, before he can hand the deed over, Gerald suffers a heart attack and dies. Al takes the deed out of his hands and declares the transaction complete. Has there been a valid transaction?

Answer: No. Real estate law requires not only that the grantor sign a deed but also that he voluntarily deliver to it the grantee. Although it seems clear from the surrounding circumstances that Gerald intended to deliver the deed, the fact that he never did so means that there can be no valid transaction. Title has not changed hands in this scenario.

---

[7] *Klouda v. Pechousek*, 414 Ill. 75, 110 N.E.2d 258 (1953).

To have a valid transaction, the deed must be both delivered and accepted.

ISSUE AT A GLANCE

a. Proving Delivery

In some cases, it may be necessary for the parties to prove that a valid delivery and acceptance actually occurred. The elements that the parties must prove are the following:

- The grantor intended that the deed transfer real property to the grantee.
- The grantor's action placed the deed beyond her possession and control.
- The grantee accepted the deed.[8]

Just as important as the grantor's delivery is the grantee's acceptance of the deed. When the grantee accepts the deed, she is bound by the terms contained in the deed. As we have already seen, there is no requirement that the grantee must sign the deed. When the deed is recorded, courts will usually presume that a valid delivery and acceptance occurred.

Tech Topic
ELECTRONIC RECORDING

The act of recording means to physically enter into the public record executed real estate records, including deeds, mortgages, easements, and other instruments that affect title. The purpose of recording is to detail the various interests that people have in a particular property. Recording establishes a priority; in other words, who holds the dominant legal interest in a property.

Until recent years, the executed documents involved in a real estate transaction would be transported to the recording entity either by mail or in person. Nowadays, e-recording is supplanting the traditional method.

The difference between traditional recording and e-recording is that the documents are delivered to the recording office via the Internet, usually through a third-party document service. The benefit of e-recording is that the recording entity can process the information more quickly and speed the return of an image of the recorded documents.

In general, this is how e-recording works:

- After closing, the lender or the title company scans the executed and notarized documents into a PDF file.
- Next, the PDF file is uploaded to the third party's web site.
- The documents are then submitted (along with appropriate indexing information) to the appropriate county.
- The county records the documents and returns an electronically stamped copy — sometimes within a couple of hours. (When recording is done using the traditional method, the wait for returned documents can take weeks.)

Not all lenders and title companies have fully embraced e-recording, but it is only a matter of time before it completely replaces traditional methods.

---

[8] *Jones v. Saunders*, 254 N.C. 644, 119 S.E.2d 789 (1961).

b. Delivery in Escrow

An escrow closing allows the grantor to deliver the deed prior to the actual date of closing and relieves the grantor of the responsibility of being present at the actual closing. We discuss escrow closings in greater detail in Chapter 13.

8. THE DEED MUST BE ATTESTED AND ACKNOWLEDGED

In order for a deed to be valid, it must be both attested and acknowledged. These are somewhat archaic terms that refer to signatures and witness provisions.

FIGURE 8-9

Attestation Clause from a Deed

IN WITNESS WHEREOF, the grantor has executed this deed on the date set forth above.

_____

Mark Goodson

---

a. Attestation

Attestation
Signing a document.

A deed must be attested. **Attestation** is another word for signature. Although these days most people sign a deed by writing their name, attestation originated in previous times when most people were illiterate and they were therefore allowed to sign with a thumbprint or mark as a way to attest the deed.

b. Acknowledgment

Acknowledgment
Proof that the person who signed a document is who she claims to be.

When grantors **acknowledge** a deed, they are presenting proof that they are who they claim to be. The best way to acknowledge a deed is to appear before a notary public and sign the deed in the notary's presence. Notaries are supposed to ask for identification and then witness signatures on deeds. Although there are other provisions that satisfy the acknowledgment requirement, such as appearing before the clerk of court or, in some cases, before a judge, notarizing a signature is the most common way to prove acknowledgment. These days, acknowledgments are usually not an official requirement under state law.

9. OTHER DEED PROVISIONS

So far, we have outlined the minimum legal requirements for a deed. However, state law may also impose other provisions. For instance, state law might also require that deeds should contain:

- Seals
- Consideration recitals
- Exceptions and exclusions

a. Seals

The use of seals in important documents goes back centuries. In many states, seals were required on all deeds before they could be filed. Placing a seal on a document

FIGURE 8-10

Acknowledgment Provision from a Deed

STATE OF GEORGIA)
)ss:
COUNTY OF COBB   )

The foregoing instrument was acknowledged before me this 30th day of October, 2001 by the persons to me known as the person(s) described in and who executed the foregoing instrument and Acknowledged before me that (s)he executed the same.

Witness my hand and official seal

April Barnard
NOTARY PUBLIC

had a very particular legal significance. For instance, a document under seal did not have to be supported by consideration and was protected by other presumptions under the law. However, seals have steadily lost importance over the years. In fact, most states no longer require a seal on a deed or they make a provision that the person's signature will substitute for the seal requirement.

b. Consideration

Consideration is a requirement for contracts. In the context of a commercial transaction, consideration establishes that both parties have surrendered something of value in exchange for something else of value. Because deeds resemble contracts, many states have provisions in their deeds for a recital of the consideration between the grantor and the grantee. Rather than requiring a specific monetary sum as consideration in the deed, most states simply fall back on a requirement that the deed is given for "valuable consideration" or "good consideration." The issue of consideration usually only rears its head in situations in which a grantor has made a gift of a parcel of real estate. Because this gift may have important tax consequences, courts often look very closely at the consideration involved in a gift transaction.

c. Exceptions and Exclusions

The deed may also contain exceptions and exclusions. These are statements inserted by the grantor that seek to limit the grantor's promises or warranties made to the grantee. A grantor might, for example, include an exception in a deed stating that the property is free and clear of all encumbrances with the exception of an existing easement. These exceptions and exclusions serve two purposes: They put the grantee on notice of specific situations and insulate the grantor from claims that she failed to provide full disclosure about the nature of the title.

10. NONESSENTIAL DEED PROVISIONS

Deeds often contain additional information and entries that are not strictly required by state law. Among these nonessential deed provisions are witness signatures and dates.

Sidebar

Although dates are not required on deeds, the presence of a date on a deed creates a rebuttable presumption that the deed was delivered.

FIGURE 8-11

Sample Exceptions and Exclusion from a Deed

The property hereinabove described was acquired by Grantor by instrument recorded in ...the Stanly County Public

Registry in Deed Book 360, at Page 482.

A map showing the above described property is recorded in Plat Book .....N/A...... page.............. .

TO HAVE AND TO HOLD the aforesaid lot or parcel of land and all privileges and appurtenances thereto belonging to the Grantee in fee simple.

And the Grantor covenants with the Grantee, that Grantor is seized of the premises in fee simple, has the right to convey the same in fee simple, that title is marketable and free and clear of all encumbrances, and that Grantor will warrant and defend t a title against the lawful claims of all persons whomsoever except for the exceptions hereinafter stated.
Title to .he property hereinabove described is subject to the following exceptions:

> (1) Easements, conditions and restrictions of record in the chain of
>   title;
> (2) 1989 ad valorem taxes, which have been assumed by the Grantees.

a. Witnesses

In most situations, there is no requirement for a deed to be witnessed by someone other than the person who acknowledged the grantor's signature. In contrast to wills, which require more than one witness, the person who witnesses the grantor's signature is sufficient.

b. Date

There is also no requirement that the deed contain a date. Obviously, a date is helpful in fixing time periods and determining exactly when certain actions occurred, but the only date that is absolutely essential is the date that the deed was recorded. Other date provisions are generally irrelevant.

TYPES OF DEEDS

There are numerous types of deeds and they all serve different functions. Among the most important are:

- General warranty deeds
- Special warranty deeds
- Deeds of trust/mortgages
- Quitclaim deeds

A. GENERAL WARRANTY DEEDS

When a grantor wishes to convey fee simple absolute rights to the grantee, the deed that does so is the general warranty deed. This deed contains a series of promises or warranties that make specific assertions. Among the warranties made in a general warranty deed are the covenants of:

- Seizin
- Quiet enjoyment
- Against encumbrances
- Further assurance
- Warranty forever

1. SEIZIN

When a general warranty deed provides a covenant of **seizin**, it simply means that the grantor is in full possession of the property and has the right to convey it to another. Seizin usually refers to ownership.[9]

Seizin
(French) Possession of real property.

2. QUIET ENJOYMENT

The covenant or promise of quiet enjoyment is the grantor's assurance that the grantee can take possession of the premises secure in the knowledge that no other person can claim an ownership interest in the property. The covenant of quiet enjoyment ensures that the new owner has full right to possess the property.

3. AGAINST ENCUMBRANCES

The warranty against encumbrances is the grantor's promise that there are no outstanding encumbrances on the property that will affect the title. Examples of encumbrances include liens, assessments, foreclosure actions, judgments, or any other legal action that could interfere with the grantee's possession of the land.

4. FURTHER ASSURANCE

The grantor's warranty of further assurance is the grantor's promise that should any claims arise against the property, the grantor will provide evidence that the title passed to the grantee was free and clear.

5. WARRANTY FOREVER

Finally, the covenant of warranty forever is simply the grantor's guarantee that she will continue to support the grantee's claims at any point in the future, should it become necessary.

General warranty deeds make the most promises or warranties to the grantee.

ISSUE AT A GLANCE

B. SPECIAL WARRANTY DEEDS

Special warranty deeds resemble general warranty deeds, but while general warranty deeds provide several different promises, a special warranty deed usually only makes a single warranty. This single promise is often as simple as stating that the grantor has taken no action during the time that the property was in the grantor's possession that will affect the grantee's rights.

---

[9] *Scott v. Fairlie*, 81 Fla. 438, 446, 89 So. 128 (1921).

SPECIAL WARRANTY DEED

THIS INDENTURE, made the 21st day of May, 2004, between Marge Simpson and Homer Simpson of the County of Springfield, State of Placid, hereinafter called "Grantor," and Ester Jenkins, whose address is 20 Robinwood Ave, Asheville, North Carolina, of the County of Buncombe, hereinafter called "Grantee" (the terms "Grantor" and "Grantee" designate both the singular and plural, as the context demands).

WITNESSETH that: Grantor, for and in consideration of Ten Dollars ($10.00) and other good and valuable considerations to said Grantor in hand paid by said Grantee, the receipt which is hereby acknowledged, has granted, bargained and sold and by these presents does grant, bargain and sell unto the said Grantee, and Grantee's heirs and assigns forever, land situate, lying and being in Springfield County, Placid and more particularly described as follows:

Tract 10-1254 in Springfield County Tract Index

TO HAVE AND TO HOLD the said tract or parcel of land, with all and singular the rights, members and appurtenances thereof, to the same being, belonging, or in anywise appertaining, to the only proper use, benefit and behalf of the said Grantee forever in FEE SIMPLE.

This conveyance and the warranties are limited to the issues of a mortgage found at DB 101/123 and by this special warranty, grantor hereby releases any claims under that document.

AND THE SAID Grantor will only warrant and forever defend the right and title to the above described property unto the said Grantee against the claims of those persons claiming by, through or under Grantor, but not otherwise.

IN WITNESS WHEREOF, the Grantor has signed, sealed and delivered this Deed, the day and year above written.

WITNESSES:
Grantor(s)

_____

_____

STATE OF PLACID
COUNTY OF SPRINGFIELD

THE FOREGOING INSTRUMENT was acknowledged before me this _(17)_ day of 22nd day of May, 2004, by Troy McClure.

_____
Notary Public
My Commission Expires: _____

C. DEEDS OF TRUST/MORTGAGES

A deed of trust is the deed that specifies the lender's rights to the property in the event that the buyer defaults on her mortgage. Also referred to as mortgages, this document sets out the rights of the lender, creates a promissory note between the buyer and the lender, and also gives the lender the right to foreclose on the property in the event of the buyer's default. We discuss deeds of trust and mortgages in greater detail in Chapter 9.

Mortgages and deeds of trust set out the rights of the lender.

ISSUE AT A GLANCE

D. QUITCLAIM DEED

A quitclaim deed does exactly what its name suggests: It surrenders any rights that the grantor may have in the property. Quitclaim deeds do not make any representations about the nature or quality of the rights that the grantor has; it simply surrenders them to the grantee.

FIGURE 8-13

Quitclaim Deed

2003-120226-0
Recording Dist: 301 - Anchorage
11/17/2003 8:39 AM Pages: 1 of 1

ALASKA

Filed for Record at Request of:
  First American Title of Alaska

AFTER RECORDING MAIL TO:

Name	John H.B. Smith
Address	3670 Richard Evelyn Byrd Street
City, State Zip	Anchorage, AK 99517

Escrow Number: 0310041 25

Statutory Warranty Deed

THE GRANTOR   The Petersen Group, Inc., an Alaska corporation

whose mailing address is: 3820 Lake Otis Parkway #204, Anchorage, AK 99508

for and in consideration of   TEN DOLLARS AND OTHER GOOD AND VALUABLE CONSIDERATION

in hand paid, conveys and warrants to   John H.B. Smith and Barbara A. Smith, husband and wife

the following described real estate, situated in the Recording District of   Anchorage
State of Alaska:

Lot 7, Block 1, BROADMOOR ESTATES WEST ADDN. NO. 1, according to the official plat thereof, filed under Plat Number 73-63, Records of the ANCHORAGE Recording District, THIRD Judicial District, State of ALASKA.

SUBJECT TO reservations, exceptions, easements, covenants, conditions and restrictions of record, if any.

Dated this   14th   day of   November , 2003   .

The Petersen Group, Inc.

BY:
Robert C. Petersen, President

FIGURE 8-14

Deed Checklist

- What type of deed is it?
- Who are the parties to the transaction?
- What is the complete, legal name of the grantor?
- Is the grantee clearly identifiable?
- Does the deed contain habendum and granting clauses?
- Is the deed signed by the grantor(s)?
- If the deed is a warranty deed, does it contain the appropriate covenants?
- Covenant of seizin?
- Covenant of quiet enjoyment?
- Covenant against encumbrances?
- Covenant of further assurance?
- Covenant of warranty forever?
- Has the deed been notarized?
- Has it been acknowledged?
- Does the deed contain the appropriate words of conveyance?
- Is this a standard deed form, such as one approved by the state bar, or did the parties develop it?

IV RECORDING STATUTES

Recording statutes were an invention of early American law. England, the source of most of our laws, had no recording statutes that set priorities. There, the rule was simple: Whoever filed first had priority over anyone else. However, various states in the United States have created several different models for recording title to land and the consequences of that recording. There are three general approaches:

1 Notice
2 Race-notice
3 Race

A. NOTICE RECORDING STATUTES

Under a pure notice system, a party who has given notice of a claim, but who has not yet filed it, will receive priority over others who have filed.

B. RACE-NOTICE RECORDING STATUTES

Race-notice statutes, on the other hand, allow the first person to record a claim that does not have notice of pending claims to receive the highest priority.

C. RACE RECORDING STATUTES

Pure race statutes allow a party to have a superior claim if she is the first to record, whether or not the party has notice of any other outstanding, but unfiled, claims. Only three states follow a pure race system for recording claims.

GENERAL WARRANTY DEED  **ANNOTATED DOCUMENT**

<u>WARRANTY DEED</u>

Identifies grantor and grantee

KNOW ALL MEN BY THESE PRESENTS, that CAROLYN DRAPER MCCALL, an unmarried woman, hereinafter called the "Grantor", for and in consideration of the sum of TEN AND NO/100THS ($10.00) DOLLARS in cash and other good and valuable consideration, in hand paid to the Grantor by BILLY L. JOHNSTON, JR. and DIANE B. JOHNSTON, hereinafter called the "Grantees", the receipt and sufficiency of which is hereby acknowledged, subject to all matters and things hereinafter set forth, has this day bargained and sold and by these presents does hereby GRANT, BARGAIN, SELL AND CONVEY unto the said Grantees, for and during their joint lives, and upon the death of either of them, then to the survivor of them, in fee simple, together with every contingent remainder and right of reversion, all that real property situated in the County of Baldwin, State of Alabama, described as follows, to-wit:

Describes property

Lot 32, First Addition to Cooper's Landing Subdivision, according to the map or plat thereof recorded in Map Book 4, page 95 in the records in the Office of the Judge of Probate of Baldwin County, Alabama.

LESS AND EXCEPT such oil, gas, and other mineral interests and all rights and privileges in connection therewith as may have been reserved or conveyed by prior owners, if any.

THIS CONVEYANCE IS MADE SUBJECT TO THE FOLLOWING:

1. Oil, gas and mineral lease, and all rights in connection therewith, by Vanway V. McRaven to Shell Oil Company, dated January 7, 1981 and recorded in Real Property Book 86, page 276.

2. Rights of other parties, the United States of America or State of Alabama in and to the shore, littoral or riparian rights to the property described above lying adjacent to unnamed canal.

TOGETHER WITH ALL AND SINGULAR, the rights, members, privileges and appurtenances thereunto belonging, or in anywise appertaining.

Habendum clause

TO HAVE AND TO HOLD the said above described property unto the said Grantees during the term of their joint lives, and upon the death of either of them, then to the survivor of them, in fee simple, and to the heirs and assigns of such survivor, forever, together with every contingent remainder and right of reversion.

Exceptions

And except as to taxes hereafter falling due which are assumed by the Grantees, and except as to the above mentioned encumbrances, the Grantor does, for herself and her heirs and assigns, hereby covenant with the Grantees that she is seized of an indefeasible estate in fee simple in said property, is in peaceable possession thereof, that said property is free and clear of all encumbrances, and that she does hereby WARRANT AND WILL FOREVER DEFEND the title to said property and the peaceable possession thereof, unto the Grantees, and to the survivor of them, and to the heirs and assigns of such survivor, against the lawful claims of all persons whomsoever.

Carolyn Draper McCall
CAROLYN DRAPER MCCALL

STATE OF _Alabama_

COUNTY OF _Baldwin_

I, _Cleveland L. Landreth_, the undersigned
authority, a Notary Public in and for said County in said State,
hereby certify that CAROLYN DRAPER MCCALL, whose name is signed
to the foregoing conveyance and who is known to me, acknowledged
before me on this day, that being informed of the contents of
said conveyance, she has executed the same voluntarily on the day
the same bears date.

Given under my hand and seal this the _10th_ day of
April, 1995.

Cleveland L. Landreth
Notary Public

My Commission Expires:
My Commission Expires
April 14, 1997

This Instrument Prepared by:

G. DAVID CHAPMAN III, P.C.
Attorney at Law
Post Office Box 1508
Gulf Shores, Alabama   36547
File 95.2373

Grantor's Address:

P.O. Box 207
Bon Secour, AL 36511

Grantees' Address:

375 Rock Products Road
Heber Springs, AR 72543

dgg21;2373.wd

Notary public provision →

REAL 0823 PAGE 1043

◆ **ETHICS**   ## USE OF FORMS

With the subject of deeds, there is always a question about the use of preprinted forms. There are some companies that sell preprinted deed forms that they claim are perfectly valid in all areas of the country. However, before using such a form, you should review it carefully to make sure that it conforms to your state's rules about deeds. A deed form that is sufficient for California may not be sufficient in New York. This can raise an ethical problem because attorneys who rely on faulty preprinted forms can open themselves up to a legal malpractice claim. Some states have preprinted forms that have been approved by the state bar. You can generally rely on these forms without any further research, but you should still be on guard whenever you use any preprinted forms. The Internet has only made this problem worse. You can find a wealth of "legal forms," including deed forms, on the Web. A form downloaded from the Internet is not guaranteed to meet your state's legal requirements.

ESTATE OF DYKES v. ESTATE OF WILLIAMS

CASE EXCERPT

ESTATE OF DYKES v. ESTATE OF WILLIAMS
864 So. 2d 926 (Miss. 2003)

McRae, Presiding Justice, for the Court.

The Estate of Johnnie Eloise Hodges Dykes filed an action in the Chancery Court of Amite County to set aside a deed that Dykes had . . . executed to her grandson, Michael A. Williams. A trial was held before the chancellor, who refused to set aside the deed and ruled in favor of the defendant, Kathryn F. Tonguis, former wife of the now deceased Michael A. Williams. Dykes's estate appeals the decision of the chancellor and argues that the chancellor erred because (1) the deed was never delivered; (2) the deed was not properly executed, notarized, and acknowledged; (3) no consideration was paid by the grantee; (4) no power of attorney existed to properly convey the land; and (5) an agent acting under power of attorney cannot make a gift when the instrument conferring power of attorney does not authorize such. We affirm.

FACTS

In February of 1982, Johnnie E. Hodges Dykes ("Johnnie") and her husband, Milford L. Dykes, executed a deed to their grandson, Michael A. Williams ("Michael"), conveying to him the family's 80-acre hunting camp near Liberty, Mississippi, while reserving a life estate in the same property for themselves. The deed was filed in the land records of Amite County, Mississippi, that June. Michael, who was 18 at the time of the conveyance, paid nothing in exchange and never even knew of the conveyance. However, the deed did state that the grantor received "ten dollars ($10.00), cash in hand paid, and other good and valuable consideration, the receipt of which is hereby acknowledged." In October of 1993, Michael and his mother, Ginger Dykes Williams ("Ginger"), executed a quitclaim deed conveying the 80 acres back to Johnnie (Milford had previously died). The deed was filed for record that November and indicated that Michael and Ginger maintained the same address in Pensacola, Florida, while Johnnie maintained residence in Mississippi.

In June of 1995, Ginger executed a quitclaim deed conveying the 80 acres back to Michael.[1] While the deed bore the name Johnnie Hodges Dykes as the grantor, it was signed "Johnnie Hodges Dykes by Ginger D. Williams, Power of Attorney." The notary public in this instance, Michelle Musselwhite ("Michelle"), typed the following at the end of the acknowledgment: "Ginger D. Williams appeared for Johnnie E. Hodges Dykes by Power of Attorney." The deed was executed in Escambia County, Florida, on June 1, 1995, and was filed in the Amite County land records on June 5, 1995. Ginger continued to pay the taxes on the land until 1999.

---

[1] This was done in an attempt to prevent the land from being taken to reimburse Medicaid expenses upon Johnnie's death.

Sometime after the June 1, 1995, execution of the deed, Johnnie passed away. On March 18, 1999, Michael married Kathryn (now Kathryn Tonguis, hereinafter "Kathryn"). Roughly four months later, Michael died. Shortly thereafter, Kathryn took over ownership and began paying taxes on the land.

On February 17, 2000, Ginger,[2] as executrix of Johnnie's estate ("the Estate"), filed a complaint against the Estate of Michael A. Williams in the Chancery Court of Amite County to cancel the 1995 deed. However, all responsive pleadings were filed by Kathryn. By agreement, Kathryn was later substituted as party defendant and waived any and all procedural errors.

At trial, the Estate sought to have the deed set aside as invalid on the grounds that (1) there was no consideration; (2) the deed was never delivered; (3) Dykes did not have the mental capacity to make a gift at the time of the deed's execution; (4) no valid power of attorney existed at the time of the deed's execution for Ginger to have properly conveyed the land; and (5) the alleged power of attorney was not recorded. On May 13, 2002, the chancellor found for Kathryn on all issues. The Estate subsequently filed its notice of appeal on June 11, 2002, after which, the case was assigned to this Court. While the Estate renews the argument that there was no valid power of attorney to effectuate the deed and the argument that the deed, itself, was invalid, we affirm the decision of the trial court that the land properly belongs to Kathryn.

STANDARD OF REVIEW

This Court will not disturb the factual findings of a chancellor unless such findings are manifestly wrong or clearly erroneous. If there is substantial evidence to support the chancellor's findings of fact, those findings must be affirmed.

DISCUSSION

I. Whether a purported deed is void ab initio when it is not delivered by the Grantor to the Grantee during the lifetime of the Grantor?

For a deed to be valid in Mississippi, the grantor must deliver it to the grantee. To show that the delivery, itself, is valid, there must be (1) "a complete and unequivocal delivery of the deed" and (2) "an actual intent by the grantor to deliver the deed," shown by the words and acts of the grantor and the context of the transaction. However, the recording of a deed creates the rebuttable presumption that it was delivered.

In (a previous case), this Court noted that where grantors retain control and possession of a deed until death, without any indication of any intent to deliver the deed, the deed is void for non-delivery. There, a woman was found not to have delivered deeds to her children where the children not only denied ever accepting the deeds, but the deeds were found in the woman's purse at the time of her death.

A somewhat similar situation occurred in Grubbs v. Everett, 236 Miss. 698, 111 So. 2d 923, 924 (1959). There, this Court affirmed the ruling of the chancellor, that there was no delivery where the purported deeds in question were found in the trunk of the

---

[2] Ginger is now Johnnie's only surviving heir and would inherit the property if the Estate's claim were successful.

deceased after his death and there was no evidence of his intention to have the deeds delivered until after his death.

In the case at bar, the record is clear that the deed in question was executed in Pensacola, Florida, on June 1, 1995, and then recorded in Liberty, Mississippi on June 5, 1995. Therefore, the rebuttable presumption has been raised that there was a valid delivery of the deed to the son.

The Estate argues that Ginger's testimony successfully defeated this presumption. Ginger stated "I did not record that deed. I did not. And if I need to take a lie detector test to swear — I don't know how it got recorded. I did not record it." The Estate claims that, since Kathryn failed to present any witness to rebut that testimony, Ginger's testimony was uncontroverted and should have carried the day.

However, the chancellor found that Ginger's testimony, itself, provided enough contradiction and, thus, Kathryn's assistance was unnecessary. Because it was Ginger's word versus the evidence, the chancellor was required to make a determination as to her credibility, which is well within his authority.

The chancellor took note of the inconsistencies between Ginger's testimony and claims at trial compared to the actions that the evidence clearly showed that she took. It was also apparent to the chancellor that the Estate's witnesses were not free of bias, and he found it notable that Ginger never challenged the validity of the deed during the four years between the execution and recording of the deed and her son's death.

Again, because the deed was recorded, the presumption of delivery was raised, and the burden was placed on the Estate to rebut. However, despite the Estate's contention that Ginger brought forth uncontroverted evidence that there was no delivery, it is clear that the chancellor considered such evidence and Ginger's credibility and found them both wanting. Considering the deference given to a chancellor's finding of fact, we affirm the chancellor's finding that the deed was delivered.

II. Whether a purported deed is patently void when it is not properly executed, notarized, and acknowledged according to Mississippi Code Sections 87-3-3, 89-3-1, and 89-3-7(f)?

An acknowledgment is simply a formal statement, made by the person executing a deed to an official who is authorized to take the acknowledgment, that the execution of the deed was of that person's own free will and accord. Not only must deeds be properly acknowledged before they may be recorded, but if the acknowledgment is for a conveyance of land by an attorney in execution of letters of attorney, the acknowledgment must reflect the representative capacity in which the signatory is acting. The Legislature has even provided a form for acknowledgments dealing with real property. Miss. Code Ann. § 89-3-7(f) (Supp. 2003). However, Mississippi gives a liberal interpretation to acknowledgments whereby an acknowledgment will not be held "fatal" for an omission that can be filled in from the body of the deed itself.

In *White*, this Court found an acknowledgment in an instrument defective because it was ambiguous and unclear. There, the instrument was so ambiguous that it was not clear which of two possible corporations was executing the instrument. Therefore, the acknowledgment was defective and the instrument void.

In the case at hand, the Estate claims that the acknowledgment was defective not only for failing to strictly follow the form provided by statute, but also because Ginger did not write the acknowledgment on her own accord, but at the instruction of the notary. However, the chancellor found that Ginger signed the acknowledgment of her own free will. Additionally, the Estate fails to cite any authority that an acknowledgment is fatally defective for not precisely adhering to form.

Notwithstanding the failure to strictly follow form, the acknowledgment contains all the necessary information and, therefore, should not be held fatal pursuant to *White*. Furthermore, it is clear from the deed that Ginger was acting on behalf of Johnnie, the grantor, and, thus, there was no ambiguity. In addition, we are guided by the chancellor's determination that Ginger signed the acknowledgment of her own free will and not at the command of Michelle, the notary. Because the chancellor was not manifestly wrong, we affirm the chancellor's finding as to this issue.

III. Whether a purported deed is void ab initio when no consideration is paid to the Grantor by the Grantee?

Offering a deed as a gift is a "perfectly respectable mode of conveyance." Furthermore, one may execute a deed for any reason seen fit, such as "love, affection, gratitude, partiality, prejudice, or even a whim or caprice." As to this issue, the only legal theory provided by the Estate is an uncited sentence that merely states that a deed is a form of a contract, followed by a citation to the rule of contract requirements. We find this issue without merit and uphold the ruling of the chancellor.

IV. Whether a purported deed is void ab initio when signed by a purported agent, where no power of attorney exists?

"Where a conveyance by an attorney is in execution of letters of attorney, so acknowledged or proved and recorded, it shall pass the interest of the principal though not formally executed in his name." Miss. Code Ann. § 87-3-3 (1999). Before one operating through letters of attorney may execute and deliver a valid deed "prior in right to the interests of (a) subsequent purchasers for value and without notice or (b) subsequent judgment lien creditors, the written power of attorney must be acknowledged and recorded in conformity with the requirements generally applicable to instruments of conveyance of interests in land." However "it is one of the oldest maxims of the law that no man shall, in a court of justice, take an advantage which has his own wrong as a foundation for that advantage." To employ this maxim, the conduct need not be of such a nature as to be criminal or justify any legal proceedings, but there must simply be a "wilful act concerning the cause of action which can be said to transgress equitable standards of conduct." In *Kountouris*, a man granted his son-in-law powers of attorney. The son-in-law consequently deeded a parcel of the father's land back in Greece to his wife, the man's daughter. Upon the father's death, it was noted that the father had actually devised the property to his son. One of the major grounds upon which this Court nullified the transaction was that the son-in-law had failed to record the letters of attorney as required by § 87-3-3.

The Estate argues that *Kountouris* mirrors the case at hand and, thus, the conveyance to Michael should be void because Ginger failed to record the letters of attorney. On the other hand, Kathryn contends that, as the chancellor held, to allow Ginger to discredit actions that she took flies in the face of the equity power with which the chancellor is vested.

It is plainly apparent that, since the letters of attorney were never recorded, . . . that § 87-3-3 was not satisfied and . . . Ginger did not have the ability to "pass the interest of the principal." While *Kountouris* appears to limit § 87-3-3 to a situation not found here, the language of the statute is simple and clearly stated. Therefore, Kathryn is not saved from Ginger's failure to record simply because this transaction does not involve a third party.

However, as the chancellor pointed out, to allow Ginger to benefit from her behavior "flies in the face" of equity. Not only is Ginger (as executrix of the Estate) trying to discredit her own actions, the entire conveyance was performed to ensure that the government did not take the land as part of any Medicaid reimbursement that might be required of the Estate.

While the chancellor erred in his analysis of § 87-3-3, he was correct as to his analysis of the impact of equitable principles on this case, and we affirm the ruling of the chancellor as to this issue.

Ensuring that the land would go to Michael untouched by Medicaid protected the wishes and best interests of Johnnie. Therefore, it cannot be said that the chancellor committed manifest error by finding that Ginger was not acting against the best interests of Johnnie nor outside her scope of authority. We affirm the ruling of the chancellor.

Conclusion

The Estate has failed to show manifest error in any of the factual findings made by the chancellor. Furthermore, while the chancellor may have incorrectly analyzed the law in regards to recording letters of attorney, principles of equity still apply and prevent any relief to the Estate. Because the Estate has failed to invalidate either Ginger's power of attorney or the deed itself, we find that the property properly belongs to Kathryn Tonguis and affirm the judgment of the chancellor.

AFFIRMED.

CASE QUESTIONS

1   What legal grounds did Dykes's estate raise to challenge the deed in this case?
2   According to the court, what must a litigant prove to show proper delivery of a deed?
3   Why did the chancellor find Ginger's testimony unconvincing?
4   Why is recordation so important to the issue of delivery?
5   Was the acknowledgment in the deed proper?

SKILLS YOU NEED IN THE REAL WORLD

LOCATING DEEDS IN THE PUBLIC RECORDS

One of the most fundamental skills that you need in real estate practice is the ability to locate specific deeds quickly. No matter how deeds are organized in your state, whether on a tract index or by grantor's names, you should take the time to master locating deeds. The first step is to visit your local courthouse to see where the deeds are stored. In some states, there is a separate office referred to as the registrar of deeds office, while in other states it is referred to as the land office or the deed room. Whatever the name, the function remains the same. This office is primarily responsible for housing all real estate records. When people come in to transfer title to real estate, they do so in this office. You should learn how the deeds are indexed. In some rural areas, deed information is still maintained by handwritten entries in a deed index. In those offices, researching deeds can be a time-consuming process. Fortunately, most deed rooms are now computerized and have as much as the last ten years' real estate transactions available in a computer database. Computer databases allow you to cross-reference grantor's or grantee's names in order to locate deeds.

In addition to the deed room, you should also visit the local tax office. The tax office is responsible for keeping track of real property tax payments and it usually has up-to-date records about not only a particular parcel, but also the most current deed references where this parcel was bought or sold. Investing a few hours now learning your local system will pay big dividends in the future.

CHAPTER SUMMARY

Deeds have basic, legal requirements. For instance, they must be in writing in order to satisfy the Statute of Frauds. They must also be signed by the grantor and have clearly identifiable parties. Deeds must also contain an adequate property description, often in the form of a metes and bounds description or reference to a government survey.

There are several different types of deeds. General warranty deeds contain numerous warranties from the grantor to the grantee, such as the assurance that the grantor is in legal possession of the property (seizin) and that there are no encumbrances against the title. A quitclaim deed, on the other hand, is a deed by the grantor to the grantee where the grantor surrenders any rights that she may have to the real estate with no promises or warranties of any kind.

REVIEW QUESTIONS

1 List and explain at least five minimum requirements that any deed should have.
2 Who is required to sign a deed and why?
3 Is the grantee required to sign the deed? Explain your answer.
4 What constitutes a valid legal description of the property conveyed in a deed?
5 What is a habendum clause and what purpose does it serve?
6 What is the difference between a habendum clause and a granting clause?
7 Provide an example of "words of conveyance" that should be found in a deed.

8 What is the significance of delivery and acceptance of a deed?

9 Compare and contrast attestation and acknowledgment.

10 What is a seal?

11 Is consideration required in a deed? Explain your answer.

12 What is the covenant of seizin?

13 What is the covenant against encumbrances?

14 What is the covenant of warranty forever?

15 What is the difference between a special warranty deed and a general warranty deed?

16 What are deeds of trust?

17 What function does a quitclaim deed serve?

18 Under what circumstances would a quitclaim deed be used?

19 Why would a buyer prefer a general warranty deed to a quitclaim deed?

20 Describe the three statutory approaches to recording title.

DISCUSSION QUESTIONS

Explain the court's reasoning in this chapter's case excerpt.

PRACTICAL APPLICATIONS

Locate a deed from your state and then answer the following questions:

What language does the deed have concerning consideration?
Does the deed contain a covenant of seizin?
Does the deed make reference to "quiet enjoyment"?
What language in the deed qualifies as a "granting" clause?

WEB SITES

Deed Basics
http://www.saclaw.lib.ca.us/pages/deeds.aspx#basics

Delivery and acceptance of deeds – Lexis-Nexis outline
http://www.lexisnexis.com/lawschool/study/outlines/html/prop/prop23.htm

General warranty deed – Ohio
http://codes.ohio.gov/orc/5302.05

Special warranty deed – New Mexico
http://www.emnrd.state.nm.us/mmd/marp/Documents/AlamoHueco3.pdf

Deeds of trust – Legal Information Institute
http://www.law.cornell.edu/wex/deed_of_trust

Quitclaim deed – California
http://www.lawlibrary.co.riverside.ca.us/quitclaimdeed2.pdf

TERMS AND PHRASES

Acknowledgment	Grantor	Habendum clause
Attestation	Grantee	Seizin
Deed	Granting clause	

SIGNIFICANT CASES

Midfirst Bank v. Abney, 850 N.E.2d 373 (Ill. App.2. Dist., 2006)
Stewman Ranch, Inc. v. Double M. Ranch, Ltd., 192 S.W.3d 808 (Tex. App., 2006)
— *Orud v. Groth,* 652 N.W.2d 447 (Iowa, 2002)
Martin v. Martin, 720 N.W.2d 732 (Iowa, 2006)
Young v. Young, 78 Conn.App. 394 (Conn. App., 2003)
Field v. Mednikow, 631 S.E.2d 395 (Ga. App., 2006)
In re Conservatorship of McGowen, 752 So.2d 1078 (Miss. App., 1999)

Mortgages and Financing the Purchase of Real Estate

⑨

Focus of This Chapter

Mortgages are the lifeblood of real estate sales. This chapter examines mortgages (deeds of trust) in great detail, concentrating not only on the basic legal requirements of a mortgage, but also on the clauses commonly found in mortgages.

Chapter Learning Objectives

After completing this chapter, you should be able to:

■ Describe the important role played by mortgage lenders in the real estate market
■ Define the purpose of the secondary mortgage market
■ List and explain the function of corporations such as Fannie Mae, Ginnie Mae, and Freddie Mac
■ Explain the common clauses and provisions found in mortgages and deeds of trust
■ Describe the various types of mortgages available to fund the purchase of real property

INTRODUCTION

Purchasing a home is the single largest investment that most people will ever make in their lives. Because few people are able to purchase a home for cash, financing the purchase is the only way to own a home. The method used to finance the purchase of real estate is the **mortgage** (also called a deed of trust). Whatever the name, the arrangement is essentially the same: The borrower transfers some rights to the lender in exchange for the money to purchase the property. The borrower not only transfers important rights, such as the right to foreclose, but also makes additional promises, such as to make monthly mortgage payments, pay real estate taxes, and maintain appropriate insurance on the premises. In this chapter we examine the ways that mortgages are created, the rights and duties imposed by

Mortgage
A contractual agreement in which a borrower transfers specific real property rights to a lender in exchange for the lender's pledge of funds to purchase the real estate.

217

the arrangement, the different types of mortgages available, and the consequences when a borrower defaults on a mortgage.

In some ways, financing the purchase of real estate resembles financing the purchase of any expensive item. When individuals purchase a new car, for instance, the purchaser borrows money from a lender to provide the funds. There is a temptation to assume that real estate financing is similar to other types of financing. Actually, real estate financing is quite different. When a person finances a car purchase, for example, the lender retains title to the automobile until the last payment is made. When a person buys a home, however, he will receive the title at the closing. The lender does not own the property. Instead, the lender receives a specific set of rights and holds those rights until the mortgage is paid off or the house is sold to someone else. Mortgage financing can be a complex issue. We begin by exploring the business of mortgages and then proceed to the features of mortgages.

In some states, a mortgage resembles a lien. If the borrower fails to make payments on the loan, the lien gives the lender the right to bring a foreclosure action to pay off the outstanding indebtedness. Mortgage lending is regulated on both the state and federal level. Many states regulate not only how mortgages can be made, but also their basic contents. Consider Figure 9-1.

FIGURE 9-1	
Mortgage Statute (Ohio)*	A mortgage in substance following the form set forth in this section, when duly executed in accordance with Chapter 5301 of the Revised Code, has the force and effect of a mortgage to the use of the mortgagee and the mortgagee's heirs, assigns, and successors, with mortgage covenants and upon the statutory condition, as defined in sections 5302.13 and 5302.14 of the Revised Code, to secure the payment of the money or the performance of any obligation specified in the mortgage. The parties may insert in the mortgage any other lawful agreement or condition.

MORTGAGE

_____, _____ (marital status), of _____ (current mailing address), for _____ Dollars paid, grant(s), with mortgage covenants, to _____, of _____ (current mailing address), the following real property:

(Description of land or interest in land and encumbrances, reservations, and exceptions, if any.)

(A reference to the last recorded instrument through which the mortgagor claims title. The omission of the reference shall not affect the validity of the mortgage.)

This mortgage is given, upon the statutory condition, to secure the payment of _____ dollars with interest as provided in a note of the same date.

"Statutory condition" is defined in section 5302.14 of the Revised Code and provides generally that, if the mortgagor pays the principal and interest secured by this mortgage, performs the other obligations secured by this mortgage and the conditions of any prior mortgage, pays all the taxes and assessments, maintains insurance against |

* Ohio Rev. Code Ann. § 5302.12.

fire and other hazards, and does not commit or suffer waste, then this mortgage shall be void.

_____, wife (husband) of the mortgagor, releases to the mortgagee all rights of dower in the described real property.

Executed this _____ day of _____.

_____

(Signature of Mortgagor)

 MORTGAGE MARKETS

When we discuss mortgage markets we are referring to lending institutions, banks, savings and loans, and a myriad of other organizations that make some or all of their income from lending money to others. The mortgage market has two levels: the primary mortgage market, consisting of lenders and borrowers, and a secondary mortgage market, consisting of governmental agencies and others who are in the business of purchasing mortgages from lenders.

A. PRIMARY MORTGAGE MARKET

When we think of the process of acquiring a mortgage to buy a house, we are focused exclusively on the primary mortgage market. Banks and other lending institutions are in the business of loaning money. They earn interest on the money that they loan out to others. Essentially, a mortgage is a simple proposition: The lender gives the borrower money that the borrower can then use to purchase something. In exchange for lending the money, the borrower gives the lender certain rights and pledges the item as collateral for the loan. When the loan arrangement concerns personal property, these rights include the power to repossess the collateral if the borrower defaults. When the loan concerns real property, the lender does not have the right to repossess, but does have an equally powerful tool: the right to foreclose.

Loaning money to individuals is both risky and lucrative. If the individual makes regular monthly payments, the interest that the bank earns can be used to finance other ventures. On the other hand, if the individual defaults on the loan the bank may be forced to go through a long and costly process of foreclosing on property that may not be worth the amount owed on the loan. As a result, all lenders screen potential borrowers and attempt to reduce the risk of loan defaults.

Tech Topic
SOCIAL MEDIA MONITORING

Real estate lenders have greatly increased the scrutiny with which they evaluate mortgage applications. Partly fueled by the mortgage scandal of 2008 and partly by changing times, lenders now use a peculiar combination of techniques to determine the fiscal soundness of borrowers.

The most obvious factors — where you live and work, your income, and how you use credit — are still of primary importance. But lenders also now check to see if a borrower's name is on any government terrorist list. Furthermore, they do not check this information only one time; they check it again before closing to see if anything has changed.

Yet another evaluation tool that lenders use is social media. Lenders routinely scour Facebook, Twitter,

LinkedIn, and other social media sites to look for discrepancies between what they find there and information contained on a borrower's application. Exchanges between friends, status updates, and even photos are analyzed to give financial organizations greater accuracy in creating a credit profile. For example, a borrower who has a high credit score but who posts a Facebook status update that he is looking for a new job raises a red flag.

Lenders generally deny that they make loan decisions based on what they discover on social media web sites because they run the risk of violating the Fair Credit Reporting Act. Nevertheless, many industry insiders claim that it does happen and is happening with increased frequency.

In an oversimplified version, a bank earns profits by taking in deposits from investors. Suppose, for example, that First Bank pays a rate of 1 percent on all deposit accounts. It then takes the money from those accounts and lends it out to borrowers at 5 percent. The difference between what the bank pays out and what it earns is the bank's profit.

If we examine the basic financial model in the previous paragraph, we will see an obvious flaw in the system. If First Bank takes in deposits and then lends those funds out to borrowers, the bank will soon run out of funds. After all, it only has so much money on hand from savings accounts and when those funds are exhausted the bank is unable to lend any additional money. This leads us to the world of the secondary mortgage market.

ISSUE AT A GLANCE

The primary mortgage market is where lenders and borrowers arrange financing for home purchases.

B. SECONDARY MORTGAGE MARKET

In 1929, the United States, like many other countries, experienced a financial catastrophe. Although there were many causes for the Great Crash, one of the most important involved the simple paradigm of home mortgages. As the previous section suggested, when a bank loans all its funds, it can neither make new mortgage arrangements nor pay passbook accounts if there should be a sudden run on the bank. In 1929, with the economy going downhill very quickly, many banks found themselves faced with hundreds of customers demanding the balance of their accounts, sometimes all on the same day. When the banks couldn't pay out that money, primarily because it had been loaned to others, they failed. Individuals lost their life savings and a financial downturn became a full-blown panic as passbook savers across the country rushed to their banks to redeem their savings before that money disappeared as well. This run on banks had a series of consequences: banks failed, businesses closed, individuals were unable to make their mortgage payments, and banks foreclosed. The United States teetered on the brink of total financial collapse.

The road out of the Great Depression was long and bumpy. President Franklin D. Roosevelt proposed a series of reforms to avoid a similar catastrophe in the future. One of the most far-reaching, at least in terms of real estate, was the creation of governmental agencies that would purchase mortgages from banks.

The idea of a secondary mortgage market was elegantly simple: The federal government would purchase mortgages from banks, giving them additional funds that they could use to repay passbook accounts or loan to other borrowers. Each mortgage arranged by the bank would be bought up by a governmental agency, creating a cycle whereby banks would never have all their money tied up in outstanding loans. The federal government also shored up confidence in passbook accounts by creating the Federal Deposit Insurance Corporation, which guaranteed payment on accounts in member banks.

ABC Bank has a pool of $1 million in funds available to disburse to mortgage borrowers. If it makes ten mortgages, each at $100,000, ABC Bank will have used all its available funds. Without some arrangement to obtain new funding, ABC Bank cannot arrange any new mortgages.

EXAMPLE 9-1

The secondary mortgage market consists of federal agencies that purchase mortgages from primary lenders.

ISSUE AT A GLANCE

1. FEDERAL AGENCIES IN THE SECONDARY MORTGAGE MARKET

In 1934, the Great Depression still had a stranglehold on the U.S. economy, but there were some bright spots. For instance, Congress had passed the national Housing Act that authorized the creation of governmental agencies whose sole purpose was to improve the mortgage market. The first of these agencies was the Federal National Mortgage Association, FNMA, created in 1938. Quickly nicknamed "Fannie Mae," this agency began buying up mortgages. The procedure was simple: Banks would approach Fannie Mae and offer to sell it mortgages that the bank had recently negotiated. Fannie Mae would purchase these mortgages and administer them for the life of the loan.

In a somewhat simplified version, suppose that First Bank has negotiated a mortgage for $50,000, at 4 percent for 30 years. If the bank were to hold that loan for the full 30 years, it would receive something on the order of $120,000 with interest payments on the original $50,000 factored in. However, the bank would have to wait the full 30 years to receive that amount. On the other hand, if First Bank sold the mortgage to Fannie Mae for $80,000, it would have the immediate benefit of extra cash that it could loan out to others. Fannie Mae would then receive the mortgage payments and would be responsible for the mortgage from that point on. The borrower might not even be aware of, or care, that Fannie Mae now owned the mortgage. In fact, the bank might continue to receive the monthly mortgage payments, charge a minimal fee to Fannie Mae for the administrative costs, and then forward the mortgage payment.

a. Fannie Mae

Fannie Mae had an enormous impact on the mortgage market. Because banks were anxious to sell mortgages to Fannie Mae, they followed its policies in regard to risk analysis, forms, and procedures. This created, over time, a uniform system across the United States. Almost incidentally, Fannie Mae also began to earn huge profits. After all, the agency had purchased mortgages at a discount, and as mortgage payments poured in from across the country, Fannie Mae found itself in the enviable position of having too much money. The more mortgages it purchased, the more money it made. However, these profits generated new problems. The government is not supposed to be a for-profit business. In 1968, Congress severed all ties with Fannie Mae and authorized it to become a private, for-profit business. Fannie Mae's success spawned new governmental agencies, including the Government National Mortgage Association (Ginnie Mae) and Freddie Mac.

In September 2008, both Fannie Mae and Freddie Mac were taken over by the federal government and placed into conservatorship. During this phase, the day-to-day business of both companies was regulated by government officials.

 **ISSUE AT A GLANCE** **Fannie Mae is the largest member of the secondary mortgage market. Recent downturns in the real estate market have called many of its decisions into question.**

Example 9-2

Fannie Mae contacts ABC Bank and inquires about its ten mortgages, each for $100,000. If ABC Bank had kept the loans for their full duration, it would have received $350,000 for each in combined principal and interest payments. Fannie Mae offers to purchase these mortgages from ABC for $275,000 each. ABC Bank agrees and receives $2.75 million for its ten mortgages. It now has new funds to loan to other mortgagors.

b. Ginnie Mae

Like Fannie Mae, the Government National Mortgage Association is a government agency that plays a substantial role in mortgages. It guarantees timely payment of principal and interest on mortgages backed by the Federal Housing Administration or the Department of Veterans' Affairs. Ginnie Mae operates under the authority of the Department of Housing and Urban Development (HUD). Besides administering Ginnie Mae and similar secondary mortgage agencies, HUD also plays a huge role in the housing market through its rules and regulations and its closing settlement form, which we examine in detail in Chapter 13.

c. Freddie Mac

The Federal Home Loan Mortgage Corporation was created in 1970 to provide another vehicle for the purchase of mortgages. A government-sponsored corporation, it is publicly owned and traded. It was designed to purchase single and multi-family mortgages in order to encourage that market. Freddie Mac reviews and approves individual loans. It continues to play an active role in the secondary mortgage market.

d. HUD

Originally authorized in the 1937 U.S. Housing Act, the Department of Housing and Urban Development was raised to a cabinet-level department in 1965. HUD plays an important role in many different phases of real estate financing. For instance, it regulates Fannie Mae and Ginnie Mae and insures mortgage loans to help people buy or refinance their current homes. It also provides borrowers with a list of approved lenders who often help individuals purchase a home with little or no money down.

e. The Role of the Federal Reserve Board

Along with governmental agencies such as Freddie Mac and private corporations such as Fannie Mae, there is another federal agency that plays an important role in the home mortgage market. The Federal Reserve System, usually referred to as the Federal Reserve, is the nation's central bank. Created in 1913, the role of the Federal

> **Sidebar**
>
> *Fannie Mae also runs other programs, such as the Maxwell Awards of Excellence Program, which invests in affordable housing, and the James A. Johnson Community Fellowship Program, which helps affordable housing activists achieve personal and professional goals.*

> **Sidebar**
>
> *Fannie Mae has provided financing for the purchase of over 63 million homes since 1938.*

The benefits provided by the secondary mortgage market are that it:
- Makes capital available to lending institutions
- Permits lenders to originate more loans
- Keeps capital flowing
- Stabilizes the U.S. economy

FIGURE 9-2

The Importance of the Secondary Mortgage Market

Reserve has changed over time. Originally intended to create a stable foundation for the U.S. financial system, the "Fed" now sets the country's monetary policy, regulates the banking industry, and sets short-term interest rates. This last responsibility puts the Fed in an extremely important position as far as home mortgage interest rates are concerned. When the Fed raises short-term interest rates, most lending institutions follow suit. The practical result is that a borrower will pay more money in interest over the life of a loan because the Fed adjusted its rate upward. Of course, the opposite is also true. When the Fed lowers its short-term interest rate, lenders quickly follow. In recent years, the Fed has been credited with softening the economic recession by moving its interest rates to historic lows.

f. Troubled Asset Relief Program

Signed into law by President Bush in 2008, the Troubled Asset Relief Program (TARP) was designed to assist financial institutions in liquidating real estate assets that had lost their value and had begun to drag on the rest of the economy. Under TARP, the U.S. government pledged $700 billion to various lenders to assist them in jump-starting the lending process. Although much of the money lent to financial institutions has been paid back, many Americans see TARP as a failure.

FIGURE 9-3

Summary of Important Federal
Legislation Related to Housing
and Real Estate Financing

- **Federal Home Loan Bank System (1932)**
  This legislation created 12 regional banks and also authorized the creation of the Federal Home Loan Bank Board that provided short-term credit to lending institutions.
- **Home Owners' Loan Corporation (1933)**
  During the Great Depression, it provided refinancing for mortgages across the country.
- **Housing Act of 1934**
  Brought the Federal Housing Administration (FHA) into existence. This governmental agency insured private mortgage loans and helped encourage lending institutions to provide more long-term mortgages to borrowers.
- **Housing Act of 1937**
  Authorized the financing of low-rent housing.
- **Federal National Mortgage Association (FNMA, or "Fannie Mae") (1938)**
  A governmental agency created to provide a secondary market for mortgages.
- **Servicemen's Readjustment Act of 1944 (the GI "Bill of Rights")**
  Created the VA mortgage loan program for veterans.
- **Housing and Urban Development Act of 1968**
  Created the Government National Mortgage Association (GNMA, or "Ginnie Mae"), which took over the duties of the recently privatized Fannie Mae.

Example 9-3

When the Federal Reserve board meets, many lenders closely follow its activities. If the Fed raises interest rates, most lenders follow suit. If the Fed decides to raise interest rates by one-fourth of a percentage point, most lenders will raise their rates by at least the same amount or even more.

2. IMPORTANT FEDERAL LEGISLATION THAT GOVERNS REAL ESTATE FINANCING

There are several federal laws that govern real estate financing. The two most important are the federal Truth in Lending Act and the Real Estate Settlement Procedures Act.

a. Federal Truth in Lending Laws

Enacted in 1968, the Truth in Lending Act (15 U.S.C.A. § 1601) requires that borrowers be given specific types of information so that they can make informed choices about their borrowing options. The Truth in Lending Act was designed to protect consumers by requiring lenders to give specific types of disclosures about the key terms of all types of lending agreements, including mortgages, and to disclose specific facts to borrowers, including the total cost of the credit arrangement and the annual percentage rate. The disclosures are supposed to be made in plain English that a layperson can understand and use as a means to compare one lender's terms to another's.[1]

Federal Truth in Lending laws require that consumers and borrowers receive specific information about mortgages and other loans.

ISSUE AT A GLANCE

b. Real Estate Settlement Procedures Act

Although we discuss the Real Estate Settlement Procedures Act in greater detail in Chapter 13, it is important to point out that RESPA plays an important role when it comes to mortgage financing. For instance, RESPA requires that mortgage borrowers be given specific information about the estimation of charges that they will incur in taking on the mortgage. See Figure 9-5.

---

[1] 15 U.S.C.A. § 1631(a).

FEDERAL TRUTH-IN-LENDING DISCLOSURE STATEMENT
(THIS IS NEITHER A CONTRACT NOR A COMMITMENT TO LEND)

Applicants: Prepared By:

Property Address:

Application No:
Check box if applicable: Date Prepared:

ANNUAL PERCENTAGE RATE	FINANCE CHARGE	Amount Financed	Total of Payments
The cost of your credit as a yearly rate	The dollar amount the credit will cost you	The amount of credit provided to you or on your behalf	The amount you will have paid after making all payments as scheduled
%	$	$	$

☐ REQUIRED DEPOSIT: The annual percentage rate does not take into account your required deposit
PAYMENTS: Your payment schedule will be:

Number of Payments	Amount of Payments **	When Payments Are Due	Number of Payments	Amount of Payments **	When Payments Are Due	Number of Payments	Amount of Payments **	When Payments Are Due

☐ DEMAND FEATURE: This obligation has a demand feature.
☐ VARIABLE RATE FEATURE: This loan contains a variable rate feature. A variable rate disclosure has been provided earlier.

CREDIT LIFE/CREDIT DISABILIY: Credit life insurance and credit disability insurance are not required to obtain credit, and will not be provided unless you sign and agree to pay the additional cost.

Type	Premium	Signature	
Credit Life		I want credit life insurance.	X
Credit Disability		I want credit disability insurance.	X
Credit Life and Disability		I want credit life and disability insurance.	X

INSURANCE: The following insurance is required to obtain credit:
☐ Credit life insurance ☐ Credit disability ☐ Property insurance ☐ Flood insurance
You may obtain the insurance from anyone you want that is acceptable to creditor
☐ If you purchase ☐ property ☐ flood insurance from creditor you will pay $ for a one year term.
SECURITY: You are giving a security interest in:
☐ The goods or property being purchased ☐ Real property you already own.
FILING FEES: $
LATE CHARGE: If a payment is more than   days late, you will be charged   %
PREPAYMENT: If you pay off early, you
☐ may ☐ will not have to pay a penalty.
☐ may ☐ will not be entitled to a refund of part of the finance charge.
ASSUMPTION: Someone buying your property
☐ may ☐ may, subject to conditions ☐ may not assume the remainder of your loan on the original terms.

(c) Estimate of charges

Each lender shall include with the booklet a good faith estimate of the amount or range of charges for specific settlement services the borrower is likely to incur in connection with the settlement as prescribed by the Secretary.

(d) Distribution by lenders to loan applicants at time of receipt or preparation of applications

Each lender referred to in subsection (a) of this section shall provide the booklet described in such subsection to each person from whom it receives or for whom it prepares a written application to borrow money to finance the purchase of residential real estate. Such booklet shall be provided by delivering it or placing it in the mail not later than 3 business days after the lender receives the application, but no booklet need be provided if the lender denies the application for credit before the end of the 3-day period. [2]

(a) Preparation and distribution

The Director of the Bureau of Consumer Financial Protection (hereafter in this section referred to as the "Director") shall prepare, at least once every 5 years, a booklet to help consumers applying for federally related mortgage loans to understand the nature and costs of real estate settlement services. The Director shall prepare the booklet in various languages and cultural styles, as the Director determines to be appropriate, so that the booklet is understandable and accessible to homebuyers of different ethnic and cultural backgrounds. The Director shall distribute such booklets to all lenders that make federally related mortgage loans. The Director shall also distribute to such lenders lists, organized by location, of homeownership counselors certified under section 1701x(e) of this title for use in complying with the requirement under subsection (c) of this section.

(b) Contents

Each booklet shall be in such form and detail as the Director shall prescribe and, in addition to such other information as the Director may provide, shall include in plain and understandable language the following information:

(1) A description and explanation of the nature and purpose of the costs incident to a real estate settlement or a federally related mortgage loan. The description and explanation shall provide general information about the mortgage process as well as specific information concerning, at a minimum—

(A) balloon payments;

(B) prepayment penalties;

(C) the advantages of prepayment; and

(D) the trade-off between closing costs and the interest rate over the life of the loan.

(2) An explanation and sample of the uniform settlement statement required by section 2603 of this title.

(3) A list and explanation of lending practices, including those prohibited by the Truth in Lending Act or other applicable federal law, and of other

---

[2] Real Estate Settlement Procedures Act, 12 U.S.C.A. § 2604.

unfair practices and unreasonable or unnecessary charges to be avoided by the prospective buyer with respect to a real estate settlement.

(4) A list and explanation of questions a consumer obtaining a federally related mortgage loan should ask regarding the loan, including whether the consumer will have the ability to repay the loan, whether the consumer sufficiently shopped for the loan, whether the loan terms include prepayment penalties or balloon payments, and whether the loan will benefit the borrower.

(5) An explanation of the right of rescission as to certain transactions provided by sections 125 and 129 of the Truth in Lending Act.

(6) A brief explanation of the nature of a variable rate mortgage and a reference to the booklet entitled "Consumer Handbook on Adjustable-Rate Mortgages," published by the Director, or to any suitable substitute of such booklet that the Director may subsequently adopt pursuant to such section.

(7) A brief explanation of the nature of a home equity line of credit and a reference to the pamphlet required to be provided under section 127A of the Truth in Lending Act.

(8) Information about homeownership counseling services made available pursuant to section 1701x(a)(4) of this title, a recommendation that the consumer use such services, and notification that a list of certified providers of homeownership counseling in the area, and their contact information, is available.

(9) An explanation of the nature and purpose of escrow accounts when used in connection with loans secured by residential real estate and the requirements under section 2609 of this title regarding such accounts.

(10) An explanation of the choices available to buyers of residential real estate in selecting persons to provide necessary services incidental to a real estate settlement.

(11) An explanation of a consumer's responsibilities, liabilities, and obligations in a mortgage transaction.

(12) An explanation of the nature and purpose of real estate appraisals, including the difference between an appraisal and a home inspection.

(13) Notice that the Office of Housing of the Department of Housing and Urban Development has made publicly available a brochure regarding loan fraud and a World Wide Web address and toll-free telephone number for obtaining the brochure.

THE LEGAL REQUIREMENTS OF A MORTGAGE/DEED OF TRUST

Mortgages share some common features. Regardless of the terms, a borrower (the mortgagor) transfers rights to the lender (the mortgagee) in exchange for money. In this example, there are two parties: the borrower and the bank. However, there is another type of financial arrangement that is popular in many states — the deed of trust.

A. MORTGAGES VERSUS DEEDS OF TRUST

In most situations there is no practical difference between a mortgage and a deed of trust. They are both financial arrangements used to finance the purchase of real estate. However, there are some important differences when you look below the surface. For one thing, deeds of trust involve three parties, while mortgages only involve two. There are also important differences when it comes to issues such as foreclosure.

1. DEEDS OF TRUST

Unlike mortgages, which usually only have two parties, the lender and the borrower, a **deed of trust** has three parties: the lender, the borrower, and the trustee. In this arrangement, the trustee acts as an intermediary between the borrower and the lender. When the deed of trust is created, the borrower transfers rights to the trustee, who holds them for the lender, unlike a mortgage relationship, in which the borrower transfers these rights to the lender. In the event of a default by the borrower, the trustee acts on behalf of the lender to institute foreclosure. The advantage of a deed of trust arrangement is that the process of foreclosure is more streamlined and requires less contact with the legal system than does the foreclosure of a mortgage.

Deed of trust
A type of real estate financing in which a lender and a borrower authorize a third party, the trustee, to act on their behalf in the event of a loan default.

The deed of trust arrangement is only followed in a few states, but it does offer significant advantages over mortgages, at least from the bank's perspective. As we will see later in this chapter, foreclosing a mortgage can be a time- and money-consuming enterprise. Deeds of trust offer distinct advantages when it comes to foreclosing on property. Instead of several months of civil actions, the trustee can begin a foreclosure action as soon as the bank determines that the borrower is in default. The only requirement is a notice of sale and a brief hearing before the local clerk of court.

Sidebar

Deeds of trust are popular in states such as Virginia and North Carolina.

Deeds of trust and mortgages closely resemble each other.

ISSUE AT A GLANCE

B. THE ELEMENTS OF A MORTGAGE

Although there are important differences between mortgages and deeds of trust when it comes to foreclosure, they share many of the same elements when it comes to other aspects. In this next section, we do not make any distinction between mortgages and deeds of trusts when discussing their components. For the sake of clarity, we will use the term "mortgage" here to include deeds of trust.

Whether a financing arrangement is deemed a deed of trust or a mortgage, some basic elements apply to each. These elements include:

- The mortgage must be in writing.
- The parties must be properly identified by name.

- The mortgage must contain specific clauses, such as:
  - ❑ Granting clause
  - ❑ Promissory note
  - ❑ Description of the debt
  - ❑ Power of sale provision
  - ❑ Priority clause
  - ❑ Provisions for taxes and insurance
  - ❑ Estoppel certificate
  - ❑ Acceleration clause
  - ❑ Due on sale clause
  - ❑ Interest escalation clause
  - ❑ Prepayment clause
  - ❑ Attorneys' fees
  - ❑ Subordination agreement

1. MORTGAGES MUST BE IN WRITING

In our discussion on deeds in the last chapter, we pointed out that each state has a version of the Statute of Frauds. This statute requires that certain types of contracts must be in writing before a court will enforce them. As we saw in that chapter, any contract that conveys a real estate interest must be in writing. Because mortgages involve the transfer of rights between the borrower and the lender, the mortgage must be in writing to be enforceable.

Mortgages are often filed with general warranty deeds. The general warranty deed conveys fee simple title to the buyer and the contemporaneous filing of the mortgage assures that no other claim will have priority over the mortgage holder. We discuss the issue of priority in greater detail later in this chapter.

2. THE PARTIES MUST BE IDENTIFIED

Just as we saw in our discussion on deeds, the parties to a mortgage must be identified. The borrower's name must be listed in order to bind him to the agreement and the lender's name must appear in order to substantiate its claim on the collateral.

FIGURE 9-6

Florida Statute Requiring Mortgages to Be in Writing

A debtor may not maintain an action on a credit agreement unless the agreement is in writing, expresses consideration, sets forth the relevant terms and conditions, and is signed by the creditor and the debtor. [3]

---

[3] Fla. Stat. Ann (West's) F.S.A. § 687.0304.

3. SPECIFIC CLAUSES IN MORTGAGES

In addition to the general requirements of writing and identified parties, mortgages have several other clauses that are required in order to make the document binding on all parties. The first of these requirements is that the property must be listed as collateral for the loan.

a. Property as Collateral

Collateral is the security for a loan. When a borrower defaults on a loan, the lender is authorized to seize the collateral in lieu of further payments. Although lenders can routinely repossess personal property posted as collateral for a loan, the situation is more complicated when real property is the loan collateral. In that situation, the lender must institute foreclosure proceedings.

Collateral
Any type of asset that is used to secure a loan.

b. Promissory Note

A **promissory note** is a borrower's agreement to repay a specific amount of money. Promissory notes are seen in a wide variety of loan agreements, and they all have the same elements:

Promissory note
A written document that binds the borrower to pay a specific amount at a specific time.

- The borrower agrees to repay a specific sum.
- The note sets out the terms of the indebtedness.
- The note bears the borrower's signature.

Mortgages should contain specific details about the amount that has been borrowed, including the interest rate, the total amount to be repaid (including interest payments), and the total term of the mortgage.

All mortgages must contain a promissory note, or a promise to pay back a specific amount, before they will be considered legally sufficient.

 ISSUE AT A GLANCE

---

c. Granting Clause

We have already encountered granting clauses in our discussion on deeds. There we saw that a granting clause indicates the parties' intentions to transfer rights. The granting clause in a mortgage serves a similar purpose. Here, it substantiates the borrower's intention of transferring the right to foreclose to the lender in exchange for the money provided for the purchase of the real estate.

d. Description of the Debt

The law is flexible about how the debt is described. The parties are free to negotiate their own terms, and courts will not interfere with their negotiations unless they are clearly insufficient. Although the debt terms can be described somewhat loosely, there must be sufficient specificity to identify the amount borrowed, the collateral for the loan, and the terms of repayment.

e. Power of Sale Provision

The power of sale provision authorizes the lender to begin foreclosure proceedings in the event of loan default. The lender can auction off the property for the total debt owed by the borrower. If this provision is missing, the lender has no right to institute a foreclosure action.

f. Taxes and Insurance

The lender may also require as a condition of the mortgage that the borrower pay all taxes and assessments made on the property. Because property can be auctioned off by the local government for failure to pay real estate taxes, lenders require the borrower to keep all tax payments current. The mortgage also provides the lender with the authority to pay the taxes for the borrower in order to stave off further action and to assess these fees back against the borrower.

In addition to taxes, the borrower must also maintain hazard insurance on the premises. The insurance will pay the balance of the loan in the event that the house is destroyed.

g. Estoppel Certificate

Estoppel certificate
The borrower's acknowledgment of the total amount borrowed in the mortgage.

An **estoppel certificate** is the borrower's certification of the amount that has been borrowed from the lender. This acts as a bar to any claim that the borrower was not aware of the total amount of the loan and also provides additional information about the loan terms.

h. Acceleration Clause

An acceleration clause allows the lender to request payment in full for the entire balance of the loan in the event of the borrower's default. This demand is usually the first step in bringing a foreclosure action. By requesting the entire amount due, the lender is establishing the exact figure owed on the loan. Of course, if the borrower is unable to make regular monthly payments on the loan and has defaulted on the mortgage, it is highly unlikely that he will be able to pay the entire balance of the loan.

i. Due on Sale Clause

A due on sale clause requires payment of the entire loan balance in the event that title to the property shifts to another individual. This provision bars a borrower from transferring title to the premises as a way of avoiding responsibility for the debt, or, more likely, to have someone else take over payments on a mortgage. The due on sale provision requires the payment of the entire loan balance before title can change hands.

j. Interest Escalation Clause

The interest escalation clause allows the lender to increase the amount of interest charges on the loan when it goes into default. The provisions allowing interest escalation must appear in the mortgage and cannot violate other state or federal laws concerning maximum permissible annual percentage rates.

k. Prepayment Clause

The prepayment clause specifies how payments on the loan will be assessed. For instance, if the borrower overpays on his monthly mortgage payment, the prepayment clause may dictate that the overage must be applied to the principal, instead of future interest payments. There are also important federal laws that bear on the issue of prepayment, which we discuss in greater detail in Chapter 13.

l. Attorney's Fees

The attorney's fees provision authorizes the lender to seek reimbursement from the borrower for any legal actions required to foreclose on the loan. These fees can include billing for the attorney's time to institute the foreclosure action and to bring it to a successful conclusion.

C. RECORDING MORTGAGES

In the previous chapter we discussed the role of recording statutes regarding deeds. The same recording statutes also govern mortgages. As a general rule, for a mortgage to have priority over other claims, it must be recorded first. The general rule, "first in time — first in line" applies in almost all scenarios. Under this rule, the first mortgage to file receives the highest level of priority. This means that, in the event of a foreclosure or other judgment, this mortgage will be paid before any others.

1. PRIORITY OF MORTGAGES

Priority is an important issue when dealing with mortgages for a very practical reason: If there is more than one claim on real estate, the claim holder who has the highest priority will be paid first. Only after this claim is paid in full will other claims be paid. Because of this rule, lenders are always eager to file their mortgages contemporaneously with the general warranty deed in the transaction. This gives the lender the highest priority against any other claims that might be brought on the property.

a. Subordination Agreement

There are times when the parties can alter the rules about priority. Suppose, for example, that the parties are in agreement that a mortgage that is subordinate to another mortgage can simply change places. This would give the formerly subordinate mortgage a higher priority. Why would the parties agree to such an action? Consider Example 9-4.

> **Sidebar**
>
> *The rule about priority in mortgages applies in many other contexts as well. In fact, there is an old Latin proverb that sets this rule: prior in tempore, potior in jure (first in time, superior in right).*

Example 9-4

Maria has advertised her house for sale. Her asking price is $125,000. In her advertisement she includes the following language: "owner financing possible." Kendra sees the ad and contacts Maria. Maria presents the following terms: She will "take back"$10,000 as an owner-financed mortgage, as long as Kendra can get the balance of the mortgage from another lender. The advantage of this arrangement is that when Kendra approaches a local bank to seek a mortgage, she will only be requesting to borrow $115,000 on a house that is worth $125,000. This should help Kendra qualify for a mortgage more easily. However, the lender has some concerns, not the least of which is the priority of the mortgages. Because Maria is providing a purchase-money mortgage in the amount of $10,000, her mortgage will take priority over the lender's loan, even though the bank is providing most of the purchase price. The lender insists on a subordination agreement before it will provide the purchase price to Kendra. Maria agrees to subordinate her mortgage to the lender's mortgage and the sale goes through.

IV TYPES OF MORTGAGES

There are many different types of mortgages, with new variations created almost daily. However, we can organize the vast field of mortgages into some basic categories. For instance, mortgages can be classified in one of two ways: fixed-rate and adjustable-rate.

FIGURE 9-7

Benefits of Fixed-Rate Mortgages

- They are inflation-proof: Monthly payments remain the same for the life of the loan, regardless of what happens to interest rates.
- They help with long-term planning: Borrowers can predict exactly what their payments will be and how long it will take to pay off the mortgage.
- They are low risk: The chances of the lender going into bankruptcy are virtually zero, because most lenders are backed by agencies such as FDIC, Fannie Mae, Ginnie Mae, and others.

FIGURE 9-8

Examples of Fixed-Rate Mortgages

- Conventional 30 years fixed
  - ☐ Maximum amount that can be borrowed: $349,999
  - ☐ Rate: 5.875%
- Conventional 20 years fixed with the same amount. Rate: 5.75%
- Conventional 15 years fixed with the same amount. Rate: 5.625%
- Conventional 10 years fixed with the same amount. Rate: 5.625%

A. FIXED-RATE MORTGAGES

Fixed-rate mortgages are the more traditional type of mortgage. In a fixed-rate mortgage, all terms remain the same throughout the loan repayment period. The term of the loan is usually 30 years and the monthly payment and interest rate remain constant over the entire life of the loan. Fixed-rate mortgages are attractive to many borrowers because they are predictable. The borrower will always know exactly what his monthly payment will be and can reference an amortization schedule to see how each monthly payment is apportioned between interest payments and principal reduction.

However, along with the advantages listed in Figure 9.7, there are also some disadvantages to fixed-rate mortgages. Their biggest disadvantage is that if the borrower gets his mortgage when interest rates are high, those rates will remain with the loan, even when interest rates fall for new loans.

Banks and other lenders usually offer incentives for first-time buyers, such as fixed-rate mortgages with financing up to 95 percent of the purchase price. This means that the buyers will only have to come up with 5 percent of the purchase price from their own funds.

1. AMORTIZATION

The month-by-month allocation of a monthly mortgage payment to the interest charges and outstanding principal is called an **amortization** schedule. Amortization refers to the process of balancing out payments on the loan principal with the interest payments on the loan. Amortization can be arranged in any number of ways. For instance, the lender might simply apply 50 percent of each payment to the principal and 50 percent to the interest charge. However, most lenders use a different approach. Instead of balancing each payment over the life of the loan, banks vary the percentage of payment, weighing early payments toward interest and later payments toward principal. Banks realize that most people sell their homes in seven years or less and skewing the payments in this way maximizes the bank's profits. On the other hand, if the borrower continues to make payments on the loan, by the time the halfway point has been reached, a larger proportion of the payment will go toward principal reduction.

Amortization
The gradual paying down and elimination of a debt through an application of payments toward both principal and interest.

When economic times are good and interest rates are low, fixed-rate mortgages are the most popular choice for borrowers.

ISSUE AT A GLANCE

B. ADJUSTABLE-RATE MORTGAGES

Unlike fixed-rate mortgages, adjustable-rate mortgages have one or more of their terms that fluctuate over time. The most common example of an adjustable-rate mortgage is one in which the interest rate fluctuates according to a predetermined

Adjustable-rate mortgages often have interest rates that are lower than the rates available for fixed-rate mortgages.

formula. An adjustable-rate mortgage might be based on any index, but many are based on the national prime lending rate. As this lending rate rises or lowers, so too does the interest rate assessed on the borrower's mortgage. Adjustable-rate mortgages are extremely attractive when the economy is uncertain and the possibility of rapid interest rate changes makes the logic of obtaining a fixed-rate mortgage questionable.

Adjustable-rate mortgages are also good alternatives for individuals whose income may vary over time. If the borrower believes that he will be making more money in the next few years, an adjustable-rate mortgage might make a great deal of sense. After all, if the borrower's salary increases, he can afford higher monthly mortgage payments should the adjustable-rate climb.

There are a wide variety of formats for adjustable-rate mortgages. They usually come in variations such as 3/27, 5/25, and other variations. The first number before the slash refers to the number of years that the rate may adjust before being locked in. Most adjustable-rate mortgages have provisions that allow for adjustable-rates for only a percentage of the total life of the loan. When that point is reached, the adjustable-rate mortgage converts into a fixed-rate mortgage.

The feature that makes adjustable-rate mortgage so attractive can also be a substantial downside. If the index on which the adjustable-rate mortgage is based increases over time, this means that the interest rate charged to the borrower also increases. This will result in either a higher mortgage payment per month, or if the payment is fixed, less money going toward paying off the principal and more going toward paying the interest charges. One way of avoiding dramatic shifts in interest rates over time is through the use of rate caps.

1. RATE CAPS

All adjustable-rate mortgages have rate caps. Sometimes known as "ceilings" or "floors," these are limitations on the degree of change that an adjustable-rate mortgage can undergo in a particular time frame. For instance, an adjustable-rate mortgage might come with a 1 percent cap. This means that during a specified period, the most that the interest rate could change either upward or downward is 1 percent. Many adjustable-rate mortgages also have lifetime caps that limit the total amount that the interest rate could change during the course of the loan. Rate caps help provide some measure of predictability to mortgages that are, by their very nature, variable. A variation of a cap, called a floor, keeps the interest rate from falling below a specific amount during a specified time period. Ceilings, on the other hand, keep interest rates from climbing above a specified amount.

C. OTHER TYPES OF MORTGAGES

In addition to fixed-rate mortgages and adjustable-rate mortgages, there are numerous other types of real estate financing available. They include:

- Balloon mortgages
- Purchase-money mortgages

- Wraparound mortgages
- Second mortgages
- Equity lines of credit

1. BALLOON MORTGAGES

A balloon mortgage is one in which the borrower pays regular monthly payments for a predetermined time period. At the end of that time period, which could be up to seven years, the balance of the loan would become due. The borrower can then either pay the entire balance or refinance the loan to create a new mortgage. The large amount that is due at the end of the seven-year period is the balloon note that must be satisfied. The advantage of balloon mortgages is that they normally have a lower interest rate than other types of mortgages. The disadvantage is obvious: If the borrower is unable to pay the entire amount when due, he will have to arrange a new mortgage. This might be difficult if the borrower's financial condition has worsened or the economy has gone into a downturn.

2. PURCHASE-MONEY MORTGAGES

Purchase-money mortgages are commonly seen in "owner financing." When a seller advertises his house for sale and includes a provision that allows for owner financing, it means that the owner is offering to finance part of the sale. The buyer could then obtain another mortgage for the remaining balance of the sale price. Owners typically offer some percentage of the total sale price under owner financing terms, meaning that the buyer would make two mortgage payments: one to the seller and another to the bank. Here, a purchase-money mortgage literally allows the purchase of the property through an owner-financed mortgage.

Purchase-money mortgages can also come in other forms, such as installment contracts. In this arrangement, the seller retains title to the property until the borrower makes the final payment. When that final payment is made, the seller transfers the title to the borrower.

3. WRAPAROUND MORTGAGES

A wraparound mortgage consists of two mortgages. Suppose that the seller has a mortgage that is a non-qualifying assumable loan with a favorable interest rate. The buyer would like to take over that loan, but the amount owed does not reflect the actual sale price. In this situation, the buyer would obtain another mortgage that would encompass the terms of the first and make up the difference between the original mortgage and the new sale price. The buyer would then make one mortgage payment and this payment would be divided between the two mortgages. For an example of a wraparound mortgage, see Example 9-5.

Example 9-5	Sue purchased her home 15 years ago. She has a 30-year non-qualifying assumable loan at a 1 percent interest rate. Paula wants to buy Sue's home and likes the fact that she can take over the payments on Sue's mortgage. However, Sue currently owes $15,000 on that loan and the sale price of the home is $50,000. Paula can take over the payments on the first loan, but she will still need to come up with an additional $35,000 to meet Sue's price for the property. Paula goes to a bank and obtains a loan for $35,000 and creates a wraparound mortgage that allows her to keep the original loan and make payments on both.

These days, the chances of coming across a non-qualifying assumable loan are very rare. Banks and other lenders have slowly weeded out these loans to avoid the precise circumstance set out in Example 9-5.

4. SECOND MORTGAGES

A second mortgage isn't really a mortgage in the conventional sense. So far, our discussion of mortgages has focused on the initial financing necessary to purchase property. A second mortgage, however, allows the current owner the chance to borrow against the equity that he has built up over time. Suppose that the homeowner has been making regular monthly payments on the property for ten or more years. The homeowner's payments have been steadily reducing the outstanding principal on the loan. But the situation has not remained static. In those ten years, the house may have appreciated in value considerably. In fact, most homes appreciate about 6 percent in value each year. The difference between the value of the home and the amount owed on it is equity.

An owner can borrow against that equity, taking out money to use for additional improvements on the property, college tuition, or any other purpose. The advantage of taking out a second mortgage on a home is that this second mortgage usually enjoys the same advantages as the first mortgage: The homeowner can deduct the amount of interest payments from his personal income tax return. However, the disadvantages apply with the same force. A lender is permitted to foreclose on a second mortgage just as easily as it can foreclose on a first mortgage.

5. EQUITY LINES OF CREDIT

An equity line of credit is a variation on a second mortgage. In this scenario, the owner negotiates a new loan using the accumulated equity in his home as collateral. However, instead of taking out a specific amount, the owner negotiates a possible maximum and then has the option of withdrawing that amount in smaller increments. An equity line of credit can function like a second bank account, acting as a financial reserve that the owner can tap into whenever he has monetary needs. Like any other form of mortgage, an equity line of credit can result in foreclosure if the borrower defaults on the loan.

 **V** **QUALIFYING FOR A MORTGAGE**

When a borrower approaches a bank to obtain financing, there are several important steps that occur. The borrower will fill out an application and part of that application will provide personal information about the borrower that the bank can use to evaluate the risks of lending money to the borrower. The process of evaluating risk is referred to as underwriting.

A. UNDERWRITING

Before any lending institution loans money to a borrower, it must evaluate the risk of the investment. Underwriters are professionals who review a borrower's history, credit rating, current income, and other factors to determine how much of a risk a particular borrower is. If the risk is acceptable, the underwriters approve the loan. If the borrower has a bad credit history or other negative factors, the underwriters will not approve the loan.

1. RISK ASSESSMENT

Underwriting is all about assessing potential risks to the lender. In order to fully evaluate the potential risk of a mortgage loan, the lender must know a great deal about the borrower and the property. Evaluating the borrower centers on reviewing the borrower's credit history. Evaluating the property involves appraisals and inspections.

2. BORROWER'S CREDIT HISTORY

One of the most important elements in underwriting is evaluating the potential risk of foreclosure if the lender enters into a mortgage arrangement with the borrower. One way of evaluating that risk is to review the borrower's credit history. Credit histories are maintained by consumer reporting agencies, such as credit bureaus.

a. Consumer Reporting Agencies

Consumer reporting agencies (CRA) are in the business of compiling information on anyone who might apply for any type of credit. Whenever a person applies for a credit card, a personal loan, or even obtains insurance, a file is created in a CRA database. These companies are in the business of selling this information to merchants so that they can make informed decisions about the people to whom they should extend credit. Consumer reporting agencies fall under the jurisdiction of the Fair Credit Reporting Act.

b. The Fair Credit Reporting Act

The Fair Credit Reporting Act (FCRA) was designed to improve accuracy and privacy of credit reports. It imposes specific responsibilities on consumer credit reporting agencies, such as Equifax and Experian. The act gives consumers the right to know exactly what is in their credit reports. Credit reporting agencies collect enormous amounts of information, including the consumer's name, birth date, Social Security number, places of employment, payment histories, addresses where the consumer has lived in recent years, and a great deal of additional information besides. Credit reports may also contain information from the public record, such as tax liens, judgments, bankruptcies, and foreclosures.

Lenders use information provided by credit bureaus to assess a potential borrower before entering into a loan agreement with him. The credit report plays a significant role in this process. However, it is not the only element that lenders use in order to assess the potential risk of an investment. Lenders also insist on appraisals.

3. POINTS

Points are fees that mortgage lenders assess against borrowers as part of the loan application process. A point equals 1 percent of the loan balance. Suppose that a borrower has obtained a loan for $100,000 and must pay two points as part of the application fee. The borrower would be obligated to pay a fee of $2,000 in addition to any other fees associated with applying for and obtaining the mortgage. Points are assessed in a wide variety of ways and are often negotiable. Some lenders assess points to justify a lower interest rate on the loan. There are plenty of mortgages where no points are assessed at all, but the interest rate is usually higher. If the borrower has a questionable credit history, he may be required to pay higher points on a mortgage.

B. APPRAISAL

In addition to underwriting and risk assessment of the individual, the lender will also want an independent analysis of the value of the real estate. This is where an appraiser enters the picture. An appraiser is in the business of providing estimates of the value of homes and real estate. Appraisers inspect the premises, compare it to others with similar features, and reach a consensus about the value of the property under consideration. Some lenders will not loan money unless the appraiser can establish conclusively that the home is worth the amount requested by the borrower. We discuss the role of appraisers in greater detail in Chapter 11.

Uniform Residential Loan Application

FIGURE 9-9

Uniform Residential Loan Application: Fannie Mae

This application is designed to be completed by the applicant(s) with the Lender's assistance. Applicants should complete this form as "Borrower" or "Co-Borrower," as applicable. Co-Borrower information must also be provided (and the appropriate box checked) when ☐ the income or assets of a person other than the Borrower (including the Borrower's spouse) will be used as a basis for loan qualification or ☐ the income or assets of the Borrower's spouse or other person who has community property rights pursuant to state law will not be used as a basis for loan qualification, but his or her liabilities must be considered because the spouse or other person has community property rights pursuant to applicable law and Borrower resides in a community property state, the security property is located in a community property state, or the Borrower is relying on other property located in a community property state as a basis for repayment of the loan.

If this is an application for joint credit, Borrower and Co-Borrower each agree that we intend to apply for joint credit (sign below):

Borrower	Co-Borrower

I. TYPE OF MORTGAGE AND TERMS OF LOAN

Mortgage Applied for:	☐ VA ☐ FHA	☐ Conventional ☐ USDA/Rural Housing Service	☐ Other (explain):		Agency Case Number	Lender Case Number
Amount $	Interest Rate %	No. of Months	**Amortization Type:**	☐ Fixed Rate ☐ GPM	☐ Other (explain): ☐ ARM (type):	

II. PROPERTY INFORMATION AND PURPOSE OF LOAN

Subject Property Address (street, city, state & ZIP)	No. of Units
Legal Description of Subject Property (attach description if necessary)	Year Built

Purpose of Loan	☐ Purchase ☐ Refinance	☐ Construction ☐ Construction-Permanent	☐ Other (explain):	Property will be: ☐ Primary Residence ☐ Secondary Residence ☐ Investment

Complete this line if construction or construction-permanent loan.

Year Lot Acquired	Original Cost $	Amount Existing Liens $	(a) Present Value of Lot $	(b) Cost of Improvements $	Total (a + b) $

Complete this line if this is a refinance loan.

Year Acquired	Original Cost $	Amount Existing Liens $	Purpose of Refinance	Describe Improvements ☐ made ☐ to be made Cost: $

Title will be held in what Name(s)	Manner in which Title will be held	Estate will be held in: ☐ Fee Simple ☐ Leasehold (show expiration date)
Source of Down Payment, Settlement Charges, and/or Subordinate Financing (explain)		

III. BORROWER INFORMATION

Borrower	Co-Borrower
Borrower's Name (include Jr. or Sr. if applicable)	Co-Borrower's Name (include Jr. or Sr. if applicable)

Social Security Number	Home Phone (incl. area code)	DOB (mm/dd/yyyy)	Yrs. School	Social Security Number	Home Phone (incl. area code)	DOB (mm/dd/yyyy)	Yrs. School

☐ Married ☐ Unmarried (include ☐ Separated single, divorced, widowed)	Dependents (not listed by Co-Borrower) no. ages	☐ Married ☐ Unmarried (include ☐ Separated single, divorced, widowed)	Dependents (not listed by Borrower) no. ages
Present Address (street, city, state, ZIP) ☐ Own ☐ Rent ___ No. Yrs.		Present Address (street, city, state, ZIP) ☐ Own ☐ Rent ___ No. Yrs.	
Mailing Address, if different from Present Address		Mailing Address, if different from Present Address	

If residing at present address for less than two years, complete the following:

Former Address (street, city, state, ZIP) ☐ Own ☐ Rent ___ No. Yrs.	Former Address (street, city, state, ZIP) ☐ Own ☐ Rent ___ No. Yrs.

IV. EMPLOYMENT INFORMATION

Borrower			Co-Borrower		
Name & Address of Employer	☐ Self Employed	Yrs. on this job	Name & Address of Employer	☐ Self Employed	Yrs. on this job
		Yrs. employed in this line of work/profession			Yrs. employed in this line of work/profession
Position/Title/Type of Business	Business Phone (incl. area code)		Position/Title/Type of Business	Business Phone (incl. area code)	

If employed in current position for less than two years or if currently employed in more than one position, complete the following:

Uniform Residential Loan Application
Freddie Mac Form 65   7/05 (rev.6/09)

Page 1 of 5

Fannie Mae Form 1003   7/05 (rev.6/09)

FIGURE 9-9

Uniform Residential Loan
Application: Fannie Mae
(continued)

Borrower			IV. EMPLOYMENT INFORMATION (cont'd)	Co-Borrower		
Name & Address of Employer	☐ Self Employed	Dates (from – to)	Name & Address of Employer	☐ Self Employed	Dates (from – to)	
		Monthly Income $			Monthly Income $	
Position/Title/Type of Business		Business Phone (incl. area code)	Position/Title/Type of Business		Business Phone (incl. area code)	
Name & Address of Employer	☐ Self Employed	Dates (from – to)	Name & Address of Employer	☐ Self Employed	Dates (from – to)	
		Monthly Income $			Monthly Income $	
Position/Title/Type of Business		Business Phone (incl. area code)	Position/Title/Type of Business		Business Phone (incl. area code)	

V. MONTHLY INCOME AND COMBINED HOUSING EXPENSE INFORMATION

Gross Monthly Income	Borrower	Co-Borrower	Total	Combined Monthly Housing Expense	Present	Proposed
Base Empl. Income*	$	$	$	Rent	$	
Overtime				First Mortgage (P&I)		$
Bonuses				Other Financing (P&I)		
Commissions				Hazard Insurance		
Dividends/Interest				Real Estate Taxes		
Net Rental Income				Mortgage Insurance		
Other (before completing, see the notice in "describe other income," below)				Homeowner Assn. Dues		
				Other:		
Total	$	$	$	Total	$	$

* Self Employed Borrower(s) may be required to provide additional documentation such as tax returns and financial statements.

Describe Other Income   *Notice:*   Alimony, child support, or separate maintenance income need not be revealed if the Borrower (B) or Co-Borrower (C) does not choose to have it considered for repaying this loan.

B/C		Monthly Amount
		$

VI. ASSETS AND LIABILITIES

This Statement and any applicable supporting schedules may be completed jointly by both married and unmarried Co-Borrowers if their assets and liabilities are sufficiently joined so that the Statement can be meaningfully and fairly presented on a combined basis; otherwise, separate Statements and Schedules are required. If the Co-Borrower section was completed about a non-applicant spouse or other person, this Statement and supporting schedules must be completed about that spouse or other person also.

Completed ☐ Jointly ☐ Not Jointly

ASSETS Description	Cash or Market Value	Liabilities and Pledged Assets. List the creditor's name, address, and account number for all outstanding debts, including automobile loans, revolving charge accounts, real estate loans, alimony, child support, stock pledges, etc. Use continuation sheet, if necessary. Indicate by (*) those liabilities, which will be satisfied upon sale of real estate owned or upon refinancing of the subject property.		
Cash deposit toward purchase held by:	$			
List checking and savings accounts below		LIABILITIES	Monthly Payment & Months Left to Pay	Unpaid Balance
Name and address of Bank, S&L, or Credit Union		Name and address of Company	$ Payment/Months	$
Acct. no.	$	Acct. no.		
Name and address of Bank, S&L, or Credit Union		Name and address of Company	$ Payment/Months	$
Acct. no.	$	Acct. no.		
Name and address of Bank, S&L, or Credit Union		Name and address of Company	$ Payment/Months	$
Acct. no.	$	Acct. no.		

VI. ASSETS AND LIABILITIES (cont'd)				
Name and address of Bank, S&L, or Credit Union		Name and address of Company	$ Payment/Months	$
Acct. no.	$	Acct. no.		
Stocks & Bonds (Company name/ number & description)	$	Name and address of Company	$ Payment/Months	$
		Acct. no.		
Life insurance net cash value	$	Name and address of Company	$ Payment/Months	$
Face amount: $				
Subtotal Liquid Assets	$			
Real estate owned (enter market value from schedule of real estate owned)	$			
Vested interest in retirement fund	$			
Net worth of business(es) owned (attach financial statement)	$	Acct. no.		
Automobiles owned (make and year)	$	Alimony/Child Support/Separate Maintenance Payments Owed to:	$	
Other Assets (itemize)	$	Job-Related Expense (child care, union dues, etc.)	$	
		Total Monthly Payments	$	
Total Assets a.	$	Net Worth (a minus b) ▶ $	**Total Liabilities b.**	$

Schedule of Real Estate Owned (If additional properties are owned, use continuation sheet.)

Property Address (enter S if sold, PS if pending sale or R if rental being held for income) ▼	Type of Property	Present Market Value	Amount of Mortgages & Liens	Gross Rental Income	Mortgage Payments	Insurance, Maintenance, Taxes & Misc.	Net Rental Income
		$	$	$	$	$	$
Totals		$	$	$	$	$	$

List any additional names under which credit has previously been received and indicate appropriate creditor name(s) and account number(s):

Alternate Name	Creditor Name	Account Number

VII. DETAILS OF TRANSACTION			VIII. DECLARATIONS					
			If you answer "Yes" to any questions a through i, please use continuation sheet for explanation.	Borrower		Co-Borrower		
				Yes	No	Yes	No	
a.	Purchase price	$	a. Are there any outstanding judgments against you?	☐	☐	☐	☐	
b.	Alterations, improvements, repairs		b. Have you been declared bankrupt within the past 7 years?	☐	☐	☐	☐	
c.	Land (if acquired separately)		c. Have you had property foreclosed upon or given title or deed in lieu thereof in the last 7 years?	☐	☐	☐	☐	
d.	Refinance (incl. debts to be paid off)		d. Are you a party to a lawsuit?	☐	☐	☐	☐	
e.	Estimated prepaid items		e. Have you directly or indirectly been obligated on any loan which resulted in foreclosure, transfer of title in lieu of foreclosure, or judgment?	☐	☐	☐	☐	
f.	Estimated closing costs		(This would include such loans as home mortgage loans, SBA loans, home improvement loans, educational loans, manufactured (mobile) home loans, any mortgage, financial obligation, bond, or loan guarantee. If "Yes," provide details, including date, name, and address of Lender, FHA or VA case number, if any, and reasons for the action.)					
g.	PMI, MIP, Funding Fee							
h.	Discount (if Borrower will pay)							
i.	Total costs (add items a through h)							

FIGURE 9-9

Uniform Residential Loan Application: Fannie Mae (continued)

VII. DETAILS OF TRANSACTION		VIII. DECLARATIONS				
			Borrower		Co-Borrower	
		If you answer "Yes" to any questions a through i, please use continuation sheet for explanation.	Yes	No	Yes	No
j. Subordinate financing		f. Are you presently delinquent or in default on any Federal debt or any other loan, mortgage, financial obligation, bond, or loan guarantee?	☐	☐	☐	☐
k. Borrower's closing costs paid by Seller		g. Are you obligated to pay alimony, child support, or separate maintenance?	☐	☐	☐	☐
l. Other Credits (explain)		h. Is any part of the down payment borrowed?	☐	☐	☐	☐
		i. Are you a co-maker or endorser on a note?	☐	☐	☐	☐
m. Loan amount (exclude PMI, MIP, Funding Fee financed)		j. Are you a U.S. citizen?	☐	☐	☐	☐
n. PMI, MIP, Funding Fee financed		k. Are you a permanent resident alien?	☐	☐	☐	☐
o. Loan amount (add m & n)		l. Do you intend to occupy the property as your primary residence? If Yes," complete question m below.	☐	☐	☐	☐
p. Cash from/to Borrower (subtract j, k, l & o from i)		m. Have you had an ownership interest in a property in the last three years?	☐	☐	☐	☐
		(1) What type of property did you own—principal residence (PR), second home (SH), or investment property (IP)?	_____		_____	
		(2) How did you hold title to the home— by yourself (S), jointly with your spouse (SP), or jointly with another person (O)?	_____		_____	

IX. ACKNOWLEDGEMENT AND AGREEMENT

Each of the undersigned specifically represents to Lender and to Lender's actual or potential agents, brokers, processors, attorneys, insurers, servicers, successors and assigns and agrees and acknowledges that: (1) the information provided in this application is true and correct as of the date set forth opposite my signature and that any intentional or negligent misrepresentation of this information contained in this application may result in civil liability, including monetary damages, to any person who may suffer any loss due to reliance upon any misrepresentation that I have made on this application, and/or in criminal penalties including, but not limited to, fine or imprisonment or both under the provisions of Title 18, United States Code, Sec. 1001, et seq.; (2) the loan requested pursuant to this application (the "Loan") will be secured by a mortgage or deed of trust on the property described in this application; (3) the property will not be used for any illegal or prohibited purpose or use; (4) all statements made in this application are made for the purpose of obtaining a residential mortgage loan; (5) the property will be occupied as indicated in this application; (6) the Lender, its servicers, successors or assigns may retain the original and/or an electronic record of this application, whether or not the Loan is approved; (7) the Lender and its agents, brokers, insurers, servicers, successors, and assigns may continuously rely on the information contained in the application, and I am obligated to amend and/or supplement the information provided in this application if any of the material facts that I have represented herein should change prior to closing of the Loan; (8) in the event that my payments on the Loan become delinquent, the Lender, its servicers, successors or assigns may, in addition to any other rights and remedies that it may have relating to such delinquency, report my name and account information to one or more consumer reporting agencies; (9) ownership of the Loan and/or administration of the Loan account may be transferred with such notice as may be required by law; (10) neither Lender nor its agents, brokers, insurers, servicers, successors or assigns has made any representation or warranty, express or implied, to me regarding the property or the condition or value of the property; and (11) my transmission of this application as an "electronic record" containing my "electronic signature," as those terms are defined in applicable federal and/or state laws (excluding audio and video recordings), or my facsimile transmission of this application containing a facsimile of my signature, shall be as effective, enforceable and valid as if a paper version of this application were delivered containing my original written signature.

Acknowledgement. Each of the undersigned hereby acknowledges that any owner of the Loan, its servicers, successors and assigns, may verify or reverify any information contained in this application or obtain any information or data relating to the Loan, for any legitimate business purpose through any source, including a source named in this application or a consumer reporting agency.

Borrower's Signature	Date	Co-Borrower's Signature	Date
X		X	

X. INFORMATION FOR GOVERNMENT MONITORING PURPOSES

The following information is requested by the Federal Government for certain types of loans related to a dwelling in order to monitor the lender's compliance with equal credit opportunity, fair housing and home mortgage disclosure laws. You are not required to furnish this information, but are encouraged to do so. The law provides that a lender may not discriminate either on the basis of this information, or on whether you choose to furnish it. If you furnish the information, please provide both ethnicity and race. For race, you may check more than one designation. If you do not furnish ethnicity, race, or sex, under Federal regulations, this lender is required to note the information on the basis of visual observation and surname if you have made this application in person. If you do not wish to furnish the information, please check the box below. (Lender must review the above material to assure that the disclosures satisfy all requirements to which the lender is subject under applicable state law for the particular type of loan applied for.)

BORROWER ☐ I do not wish to furnish this information			CO-BORROWER ☐ I do not wish to furnish this information		
Ethnicity: ☐ Hispanic or Latino ☐ Not Hispanic or Latino			Ethnicity: ☐ Hispanic or Latino ☐ Not Hispanic or Latino		
Race: ☐ American Indian or Alaska Native ☐ Native Hawaiian or Other Pacific Islander	☐ Asian ☐ White	☐ Black or African American	Race: ☐ American Indian or Alaska Native ☐ Native Hawaiian or Other Pacific Islander	☐ Asian ☐ White	☐ Black or African American
Sex: ☐ Female ☐ Male			Sex: ☐ Female ☐ Male		

To be Completed by Loan Originator:
This information was provided:
☐ In a face-to-face interview
☐ In a telephone interview
☐ By the applicant and submitted by fax or mail
☐ By the applicant and submitted via e-mail or the Internet

Loan Originator's Signature X		Date
Loan Originator's Name (print or type)	Loan Originator Identifier	Loan Originator's Phone Number (including area code)
Loan Origination Company's Name	Loan Origination Company Identifier	Loan Origination Company's Address

Uniform Residential Loan Application
Freddie Mac Form 65   7/05 (rev.6/09)   Page 4 of 5   Fannie Mae Form 1003   7/05 (rev.6/09)

CONTINUATION SHEET/RESIDENTIAL LOAN APPLICATION		
Use this continuation sheet if you need more space to complete the Residential Loan Application. Mark **B** for Borrower or **C** for Co-Borrower.	Borrower:	Agency Case Number:
	Co-Borrower:	Lender Case Number:

I/We fully understand that it is a Federal crime punishable by fine or imprisonment, or both, to knowingly make any false statements concerning any of the above facts as applicable under the provisions of Title 18, United States Code, Section 1001, et seq.

Borrower's Signature	Date	Co-Borrower's Signature	Date
X		X	

Uniform Residential Loan Application
Freddie Mac Form 65   7/05 (rev.6/09)   Page 5 of 5   Fannie Mae Form 1003   7/05 (rev.6/09)

C. THE RISE OF INTERNET LENDERS

In the era before the Internet and the World Wide Web, the idea that a lender in one part of the country would finance a home purchase in another part was virtually unheard of. However, the Internet has provided new resources for borrowers. These days, a borrower has the option of going not only to local lenders, but also to online lenders to arrange for mortgages, equity lines of credit, and second mortgages.

DISCHARGING A MORTGAGE

The term "discharge" means to satisfy a contractual obligation. A borrower can discharge a mortgage in one of two ways: He can make all monthly payments until the loan amount is paid off or he can sell the house and pay off the outstanding balance. The second situation is far more common than the first. When we discuss the closing process, we will see how the outstanding mortgage is discharged as part of the real estate settlement.

 FORECLOSURE

Although we discussed foreclosure in Chapter 4, it is important to point out some important features of foreclosure as it applies to mortgages and deeds of trust. The process of foreclosure varies from state to state, but there are some general guidelines that are followed in all states. For instance, a foreclosure is authorized when the borrower defaults on the loan. The most common reason to default is failing to make regular monthly payments. When borrowers fall on hard times, they often try to maintain their mortgages at the expense of other financial commitments, but eventually they begin to fall behind on their mortgage payments. When the borrower becomes 90 or 120 days late on a mortgage, the lender is authorized to institute foreclosure proceedings. As we saw earlier in this chapter, the mortgage itself provides the framework for the foreclosure process. There are two general types of foreclosure actions: judicial foreclosure and power of sale foreclosure.

A. JUDICIAL FORECLOSURE

A judicial foreclosure is the process used in the majority of states. The lender institutes a civil action, after giving notice to the borrower of his default and after demanding the balance of the loan be paid by a specific date. The lender essentially brings a civil complaint against the borrower and requests a judge to rule that the borrower is in default and that the lender has the authority to auction off the property for the outstanding balance on the loan.

FIGURE 9-10

Most Common Reasons for a Default on a Mortgage

- Failure to pay monthly
- Failure to pay property taxes
- Failure to obtain hazard insurance

B. POWER OF SALE FORECLOSURE

Power of sale foreclosures are seen in states that follow the deed of trust model for financing real estate. The deed of trust contains a provision that allows the trustee to institute foreclosure proceedings and initiate an auction once apprised of the borrower's default by the lender. Power of sale foreclosures have several distinct advantages over judicial foreclosures. For one thing, these types of foreclosures do not require a judicial proceeding. In order to conduct a foreclosure under power of sale, the trustee must give notice of default to the borrower, advertise the auction for a specified number of weeks in the local paper, and then conduct the auction on the courthouse steps. Many would argue that the reason for the continued viability of deeds of trust is that they offer lenders expedited foreclosures.

1. THE FORECLOSURE AUCTION

Foreclosure sales must be held in the county where the property is located. When the day for the auction arrives, the bank's representative will read out the foreclosure notice. These auctions often occur at the entrance to the courthouse, although there are provisions that allow them to be held at the property as well. Many individuals attend foreclosure auctions in hopes of purchasing a property well below fair market value. However, the chances that a prime piece of real estate will sell for pennies on the dollar is more urban myth than reality. Usually there are plenty of bidders on choice real estate, and they will bid up the price until someone prevails.

Once the auction is completed, the lender will take its outstanding debt from the sale price. If the auction resulted in more money than the lender was owed, the balance will go to the former owner. If the auction failed to bring in enough money to satisfy the mortgage, the lender may institute a deficiency action against the former owner for the balance. The chances of succeeding on such an action are usually slim.

2. RISING FORECLOSURE RATES

In 2007 and 2008, many lenders began noting an increase in foreclosure rates. Various private foreclosure companies have listed foreclosure rates rising as high as 90 percent, but at least one has backtracked on its claim of the highest foreclosure rates in fifty years.[4] Companies such as RealtyTrac (realtytrac.com) have gone on record describing increases in foreclosure rates of 88 percent in states such as Ohio. On the other hand, U.S. Census figures report no statistical difference in housing occupancy from previous years.[5] While the final figures may, and in some cases already have, undergo a downward revision in final

---

[4] http://www.washingtonpost.com/wp-dyn/content/article/2007/06/14/AR2007061400513.html
[5] http://www.census.gov/hhes/www/housing/hvs/qtr407/q407press.pdf

numbers, there can be little doubt that for many Americans, 2007 and beyond saw an increase in the number of foreclosed homes. The question is: what has caused this increase?

Many point to questionable lending practices by marginal lenders. Conventional wisdom points to lowered underwriting standards by greedy companies easy to cash in on the booming real estate market. These companies offered attractive terms with uglier terms buried in fine print. Such practices undoubtedly exist. Some companies have come under government scrutiny for a wide range of questionable — if not illegal — practices such as disguising interest rates, balloon payments, and excessive fees.

Sidebar

"In Ohio . . . As income levels have gone down, foreclosure rates have gone up, rising 88 percent in 2007."[6]

ANNOTATED DOCUMENT   RESIDENTIAL MORTGAGE

MORTGAGE

This paragraph identifies the parties to the mortgage

THIS INDENTURE, this the 22nd day of May, 2004, between Homer and Marge Simpson, hereinafter referred to as "Mortgagor", and First National Bank, hereinafter referred to as "Mortgagee," recognizing that for the purpose of this document singular and plural references shall constitute references to the above-named parties and that any gender references also be applied to the individuals parties.

WITNESSETH

"NOTE"

WHEREAS, Mortgagor is justly indebted to Mortgagee in the sum of one hundred and forty-nine thousand DOLLARS ($149,000) in U.S. currency and mortgage has and by these presents does agree to repay the same, with interest, according to the terms of said indenture, and by the terms of a note hereinafter referred to as the "Note," given by the Mortgagor to Mortgagee, bearing the date set out below.

The amount borrowed for the purchase of the home

DESCRIPTION OF THE PROPERTY SUBJECT TO THE NOTE:

In consideration of the sum set out above in the note provision and the premises that secure such note, Mortgagor has granted, bargained, sold and conveyed, and by these presents does grant, bargain, sell and convey unto Mortgagee a parcel of real estate situated in Springfield County, State of Placid, more particularly described in Exhibit "A" attached hereto and by this reference made a part hereof;

The property is described in a separate and attached document

---

[6] Remarks prepared for Alphonso Jackson, Secretary of Housing and Urban Development, Housing Roundtable at the Columbus Board of Realtors, Opening statement, February 21, 2008.

TOGETHER with all buildings, structures, fixtures and other improvements now or which will hereafter be located on, above or below the surface of the property described in Exhibit "A," or any part and parcel thereof; and,

TOGETHER with all and singular tenements, hereditaments, easements, riparian and littoral rights, and appurtenances thereunto belonging or in anywise appertaining, whether now owned or hereafter acquired by Mortgagor, and including all rights of ingress and egress to and from adjoining property (whether such rights currently lender's exist or subsequently arise) together with the reversion or reversions, remainder and remainders, rents, issues and profits thereof; and also all the rights, titles, interests, claims and demands whatsoever of Mortgagor of, in and to the same and of, in and to every part and parcel thereof; and,

> Here the parties describe the nature of the lender's interest in the property

TOGETHER with all the common elements appurtenant to any parcel, unit or unit which is all or part of the Premises; and,

ALL the foregoing encumbered by this Mortgage being hereinafter referred to as "Premises";

TO HAVE AND TO HOLD the Premises hereby granted to the use, benefit and behalf of the Mortgagee, forever.

EQUITY OF REDEMPTION

This agree is subject to the following conditions: If Mortgagor shall promptly pay or cause to be paid to Mortgagee, at its address listed in the Note, or at such other place which may hereafter be designated by Mortgagee, its or their successors or assigns, with interest, the principal sum of one hundred and forty nine thousand DOLLARS ($149,000) with final maturity, if not sooner paid, as stated in said Note unless amended or extended according terms of the Note executed by Mortgagor and payable to the order of Mortgagee, then these presents shall cease and be void, otherwise these presents shall remain in full force and effect. Said right is granted to Mortgagor as set out in state statute PL 3-25-14 and in accordance therewith.

> This provision gives the borrower the right to pay off the loan balance before the property goes to foreclosure

I. COVENANTS OF MORTGAGOR

Mortgagor covenants and agrees with Mortgagee as follows:

1-1. Secured Indebtedness.

This Mortgage is given as security for the Note and also as security for any and all other sums, indebtedness, obligations and liabilities of any and every kind arising, under the Note or this Mortgage, as amended or modified or supplemented from time to time, and any all renewals, modifications or extensions of any or all of the foregoing (all of which are collectively referred to herein as the "Secured Indebtedness"), the entire Secured Indebtedness being equally secured with and having the same priority as any amounts owed at the date hereof.

> This paragraph details the actual obligation to repay the amount borrowed

1-2. Performance of Conditions Set out in Note, Mortgage

Mortgagor shall perform, observe and comply with all provisions hereof and of the Note and shall promptly pay, in lawful U.S. currency, to Mortgagee the Secured Indebtedness

Borrower also agrees to keep the insurance and property taxes during the period of the mortgage

with interest thereon as provided in the Note, this Mortgage and all other documents constituting the Secured Indebtedness.

1-3. Payments Other Than Principal and Interest.
Mortgagor shall pay, when due and payable, (1) all taxes, assessments, general or special, and other charges levied on, or insurance and assessed, placed, or made against the property taxes Premises, this instrument or the Secured during the period Indebtedness or any interest of the Mortgagee of the mortgage, in the Premises or the obligations secured hereby; (2) premiums on policies of fire and other hazard insurance covering the Premises, as required herein; (3) ground rents or other lease rentals; and (4) other sums related to the Premises or the indebtedness secured hereby, if any, payable by Mortgagor.

1-4. Hazard and Property Insurance.
Mortgagor shall, at its sole cost and expense, keep the Premises insured against all hazards as is customary and reasonable for residential properties of similar type and nature located in Springfield County, State of Placid.

1-5. Care and Maintenance of Pledged Property.
Mortgagor shall maintain the Premises in good condition and repair and shall not commit or suffer any material waste to the Premises.

1-6. Prior or Pre-Existing Mortgages.
With regard to prior or pre-existing mortgages, lines of credit, second mortgages or other indentures for which premises are pledged as security, Mortgagor hereby agrees to: (i) Pay promptly, when due, all installments of principal and interest and all other sums and charges made payable by the Prior Mortgage; (ii) Promptly perform and observe all of the terms, covenants and conditions required to be performed and observed by Mortgagor under the Prior Mortgage, within the period provided in said Prior Mortgage; (iii) Promptly notify Mortgagee of any default, or notice claiming any event of default by Mortgagor in the performance or observance of any term, covenant or condition to be performed or observed by Mortgagor under any such Prior Mortgage. (iv) Mortgagor will not request nor will it accept any voluntary future advances under the Prior Mortgage without Mortgagee's prior written consent, which consent shall not be unreasonably withheld.

II. DEFAULT

2-1. Definition of Default.

A default is triggered by any of these conditions and is the first step in putting the property up for auction through foreclosure

The occurrence of any one of the following events which shall not be cured within ten (10) days after written notice of the occurrence of the event, if the default is monetary, or which shall not be cured within ten (10) days after written notice from Mortgagee, if the default is non-monetary, shall constitute a "Default": (a) Mortgagor fails to pay the Secured Indebtedness, or any part thereof, or the taxes, insurance and other charges, as herein before provided, when and as the same shall become due and payable; (b) Any material warranty of Mortgagor herein contained, or contained in the Note, proves untrue or misleading in any material respect; (c) Mortgagor materially fails to keep, observe, perform, carry out and execute the covenants, agreements, obligations and conditions set out in this Mortgage, or in the Note; (d) Foreclosure proceedings (whether judicial or otherwise) are instituted on any mortgage or any lien of any kind secured by any portion of the Premises and affecting the priority of this Mortgage.

2-2. Options Of Mortgagee in the Event Of Default.

Upon the occurrence of any default, as that term is described in paragraph 2-1, the Mortgagee may immediately do any one or more of the following: (a) Declare the total Secured Indebtedness, including without limitation all payments for taxes, assessments, insurance premiums, liens, costs, expenses and attorney's fees herein specified, without notice to Mortgagor (such notice being hereby expressly waived by Mortgagor), to be due and collectible at once, by foreclosure or otherwise; (b) In the event that Mortgagee elects to accelerate the maturity of the Secured Indebtedness and declares the Secured Indebtedness to be due and payable in full at once as provided for in Paragraph 1.02(a) hereinabove, or as may be provided for in the Note, or any other provision or term of this Mortgage, then Mortgagee shall have the right to pursue all of Mortgagee's rights and remedies for the collection of such Secured Indebtedness, whether such rights and remedies are granted by this Mortgage, any other agreement, law, equity or otherwise, to include, without limitation, the institution of foreclosure proceedings against the Premises under the terms of this Mortgage and any applicable state or federal law.

III. MISCELLANEOUS PROVISIONS

3-1. Prior Liens.

Mortgagor shall keep the Premises free from all prior liens (except for those consented to by Mortgagee).

3-2. Notice, Demand and Request.

Every provision for notice and demand or request shall be deemed fulfilled by written notice and demand or request delivered in accordance with the provisions of the Note relating to notice.

3-3. Construction of Terms and Phrases.

The words "Mortgagor" and "Mortgagee" whenever used herein shall include all individuals, corporations (and if a corporation, its officers, employees or agents), trusts and any and all other persons or entities, and the respective heirs, executors, administrators, legal representatives, successors and assigns of the parties hereto, and all those holding under either of them. The pronouns used herein shall include, when appropriate, either gender and both singular and plural. The word "Note" shall also include one or more notes and the grammatical construction of sentences shall conform thereto.

3-4. Severability.

In the event that any provision of this Mortgage or any other Loan Document or the application thereof shall, for any reason and to any extent, be deemed invalid or unenforceable by a court of law, neither the remainder of the instrument in which such provision is contained, nor the application of the provision to other persons, entities or circumstances, nor any other instrument referred to hereinabove shall be affected thereby, but instead shall be enforced to the maximum extent permitted by law. Clauses shall be construed in order to give effect to the clauses as individually set out.

This clause is found in many contracts; it allows courts to construe the clauses independently and will not result in a void contract if one clause is illegal

3-5. Applicable Law.

The terms and provisions of this Mortgage are to be governed by the laws of the State of Placid. No payment of interest or in the nature of interest for any debt secured in part by this Mortgage shall exceed the maximum amount permitted by law. Any payment in excess of the maximum amount shall be applied or disbursed as provided in the Note in regard to such amounts that are paid by the Mortgagor or received by the Mortgagee.

3-6. Descriptive Headings.

The descriptive headings used herein are for convenience of reference only, and they are not intended to have any effect whatsoever in determining the rights or obligations of the Mortgagor or Mortgagee and they shall not be used in the interpretation or construction hereof.

3-7. Attorneys' Fees.

As used in this Mortgage, attorneys' fees shall include, but not be limited to, fees incurred in all matters of collection and enforcement, construction and interpretation, before, during and after suit, trial, proceedings and appeals. Attorneys' fees shall also include hourly charges for paralegals, law clerks and other staff members operating under the supervision of an attorney.

3-8. Exculpation and Release.

Notwithstanding anything contained herein to the contrary, the Note which this Mortgage secures is a non-recourse Note and such Note shall be enforced against Mortgagor only to the extent of Mortgagor's interest in the Premises as described herein and to the extent of Mortgagor's interest in any personal property as may be described herein.

IN WITNESS WHEREOF, the Mortgagor has caused this instrument to be duly executed as of the 22nd day of May, 2004.

Witnessed by:

_____

_____

STATE OF PLACID

COUNTY OF SPRINGFIELD

THE FOREGOING INSTRUMENT was acknowledged before me this day of 22nd day of May, 2004, by Troy McClure.
Notary Public

_____

My Commission Expires: _____

PREDATORY LENDING

With the tremendous expansion in the availability of capital funding for all levels of income, there have also been some problems. Unfortunately, some unscrupulous lenders are taking advantage of individuals by engaging in practices that fall under the heading of "predatory lending." All legal professionals should be aware of predatory lending practices, which can include any of the following:

- Excessive fees to process loan paperwork
- Excessive interest rates
- Single-premium credit insurance
- Loans made to individuals without inquiring into their ability to repay the loan
- Loan "flipping" or refinancing the same loan several times within a short period of time
- Prepayment penalties[7]

Predatory lenders often strip away the one remaining asset that low- and middle-income individuals still have: the equity in their homes. After being assessed with excessive interest rates, hidden fees, and other penalties, the predatory lender then institutes a foreclosure action against the individual. Legal professionals should work hard to make sure that predatory lenders are reported to the appropriate state and federal agencies and should not work with such lenders not only because of the ethical concerns, but also because predatory lenders are often prosecuted.

BAYVIEW LOAN SERVICING, LLC v. SIMMONS.

CASE EXCERPT

BAYVIEW LOAN SERVICING, LLC v. SIMMONS
654 S.E.2d 898 (Va., 2008)

OPINION BY Justice G. Steven Agee.

Bayview Loan Servicing, LLC appeals from the judgment of the Circuit Court of Rockingham County, awarding Janet M. Simmons $156,809.46 in damages resulting from the foreclosure sale of Simmons' property. The circuit court determined Bayview breached a notice obligation under a deed of trust securing her property. On appeal, Bayview argues that the circuit court erred in holding that Bayview breached any obligation to Simmons because, under Code § 55-59.1(A), a properly executed notice of a foreclosure sale subsumed any contractual notice obligation in the deed of trust.

For the reasons set forth below, we will affirm the judgment of the circuit court.

I. RELEVANT FACTS AND PROCEEDINGS BELOW

Donald and Janet Simmons owned a 3.08-acre parcel of land situated in Rockingham County ("the Parcel"), which they conveyed by deed of trust on May 8, 1998, ("the Deed

---

[7] Government Accounting Office, http://www.gao.gov/new.items/d04280.pdf

of Trust") to Arthur Friedman, trustee, for the benefit of CommonPoint Mortgage Co. to secure a note in the principal amount of $134,532.00, plus interest ("the Note"). On September 18, 2002, after several intervening assignments, Wachovia Bank, N.A. ("Wachovia"), apparently became the assignee and beneficiary of the Deed of Trust and Bayview became the holder of the Note. Bayview acted as Wachovia's servicing agent for the Deed of Trust.

By April 2004, Simmons was substantially in arrears on the monthly payments due under the Note. On February 23, 2005, Bayview purportedly sent Simmons a letter by first-class mail notifying her that her account was past due in the amount of $31,942.23 and that the Note would be accelerated, the full balance would be due and payable, and foreclosure proceedings would begin if the past due amount was not paid within thirty days. Simmons denied ever receiving the letter.

On May 19, 2005, pursuant to Code § 55-59(9), Bayview substituted Specialized, Inc. of Virginia ("Specialized") as trustee under the Deed of Trust. On June 28, 2005, Specialized notified Simmons by letter that her account was in default, that payment had been accelerated due to that default, and that the Parcel would be sold at foreclosure on July 13, 2005. Although the June 28 letter was sent by certified mail, it was not claimed and was returned to Specialized by the United States Postal Service.

On July 13, 2005, the Parcel was sold at foreclosure auction to a third-party bidder for $172,000.00. Simmons did not learn of the foreclosure sale until two days later, on July 15, 2005. On the date of the foreclosure sale, the Parcel had a fair market value of $358,000.00.

Simmons timely filed an amended Complaint in the Circuit Court for Rockingham County alleging breach of contract by Bayview under the Deed of Trust. Simmons alleged that Paragraph 17 of the Deed of Trust required a pre-acceleration notice of breach and the action required to cure the breach prior to acceleration of any indebtedness secured by the Deed of Trust and that Paragraph 12 of the Deed of Trust required that notice be delivered or sent by certified mail. Simmons then alleged neither personal nor certified mail delivery of the pre-acceleration notice was made and therefore no right to accelerate the indebtedness secured by the Deed of Trust had accrued. Consequently, Simmons claimed no right to foreclose had matured.

Paragraph 12 provides, in relevant part, that:

> Except for any notice required under applicable law to be given in another manner, (a) any notice to Borrower provided for in this Deed of Trust shall be given by delivering it or by mailing such notice by certified mail addressed to Borrower at the Property Address.

Bayview responded that its letter of February 23, 2005, constituted substantial compliance with the requirements of the Deed of Trust; that Simmons had not provided credible evidence to overcome the presumption that she had received the February 23 notice; that Simmons had actual knowledge of delinquency and had evaded receipt of notice; and that the notice of foreclosure sale under Code § 55-59.1(A), which was sent by certified mail, satisfied the pre-acceleration notice required by the Deed of Trust. Bayview did not contest that the February 23, 2005, letter was not sent by certified mail.

After a hearing, the circuit court made the specific factual finding that Simmons presented credible evidence that she had not received the February 23 letter. Bayview was thus "required to prove that Plaintiff had actual knowledge of the pre-acceleration notice of the foreclosure sale." The circuit court determined that Bayview failed in its proof that Simmons had actual knowledge of the pre-acceleration notice. The circuit court then held that Bayview breached its obligations under the Deed of Trust as the right to accelerate the indebtedness and sell the Parcel at foreclosure had never matured due to Bayview's failure to give the pre-acceleration notice required under Paragraph 17 of the Deed of Trust in the manner required by Paragraph 12 of that instrument. The circuit court also concluded that Simmons had not waived her right to notice and opportunity to cure default; that Code § 55-59.1(A) did not protect Bayview from liability by merging the pre-acceleration notice with the notice of foreclosure sale Specialized sent Simmons by certified mail; and that Bayview's breach was the proximate cause of Simmons's loss of $156,809.46 equity in the Parcel. The circuit court then entered judgment for Simmons against Bayview in the amount of $156,809.46. We awarded Bayview this appeal.

II. ANALYSIS

Bayview argues in its sole assignment of error that the circuit court erred in failing to hold that, under Code § 55-59.1(A), the notice of proposed foreclosure sale from Specialized "effectively exercise[d] the right of acceleration expressly contained in the deed of trust."

Bayview relies on Code § 55-59.1(A), which provides, in pertinent part, that:

> The written notice of proposed sale when given as provided herein shall be deemed an effective exercise of any right of acceleration contained in such deed of trust or otherwise possessed by the party secured relative to the indebtedness secured. The inadvertent failure to give notice as required by this subsection shall not impose liability on either the trustee or the secured party.

Bayview argues that Specialized's notice "exercise[d] the right of acceleration" in the Deed of Trust by virtue of the specific language in that statute, thus obviating any requirement to meet the certified mail provision in Paragraph 12 of the Deed of Trust. Neither Bayview nor Simmons disputes that the notice of foreclosure sale that Specialized sent on June 28, 2005, to Simmons by certified mail satisfied the requirements of Code § 55-59.1(A), but Simmons contends the statute does not apply in this case.

Bayview concedes that the pre-acceleration notice is "a contractual condition on the acceleration of defaulted debt." However, Bayview contends that such a contractual condition is superseded by Code § 55-59.1(A). Bayview contends the pertinent language in that statute, "[t]he written notice of proposed sale . . . shall be deemed an effective exercise of any right of acceleration contained in such deed of trust," was added by the General Assembly in 1976 to derogate the decision of this Court in Sharpe v. Talley, 215 Va. 615, 212 S.E.2d 273 (1975).

Sharpe, Bayview argues, is closely analogous to the case at bar. There, this Court held that notice of acceleration must be complete and effective prior to a foreclosure sale, found the notice provided to the debtor ineffective, and remanded the case for an award of monetary damages to the debtor against the beneficiary of the deed of trust. Sharpe, 215 Va. at 622-23, 212 S.E.2d at 277-78. Bayview asserts the General Assembly modified former Code § 55-59(6), subsequently recodified as Code § 55-59.1(A), to include the current statutory language cited above and allow notice of acceleration to be merged with the notice of foreclosure sale, notwithstanding any contrary provision in the Deed of Trust.

Bayview misreads the scope of Code § 55-59.1(A) and any analogy to the Sharpe case. While Bayview is correct that a notice of foreclosure sale, as represented by Specialized's June 28, 2005, letter to Simmons, could act as the exercise of the "right of acceleration" under the Deed of Trust, Code § 55-59.1(A) does not establish a statutory mandate as to whether such "right of acceleration" is in existence and capable of being exercised by the foreclosure notice. Such a determination remains a matter of contract between the parties, as represented by Paragraph 17 of the Deed of Trust.

In Paragraph 17 of the Deed of Trust, the parties agreed no right of acceleration would be in existence to exercise (in other words, that no such right would have accrued to Bayview) until the condition precedent of providing the pre-acceleration notice had been satisfied. That condition precedent required a notice by personal delivery or certified mail specifying:

> (1) the breach; (2) the action required to cure such breach; (3) a date, not less than 10 days from the date the notice is mailed to Borrower by which such breach must be cured; and (4) that failure to cure such breach on or before the date specified in the notice may result in acceleration of the sums secured by this Deed of Trust and sale of the Property.

As noted above, this required notice was not given and thus the condition precedent to Bayview's right of acceleration was never met. Because Bayview did not comply with the specific condition precedent under the Deed of Trust, prior to the notice of foreclosure sale by Specialized, Bayview had not acquired the right to accelerate payment under the terms of the Deed of Trust. Thus, Specialized's June 28, 2005, letter could exercise no right of acceleration because no such right had then accrued to Bayview.

Bayview had no right of acceleration at the time that the notice of foreclosure sale was sent. Accordingly, Code § 55-59.1(A) does not cure Bayview's contractual breach under the Deed of Trust or immunize Bayview from its liability to Simmons for her lost equity in the Parcel sold in foreclosure. Therefore, the circuit court did not err by entering judgment in favor of Simmons.

CONCLUSION

For the foregoing reasons, we will affirm the judgment of the circuit court. Affirmed.

CASE QUESTIONS

1 How did the property in this case come to be foreclosed?
2 When did Simmons learn of the foreclosure sale, and what details emerged about the sale?
3 What grounds did Simmons raise in her complaint against Bayview?
4 What findings did the trial court make?
5 What conclusion did the appellate court reach as to Bayview's claim of substantial compliance with the statute?

SKILLS YOU NEED IN THE REAL WORLD

DECIPHERING MORTGAGES

One the most important skills you can develop in a real estate practice is the ability to locate and decipher mortgage agreements. Because mortgages are recorded, they are a matter of public record. They may be cross-referenced by the borrower's name or by the particular tract index, but whatever method is used in your area, you should spend some time learning how to quickly and efficiently locate mortgages. Once located, you should review the entire mortgage, clause by clause, and decipher the important features of that mortgage, including:

- Default provisions
- Type of foreclosure authorized
- Interest and other acceleration clauses
- Redemption rights

This list is not meant to be exhaustive. Most of the features are self-explanatory, except the last one. "Redemption rights" refer to the borrower's ability to redeem or pay off the loan balance at or before the foreclosure auction. Sometimes these redemption rights also give the borrower the right to challenge the foreclosure auction or even to bid at the auction. You should be familiar with all the terms of mortgages in your state and keep a folder of some of the more unusual mortgages that you come in contact with. This will be time well spent and will help you master mortgage law in your state.

CHAPTER SUMMARY

Real estate purchases are financed through the use of mortgages and deeds of trust. Although the issues involved in real estate financing can be complex, the basic arrangement is relatively simple. A borrower applies to a lender for funds that the borrower will use to purchase the real estate. In exchange for these funds, the lender requires that the borrower transfer certain rights to it. Among these rights is the right to foreclose on the property if the borrower defaults on the mortgage. There are two mortgage markets, the primary and secondary. The primary mortgage market consists of lenders who are in the business of loaning funds to individuals to purchase real estate. These lenders can be institutions as varied as banks, savings and loan associations, credit unions, and insurance companies. But there is also a secondary mortgage market. This market consists of both governmental and private corporations that are in the business of purchasing mortgages from lenders. The agencies purchase mortgages at a discount from lenders, freeing up funds that the lenders can then use for other mortgagors. The secondary mortgage market is a vital component of the American economy and ensures the continued vitality of the American mortgage market.

Whether a particular state follows a mortgage or deed of trust arrangement in real estate financing, the legal elements used to create these documents are generally the same. Mortgages must be in writing; they must contain specific clauses, including the granting clause, promissory note clause, and power of sale provision. The lender's right to foreclose on the loan is also a common provision found in both mortgages and deeds of trust.

There are numerous types of mortgages, all of which have radically different features. The two broadest categories of mortgages include fixed-rate mortgages and adjustable-rate mortgages. In a fixed-rate mortgage, all of the terms, including interest rate, monthly payment, and borrowed amount remain the same for the life of the loan. In an adjustable-rate mortgage, on the other hand, one or more of the terms fluctuates. It is very common for adjustable-rate mortgages to have fluctuating interest rates that are indexed to some other figure, such as the national prime lending rate or other national index.

REVIEW QUESTIONS

1. How is the secondary mortgage market different from the primary mortgage market?
2. What is Fannie Mae?
3. Explain the significance of the secondary mortgage market.
4. How does the Truth in Lending Act Protect consumers?
5. What is the difference between a mortgage and deed of trust?
6. What is a granting clause in a mortgage?
7. What is the promissory note provision in a mortgage?
8. What is a power of sale provision?
9. What is an estoppel certificate?
10. What are the rules of priority when it comes to mortgages?
11. What is a subordination agreement?
12. What is the difference between a fixed-rate mortgage and an adjustable-rate mortgage?
13. What is a balloon mortgage?
14. What is a wraparound mortgage?
15. What is mortgage underwriting?
16. What qualifies as a default under mortgage?
17. What are some of the common reasons for a borrower to default on a mortgage?
18. Explain the difference between judicial and power of sale foreclosure.

19 Explain the holding in this chapter's case excerpt. What are the issues in this case? What result did the court reach?

20 What is predatory lending?

DISCUSSION QUESTIONS

Does your state allow mortgages, deeds of trust, or both types of real estate financing? What are the advantages of one over the other?

PRACTICAL APPLICATIONS

Go to your local courthouse, locate a mortgage or deed of trust and answer the following questions:

What is the borrower's full name?
What is the lender's name?
What is the total amount financed?
When is the final payment due?

WEB SITES

Freddie Mac
http://www.freddiemac.com/index.html

Fannie Mae
http://www.fanniemae.com

Ginnie Mae
http://www.ginniemae.gov/index.asp

Massachusetts Housing Finance Agency
http://www.masshousing.com

Maryland Commissioner of Financial Regulation Division
http://www.dllr.state.md.us/finance

Equifax
http://www.equifax.com

Experian
http://www.experian.com

TERMS AND PHRASES

Amortization	Deed of trust	Mortgage
Collateral	Estoppel certificate	Promissory note

SIGNIFICANT CASES

Garretson v. Post, 68 Cal. Rptr. 3d 230 (2007)

Louise → *Carolina Bank v. Chatham Station, Inc.*, 651 S.E.2d 386 (N.C.App., 2007)

Royal Thrift and Loan Co. v. County Escrow, Inc., 20 Cal. Rptr. 3d 37 (2004)

Gilroy v. Ryberg, 266 Neb. 617 (Neb., 2003)

Public and Private Restrictions on the Use of Land

Focus of This Chapter

This chapter explores both public and private restrictions on the use of real estate by landowners. Public restrictions, such as zoning, are explained. Private restrictions, such as restrictive covenants, are examined in detail. Special emphasis is placed on the role of the paralegal in researching, preparing, and locating various public and private land use restrictions.

Chapter Learning Objectives

After completing this chapter, you should be able to:

■ Describe the nature and purpose of zoning regulations
■ Explain the importance of urban planning
■ Define important state and federal laws that affect the rights of private landowners
■ Explain the importance of restrictive covenants
■ Describe the area of nuisance law

INTRODUCTION

In this chapter we examine the many ways that a landowner's use of her land can be restricted. Public laws, such as zoning, and federal environmental laws can have a huge impact on what a private landowner is permitted to do with her property. In addition to these legislative restrictions, there are also private restrictions placed on use. These usually come in the form of restrictive covenants. We begin our discussion with an exploration of the legislative, or public, restrictions on land use.

PUBLIC RESTRICTIONS ON PRIVATE LAND

Your home may be your castle, but that does not mean that you are free to carry out any activity you wish there. In fact, local, state, and federal governments have the right to impose any number of restrictions on the way that private individuals use their property. We examine these public restrictions by starting with local ordinances, such as zoning regulations, and then proceed through state and federal legislation that also limits how a private landowner may use her land.

A. ZONING

Zoning
The division of land in a local area into separate districts that are regulated by their use and development.

Local governments have the right to impose **zoning** rules and regulations as part of the police power vested in the government through state and federal constitutions. Zoning regulations restrict the way that both private and business landowners may use their property. Of course, not all property in United States falls under zoning ordinances. In fact, there are vast tracts of land in the country that are not regulated by any type of zoning. Generally speaking, zoning ordinances are enacted by municipalities and towns that have reached a certain level of development. Farming communities and vast tracts of unimproved land generally do not have local zoning boards to contend with. When a city or town does have a zoning board, zoning regulations are designed to serve four primary purposes:

1 Promote health and morals
2 Reduce traffic congestion and improve traffic flow
3 Emphasize safety from fire and other potential hazards
4 Provide adequate heat, light, and air flow for residents

Local governments often use zoning regulations as a means to control development and to make effective use of available space. Zoning is often seen as an effective planning tool for local governments. Through zoning ordinances, municipal governments can concentrate industry and commercial development in particular parts of town, while designating other parts for residential use only. This has the benefit of keeping residential areas as far away as possible from industrial and commercial enterprises.

 The authority to issue zoning ordinances arises under a city's or town's police powers.

ISSUE AT A GLANCE

A zoning ordinance is usually enacted as some form of protective legislation. For example, a zoning regulation might attempt to protect general health and safety, or help ensure property values. For instance, a zoning ordinance will specify that structures must have a minimum setback distance from the road or that only specific types of materials may be used for buildings. The most common example of a zoning ordinance is a limitation on the use of the property, such as designating an area for residential use only, while other areas are zoned as commercial use only. Zoning regulations also carry with them enforcement provisions that allow the zoning board to issue citations against landowners who do not conform to the ordinance. The citation can result in a prosecution if the landowner fails to abide by the zoning regulations.

1. AESTHETIC ZONING

Some cities and towns enact **aesthetic zoning** ordinances to maintain a general overall appearance for their structures. These ordinances may require all architecture to meet specified standards. Asheville, North Carolina, has set aside an area referred to as "Biltmore Village," where all commercial structures must have mission-style architectural features.

Aesthetic zoning
The requirement that all commercial and residential structures in a specified area have the same general appearance.

The most common function of zoning ordinances is to control physical aspects of buildings. For instance, a zoning ordinance might require a minimum setback that a building must have from the road. Any structure that is closer to the road than this minimum distance would be in violation of zoning ordinances and would be cited.

Although zoning is an interference with a private individual's use of property, courts have ruled that it is a constitutional interference and that most zoning ordinances are perfectly legal.[1] However, there are certain zoning regulations that have been ruled unconstitutional. A zoning ordinance that prohibited individuals from certain ethnic groups or races from owning property would obviously be a violation of the Constitution.

It is important to draw a distinction between zoning and other types of municipal ordinances. For instance, building codes, which limit the manner in which buildings can be erected or rehabilitated, are not a form of zoning. Building codes focus on safety and health issues and therefore have greater latitude than zoning ordinances, which are usually more general in nature.

Sidebar

The city of Helen, Georgia, has a set of zoning ordinances that requires all commercial structures to maintain a Bavarian theme.

2. ENFORCING ZONING REGULATIONS

Courts consistently require zoning regulations to be limited in their focus to specific areas, such as safety, health, and general welfare. When a zoning ordinance goes beyond one of these issues, courts may strike down the regulation as excessive or overbroad.[2] The general limitation on any zoning ordinance or regulation is that it must serve a justifiable governmental purpose. Examples of permissible governmental purposes include regulations that control traffic, noise, or pollution. If the

---

[1] *King v. Caddo Parish Commission*, 719 So. 2d 410 (La. 1998).
[2] N.C. Gen. Stat. § 153A-341.

city can show that a zoning ordinance meets a justifiable goal, courts will usually uphold the ordinance as constitutional.

3. TYPES OF ZONING CATEGORIES

Zoning categories come in three broad categories: residential, commercial, and industrial. By limiting use in particular areas, zoning boards hope to control development and provide greater health and safety for residents. When an area is zoned for commercial use, it means that private owners in that area may only operate businesses there. They cannot, for example, build a home there. Although there are three broad zoning categories, most cities have numerous additional zoning classifications and sub-classifications that can complicate the issues. In each of these zones, use is limited to the specific classification. For instance, residential zoning classifications can contain numerous categories, from single-family homes to apartments and multi-family homes.

a. Residential

Residential classifications can include a number of different types of dwellings. For instance, residential classifications can include detached homes, single-family residences, townhouses, apartments, group living structures (such as assisted-living facilities), as well as public accommodations from college dormitories to fire departments. Zoning ordinances establish minimum square footage for each of these classifications, including a general percentage of how much floor space can be devoted to a particular type of use.

b. Commercial

Commercial designations cover a number of different types of business establishments. Here, the focus of the zoning ordinances is on total square footage, fire and safety issues, and minimum setbacks. Business and commercial district zoning may also include requirements pertaining to the materials used in constructing the buildings as well as the placement of firewalls and the width of walls adjoining other businesses.

c. Industrial

Industrial classifications can include light, medium, and heavy industry with appropriate regulation governing the placement of the structures in relation to residential areas as well as limitations on the types of chemical and manufacturing processes that are allowed on site.

 Although there are three general categories of zoning regulations, many local governments create numerous other sub-categories.

FIGURE 10-1

City of Chicago Zoning
Ordinance for Townhouses

17-9-0120 Townhouse Developments

17-9-012001-A   Purpose

The purpose of these standards is to establish setback, building spacing, landscaping and design standards that are tailored to *townhouse developments*. Such standards are intended to ensure that *townhouse developments* are compatible with the traditional character of Chicago's neighborhoods.

17-9-0120-B   Applicability

The *townhouse development* standards of this section apply in all districts in which townhouses are allowed.

17-9-0120-C   Number of Buildings on Zoning Lot

Multiple townhouse buildings are expressly allowed on a single zoning lot in those townhouse developments that comply with the townhouse development standards of this section (Sec. 17-9-0120), provided that each building contains no more than 9 townhouse units.

17-9-0120-D   Lot Frontage

The minimum *lot frontage* for a *townhouse development* is 35 feet.

(See Sec. *17-17-0303* for rules governing the measurement of *lot frontage*.)

17-9-0120-E   Building Setbacks for Front and Rear Walls

1. **Front and Rear Walls Defined**
    Front walls and *rear walls* are those walls that are generally perpendicular to party walls. These walls are typically the primary sources of light and air for a *townhouse* unit.

2. **Front or Rear Walls Facing a Public Street**

    a. *Front walls* and *rear walls* that face a public street must be set back from the *street property line* as follows:

District	Minimum Setback (feet)
RT3.5	12
RT4	12
RM4.5	12
B/C dash 1	12
B/C dash 1.5	12
B/C dash 2	12
All other districts	10

    b. Required *front wall* and *rear wall* setbacks may be reduced to match the predominant setbacks of adjoining structures on the same side of the *street* between the nearest intersecting *streets* or *alleys*, provided that a minimum setback of 3 feet is provided in all cases. Landscaping must be installed within these required setbacks.

3. **Front or Rear Walls Facing a Side or Rear Property Line**

http://developmentcode.com/ChicagoNew/maintain/ViewCode.asp?recIndex=5355

4. EXCEPTIONS TO ZONING CLASSIFICATIONS

Although zoning boards have the power to enforce their rules and regulations by issuing citations, there are often structures within zoned areas that do not conform to the existing ordinances. They may not conform because the structure existed prior to the enactment of the zoning regulation, or the zoning board may have made an exception that allows a structure to be built that does not conform to the zoning regulations. There are three different categories of structures that may continue to be used even when they do not conform to zoning rules and regulations:

- Nonconforming use
- Conditional use permit
- Variance

a. Nonconforming Use

Nonconforming use
A structure that violates a zoning classification, but predated the enactment of the zoning rule.

The classification of **nonconforming use** is reserved for a structure that predates the enactment of a zoning regulation. A new zoning ordinance cannot force the closure of a preexisting business, or force an individual out of her home. When the structure is already in existence at the time the zoning ordinance is created, it is allowed to stand even though its use violates the new rule and the general classification for the entire area.

b. Conditional Use Permit

Conditional use permit
An exception to a zoning classification granted by a zoning board, usually to benefit area residents.

There are times when a city wishes to encourage business development for commercial services within a residential area. In such a situation, the board might issue a **conditional use permit** that allows a business entity to operate in an area that has been reserved for residential use. Conditional use permits allow the property to be used in a way that is not in strict compliance with the zoning classification, but that does provide an essential service. Examples of conditional use permits would include authorizing a grocery store or gas station to operate in a residential area for the convenience of local residents. There are strict limitations on the issuance of conditional use permits, however. The zoning board cannot act in an unreasonable or capricious way. For instance, the zoning board cannot limit conditional use permits to members of a zoning board member's family or to a specific company.

c. Variance

Variance
An exception to a zoning classification granted by a zoning board.

In addition to conditional use permits, boards are also authorized to make exceptions to zoning classifications. An exception is referred to as a **variance**. A landowner might, for example, request a variance to operate her home-based business in an area reserved for residential use only. In this situation, the landowner would have to apply to the zoning board for a variance that would allow her to conduct a commercial enterprise in a residential area. Zoning boards issue variances to allow

FIGURE 10-2

Las Vegas, Nevada
Ordinance Code Definition
of Nonconforming Use

19.16.030 REGULATIONS

   A. Nonconforming Use of a Conforming Building

      1. Expansion or Redevelopment of Use. A nonconforming use of a conforming building shall not be continued following redevelopment of the property nor extended or expanded into any other portion of the conforming building; provided, however, that an existing use which was made nonconforming by one or more of the following may be continued following redevelopment or expanded in accordance with Subsection (2) of this Section (A):

         a.   The adoption of a Special Use Permit requirement for that type of use;

         b.   The adoption of a 400-foot or 1500-foot separation requirement between that type of use and a protected use;

         c.   The adoption of a 1500-foot separation requirement between two uses of that type;

         d.   The establishment of a protected use that, by virtue of a 400-foot or 1500-foot separation requirement, would otherwise prohibit the existing use from expanding or from continuing following redevelopment; or

         e.   The adoption of a different method of measuring distance for purposes of a separation requirement.

a degree of flexibility in zoning regulations, recognizing that it is extremely difficult to limit use entirely. If the zoning board allows a variance, it means that property located in one designated area can be used in a different way. Individuals and companies request variances all the time, and this is often the main item of business at zoning board meetings.

d. Unconstitutional or Illegal Zoning Regulations

At times in the past, some zoning rules and regulations have been used to discriminate against some members of society. For example, in the early twentieth century, there were zoning ordinances that prohibited African Americans from living in predominantly white neighborhoods. Eventually those zoning ordinances were struck down as unconstitutional. However, the history of unconstitutional or illegal zoning regulations did not end there.

Interestingly enough, there is no prohibition against enacting zoning rules and regulations that discriminate on neutral grounds. What is illegal is the basis of discrimination. Zoning ordinances are, by their very nature, prohibitions on the ways that landowners can use their land and thus could be construed as discriminatory in any form. However, as long as zoning rules and regulations apply equally to everyone in the same territory, and are not based on unconstitutional practices, the zoning ordinance will be upheld by the courts. Zoning boards must always justify their zoning ordinances by the "rational basis" test. Under this test, courts require zoning boards to demonstrate that there is a connection between the zoning ordinance and the ultimate goal of that ordinance. If the ultimate goal is to promote safety, health, or any other justifiable goal, there is a strong likelihood that the zoning ordinance will be upheld as constitutional. However, there are certain classifications that are considered to be suspect. For instance, any zoning ordinance based on race, religion, or ethnic origin would automatically fall into a suspect classification and would most likely be ruled unconstitutional.[3] Zoning boards must demonstrate that they balance the interests of individual homeowners against the needs of society.

EXAMPLE 10-1

The town of Springfield has recently enacted a new zoning ordinance that limits bill-boards and landscaping along a newly constructed street. This zoning ordinance does not apply to other streets in the town. Landowners on the newly constructed street have filed suit alleging that this new zoning ordinance violates the Constitution. The zoning board counters that the new regulation is designed to ease traffic flow, promote traffic safety, and also meet aesthetic requirements. Based on what you have learned so far about zoning rules and regulations, who will win this lawsuit?

Answer: The town should win. Because the town can satisfy the rational basis test by showing that the new regulation is based on legitimate concerns of traffic safety and aesthetics, the court will most likely rule in favor of the town.[4]

i. "Spot" Zoning

Spot zoning
A practice that is often ruled unconstitutional, in which a particular parcel is singled out for special treatment that does not further any of the stated goals of zoning regulations.

Spot zoning is a practice used by zoning boards to single out a particular parcel for special treatment. Courts generally take a dim view of spot zoning, because it places greater emphasis on individual parcels instead of the general community. An example of spot zoning would be the zoning board's action in selecting a particular residence and changing the zoning for that property but not the rest of the area. Spot zoning was often used as a way of forcing out criminal activity and other undesirable elements in neighborhoods. Many states consider spot zoning to be illegal, no matter how good the intentions. Courts have created the following criteria to identify instances of illegal spot zoning:

- The zoning ordinance is aimed at a single parcel or a limited area.
- The ordinance is inconsistent with surrounding zoning classifications.
- The ordinance was not created to benefit the community as a whole or to further public health, safety, or other permissible reasons and is arbitrary or capricious.[5]

---

[3] *Corn v. City of Lauderdale Lakes*, 997 F.2d 1369 (11th Cir. 1993).
[4] *Craft v. City of Fort Smith*, 335 Ark. 417, 984 S.W.2d 22 (1998).
[5] *Griswold v. City of Homer*, 925 P.2d 1015 (Alaska 1996).

Tech Topic
VIRTUAL PLANNING

Along with population increases comes the need for expanded development, both residential and commercial. Residents not only like to know about plans for development, but they also prize having input to help shape the future of their community.

Historically, this has meant a long process of public meetings designed to allow residents the opportunity to learn about prospective development projects and deliver their support or opposition in person. Typically, most of those in attendance represent organized groups on both sides, and the measure of legitimate support or opposition by the public in general is hard to come by.

Although the length of the process has not changed much, the method of gathering public opinion has.

Nowadays, residents are often invited to express their opinions on planned projects by visiting web sites designed expressly for that purpose. Carefully created surveys collect and sort data, producing an overview of how the public is reacting to a proposed project. Even though the results might not qualify as statistically valid because of the voluntary nature of the process, they are every bit as reliable as opinions gathered from a public meeting. Furthermore, it affords those unable to attend a public meeting the chance to weigh in, thereby increasing the number of people involved in the process.

It is doubtful that virtual planning meetings will completely supplant public meetings anytime soon, but they have provided a welcome adjunct to the process.

B. BUILDING CODES

Building codes are different from zoning ordinances. Building codes are local or state rules and regulations that have specific restrictions on the way that buildings can be constructed, heating and air-conditioning systems can be installed, and plumbing and electrical work can be completed. Building codes are designed to protect the health, safety, and general welfare of the community. Because these codes are focused on safety and health issues, courts generally enforce them, even when building contractors and others claim the regulations are onerous.

C. PLANNING BOARDS

In addition to zoning boards, many communities also have planning boards. These boards are responsible for managing the development of the local community. They engage in long-term studies and work closely with the zoning board to effectuate an overall plan to benefit the local citizens, reduce congestion, noise, and air pollution, and also maintain real estate values.

D. HISTORICAL DISTRICTS

Many communities have areas of historical significance. When a particular area is designated as a historical district, it receives special protection on both the local and state level. This protection can come in the form of special tax incentives for individuals who own designated historic sites as well as limitations on the repair and refurbishment of these structures.

E. URBAN PLANNING

Entire texts are written on the topic of urban planning; we only touch on the highlights in this chapter. At its simplest, urban planning consists of any short- or long-term planning that seeks to conserve the value of a community or to enhance its living standards over time. However, that simple explanation belies some very complicated issues. Whether addressing water use, urban landscaping, traffic flow patterns, census data, birth rates, or any of a number of other issues, urban planners attempt to control growth or at least to give it an appropriate outlet. Without such planning, the local community would soon suffer an overload of people, traffic, pollution, as well as depleted resources.

Urban planners must take into account not only the current state of the community but also the likely complexion of the area in ten, 20, or even 50 years. Along with the issues surrounding population growth, there are also issues of resource allotment, tax incentives to bring in more businesses, and the most

---

FIGURE 10-3	Legislative findings. The historical heritage of our State is one of our most valued and important assets. The conservation and preservation of historic districts and landmarks stabilize and increase property values in their areas and strengthen the overall economy of the State. This Part authorizes cities and counties of the State within their respective zoning jurisdictions and by means of listing, regulation, and acquisition: (1) To safeguard the heritage of the city or county by preserving any district or landmark therein that embodies important elements of its culture, history, architectural history, or prehistory; and (2) To promote the use and conservation of such district or landmark for the education, pleasure and enrichment of the residents of the city or county and the State as a whole.
Authorization of Historic Districts	

Character of historic district defined. Historic districts established pursuant to this Part shall consist of areas which are deemed to be of special significance in terms of their history, prehistory, architecture, and/or culture, and to possess integrity of design, setting, materials, feeling, and association.

Designation of historic districts. Any municipal governing board may, as part of a zoning or other ordinance enacted or amended pursuant to this Article, designate and from time to time amend one or more historic districts within the area subject to the ordinance.[6]

---

[6] N.C. Gen. Stat. § 160A-400.1.

appropriate method to use local government budgets to anticipate future problems. These days, urban planners must also take into account technological aspects that did not figure into local government plans even ten years ago. For instance, what is the distribution of broadband Internet access and cell phone towers? Without such access, a community would be hard-pressed to attract new businesses to the area.

F. INTERSTATE LAND SALES FULL DISCLOSURE ACT

So far, our discussion concerning public restrictions on land has been limited to topics such as zoning or urban planning. Both of these are local government concerns, often handled at town council or other meetings. However, there are several important pieces of federal legislation that can play an important role in the way that landowners can use their property. One such federal act is the Interstate Land Sales Full Disclosure Act.[7] Passed in 1968 after a notorious series of frauds committed by individuals with access to prior knowledge of the planned route of the new U.S. interstate system, this legislation requires land promoters to make specific disclosures about land on or near the interstate highway system. For instance, any promoter who plans to sell 25 or more lots must disclose:

- The identity of the owners of the land that is being subdivided and offered for sale
- A description of the physical properties of the land (farm land, swamp land, partially covered by timber, etc.)
- A description of the access and availability of utilities for the new lots
- A statement about the condition or existence of access roads to the new lots

The act also requires promoters to register their land sales with appropriate government agencies to provide buyers with disclosures at least 48 hours prior to purchase, and allow buyers a seven-day period to change their minds about the sale. The act establishes stringent guidelines about fraud and misrepresentation, and authorizes federal prosecutions for land promoters who violate the act's provisions.

G. ENVIRONMENTAL ISSUES

Besides the Interstate Land Sales Full Disclosure Act, there are other important federal laws that can have an impact on a landowner's use of her property. A common example is the Clean Water Act. This act provides strict guidelines for the use of wetlands and imposes limitations on the way that areas that qualify as wetlands can be used. Under the Clean Water Act, a wetland is described as "those areas that are inundated or saturated by surface or ground water at a frequency and

---

[7] 15 U. S. C. § 1701.

duration sufficient to support, and that under normal circumstances do support, a prevalence of vegetation typically adapted for life in saturated soil conditions. Wetlands generally include swamps, marshes, bogs and similar areas." On the basis of that definition, many areas fall under the jurisdiction of the Clean Water Act.

The Environmental Protection Agency is the branch of the federal government that is responsible for enforcing various environmental rules and regulations, including the Clean Water Act.

Section 404 of the Clean Water Act, for instance, prohibits the discharge of dredged or other materials into an aquatic environment if the release would significantly degrade the water supply. Owners often must apply for permits from the Environmental Protection Agency before they are allowed to discharge substances into the nation's water supply.

1. THE SUPERFUND

The Comprehensive Environmental Response, Compensation, and Liability Act (CERCLA), which is commonly known as the environmental Superfund, became law in 1980. The act created a tax that is imposed on chemical and petroleum industries to help defer the costs associated with cleaning up hazardous chemical spills. Among other things, CERCLA has:

- Created rules that prohibit the development of certain sites that were formerly hazardous waste sites
- Created a fund to assist in the cleanup of these sites
- Imposed liability on companies and individuals who had created the hazardous sites in the first place

PRIVATE RESTRICTIONS ON LAND USE

So far, our discussions have centered on governmental restrictions on the ability of private landowners to use their lands. In the following sections, we examine private actions that individuals can bring against one another to control the way that land is used. The most common form of private restriction on land use is the restrictive covenant. In many ways, restrictive covenants resemble zoning regulations, except that they are both imposed and enforced by private individuals.

A. RESTRICTIVE COVENANTS

Restrictive covenant
A condition or restriction on the way that land may be used that is imposed by private individuals.

Like zoning regulations, **restrictive covenants** control issues such as minimum setbacks from roadways, appearance, architecture, minimum lot sizes, and a host of other issues. However, the important difference between restrictive covenants and zoning regulations is that restrictive covenants are imposed by private individuals on other private individuals.

Restrictive covenants are imposed through deeds or other public record documents. They are said to "run with the land," which means that once a restrictive covenant is imposed on a parcel of land, it remains with that parcel no matter how many times ownership of the land changes hands. Restrictive covenants imposed on present owners will be binding on future owners.

Developers often use restrictive covenants as a way to control use in planned communities, such as subdivisions or other commercial developments. Landowners often create restrictive covenants when there are no zoning rules or regulations imposed by the local government. Courts have recognized the rights of landowners to create restrictive covenants of property, as long as they fall within certain guidelines. For instance, restrictive covenants cannot be used to discriminate against potential owners any more than zoning rules or regulations can.[8]

Restrictive covenants are used by private individuals to control how property can be used, even to the extent of what structures can be placed on the land, how far the house can be set back from the road, and even the minimum and maximum square footage of residences.

ISSUE AT A GLANCE

---

1. CREATING COVENANTS

A restrictive covenant is, in essence, a contract.[9] A seller can create a series of covenants and record them, or put them in a deed, and the new owner takes the property subject to these limitations. The new owner does not have the option of ignoring these conditions. The most common ways to create restrictive covenants are:

- Including them in a deed from the grantor to the grantee
- Recording the restrictive covenants in the public records
- Recording a plat that contains the restrictive covenants

Just as we have seen in other contexts dealing with real property, restrictive covenants must be in writing to satisfy the Statute of Frauds. If they are not in writing, they cannot be enforced.

2. RESTRICTIVE COVENANTS "TOUCH AND CONCERN"

When valid restrictive covenants are created, they impose conditions on the way that the property can be used, which must touch and concern the land. This colorful phrase means that the conditions placed on the new owner must concern the real estate, not the parties. A restrictive covenant cannot, for example, forbid

---

[8] *Sheets v. Dillon*, 221 N.C. 426, 431, 20 S.E.2d 344, 347 (1942).
[9] *Beall v. Hardie*, 177 Kan. 353, 279 P.2d 276 (1955).

the new owner from practicing a particular religion or from espousing particular politics. Instead, the conditions must apply to the parcel.

3. TYPICAL COVENANTS

Restrictive covenants can come in an enormous variety, but there are some basic principles that they all must follow. As we have already seen, each covenant must touch and concern the land. Because of this rule, the most common restrictive covenants:

- Establish minimum lot sizes
- Limit use of the property, such as to residential use only
- Limit the number of outbuildings on the parcel
- Restrict the types of animals that can live on the premises, such as forbidding farm animals
- Require that all buildings conform to a general architectural theme

4. ILLEGAL OR UNCONSTITUTIONAL COVENANTS

We have seen that restrictive covenants must touch and concern the real property and cannot be used as a vehicle to carry out discriminatory policies. Under this rule, restrictive covenants cannot be used to prevent people of a certain race, religion, or national origin from owning property in specific neighborhoods. Restrictive covenants were once used in this way, but were eventually abolished by the U.S. Supreme Court. In *Shelley v. Kraemer*,[10] the Court ruled that restrictive covenants were being used as a method to keep African Americans out of white neighborhoods. In that case, white neighbors banded together and recorded the following restrictive covenant:

> The said property is hereby restricted to the use and occupancy for the term of Fifty (50) years from this date, so that it shall be a condition all the time and whether recited and referred to as (sic) not in subsequent conveyances and shall attach to the land, as a condition precedent to the sale of the same, that hereafter no part of said property or any portion thereof shall be, for said term of Fifty-years, occupied by any person not of the Caucasian race, it being intended hereby to restrict the use of said property for said period of time against the occupancy as owners or tenants of any portion of said property for resident or other purpose by people of the Negro or Mongolian Race.[11]

The Supreme Court ruled that such a condition was unconstitutional and a denial of equal protection under state and federal laws. The restrictive covenant was struck down.

---

[10] 334 U.S. 1, 68 S. Ct. 836, 92 L. Ed. 1161 (1948).
[11] *Shelley v. Kraemer*, 334 U.S. 1, 68 S.Ct. 836, 92 L. Ed. 1161 (1948).

FIGURE 10-4

Restrictive Covenants

1. These covenants are to run with the land and shall be binding on all parties and all persons claiming under them until January 1, 2003, at which time said covenants shall be automatically extended for successive periods of ten (10) years, unless by vote of those persons then owning a majority of said lots it is agreed to change said covenants in whole or in part.

2. If the parties hereto, or any of them or their heirs, or successors or assigns shall violate or attempt to violate any of the covenants herein, it shall be lawful for any other person or persons owning any real property situated in said subdivision as shown on said plat to prosecute any proceedings at law or in equity against the person or persons violating or attempting to violate any such covenant and either to prevent him or them from so doing, or to recover damages or other dues for such violation.

3. Invalidation of any one of these covenants by judgment or court order shall in no wise effect any of the other provisions which shall remain in full force and effect.

4. All numbered lots in said subdivision as shown on said plat shall be known and described as residential lots and no part of said lots shall be used for any type of business or stores. No structure shall be erected, altered, placed or permitted to remain on any lot other than one detached single family dwelling, except storage buildings which are of the same construction as the residence located on said lot.

5. None of said numbered lots as shown on said recorded plat shall be re-subdivided so as to create an additional building lot. Where a residence has been erected on a plot consisting of two or more lots, none of said lots shall thereafter be sold separately if such sales would result in a violation of Paragraph 8 below.

6. No trailer, basement, garage, or other outbuildings erected on these residential lots shall be, at any time, used as a residence temporarily or permanently, nor shall any residence be moved onto a building plot in the subdivision. No mobile homes, either temporary or permanent, shall be allowed on any lot in this subdivision.

7. That no single-family residence having less than 1,200 square feet of heated floor space exclusive of garage, carport, basement, or other auxiliary structure shall be erected on the lot. Any residence having living quarters on more than one floor must contain at least 1,000 square feet of heated floor space on the principal floor and a total of not less than 1,600 square feet of heated floor space exclusive of garage, carport, basement, or other auxiliary structure.

For a restrictive covenant to have legal impact, the restrictions must focus on how the property is used, not the religious, racial, or ethnic origin of the people owning the land.

ISSUE AT A GLANCE

5. ENFORCING COVENANTS

Enforcing restrictive covenants is a relatively straightforward affair. Unlike zoning regulations, which allow the local government to cite the offending homeowner, restrictive covenants must be enforced through civil lawsuits by adjoining landowners. These landowners, who must be bound by the same restrictive covenants, are permitted to sue the offending landowner to enforce the restrictive covenants that they agreed to when they purchased the property.

6. TERMINATING RESTRICTIVE COVENANTS

Restrictive covenants can be terminated in any of several ways. They may expire by their own terms, such as when the restrictive covenant contains language providing a termination date. The most common ways for restrictive covenants to terminate are:

- When the restrictive covenants have a stated time period
- When the restrictive covenants have been abandoned
- When the neighborhood has undergone substantially changed conditions
- When the properties affected have merged

a. Stated Time Period

It is not uncommon for restrictive covenants to have a predetermined time period. For instance, the owners might simply state that the conditions will only apply for 20 years. There is no requirement that restrictive covenants give a specific time period. When they fail to do so, they are considered binding in perpetuity.

b. Abandonment

Restrictive covenants terminate when they have been abandoned by the people they were designed to protect. Abandonment can occur in a number of ways. Suppose, for example, that the local owners have been disregarding the restrictive covenants for years. When it has become obvious that the restrictive covenants no longer have any legal significance, courts will not enforce them. In one case, a court stated that, "Restrictive covenants will not be enforced merely to harass and annoy some particular person, when it is clear to the court that the objective for which the restrictive covenants were originally entered into have already failed."[12]

c. Changed Conditions

Restrictive covenants may also be extinguished when the conditions existing on the real property no longer have any bearing to the original conditions. Suppose, for

---

[12] *Logan v. Sprinkle*, 256 N.C. 41, 123 S.E.2d 209 (1961).

example, that when the original restrictive covenants were enacted, the entire area consisted of farmland and groves. However, what was once farmland now consists of retail establishments and apartment buildings. In this case, subsequent owners have abandoned the original intent of the restrictive covenants. The standard that courts use to determine if there has been a sufficient change of conditions to terminate restrictive covenants is that there is a fundamental change in the use of the property to such an extent that the original purpose of the restrictive covenants no longer applies.[13]

d. Merger

Merger is a doctrine we have encountered in several situations already. For instance, we saw in life estates that when a person is both the remainderman and a life tenant, the estate merges into one complete unit owned by the single individual. The idea behind merger in the context of restrictive covenants is relatively simple: When a single individual owns all affected parcels, there no longer are any outside interests involved, and the individual is free to dispose of the restrictive covenants. In this case, merger would apply only if a single individual owns every parcel affected by the restrictive covenants. Even if this individual owns all but one parcel, merger would not apply and restrictive covenants would not be terminated.

B. SUBDIVISION RULES AND REGULATIONS

Many cities and towns across the country have been vested with the power to adopt subdivision regulations for neighborhoods in their areas. Towns can adopt ordinances that require a real estate developer to create a plat designating the streets, easements, rights of way, and boundary lines for all tracts contained in a particular subdivision, as well as any other limitations that are reasonable for safety or health reasons.

C. NUISANCE ACTIONS

Nuisance actions are a type of civil lawsuit that give one landowner the right to sue another. A landowner might sue her neighbor when the neighbor is engaging in activities that make it difficult or impossible for other neighbors to enjoy their property. A civil nuisance action would be authorized, for instance, when the neighbor is engaged in some chemical or manufacturing process that involves loud noises or odors that interfere with the enjoyment of property. Nuisance

> ### Sidebar
>
> "*It is to be remembered that there are two basic devices for urban planning and development; community zoning and restrictive covenants among private individuals. The beneficial results of private land-use controls are readily apparent throughout the country and are not merely confined to residential subdivisions. Use of restrictions are encouraged by most planning agencies. Indeed, restrictive covenants are held to be superior to zoning laws which rest on police power.*"[14]

Nuisance
A cause of action that is authorized when the defendant's behavior results in a loss of enjoyment or value in the plaintiff's property.

---

[13] *Gladstone v. Gregory*, 95 Nev. 474, 596 P.2d 491 (1979).
[14] *Meredith v. Washoe County. Sch. Dist.*, 84 Nev. 15, 19, 435 P.2d 750 (1968).

actions are commonly seen in situations in which fumes, liquids, or other substances are leaking from one person's property to another's.

1. PUBLIC NUISANCE

There are actually two different types of nuisance actions: public and private. A public nuisance is some condition that affects rights of citizens in general. This condition could be a health risk or a general annoyance. When a condition is classified as a public nuisance, local government officials are authorized to bring an action for the good of the community. New federal statutes have made the use of nuisance actions even more valuable to those claiming that large corporations are polluting groundwater or dumping hazardous waste. Working through the EPA, many agencies use federal statutes to force companies to pay for the complete cost of cleaning up a site that has been designated hazardous.

Private individuals are usually prevented from bringing a claim under public nuisance laws; such actions are generally reserved for the government. Placing such limitations on public nuisance lawsuits is a direct reflection of the fact that there are many things in life that we must all put up with, and allowing a private person to bring a public nuisance suit for these things would grind the legal system to a halt. However, the same limitations disappear when the allegation is a private nuisance.

2. PRIVATE NUISANCE

Private nuisance actions, on the other hand, have fewer limitations than public nuisance actions. Neighbors are free to sue other neighbors for actions that affect the quality, use, and enjoyment of their property. Consider Example 10-2.

EXAMPLE 10-2

Juan lives on a typical suburban street. His next-door neighbor Chip has recently acquired 100 rabbits and keeps them in cages in his backyard. That number of rabbits produces a strong odor and Juan wants to know if he can bring a civil nuisance action against Chip to force Chip to get rid of the rabbits. Will his suit be successful?

Answer: Most likely. If Juan can establish that the odor from the rabbits is affecting his ability to use and enjoy his property, he may be able to prove his suit and have a judge order Chip to get rid of the rabbits.

Elements of a Private Nuisance Action

- The defendant maintains a condition that
- Substantially interferes with the plaintiff s right
- To use and enjoy his property

RESTRICTIVE COVENANTS

ANNOTATED DOCUMENT

1. These covenants are to run with the land and shall be binding on all parties and all persons claiming under then until January 1, 2003, at which said covenants shall be automatically extended for successive periods of ten (10) years, unless by vote of those persons then owning a majority of said lots it is agreed to change said covenants in whole or in part.

2. If the parties hereto, or any of them or their heirs, or successors or assigns shall violate or attempt to violate any of the covenants herein, it shall be lawful for any other person or person owning any real property situated in said subdivision as shown on said plat to prosecute any proceedings at law or in equity against the person or persons violating or attempting to violate any such covenant and either to prevent him or them from so doing, or to recover damages or other does for such violation.

3. Invalidation of any one of these covenants by judgment or court order shall in no wise affect any of the other provisions which shall remain in full force and effect.

4. All numbered lots in said subdivision as shown on said plat shall be known and described as residential lots and no part of said lots shall be used for any type of business or stores. No structure shall be erected, altered, placed or permitted to remain on any lot other than one detached single family dwelling, except storage buildings which are of the same construction as the residence located on said lot.

5. None of said numbered lots as shown on said recorded plat shall be re-subdivided so as to create an additional building lot. Where a residence has been erected on a plot consisting of two or more lots, none of said lots shall thereafter be sold separately if such sales would result in a violation of Paragraph 8 below.

6. No trailer, basement, garage, or other outbuildings erected on these residential lots shall be, at any time, used as a residence temporarily or permanently, nor shall any residence be moved onto a building plot in the subdivision. No mobile homes, either temporary or permanent, shall be allowed on any lot in this subdivision.

7. That no single-family residence having less than 1,200 square feet of heated floor space exclusive of garage, carport, basement, or other auxiliary structure shall be erected on the lot. Any residence having living quarters on more than one floor must contain at least 1,000 square feet of heated floor

This provision sets the time limit for the restrictive covenants

This clause allows civil action to enforce the restrictive covenants

Here, the lot use is restricted to residential only

This provision prohibits the use of mobile homes on the lots space on the principal floor and a total of not less than 1,600 square feet of heated floor space exclusive of garage, carport, basement, or other auxiliary structure.

8. All dwellings constructed shall have a setback of a minimum of 40 feet from the front property line and 12 feet from either side line. On corner lots, all dwellings constructed shall have a setback line of a minimum of 20 feet from the side street.

9. No signs of any kind shall be displayed to the public view on any lot, except one sign of not more than 5 ft. advertising property for sale or rent, or signs used by a builder to advertise the property during the construction and sales term.

10. No lots shall be used or maintained as a dumping ground for rubbish, trash, garbage or other waste. All trash and garbage must be kept in a sanitary container. All trash containers shall be maintained in a location that is not visible from the street.

11. Grass and weeds are to be kept down on all vacant lots to prevent an unsightly and unsanitary condition. This is an obligation of the owner and is to be done at his or her expense.

12. All homes constructed in this subdivision shall be principally of brick, stone or wood siding of 4 inches or larger. No concrete or cinder blocks shall appear.

13. The grantors reserve an easement of 10 feet along the rear property line, and 5 feet along the side property line of each and every lot for present or future utility needs, such as telephone, electricity, water, sewer, gas lines, and drainage from streets and slopes. Any easements which have heretofore been granted by the grantors are also reserved. The easement area of each road and all improvements on it shall be maintained continuously by the owner of the road except for improvements for which a public authority or utility company is responsible.

14. No animals, livestock or poultry shall be raised, or kept on any lot, except that dogs, cats or other household pets may be kept, provided that they are not kept, bred, or maintained for any commercial purposes.

Here, the restrictive covenants limit the type of material that can be used in building a home

ETHICS — DISCRIMINATORY RESTRICTIVE COVENANTS

Legal professionals should always be on guard against unscrupulous or unconstitutional practices. In the area of restrictive covenants, with its long history of discriminatory practices, it is always a good idea to review proposed restrictive covenants for any clause that could be used to discriminate against a particular group. Unlike the early twentieth century, when covenants contained clauses that were clearly discriminatory, modern covenants may be more subtle. For instance, a discriminatory covenant might require a "sponsor" before a person will be allowed to live in a specific neighborhood. Other covenants might contain provisions establishing minimum income limits for ownership or control who can be a member of the neighborhood association. Any such provision should be viewed with skepticism and when doubt exists, the provision should be thoroughly researched to make sure that it is not an unconstitutional infringement on a buyer's right to live in a certain place.

HAWKINS VIEW ARCHITECTURAL CONTROL COMMITTEE v. COOPER

CASE EXCERPT

241 Or.App. 269, 279, 250 P.3d 380, 385 (Or.App., 2011)

WOLLHEIM, J.

Plaintiff is the Architectural Control Committee of Hawkins View, a planned neighborhood in Eugene. Defendants own a lot in Hawkins View that is subject to the Conditions, Covenants, and Restrictions (CCRs) of Hawkins View. Plaintiff initiated this case, seeking a declaration that the CCRs preclude defendants from building more than one house on their lot and an injunction enjoining defendants from subdividing their lot without homeowner approval as required by the CCRs. The parties filed cross-motions for summary judgment, and the trial court granted summary judgment to plaintiff, along with attorney fees. The judgment declared that defendants could build only one house on their lot and enjoined defendants from subdividing their lot without obtaining the requisite homeowner approval. Defendants appeal, contending that the CCRs are ambiguous and, thus, that issues of material fact preclude summary judgment. We affirm.

The Hawkins View subdivision was created in two phases. In 1996, the developer recorded a declaration that created the original subdivision, Phase I. Included in that declaration were the original CCRs, along with a definition of the property subject to the CCRs. The declaration recited: "Declarant owns certain real property in Eugene, Oregon known as Hawkins View more particularly described in Exhibit 'A' attached hereto and incorporated herein ('the Property')." Exhibit A referred to a plat of Hawkins View and provided, "Lots 1–102 of Hawkins View PUD as platted and recorded in File 75 Slides 300–303, Lane County, Oregon, Plat Records, Lane County, Oregon." The plat map referred to depicts lots 1 to 102 of Hawkins View and an additional lot, 103. The declaration subjected "all the Property, together with any and all properties which may hereafter be added to the planned community pursuant to Section 2.2 hereof to the Covenants, Conditions and Restrictions contained herein." The CCRs defined "Property" as "all real property, improvements and fixtures as described in Exhibit 'A.'"

In Section 2.2, the declarant reserved the right to add additional property to Hawkins View. That section provided:

"Additions to Property. The Development shall initially consist of Property. The Development may be expanded by filing a supplement to this Declaration together with a plat with the County Recorder of Lane County, designating that property to be added to and become subject to the Covenants contained herein. At any time within seven (7) years from the date of filing hereof, the Declarant may add additional property to the Development without the consent of any party. There shall be no limitation on the number of Lots and/or Lots which may be developed in the Development."

In 1997, as part of Phase 2 of the development, the declarant exercised his authority to add property to Hawkins View by amending Exhibit A, as follows:

"Pursuant to paragraph 2.2 of the Declaration, Exhibit A is amended and supplemented to add the following described real property as within the Property covered by the Declaration:

"Lots 1–14 inclusive of Hawkins View PUD, Phase 2, as platted and recorded in File 75, Slides 571 & 572, Lane County Plat Records, Lane County, Oregon."

The amendment to Exhibit A that incorporated Phase 2 into Hawkins View subdivided lot 103 into 14 lots, which are referred to in Section 9 of the fourth amendment as "Lots 1–14." Lots 1 to 13 are one-third of an acre on average. By contrast, lot 14 is nearly 10 acres.

The CCRs created an Architectural Control Committee (ACC), defining the ACC as "the Committee initially formed by the Declarant and later elected by the Homeowners, to review and approve or deny plans and specifications for the design and construction of Improvements within the Development and to undertake such other tasks as may be specified by the Declarant or the Homeowners." The declaration charged the ACC with the exclusive "responsibility and authority for enforcing the Covenants Conditions and Restrictions of this Declaration." The declaration also gave the ACC the specific duty of reviewing "plans, specifications, design, construction, and alterations of all Improvements built within the Property."

In October 2007, defendants purchased lot 14 from the declarant. The declarant had marketed lot 14 as having "development potential." After reviewing the CCRs attached to that lot, defendants agreed that it had that potential. However, one restriction imposed by the CCRs is that only one house may be built on each lot. A "lot" is defined as "a distinct parcel of real property designated as a Lot on the final Plat recorded with Lane County, containing a separate tax lot number." Nonetheless, defendants believed that the CCRs permitted them to subdivide lot 14 into multiple lots by recording a new plat with Lane County. In defendants' view, once lot 14 was subdivided, they could build one house on each new lot without violating the one-house-per-lot rule contained in the CCRs.

Plaintiff objected to defendants' development plans. Plaintiff notified defendants that their development plan violated the one-house-per-lot rule because, even if defendants subdivided their lot by recording a new plat with the county, defendants' unilateral action would not transform their single lot into multiple lots as defined by the CCRs. Rather, in plaintiff's view, defendants could effectuate their plan only by amending the CCRs, which required approval by 85 percent of Hawkins View homeowners.

Defendants went forward with their development plans despite the dispute and communicated with the county about subdividing their lot. Plaintiff responded by filing this action seeking a declaration that defendants could build only one house on their lot and an injunction preventing defendants from filing a new plat with the county unless defendants obtained the necessary homeowner approval to amend the CCRs. Defendants answered and filed a cross-claim, seeking a declaration that the CCRs did not preclude them from subdividing their lot and that "the ACC has no jurisdiction" to stop defendants' plan to subdivide their lot. The parties also sought attorney fees.

The parties filed cross-motions for summary judgment. Plaintiff argued that defendants were limited to building one house on their lot and that defendants could not effectively file a new plat without amending the CCRs, which required 85 percent homeowner approval. Defendants conceded that they were limited to building one house per lot, but argued that there was no restriction on subdividing their lot. The trial court granted plaintiff's motion for summary judgment and entered a general judgment declaring that defendants could not build more than one house on their lot and enjoining defendants from filing a plat that subdivided their lot without approval from 85 percent of the Hawkins View homeowners. The court also entered a supplemental judgment awarding plaintiff attorney fees.

Defendants appeal, assigning error to the trial court's granting of plaintiff's motion for summary judgment and to the court's denial of defendants' motion for summary judgment. Defendants also assign error to the trial court's supplemental judgment awarding plaintiff attorney fees, arguing that, if the trial court erred on the merits, then the award of attorney fees is also error.

The parties renew the arguments that they made to the trial court. Because defendants agree that the CCRs limit lot owners to building one house per lot, we understand the dispute to be whether the CCRs restrict defendants from unilaterally subdividing their lot. Our task, then, is to determine the meaning of the CCRs, using the method described in Yogman v. Parrott, 325 Or. 358, 361–64, 937 P.2d 1019 (1997). We begin by examining the text of the relevant provisions in the context of the document as a whole. If the meaning is unambiguous, our analysis ends. Id. at 361, 937 P.2d 1019. "'Whether the terms of a contract are ambiguous is a question of law. In the absence of an ambiguity, the court construes the words of a contract as a matter of law.'" Id. (quoting Eagle Industries, Inc. v. Thompson, 321 Or. 398, 405, 900 P.2d 475 (1995)).

If, however, we determine that the text in context is ambiguous, our next step is to examine extrinsic evidence of the contracting parties' intent. Id. at 363, 937 P.2d 1019. The practical construction of the contractual provision applied by the contracting parties and their successors — that is, the manner in which the parties applied the contractual term at issue — is a useful clue to the meaning of a textually ambiguous provision. Id. at 364, 937 P.2d 1019.

Finally, if extrinsic evidence fails to clarify the ambiguity, we turn to maxims of construction. Id. The maxim ordinarily applied in this context is that restrictive covenants are to be construed strictly. Id. at 366, 937 P.2d 1019.

We begin, then, with the text of the provisions. As a threshold issue, defendants argue that plaintiff, the ACC, is not authorized to bring this action. Four sections of the CCRs discuss plaintiff's authority.

Section 6.1 provides:

> "Architectural Control Committee. The responsibility and authority for enforcing the Covenants Conditions and Restrictions of this Declaration shall rest exclusively with the Architectural Control Committee in order to foster uniformity of enforcement and to further the best interests of the Development as a whole. Enforcement may take the form of injunctive or declaratory relief to require compliance without the necessity of proving special or specific harm or the necessity of posting a bond."

That section's broad grant of authority to plaintiff — assigning it exclusive responsibility and authority to enforce the CCRs — appears to answer defendants' argument. Plaintiff brought this action for the purpose of enforcing the CCRs, a responsibility that rests exclusively with plaintiff under Section 6.1. Section 6.3 confirms that interpretation. It provides:

> "Homeowners' Enforcement. All requests by Homeowners for enforcement or interpretation of the Covenants, Conditions, and Restrictions shall be submitted for consideration to the Architectural Control Committee."

Thus, if any homeowner perceives a violation of the CCRs, the homeowner must submit a request to plaintiff for the enforcement or interpretation of the CCRs.

Nonetheless, defendants argue that two other sections of the CCRs, Sections 1.1 and 4.2, assign more narrow duties to plaintiff and limit the authority granted under Section 6.1. Section 1.1 defines "Architectural Control Committee" to mean "the Committee initially formed by the Declarant and later elected by the Homeowners, to review and approve or deny plans and specifications for the design and construction of Improvements within the Development and to undertake such other tasks as may be specified by the Declarant or the Homeowners."

Defendants contend that that definition limits plaintiff's authority to reviewing and approving or denying plans and specifications for the design and construction of improvements within Hawkins View because "there was no evidence that the Declarant or the Homeowners had ever specified any other 'tasks' for plaintiff to perform." We disagree, because Section 6.1, quoted above, assigns plaintiff the additional task of enforcing the CCRs.

Next, defendants argue that Section 4.2 also limits plaintiff's authority to approving and denying plans for improvements built in Hawkins View. That section provides:

> "Duties. The Architectural Control Committee (herein 'Committee') shall be established to review and approve or deny plans, specifications, design, construction, and alterations of all Improvements built within the Property, pursuant to design specifications set out in these Covenants Conditions and Restrictions. The Committee shall consist of three members, at least one of whom shall be an architect, engineer, or contractor or shall have such other similar qualifications. The Committee shall consider the recommendations, if any, of the Declarant and Homeowners for design control and site approval for proposed Improvements, but it shall exercise its own judgment regarding the proposed Improvements. In approving or denying proposed Improvements, the Committee shall consider whether the Improvement complies with this Declaration, the design guidelines contained herein, and the overall aesthetic quality and feeling of continuity of the Development."

It is true, as defendants contend, that Section 4.2 describes plaintiff's responsibility to review and approve or deny development plans. However, there is no inconsistency between that section and Section 6.1, which assigns exclusive authority to enforce the CCRs to plaintiff. Indeed, many sections of the CCRs set out design standards for the neighborhood that are to be enforced, pursuant to Section 6.1, by plaintiff. Accordingly, we conclude that Sections 1.1, 4.2, and 6.1 are not contradictory and that Section 6.1 expressly grants plaintiff exclusive authority to enforce the CCRs.

We next consider whether the CCRs preclude defendants from subdividing their lot without homeowner approval. Section 8.3 provides:

"This Declaration may be amended at any time by an instrument signed by 85% of the total Homeowners of the Property. Any amendment must be properly recorded, if necessary, under the laws of the state of Oregon."

The CCRs define the term "declaration" to mean "the Covenants, Conditions, and Restrictions and all other provisions herein set forth in this entire document, including any amendments or supplements." Thus, the declaration includes the CCRs as well as any provisions set forth in the entire document containing the CCRs, along with any amendments or supplements, and may be amended only with 85 percent homeowner approval. The homeowner approval rule applies not only to the CCRs, but to the entire declaration. Thus, if defendants' lot 14 is part of the declaration, then a subdivision of lot 14 would be subject to the homeowner approval rule of Section 8.3. Whether lot 14, as platted, is part of the declaration is resolved by reference to the 1997 amendment to the declaration, which amended Exhibit A. The declarant filed that amendment when he added property to Hawkins View. Section 9 of the amendment provides:

"Pursuant to paragraph 2.2 of the Declaration, Exhibit A is amended and supplemented to add the following described real property as within the Property covered by the Declaration:

"Lots 1–14 inclusive of Hawkins View PUD, Phase 2, as platted and recorded in File 75, Slides 571 & 572, Lane County Oregon Plat Records, Lane County, Oregon."

That section added lot 14, as platted and recorded, to "the Property Covered by the Declaration." Accordingly, the declaration brought lot 14 within Hawkins View "as platted and recorded." Thus, any subsequent plat that subdivides lot 14 would eliminate the lot 14 that is included within the declaration "as platted and recorded." Put another way, a subdivided lot 14 would be platted differently than lot 14 is currently platted and recorded. Because defendants seek to amend the declaration by recording a new plat, they must comply with Section 8.3, which requires 85 percent homeowner approval before amending the declaration.

Context confirms our interpretation. The original declaration created Phase I of the development, which included lots 1 to 102. The declarant left lot 103 outside of the development. However, in Phase 2 of the development, the declarant subdivided lot 103 and brought the subdivided lots, including lot 14, inside the development, expressly pursuant to Section 2.2.

Because we conclude that the CCRs expressly and unambiguously preclude defendants from subdividing their lot without the mandated homeowner approval, we do not need to address the additional steps of contract interpretation set out in Yogman.

In view of our conclusion that the trial court correctly interpreted the CCRs to require homeowner approval for subdivision of lot 14, we conclude that the trial court did not err when it granted plaintiff's motion for summary judgment and declared that defendants could not build more than one house on their lot and enjoined defendants from subdividing their lot without 85 percent homeowner approval. In light of our disposition on the merits, we reject defendants' assignment of error contending that the trial court erred in awarding plaintiff attorney fees.

Affirmed.

CASE QUESTIONS

1   What is a CCR?
2   According to the CCRs, what is the Architectural Control Committee?
3   What is the plaintiff's complaint in this suit?
4   According to the court, what is the process by which it determines the meaning of the CCRs?
5   What was the court's decision in this case?

 SKILLS YOU NEED IN THE REAL WORLD

LOCATING RESTRICTIVE COVENANTS

The process of locating restrictive covenants isn't always as easy and straightforward as you might think. In some cases, restrictive covenants are filed with the general warranty deeds. However, in other situations, they are filed as a separate document and the deeds are cross-referenced to the filing. In still other situations, the restrictive covenants may be contained on a plat or some other document. In any event, you should develop your skills in locating restrictive covenants. Talk to courthouse personnel: They are a gold mine of information and can often recall details about certain areas that aren't clearly reflected in the public records. They can also save you a lot of time by directing you to the correct filing. Once you have located a copy of the restrictive covenants for a particular neighborhood, make a copy of all clauses and review them. Also note any property to which these restrictive covenants apply. If a question comes up about the application, constitutionality, or validity of the covenants, others will certainly want to see a hard copy of them.

CHAPTER SUMMARY

In this chapter we have seen that there are numerous restrictions on a private individual's ability to use her land. Zoning is one of the most common types of local governmental control on private property use. Zoning rules and regulations must have a rational basis and must attempt to enforce safety, health, or other concerns. Zoning rules and regulations can be enforced through citations. There are three broad categories of zoning: residential, commercial, and industrial. When a structure predates the enactment of a zoning regulation, it is referred to as a nonconforming use. If a landowner wishes to use property in a way that is inconsistent with existing zoning rules and regulations, she can apply for a zoning variance. Zoning boards occasionally grant exceptions, called conditional use permits, to encourage businesses to go into residential areas. Zoning cannot be used to discriminate against individuals. An example of a potentially discriminatory zoning practice is "spot" zoning. In addition to zoning rules and regulations, individuals are also bound by state and federal laws that can severely limit how an individual uses her property.

Restrictive covenants are a way of regulating use by private individuals. Restrictive covenants are created by previous owners and act as conditions that limit use for future owners. The typical provisions of restrictive covenants include minimum lot sizes, minimum square footage in houses, and other issues. Restrictive covenants can be terminated by their own terms if they are abandoned, if a court rules that conditions have changed to such extent that they are no longer applicable, or if merger has occurred. In addition to restrictive covenants, private individuals can also bring nuisance actions against neighbors who are engaging in practices that limit a person's use and enjoyment of her property.

REVIEW QUESTIONS

1. What is zoning?
2. What is aesthetic zoning?
3. How are zoning regulations enforced?
4. What are the three broad categories of zoning regulations?
5. What is a nonconforming use?
6. What is a conditional use permit?
7. What is a variance?
8. What are some examples of unconstitutional zoning regulations?
9. What is the "rational basis test" as it applies to zoning?
10. What is "spot" zoning?
11. How do building codes compare with zoning rules and regulations?
12. What is a historical district?
13. What is the Interstate Land Sales Full Disclosure Act?
14. What is the role of environmental issues in restricting a private landowner's use of property?
15. Explain restrictive covenants.
16. What are some of the methods used to create restrictive covenants?
17. How can restrictive covenants be terminated?
18. Provide examples of some of the typical provisions found in restrictive covenants.

19 What does it mean when we say that restrictive covenants must "touch and concern" the land?

20 What are some examples of unconstitutional restrictive covenants?

DISCUSSION QUESTIONS

Having zoning regulations that regulate health and safety seems like a good idea, but what about aesthetic zoning? Why should a local government be able to dictate to a private landowner or businessperson how a particular structure should look? Is there a good reason for such zoning regulations? Explain your answer.

PRACTICAL APPLICATIONS

At your local deed office or land registry office, locate a copy of restrictive covenants. What types of limitations are contained in these restrictive covenants?

WEB SITES

New York City Department of City Planning
http://www.nyc.gov/html/dcp/html/subcats/zoning.html

Washington, D.C. Office of Zoning
http://www.dcoz.dcgov.org/main.shtm

New Hampshire Office of Energy and Planning
http://www.nh.gov/oep/programs/MRPA/ZoningBoardFAQs.htm

City of Chicago, IL Zoning
http://www.cityofchicago.org/city/en/depts/dcd/provdrs/admin.html

TERMS AND PHRASES

Aesthetic zoning	Nuisance	Variance
Conditional use permit	Restrictive covenant	Zoning
Nonconforming use	Spot zoning	

SIGNIFICANT CASES

Wise v. Harrington Grove Community Ass'n, Inc., 584 S.E.2d 731 (N.C., 2003)

Samms v. Autumn Run Community Improvement Ass'n, Inc., 23 S.W.3d 398 (Tex. App. Houston. 1.Dist., 2000)

Berg v. Bridle Path Homeowners Ass'n, Inc., 809 So. 2d 32 (Fla. App. 4.Dist., 2002)

County Commissioners of Charles County v. St. Charles Associates Limited Partnership, 784 A.2d 545 (Md., 2001)

Duffy v. Landings Association, Inc., 536 S.E.2d 758 (Ga. App., 2000)

Hill v. Palm Beach Polo, Inc., 717 So. 2d 1080 (Fla. App. 4.Dist., 1998)

Maryland Overpak Corp. v. Mayor and City Council of Baltimore, 909 A.2d 235 (Md., 2006)

Mueller v. People's Counsel for Baltimore County, 934 A.2d 974 (Md. Spec. App., 2007)

McDowell v. Randolph County, 649 S.E.2d 920 (N.C. App., 2007)

Schafer v. Deuel County Bd. of Com'rs, 725 N.W.2d 241 (S.D., 2006)

Real Estate Professions

Focus of This Chapter

Various real estate professions are profiled in this chapter, from real estate brokers to law firms that specialize in real estate issues. The chapter also addresses the day-to-day activities of real estate paralegals.

Chapter Learning Objectives

After completing this chapter, you should be able to:

- Identify the various real estate professions
- Define the role played by real estate brokers in the sale of property
- Explain the importance of agency law for real estate brokers
- Describe the function of real estate inspectors and surveyors
- Identify the important duties of the legal professionals in a real estate practice

 **INTRODUCTION**

There is a dizzying array of professions tied directly or indirectly to real estate. In this chapter, we examine not only the rules and regulations associated with real estate brokers, but also the role of appraisers, surveyors, loan officers, and last, but not least, the legal professionals who specialize in real estate law, especially paralegals.

The most well-known example of professionals who work in real estate everyday is real estate brokers. These professionals are regulated by state law, have their own code of ethics, and are bound by the law of agency. But there are many others who are closely involved in real estate law. For instance, there are loan officers at lending institutions whose job it is to evaluate prospective borrowers. There are also appraisers, surveyors, investors, and many others. We begin our examination of real estate professions by exploring an area of law that is closely intertwined with many of these professions: the law of agency.

THE LAW OF AGENCY

Agency
A business relationship between a principal (who is the source of the authority for the transaction) and the agent (who has the power to carry it out).

Principal
The person for whom an agent works.

Agents have existed in one form or another for centuries. Essentially, an **agency** relationship is created when a person is unable or unwilling to conduct business on his own behalf and instead retains another person to act for him. The person who hires an agent is referred to as the **principal**. The principal works out an arrangement with an agent, giving this agent the power to conduct certain transactions and the authority to see these transactions through to completion. The law of agency is very fluid and allows for a multitude of different relationships.

Once an agency arrangement is created, the agent has the power to legally bind the principal to contracts and other relationships. The agent can negotiate on behalf of the principal and, depending on the nature of the agreement between the agent and the principal, carry out an entire series of business transactions without the principal's direct involvement. Because this arrangement can bind the principal to serious legal obligations, most agency relationships are carefully crafted and written out. The agency agreement usually states the exact parameters of the agent's responsibility and authorization. One of the best examples of an agency relationship in real estate practice is the listing agreement between a home seller and a real estate broker, discussed in Chapter 6. How is this arrangement created?

A. CREATING AN AGENCY RELATIONSHIP

Although agency relationships can be created in a wide variety of ways, the most common way is by the express agreement between the principal and agent. In this agreement, which is often written out, the principal provides the exact parameters of the agent's authority, including details about particular transactions. The agent, for his part, will also want details about compensation and authority spelled out clearly to avoid any misunderstandings and potential legal liability. Putting an agency relationship into writing makes a great deal of sense, but there are numerous situations in which the principal-agency relationship rests completely on a verbal agreement.

 **An agency relationship can be created in a number of ways.**

Fiduciary
A person who holds a special position of trust and confidence in relation to another.

1. AGENT'S DUTY TO THE PRINCIPAL

As soon as the principal-agency relationship is created, certain duties are imposed on both parties. Agents are fiduciaries to principals. A **fiduciary** is someone who owes legal and ethical duties to another. The fiduciary relationship has been recognized under American and English law for centuries. Because an agent is a principal's fiduciary, the law imposes several key duties on the agent, including:

■ Obedience
■ Care
■ Loyalty
■ Accounting

a. Obedience

An agent's first, and some would argue most important, duty is to obey the principal's instructions. The entire reason for a principal-agency relationship is so that the principal can have some transaction carried out. Obviously, the principal must have faith that the agent will follow the instructions given. The law reinforces this duty by making obedience to the principal's instructions one of the core responsibilities of an agent. Disobedience of a principal's instructions is a primary ground for a successful lawsuit by the principal against the agent. There is a certain amount of flexibility under agency law when it comes to the principal's instructions. A principal might, for example, spell out the exact parameters and directions that the agent must follow. However, there are numerous situations in which the principal is either unable or unwilling to dictate all of the agent's actions. In fact, in situations in which the agent has special training and education, the principal would not want to control the agent's actions because the principal might make an elementary error. Beyond that, the principal uses an agent in order to take advantage of the agent's training and experience.

b. Care

In addition to obedience, the agent must also demonstrate diligence and due care in performing his duties. If the agent fails to live up to this standard, the principal would be authorized to bring a civil action against the agent. The standard of care that an agent must follow is not determined on a case-by-case basis. Instead, the agent's actions are compared with the actions that other reasonable and prudent agents in the same situation would have taken. If the agent fails to live up to the duty of care created by other agents, he is liable to the principal.

c. Loyalty

The duty of loyalty is considered one of the most important duties that an agent owes to a principal. This duty requires the agent to act in the best interests of the principal and to avoid situations in which there is a conflict of interest between the agent's desires and the principal's needs. If such a conflict arises, the agent must at least inform the principal of the potential conflict of interest and may also be required to withdraw from representing the principal in any way. The duty of loyalty requires the agent to place the business interests of the principal ahead of other considerations.

The duty of loyalty also imposes on an agent the requirement to avoid self-dealing. This term refers to the agent's unethical use of confidential information related to the principal that helps enrich the agent at the principal's expense. Consider Example 11-1.

EXAMPLE 11-1

Sally is Mario's agent. While working for Mario, she learns that he intends to purchase hundreds of acres of farmland in order to build an amusement park. Mario has understandably kept his plans secret to avoid a run-up in price on local farmland. Sally negotiates with local farmers and purchases the property herself, and then approaches Mario with an offer to buy the land at a substantially increased price. Can Mario bring suit against Sally alleging that she has violated her duty of loyalty? If so, who will win this suit?

Answer: Mario. Because Sally was Mario's agent, she cannot use information gathered from that relationship to personally enrich herself, especially at her principal's expense.

---

d. Accounting

Our discussion of the duties that an agent owes the principal would not be complete without including some of the more practical aspects of the relationship. An agent must make a full accounting of all financial arrangements and distributions that have arisen in the principal-agency relationship.

2. AGENT'S DUTY TO THIRD PARTIES

We have seen that agents have specific duties that they owe to their principals. However, questions often arise about an agent's duty to individuals who are outside the principal-agency relationship. Agents are not fiduciaries to third parties, so they obviously do not owe the same duties to them that they owe to their principals. So what duties does an agent owe to third parties? Under these circumstances, agents have the following duties:

- The duty of honesty and fair dealing
- The duty not to commit fraud
- The duty to avoid negligent misrepresentation

a. The Duty of Honesty and Fair Dealing

Although agents do not have fiduciary duties to third parties, they do have general duties. Perhaps most important of these is the duty of honesty and fair dealing. Agents must avoid using deceptive trade practices, fraud, or any other illegal practices. As we will see later in this chapter, this duty requires that real estate agents make certain disclosures to potential buyers. It also imposes upon them the obligation to make sure that buyers understand that real estate agents work for and are paid by sellers

b. Duty Not to Commit Fraud

The word **fraud** is used in everyday conversation and can have a wide variety of meanings. However, in the legal context, fraud has a very specific meaning. Fraud is deliberate concealment or deceit that causes injury to a third party or gives the agent an unconscionable advantage in a business transaction. If an agent conceals or actively deceives someone about a material fact, this constitutes fraud.

Fraud
An intentional deception that causes injury to another person.

FIGURE 11-1

Legal Elements of Fraud

- An agent made a representation of a material fact or concealed a fact

- The representation was false

- The agent knew that the representation was false

- The agent made the representation with the intent that a third party would rely on the representation

- The third party's reliance on the representation was reasonable under the circumstances

- The other party suffered injury from his reliance on the representation

i. Material Facts

Fraud can be both a criminal and a civil action. As you can see in Figure 11-1, there are several elements involved in proving a fraud action. These elements do not change in any significant way from civil cases to criminal cases. Both require the intentional misrepresentation of a **material fact**. A material fact is a critical negotiating point or understanding that, if changed, would likely alter the outcome of the business transaction. For instance, a person claims that he has title to an object and proposes to sell that object to another person when in fact he does not have title. His ownership is a material fact and the defrauded party would be entitled to bring either a civil or criminal act against him.

Material fact
An important or central fact in the contract or business negotiations that if fully revealed would change the outcome of the transaction.

ii. Sales Tactics

There is an important limitation on the law of representations and material facts. The law makes exceptions for statements that are normally associated with salesmanship. When a salesperson makes a claim such as, "this is the prettiest property I have ever seen in my entire life," such a comment is not intended to be taken literally. Put another way, the salesperson's opinion about the beauty of the property is not a material fact. The buyer would have a difficult time proving that the salesperson had seen prettier tracts at other times. As a result, many of the comments and statements that all consumers hear from salespersons are usually not taken literally unless they are presented as facts. Consider Example 11-2.

EXAMPLE 11-2

Arnold is an agent representing Alberta. Alberta wishes to sell her home. One day, while Arnold is showing the house to prospective buyers, he makes the following statements:

"This house has some of the finest craftsmanship you'll ever hope to see."

"Look at those windows — they are double paned and the best that money can buy."

"Take a look at those floors. They are so clean you could eat off them."

If any of these comments proved to be inaccurate, which one could be the basis of a fraud allegation?

Answer: Only the second. The first and third comments are opinions and are not actionable as fraud. However, if it turns out that the windows are not double paned or are not the best that money can buy, the buyers would have an action against Arnold for fraudulent statement.

c. Duty to Avoid Negligent Misrepresentation

Negligent misrepresentation
Liability for a statement that proved to be untrue when the person making the statement had no reasonable belief in its accuracy.

In addition to avoiding fraud, agents must also be aware that they face potential liability for **negligent misrepresentation**. There is a fine line between fraud and negligent misrepresentation. Both involve the communication of facts that are not correct, but there is an important difference. Fraud is considered to be an intentional action, while negligent misrepresentation is considered to be unintentional. As a result, fraud is always punished more severely than negligent misrepresentation. When we say that an agent has the duty to avoid negligent misrepresentation, what we are actually saying is that an agent must be aware of the truth about statements that he makes before making them. If an agent is not sure about the veracity of the statement and makes it anyway, and the statement proves to be untrue, the agent would be liable under the theory of negligent misrepresentation. This is true even if the agent believes that the statement is true, but has made no effort to verify it. An action for negligent misrepresentation can also be brought when an agent makes a statement with reckless disregard for its truth. Under any of these circumstances, an agent can be liable to a third party and may end up paying substantial monetary damages to the people who rely on the statements.

 Fraud is an intentional action; negligent misrepresentation is an unintentional action.

3. PRINCIPAL'S DUTY TO AGENT

Now that we have discussed the duties that agents owe to principals and third parties, we focus on the duties that principals owe to agents. Given the nature and quantity of duties that agents owe to their principals, it may be surprising to learn that principals have very few legal obligations to their agents. Generally speaking, principals have only three duties to their agents:

- Duty to compensate the agent
- Duty to cooperate
- Duty not to unfairly injure the agent's reputation

a. Duty to Compensate the Agent

It should come as no surprise that the primary duty the principal owes to an agent is to compensate the agent for his actions on behalf of the principal. The agent's

FIGURE 11-2

Elements of Negligent
Misrepresentation

- A false statement made by an agent

- But that the agent had not verified, or made with reckless disregard as to its truth

- That the agent believed was true

- That resulted in a financial loss to a third party relying on the statement

compensation can come in a wide variety of forms. An agent might be paid a flat fee for a service, or receive an hourly rate. As we will see later in this chapter, real estate agents are often paid on a commission basis. A commission is a percentage of the sale price. If a principal refuses to pay an agent's commission, the agent is entitled to sue the principal for the outstanding amount plus any additional charges that the agent has incurred in attempting to receive payment. Principals are often responsible for paying not only for an agent's services, but also for any expenses incurred by the agent during his representation.

b. Duty to Cooperate

In addition to paying the agent, the principal also has the duty to cooperate with the agent. Although this would seem to be a duty that should go without saying, there are situations in which a principal might choose not to cooperate with an agent in order to avoid paying the agent's fee. In such a situation, the agent could bring a civil action against the principal alleging a failure of the principal to abide by the duty to cooperate. Consider Example 11-3.

EXAMPLE 11-3

Arnold has been representing Alberta in her attempt to sell her house. Unfortunately, the market is depressed in her area and there have been few offers on Alberta's house. There is less than two weeks to go on the contract that Arnold signed with Alberta to represent her. When those two weeks are up, Alberta is free to hire another agent or to sell the house herself. A potential buyer, Calvin, approaches Alberta with the following proposition: If Alberta will stop cooperating with Arnold and wait for the two-week period to pass, she can avoid paying Arnold's commission when she sells the house to Calvin. Alberta refuses to show the house anymore and cuts off all contact with Arnold. Later, Arnold learns that Calvin had approached Alberta prior to the expiration of his listing agreement with her. Arnold sues for his commission. Will he get it?

Answer: Yes. Because Alberta violated her duty of cooperation with Arnold and engaged in an agreement with Calvin to cheat Arnold out of his commission, Arnold will receive his commission anyway, despite the fact that the sale occurred after Arnold's contract of representation terminated.

The duty to cooperate means not only that the principal must pay the agent's commission, but also that the principal should not terminate the agency relationship for an unjust or capricious reason. The principal is required to act reasonably to assist the agent in carrying out his duties and not to impose unreasonable demands on the agent.

c. Duty Not to Unfairly Injure the Agent's Reputation

In addition to the principal's other duties to compensate and cooperate, the principal is also under the obligation to refrain from unfairly injuring the agent's reputation. In many ways, this obligation resembles a defamation suit, in which a person is sued for making false statements about another. Here, however, the suit would be specific to the principal-agency relationship and would depend on the nature of the statements made by the principal. The principal is permitted to use the same defense that defendants use in defamation cases: that the statement was true.

B. INDEPENDENT CONTRACTORS

In our discussion of agency relationships, it is important to point out other relationships that do not follow the agency pattern. When a person is classified as an independent contractor, he is not an agent. Independent contractors are specialists. They make their own decisions about how the job will be completed, and other than cursory instructions from the employer, they do not take direction about how they should complete their jobs. They are truly independent, and with this independence comes the freedom from being classified as an agent, with the attendant legal and ethical duties that arise from that classification. There are times when the line between being an agent, an independent contractor, and or having some other business relationship is unclear. For an example of such a situation, read this chapter's case excerpt.

ISSUE AT A GLANCE

Independent contractors do not qualify as agents and do not have the same level of responsibility or duties as agents.

APPLYING AGENCY LAW TO REAL ESTATE TRANSACTIONS

So far, our discussions about agency law have been very general. But this is a book about real estate law and this chapter focuses on real estate professions. It is time for us to apply the general law of agency to the specialized world of real estate professionals.

The most common example of an agency relationship in real estate is the real estate agent. A real estate agent is, in every legal sense of the word, an agent. The real estate agent has a principal, has both ethical and legal duties to that principal, and receives his compensation from the principal. In a typical real estate agency relationship, a person who is legally authorized to act as a real estate agent enters into an agreement with a person who wishes to sell a home. In this scenario, the seller is the principal. The seller negotiates specific details of the agent's representation, including how long the relationship will last, what the agent is authorized to tell others about the home, when and how the agent will show the house to prospective buyers, and the amount of the agent's compensation. In most real estate transactions, a real estate agent works on a straight commission basis. The agent's compensation is a percentage of the final sale price.

Real estate agents owe the same duties to their principals as any other agent. However, because they are state licensed, real estate agents often owe additional duties to their principals. These differences also extend to the standard of care that is imposed on real estate agents.

Randy has produced a buyer who is ready, willing, and able to purchase Sandy's home. By the terms of their agency relationship, Sandy has agreed to pay Randy a 6 percent commission on the sale price. The sale price of the home is $120,000. What is Randy's commission?

    Answer: Randy's commission is $7,200.

EXAMPLE 11-4

A. A REAL ESTATE AGENT'S DUTY OF CARE

Real estate agents actually have a more rigorous standard of care than that seen with other agency relationships. State laws impose on them the duty to use skill, care, and diligence in the performance of their duties. They must demonstrate the same level of skill and care as other real estate agents. It isn't enough for a real estate agent to meet a general standard of skill and care. When it comes time for a court to weigh the real estate agent's actions, he will be compared to the standards of other real estate agents and held to the same high standards, regardless of the fact that he may be a novice in the profession. When it comes to diligence, courts are even more specific. To demonstrate diligence, a real estate agent must show that he acted with reasonable diligence in obtaining the most advantageous result for the principal. In a real estate context that translates into two factors: The agent obtained the best possible price and the best possible terms for the principal. Failure to do either may make the agent liable to the principal.

B. AN AGENT'S RESPONSIBILITY TO DISCLOSE INFORMATION

A real estate agent is required to make a complete disclosure to the principal of any information that potentially could be relevant to the transaction. In fact, most states require a real estate agent to make full disclosure not only to the principal but also to the prospective buyers. Among these disclosures, real estate agents must inform the buyers that the agent is working for and is paid by the seller. Although many states allow real estate agents to represent both the buyer and seller in a transaction, this arrangement is only allowed when there has been full disclosure to both sides and the arrangement is made with the informed consent of both parties.[1] The arrangement is referred to as dual agency and is a violation of state regulations unless fully disclosed to both sides. In the states where dual agency is permitted, the parties must agree to the representation in writing. Real estate agents not only have a legal obligation to disclose certain information, they also have an ethical obligation to preserve confidential information. Because the real estate agent represents the seller, the agent is not permitted to disclose to the buyer the seller's absolute lowest sale price or any other confidential information that the seller has relayed to the agent.

C. CLASSIFICATIONS OF REAL ESTATE AGENTS

So far, our discussion about the duties of real estate agents has presumed that there is only one classification: the agent. However, there are actually two different classifications of real estate professionals: real estate brokers and real estate agents.

1. REAL ESTATE BROKERS AND REAL ESTATE AGENTS

A real estate broker carries out the full range of activities normally associated with real estate transactions that fall under the category of agent. A real estate broker is someone who is licensed by the state and is authorized to earn a commission. A real estate agent, on the other hand, is usually a person who works under the authority of the real estate broker. The agent assists the broker and in exchange earns part of the commission. It is important to remember that the terminology used here can vary considerably from state to state. For instance, some states may recognize the two classifications as brokers and salespersons, while another state would refer to these individuals by other titles. In some instances, states have eliminated entire categories, such as real estate agents, and now refer to all members of their profession as brokers. For the sake of clarity, we will refer to these two categories as real estate brokers and real estate agents.

   Both the broker and the agent often work for a company that has other staff, including other real estate brokers, agents, salespersons, secretaries, and office managers. Whether a broker works for a firm or is self-employed, the broker's responsibilities to the seller remain the same.

   Although working as a real estate broker or agent offers a certain measure of freedom, there are downsides. For one thing, brokers and agents often work evenings and weekends and may also be on call to their clients at other times. Novice agents also face stiff competition from older, more established real estate agents who have better connections in the community.

   In addition to locating buyers, real estate brokers may also be responsible for arranging title searches and coordinating closings between buyers and sellers.

Sidebar

In 2002, there were 99,000 real estate brokers in United States. This compares to 308,000 real estate agents. Six out of ten real estate agents are self-employed.[2] By 2006, the number of real estate brokers had dropped to 40,480. Real estate sales agent numbers suffered an even sharper drop. By 2006, the total number had dropped to 128,140.[3]

---

[1] National Association of Realtors, Standard of Practice 1-5.
[2] Bureau of Labor Statistics, U.S. Department of Labor, Occupational Outlook Handbook, 2004-05 Edition.
[3] U.S. Department of Labor, Bureau of Labor Statistics, 2008.

Brokers often have a network of loan officers and mortgage brokers who can help the borrower begin the process of qualifying for a loan. In addition to meeting with prospective buyers, brokers also spend a great deal of time meeting with prospective sellers to sign listing agreements. Depending on the state, the broker may be the person responsible for coordinating the entire transaction, from the initial meeting of the buyer and seller to the closing or settlement. In other states, real estate attorneys handle these details.

Brokers also meet with prospective buyers and ask them questions in order to determine the best possible match between what the buyer can afford and the properties currently available. The broker will then turn to the "hot sheet" or, more likely, a computer database, to investigate the properties currently listed for sale to meet the buyer's specifications. We discuss how properties are advertised in the section on Multiple Listing Services.

Although brokers work for sellers, they may spend days or even weeks with a particular buyer. This sometimes creates a false impression for the buyer. The buyer may believe that the real estate broker has his best interests in mind, forgetting the basic agency relationship that exists between the real estate broker and the owner of the property that is eventually sold.

2. BECOMING A REAL ESTATE BROKER OR AGENT

Every state requires real estate brokers and agents to be licensed. There are some minimum requirements that all applicants must meet. They include:

- Must be a high school graduate
- Must be at least 18 years of age
- Must pass a written examination[5]

In addition to these minimum requirements, most states also require:

- Proof of good moral character
- Successful completion of real estate education requirements

Most states require that candidates complete a minimum number of hours of classroom instruction. For instance, some states require a minimum of 60 hours of classroom instruction before an applicant is allowed to take the written examination.[6] Once a real estate broker or agent obtains a license, he must also complete continuing education credits to maintain standing with the state. Notice that we have not used the term "Realtor." This term is a trademark symbol owned by the National Association of Realtors and can only be used by members of that organization. The NAR has been in existence since 1913, and the vast majority of real estate brokers and agents in the United States are members.

> **Sidebar**
>
> *Employment of real estate brokers and sales agents is expected to grow more slowly than the average for all occupations through the year 2012.*[4]

---

[4] Bureau of Labor Statistics, U.S. Department of Labor, Occupational Outlook Handbook, 2004-2005.
[5] Bureau of Labor Statistics, U.S. Department of Labor, Occupational Outlook Handbook, 2004-2005.
[6] Bureau of Labor Statistics, U.S. Department of Labor, Occupational Outlook Handbook, 2004-2005.

3. REGULATIONS THAT GOVERN REAL ESTATE AGENTS

Because states require real estate brokers and agents to be licensed, all states have some form of real estate commission that is responsible not only for admitting new members, but also for sanctioning brokers and agents who violate state regulations. State real estate boards are authorized to take disciplinary action against brokers and agents who violate rules and regulations. Among the more common actions that can result in sanctions are:

- Negligent misrepresentation
- Fraud
- Making false promises designed to influence or persuade a person
- Dual agency
- Failing to account for client funds
- Absconding or embezzling settlement funds

FIGURE 11-3

Annual Mean Wage, Real Estate Brokers, Bureau of Labor Statistics, 2011[7]

Occupation: Real Estate Brokers (SOC code 419021)	
Period: May 2010	
Area name	**Annual mean wage(2)**
National	**$76,060**
Footnotes: (2) Annual wages have been calculated by multiplying the hourly mean wage by 2080 hours; where an hourly mean wage is not published the annual wage has been directly calculated from the reported survey data.	
SOC code: Standard Occupational Classification code—see http://www.bls.gov/soc/home.htm	
Data extracted on December 18 2011	

If the state agency that governs real estate brokers and agents finds that a member has committed these or any other infractions, it is entitled to bring disciplinary action. A real estate broker or agent may have his license permanently suspended for serious infractions. State agencies are also authorized to temporarily suspend an agent's license for a less serious violation. For a summary of other possible sanctions against real estate agents, see Figure 11-4.

---

[7] Bureau of Labor Statistics, U.S. Department of Labor, Occupational Outlook Handbook, 2004-2005.

FIGURE 11-4

■ Temporary or permanent
suspension of license

■ Criminal liability

■ Civil liability to the client or third party

Summary of Possible Sanctions Against Real Estate Agents

4. SERVICES PROVIDED BY REAL ESTATE AGENTS AND BROKERS

Buyers and sellers turn to real estate agents because of their training, education, and experience with the real estate market. A real estate broker can be an invaluable asset to a seller by providing several services that are unavailable anywhere else. Not only will a real estate broker be able to advertise the property, but also, in most circumstances, the broker will list the property in the Multiple Listing Service.

a. Multiple Listing Service

The Multiple Listing Service (MLS) is a feature provided by real estate agents and brokers. Essentially the MLS is a database listing all available properties. The MLS both advertises these properties and offers to split commissions with other agents in the area. Listings in the MLS contain extensive descriptions, along with exterior photographs and other information, such as lot size, internal and external features of the residence, information about total square footage, bathrooms, bedrooms, and many other aspects. But the MLS is more. By offering to split the commission with other real estate agents, the MLS essentially puts all real estate agents in the community to work for the house seller. Although the MLS was once only a printed document, these days members of the local MLS can access property listings online. In the days before the widespread ability to access of the World Wide Web, the most recent postings in the MLS were referred to as the "hot sheet." The hot sheet would be printed once a week and distributed to local real estate agents. These days, a hot sheet is usually found online, not in hard copy. Because the MLS is only available to real estate brokers and agents, it continues to be an extremely valuable resource.

A multiple listing service is both an advertisement of available properties and an offer to other brokers to share in a commission.

ISSUE AT A GLANCE

b. Locating and Prequalifying Buyers

The primary purpose for the existence of a real estate broker or agent is to bring buyers and sellers together. To that end, real estate brokers not only enter into listing agreements with sellers to advertise and promote the sale of the property, but also actively seek potential buyers. It is not unusual for brokers and agents to

Tech Topic
ADVERTISING REAL ESTATE

Savvy real estate agents have come up with innovative ways to use technology and the Web to give buyers a comprehensive view of properties for sale. For example, special 360-degree cameras, or cameras with panorama attachments, can turn still photos into a sweeping panoramic view of a property. Likewise, a collection of still shots can be turned into a slide show, offering interior and exterior views from all angles. Uploaded to a web site, prospective buyers merely click a button to see the panoramic shots or a slide show that displays a property from every perspective, inside and out.

Some web sites include a map of a community, which buyers can customize to pinpoint the location of all properties for sale in a specific area. Buyers can further customize their search by specifying price, number of bedrooms and bathrooms, and additional amenities. All of it is automated; the agent needs only to input the basic information from the MLS listing.

Google Earth and Google maps have added another layer to search technology. Buyers can view not only the property they're interested in, but also the surrounding neighborhood. Armed with such extensive information, buyers can discard properties they might otherwise have had to visit. Conversely, they can approach the in-person property search with greater optimism that a prospective property meets their needs.

pre-qualify buyers, by meeting with them in person and asking them general questions about their financial condition and putting them in contact with local lenders. Obviously, it is in the broker's best interest to ensure that a buyer can produce the funds necessary to complete the transaction. The broker's ultimate responsibility is to produce a buyer who is ready, willing, and able to complete the transaction. The phrase "ready, willing, and able" has particular legal significance. If a broker or agent produces such a buyer and the seller reneges on the transaction, the real estate agent is still entitled to his commission. Even if the transaction never occurs, the real estate agent would be entitled to a commission based on the negotiated sale price, regardless of the fact that the sale never went through.[8]

OTHER REAL ESTATE PROFESSIONS

In this section we examine many other types of real estate professions, including:

- Real estate investors
- Loan officers
- Appraisers
- Inspectors

---

[8] *Bigman Assoc. v. Fox*, 133 A.D.2d 93, 518 N.Y.S.2d 630 (1987).

A. REAL ESTATE INVESTMENTS

At one time or another, we have all heard the general statement that real estate makes a good investment. There are many appealing aspects to real estate as part of a financial portfolio, but there are also considerable risks that can prove to be disasters for the uninformed investor. We begin our discussion by addressing the issue of home ownership and then proceed to individuals who invest in real estate and others who earn their income directly from the real estate market.

1. ADVANTAGES OF REAL ESTATE INVESTMENTS

In general, real estate is a wise investment. Houses and land generally appreciate in value over time and offer other advantages. The advantages of real estate include:

- Generally appreciates in value
- Improves a homeowner's credit rating
- Provides a ready source of funds for equity loans
- Offers tax write-offs

a. Appreciation in Value

Real estate makes a good investment because it generally appreciates in value. When something appreciates, it gains in value over time without substantial reinvestment on the part of the owner. There are several reasons why land appreciates in value. For one thing, a growing population demands more housing. As the population becomes more affluent, individual buyers seek bigger and more expensive properties. Finally, although the population steadily increases, the supply of land is fixed and the laws of supply and demand dictate that prices rise in this situation. However, simply because land generally appreciates in value, this does not mean that all parcels will be worth more next year than they are worth this year. Periodically land sales have dipped dramatically and prices have fallen, causing great economic hardship for individual homeowners.

b. Impact on Credit Rating

Homeownership is a great way of improving an individual's credit standing. Regular payments on a monthly mortgage contribute to a positive credit history for an individual, allowing him to borrow additional funds for other purchases.

c. Potential Source of Funds

As a homeowner slowly builds equity in land, this provides a ready source of cash if the homeowner chooses to borrow against the equity. As we have already seen in previous chapters, equity is the difference between the value of the property and the amount that is owed on it. If a person has $20,000 equity in his home, lenders will use this equity as collateral for a new loan. A homeowner can take advantage of this equity in order to borrow to make improvements on a home, take an expensive vacation, or to fund a child's college education.

d. Tax Advantages

One of the best advantages that come from homeownership is the tax advantage it gives individual taxpayers. The Internal Revenue Service allows homeowners to deduct interest charges on monthly mortgage payments from their annual income tax returns. This gives mortgage loans an advantage not seen with other types of lending. The ability to write off mortgage interest is a powerful incentive to purchase a home to help reduce an individual's personal income tax liability in any given year. However, this advantage is only available to individuals who own and live on the property. Real estate investors and others do not receive this favorable tax treatment.

2. DISADVANTAGES OF REAL ESTATE INVESTMENTS

Although there are numerous advantages to investing in real estate, there are also some important disadvantages. Among these disadvantages are:

- Poor liquidity
- Property taxes
- Maintenance costs
- Financing and down payment costs

a. Poor Liquidity

One of the biggest disadvantages to homeownership is the lack of liquidity in the investment. Liquidity refers to the ease with which an investor can convert funds for use in other investments. Because the sale of a home can take weeks or months, it is not easy for a homeowner to take profits out of a real estate investment. If an individual needs cash quickly, tying up money in a real estate investment is a bad choice.

b. Property Taxes

In addition to poor liquidity, an individual homeowner is also responsible for paying property taxes. These taxes are assessed on an annual basis and can run to thousands of dollars per year. If a homeowner is unable to pay these taxes, the local government is authorized to foreclose on the property to satisfy the tax bill.

c. Maintenance Costs

Unlike rental situations, a homeowner is responsible for all maintenance costs to keep the premises in good repair. Depending on the quality of the home, maintenance costs can easily take more out of a homeowner's budget than property taxes and mortgage payments combined. Some homes are in such poor shape that they require tremendous capital investment. The homeowner is responsible for all these maintenance costs, and if the homeowner is unable to meet upkeep costs, the house will slowly deteriorate, losing value over time.

d. Financing and Down Payment Costs

Last, but certainly not least, there are many costs associated with purchasing the house. A potential homeowner may have to come up with as much as 10 percent of the total purchase price as a down payment before a lender will even consider providing a mortgage. In addition to down payment costs, banks also assess other fees as part of the lending process. Many of these fees can cause substantial financial hardship for individuals with limited financial resources.

3. REAL ESTATE INVESTMENT TRUSTS

A real estate investment trust (REIT) is a security that trades like a stock on any of the major national stock exchanges. In many ways, it resembles a mutual fund. The trust devotes itself to the business of purchasing, managing, and selling tracts of real estate for profit. Investors buy shares in the trust and this money is then used to purchase real property around the nation. Profits from real estate investment are then passed back to the investors based on the number of shares that they have purchased in the trust. Real estate investment trusts can be an attractive alternative for individuals who wish to take advantage of the generally positive investment potential for real estate, while avoiding many of the disadvantages. REITs usually receive special tax considerations, while also providing the investor with the kind of high liquidity that is normally not found in individual real estate ownership. Individual investors can buy and sell their shares on an open market in the same way that other investors buy and sell stocks and bonds. There are numerous types of REITs, including some that specialize in mortgages, commercial property, and apartment complexes, among many others.

> **Real estate investment trusts offer many of the advantages of real estate investing while avoiding some of the common disadvantages.**

ISSUE AT
A GLANCE

4. SMALL INVESTORS AND "DO IT YOURSELFERS"

There are some individuals who specialize in buying and selling individual parcels of real estate. Some of them purchase distressed real estate with the idea of making improvements to it and then selling it for a profit. Others acquire properties to hold as rental units. This can be an attractive investment alternative for individuals who know a lot about construction and can do much of the work themselves. For individuals who lack those skills, many of the profits that could come from the sale of a "fixer-upper" are lost in labor costs to pay others to improve the property. And as we will see in Chapter 14, there are important tax considerations that go into any decision to buy, fix up, and resell real estate. State and federal capital gains taxes can eat into any potential profit.

| EXAMPLE 11-5 | Juan posts signs around town reading, "I buy ugly houses." He wants to buy houses that may not be considered to be as desirable as others. Why would Juan do such a thing? |

Answer: If Juan chooses correctly, it can be a lucrative business. Even with the costs associated with fixing up the home, and factoring in capital gains taxes, Juan may still make $10,000–$20,000 per home. It only takes several homes per year to earn him a substantial salary.

B. LOAN OFFICERS

Although the classification of real estate investors covers several important areas, these are not the only individuals who earn their income directly or indirectly from the real estate profession. Loan officers are another important category. They play a critical role in the sale and purchase of real estate for the simple reason that most people do not have thousands of dollars of ready cash on hand to purchase real estate. Buyers must go to a local banker or other lending institution and borrow funds for the purchase. The problem with a term such as "loan officer" is that it is very broad. In any typical residential mortgage situation, there are literally dozens of individuals who are involved in various phases of the transaction. Lenders have individuals who act as customer service representatives who meet with potential borrowers, underwriters to evaluate the risk of extending credit to the buyer, and committees that are responsible for reviewing loan applications and making decisions about mortgages. All these individuals earn their living either directly or indirectly from real estate.

1. ONLINE LOAN APPLICATIONS

Many lenders have moved to an Internet-based loan application process. Even traditional banks have Web pages on which prospective borrowers may complete an application and submit it to the loan department, all without ever having to step inside the bank itself.

2. INTERNET MORTGAGE LENDERS

Traditional lenders are also getting stiff competition from lenders that are entirely Web-based. In previous years, borrowers would go to lenders in the community in order to finance the purchase of a home. These days, a borrower can just as easily obtain a mortgage from an Internet-based mortgage lender with offices on the other side of the country.

C. APPRAISERS

The topic of appraisal is complicated enough to fill a book by itself. Appraisers are professionals who evaluate properties and assess fair market value of real estate. Like real estate brokers, appraisers are state certified and licensed. Banks and lenders often require an appraisal before loaning money in a particular transaction. After all, the lender is providing funds based on the value of the property and it would be foolish to do so without determining that the property is worth the amount loaned.

Appraisers usually visit the seller's house and inspect it. They list the various features and also evaluate the neighborhood. They use several different methods to determine a final value for the real estate. Among the techniques used by appraisers is a comparison of the property for sale with other, similar parcels. They will seek out information about recent sale prices of similarly situated properties and use this as one element of an appraisal. They may also use other techniques, such as:

- Reviewing tax records
- Examining deeds and recent sales
- Measuring property boundaries
- Reviewing MLS listings

The appraiser may also visit several different local government offices, including:

- Registrar of deeds office (land office or registry office)
- Property tax office
- Zoning board
- Permits and applications department, among many others

Once the appraiser puts together his report, he forwards it to the lender. Many lenders require that the appraisal amount meet or exceed the amount of the mortgage before authorizing a release of funds in the closing.

1. THE IMPORTANCE OF REAL ESTATE VALUATION

Even before an appraiser enters the picture, the seller and listing agent will attempt to come up with a reasonable sale price for the home. Putting a price on real estate is also important for other reasons. For instance, real property taxes are based on property value. Without an appraisal, how do real estate agents value property? Generally, they prepare a comparative market analysis.

a. Comparative Market Analysis

When a real estate broker or agent prepares a comparative market analysis (CMA), it is not the same thing as an appraisal. CMAs are meant to be more general than the specific report provided by an appraiser. They are prepared for real estate clients to provide guidance in setting the sale price. A CMA is a summary of recent sales of similar properties, based on the sale price of homes with similar features, amenities, and locations as the house currently up for sale. The CMA uses this as a means to provide a general framework to set a price for the current home. In some states, brokers can charge a fee for the CMA, while in others the report is prepared as part of the duties that the broker carries out for the seller.

D. SURVEYORS

Surveyors physically check the accuracy of property boundary lines. Surveying requires careful attention to detail. A surveyor must go to the property and measure off distances and directions with carefully calibrated equipment. When they have completed the physical measurements, they prepare a drawing showing the property boundaries.

E. THE LEGAL TEAM

Lawyers and paralegals often play a significant role in real estate transactions. In some states, lawyers draft the deeds of conveyance, while paralegals conduct the title search, under the supervision of lawyers. In other states, brokers or others may perform these tasks, but there is no denying the importance that sound legal advice can have on a real estate transaction.

1. REAL ESTATE ATTORNEYS

Real estate attorneys are often called upon to draft general warranty deeds and to advise lenders about the legal aspects of mortgages or deeds of trust. In many states, attorneys also conduct closings or real estate settlements during which all funds between the buyer and the seller are distributed.

2. REAL ESTATE PARALEGALS

Real estate paralegals play an absolutely essential role in real estate transactions. They carry out many of the daily activities associated with a real estate practice, from preparing deeds to confirming closing dates. Paralegals, in some states, also conduct title examinations to determine the marketability of title for a particular parcel. In addition to these activities, paralegals also coordinate many of the events that are part of a real estate transaction. They work closely with real estate brokers, agents, loan officers, title insurance agents and many others. In the next several chapters, we outline the role played by paralegals in areas such as title insurance, title examinations, and the closing process.

3. REAL ESTATE TITLE SEARCHERS

Some real estate professionals earn their living by performing title examinations. Commonly referred to as "title searchers," this group includes not only lawyers and paralegals, but also other individuals who have learned how to carry out these activities and market them to law firms and title insurance companies. In other states, individuals might work to prepare abstracts of title documents. The methods used to compensate these individuals vary. In some cases, they are paid by the job, while in others they are paid by the hour. We discuss the role of title searchers and abstractors in greater detail in the next chapter.

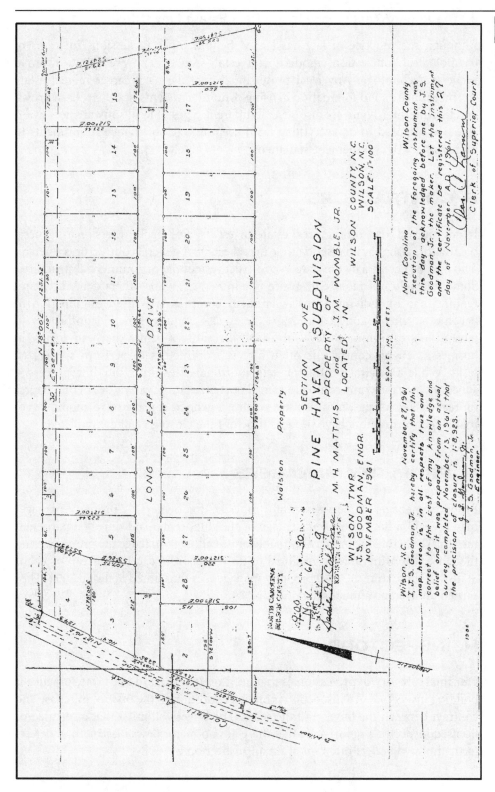

FIGURE 11-5

Survey of Pine Haven
Subdivision

a. The Role of Technology in the Real Estate Law Office

Although the practice of law has lagged behind other professions in terms of technological innovation, modern real estate practice now employs a broad range of technology. Any legal professional considering a career in real estate law must have a solid foundation in using computer systems, scanners, flash drives, and the Internet. There are also several different types of legal software now available that are used to do everything from keeping track of client appointments to preparing a HUD settlement statement.

F. CONTRACTORS

In addition to loan officers, real estate investors, and legal professionals, general contractors also play an essential role in real estate. A general contractor is a person who may be licensed by the state to construct residential or commercial structures. Some states do not require licensure of contractors, while others do. Most states require that an individual post a bond or complete a written examination to become a general contractor. Most states also require general contractors to have at least a minimum level of financial resources before they can engage in business. General contractors often hire subcontractors to perform specialized tasks. While a general contractor may coordinate the entire building process, a subcontractor may only complete a small portion of it. As we will see in the chapter on real estate closings, most lenders require a general contractor to submit proof that all subcontractors have been paid before the closing can be completed.

G. PROPERTY MANAGERS

Property managers supervise rental properties for owners. A property manager may be paid a flat fee or a percentage of the total rents paid during a particular month. The actual owner may be unable or unwilling to manage the properties and therefore will bring in a professional to do it. According to the Bureau of Labor Statistics, there were 293,000 property managers in the United States in 2002. They earned an average annual salary of $36,880.[9]

H. INSPECTORS

Our final category of professionals that are closely related to real estate practice is building inspectors. An inspection is often a condition in the offer of purchase and contract between the buyer and the seller. The buyer will insist that a certified or licensed inspector's report state that there are no major flaws or structural defects in the home. Lenders often insist on an inspection as well.

---

[9] Bureau of Labor Statistics, U.S. Department of Labor, Occupational Outlook Handbook, 2004-2005.

1. CONDUCTING A REAL ESTATE INSPECTION

Real estate inspectors examine properties in painstaking detail to come up with an accurate overview of the condition of the premises. Thorough real estate inspections ensure that buyers will not discover any major problems with the home after taking possession. Inspections also protect the interests of the mortgage lender. A real estate inspection resembles an appraisal, but there are important differences. The purpose of an appraisal is to determine the value of the property. An inspection, on the other hand, is designed to discover any major or minor flaws with the premises. It is important to make a distinction here between private inspectors and government inspectors. Private inspectors are in the business of inspecting residential properties and issuing reports to buyers and sellers as part of the real estate transaction. However, there is an entirely separate class of inspectors who work for local governmental agencies and are responsible for inspecting new construction to make sure that it complies with building codes. We have discussed the role of governmental inspectors in previous chapters. They are usually not involved in a typical real estate transaction in which there is a preexisting structure on the property.

Real estate inspectors produce a final report listing all of the important house systems and any major or minor problems with those systems. For an example of a real estate inspector's checklist, see Figure 11-6. Unlike the example provided here, the final report will often run to dozens of pages and provide detailed information on every aspect of the house.

Exterior	Good	Fair	Poor	Bad	Comments
		Condition			
Windows					
Siding type Vinyl Composite Wood siding Other					
Doors					
Chimneys					
Roof ventilation					
Interior					
Overall appearance					
Ceiling					
Walls					
Systems: Heating/Air conditioning Electrical (Amp service) Water Sewage					

FIGURE 11-6

Typical Inspection Checklist

ANNOTATED DOCUMENT — REAL ESTATE APPRAISAL

Uniform Residential Appraisal Report   File

The purpose of this summary appraisal report is to provide the lender/client with an accurate, and adequately supported, opinion of the market value of the subject property.

Property Address **21 MAPLE DRIVE**   City **ANYTOWN**   State **PL**   Zip Code **003300**
Borrower **BILL BORROWER**   Owner of Public Record **SAME**   County **BARLES**
Legal Description **SEE ATTACHED**
Assessor's Parcel # **BA-12350**   Tax Year **2005**   R.E. Taxes $ **2012**
Neighborhood Name **SIMPSON ESTATES**   Map Reference   Census Tract
Occupant ☑ Owner ☐ Tenant ☐ Vacant   Special Assessments $ **0**   ☐ PUD   HOA $ ☐ per year ☐ per month
Property Rights Appraised ☐ Fee Simple ☐ Leasehold ☐ Other (describe)
Assignment Type ☑ Purchase Transaction ☐ Refinance Transaction ☐ Other (describe)
Lender/Client **FIRST NATIONAL BANK**   Address **123 ELM STREET**
Is the subject property currently offered for sale or has it been offered for sale in the twelve months prior to the effective date of this appraisal? ☐ Yes ☑ No
Report data source(s) used, offering price(s), and date(s). **N/A**

I ☐ did ☑ did not analyze the contract for sale for the subject purchase transaction. Explain the results of the analysis of the contract for sale or why the analysis was not performed.

Contract Price $ **N/A**   Date of Contract   Is the property seller the owner of public record? ☐ Yes ☐ No Data Source(s)
Is there any financial assistance (loan charges, sale concessions, gift or downpayment assistance, etc.) to be paid by any party on behalf of the borrower? ☐ Yes ☐ No
If Yes, report the total dollar amount and describe the items to be paid.

Note: Race and the racial composition of the neighborhood are not appraisal factors.

Neighborhood Characteristics	One-Unit Housing Trends	One-Unit Housing		Present Land Use %	
Location ☐ Urban ☑ Suburban ☐ Rural	Property Values ☑ Increasing ☐ Stable ☐ Declining	PRICE	AGE	One-Unit	**100** %
Built-Up ☑ Over 75% ☐ 25-75% ☐ Under 25%	Demand/Supply ☐ Shortage ☑ In Balance ☐ Over Supply	$ (000)	**25**(yrs)	2-4 Unit	**0** %
Growth ☐ Rapid ☑ Stable ☐ Slow	Marketing Time ☐ Under 3 mths ☐ 3-6 mths ☐ Over 6 mths	**100** Low		Multi-Family	**0** %
Neighborhood Boundaries **.25 - .5 ACRE LOTS**		High		Commercial	**0** %
		Pred.		Other	**0** %

Neighborhood Description **GENERALLY, 2-3 BEDROOM HOMES OLDER NEIGHBORHOOD, GOOD CONDITION, NEIGHBORS KEEP GOOD YARDS**

Market Conditions (including support for the above conclusions) **FAVORABLE, SEE ATTACHED REPORT SUMMARY**

→ Neighborhood description

Dimensions **52 × 35**   Area **1900**   Shape **L SHAPE**   View **1980**
Specific Zoning Classification **R-1**   Zoning Description **RESIDENTIAL ONLY**
Zoning Compliance ☑ Legal ☐ Legal Nonconforming (Grandfathered Use) ☐ No Zoning ☐ Illegal (describe)
Is the highest and best use of the subject property as improved (or as proposed per plans and specifications) the present use? ☑ Yes ☐ No If No, describe

Utilities	Public	Other (describe)		Public	Other (describe)	Off-site Improvements—Type	Public	Private
Electricity	☑		Water	☑		Street	☑	☐
Gas			Sanitary Sewer	☑		Alley		☐

FEMA Special Flood Hazard Area ☐ Yes ☑ No FEMA Flood Zone   FEMA Map # **N/A**   FEMA Map Date **N/A**
Are the utilities and off-site improvements typical for the market area? ☑ Yes ☐ No If No, describe
Are there any adverse site conditions or external factors (easements, encroachments, environmental conditions, land uses, etc.)? ☐ Yes ☐ No If Yes, describe
ELECTRICAL EASEMENT (FRONT YARD), NO OTHER EASEMENTS

General Description	Foundation	Exterior Description materials/condition	Interior materials/condition
Units ☑ One ☐ One with Accessory Unit	☐ Concrete Slab ☐ Crawl Space	Foundation Walls **C-BLOCK**	Floors **HARDWOOD**
# of Stories	☑ Full Basement ☐ Partial Basement	Exterior Walls **SIDING (W)**	Walls **DRY WALL**
Type ☐ Det. ☑ Att. ☐ S-Det./End Unit	Basement Area **700** sq. ft.	Roof Surface **ASPHALT SH.**	Trim/Finish **PAINT**
☐ Existing ☐ Proposed ☐ Under Const.	Basement Finish **BLOCK 100**%	Gutters & Downspouts **GOOD COND.**	Bath Floor **TILE**
Design (Style) **RANCH**	☑ Outside Entry/Exit ☐ Sump Pump	Window Type **DOUBLE PANE**	Bath Wainscot **NONE**
Year Built **1980**	Evidence of ☐ Infestation **NONE**	Storm Sash/Insulated ✓	Car Storage ☐ None
Effective Age (Yrs) **25**	☐ Dampness ☐ Settlement	Screens ✓	☑ Driveway # of Cars **2**
Attic ☐ None	Heating ☑ FWA ☐ HWBB ☐ Radiant	Amenities ☐ Woodstove(s) #	Driveway Surface **ASPHALT**
☑ Drop Stair ☐ Stairs	☐ Other Fuel	☑ Fireplace(s) # **1** ☑ Fence	☑ Garage # of Cars **1**
☐ Floor ☐ Scuttle	Cooling ☑ Central Air Conditioning	☑ Patio/Deck **3** ☑ Porch	☐ Carport # of Cars
☐ Finished ☐ Heated	☐ Individual ☐ Other	☑ Pool **1** ☐ Other	☐ Att. ☐ Det. ☑ Built-in

Appliances ☑ Refrigerator ☑ Range/Oven ☑ Dishwasher ☐ Disposal ☑ Microwave ☑ Washer/Dryer ☐ Other (describe)
Finished area above grade contains: **6** Rooms **3** Bedrooms **2** Bath(s) **1800** Square Feet of Gross Living Area Above Grade
Additional features (special energy efficient items, etc.)

Describe the condition of the property (including needed repairs, deterioration, renovations, remodeling, etc.) **WATER DAMAGE ON N. SIDE PORCH NEAR DOWNSPOUT**

Are there any physical deficiencies or adverse conditions that affect the livability, soundness, or structural integrity of the property? ☐ Yes ☑ No If Yes, describe

Does the property generally conform to the neighborhood (functional utility, style, condition, use, construction, etc.)? ☑ Yes ☐ No If No, describe

→ Adverse site conditions or external factors

→ Condition of property

REAL ESTATE PROFESSIONALS' CODES OF ETHICS

The National Association of Realtors has its own code of ethics. As a legal professional, it is not enough for you to be aware of your own ethical code, you must also understand the ethical codes imposed on other professionals. For instance, you should review the National Association of Realtors' ethical code, which can be found online at the Web site provided at the end of this chapter. Individual states also have their own ethical rules and standards of practice that you should review to make sure that you do not inadvertently violate a real estate agent's ethical codes.

WHEAT v. LINDSLEY

WHEAT v. LINDSLEY,
906 So.2d 782 (2004)

Irving, J., for the Court.

Debbie Wheat, a real estate agent, appeals from an adverse judgment rendered by the Chancery Court of Lamar County which found that the relationship between her and Pamela Lindsley, a land purchaser, was that of principal and agent; that Wheat owed a fiduciary duty to Lindsley; and that Wheat owed Lindsley $91,266.02 resulting from the conversion by Wheat of $81,000 in loan proceeds intended for Lindsley's benefit and the failure by Wheat to repay $10,266.02 of a $15,000 loan from Lindsley to her. Feeling aggrieved by this decision, Wheat appeals and asserts the following issue: (1) whether or not the chancellor ruled against the overwhelming weight of the evidence in finding that there was not a joint venture between Wheat and Lindsley and that Lindsley was entitled to recover from Wheat.

Ascertaining no error, we affirm.

FACTS

The underlying dispute giving rise to this appeal involves transactions between Debbie Wheat and Pamela Lindsley regarding a $15,000 loan from Lindsley to Wheat and a business arrangement between Lindsley and Wheat involving the purchase of two lots by Lindsley and the supervision by Wheat of the construction of residential houses on the lots. These lots are referred to in this opinion as Lots 39 and 40.

Lindsley, a nurse, received a substantial sum of money as a result of an accidental injury around 1985. After her injury, she left the nursing profession and concentrated on investment opportunities. Wheat is a licensed and experienced real estate sales person. Lindsley and Wheat became acquainted several years prior to their entering into several real estate transactions and the loan which are the genesis of this litigation.

On March 18, 1998, Lindsley issued to Wheat a check for $15,000 which Wheat cashed. The check was drawn on a joint account which they maintained at First National Bank. Lindsley initially wrote the word, "loan," on the memo portion of the check but later added the notation, "advance to be repaid 1 month." Wheat did not deny receiving and retaining the money and that it was an amount to be repaid. However, the women disagreed as to whether this amount was repaid. Wheat pointed to deposits of $6,000 and $9,000 to the joint account as being repayment of the loan, while Lindsley's interpretation of those deposits was totally contrary. Lindsley did confess, however, that Wheat was entitled to a credit on this debt in the sum of $4,766.02 resulting from a payment made by Wheat in settling the account between them on Lot 40.

The two specific deals which have produced the conflict between the parties center around the purchase by Lindsley, at the suggestion of Wheat, of two lots in a development area called Fieldstone, Lots 39 and 40. It was the parties' intention that these two lots be purchased by Lindsley and a "spec" house constructed on each lot. The houses would then be sold for a profit. As between the two women, there was not, and never was, any written definitive agreement between them as to the relationship, rights, obligations, and ultimate expectations of receipts by either of them as a result of the projects undertaken.

In early February 1992, Lindsley purchased and took title to lots 39 and 40. At Wheat's suggestion, Lindsley transferred title in Lot 40 to Wheat. Wheat served as primary supervisor for the construction of the house and operated through a bank account established for her use in completion of the house.

When the closing of the Lot 40 transaction occurred on June 8, 1998, Lindsley was present and participated in the transaction although the closing papers listed Wheat as the seller and settler of the closing, with all documents being duly signed by Wheat. The sales commission from the sale was paid to Re/Max Real Estate, the agency with which Wheat was an operating salesperson. The net proceeds from the sale were paid to and received by Lindsley as the acknowledged principal in the deal.

Lot 39, owned by Lindsley, was likewise scheduled to have a house constructed on it. As was the case with the construction of the house on Lot 40, the construction of the house on Lot 39 was to be supervised and sold by Wheat. As was done in the Lot 40 transaction, Lindsley, at Wheat's suggestion, transferred title of Lot 39 to Wheat on May 5, 1998. On the same day, Wheat negotiated a loan from Lamar Bank for the principal sum of $100,000, securing the loan by a deed of trust on Lot 39. The loan proceeds were ultimately credited to the Lot 39 checking account. Wheat thereafter reconveyed Lot 39 back to Lindsley on June 3, 1998. Thereafter, Wheat made an $81,000 withdrawal from the Lot 39 account, leaving $19,000 in the account. This withdrawn amount was never replaced into the account. Lamar Bank subsequently foreclosed on the deed of trust with a purported purchase by Wheat, but this transaction was set aside by an agreed judgment. The judgment further deeded Lot 39 to the Bank. The Bank completed the construction of the house and subsequently sold the property with a relatively substantial deficiency.

On September 30, 1998, Lindsley filed a petition for accounting of funds and other relief against Wheat. She subsequently filed an amended petition for damages for breach of contract, cancellation of contract, accounting of funds, permanent injunction and other relief. Wheat filed her answer and counterclaimed for specific performance and injunctive relief, an accounting, actual damages, punitive damages, and attorney's fees.

The Chancery Court of Lamar County bifurcated the causes of action and rendered decisions on two issues: the contractual relationship which existed between Wheat and Lindsley and the amount of money owing between the two parties. In a memorandum opinion dated August 8, 2000, the court found that the relationship between Wheat and Lindsley was that of principal and agent with Lindsley being the principal and Wheat as her real estate agent. The court also found that Wheat was in a fiduciary relationship with Lindsley, subject to the Rules and Regulations of the Mississippi Real Estate Commission. In a subsequent memorandum opinion, the court found that Lindsley was entitled to a monetary judgment against Wheat in the amount of $91,266.02 plus pre-judgment and post-judgment interest.

ANALYSIS AND DISCUSSION OF THE ISSUES

This Court employs a limited standard of review on appeals from the chancery court. "If the substantial credible evidence supports the chancellor's decision, it will be affirmed." Reddell v. Reddell, 696 So. 2d 287, 288 (Miss. 1997). "This Court will not interfere with the findings of the chancellor unless the chancellor was manifestly wrong, clearly erroneous or a wrong legal standard." Id. "A chancellor sits as fact-finder and in resolving factual disputes, is the sole judge of the credibility of witness." Murphy v. Murphy, 631 So. 2d 812, 815 (Miss. 1994).

Wheat argues that the chancellor abused his discretion when he found that there was no joint venture between her and Lindsley regarding the real estate transactions. She explains that the chancellor's ruling was against the weight of the evidence because (1) Lindsley admitted that a joint venture existed between them, (2) the parties maintained a joint bank account to which each had access, (3) Lindsley voluntarily deeded both Lot 39 and 40 to her in order to obtain loans and benefits from the bank, and (4) they previously shared profits from properties they sold in the past. Lindsley counters that the chancellor correctly found that the parties' relationship was that of agent and principal.

In Pittman v. Weber Energy Corp., 790 So. 2d 823, 826 (Miss. 2001), our supreme court explained the concept of a joint venture: This Court first observed no exact definition could be given of a joint venture, the answer in each case depended upon the terms of the agreement, the acts of the parties, the nature of the undertaking and other facts. We broadly defined a joint venture as an association of persons to carry out a single business enterprise for profit, for which purpose they combine their property, money, efforts, skill and knowledge. We said it exists when two or more persons combine in a joint business enterprise for their mutual benefit with an understanding that they are to share in profits or losses and each to have a voice in its management. We noted a condition precedent for its existence was a joint proprietary interest in the enterprise and right of mutual control.

On the other hand, an agency relationship between broker and owner is personal and fiduciary. Smith v. H.C. Bailey Companies, 477 So. 2d 224, 235 (Miss. 1985). Real estate brokers have a duty to act solely for the benefit of their principals in all matters connected with the agency. Century 21 Deep South Properties, Ltd. v. Corson, 612 So. 2d 359, 368 (Miss. 1992). Any breach by agent of his duty of good faith to principal, whereby principal suffers any disadvantage and agent reaps any benefit, is fraud, for which agent is accountable, either in damages or by judgment precluding agent from taking or retaining benefits so obtained. Van Zandt v. Van Zandt, 227 Miss. 528, 86 So. 2d 466, 470 (1956).

Throughout her testimony, Lindsley asserted that Wheat was functioning as her agent to find various properties that could be acquired by Lindsley and subsequently sold after necessary repair, renovation, and/or new construction. She further explained that Wheat was to assist and participate in the promotion of selling those properties as appropriate to her experience, training, and knowledge as a real estate salesperson, with Wheat obtaining compensation by way of sale commissions or other appropriate compensation. Wheat, on the other hand, asserted that the relationship with Lindsley was a "50/50" joint venture partnership. She explained that they would buy properties, build houses or make other improvements on the property and that she would assist in overseeing the construction and use her expertise to sell the properties.

In its review of the evidence, the chancery court concluded:

> The relationship (between Lindsley and Wheat) is not a partnership, nor is it a joint venture endeavor with equal interest and equal sharing aspect, but rather is best characterized as a principal and Wheat in the position of agent. . . . The relationship was obviously a fiduciary one, but the Court finds no credible basis for concluding that it was a relationship in which Wheat was to share in profits, nor was she to share with Lindsley the "profits," i.e. sales commissions, she realized in the various transactions.

We find that the chancellor's decision that the parties were engaged in a principal and agent relationship is supported by substantial evidence. Here, we first note that there was no express agreement between Lindsley and Wheat, although both acknowledge the existence of an oral agreement to buy and sell properties. Although Wheat testified that she and Lindsley had a "50/50" joint venture partnership, she admitted that she did not recall the terms "50/50" or "half" being used by Lindsley in their agreement. While Lindsley characterized their relationship as a "joint venture," she explained that she understood their agreement to be that Wheat would receive commissions on the sale of Lindsley's properties and that Lindsley would retain any profit from those sales.

The evidence further confirms that Wheat was noted on the listing agreements for the Lot 39 and Lot 40 properties to receive a 6% commission if those properties sold. While Lindsley and Wheat had access to a joint banking account for construction expenditures, all money deposited or withdrawn by either party originated from personal funds of Lindsley or from loans acquired from her properties being used as collateral. Wheat contributed no personal funds to the account. Wheat also testified that she had written very few checks on the account and affirmed that Lindsley was the primary handler of the account.

While Wheat contended that Lindsley deeded her Lot 39 and Lot 40 to help Lindsley secure loans with the Bank, Lindsley testified that her deeding of Lot 39 and Lot 40 to Wheat was not for the purpose of conveying her any interest of a gift to those properties.

It appears that neither party kept the other fully informed as to her individual actions. Moreover, all money obtained by Wheat from the Lot 39 transaction was the result of her actions in withdrawing funds from the joint bank account maintained for the construction of Lot 39. It is clear that in their past transactions that the only money received by Wheat was the standard sales commission and that Lindsley and Wheat never actually engaged in a division of profits realized from any of their past transactions. In fact, in the Lot 40 transaction, a deal in which Wheat had participated and the closing of which was attended by Lindsley, the entire proceeds of the sale were paid to Lindsley with no questions asked or objection made by Wheat.

We therefore find that the chancellor did not err in finding that the parties were engaged in a business relationship whereby Lindsley was the owner/principal and Wheat was her agent. As to the transactions which gave rise to the judgment against Wheat, it is undisputed that Wheat did not have the authority to withdraw for her personal use $81,000 from the Lot 39 construction account. We note that during cross examination, Wheat even admitted that she used the $81,000 for her own personal benefit. Furthermore, Wheat did not provide any explanation of why she was entitled to the $81,000, nor did she present any evidence that the money had been repaid. The remainder of the judgment was for the balance owed on a $15,000 loan from Lindsley to Wheat. As previously observed, Wheat admitted that Lindsley loaned her $15,000. However, Wheat contends that the loan was repaid. The chancellor, as the trier of fact, found against Wheat on this issue. From our review of the record, he was fully justified in doing so.

Therefore, we find that the judgment of the chancery court finding that Lindsley is entitled to recover $91,266.02 from Wheat is not against the overwhelming weight of the evidence.

JUDGMENT OF THE LAMAR COUNTY CHANCERY COURT IS AFFIRMED. STATUTORY DAMAGES AND INTEREST ARE AWARDED. ALL COSTS OF THIS APPEAL ARE ASSESSED TO THE APPELLANT.

CASE QUESTIONS

1   What was the basic contention between Wheat and Lindsley?
2   What allegations did Lindsley make against Wheat?
3   What did the trial court determine was the relationship between Lindsley and Wheat?
4   How did this determination affect the interpretation of the case?
5   Was Wheat authorized to make withdrawals from Lindsley's personal account and to retain these funds?

SKILLS YOU NEED IN THE REAL WORLD

UNDERSTANDING COMMISSIONS

If the calculations in real estate commissions make it appear that real estate agents are earning a lot of money for relatively little effort, take a closer look not only at the numerous duties that the agents carry out, but also at the reality of how commissions are paid.

A real estate agent who produces a buyer who is ready, willing, and able to purchase the property has earned a commission. As we know, the commission is usually 6 percent of the sale price. However, we also know that one of the main advantages to using a real estate broker is his access to the Multiple Listing Service. This service essentially advertises homes for sale with the promise of splitting the commission with an agent who can produce a buyer. The chances of the listing agent also being the person who produces the buyer are very slim. Instead, most transactions involve at least two brokers: the listing agent and the procuring agent. If we assume that the final sales price for a home is $100,000, the commission is $6,000. This amount is split between the two agents, resulting in a net of $3,000 apiece. However, the calculations are not over. Because most agents work for companies, they have arrangements to split their earned commission with the company in exchange for providing office space, secretarial services, and other amenities. This can mean that the agent ends up splitting 50 percent of his earned commission with the company for whom the agent works. That means that of the $3,000 that the agent earned, he may only end up pocketing only $1,500. (Even this math is a little misleading, given the fact that agents may also have to pay other expenses and they will certainly have to pay both state and federal income tax.) If you understand how real estate commissions are actually doled out, you will have a better understanding of the system — and possibly more empathy for real estate agents.

CHAPTER SUMMARY

An agency relationship is created between an agent and a principal. An agent has strict duties that he must comply with while representing the principal. Among these duties is the duty of obedience, loyalty, and accounting. The most common example of an agency relationship in real estate law is the real estate broker-seller relationship. In this relationship, a real estate broker represents the interests of a home seller. When the agent locates a buyer who is ready, willing, and able to purchase the home, the agent is entitled to a commission, which is based on a percentage of total sale price.

There are several other important professions closely related to real estate practice. Investing in real estate can be a lucrative business on both a large and small level. Real estate investment trusts are publicly traded securities that pool funds in order to manage and sell large parcels of real estate. Individual investors can also purchase real estate in order to fix it up and resell it or to manage it as rental property. Other professions closely tied to real estate practice include loan officers, appraisers, and surveyors. Loan officers evaluate potential borrowers and handle paperwork associated with a mortgage. Appraisers are professionals whose duty is to evaluate real estate for value. Surveyors are responsible for determining the exact physical boundaries of a particular parcel of real estate. Real estate inspectors are responsible for examining structures on the premises and making a complete and detailed report to the buyer and the lender to assure both that the property has no major flaws.

REVIEW QUESTIONS

1 What is an agent?

2 Are agency relationships required to be in writing? Why or why not?

3 List and explain the four duties that an agent owes to a principal.

4 What is a fiduciary?

5 What is "self-dealing"?

6 List and explain the three duties that agents owe to third parties.

7 What is fraud in the legal context?

8 What duties does a principal owe to an agent?

9 What is the difference between an agent and an independent contractor?

10 In a typical real estate transaction, who is the principal, who is the agent, and who is the third party?

11 What is the difference between a real estate broker and a real estate agent?

12 What is a Multiple Listing Service?

13 What are some of the advantages of real estate as an investment?

14 What are some of the disadvantages of real estate as an investment?

15 What are Real Estate Investment Trusts?

16 Explain the role of a real estate appraiser.

17 What is a comparative market analysis?

18 What are some of the duties carried out by real estate paralegals?

19 Explain the role of a real estate inspector.

20 Explain the commission system for paying real estate agents.

DISCUSSION QUESTIONS

Given the fact that most real estate agents work for sellers, should there be a larger class of buyer's agents? What advantages and disadvantages do buyer's agents bring to a real estate transaction?

PRACTICAL APPLICATIONS

Contact a local real estate agent and interview this person. What got him interested in real estate as a profession? What are the advantages and disadvantages of a career as a real estate agent? What is the biggest misconception about real estate agents? Would this person recommend it as a profession? Why or why not?

WEB SITES

National Association of Real Estate Investment Trusts
http://www.nareit.com

National Association of Realtors
http://www.realtor.org

California Real Estate Inspection Association
http://www.creia.org

Ohio, Division of Real Estate and Professional Licensing
http://com.ohio.gov/real/

Texas Real Estate Commission
http://www.trec.state.tx.us/

TERMS AND PHRASES

Agency	Material fact	Principal
Fiduciary	Negligent	
Fraud	misrepresentation	

SIGNIFICANT CASES

Killearn Partners, Inc. v. Southeast Properties, Inc., 611 S.E.2d 26 (Ga., 2005)
Edwards Bros., Inc. v. Overdrive Logistics, Inc., 581 S.E.2d 570 (Ga. App., 2003)
Sharon Ava & Co., Inc. v. Olympic Tower Associates, 686 N.Y.S.2d 422
   (N.Y.A.D. 1 Dept., 1999)
Fraser v. Bovino, 721 A.2d 20 (N.J. Super. App., 1998)
Keahey v. Plumlee, 226 S.W.3d 31 (Ark. App., 2006)

Title Insurance and Title Examinations

Focus of This Chapter

Title examinations are treated in a separate chapter because states have radically different approaches to this issue. Regional differences in the method (and even the role) of title examinations in real property transactions are examined closely. This chapter emphasizes the role of the legal team in general and the paralegal in particular in carrying out the various steps of a real estate title examination. The chapter also provides basic forms for title examinations.

Chapter Learning Objectives

After completing this chapter, you should be able to:

- Explain the importance of title insurance
- List and explain the basic steps involved in carrying out a title examination
- Describe why a title examination is necessary
- Describe the impact of legal malpractice claims on title searches
- Explain the extent of information that can be located through public records

INTRODUCTION

In this chapter, we explore the importance of title insurance and explain the basic steps involved in a title examination. The manner and method used to carry out a title examination varies considerably from state to state. As a result, we examine the basic reasons why such a search is necessary and then discuss how these examinations are carried out in different states. We also examine the important role played by attorneys and paralegals, both in states that require attorney-certified title searches and in states where attorney involvement is not required. Throughout this chapter, we also demonstrate the vitally important role played by real estate paralegals across the country. However, before we explore the issue of title examinations, let's begin with the role of title insurance in modern real estate practice.

TITLE INSURANCE

Title insurance
An insurance policy that protects against legal claims on title to real property.

Title insurance is an insurance policy similar to automobile or life insurance. However, title insurance focuses on a very narrow issue: the marketability of the title to property. A title insurance policy is designed to pay for any costs associated with claims raised against a title after the transaction has been completed. It is title insurance that accounts for the need for a title examination.

A. WHAT TITLE INSURANCE DOES

Title insurance is a simple concept with profound implications for real estate law. What a title insurance company agrees to do in its policy is to pay the legal costs associated with defending any claim against the property by someone who purports to have a title interest. Example 12-1 provides a typical scenario.

EXAMPLE 12-1

Uncle Harry decided to put his house and surrounding property up for sale last year. Demetria liked the house and put in a bid on the property. They haggled over the price and eventually settled on a figure that both found acceptable. Demetria went to a local bank to arrange financing and the bank insisted that Demetria obtain a title insurance policy, which she did. After the transaction was complete, Uncle Harry's long-lost son, Micah, arrived in town and claimed that he had a half interest in the property. He brought suit against Demetria. Fortunately, she had a title insurance policy and the insurance company hired a local attorney to represent her. The case went to trial and the jury eventually found in Demetria's favor. Had Demetria been forced to pay her legal fees, she would never have been able to hire an attorney. Hence the need for title insurance.

Title insurance protects not only the buyer, but also the lender. If a claim suddenly arises that affects the buyer's interest in the land, the lender's claim is also in jeopardy. This is the simple reason why many lenders also require title insurance.

 **A title insurance policy protects against any claim that someone else has title rights to the buyer's property.**

B. OBTAINING TITLE INSURANCE

Obtaining title insurance resembles the process of obtaining any other type of insurance. However, while an applicant might be required to submit to a medical examination before a health insurer issues a policy, a title insurance company is concerned with the specific issue of title to the property. As a result, the insurer needs to know exactly what legal actions have been taken against the property that could have an effect on the title. A title insurer will want to know:

- Who has an interest in the property?
- Have all of these interests been properly conveyed to the buyer?
- Are there any outstanding issues in the public records that could affect title to the property, such as:
  - Outstanding or unpaid taxes
  - Liens or assessments
  - Judgments
  - Federal tax liens
  - Complications from divorce or probate

This list provides only a general outline of the types of problems that could have an impact on the title. As a result, the title insurance company will require a title examination to determine that none of these problems exist. If they do, the insurer probably will not issue a policy. In some cases, the title insurance company will insist that a potential legal problem be cleared up before it will issue a policy.

There are two general types of title insurance: owners' policies and lenders' policies. Owners' policies are obviously designed to protect the owner from any legal claim made against the property, while a lender's policy protects the lender's interest.

1. TITLE INSURANCE POLICY

Before a title insurer will issue a **policy**, it must have some indication about the current state of the title. In some states, title insurance companies rely on attorneys to give legal opinions about the title before they will issue a **binder**. In other states, this duty may fall to the title insurance company itself, or to some other legal professional.

Policy
The contract of insurance between the insurance company and the insured.

Binder
A preliminary agreement to issue an insurance policy.

Title insurance works just like any other insurance; a policyholder pays a premium and receives a policy that binds the insurance company to take certain actions on the policyholder's behalf.

 ISSUE AT A GLANCE

Once the title insurance company is satisfied about the legal status of the property, it will issue a policy. An insurance policy is a contract between the insurance company and the insured. The policy sets out the duties and limitations for both parties. The title insurance company, for instance, declares that it will defend a suit brought about the property for a title defect. The insured, for her part, pays a onetime premium in exchange for this service. The American Land Title Association creates general forms that are followed in most states. The insurance policy sets out what property is covered and any exceptions to coverage. For an example of a title insurance policy, see the Appendix.

Exceptions include matters of record or other legal claims for which the title insurance company will not provide coverage. Examples of exceptions could be claims by a spouse during a divorce proceeding or foreclosure provisions in a mortgage. Any other exceptions must be prominently noted on the policy.

2. TITLE INSURANCE PREMIUM

Premium
The periodic payment to keep an insurance policy in effect.

Unlike other forms of insurance, title insurance has only a one-time **premium**. This premium is paid as part of the closing or settlement on the property and no additional premiums are ever paid. The amount of the policy is often a percentage of the total sale price, such as one-half of 1 percent. See Example 12-2.

EXAMPLE 12-2

Vondra wants to obtain a title insurance policy to cover the purchase of her new home. The sale price is $125,000. How much is Vondra's title insurance premium?
   Answer: Multiply $125,000 by .5%. The answer is $625.

---

3. TERMINATING THE POLICY

Title insurance remains in effect as long as the owner who purchased the property continues to hold title. However, it automatically terminates when the owner sells the property or has title taken away, such as through a foreclosure process. Policies are not transferable from one owner to another. The new owner must obtain a new insurance policy.

As we will see, the title insurance company is the institution primarily responsible for forcing the parties to review the public records to make sure that there are no outstanding claims on the property and that title is free and clear. Title insurance companies require a title examination.

 ## TITLE EXAMINATIONS

Title examination
The process of reviewing public records to determine whether there are any outstanding claims that will affect the marketability of title to real property.

Although not all states use the **title examination** process to determine the marketability of titles, or even use the term "title examination," all states have some process for recording claims against property in the public records. Whether this recordation process involves a grantor-grantee index or a tract system, there are many types of claims that can adversely affect title to property. This is one of the main reasons to conduct a title examination.

A. WHAT IS A TITLE EXAMINATION?

Title examinations are necessary in order to determine the legal status of a parcel of real estate. As we have seen throughout this book, there are many actions that a real estate owner can take which will have a significant impact on future owners. A title examination (or title search) is the method used to discover any claims on the current owner or the property that could have an adverse affect on the transaction. There are some parcels that have so many attendant legal problems that they are virtually impossible to sell. The reason for this is that it would take so much time, money, and effort to clean up the title that a prospective buyer would just as soon buy another parcel that does not have such problems. The primary purpose of a title examination is to discover any legal problems and to solve them before the closing.

In some states, the final product of a title examination is an attorney's legal opinion about the current state of the property. When an attorney issues an opinion stating that the title is free and clear of all encumbrances, this is an assurance that the buyer can take the property without fear of losing it to some adverse claim. It also gives the title insurance company justification in issuing a policy. In states that do not use the attorney-certification process, a title examination is still conducted. However, instead of an attorney, a professional title searcher will review the public records and make a report to the prospective buyer and the title insurance company.

Title searches are necessary in order to ensure that title to property is free and clear of all liens, judgments, assessments, and other actions that could cloud a title.

B. BEGINNING A TITLE SEARCH

The title search usually begins when a law office or professional title examiner is contacted by a real estate broker, lender, or buyer and asked to review the title for the land in question. In almost all situations, the borrower will ultimately pay for the title examination, either directly or indirectly.

To begin a title search, the examiner must know the street address, parcel number, tax map ID number, or some other information that helps to identify the parcel. Once the examiner has this information, she can review the real estate records for any filing that might affect legal title to the property. At its simplest, title examination involves a review of the public records. To do as complete a job as possible, a title examiner should have the following information:

- The names of the current property owners
- A legal description of the real property that is the subject of the transaction
- Street address
- Parcel number, tax ID number, or other identifying information
- The time period that the title search must cover
- Deed book and page number, if available

A title examiner can begin a search with very little information, perhaps only the sellers' names and the property street address, although having more information is always helpful.

FIGURE 12-1	Title Examination Worksheet

Title Search Form

Examination prepared for: _____

Date of title examination: _____

Type of loan: _____

CHAIN OF TITLE

1.

Book: _____ **page:** _____

Grantors: _____

Grantees: _____

Type of transaction: _____

Date of transaction: _____

Date recorded: _____ **time of recording:** _____

Acreage: _____

Brief description: _____ _____

_____

2.

Book: _____ **page:** _____

Grantors: _____

Grantees: _____

Type of transaction: _____

Date of transaction: _____

Date recorded: _____ **time of recording:** _____

Acreage: _____

Brief description: _____

UNCANCELLED DEEDS OF TRUST/MORTGAGES

Book: _____ **page:** _____

Date of transaction: _____

Date recorded: _____ **time of recording:** _____

Lender: _____

Amount: $ _____

Book: _____ **page:** _____

Date of transaction: _____

Date recorded: _____ **time of recording:** _____

Lender: _____

Amount: $ _____

1. NAMES OF THE CURRENT OWNERS

It is essential to get the current owners' names to begin a title search. The current owners are the ones who will be transferring title to the buyer. Getting the owners' names not only ensures that the title searcher is researching the correct parcel, but also guards against early misunderstandings, such as when the people involved own more than one parcel of real estate. In states where the parcel is cross-referenced by address or ID number, having the owners' names also serves as a means to double-check that the title examiner received the right information in the first place.

a. Grantor-Grantee Index

In many states, properties are listed by owners' and buyers' names only, under a system known as the **grantor-grantee index**. In those states, the only way to research the title is to work through the names of the previous owners to see if any action taken by or against them could have a possible impact on the legal status of the property.

Grantor-grantee index
A listing of all property by the names of individuals who buy and sell it.

b. Tract Index

In other states, property is indexed by parcel number. In those states, any judgments or other actions that could affect the property are listed on a card (or a database entry). Whatever the method used, it is always helpful to have additional information about the parties involved in the transaction. Not all this information can be found on a property card, so it involves researching other public records. Examples of helpful information about the parties include:

- What are the ages of all parties? (Is everyone involved a legal adult?)
- Have any of the parties been declared mentally incompetent?
- Are any of the parties married? If so, what are the complete legal names of their spouses? Have the spouses also signed all deeds and other documents?
- When did the grantor/current owner acquire the property and from whom? (It helps to double-check information.)

2. DESCRIPTION OF THE PROPERTY TO BE CONVEYED

It is vitally important to a legal professional to properly identify the property in question before beginning the search. Sometimes street addresses are incorrect and the parties' descriptions may not have sufficient detail to correctly identify the property in question. It is extremely easy to confuse different real estate tracts, especially when the only information available is a poorly drafted description. Pinpointing the actual tract involved in the transaction is an absolute necessity to a successful title search.

3. TIME PERIOD

When a title searcher reviews the public records concerning property and owners, the normal search period is at least 30 years. The reason for conducting such a lengthy search through the records is to ensure that a title searcher locates any document that could potentially have a legal impact on the property today. Although many practitioners search back 40 years or more, most states have provisions that invalidate judgments that are older than three or four decades.

Some title searchers not only search the period that each owner possessed the property, but also extend the search period up to two years beyond that time. This acts as a safety precaution to catch any probate matters that might not have arisen during the actual term of ownership.

4. TAX ID NUMBER

The local tax office assigns tax ID numbers or other identifiers to every parcel of real estate in the county. This tax ID number can be extremely helpful to a title searcher not only in helping to identify the property, but also in taking advantage of the enormous amount of information available in the tax office. We discuss the role of the tax office, and the information that it collects, in the final chapter of this book.

5. DEED BOOK AND PAGE NUMBER

One of the best starting places for a title examiner is the last deed that conveyed an interest in the property. This information, coupled with the tract index or grantor-grantee index, will provide a wealth of information. Unfortunately, most clients do not realize the significance of the previous deeds and usually fail to provide one to the title examiner. Deed book volume and page numbers are always helpful in beginning a title examination. The format for a deed book reference varies from state to state, but most states follow a formula such as DB 909, Page 102. The first number in this cite gives the title examiner the volume number of the book in which a copy of the deed can be found. The second number is the page of that volume that corresponds to the deed. These days, the growing use of digital technology has made substantial inroads in storing deeds and other information, but most title examiners find that the ancient system of categorization is still used, despite the fact that deeds may not even be stored in actual books anymore.

A copy of the deed for the prior transactions is a gold mine of information. As we saw in Chapter 8, a general warranty deed not only identifies the parties, but also describes the property, lists geographic features, and even explains unusual aspects of the deed's history. In addition to all of this information, a previous title examiner may have included helpful information to explain some unusual aspect of the legal title and thus help clear up a potential problem.

6. SURVEYS AND PLATS

In addition to the basic information outlined above, it is also helpful to have a copy of the most recent plat or survey of the property. Human begins have a strong bias toward visual information, and a well-drawn plat can clear up many issues that written deed provisions only obscure. If the title examiner can also obtain a copy of the most recent title insurance policy, that is always a huge help. That policy will list any features that the parties considered to be important enough to explain and may save hours of work sorting through the public records to explain a feature that a previous title examiner cleared up in the notes or exclusions accompanying a title insurance policy.

Many title insurance companies offer this information to a title examiner with directions to simply "bring the title current." This phrase means that a title insurance company only wishes a title examiner to research the public records from the time that the last title insurance policy was issued through to the present. The theory is that the previous title examination would have discovered any legal problems and the only real concern is what has happened since. There are many who dispute this approach, pointing out that something that was missed in the first title search will not be discovered in the second if the examiner is not permitted to prepare a complete title search.

A survey or plat is a drawing based on the property boundaries.

ISSUE AT
A GLANCE

STEPS IN A TITLE SEARCH

Title examination can be a very rewarding and interesting profession. It can also be tedious and dull. A title examiner must employ many different legal skills, from interpreting probate and divorce records to chasing down civil judgments and criminal convictions. Another attractive feature of working as a real estate title examiner is the assurance of being paid. The work is necessary because lenders and title insurance companies need it, and because of that need, the title examiner will be paid for performing this important service. The level of pay, however, varies considerably, not only from state to state, but also even from city to city.

There are different ways of conducting a title search. The reason for these variations has a lot to do with the way that real estate records are stored. In some states, searching a title is a relatively straightforward manner. All information relevant to a particular tract is recorded on a card that corresponds to the property. However, in other states, information must be gleaned from a wide variety of sources. Because this second process is more involved than the first, in the next sections we outline how it is done. Even if this method is not the procedure used in your state, you may find some helpful suggestions about information stored in the public records that can prove to be extremely valuable.

A. CREATING A CLIENT FILE

No matter what system a state uses to store land records, there is a practical step that all title examiners follow: creating a client file. This file contains the following information:

- The client's name
- The date that the title examination is due
- The street address/plat number/ID number of the property
- The method of payment for the search

- Notes from previous title insurance policies or old title examinations
- Unusual or noteworthy information about this particular tract

Some or all of this information will be stored in a physical file or, more likely, in a client file on the company computer. Title examiners should remember that some or all of this information may contain confidential information and should not be shared with others.

B. STEP 1: CREATING THE CHAIN OF TITLE

Chain of title
A complete listing of all owners of a particular parcel of real estate for a specified time period.

Once the client file has been created, and the necessary basic information has been gathered, the title searcher is ready to begin the actual title search. In states that do not follow the tract information system, which records all important information for a parcel in one place, the title examiner must create a chain of ownership, also known as a **chain of title**, listing every owner for the property going back a specific period of time. Most title examiners search back at least 30, if not 40, years. Although you might think that the land office or deed room is the best place to start, actually one of the best sources of information is the local tax office.

ISSUE AT A GLANCE

The chain of title establishes each owner and the time period that each possessed the property going back for 30 or 40 years.

1. THE TAX OFFICE

The local tax office contains a wealth of information about real estate in the area, including owners' names, total acreage, PIN (parcel identification number) or parcel ID numbers, tax maps, tax ID numbers, and deed references. In some states, this information is still stored on a paper "tax card," but in most it is available in a computer database that provides not only all the information set out above, but also basic floor plans, square footage, and even digital photos of the property in question. Some states even provide this information on the Web. (There are references to such web sites at the end of this chapter.) The tax office is also a great resource because it keeps complete records about all real property located in the city or county and has its own set of tax maps. These maps can be cross-referenced with plats or surveys of the property to help clear up confusing issues, or even to help identify the exact parcel in question. In some states, the tax office is also cross-referenced with the land office or deed office, and provides information such as deed book references and other information that can be a big time-saver later on.

Another reason to begin a title examination with tax records is that the title examiner must check on the status of the property taxes. If the current owner is in default on her taxes, this may stop the entire transaction. If the property were facing tax foreclosure, no buyer would invest the time and energy to purchase the property when it might be auctioned off within days. The title examiner must also know the amount of taxes paid so that the amount can be prorated between the buyer and seller during the closing. We discuss prorations in greater detail in the next chapter.

2. CREATING THE LINKS IN THE CHAIN OF OWNERSHIP

In states that follow a grantor-grantee index model, the title examiner's first step is to search the grantee index and look up the name of the current owner of the property. The grantee index lists all conveyances through which a party received an interest in real estate. Because the current owner received her title from the previous owner of this particular parcel, that person's name will be listed here. The entry in the grantee index will give a deed book and page number reference. Using that reference, the title searcher finds the deed. This deed will provide the name of the previous owner and the title searcher will repeat the process, looking up the previous owner's name in the grantee index to see from whom she purchased the property and so on, going back through the records until the title searcher has covered the specified time period.

The purpose of creating a chain of title is to learn both the names of each owner and the dates of ownership. A title searcher should make sure to note the exact date that each owner acquired the property and the exact date that each sold the property. These dates are important because they not only determine the time periods that each owner held the property, but they also form the basis for the next phase of the search: checking the "outs" or adverse entries for each owner.

Grantor Name(s):

Grantee Name(s):

Date of Transaction:

Deed Book Reference:

(volume and page number)

Brief description of the property:

FIGURE 12-2

Chain of Title Form

3. TECHNOLOGICAL INNOVATIONS IN LAND RECORDS

Before the widespread use of computers in land record offices, information about parcels was manually recorded, sometimes handwritten. This added a new level of complexity to title searches: A title examiner had to know not only how to find information, but also how to decipher it. Modern innovations such as computer databases have taken away that tedious aspect of title examinations. Nowadays, a title examiner can simply type in a person's name or a tract reference, and pull up all the information needed to complete the search. However, although the computer solved many old problems, it also created some new ones. For example, if a person's name or reference number has been incorrectly entered into the computer database, finding it again may prove to be a challenge. Title examiners should keep in mind common misspellings of names and also remember that numbers can easily be transposed.

FIGURE 12-3

Common Problems in Title Examinations

■ The previous owner's name has changed (through marriage, name change)
■ The parties' names have been incorrectly entered into the database
■ The party used a common nickname to sign a document ("Jack" for John, for example)

FIGURE 12-4

Completed Chain of Title Form

Current Owner(s): Bryan and Beth Gartman

Grantor Name(s):	Rod and Lisa Burnett
Grantee Name(s):	Bryan and Beth Gartman
Date of Transaction:	November 4, 2003
Date Recorded:	November 18, 2003
Deed Book Reference:	4678/pp. 10–06
Brief description of the property:	.25 acres, Burke Estates Subdivision
Subdivision	

Prior Transaction:

Grantor Name(s):	Leslie and George McKesson
Grantee Name(s):	Rod and Lisa Burnett
Date of Transaction:	April 26, 1996
Date Recorded:	April 26, 1996
Deed Book Reference:	4563/pp. 9–12
Brief description of the property:	.25 acres, Burke Estates Subdivision

Prior Transaction:

Grantor Name(s):	Tara Bevans
Grantee Name(s):	Leslie and George McKesson
Date of Transaction:	May 2, 1985
Date Recorded:	May 4, 1985
Deed Book Reference:	3476/p. 122
Brief description of the property:	.25 acres, Burke Estates Subdivision
Subdivision	

Prior Transaction:

Grantor Name(s):	Marvin and Paula Barnes
Grantee Name(s):	Tara Bevans
Date of Transaction:	October 13, 1981
Date Recorded:	October 13, 1981
Deed Book Reference:	2163/p. 208
Brief description of the property:	.25 acres, Burke Estates Subdivision

Tech Topic
ONLINE TITLE SEARCHES

Much of the business of real estate has been automated, thanks to technology advances that allow for the marketing and sale of properties largely online. Virtually everything real estate–related can be accomplished online — with one notable exception: title searches.

Researching the history and provenance of a piece of property could easily be accomplished online. All the relevant information has long been computerized in searchable databases, and one could theoretically perform an accurate title search with little more than a laptop and a Wi-Fi connection.

Why has this not become standard practice? The answer is that the title companies have enormous political power and have blocked efforts to modernize title searching. They oppose such efforts because of the fees they collect from buyers for every real estate transaction, fees in the thousands of dollars for the title search and then for the insurance in case of error. Title fees amount to almost half of the fees associated with buying a property and could be greatly reduced if the title companies would agree to reform.

The technology exists, but the title companies' grip on the process is not likely to allow reform anytime soon.

Law firms that specialize in closings and title examinations often use their own forms to check the accuracy of a title search.

ISSUE AT
A GLANCE

C. STEP 2: ESTABLISHING THE OUT OR ADVERSE CONVEYANCES

When the chain of ownership has been established, the next step in the title search is to review the adverse conveyances, sometimes referred to as the "out" conveyances. This is a search of the records to see what actions the individual owners took during the time that they owned the property and also to determine if any of these actions have had an effect on the property. Previous owners can do any of a number of actions that can have repercussions extending into the future. An owner might have granted an easement to a neighbor. She might have failed to pay real estate taxes. There are dozens of actions that previous owners could have taken that could have an adverse impact on the property. All of these are good reasons to check the public records.

In states with grantor-grantee indexes, there are two primary sources for information to complete the adverse conveyance worksheet. The first is the grantor index itself. This is the index in which any out conveyance is recorded, even if the conveyance was not done voluntarily. Foreclosures will be listed here, with the previous owner's name as grantor. If a lien has been recorded, it will be indexed under the name of the owner at the time that the lien was given. Because all these actions must be recorded in order to be effective, the title searcher can feel confident that the grantor index will show entries for such actions.

The other place to look for adverse conveyances in states that follow the grantor-grantee model is the clerk's office. We address the clerk's office in detail under the section dealing with judgments.

In states that follow a property card or tract index, actions that affect legal title to property will be listed for that property. This makes checking out conveyances an easy and straightforward activity.

When a title examiner finds any adverse listing, the best practice is to look up the actual document and to review its provisions to make sure that it has no legal impact on the property.

1. REVIEWING TITLE DOCUMENTS

Each document that contains an owner's name should be reviewed to ensure that the listing does not involve the property for which the title examiner is searching or, if it does, that it causes no legal problems for the current title. Any questionable document should be copied and discussed with the title insurance company or real estate attorney to determine its legal significance.

Among the title documents that title examiners routinely encounter are:

- Mortgages or deeds of trust
- Assignments
- Easements for utility companies
- Rights of way
- Restrictive covenants
- Leases
- Water rights declarations
- Subordination agreements

a. Mortgage or Deed of Trust Issues in Title Examinations

One of the most important items to track down in checking the adverse conveyances are the financing documents. As we saw in Chapter 9, there are two preferred methods used to finance the purchase of real estate: mortgages and deeds of trust. Mortgages are the most common method, but it is always important to understand the function of deeds of trust. A title searcher must be able not only to locate a copy of a mortgage, but also to show that each previous mortgage was paid in full or satisfied. In some cases, the mortgage or deed of trust may actually be stamped with the word, "Satisfied." In other situations a separate document will be filed indicating that the mortgage was paid in full. In every situation, the title searcher must show that the financial document for prior transactions was cancelled or satisfied. Without such proof there may be an outstanding and unsatisfied mortgage on the property. In such a situation, a new buyer might be purchasing more than she bargained for.

Outstanding or unpaid mortgages are a problem for the transaction; many lenders will not approve disbursement of funds until these questions are cleared up.

2. LIENS

Another important item that is located during the adverse conveyances part of a title search is the presence of liens on the property. We discussed the legal importance of liens in Chapter 5. In that chapter, we saw that a lien is a mechanism that allows creditors to place encumbrances on titles that must be satisfied before title to the property can be transferred. A proper title examination must always seek to uncover any and all liens and ensure that the parties satisfy these liens before the transaction can resume.

Any liens located in checking the out conveyances should be noted prominently on the title search forms. See Figure 12-5 for an example of an adverse conveyances worksheet.

3. UCC LISTINGS

The Uniform Commercial Code listings are required whenever a borrower pledges personal property as collateral for a loan. The most common example is a car loan. When a person finances an automobile purchase, she executes a document that lists the automobile as collateral for the loan. Under this arrangement, if the borrower defaults on the loan, the lender is authorized to repossess the collateral. The document that records a creditor's interest in personal property is a UCC filing. Why would it be necessary to check UCC filings when conducting a title examination? There are times when a UCC filing is recorded on a fixture. As we saw in Chapter 5, a fixture is an item of personal property that becomes permanently attached to real property. When this happens, the property is reclassified from personal property to real property. The practical effect of this is that a UCC filing for personal property suddenly has implications for real estate. Consider Example 12-3.

Shana has been working construction for years and last year she formed her own company, called "Decks 'R Us." Shana's innovation is that she will finance the construction of a deck in the same way that the purchase of a car or a boat is financed. In order to properly record her interest in the deck that she builds for her customers, Shana files UCC statements on all the decks that she builds on the installment plan. Does this UCC filing have a potential impact on the real estate?

EXAMPLE 12-3

Answer: Yes. Because a deck is, by its very nature, permanently attached to real property, Shana's UCC filing might ripen into a lien or other encumbrance that could have a substantial impact on the property. As a result, the title examiner should note any UCC filing from Decks 'R Us.

---

4. MARRIAGE, BIRTH, AND DEATH RECORDS

Marriage, birth, and death records can provide vital information for a title examiner. Marriage records can show that a previous owner was married and can clear up an issue of whether the spouse should have signed the deed conveying it to the next owner in the chain. Birth and death records can establish family relationships

FIGURE 12-5

Adverse Conveyances Worksheet

Out Conveyances

Current Owner:

John Farthing

Period checked: 10-10-03 to present

a. Out conveyances:	None
b. Lawsuits:	None
c. Taxes paid:	Yes; 2003—$546.43; taxes are current
d. UCC listings:	Yes; for J. Farthing, 2005 Ford Fiesta; dollar amount not listed

Previous Owner:

Katie Burnett

Period checked: 6-17-94 through 10-10-03

a. Out conveyances:	None
b. Lawsuits:	None
c. Taxes paid:	No past due notices
d. UCC listings:	N/A, beyond 5-year limit

Previous Owner:

Michele Saw

Period checked: 2-2-90 through 6-17-94

a. Out conveyances:	None
b. Lawsuits:	Yes; 4-17-01, Equity One $3,062.89
	2-02-01, Weary Regional Medical Center $1,188.25
	Judgment outstanding and unpaid
c. Taxes paid:	N/A
d. UCC listings:	N/A, beyond 5-year limit

and can clear up who has title to lands that have been transferred from family member to family member over the years. They can also indicate when a person is a "junior" or a "senior." Men have a tendency to drop the "junior" designation after their names upon the deaths of their fathers. This can cause a great deal of confusion in the records that can be cleared up by reference to birth certificates.

5. PROBATE RECORDS

Probate records are essential when dealing with any real estate that has passed by testate or intestate proceedings. As we saw in Chapter 4, when a person dies with a will, she is said to have died testate. In such a case, the courts will attempt to give effect to the provisions of the person's will, passing title to real estate to whoever is designated. Once probated, a will becomes a matter of public record. The will can explain how and when a person obtained title to property. When a person dies without a will, she has died intestate. In that situation, a probate court will appoint an administrator who will distribute the decedent's property according to state law. Records of real estate transferred pursuant to intestate proceedings will also be a matter of public record.

6. JUDGMENTS

Establishing out conveyances involves not only the deed room, but also other government records. A title searcher will spend a great deal of time in the clerk of court's office in order to make sure that there are no pending civil actions, or judgments that have been assessed against the owners or the property.

a. The Clerk of Court's Office

Title searchers go to the clerk of court's office to look for liens, judgments, delinquencies, assessments, foreclosures, and any other actions. A title examiner may also need to visit the federal courthouse to look up information on bankruptcies or federal tax liens. Any of these actions could have a potential impact on the property. These days, most of this information is available on terminals inside the clerk's office and, in many cases, through databases provided on the Web.

The clerk's office is the office responsible for maintaining records for all civil and criminal actions in the county. Almost all the records in the clerk's office are open to the public. Juvenile and adoption records are usually sealed, but other proceedings, from divorce to criminal actions, are all open to the public for review.

Title examinations involve sifting through many different types of public records.

ISSUE AT A GLANCE

D. STEP 3: COMPILING THE INFORMATION

The final step of a title examination is to compile all the information into a final report. The information must be complete and provide answers to obvious questions. Are there taxes outstanding for the year, and if so, in what amount? Are there any outstanding or unsatisfied mortgages? In many ways, a title examiner must have a practical, no-nonsense attitude about the search. If there are any problems with the title, these must be addressed and cleared up or the sale will not be completed. Many title examiners take the attitude that, in the absence of proof that a problem has been resolved, one should assume that it has not.

There are numerous forms provided in this chapter and in the Appendix concerning title examination. However, the job is not about forms; it is about details. No matter how good the form is, the title examination will be a failure if the title examiner does not to pay close attention to details.

Throughout this chapter, you will find various title search forms and abstracts. Different firms use different forms and if you go to work as a title searcher, your firm will use its own forms. Again, the important aspect of a title search is not what form you use, but how thorough you are in your research.

1. TITLE ABSTRACTS

Title abstract
Forms that summarize important information about title to a particular piece of real estate.

The forms provided in this book are merely a guide to help someone who is conducting a title search double-check certain information. Many title insurance companies and title attorneys require a title examiner to use particular forms, called **title abstract** forms. These forms summarize the important features of a parcel, and encapsulate all the important information in such a way that it is readily available.

E. PRELIMINARY AND FINAL TITLE CERTIFICATES

In states that require attorneys to certify the marketability of title, the end result of a title search is a final title certificate. See Figure 12-6. The preliminary title certificate is issued prior to the closing and details any potential problems with the title and what actions the legal team will take to clear up these problems. The final title certificate details the exact legal nature of the title and offers the attorney's legal opinion that the title is free and clear of any encumbrance that would affect the transaction. A title search must be exacting because an attorney who offers an opinion about the legal status of a real estate title is putting her reputation on the line. More important, an inaccurate title opinion can result in a claim of legal malpractice.

1. LEGAL MALPRACTICE AND TITLE EXAMINATIONS

When an attorney offers a final opinion on the nature of a real property title, the attorney is certifying that there are no legal impediments to the sale. If the attorney's opinion is wrong because the legal team has missed an important entry, or failed to notice an outstanding legal claim against the property, the borrower, lender, and title insurance company all may have causes of action against the attorney for legal malpractice. In previous decades, legal malpractice was a very rare action. These days, it is quite common. Title insurance companies no longer hesitate to sue attorneys for malpractice when the attorney certifies a title and then the insurance company must pay out a large settlement in an action that was clearly a matter of public record.

FIGURE 12-6

Final Title Opinion Letter

FINAL OPINION ON TITLE FOR

AMERICAN TITLE INSURANCE COMPANY

The undersigned has examined the record title on the Barnes County records (and

municipal tax and assessment records if within a municipality) for the period shown below relative

to title to the real property described below, and gives the following opinion of status:

Owner(s): **Rod S. Burnett and wife, Lisa M. Burnett**
Interest or estate: **Marketable Fee Simple**
Property Description: (or attach copy of legal description)

Being all of **Lot 7 of Mimosa Hills, Section I as shown on a plat recorded in Plat Book 10, Page 11A of the Barnes County Registry.**

Subject to the un-initialed **STANDARD EXCEPTIONS** on reverse side hereof.
Also subject to the following **SPECIAL INFORMATION AND EXCEPTIONS:**
Taxes:

1.	Ad valorem taxes are paid through and including those for the year:	**2001**.
2.	Taxes now due and payable:	**2004 taxes for $854.02**.
3.	Taxes, a lien, deferred or otherwise, but not yet due and payable:	**2004 & subsequent years**
4.	Special levies or assessments now due or payable in future installments:	**0.00**.
5.	Estate or inheritance taxes:	**0.00**.

Restrictive Covenants? No (Attach Copy).
1. Book, Page.
2. Burnett's survey and/or public record indicate a violation?
3. Contain reversionary or forfeiture clause?
4. Building Setback Line(s)
5 Easements/Other Matters: **None recorded**

Survey and Inspection Report Attached? NO

Recorded Plat? Yes
1. **Plat Book 10, Page 11A**.
2. Building Setback Line(s): **25 feet from side street**
3. Violated? **Unknown**
4. Easements/Other Matters: _____.

Access to Public Right of Way? Yes
Direct (If private easement, attach copy).
If over a private easement, has a search been made of adjoining property on which easement

crosses? N/A

Property Occupied By: Owners

Updating from Previous Title Insurance Policy? Yes (Attach Copy). If "Yes", has a search of

the public records been accomplished for such period of time within which judgments, liens or other

matters could affect the property, regarding the owner(s) of the property on and after the date of

said policy? **Yes**

Title Ins. Co. Policy #12X456

Other Easements, Liens, Deeds of Trust, Objections or Defects:

Deed of Trust from John S. Burnett and wife, Jane A. Burnett for Clarence D. Arrow, Trustee for First National Bank, dated May 15, 2001 at 2:00 p.m. in Book 1101, page 45, in the Office of the Register of Deeds for Barnes County, North Carolina, and securing the amount of $135,000.00 (To Be Paid and Cancelled).

This opinion of title is for the parties to whom it is furnished, is not transferable, and may not be

used by any other person or entity without the prior written consent of the undersigned.

FIGURE 12-6

Final Title Opinion Letter
(continued)

TITLE INSURANCE APPLICATION

1. Owner's Insurance: **$ 50,000.00**
   a) Insured: **Rod S. Burnett and Lisa M. Burnett**
   b) Use of Property: **Residential**

2. Mortgagee insurance: **$ 50,000.00**
   a) Insured: **FIRST NATIONAL Bank**
   b) Loan is: **Permanent**
   The following Standard ALTA Endorsements are requested: **8.1 (Environmental Lien Protection)**
Send original Binder to: **Clarence D. Arrow, Atty. 123 Main Street, Anywhere, PL 22222**

Page 2

STANDARD EXCEPTIONS

The attorney should initial any exceptions that are to be eliminated on the line to the left of the exception.

____1. Interest or claims not disclosed by public records, including but not limited to:
(a) Unrecorded Mechanics' or Materialmen's liens. (Liens may be filed by persons or entities furnishing labor or materials to any improvements of real property within 120 days from the last day of performance and will upon perfection relate in priority to the first day of performance as a valid lien on real property.)
(b) Unrecorded leases. (Under North Carolina law, parties in possession of the premises under a verbal or unrecorded lease of three years or less duration may remain in possession under terms of the tenancy.)
(c) Matters that may defeat or impair title which do not appear on the record. (Evidence revealing missing heirs, forgeries, etc. may not be on the public records, but such facts if properly established may impair or defeat what appears to be a good title on the record.)
(d) Taxes, special assessments and other governmental charges that are not shown as existing liens by the public records. (Governmental charges may be made for acreage fees, tap-on fees, cost of weed cutting, demolition of condemned buildings and other matters that are not shown as existing liens on the property by the public records.)
(e) Unlisted personal property taxes. (If discovered, such taxes and any penalties may be assessed as a lien on the subject property.)

____2. Matters occurring prior to and subsequent to the inclusive dates of examination.

____3. Matters which would be revealed by a review of the public records regarding the proposed purchaser/borrower, who is not a current owner of the property.

____4. Any inaccuracies and discrepancies which an accurate survey of the property may disclose. (A survey, if procured from a competent surveyor or civil engineer, will normally determine whether improvements lie within the boundaries of the property, whether existing utility lines, roads or other easements cross the premises, and whether there are any encroachments.)

____5. Security interests that may have attached to fixtures on the subject property as provided in Article 9 of the Uniform Commercial Code of North Carolina.

____6. Compliance with any local, county, state or federal government law or regulation relative to environment, zoning, subdivision, occupancy, use, construction or development of the subject property.

____7. Federal judgments, liens, and proceedings filed only in the Federal Court. (Upon the filing of a petition in Bankruptcy, title to real property vests in the Trustee in Bankruptcy and notice thereof is not always required to be filed in the County in which the Bankrupt owns property; federal condemnation proceedings may vest property in the federal government and notice thereof is not required to be recorded among the County records.)

____8. Civil actions where no notice of *lis pendens* against subject property appears of record.

Note: The matters included in Standard Exceptions Number One (1) above set forth are items that cannot be checked. Standard Exceptions numbered 2,3,4,5,6,7 and 8 are not included in a normal search of the County records during examination of title. Upon special request, additional investigation may be made, and Standard Exceptions numbered 2, 3, 4, 5, 6, 7 and 8 can be eliminated. Any such elimination is evidenced by the initialing of such exception in the left margin by the attorney.

(Continued from front)

There are also some practices engaged in by legal professionals that may put the attorney in danger of a legal malpractice action, including "tacking."

a. Tacking

Tacking
The process of updating a previous title search.

Tacking refers to the process of relying on a previous title search and simply conducting a review of the public records since the last title search was conducted. We discussed this practice earlier in our discussion of title insurance. Tacking is permissible when the title insurance company is aware of the process and even suggests it. However, tacking can be an ethical violation if an attorney or title examiner submits a full title search without explaining that all she really did was to review the last few years' public records. The appeal of tacking is obvious: It saves time. When there is a preexisting title insurance policy, and the property is being refinanced, a title insurance company might not wish to have a complete title search done. Instead, the title insurance company might simply authorize a check of the records from the date of the last title search. This is usually referred to as "bringing the title forward." Tacking presents legal and ethical problems, however, when the client is not aware that it is being done.

F. THE PARALEGAL'S ROLE IN TITLE SEARCHES

In states where attorneys certify real estate titles, it often falls to paralegals to actually conduct the work involved. Paralegals or legal assistants review the public records, and title documents and even prepare the preliminary and final title opinions (but do not sign them). The process of using paralegals to carry out all phases of an attorney's certification short of actually signing the certification letter raises a host of ethical issues. In states where attorneys do not certify titles, paralegals may still work as title examiners. There the potential ethical dilemmas between attorneys and paralegals, at least on this topic, disappear.

With all of the advances in computers, software, and digital storage, it should come as no surprise that advanced technology has begun to come to the rescue of the title searcher. At the beginning of the millennium, a title searcher would carry out his or her duties in much the same way that a title searcher in the 1970s would have. But there have been recent and, some would argue, long overdue changes in title search work. For instance, many of the preliminary steps of a title search can be carried out online without even visiting the courthouse in person.

It is fairly common practice for a title searcher to access recent Deed Room or Land Office records through local county web sites. These web sites offer a huge time saving feature for title searchers. Instead of having to wait until the title searcher can physically visit the courthouse, he or she can access these public documents through the Internet, any day of the week and at any time of day. Tax offices are also now routinely providing high-quality data for title searchers that may obviate the need to visit to the tax office entirely.

But recent innovations in title search work go beyond limited online access to deeds, mortgages, and tax records. Other innovations are more sweeping. Consider the program Eflite, for example. Created by Investor's Title (https://eflite.invtitle. com/Login.aspx), this program has quietly revolutionized the historical approach to title search. This program allows title searchers to complete online forms and then store them on servers for later retrieval by attorneys. The long-anticipated paperless title search might actually become a reality. Using this program, a title searcher can effectively work from his or her home, submit materials to the attorney online and then move on to the next assignment. The attorney can review the entire search, including documents, online and when satisfied, generate preliminary and final title opinions that can then be automatically forwarded to the title insurance company for review. Eflite even interfaces with SoftPro® to generate many of the typical forms used in closings.

COMMON PROBLEMS IN TITLE SEARCHES

In this last section of the chapter, we will explore some of the most common problems encountered by title examiners and also address some methods of overcoming these problems.

A. SUBDIVIDED PROPERTIES

It is a common practice to carve out smaller tracts from much larger ones. Real estate developers do this all the time. However, subdivided properties sometimes cause problems. For instance, the smaller properties may not be properly identified, leading to confusion about which property is which. It can be difficult to sift through all the properties to identify a particular parcel, especially in large developments.

When faced with this situation, always start with the most recent deed, if it is available. Many times the deed will contain language explaining how the original property was subdivided and how this particular tract was created (and when). It is also helpful to locate the plat or survey of the subdivision. Besides presenting a visual depiction of the entire area, these drawings often contain additional information, such as bordering properties, existing easements, and water and sewer lines that can help clear up many problems.

B. HOLES OR BREAKS IN THE CHAIN OF TITLE

In states that follow the grantor-grantee model, it is a common problem to have an apparent hole in the chain of title. A title examiner will begin tracing back each of the owners until suddenly she cannot find a previous owner. There appears to be no deed granting property to a particular owner. In areas that follow the tract system, this is not a common problem. What can cause this apparent break in the chain of title? The most common reason is that the owner changed names while possessing the property. The property was conveyed to the owner under one name and was then conveyed out from that owner under a different name. This happens more often than you might think. If a woman is single when she acquires property, marries and takes her husband's last name, when she sells the property, her last name will be different.

What most title examiners do when they find an apparent missing transaction in the chain of title is to go to the marriage records. More often than not, they will discover that the missing transaction is a result of someone getting married. Less frequently, the missing transaction may be caused by incorrectly indexing the owner's name in the first place.

CHAIN OF TITLE

Current Owners Cynthia Thompson Epps of 5402 Burkemont Road Morganton, NC 28655

Grantor Names:	Colin D. Epps and wife Cindy Thompson Epps
Grantee Names:	Cynthia Thompson Epps
Date of Transaction:	October 14, 2004
Date Recorded:	November 5, 2004
Deed Book Reference:	Book 1412 pg 443–446
Brief description of property:	1.32 acres Southside of State RD 1957, Burkemont Mountain Rd.

Current owners

Prior Transaction:

Grantor Names:	W.V. Home and wife Eula Denton Home, Wanda Home Elliot Nesbitt, Debbie Thompson McPeters, legally separated, and Cindy Thompson Epps and her husband Colin D. Epps
Grantee Names:	Colin D. Epps and wife Cindy Thompson Epps
Date of Transaction:	February 14, 2000
Date Recorded:	February 28, 2000
Deed Book Reference:	Book 942 pg 1599
Brief description of property:	1.32 acres Southside of State RD 1957, Burkemont Mountain Rd.

Prior Transaction:

Grantor Names:	W.V. Home and wife Eula Denton Home, Wanda Home Elliot Nesbitt, Debbie Thompson McPeters, legally separated, and Cindy Thompson Epps
Grantee Names:	Colin D. Epps and wife Cindy Thompson Epps
Date of Transaction:	December 17, 1999
Date Recorded:	December 30, 1999
Deed Book Reference:	Book 939 pg 2315
Brief description of the property:	1.32 acres Southside of State RD 1957, Burkemont Mountain Rd.

* Note W.V. Home and wife Eula Denton Home gave their children Wanda and David Nesbitt, Debbie Thompson McPeters who is legally separated, and Cindy Thompson Epps and her husband a 1/3 undivided interest then the children signed their 1/3 undivided interest back to Cindy Thompson Epps and her husband Colin D. Epps.

Prior Transaction:

Grantor Names:	W.V. Home
Grantee Names:	W.V. Home and wife Eula Denton Home

Notes clarify portions of the chain of title

(Continued on p. 346)

Date of Transaction: November 2, 1981
Date Recorded: February 16, 1982
Deed Book Reference: Book 615 pg 536
Brief description of the property: 6.88 acres of S.R. 1957 on
                                        Burkemont Mountain Rd.

* Note W.V. Home transferred his half interest to his wife Eula Denton Home so her name can be on the deed after they were married.

Prior Transaction:

<table>
<tr><td>Notes clarify portions of the chain of title</td><td>Grantor Names:</td><td>Sherill H. Green and wife Quinn H. Green and Burlie
L. Houk and his wife Grace G. Houk.</td></tr>
</table>

Grantees Names: W.V. Home
Date of Transaction: July 21, 1980
Date Recorded: July 24, 1980
Deed Book Reference: Book 589 pg 446
Brief description of property: 6.88 acres of S.R. 1957 on
                                        Burkemont Mountain Rd.

Prior Transaction:

Grantor Names: lssiah Carswell and Wachovia Bank and
                                        Trust Company
Grantee Names: Sherill H. Green and Burlie L. Houk
Date of Transaction: August 1, 1979
Date Recorded: August 14, 1979
Deed Book Reference: Book 572 pg 808
Brief description of property: Southwestern corner on Burkemont Rd.
Prior Transaction:
Grantor Names: Iola P. Mace
Grantee Names: Issiah Carswell
Date of Transaction: August 9, 1960
Date Recorded: August 10, 1960
Deed Book Reference: Book 205 pg 628

Brief description of property: Southwestern corner on Burkemont Rd.

* Note Iola P. Mace died and Issiah Carswell and Wachovia bank transferred the property to the Greens and Houks.

                                        Out Conveyance

Owners: Colin D. Epps and wife Cindy Thompson Epps
                                        5402 Burkemont Road
                                        Morganton, NC 28655
                                        Taxes Paid on 7/30/2004 in the amount of
                                        $522.91
Out Conveyance   Checked 3/15/05 at 9:00 am

Period checked: The period was checked from 1/1/1998 to
3/15/2005

Deed of Trust: Recorded 6/25/03 in Book 1255 pg 772–788

This deed has not yet been cancelled.
Right of Way Agreement — recorded 8/18/1998 in Book 908 pg 2301
I checked the Clerk's office from 1/1/1998 to 3/15/05 and nothing was found except that
they had divorced.

TACKING AND OTHER SHORTCUTS

There is always a temptation to take shortcuts. This is especially true in title work.
The reasoning that some title examiners use is, "If there is a problem with this
property, it would have cropped up by now." So they decide to shortcut the process
and submit the title as free of any encumbrances so that they can shave some time
off a title search and move on to the next one. This is an especially strong temptation when you consider that most title examiners are paid by the search, not by
the hour. However, these shortcuts can have profound effects on other people.
A missed lien, judgment, or assessment can mean that the new owner will be forced
to pay thousands of dollars, or the title insurance company will have to pay thousands of dollars in defending the owner. In either event, the title examiner's reputation will be ruined. No matter how big a city you are in, the legal community is
always small and word gets around quickly. Title examiners who skimp on the
details and take chances on missing crucial information eventually get weeded out
of the profession. Title insurance companies will refuse to work with them; attorneys will refuse to hire them and what was a promising and potentially lucrative
career has now been closed off forever, all for the sake of saving a little time on a
single title search.

ESTATE OF FLEMING v. NICHOLSON

ESTATE OF FLEMING v. NICHOLSON
168 Vt. 495, 724 A.2d 1026 (1998)

JOHNSON, J.

Defendants, David Nicholson and the law firm of Nicholson & Taylor, P.C., appeal
an order of the superior court granting partial summary judgment to plaintiff, estate of
Edward Fleming, and an order awarding plaintiff prejudgment interest on damages. In

granting summary judgment to plaintiff, the court found defendants negligent as a matter of law for failing to disclose a lack of a subdivision permit discovered while performing a title search on property plaintiff contemplated purchasing. After an evidentiary hearing was held regarding the computation of damages, the court calculated and awarded damages to plaintiff in the amount of $55,766.00 and prejudgment interest in the amount of $59,695.60. Defendants now argue that the trial court erred in granting summary judgment to plaintiff because there was no expert testimony presented concerning the standard of care for attorneys in Vermont and because defendant Nicholson was reasonable in not disclosing the defect in title. In addition, defendants argue that the court should not have granted prejudgment interest because the plaintiff's damages were not readily ascertainable. We affirm the grant of summary judgment and the award of prejudgment interest.

In 1988, Edward Fleming retained the law firm of Nicholson & Taylor, P.C., to conduct a title search on a parcel of land he was considering purchasing. While performing the search, defendant Nicholson discovered that the parcel was carved out of a larger piece of land in 1976 with the aid of a deferral of subdivision permit issued by the Department of Environmental Conservation (DEC). Defendant also discovered that in the late 1970's a dwelling and wastewater system were constructed on the property without a subdivision permit and in violation of the deferral of permit. At the time of the title search, the DEC followed a 1984 nonenforcement policy with regard to subdivision violations. Relying on this nonenforcement policy, defendant decided not to inform Fleming of the subdivision violation. Fleming, believing there were no title defects, purchased the property for $66,500.00. Unbeknownst to Fleming, the DEC rescinded the nonenforcement policy in 1989. In 1991, Fleming refinanced his mortgage on the property and died a year later. In 1994, Fleming's estate contracted to sell the property for $94,000.00, but the discovery of the subdivision violation terminated the contract. Fleming's mortgagee subsequently foreclosed on the property and sold the property at a decreased value of $10,734.00 in 1995.

The administrator of Fleming's estate, Grant C. Rees, then brought a legal malpractice action against Nicholson & Taylor, P.C., and against David Nicholson, Esq. and Todd Taylor, Esq. individually. Plaintiff moved for summary judgment on the issue of defendant's liability, and defendant Taylor filed a cross-motion for summary judgment. The court granted Taylor's motion, and plaintiff has not appealed the decision in favor of Taylor. The court granted summary judgment on the issue of liability as against defendants Nicholson and Nicholson and Taylor, P.C., holding defendant Nicholson negligent as a matter of law for failing to inform his client of the permit deferral and lack of a subdivision permit for the dwelling and wastewater system. An evidentiary hearing was held regarding the computation of damages (plaintiff waived trial by jury), and the court awarded plaintiff damages in the amount of $55,766.00 plus $59,695.60 in prejudgment interest.

Summary judgment is appropriate when there are no genuine issues of material fact and the moving party is entitled to judgment as a matter of law.

In a legal malpractice action, a plaintiff must prove that the attorney was in fact negligent and that this negligence was the proximate cause of the plaintiff's injury. Generally, negligence by professionals is demonstrated using expert testimony to: (1) describe the proper standard of skill and care for that profession, (2) show that the defendant's conduct departed from that standard of care, and (3) show that this conduct was the proximate cause of plaintiff's harm. If the alleged negligent conduct is a matter of judgment unique to that profession, the above elements must be established by expert testimony to assist the trier of fact in determining negligence.

There are situations, however, where expert testimony is not needed. Where a professional's lack of care is so apparent that only common knowledge and experience are needed to comprehend it, expert testimony is not required to assist the trier of fact in finding the elements of negligence.

Here, defendant's lack of care under the circumstances was so apparent that no expert testimony was required. In general, the standard of care to which an attorney is held in rendering professional services is the degree of care, skill, diligence, and knowledge commonly possessed and exercised by a reasonable, careful, and prudent attorney practicing in the jurisdiction of Vermont. Defendant argues that expert testimony was needed to assist the trier of fact in determining whether his conduct conformed to that standard, that is, whether a reasonable, careful, and prudent Vermont attorney would have disclosed the existence of the subdivision violation, taking into account the existence of the nonenforcement policy. We disagree.

Defendant relies on Tetreault to argue that a trier of fact requires the guidance of expert testimony in assessing an attorney's conduct with respect to a title search. See Tetreault, 165 Vt. at 578, 682 A.2d at 950-51. Defendant's reliance on Tetreault is misplaced, however, because the negligent conduct at issue in Tetreault is distinguishable from the conduct at issue in this case. In Tetreault, the plaintiffs brought a malpractice claim against their attorney, claiming that the attorney was negligent in failing to discover and advise them of subdivision permit violations on the property they were purchasing. See id. We held that expert testimony was required to prove both the standard of care and whether there had been a breach of the standard. The central question concerned the process and common activities performed during a title search, a task which is unique to the profession and therefore created the need for expert testimony. In the present case, defendant's aptitude in performing the title search is not at issue; rather, the finding of negligence is premised upon his failure to disclose important information to his client, namely, the permit violations that could diminish the value of the subject property.

That defendant's nondisclosure of this information proximately caused plaintiff's loss is also apparent. Defendant ultimately prevented his client from making an informed decision about whether to purchase the property. Defendant is the source from which Fleming would have expected to receive such information, and absent that information, Fleming would have necessarily misapprehended the value of the property. The issues of whether defendant had a duty to disclose the permit violation, whether he breached that duty, and whether the breach proximately caused plaintiff's injury are not technical issues that require the assistance of an expert in order for a trier of fact to be able to comprehend them. The question, then, in reviewing the grant of summary judgment, is whether defendant has raised any genuine issues of material fact concerning the elements of negligence.

Defendant argues that the majority of attorneys in Vermont, with knowledge of the non-enforcement policy, would not have disclosed the permit violations, and that his conduct was therefore reasonable. We reject the notion that the practice of the majority of attorneys conclusively establishes the standard of care. While the standard of care is based on the "degree of care, skill, diligence and knowledge commonly possessed and exercised by a reasonable, careful and prudent" Vermont lawyer, Russo, 147 Vt. at 24, 510 A.2d at

438, the conduct of the majority of Vermont lawyers does not define "reasonableness" per se. It is ultimately the role of the courts to define this standard. "Courts must in the end say what is required; there are precautions so imperative that even their universal disregard will not excuse their omission." We find that a reasonable, careful, and prudent attorney would disclose the existence of the permit violations and nonenforcement policy to a client. In conducting a title search for a client, an attorney has a duty to inform and explain to the client the implications of any clouds on the title that would influence a reasonably prudent purchaser not to purchase the property. After disclosing this information, it is possible that a reasonable attorney might advise his client to purchase the property even with the encumbrances, but that is not the issue at bar. After conducting the title search for Fleming, defendant had a duty to inform and explain to Fleming the implications of the deferral of permit, violations thereof, and the lack of a subdivision permit.

Summary judgment was therefore appropriate in this case because there are no issues of material fact in dispute. We agree with the trial court that defendant was negligent as a matter of law and affirm the grant of summary judgment. Because the trial court used a reasonable and established method to calculate damages and prejudgment interest in this case, we find no abuse of discretion and affirm the award of prejudgment interest.

Affirmed.

CASE QUESTIONS

1   For what purpose did Fleming retain the firm of Nicholson & Taylor?
2   What error does Fleming accuse Nicholson of committing?
3   What ruling did the trial court make in this case?
4   Was expert testimony required in this case to establish Nicholson's negligence?
5   According to the court, what was the proximate cause of Fleming losing his property?

 SKILLS YOU NEED IN THE REAL WORLD

DOUBLE-CHECKING YOUR OWN TITLE WORK

One of the advantages to title searching is that there is a built-in mechanism to help a title searcher double-check her work. Because the grantor and grantee indexes are mirror images of one another, when a title searcher has a question about a particular conveyance, she can double-check the work by verifying the entry in the other indexes.

For example, suppose that the current owner of the property, John Doe, shows a deed book reference of volume 900, page 32, purchased from Joseph Wilson. The grantee index will show an entry from Joseph Wilson to John Doe. The grantor index, on the other hand, will show an entry under John Doe's name, receiving property from Joseph Wilson. Once a chain of title is established, the adverse conveyance worksheet is used to double-check the entries in the chain. At some point, a person listed as an owner in the chain will also be listed in the adverse conveyances. This helps a title examiner to cross-reference her work.

CHAPTER SUMMARY

Title insurance is an insurance policy with a very specialized function. It protects owners against claims made against the title to their property. Before a title insurance company will issue a policy, it requires an examination of the public records to make sure that there are no outstanding legal claims on the property. The mechanism to check the public records is a title examination. A title examiner is someone who is trained to review all public records in order to discover any potential claims against a parcel of real estate. The title examiner must review land records and civil and criminal actions to check for any outstanding legal claims on the property. The basic reason for a title examination is to protect the new owner from any claim that might affect her enjoyment of the property. Title examinations are required not only by title insurance companies, but also by lenders who wish to safeguard their interest in the property.

A title examination is a multistep process. In states that follow the grantor-grantee index model, properties are listed by the names of the buyers and sellers. A title examiner in such a state is required to establish a chain of title, listing all the names of the owners of a particular tract going back for a specific period of time. In these states, attorneys are usually responsible for certifying the title as free and clear of all encumbrances. The attorney's opinion about the legal status of the property is grounds for a legal malpractice action if the attorney is incorrect. Not all states follow the attorney certification model. In some states, title examinations are performed by nonlawyers. Under either system, a title examiner must pay close attention to detail and make sure that all records are properly surveyed for any potential legal impact on the property.

REVIEW QUESTIONS

1   What is title insurance?
2   How can title insurance assist in completing a real estate transaction?
3   What are some of the problems that title insurance protects against?
4   How does someone acquire title insurance?
5   How often must a person pay a title insurance premium?
6   What is the grantor-grantee index?
7   How can surveys and plats of property help in a title examination?

8   What are the basic steps involved in a title search?

9   What is a chain of title?

10 What information can a title examiner gather at the local tax office?

11 What are adverse or out conveyances?

12 Why is it important to determine if a previous mortgage has been canceled?

13 What are abstract forms?

14 What are the Uniform Commercial Code filings? Why are they important for title examinations?

15 How do probate, marriage, birth, and death records assist a title examiner?

16 What is the purpose of a preliminary title opinion?

17 Why is legal malpractice an issue in title searches in some states?

18 What is "tacking"? Why does it present ethical concerns?

19 Are attorneys required to certify titles in all states? Explain your answer.

20 Explain how the attorney in this chapter's case excerpt committed legal malpractice.

DISCUSSION QUESTIONS

Should all states move to a system whereby an attorney certifies title to real property? What advantages and disadvantages would such a system bring have?

PRACTICAL APPLICATIONS

Using the forms provided in the figures throughout this chapter, prepare a title search on a piece of property. Create a chain of title going back for 40 years, then a list of adverse conveyances for each owner in the chain. Are there any Uniform Commercial Code listings for the current owner?

WEB SITES

Fidelity National Title Insurance Company
https://www.fntic.com

American Land Title Association
http://www.alta.org

Law.com Dictionary
http://www.law.com

Legal Explanations
http://www.legal-explanations.com

TERMS AND PHRASES

Binder	Policy	Title abstract
Chain of title	Premium	Title examination
Grantor-grantee index	Tacking	Title insurance

SIGNIFICANT CASES

First Midwest Bank, N.A. v. Stewart Title Guar. Co., 218 Ill. 2d 326 (Ill., 2006)
Chicago Title Ins. Co. v. Huntington Natl. Bank, 719 N.E.2d 955 (Ohio, 1999)
Kenney v. Henry Fischer Builder, Inc., 716 N.E.2d 1189 (Ohio App., 1998)
Childs v. Charske, 822 N.E.2d 853 (Ohio Com. Pl., 2004)
Linden v. Moskowitz, 743 N.Y.S.2d 65 (N.Y.A.D. 1 Dept., 2002)
Fidelity Nat. Title Ins. Co. of Tennessee v. Kidd, 99 N.C.App. 737, 394 S.E.2d 225
   (1990)

The Closing

13

Focus of This Chapter

This chapter provides a general introduction to closing/settlement procedures nationwide and then examines the specifics of this process in various locales across the country to provide specific examples of how the process is actually carried out. The paralegal's role in the closing is examined in detail.

Chapter Learning Objectives

After completing this chapter, you should be able to:

■ Describe the importance of a real estate settlement
■ Explain the basic procedures involved in completing a real estate settlement
■ List and describe the participants in the closing
■ Define the important documents required at a closing
■ Explain the ethical concerns that arise from the use of paralegals in real estate closings

INTRODUCTION

A real estate settlement, or closing, is the point at which the parties to a real estate transaction come together, sign appropriate paperwork, and disburse funds. We examine the closing process in detail in this chapter, concentrating not only on the basic procedures, but also the critically important role played by paralegals in modern real estate closings.

Before we can begin describing the process of completing a real estate closing, it is important to address an issue about terminology. In different parts of the country, the final step to bring a real estate transaction to its completion is referred to as a "closing," while in other parts, it is called a "settlement." In still other parts of the country, the process goes by another name. For the sake of clarity, we will use the term "closing" to refer to the process of finalizing a real estate sale.

A. WHAT IS A CLOSING?

Closing
Also known as a settlement, the final phase of a real estate transaction at which all deeds are signed and funds are distributed to complete the sale of real property.

A **closing** is the final step in a long process that began with a homeowner's decision to sell his house. The homeowner contacted a real estate agent who entered into a listing agreement with the homeowner, placing the house for sale. At some point, a buyer made an offer on the house and the stage was set for a closing. Between the time of the offer and acceptance, a great many things have happened. The buyer arranged for a mortgage with a lender. The house was inspected. The lender probably requested an appraisal. The buyer arranged for title insurance. The lender finalized its paperwork and prepared checks to disburse at the closing. A deed was prepared that will transfer the owner's interest in the property to the buyer. We have discussed all these aspects in previous chapters. The closing is when all of the details finally come together.

ISSUE AT
A GLANCE

A closing brings together the buyer and the seller for the final stage in a real estate transaction.

Closings can be both complicated and time-consuming. Many different individuals are involved and this is always a recipe for delay. Someone must take the responsibility of coordinating all the information to bring about the closing. In some states, attorneys are responsible for conducting closings, while in other states that duty falls to the lender or even a title insurance company representative. No matter who pulls the closing together, the actual process requires careful attention to detail. It is easy to make a mistake at a closing and such a mistake can have enormous financial consequences. In states where attorneys conduct closings, it is very common for the attorney to rely on the services of a qualified paralegal to collect all the important documents and to coordinate the physical meeting of all concerned parties.

BASIC PREPARATIONS TO CONDUCT A CLOSING

Although different states follow different rules about who is authorized to conduct closings, there are similarities in the basic processes involved no matter where the closing is conducted. For instance, the buyer will have contacted a lender and arranged for a mortgage or deed of trust in order to purchase the property. The lender will make the funds available at the closing.

A. MORTGAGES

The most obvious requirement of any transaction is payment for the property. Purchase contracts often contain express provisions requiring a loan commitment from the lender within ten days of the contract date. Without this assurance, the transaction can never be completed. Once the loan commitment is given, it is up to the lender to make the funds available to complete the transaction at the closing.

B. ATTORNEY REPRESENTATION

Although many states do not require an attorney to conduct a closing, many buyers hire one anyway, in order to safeguard their interests and to handle any legal questions that come up during the negotiations and closing. In some states, there is a question about whether a nonlawyer can conduct a closing. States are split on this, with some allowing nonlawyers to conduct the entire closing, and others states claiming that handling a closing is essentially a legal process and requires the presence of an attorney. (For a good discussion of this point, see this chapter's case excerpt.) If a buyer hires an attorney, or if the closing occurs in a state where an attorney's involvement is mandatory, the attorney's fee is paid by the buyer from the proceeds at the sale. Most attorneys who handle closings are paid a flat fee or a percentage of the sales price.

Attorneys are used in most, but not all, states to handle the details of a closing.

ISSUE AT
A GLANCE

EXAMPLE 13-1

Ricardo has entered into a contract to purchase a home. He approaches a local law firm about representing him at the closing. The attorney explains that she will handle the closing, ensure that all documents are properly signed and recorded, and ensure that the deed and mortgage are properly recorded. Her fee is one-half of 1 percent of the sale price. The sale price is $92,000. How much is Ricardo's attorney fee?

Answer: Multiply $92,000 by .5%. The answer is $460.

C. ESTABLISHING THE DATE FOR THE CLOSING

Because of the number of individuals who are involved in a typical real estate transaction, setting a closing date is not a simple matter. Many of these individuals must produce specific documents, and these documents must be completed prior to the closing date. Because many different legal professionals handle closings across the country, we will refer to this person as a "closing professional," recognizing that this term encompasses title insurers, lenders, real estate attorneys, paralegals, and real estate agents. Whoever is responsible for coordinating the closing must keep after all parties to make sure that checks, contracts, and other documents are ready in time for the closing date.

Scheduling a closing can be a very challenging part of real estate work. The final date and time of the closing must take into account the needs of several different parties, including the client, the closing attorney (if any), the real estate agents, and

A party might insist on a time is of the essence clause when he is facing a set date in another closing and must have the funds from that transaction before being able to complete the purchase of the new home.

the lender. If the funds are not available, there is little point in scheduling a closing. The seller will certainly not execute a deed and sign over his rights without receiving payment. Besides the practical issues of completing all the necessary paperwork, there is another important issue regarding closing dates: time is of the essence clauses.

1. TIME IS OF THE ESSENCE

We encountered time is of the essence clauses in Chapter 6. In that chapter, we saw that when a real estate contract contains such a clause, the closing must occur on the date set or the contract is void. Obviously all parties wish to avoid that result, and this puts even greater pressure on the participants to complete all paperwork in time for the closing date.

EXAMPLE 13-2

Renee is selling her home. She needs the funds from this sale in order to purchase a new home. She negotiated a closing date of the fifth day of the month to close on the sale of her home and a closing of the seventh for the purchase of her new home, and included a time is of the essence clause in the first contract. On the fifth, the attorney handling the closing calls to say that she has not received all the paperwork that she needs to conclude the closing. She says that the closing cannot be held until the sixth. What effect does this have on the first contract?

Answer: It voids it. A time is of the essence clause specifically provides that the contract will be voided if the closing does not occur on a specific date. The attorney has indicated that the closing cannot be performed on that date, so the contract provision is triggered.

D. GATHERING DOCUMENTS AND INFORMATION FOR THE CLOSING

The first and most important job in organizing a closing is gathering information. Many of the professionals responsible for coordinating the closing rely on forms to help them double-check all information needed to complete the closing. Not only will the closing professional need everyone's full name and address, but also their telephone, cell phone, and e-mail addresses as well. These days, it is often easier to reach someone through e-mail or by cell phone than by other means. Many of the transactions that were formally handled by couriers and faxes are now done by e-mail. To successfully complete the closing, it is necessary for the closing professional to gather information from a wide variety of sources. The most common information needed to complete a closing includes:

1 Title search
2 Legal description of property
3 Loan payoff amounts
4 Tax information
5 Termite inspection report

Closings require close attention to detail, especially in regard to particular documents needed to complete the process.

ISSUE AT
A GLANCE

1. TITLE SEARCH

The title search must be completed prior to closing. As we saw in the last chapter, a title search can be very involved and detailed. The purpose of the title search is to ensure that there are no legal claims that could affect the title to the property or prevent the finalization of the transaction. For a complete summary of title searches, see Chapter 12.

a. Title Defects

When a title search has discovered potential title defects, such as liens, judgments, or any other issue that clouds title, it is up to the seller (and the seller's attorney) to clear up these title defects before the closing. One of the conditions that buyers, lenders, and title insurance companies insist on is that the title must be free of defects.

b. Attorney Certifications

As we saw in the previous chapter, some states use a system whereby the attorney certifies the status of the title. In those states, the attorney will issue two reports: the preliminary opinion and the final opinion. The preliminary opinion details any possible problems with the title and what the legal team will do to correct them. The final title opinion confirms that any legal problem has been cleared up and certifies that the title is free and clear of encumbrances.

The preliminary and final title opinions go not only to the client, but also to the title insurance company. It is these opinions that serve as the basis for the issuance of a title insurance policy.

2. LEGAL DESCRIPTION OF THE PROPERTY

The legal description of the property is important for several reasons. It will be used in various documents, from the deed to the mortgage, to correctly identify the property. Researching and preparing the legal description often falls to the legal assistant or paralegal who works for a closing professional. As we have seen in previous chapters, there are several different methods used to identify property, from tract indexes to metes and bounds descriptions. No matter what type is used, the closing professional must make sure that the description is correct.

Understanding how property is described, either through metes and bounds or the tract system, can be a huge advantage to any legal professional, as well as consumers, investors, and home owners.

ISSUE AT
A GLANCE

3. LOAN PAYOFF AMOUNTS

Just before the actual closing, the closing professional must obtain information about the exact amount owed on the seller's mortgage. The reason that the closing professional must wait until the last possible moment is to ensure that this figure is accurate. Lenders charge daily interest rates on loans and the closing professional must confirm the amount owed up to the day of the closing so that the check written to pay off that mortgage is correct. This check will be disbursed at the closing and it is absolutely necessary that the amount is correct.

a. Seller's Information

The seller should provide complete information about outstanding mortgages, including the lender's name, address, account numbers, and estimated payoff amounts. The closing professional will pin down the actual payoff amounts, but it is always helpful to have a rough estimate from the seller. This estimate helps to double-check the information provided from the seller. It also helps to determine if there are actually a first and second mortgage. Obviously, both of these mortgages must be satisfied at the closing. When the seller's estimate is wildly divergent from the actual estimate, this can be a hint that there may be more than one mortgage on the property. One way of determining payoff amounts is by creating a standardized form that is sent to all lenders requesting this information. This letter may be followed up with a phone call shortly before the closing to determine the most up-to-the-minute payoff amount. Lenders will also often guarantee the loan payoff amount for a specific period. For instance, a lender might declare that the loan payoff amount is good for five business days only. If the closing occurs after that time, the closing professional should call back and get new information.

4. TAX INFORMATION

One of the most important pieces of information that must be obtained prior to the closing is the tax bill for the property. If the taxes have not been paid on that property, they must be paid at the closing. If they have already been paid, then the seller will want reimbursement for the part of the year for which he did not live in the house. Fortunately, a thorough title examination always seeks this information. If the seller must be reimbursed for his payment of taxes, the closing professional must prorate payments between the buyer and the seller. We discuss proration later in this chapter.

5. TERMITE AND OTHER INSPECTIONS

There are several different types of inspections that must occur prior to the actual closing. For instance, in Chapter 11 we examined the issue of the buyer's inspection of the premises by a certified housing inspector. However, the lender may also insist on a pest inspection.

A termite or pest inspection is a requirement imposed by most lenders. The reasons for the inspection are self-evident: The lender wants to make sure that there

- ■ Title search
- ■ Legal description of the property
- ■ Loan payoff amounts
- ■ Property survey
- ■ Tax information
- ■ Termite inspection and report
- ■ House inspector's report
- ■ Title insurance binder
- ■ Information on any title problems
- ■ Sewage certification or percolation test for unimproved property

are no infestations that could ultimately affect the safety or stability of the structure. Lenders insist that a certified professional must carry out this inspection. This inspector will examine the entire physical structure of the house, searching for any type of wood-boring insect. The inspector's final certification that the house is free of termites or other infestations is one of the documents that are required in order to conclude the closing.

E. LOAN-CLOSING SOFTWARE

Modern computer software has made the job of loan closing considerably easier. Before the widespread use of the Department of Housing and Urban Development's **HUD-1 Settlement Form**, closings differed from state to state and even city to city. Closing paperwork was completed by hand and often involved time-consuming calculations, especially when it came to determining prorated payments for heating oil, taxes, and other payments. Closing software has taken away much of the tedium involved in creating a settlement statement. Programs such as SoftPro and Display Soft can generate all the documents needed to complete the closing, including the HUD-1 settlement statement. The software also calculates the exact amount needed for disbursement checks, real estate commissions, and the closing professional's fee.

HUD-1 Settlement Form
A real estate settlement and disbursement form that has been widely adopted by U.S. lenders.

 THE PROCEDURE AT THE CLOSING

Immediately before the closing, the closing professional is responsible for pulling all the documents together to ensure that the closing proceeds smoothly. During the closing, the parties will meet face-to-face and sign numerous documents. Keeping all these documents and disbursement checks organized can be daunting. The parties may also have questions about the legal impact of certain aspects of the closing. This is one reason why many states require attorneys to actually conduct the closing. In states where an attorney is not required, the parties are urged to have their questions answered by an attorney and the closing professional is counseled not to give legal advice to any of the parties.

As the various documents are passed from party to party, there is often a need to have a signature notarized. Many closing professionals have notaries on staff to facilitate this aspect of the process. One of the most important aspects of the closing is the correct preparation of the loan closing package.

A. PREPARING THE LOAN PACKAGE

Loan package
A set of instructions from a lender about how financial documents should be prepared and distributed at the closing.

Several days prior to the closing, the lender should send the closing professional a **loan package** that includes all the documents that must be completed during the closing. Many lenders have specific instructions and requirements for the way that their loan documents must be prepared and finalized. The loan package will include not only the documents that must be completed, but also a complete and thorough set of instructions about how these documents should be completed and returned to the lender. Unfortunately, some lenders wait until the last minute, sometimes the actual day of the closing, before they send the loan package to the closing professional. This puts a great deal of pressure on the team.

ISSUE AT A GLANCE

The loan package contains all the documents that the lender needs the buyer to complete at the closing. It also contains instructions for the law firm handling the closing.

B. VERIFYING HAZARD INSURANCE

The closing professional must also verify that the new owner has obtained hazard insurance for the property. Hazard insurance, also known as homeowner's insurance, is required by the lender in order to safeguard the collateral for the loan. In addition to the loan package and hazard insurance, there are numerous other documents that will be exchanged during the closing.

C. DOCUMENTS EXCHANGED AT THE CLOSING

In this section we examine the most common documents that are exchanged at the closing. These documents must all be prepared prior to the closing and may require additional attention after the closing, such as filing at the local courthouse. The documents exchanged during the closing include:

1. General warranty deed
2. Mortgage
3. IRS forms
4. Lien waiver affidavits (if required)
5. HUD-1 Settlement Form
6. Bill of sale for personal property
7. Compliance agreement
8. Credit insurance documents

9   Loan application
10 USA PATRIOT Act requirements
11 PMI disclosures
12 Trust disbursement records
13 Truth In Lending documentation
14 Termite inspection letter
15 Survey

1. GENERAL WARRANTY DEED

One of the responsibilities of the closing professional is to make sure that the deed is drafted correctly. This is where having an attorney prepare the deed is absolutely essential. In states where attorneys conduct the closings, they also prepare the deeds.

a. Preparing the Deed

There are many issues involved in preparing the deed. For instance, the deed must contain the appropriate language, legal descriptions, and correctly identified parties, among other features that we discussed in depth in Chapter 8.

2. MORTGAGE

As we have already seen, the mortgage (or deed of trust) is the financing document that sets out the arrangement between the buyer and the lender. The mortgage also gives the lender the right to foreclose on the property in the event that the buyer defaults. In addition to this feature, another important aspect of the mortgage is the promissory note provision.

a. Promissory Note

The **promissory note** is the provision in a mortgage under which the borrower agrees to specific repayment terms, including the total amount of the loan, the monthly interest payment, the annual percentage rate for the loan, the length of the loan, and other features. The promissory note provision is the binding agreement between the lender and the borrower whereby the borrower promises to repay the loan. Without this provision, a lender would have no way of enforcing a loan.

Promissory note
A legal agreement whereby the borrower agrees to borrow a specific amount and also agrees to the repayment of that amount.

b. Subordination Agreements

We discussed subordination agreements in Chapter 9. In that chapter, we saw that a subordination agreement could be required in situations in which there is more than one mortgage on the property and there is an issue about priority. In situations involving owner financing, for instance, a lender might insist that the owner subordinate his mortgage to the lender's mortgage, especially when the lender is providing the bulk of the funds.

3. IRS FORMS

There are various Internal Revenue Service forms that may be required as part of the closing. One of the most important of these is form 1099. This form has been required by the IRS since 1987; it details the total amount received by the seller during the closing. This document is important because it shows any profit that the seller has taken from the sale and will have important consequences for the seller's personal income tax return.

a. IRS Form 4506

In addition to Form 1099, other IRS forms may also be required. Another common one is Form 4506. This form allows the lender to request a copy of the borrower's income tax return from the IRS. This information is important in order to evaluate the borrower for a possible loan. Without this form, the IRS will not release a copy of an individual's income tax return.

b. W-9 Form

A W-9 Form verifies the borrower's Social Security number and is important not only as a means of tracking capital gains and other taxes, but also for reporting purposes to other agencies. With modern concerns over identity theft and money laundering, the W-9 is a further safeguard that a person is who he claims to be.

4. LIEN WAIVER AFFIDAVITS

Title insurance companies routinely require lien waiver affidavits to show that there are no liens or other encumbrances against the property. This form is used as a further safety net. By requiring the owner/seller to sign such an affidavit, the title insurance company can be assured that there are no outstanding or as yet unfiled liens that could affect title to the property at some later date. When sellers sign a lien waiver affidavit, they are swearing that they know of no judgments, encumbrances, liens, or other pending matters that could act as a bar to the transaction being completed. In states that use attorneys to conduct title examinations, lien waiver affidavits are often attached to the final title certificate.

5. HUD-1 SETTLEMENT FORM

Almost all lenders and attorneys use the Housing and Urban Development Administration's Form 1 for the settlement closing statement. Although this form was not always the preferred method for accounting for the funds disbursed at closings, the prevalence of Fannie Mae and other governmental agencies in the secondary mortgage market have made the form ubiquitous. The reason is simple: Fannie Mae, Ginnie Mae, Freddie Mac, and other corporations that purchase mortgages on the secondary mortgage market insist on uniformity and have all adopted the HUD-1 form as one method of ensuring that uniformity. As a result, almost all lenders use the HUD form. It is even part of closing software programs. The form is actually generated by the software as the final step in helping to creating a closing package. There is a blank HUD-1 settlement closing form in the Appendix.

6. BILL OF SALE FOR PERSONAL PROPERTY

In some situations, the seller and the buyer may have negotiated the purchase of items of personal property in addition to the real property. If, for instance, the seller has agreed to sell furniture, appliances, or other personal property, this sale must be set out in a separate bill of sale. This bill of sale is independent of the other closing documents. Remember that the other documents are concerned with the transfer of title to real property. Any sale of personal property is separate and distinct from that transaction and must have its own supporting documentation.

7. COMPLIANCE AGREEMENT

A compliance agreement is a form signed by the borrower that permits the lender to request additional information or documents after the closing. The lender insists on this form in case there is some type of clerical error or missing paperwork from the closing. A compliance agreement is the borrower's agreement to provide any additional information requested by the lender after the closing has been completed.

8. CREDIT INSURANCE OR PROTECTION PLAN ADDENDUM

It is very common for borrowers not only to negotiate the provisions of the real estate mortgage, but also to request disability protection insurance. Disability insurance is a specific type of policy that will make a borrower's mortgage payments in the event that he is unable to meet that requirement because of illness or injury. If disability insurance is part of the mortgage packet negotiated with the lender, the first premium is usually due at the closing and will be part of the disbursements that occur at that time.

9. LOAN APPLICATION

When the borrower first approached the lender about financing the purchase of real estate, he filled out an application and presented it to the lender. What lenders often do prior to the closing is to retype that application and put it in a final (and more easily read) form. During the closing, the borrower is often asked to sign this new loan application and to confirm that it contains all the same information that the borrower originally presented in the handwritten application.

10. USA PATRIOT ACT REQUIREMENTS

The USA PATRIOT Act was passed after the terrible events of September 11, 2001. Although terrorism would seem to be completely unrelated to a typical real estate transaction, the USA PATRIOT Act became a major factor in real estate closings by virtue of language contained in one clause of the act. The provision in question, Section 352, requires that certain financial institutions create an anti-money laundering program and certify that it has complied with the Act. More than bombs and hatred, terrorism thrives on money. It takes a great deal of money to keep a terrorist group functioning, and most of the money to support these efforts comes from laundered money from illicit activities as varied as counterfeit store coupons to shady real estate deals. As a result, most closing professionals now include a provision in their closing documents to show that they have complied with the USA PATRIOT Act in determining the identities of the people involved and certifying, to the extent possible, that the transaction was not completed for money laundering purposes.

11. PMI DISCLOSURE

Private mortgage insurance
An insurance policy that protects the lender and pays a specified amount in the event that the borrower defaults on the loan.

Private mortgage insurance is insurance that protects the lender when the borrower has put down less than 20 percent of the loan purchase price. In the event that the borrower defaults on the mortgage, PMI will reimburse the lender for money lost. It is referred to as "private mortgage insurance" to distinguish it from some government programs under the FHA and VA that serve the same function. The PMI disclosure brochure is a document that explains to the borrower what PMI is. The PMI disclosure form also informs the borrower how he can remove the PMI premium from the loan and when the PMI is scheduled to terminate. PMI is not designed to help the borrower. It reimburses the lender in the event of a borrower's default. However, PMI indirectly assists a borrower. If a company is willing to issue a PMI policy in a particular transaction, it usually means that a borrower who might not have qualified for a mortgage under other circumstances will get one.

 Private mortgage insurance protects the lender in the event of a borrower default. It is required whenever the borrower finances more than 80 percent of the purchase price.

12. TRUST DISBURSEMENT RECORDS

The trust disbursement record is a way for the closing professional to keep track of all funds collected and disbursed before the closing. When the bank issues funds for the closing, they are normally deposited in the closing professional's trust account where they will remain until the day of the closing. At that time, the closing professional will issue a series of checks from that trust account. Some of these funds will pay the real estate agent commissions, while others will pay a profit to the seller. The closing professional must make a full accounting of these funds and show that none have been retained, except for the closing agent's fee. Closing software will generate these reports in a fraction of the time that it took before. See Figure 13-2 for an example of a record of trust disbursements.

13. TRUTH IN LENDING DOCUMENTATION

The Federal Truth in Lending Act ("TILA") was originally created as a way to safeguard consumers from unscrupulous lenders. Under TILA, a lender must

FIGURE 13-2

Record of Trust
Disbursements

Client: Juan Garcia

Re: Residence, purchase of

Closing date: April 6, 2004

Disbursement date: April 6, 2004

Amount received: $133,000, April 1, 2004

Disbursement Date	Payee	Amount
April 6, 2004	Bank of Placid	$508.50
April 6, 2004	Bank of Placid Escrow fee and taxes	$1,123.65
April 6, 2004	Placid County Registry	$61
April 6, 2004	Placid County tax collector (2004)	$624.22
April 6, 2004	First Citizens' Savings and Loan mortgage payoff, loan number 12345	$89,004
April 6, 2004	Attorney's fee	$824
April 6, 2004	Title insurance premium	$203.50
April 6, 2004	Cash out to seller	$8,457.20
April 6, 2004	Total disbursed amount	$100,806.07
April 6, 2004	Balance	$0

make specific disclosures to the borrower before the loan is finalized. Among the requirements of the Federal Truth in Lending Act is that a lender must display the required information:

- "Clearly and conspicuously"
- In a meaningful and proper sequence
- In writing
- In a permanent form that the consumer is allowed to retain

These disclosures are made in forms that nearly all of us have seen at one point or another. They are required in nearly all types of loan arrangements, from credit cards to car loans. Essentially, TILA requires the lender to give complete information to the borrower about the costs of borrowing money. As you can see in Figure 13-3, TILA has specific requirements.

FIGURE 13-3

Federal Truth in Lending and
Regulation Z

FEDERAL TRUTH-IN-LENDING DISCLOSURE STATEMENT
(THIS IS NEITHER A CONTRACT NOR A COMMITMENT TO LEND)

Applicants: Prepared By:

Property Address:

Application No: Date Prepared:
Check box if applicable:

ANNUAL PERCENTAGE RATE The cost of your credit as a yearly rate	FINANCE CHARGE The dollar amount the credit will cost you	Amount Financed The amount of credit provided to you or on your behalf	Total of Payments The amount you will have paid after making all payments as scheduled
%	$	$	$

☐ REQUIRED DEPOSIT: The annual percentage rate does not take into account your required deposit
PAYMENTS: Your payment schedule will be:

Number of Payments	Amount of Payments **	When Payments Are Due	Number of Payments	Amount of Payments **	When Payments Are Due	Number of Payments	Amount of Payments **	When Payments Are Due

☐ DEMAND FEATURE: This obligation has a demand feature.
☐ VARIABLE RATE FEATURE: This loan contains a variable rate feature. A variable rate disclosure has been provided earlier.

CREDIT LIFE/CREDIT DISABILIY: Credit life insurance and credit disability insurance are not required to obtain credit, and will not be provided unless you sign and agree to pay the additional cost.

Type	Premium	Signature	
Credit Life		I want credit life insurance.	X
Credit Disability		I want credit disability insurance.	X
Credit Life and Disability		I waft credit life and disability insurance.	X

INSURANCE: The following insurance is required to obtain credit:
☐ Credit life insurance   ☐ Credit disability   ☐ Property insurance   ☐ Flood insurance
You may obtain the insurance from anyone you want that is acceptable to creditor
☐ If you purchase   ☐ property   ☐ flood insurance from creditor you will pay $ for a one year term.
SECURITY: You are giving a security interest in:
☐ The goods or property being purchased   ☐ Real property you already own.
FILING FEES: $
LATE CHARGE: If a payment is more than   days late, you will be charged   %
PREPAYMENT: If you pay off early, you
☐ may   ☐ will not   have to pay a penalty.
☐ may   ☐ will not   be entitled to a refund of part of the finance charge.
ASSUMPTION: Someone buying your property
☐ may   ☐ may, subject to conditions   ☐ may not   assume the remainder of your loan on the original terms.

Federal Truth in Lending requires a lender to give specific information about percentage rates for a loan and the total amount that the borrower will repay should he make every payment for the life of the loan.

14. TERMITE INSPECTION LETTER

Lenders almost always require a termite inspection before they will finance the purchase of a residence. The termite inspector will issue a report, sometimes in the form of a letter that details exactly what the inspector found. If any evidence of termite infestation was found, the termite inspector must issue a follow-up report showing that the infestation has been dealt with and no further evidence of termites can be found. Without this report, the lender will not go through with the closing. It is up to the seller to pay for the treatments to get rid of any infestations.

15. SURVEY

Surveys are physical measurements of the property and can reveal a host of problems, from inaccurate boundaries and unrecorded easements to encroachments. Most lenders require an accurate survey of the property before disbursing funds for the closing. Many lenders require a new survey every time that a property is resold (or even refinanced). Some lenders will allow the borrower to use a survey that is only a few years old and will not require the borrower to pay for a new one. In other situations, the lender may accept a seller's affidavit in place of a new survey.

a. Seller's Affidavit

A seller's affidavit is a sworn statement that there have been no changes, improvements, or boundary line changes to the property since the date of the last survey. Sellers' affidavits are sometimes used instead of a new survey. The problem with such affidavits is that the seller may have a good faith, but mistaken view of the facts. Many sellers are also reluctant to sign such affidavits, believing that such a statement might leave them open to civil liability later on.

 ## IV CONDUCTING THE CLOSING

All closings follow the same general procedures, but closing professionals know that no two closings are ever exactly the same. Real estate law offers an almost endless variation of issues and problems to be solved and this is as true with closings as any other aspect of the practice.

In states where attorneys conduct the closings, real estate paralegals usually handle most of the details. The paralegal receives the loan packet from the lender and is responsible for making sure that all the lender's instructions are followed to the letter. It is also the paralegal who is often responsible for conducting the title examination and coordinating the attendance of the people necessary for a successful closing.

FIGURE 13-4

Termite and Wood-Boring
Insect Inspection Report

This report is prepared by a state-licensed inspector for the purposes of inspecting a residence for the presence of termites and other wood-boring insects. This inspection is not a warranty or a guarantee that no such insects exist on the premises. Instead, it is based on the inspector's access and due diligence in performing the inspection.

Section 1
Identifying Information

Seller's name: Sally Seller
Buyer's name: Brian Borrower
Property address: 1390 Placid Street, Anywhere, PL 003360
Structures inspected: <u>residence at above location</u>

Section 2
Exceptions and exclusions:

This inspection was limited because of the inaccessibility of certain portions of the residence. Inaccessible or regions included: wall, floor, and ceiling.

Section 3
Presence of termites or other wood-boring insects:

The inspector found evidence of the following: Subterranean termites, Powder post beetles

Section 4
Treatment

The above-described property was treated in the following manner:
<u>Treatment for subterranean termites</u>
<u>Treatment for powder post beetles</u>

Section 5
Damage to above-described property

There is visible damage from powder post beetles; this damage was discovered in the joists and steps leading from the basement.

Disclaimer: I have no interest in this property. My company has no interest in this property.

Signed: <u>Irving Inspector</u>
Placid Termite and Pest Company
Anywhere, PL 00330
1-912-555-1212

A. PEOPLE NORMALLY PRESENT AT A CLOSING

There are several people who are normally present at the closing. In states where nonlawyers are permitted to conduct the closing, there may not be an attorney present. However, other individuals will certainly be there. They include:

- The closing professional
- The buyers
- The sellers

1. CLOSING PROFESSIONAL

Throughout this chapter, we have referred to the "closing professional." This is the person who is responsible for organizing the documents, managing the funds, and coordinating the closing so that it runs smoothly. The identity of this person varies from state to state. In some states, as we have already seen, the closing professional must be an attorney. In other states, the closing professional may be a real estate broker, a title insurance agent, or even the lender.

a. Attorney

In states that require attorneys to conduct closings, the attorney will obviously be present and will carry out all the actions that we have so far ascribed to the closing professional. However, an attorney has one advantage over other types of closing professionals: He can answer legal questions that arise at the closing. In fact, it is this feature that many states still use as justification for permitting only attorneys to handle closings. Other closing professionals, such as lenders, title insurance agents, and real estate brokers are not permitted to explain the legal significance of documents or to describe the impact that the closing will have on the legal rights of any of the parties. If any of these individuals did that, they would be guilty of practicing law without a license. An attorney obviously does not face that impediment. Attorneys who routinely handle closings have another distinct advantage over other closing professionals: paralegals.

b. Paralegal

The paralegal who works at a real estate firm carries out much, if not all, of the preparatory work to ensure that a closing goes off without a hitch. The paralegal may have personally handled the title search and will probably have completed all the documents necessary to conclude the closing. In addition to handling the paperwork, the paralegal is also the person who usually coordinates the actual meeting, making sure that all parties know when and where they are supposed to be. Usually, the paralegal is a notary public and can notarize legal documents. Finally, the paralegal will also be the person who takes the signed documents to the courthouse for filing.

Given all of the actions that paralegals routinely carry out in a real estate closing, some people have asked: What exactly does the attorney do to justify his fee? This question has particular relevance in states where the attorney may not be present at the closing. The paralegal may actually conduct the entire closing alone, with the attorney on the premises, or available by telephone for a quick consultation. This chapter's case excerpt and ethics discussion focus on this interesting issue.

2. BUYERS

The buyers will be present at the closing because they must sign the paperwork necessary to complete the process. Even more important, they must be present to receive a signed and fully executed deed from the seller. As we have seen in previous chapters, a real estate transaction is only complete when a deed is delivered by the seller and accepted by the buyer.

3. SELLERS

The sellers will also be present for the practical reason that they will be receiving a check for their profit from the sale. The seller is also present in order to deliver the deed to the buyer.

4. REAL ESTATE AGENT

There is no requirement for the real estate agent to be present at the closing. Although real estate agents act as closing professionals in some states, there is no real need for them to be present at the closing if they are not conducting it. The closing professional will write a check to the real estate agent and will forward this check to the agent. In fact, most real estate agents contact the closing professional and request several different checks to be written, each one reflecting the percentage of the commission that goes to the various individuals involved. As we saw in the last chapter, a real estate agent's final check will reflect commission sharing with another agent and perhaps reductions for amounts paid to the real estate agent's company.

B. DISBURSING THE FUNDS

The lender deposits the mortgage money into the closing professional's trust account prior to the closing. The person conducting the closing then writes checks on that account, distributing the funds to the various parties at the closing. In this section, we detail some of the disbursements made at a typical real estate closing. Among the items that are paid at the closing include:

- The previous mortgage
- The lender's fees
- The attorney's fees
- The recording fees
- The seller's profit
- The real estate agent's commission
- The real property taxes

1. LENDER'S FEES

Among the fees that must be accounted for at the closing include the lender's fees. These include any fees associated with giving the loan, such as "points" (a fee based on a percentage of the total amount financed) and other fees assessed by the lender. The lender may also require payment of interim mortgage interest on the loan and additional monthly payments for hazard or homeowner's insurance and taxes. These are commonly referred to as "escrow accounts."

a. Escrow Accounts for Insurance and Taxes

In most mortgage situations, the lenders require a monthly payment that includes not only the monthly loan repayment, but also an additional amount that is set aside to pay the annual hazard insurance premiums and tax assessment. The lender will set aside these extra funds and then pay the insurance and taxes annually. However, not all lenders set up escrow accounts for their borrowers. Some lenders prefer to have the borrower pay his own insurance premiums and tax assessments as they come due.

Many lenders require the borrower to pay additional money each month for the annual hazard insurance premium and real property taxes.

ISSUE AT
A GLANCE

---

2. ATTORNEY'S FEES

Other fees paid at the closing include the attorney's fee for handling the closing and carrying out the title search. This fee is usually a percentage of the total loan amount, such as one-half of 1 percent of the total purchase price. The attorney may also simply charge a flat rate for the service.

3. RECORDING FEES

The land or deed office charges a fee to record deeds and mortgages. These fees are added to the amount that the borrower must pay at the closing. Recording fees vary across the nation, from less than a dollar per page recorded, to flat fees for recording specific types of documents.

4. SELLER'S PROFIT ON THE TRANSACTION

The seller's profit on the transaction will come in the form of a check drawn on the closing professional's trust account. This profit is the amount that is left over after paying off the seller's mortgage, the real estate agent's commission, and any other charges assessed against the seller.

5. CERTIFIED FUNDS FROM THE BUYER

One of the questions that buyers ask before a closing is how much money they should bring with them to the closing. Buyers are invariably required to bring certified funds to the closing. These additional funds may be required for lender fees, inspections, or any of a number of services for which the buyer is responsible. Certified funds are not the buyer's personal check. Instead, they must be in the form of a cashier's check or some other form of certified funds. The buyer may also simply pay the fees in cash, but the amount in question could be several thousand dollars.

6. REAL ESTATE AGENT'S COMMISSION

We have already discussed the fact that the real estate agent is usually not present at the closing, unless he is conducting it. One of the disbursements that must be made at the closing is the real estate agent's commission. We now know that instead of one check for the full commission amount, the commission is actually paid out in a series of smaller checks, all made out to the different individuals involved in the sale.

7. TAX PAYMENTS

If there are any outstanding real property taxes from prior years, those must be paid prior to the closing. Such payments would be the seller's responsibility. However, a different issue arises when the tax payment is for the current year's assessment. In that case, if the sellers have paid the taxes for the entire year, they would be due a partial refund from the buyers. After all, without such a refund, the buyers would be taking advantage of the seller's prepayment. The same question would arise when the taxes have not yet been paid for the year. In that situation, the buyer's payment would reflect an entire year's residence when they only occupied it for part of the year. In both situations, taxes must be prorated.

Proration
The distribution of payments based on a person's liability for the debt.

a. Proration

Proration is the process of assessing payments based on the amount paid and the quantity of time that a party resides in the premises.

| **EXAMPLE 13-3** | Placid County requires homeowners to pay their real estate taxes on the first business day of the year. This year, that day was January 3. When a homeowner pays these taxes, he is paying for the entire calendar year. |

Placid County requires homeowners to pay their real estate taxes on the first business day of the year. This year, that day was January 3. When a homeowner pays these taxes, he is paying for the entire calendar year.

On January 3 of this year, Mary paid her real estate taxes of $459.12. However, she later put her house on the market and sold it on July 3. Because she paid the entire year's taxes in advance, she wants her tax payment prorated. How much will the new owners have to reimburse Mary for her taxes?

Answer: In order to prorate the taxes, we need some information. First of all, how many days passed from the day that Mary paid her taxes until the closing? If the year is not a leap year, there are 181 days between January 3 (not counting the 3) and July 3 (including the day of the closing). If we can determine a daily rate for the year, we can determine an exact amount for the proration.

$459.12 divided by 365 days in a year yields a daily tax rate of $1.26 (rounding off). Mary lived in the house for 181 days, so her portion of the taxes is:

181 days $\times$ $1.26 daily rate $=$459.06.

Subtracting this amount from $459.12, Mary is due a refund from the buyers of $231.06. This is the amount that the buyers must transfer to Mary at the closing.

As you can see from Example 13-3, the calculations involved in proration can get complicated. To reach the answer in that example, we used the actual days method. However, there are other approaches.

i. Actual Days Method of Proration

In the actual days method of proration, the parties count the actual number of days involved and then calculate a daily rate based on that amount of time. However, there are other methods to arrive at the amount of proration. For example, there is the 30-day month method.

ii. 30-Day Month Method of Proration

In the 30-day month method of proration, the calculations assume that every month has exactly thirty days and the time period is calculated using those figures. The closing professional must work with the parties and lenders in order to determine which method of proration is preferred in a particular area. Closing software programs are also adaptable on this point. The user can select from any of a number of proration methods to calculate the final amounts.

iii. Prorating Other Bills

Although we have used taxes as an example of a billed item that is prorated during a closing, the process applies to several other types of accounts. For instance, heating oil purchased in advance would be prorated, as would utility payments, city taxes, water, sewage, and trash services, among others.

 ## V OTHER CLOSING ISSUES

In addition to disbursements and documentation, there are other issues that commonly arise at closings. Among these issues are escrow closings, the issue of dual representation and the disclosures required by state and federal laws.

A. "ESCROW" CLOSINGS

Earlier in this chapter we used the word "escrow" to describe a system set up by lenders in which a borrower pays additional fees above the mortgage payment for the annual assessments for home insurance and taxes. However, escrow also refers to a type of closing.

Although face-to-face meetings are the preferred method used to close real estate transactions in many states, there is a provision that allows one or both parties to be absent on the day of the closing. In an escrow closing, a party signs an "escrow agreement" and completes all the necessary paperwork to complete the closing prior to the actual event. State law then applies a legal fiction to the agreement: that the signatures were actually completed at the closing, not before it. The legal fiction is a necessary feature of escrow closings and is referred to as the "doctrine of relation back."

1. THE DOCTRINE OF RELATION BACK

The doctrine of relation back is used in escrow closings to satisfy specific legal requirements. As we have seen in previous chapters, a deed is not effective until it is signed by the seller, delivered, and accepted by the buyer. When one of the parties is unable to attend the closing, this procedure could never occur. However, the law has adapted over time and allowed certain actions to be completed at different times. The doctrine of relation back states that when one of the parties signs an escrow agreement and completes paperwork prior to the actual closing, the signatures and actions will not have legal effect until the closing is completed, exactly as if the person were present. The doctrine also helps settle some difficult questions. Suppose, for example, that the seller signs an escrow agreement, completes all paperwork, but is killed before the closing can take place. In most ordinary situations, the seller's death would void the transaction; however, under the doctrine of relation back, the seller's actions are deemed to have occurred at the closing, whether or not he was actually alive at that time. Escrow closings were not created to satisfy this unusual situation. The most common reason for an escrow closing is that one of the parties could not be physically present at the closing and an escrow closing allowed the transaction to be completed. Escrow closings have become so popular in some states that they are the most common type of closing, even when the parties could be present at the closing.

When the sellers and buyers place signed documents into escrow, it is usually on express conditions that certain things must occur before the closing can continue. For the seller, these conditions include presentation of the funds to conclude the transaction. For the buyer, these conditions include a signed and delivered copy of the deed and any other preconditions that were negotiated in the offer to purchase and contract.

EXAMPLE 13-4

On Tuesday, Daniel, the seller, attends an escrow closing and signs the deed and other paperwork transferring title to Miranda, the buyer. On Wednesday, Daniel suffers a catastrophic stroke and is left in a permanent vegetative state. Miranda appears at the attorney's office on Thursday to sign the paperwork and receive title to the property. Can the transaction be completed?

Answer: Because this is an escrow closing, the fact that Daniel later suffered a stroke does not affect the transaction. The doctrine of relation back protects the transaction and Miranda can receive title. Would the answer have been different if instead of suffering a stroke, Daniel had been declared mentally incompetent on Wednesday?

B. DUAL REPRESENTATION

In a typical real estate closing, both the buyer and seller may request that one attorney represent them both. This can put an attorney in a potential ethical dilemma. After all, the buyer's and seller's interests are, by definition, adverse to one another. In certain situations, the attorney is allowed to represent both parties, but only after full disclosure and agreement from both sides. Dual representation, or dual agency, is also a problem for other professionals, such as real estate agents.

In all states, full disclosure is the rule. The closing professional must disclose to all parties who the professional represents and who is paying that professional's fee.

 VI ## AFTER THE CLOSING

After the closing, the deeds and mortgages must be filed at the courthouse. The closing professional, or paralegal, will take the original deed and mortgage to the courthouse and make sure that it is properly recorded. The closing professional often makes additional copies of these recorded documents to give to the buyer and the lender.

A. FILING AND PRIORITY

When filing the general warranty deed and mortgage, the sequence is important in order to guarantee priority. The deed must be filed first, showing the transfer of rights from the seller to the buyer. Immediately afterward, the mortgage must be filed. It is important that the mortgage be filed immediately to prevent any other creditors from obtaining a superior claim to the lender. The rule in most states is that whoever files first has the highest priority when it comes to foreclosures or judgments. Because the lender has loaned thousands, or even hundreds of thousands, of dollars on the sale, the lender will want to make sure that its mortgage has higher priority than any other claim. Filing it immediately after the general warranty deed is one way of making sure that happens.

FIGURE 13-5

Closing Checklist

- Sale contract
  - ☐ Copy of tax record
  - ☐ Are there any taxes outstanding?
- Created client file?
- Names of parties
  - ☐ Complete legal name of buyer
  - ☐ Realtor(s) names
- Lender
- Seller's complete legal name
  - ☐ Seller's address:
- Title insurance binder (policy number)
- Mortgage?
- Termite letter received?
- Survey?
  - ☐ Prepared by: _____
  - ☐ Survey fee:

- Lien waiver
- W-9 form
- General warranty deed
- Restrictive covenants?
- Loan package (provided by lender)
- HUD-1 form completed
- Checks typed up and ready?
- Will a courier be required?
- Title insurance policy mailed to client and lender
- Certified copies of the general warranty deed and mortgage provided to clients and lender
- File closed out? Date:

SETTLEMENT STATEMENT

A. SETTLEMENT STATEMENT

U.S. DEPARTMENT OF HOUSING
AND URBAN DEVELOPMENT

OMB No. 2502-0285

B. Type of Loan

| 1. [ ] FHA | 2. [ ] FmHA | 3. [ ] Conv. Unins | 6. File No. | 7. Loan No. | Mortgage Insurance Case # |
| 4. [ ] VA | 5. [ ] Conv. Ins. | | | ♦ | |

C. Note: This form is furnished to give you a statement of actual settlement costs. Amounts paid to and by the settlement agent are shown. Items marked "(p.o.c.)" were paid outside the closing; they are shown here for informational purposes and are not included in the totals.

D. Name and Address of Borrower: ♦[borrower] and wife, ♦
♦

E. Name and Address of Seller: n/a

F. Name and Address of Lender: ♦[bank]
♦

G. Property Location: Tax ID #♦, Burke County, NC, ♦ Township, Deed Book ♦, Page ♦, Burke Registry
Address: ♦

H. Settlement Agent: stov♦
Place of Settlement: Daniel Law Firm, PA
P.O. Drawer 1825
Morganton, NC 28680-1825

I. Settlement Date: ♦[closing-date]

Summary of borrower's transaction

Summary of seller's transaction

J. SUMMARY OF BORROWER'S TRANSACTION:		K. SUMMARY OF SELLER'S TRANSACTION:	
100 GROSS AMOUNT DUE FROM BORROWER:		**400.** GROSS AMOUNT DUE TO SELLER:	
101. Contract Sales Price		401. Contract Sales Price	
102. Personal Property		402. Personal Property	
103. Settlement Charges to Borrower (line 1400)	♦	403.	
104. Payoff of Loan to ♦	♦	404.	
105.		405.	
106.		406.	
107.		407.	
ADJUSTMENTS FOR ITEMS PAID BY SELLER IN ADVANCE		ADJUSTMENTS FOR ITEMS PAID BY SELLER IN ADVANCE	
108. City/Town Taxes to		408. City/Town Taxes to	
109. County Taxes to		409. County Taxes to	
110. Assessments to		410. Assessments to	
111.		411.	
112.		412.	
120. Gross Amount Due From Borrower:	0.00	420. Gross Amount Due To Seller:	0.00
200. AMOUNTS PAID BY OR ON BEHALF OF BORROWER:		**500.** REDUCTIONS IN AMOUNT DUE SELLER:	
201. Deposit or Earnest Money		501. Excess Deposit (see instructions)	
202. Principal Amount of New Loan	♦	502. Settlement Charges to Seller (line 1400)	
203. Existing Loan(s) taken Subject to		503. Existing Loans Taken Subject to	
204.		504. Payoff of First Mortgage Loan	
205.		505. Payoff of Second Mortgage Loan	
206.		506.	
207.		507.	
208.		508.	
209.		509.	
ADJUSTMENTS FOR ITEMS UNPAID BY SELLER		ADJUSTMENTS FOR ITEMS UNPAID BY SELLER	
210. City/Town Taxes to		510. City/Town Taxes to	
211. County Taxes to		511. County Taxes to	
212. Assessments to		512. Assessments to	
213.		513.	
214.		514.	
215.		515.	
216.		516.	
217.		517.	
218.		518.	
220. Total Paid by/for Borrower:	0.00	520. Total Reduction in Amount Due Seller:	0.00
300. CASH AT SETTLEMENT FROM/TO BORROWER:		**600.** CASH AT SETTLEMENT TO/FROM SELLER:	
301. Gross amount due from Borrower (line 120)	0.00	601. Gross Amount Due to Seller (line 420)	0.00
302. Less amounts paid by/for Borrower (line 220)	0.00	602. Less Reductions in Amt Due Seller (line 520)	0.00
303. CASH FROM BORROWER:	0.00	603. CASH TO SELLER:	0.00

L. SETTLEMENT CHARGES

		Paid from Borrower's Funds at Settlement	Paid from Seller's Funds at Settlement
700.	**TOTAL SALES/BROKER'S COMMISSION** Based on Price $ @ % =		
	Division of Commission (line 700) as follows:		
701.	$ to		
702.	$ to		
703.	Commission paid at Settlement		
704.			
800	**ITEMS PAYABLE IN CONNECTION WITH LOAN**		
801.	Origination Fee % to	◆	
802.	Loan Discount % to		
803.	Appraisal Fee to		
804.	Credit Report to		
805.	Lender's Inspection Fee		
806.	Mortgage Insurance Application Fee to		
807.	Assumption Fee		
808.	Tax Service Fee to		
809.			
810.			
811.			
900.	**ITEMS REQUIRED BY LENDER TO BE PAID IN ADVANCE**		
901.	Interest from ◆ to ◆	◆	
902.	Mortgage Insurance Premium for months to		
903.	Hazard Insurance Premium for year		
904.	County Taxes to		
905.			
1000.	**RESERVES DEPOSITED WITH LENDER**		
1001.	Hazard Insurance ◆ Months @ $◆ per month	◆	
1002.	Mortgage Insurance Months @ $ per month		
1003.	City Property Taxes Months @ $ per month		
1004.	County Property Taxes Months @ $ per month	◆	
1005.	Annual Assessments Months @ $ per month		
1100.	**TITLE CHARGES**		
1101.	Settlement or Closing Fee		
1102.	Title Search and Examination		
1103.	Title Search, Examination, Document Prep, Closing ($ ◆)		
1104.	Fax and Long-Distance Telephone Charges ($ ◆5.00)		
1105.	Burke Registry and In-House Copying Charges ($◆(.15 ea.)		
1106.	Express Mail to Lender ($◆15.00)		
1107.	ATTORNEY'S FEES to *Daniel Law Firm, P.A.*	◆	
	(includes above item numbers: 1101, 1102, 1103, 1104, 1105)		
1108.	Title Binder: to Commonwealth Title Insurance		
1109.	Lender's Coverage $◆		
1110.	Owner's Coverage $◆		
1111.	TITLE INSURANCE to *◆Commonwealth Title Agency*	◆	
	(includes above item numbers: 1107, 1108, 1109)		
1112.			
1113.			
1114.			
1200.	**GOVERNMENT RECORDING AND TRANSFER CHARGES** (*◆Burke County*)		
1201.	Recording Fees: Deed $ Mortgage $ Releases $	◆	
1202.	State Excise Revenue Stamp:		
1203.	City/Local Tax Stamps:		
1204.			
1205.			
1300.	**ADDITIONAL SETTLEMENT CHARGES**		
1301.	Survey to	◆	
1302.	Pest Inspection to	◆	
1303.			
1304.			
1305.			
1400.	**TOTAL SETTLEMENT CHARGES** (enter on line 103, Section J and line 502, Section K)	0.00	0.00

I have carefully reviewed the HUD-1 Settlement statement and to the best of my knowledge and belief it is true and accurate statement of all receipts and disbursements made on my account or by me in this transaction. I further certify that I have received a copy of the HUD-1 Settlement Statement.

Buyer/Borrower: _____ Date: ◆   Seller: _____ Date: ◆

Buyer/Borrower: _____ Date: ◆   Seller: _____ Date: ◆

The HUD-1 Settlement Statement which I have prepared is a true and accurate account of this transaction. I have caused or will cause the funds to be disbursed in accordance with this statement.

Settlement Agent: _____ Date: ◆
    stdv◆, Attorney

Broker's commission

Title charges

Total settlement charges

DELEGATING THE CLOSING TO THE PARALEGAL

One of the most hotly contested issues in modern real estate practice concerns the use of paralegals to conduct real estate closings. As we have seen in this chapter, many states limit real estate closings to licensed attorneys. In those states, is it an ethical violation to allow the paralegal to conduct the entire real estate closing in the absence of the attorney? In some states, the answer is yes, while in other states the answer is no. The issue involves the role of the attorney and the paralegal. We have already seen that many states allow non-attorneys to conduct real estate closings. In those states, there is no ethical violation for a paralegal to conduct the closing because there is no requirement for an attorney to do it in the first place. However, in states that require an attorney to conduct the closing, must the attorney be present when the closing is held or can the attorney delegate the closing to a experienced paralegal? Unfortunately, there is no clear consensus among the states on this point either. The safest practice is to locate ethics decisions from your state bar on this question to make sure that you stay on the right side of the ethical rules.

COUNTRYWIDE HOME LOANS, INC. v. KENTUCKY BAR ASS'N

COUNTRYWIDE HOME LOANS, INC. v. KENTUCKY BAR ASS'N
113 S.W.3d 105 (Ky. 2003)

KELLER, Justice.

I. INTRODUCTION

On March 1, 2000, Movants, Countrywide Home Loans, Inc. ("Countrywide") and LandSafe Services, Inc. ("LandSafe"), Kentucky Land Title Association ("KLTA"), and Kentucky Association of Realtors, Inc. ("KAR") and Home Builders Association of Kentucky, Inc. ("HBAK"), moved under SCR 3.530(5) for this Court to review Advisory Opinion U-58, adopted by the Kentucky Bar Association ("KBA") Board of Governors in November 1999 and published in the January 2000 issue of Kentucky Bench & Bar. U-58 declares that performance of a real estate closing by a lay closing agent is the unauthorized practice of law. Movants request that the Court vacate U-58, and, in support of that request, argue that U-58 is contradictory to both public policy and U-31, a previous advisory opinion that had allowed laypersons to conduct real estate closings subject to certain limitations. We granted the motions to review U-58, allowed the parties to take evidence, and heard oral argument on the issues. We now vacate U-58 and hold that U-31 accurately states the law regarding lay closing agents' ability to perform real estate closings in Kentucky.

II. BACKGROUND

In 1981, the Kentucky Bar Association Board of Governors rendered Opinion KBA U-31, which addresses essentially the same issue that was later addressed in U-58 and that is now presented for our review. U-31 asked:

Does a real estate mortgage lender, or a title insurance company on behalf of a real estate mortgage lender, commit the unauthorized practice of law by performing the ministerial acts necessary in the closing of a real estate loan? The Board of Governors answered with a "qualified no." Essentially, U-31 permitted laypersons to conduct real estate closings so long as they avoided giving legal advice. Specifically, the opinion instructed that when a question of a legal nature is asked at a closing "the lay person should discontinue the closing and seek proper legal advice." In reaching this conclusion, the Board of Governors recognized that "a 'real estate closing' is at best ministerial in nature. Some lawyers will allow secretaries and paralegals to participate in closings. The closing, which consists mainly of financial matters, payments, schedules of payment, and insurance, is basically a nonlegal function." The Board did, however, offer a warning that "federal loans involve significant knowledge of the law, and questions as to what is meant in the documents would certainly involve the unauthorized practice of law." More than fifteen years after the Board of Governors issued that warning, the role of non-lawyer closing agents was again at issue. Marcus Carey, chairperson of the KBA's Unauthorized Practice Committee, was advised by several Kentucky real estate attorneys of their concerns that title insurance companies and title agencies might be engaged in the unlawful practice of law when they closed real estate transactions without the participation of or supervision by licensed attorneys. Carey determined that this was the type of issue that his committee was charged with addressing and raised the issue before the Unauthorized Practice Committee.

We begin our evaluation of U-58 with the text of the opinion U-58.

Question: May real estate closings be conducted by persons who are not real parties in interest without direct supervision of a licensed attorney?

Answer: No.

Question: May title agencies or title insurance companies conduct real estate closings?

Answer: No.

Unauthorized Practice of Law

Only licensed attorneys may practice law in Kentucky. The practice is regulated exclusively by the court. The compelling reason for such regulation is to protect the public against rendition of legal services by unqualified persons. Kentucky Rule of Professional Conduct (RPC) 5.5. The practice of law is defined by SCR 3.020 as any service: "involving legal knowledge or legal advice, whether of representation, counsel or advocacy in or out of court, rendered in respect to the rights, duties, obligations, liabilities, or business relations of one requiring the services."

Real Estate Closings

Real estate closings typically have either two or three real parties in interest: seller and buyer, borrower and lender, or seller, buyer-borrower, and lender. Of these three, the least complex are the two-party closings of single sale or loan transactions involving the transfer of an interest in real estate, by deed or mortgage, for purchase money or loan proceeds. The sale of real estate financed by a third party lender is the more complex because it involves separate sale and secured loan transactions in a simultaneous closing.

The "conduct" of a closing is the culmination of such transactions. Notwithstanding the standardization of real estate closing documentation, it is unrealistic and naive to assume that, in all instances, the settlement agent can present important legal documents to the seller, buyer, borrower, and/or lender at a closing without legal questions being asked and without giving legal advice. The preparation and presentation of closing documents is an implied representation that the documents fulfill the requirements of the parties' contractual commitments and the law, and that the documents have been reviewed and found to be legally sufficient. Real estate closings should be conducted only under the supervision of an attorney because questions of legal rights and duties are always involved, and there is no way of assuring that lay settlement agents would raise, or would not attempt to answer, the legal questions. Whether stated or not, the person conducting the closing vouches for the legal sufficiency of the documents, whether complex, simple, or pre-printed. It does not matter whether the instruments are deemed simple or complex. As Judge Pound said when closing transactions were much less complicated than today, "the most complex are simple to the skilled, and the simplest often trouble the inexperienced." The legal questions present at a closing, whether asked or should be asked, are endless, as demonstrated by the attached appendix of issues affecting the quality of title and enforceability of documents. In summary, the contract of sale or the loan commitment must be reviewed and interpreted for contract compliance and remedies. Sufficiency of the legal description or survey plat and access to public ways and utilities must be determined. The title opinion or title insurance commitment must be reviewed and interpreted to inform the purchaser of its meaning and potential risks, and the effect of restrictions, encumbrances, and other title exceptions. The closing documents must be explained.

By its very nature a real estate closing involves substantial rights and liabilities. The parties approach the closing having made commitments with other parties and invested time and money in anticipation of a mutual understanding of their contractual obligations and trusting that all legal issues have been properly addressed. If a problem arises during closing and there is no attorney-client relationship, the parties are without the benefit of independent counsel and may lack the leverage or will to halt a transaction that is not in their best interests.

Closing Supervision by Attorney

An attorney need not be physically present at the closing, so long as it is in fact conducted under his supervision and control, but the responsible attorney must be familiar with the documentation and be available at the time of closing for consultation. He bears ultimate responsibility for the closing and is subject to disciplinary action for any act or omission which otherwise would be misconduct by him or his closing employees, as well as being legally accountable under the duty imposed by Seigle v. Jasper, 867 S.W.2d 476 (Ky. App. 1993). By failing to attend or supervise a closing, the attorney who is responsible for the documentation or who has examined and opined on the quality of title may be guilty of aiding or assisting lay settlement agents in the unauthorized practice of law contrary to SCR 3.470.

Closing by Institutional Lender

When an institutional lender is a real party in interest to a real estate transaction as mortgagee, its lay employee or in-house attorney may preside over the mortgage closing with a customer not represented by an attorney. Though institutional lenders, namely banks, savings and loans, and Farm Credit Services are not subject to the same disciplinary action as attorneys, the public is protected to some degree by state and federal requirements for licensure, capitalization, oaths of directors and officers, insured deposits, and other regulations. The lender's employee may attend to the ministerial issues of financial matters, payments, and insurance related to the loan, as these are commonly nonlegal functions.

The lender's employee may also prepare or select and complete necessary "form" loan documents if no fee is charged, directly or indirectly, for such services, provided that the lender's own attorney or some other licensed attorney passes judgment on and is responsible for the documents as finally executed. No lender's lay employee may undertake to give legal advice to or answer any questions posed by the borrower or any other transaction party involving interpretation of legal provisions of closing documents or other matters requiring legal knowledge or skill. When a legal question is asked or becomes apparent, the institutional lender employee should suspend the closing to consult legal counsel in order to avoid the unauthorized practice of law. Such employee may not conduct any part of a real estate closing other than the mortgage loan.

Closing by Title Companies

A distinction must be made as to lay settlement agencies such as title companies and title insurance companies which are not real parties in interest to the real estate or loan transactions. Their only interest is the payment of settlement fees. They act only as a conduit to exchange funds and documents. A lay settlement agency may compile and report factual information from the public records, including abstracts of title, but may not render title opinions. They may act as an agent or broker in connection with the issuance of title insurance commitments and policies and may provide clerical services for a closing. They do not conduct a closing or examine the required documents with an eye for protecting the independent legal rights of the seller, buyer, or lender. Such agencies are not regulated and owe no legal duties to the parties other than those imposed by agency or tort law. Their employees have no mandated educational prerequisites for real estate transactions or disciplinary oversight. A title agency may not conduct real estate closings or ask legal fees for closing services under the guise of a "settlement fee" or other charge. Their conduct of a closing absent independent legal counsel constitutes the unauthorized practice of law.

III. PARTIES, ARGUMENTS, AND EVIDENCE

U-58 has a potential impact on nearly all of the regular participants in real estate transactions. The parties to this motion are representative of most of the affected individuals, although in addressing the issue before us, we must balance the concerns of these parties with the interests and largely-unvoiced concerns of real estate consumers across this state.

Countrywide and Landsafe also emphasize that the presence of lay closing agents contributes to a more competitive market for real estate consumer services, and maintain that U-58 is merely an attempt by the real estate bar to thwart competition. Accordingly, they urge us to follow the majority of other jurisdictions by clarifying that laypersons may conduct real estate closings in Kentucky without engaging in the unauthorized practice of law.

The United States of America, Department of Justice ("Department") has filed an amicus curiae brief in support of Movants. The Department states: KBA U-58 likely will cause costs for all Kentucky consumers to rise while providing them no more protection than they currently receive. On the other hand, there is no demonstrated harm from the lay closings that have taken place in Kentucky since the KBA sanctioned the practice in 1981, and less drastic measures than banning lay settlements are available if additional consumer protections are required.

U-58 provides that "the 'conduct' of a closing is the culmination of the sale and loan or secured loan transactions resulting in the transfer of an interest in real estate." As described by Professor Bratt, the closing is "that very thin slice in a continuum that starts with a listing agreement and usually ends with the closing, that it's that little sliver at the end where the parties come into the room, sit around the table, they execute and exchange the necessary documents and money to complete the transaction." This view is compatible with our understanding of the real estate closing—"the final steps of the transaction whereat the consideration is paid, mortgage is secured, deed is delivered or placed in escrow, etc"—or, as the New Jersey Supreme Court described the occasion:

> The day for closing arrives and everyone meets, usually at the offices of the title company. Seller and buyer are there, each without an attorney; the broker is there, and the title officer is there, representing both the title company and the mortgagee. The funds are there. And the critical legal documents are also on hand: the mortgage and the note, usually prepared by the mortgagee; the deed, along with the affidavit of title, prepared by the attorney selected by the broker or by the title company; the settlement statement, usually prepared by the title company, indicating how much is owed, what deductions should be made for taxes and other costs and what credits are due; and the final marked-up title binder, which evidences the obligation of the title company to issue a title policy to the buyer, and which at that point is probably practically meaningless to the buyer. All are executed and delivered, along with other documents, and the funds are delivered or held in escrow until the title company arranges to pay off prior mortgages and liens. The deal closes, satisfactory to buyer and seller in practically all cases, satisfactory both at the closing and thereafter.

We understand Kentucky real estate closings to occur in much the same fashion. Thus, in defining the operational terms, we accept that the closing is, in fact, that "final event" where the parties gather around a table to complete their transaction by signing and exchanging documents and transferring funds.

All agree that the pile of documents required at the closing has grown significantly as a result of the stringent requirements for resale of mortgages on the secondary market. Further, all agree that these documents are, in general, more standardized than they were prior to the secondary market. Most witnesses admitted that there is little or no possibility of negotiating the terms of these documents with the lender; instead, acceptance of the terms is a "take it or leave it" condition to issuance of the loan. James T. Maher described the changes:

"I would say certainly before the mid-70s residential real estate transactions, other than in the title insurance policy area, were much more idiosyncratic, if you will. The security interest agreements, certainly before 1970 when the Fannie Mae, Freddie Mac documents first came out, and their uses increased to sort of almost every year, has certainly geometrically increased since the mid-80 time frame that seems to be the focus of these questions.

"Before '75, there was no uniform settlement statement, and a lot of the certifications and mortgage credit related documentation that tends to get executed at a settlement table, was not — either not needed or was unique to each individual lender, and whatever they decided was required. Now you have a Fannie Mae or Freddie Mac sellers or guide that dictates most of these forms or the response to them."

Considerable evidence was offered concerning the types of questions that are asked at closings. Movants' witnesses testified to their opinions that virtually no legal questions are asked at closings because, in a properly conducted real estate closing, all legal issues should be resolved before the parties meet at the closing table. The KBA's witnesses, however, testified to their diametrically opposite opinions that hardly any closing occurs without one of the parties asking a question that the closer cannot answer without the exercise of legal skill and expertise. What is abundantly clear from the evidence, however, is that the appendix of "typical questions" attached to U-58 is excessive.

From the evidence, we agree with Movants that few, if any, significant legal questions arise at most residential closings. Moreover, the evidence has convinced us that in those few instances where legal questions do arise, lay closing agents are properly trained to answer only if they can do so by reading from the document itself without providing any additional explanation. If they cannot do so, they are trained to halt the closing so that the parties may seek legal counsel. Thus, the evidence demonstrates that, by and large, lay closers have been following the mandates of U-31.

B. Lay Closings and Unauthorized Practice of Law

We are asked today to decide an issue of first impression in this state. It is an issue of much less breadth than the evidence adduced by the parties would suggest: Is conducting a real estate closing the unauthorized practice of law? Based on our review of the evidence and arguments presented to us, we hold that it is not the unauthorized practice of law for a layperson to conduct a real estate closing for another party. Therefore, we vacate U-58 and adopt the reasoning of U-31.

Our Supreme Court rules define the practice of law as "any service rendered involving legal knowledge or legal advice, whether of representation, counsel or advocacy in or out of court rendered in respect to the rights, duties, obligations, liabilities, or business relations of one requiring the services." The General Assembly has criminalized the unauthorized practice of law, and our disciplinary rules prohibit attorneys from "assisting a person who is not a member of the bar in the performance of an activity that constitutes the unauthorized practice of law." The rationale for such restrictions is that "limiting the practice of law to members of the bar protects the public against rendition of legal services by unqualified persons."

Accordingly, the conduct of a closing is the practice of law if (1) it requires legal knowledge or legal advice, (2) involves representation, counsel or advocacy on behalf of another party, and (3) involves the rights, duties, obligations, liabilities, or business relations of that other party.

KBA insists that U-31 and U-58 can coexist without conflict. We fail to see any logic in this argument. In its very first line, U-31 recognizes that it is concerned with the activities of real estate mortgage lenders and title insurance companies. Quickly its text goes on to permit lay real estate closings by these groups. The opinion provides:

> A "real estate closing" is at best ministerial in nature. Some lawyers allow secretaries and paralegals to participate in closings. The closing, which consists mainly of financial matters, payments, schedules of payment, and insurance, is basically a nonlegal function. So long as the lay person avoids the giving of legal advice, there is no problem with a lay employee closing a real estate transaction. The rub which frequently arises in a real estate closing situation is that often questions of a legal nature are posed to the layman who is closing the transaction. Any response would constitute legal advice and would be the unauthorized practice of law by the person answering the questions. In such an instance, the lay person should discontinue the closing and seek proper legal advice. It should be observed that many Federal loans involve significant knowledge of the law, and questions as to what is meant in the documents would certainly involve the unauthorized practice of law.

We think this sound and fair guidance that, if followed, offers substantial protection to consumers. Today we offer this guidance to those laypersons who perform closings, but we recognize that this advice does not mean that an attorney is required in every instance, but only where it is necessary to render legal services in connection with the transaction.

We do not deny that there are some portions of the residential real estate transaction that do constitute the practice of law, i.e., the title commitment letter and the preparation of deeds and mortgages, but this case has not asked us to deal with those matters attendant to the real estate closing itself. What we have been concerned with today is merely the thin slice at the end of the real estate transaction that we refer to as the closing. Certainly, we do not doubt that legal issues arise at some real estate closings. We do not, however, believe that the rate at which these issues arise requires that only attorneys or persons under their immediate supervision conduct real estate closings. Stated otherwise, although a layperson may not dispense legal advice anywhere — not on the golf course, not in line at the grocery, not while fishing on a lake somewhere, and certainly not at a real estate closing — we do not believe that a real estate closing is a setting so fraught with the potential for unauthorized practice that U-58's blanket prohibition against lay closing agents is warranted as a prophylactic measure. Thus, we vacate U-58. In doing so, we recognize that U-31 properly states the law on real estate closings in Kentucky: laypersons may conduct real estate closings on behalf of other parties, but they may not answer legal questions that arise at the closing or offer any legal advice to the parties. If they do answer such questions, they are then engaged in the unauthorized practice of law.

V. CONCLUSION

For the above reasons, we hereby vacate U-58 and hold that U-31 accurately describes the unauthorized practice of law parameters for real estate closings conducted by non-lawyers.

CASE QUESTIONS

1 What is the basis of this suit?
2 What was the finding under advisory opinion U-31?
3 How many real parties in interest have an important stake in the closing?
4 How does the court address the issue of allowing non-attorneys to conduct closings, in an era of standardized closing documentation?
5 According to the court, is it necessary to have an attorney physically present when the closing occurs?

SKILLS YOU NEED IN THE REAL WORLD

PREPARING HUD-1 STATEMENTS

Preparing HUD-1 settlement statements can be one of the most challenging aspects of a closing. If you are the person who is responsible for tracking all the details and preparing the settlement statement, you should give consideration to acquiring one of the excellent software packages currently available. Not only will the software help you expedite a closing, but many title insurance companies and lenders have begun refusing to deal with closing professionals who do not use software. They have had too many bad experiences with settlement statements prepared by hand, and they may require you to certify which type of closing software you use before they will permit you to act as a closing professional. The skill that you need here is the ability to weed through the many different programs now available to come up with the one that meets your clients' needs, offers you solid performance, and will keep you out of trouble. Talk with other paralegals in your area. What program do they use? What are the program's advantages and disadvantages? (There are always disadvantages.) What kind of learning curve is involved in mastering the program? How user-friendly is it? What type of support does the company offer? Is the program subject to bugs or other actions that will cause it to freeze up? Does the company offer a license program that allows you to use the program on a network? These are all questions you should consider before acquiring any closing software package.

CHAPTER SUMMARY

A real estate closing is the final process in a real estate transaction that began when a homeowner decided to put his house up for sale. The closing is important for a number of reasons, not only because this is where the deed that transfers ownership to property is exchanged, but also because of the monetary disbursements that are made during the closing. Closings are handled in different ways around the country. In some states, for example, real estate attorneys and paralegals conduct closings. In other parts of the country, closings are conducted by title insurance companies, lenders, and others. No matter who conducts the closing, there are some basic features that all closings share. For example, mortgage documents will be signed at the closing. Truth in lending and other federal legislative initiatives must also be satisfied during the closing. Taxes must be paid. Real estate agents' commissions will be disbursed and several other important documents will also be exchanged during the course of the settlement process. It is important for any real estate professional to understand the legal significance of a real estate closing. In addition to legal concerns, there are also several ethical concerns that are often raised during the closing process. For instance, when a non-attorney conducts a closing, this person is barred from giving legal advice about the impact of particular documents. In states that follow an attorney model for closings, ethical issues arise about the use of paralegals to conduct the closing. In some states, the practice is permissible, while in other states it is not.

REVIEW QUESTIONS

1   List and explain the basic steps involved in conducting a closing.
2   Why is it difficult to schedule a closing?
3   Why is a contract clause that "time is of the essence" a particular challenge for closing professionals?
4   What are some of the important documents that are completed during a real estate closing?
5   What is a survey, and why is it important to the closing?
6   What are "loan payoff amounts" and why are they important?
7   Why is it important to know the tax payment status on a parcel of real estate prior to the closing?
8   What is the significance of the termite inspection report?
9   List some of the tax forms that may be required as part of the closing.
10 How has the USA PATRIOT Act affected real estate closings?
11 Explain records of trust disbursements. Describe private mortgage insurance.
12 What is a seller's affidavit, and how does it relate to surveys?
13 List the people who are typically present at the closing. What do these people normally do at the closing?
14 What impact do federal truth in lending laws have on a real estate closing?
15 List and explain the documents that are usually required at the closing.
16 "Escrow" is used in two different contexts in this chapter. Explain both.
17 What are the ethical concerns surrounding dual representation at a closing?
18 What are some of the ethical concerns about allowing paralegals to conduct real estate closings?
19 Explain the Federal Truth in Lending Act and its significance on closings.

20 According to this chapter's case excerpt, why do real estate closings generally not involve the practice of law?

21 What are the some of the concerns in choosing a closing software package?

DISCUSSION QUESTIONS

Given the fact that so many states have different approaches to the use of attorneys and non-attorneys to conduct closings, is there an argument that you can make supporting the exclusive use of attorneys (and paralegals) at real estate closings?

PRACTICAL APPLICATIONS

Using the blank form provided in the Appendix, and the example provided in this chapter, complete a basic HUD-1 settlement closing form using the following information:

It was a gloomy, dreadful August day when Lisa and Rod Burnett finally found the house of their dreams. It was a ranch with an attached garage a few miles out of town. They put in an offer for $120,000, which was promptly accepted by the owner, Sal Seller.

The Burnetts didn't have much money for a deposit, so they only came up with $750 earnest money.

Sal Seller agreed to pay $2,000 toward closing costs.

Because it is an FHA loan, the Burnetts only have to come up with a 3 percent down payment.

Other terms from the contract:

1 1.5% loan origination fee
2 1 point
3 Appraisal fee: $220
4 Mortgage insurance application fee of $966
5 Pest inspection: $60
6 Reserve of two months of hazard insurance
7 Daily interest due from closing to first of next month: $18.23
8 Title Insurance is required
9 Hazard insurance premium: $230
10 Survey: $350

The deed will cost $8 to record; the deed of trust will cost $12 to record. Attorney's fee is one-half of 1 percent of the selling price, and Sal Seller has attorney's fees of $120.00.

Real property taxes are $415, and they have not been paid for this calendar year, putting them in arrears, since Sal Seller should have paid them.

Sal has a mortgage balance of $42,233. The closing date is August 25. The commission check is being split between Ron Realtor and Sandy Salesman on a 50-50 basis.

WEB SITES

Federal Deposit Insurance Corporation
www.fdic.gov

Federal Reserve
www.federalreserve.gov

Department of Housing and Urban Development
www.hud.gov

TERMS AND PHRASES

Closing
HUD-1 settlement form
Loan package

Promissory note
Private mortgage
 insurance

Proration

SIGNIFICANT CASES

In re Barrier, 375 S.C. 490, 654 S.E.2d 85 (S.C., 2007)
Dayton Supply & Tool Co., Inc. v. Montgomery Cty. Bd. of Revision, 111 Ohio St. 3d 367, 856 N.E.2d 926 (Ohio, 2006)
Doe Law Firm v. Richardson, 371 S.C. 14, 636 S.E.2d 866 (S.C., 2006)
In re Driscoll, 447 Mass. 678, 856 N.E.2d 840 (Mass., 2006)
In re Ingalls, 369 S.C. 569, 633 S.E.2d 512 (S.C., 2006)
In re Harrell, 365 S.C. 313, 617 S.E.2d 368 (S.C., 2005)

Taxation Issues in Real Property

 ## INTRODUCTION

In this chapter we examine the important issue of real property taxation. Real estate remains an important source of tax revenue for state and local governments and may be one of the few sources of revenue for some governments. We explore not only a government's right to impose taxes, but also how tax rates are determined, the duty of tax assessors, and finally how tax regulations are enforced, including the use of tax auctions.

REAL PROPERTY TAXES

The topic of taxes has come up in several contexts throughout this book. In the chapter on title examinations, we mentioned that the status of real property taxes is one of the most important parts of a real estate title search. Taxes are important in many other contexts as well. In this chapter we examine the issue of assessing real estate taxes as well as related issues, such as the payment of capital gains taxes on profits from real estate transactions.

Ad valorem taxes
Taxes assessed according to the value of the property.

Taxation can be a complex topic and entire books are written about it. We restrict our consideration of the issue to taxes as they pertain to real estate. First, we must begin with a discussion of **ad valorem taxes.**

A. AD VALOREM TAXATION

The concept underlying an ad valorem tax scheme is that the local government assesses a tax based on an item's value. Taxing by value is an ancient concept and relatively easy to impose. Ad valorem taxes can be applied to personal property, such as imported goods or automobiles. They can also be assessed against real property. The issue in any ad valorem tax scheme is the value of the property. In most cases, the government bases the tax on the fair market value of the property. As we discuss later in this chapter, the person responsible for determining fair market value is the tax assessor. However, before we can examine the complexities of government tax schemes, we must first address a more fundamental question: Where does the government get the power to assess taxes?

 **Ad valorem taxes are based on the item's value.**

1. THE POWER TO LEVY TAXES

The power to levy a tax against citizens is set out in the U.S. Constitution, as well as in all state constitutions. State statutes authorize cities to impose taxes on real and personal property located within their geographic limits. Taxes can be assessed to pay for a wide variety of services and also to pay government salaries, service government debt, make up for government deficits, and meet law enforcement costs, among others.

B. WHAT CAN BE TAXED?

State constitutions authorize state and local governments to assess taxes against both real and personal property. This means that in addition to land, governments can tax a wide variety of other items. We restrict our discussion of taxes to the assessment of real property taxes, but keep in mind that there are many other types of taxes imposed against individuals. Essentially, the government has the power to tax anything that is not specifically exempt.

The boards of county commissioners shall have power and jurisdiction in their respective counties to levy, for the purposes prescribed by law, such amount of taxes on the assessed value of real and personal property in the county as may be authorized by law.[1]

All real property within the state shall be subject to real property taxation, special ad valorem levies and special assessments unless exempt therefrom by law. Notwithstanding any provision of this chapter or of any other general, special or local law to the contrary, personal property, whether tangible or intangible, shall not be liable to ad valorem taxation.[2]

1. TAX EXEMPTIONS

State statutes provide **exemptions** for many types of properties. When a property is exempt, it means that the property owners are not required to pay real property taxes. There are many different types of exemptions, including:

Exemption
When an owner is not obligated to pay a specific tax.

- Homestead exemption
- Charitable exemption
- Nonprofit exemption
- Governmental exemption

a. Homestead Exemption

Many states allow permanent residents to qualify for a homestead exemption under the tax code. This means that a taxpayer can exempt up to a maximum percentage of appraised value. Some states allow a homeowner to choose the larger of a maximum percentage and a total amount. To qualify for a homestead exemption, many states impose additional requirements, for example, that the taxpayer be at least 65 years of age and meet other income eligibility requirements.

b. Charitable Exemption

In all states qualifying charitable and religious organizations receive tax exemption status. The method to qualify as a charity or religious organization varies according to both state and federal law, but if an organization qualifies, it is not required to pay any real property taxes.

---

[1] Nev. Rev. Stat. § 244.150.
[2] N.Y. Real Prop. Tax Law (McKinney) § 300.

FIGURE 14-3

Nonprofit Organizations
(New York)

1. (a) Real property owned by a corporation or association organized or conducted exclusively for religious, charitable, hospital, educational, or moral or mental improvement of men, women or children purposes, or for two or more such purposes, and used exclusively for carrying out thereupon one or more of such purposes either by the owning corporation or association or by another such corporation or association as hereinafter provided shall be exempt from taxation as provided in this section.

(b) Real property such as specified in paragraph (a) of this subdivision shall not be exempt if any officer, member or employee of the owning corporation or association shall receive or may be lawfully entitled to receive any pecuniary profit from the operations thereof, except reasonable compensation for services in effecting one or more of such purposes, or as proper beneficiaries of its strictly charitable purposes; or if the organization thereof for any such avowed purposes be a guise or pretense for directly or indirectly making any other pecuniary profit for such corporation or association or for any of its members or employees; or if it be not in good faith organized or conducted exclusively for one or more of such purposes.[3]

c. Nonprofit Exemption

Many states allow not only charitable and religious organizations but also nonprofit organizations to be exempt from the tax code. Under these rules, a qualifying nonprofit organization would be exempt from any real property tax assessments. See Figure 14-3.

d. Government Exemption

In addition to exempting charities, and religious and nonprofit organizations, local governments also exempt government-owned property from taxation. For instance, federal and state property is not assessed for real property taxes. In addition to government property, some tax codes also create specially protected areas, such as enterprise zones, that may also receive favorable tax treatment.

i. Enterprise Zones

Many local governments recognize that in order to improve living conditions and raise personal incomes (and to improve the tax base), it is important to attract businesses to economically depressed areas. One way of doing that is to create special zones where businesses receive favorable tax treatment. An enterprise zone is a common example. When a local government designates an enterprise zone, it sets off a specific geographic area and advertises the fact that businesses relocating to that area will have a lower tax bill. This usually results in a gradual buildup of the enterprise zone. Ultimately, offering a tax incentive proves to be a wise investment. By encouraging new businesses, the government is actually improving its tax base. More businesses mean more people and ultimately better tax revenues. See Figure 14-4 for an example of enterprise zone legislation.

---

[3] N.Y. Real Prop. Tax Law (McKinney) 420-a.

FIGURE 14-4

Property Subject to Taxation (Ohio)

(1) An area with a single continuous boundary designated in the manner set forth in section 5709.62 or 5709.63 of the Revised Code and certified by the director of development as having a population of at least four thousand according to the best and most recent data available to the director and having at least two of the following characteristics:

(a) It is located in a municipal corporation defined by the United States office of management and budget as a principal city of a metropolitan statistical area;

(b) It is located in a county designated as being in the "Appalachian region" under the "Appalachian Regional Development Act of 1965," 79 Stat. 5, 40 App. U.S.C.A. 403, as amended;

(c) Its average rate of unemployment, during the most recent twelve-month period for which data are available, is equal to at least one hundred twenty-five per cent of the average rate of unemployment for the state of Ohio for the same period.[4]

C. HOW TAX VALUES ARE DETERMINED

Before a property can be assessed for taxes, the local government must determine its value. The tax assessor's office is responsible for assigning a value to all eligible property in the jurisdiction.

1. TAX ASSESSMENT

The tax assessor is responsible for determining the taxable value of property. Tax assessment takes into account many different factors, including:

- Zoning
- Access
- Crop value
- Acreage
- Buildings and structures

A tax assessment determines the value of all property in the jurisdiction as of a particular day. That day might be January 1 of the calendar year, or any other date selected by the government. Assessors have strict rules that must be complied with in determining the value of property. For instance, an assessor may be required to determine the fair market value of property based on a formula created by the state legislature.

---

[4] Ohio Rev. Code Ann. § 5709.61.

a. Challenging an Assessment

Taxpayers often complain about the taxes that they must pay. However, a taxpayer is allowed to challenge a tax assessment when she can show that the value reached was arbitrary or capricious. Only if the taxpayer can show that the assessor deviated from standard practices or carried out some other unauthorized activity will the taxpayer be successful in reducing the tax assessment on a particular property. Most taxpayers who challenge their assessments lose their suits.

2. CALCULATING THE TAX RATE

Millage rate
A tax rate that equates to one dollar per thousand dollars in value.

Assessment is only the first step in determining the tax bill for a particular parcel. The property value must be calculated against the local tax rate, sometimes known as the **millage rate**. When a local government creates its annual tax rates, it begins with the assessed value of all real property located within its geographic limits. Then it estimates the amount of money it will need to carry out all governmental activity for the year. Dividing one value into the other determines the tax rate. Consider Example 14-1.

ISSUE AT A GLANCE

Tax assessment takes into account several factors to calculate the value of a parcel of real estate.

FIGURE 14-5

Duties of Assessor (Ohio)

An assessor, from the maps and descriptions furnished him by the county auditor and other sources of information, shall make a correct and pertinent description of each tract and lot of real property in his district. When he deems it necessary to obtain an accurate description of any separate tract or lot in his district, he may require the owner or occupier thereof to furnish such description, with any title papers he has in his possession. If such owner or occupier, upon demand, neglects or refuses to so furnish a satisfactory description of such parcel of real property, the assessor may employ a competent surveyor to make a description of the boundaries and location thereof, and a statement of the quantity of land therein. The expense of such survey shall be returned by such assessor to the county auditor, who shall add it to the tax assessed upon such real property, and it shall be collected by the county treasurer with such tax, and when collected, shall be paid, on demand, to the person to whom it is due.[5]

---

[5] Ohio Rev. Code Ann. § 5713.02.

Cost-a-lot County has assessed all of its qualifying real property and has determined that the total value is $250 million. The county has also calculated that in order to carry out all of its services and to pay its employees, it will need $10 million. Using these numbers, the county divides $10 million by $250 million to determine its tax rate. In this case, that rate would be $.04, or $40 for every $1,000 in value. That would be a high, but not unheard of, tax rate. For a house valued at $100,000, the annual tax bill would be $4,000. Some states have passed legislation to prevent real estate tax bills from going beyond a specific millage rate. What would the tax amount be for a house worth $250,000 at $20/$1,000 millage rate?

EXAMPLE 14-1

Taxpayers can challenge a tax assessment, but only if they can show that the value reached was arbitrary.

ISSUE AT
A GLANCE

a. Reassessment

Tax assessors could go through the lengthy process of assessing property every year in order to determine accurate values for that year's budget. However, the burden of reassessing every year might easily cost more money than it would generate in new taxes. Instead, many governments authorize their tax offices to reassess every few years, with some requiring no more than eight years between each reassessment.

D. PAYING TAXES

Each state handles paying taxes differently. Some states make taxes due in the fall, while others require them to be paid at the first of the year. Regardless of when the deadline is, the taxes must be paid by that time or the taxpayer faces sanctions, including interest charges, tax liens, and tax auctions.

1. ENFORCING TAX REGULATIONS

State statutes give governments the power to enforce their tax regulations through a wide assortment of remedies, including levies, garnishment, and attachments. Governments are also authorized to issue liens on property and to enforce those liens with tax auctions of the property.

a. Tax Liens

A tax lien operates like any other lien. It prevents the sale of the property until the tax has been satisfied. But tax liens have important differences from other types of liens. The lien remains on the property and is transferred when title is transferred. This means that a tax that was not paid by a previous owner can be assessed against a current owner. Tax liens also have the advantage of higher priority.

i. Setting Priorities in Tax Liens

Tax liens have special priority status under the law. Regardless of when a tax lien is filed, it automatically takes priority[6] over other claims and must be paid in full before other judgments or liens. This gives the local taxing authority a powerful tool in collecting taxes. In addition to imposing a tax lien, the government can also foreclose on a tax lien.

FIGURE 14-6

Duty of County Commissioners and School Board in Setting Rate of Taxation (Florida)

> (1) The county commissioners shall determine the amount to be raised for all county purposes, except for county school purposes, and shall enter upon their minutes the rates to be levied for each fund respectively, together with the rates certified to be levied by the board of county commissioners for use of the county, special taxing district, board, agency, or other taxing unit within the county for which the board of county commissioners is required by law to levy taxes.[6]

FIGURE 14-7

When Taxes Due; Delinquent (Florida)

> All taxes shall be due and payable on November 1 of each year or as soon thereafter as the certified tax roll is received by the tax collector. Taxes shall become delinquent on April 1 following the year in which they are assessed or immediately after 60 days have expired from the mailing of the original tax notice, whichever is later. If the delinquency date for ad valorem taxes is later than April 1 of the year following the year in which taxes are assessed, all dates or time periods specified in this chapter relative to the collection of, or administrative procedures regarding, delinquent taxes shall be extended a like number of days.[7]

b. Foreclosing a Tax Lien

When a tax lien has been outstanding for a specific period of time and remains unpaid, the local government is authorized to begin proceedings to foreclose the tax lien. The property will literally be auctioned off for back taxes. The auction is authorized like any other foreclosure auction, but these auctions have the added appeal that a successful bidder may acquire property for only a fraction of its true value. It is common for property valued at hundreds of thousands of dollars to be auctioned for back taxes in the amount of a few thousand dollars.

However, before anyone decides to bid at a tax auction, there are some complexities to consider. For instance, the successful bidder at a tax auction does not receive a general warranty deed to the property. The successful bidder doesn't even receive title in fee simple absolute. Instead, the bidder receives a deed that is

---

[6] Fla. Stat. Ann. (West's) § 200.011.
[7] Fla. Stat. Ann. (West's) § 197.333.

Tech Topic
REAL ESTATE AND TAXATION

For the typical homeowner, property taxes are relatively straightforward. Each year, property taxes are calculated and assessed on the basis of current city, county, and state rates. Aside from the odd special assessment or incremental increase, residential property taxes remain fairly consistent from year to year.

Taxation on commercial property is vastly different, however. In an attempt to lure businesses to establish a presence, many states and localities offer tax incentives, particularly for employing advanced technology. For example, in Mississippi a property tax exemption is available for telecommunications businesses when they purchase equipment for deploying broadband technology in the state. In Prince George's County, Maryland, any business primarily involved with the application of computer sciences can be eligible to receive a property tax credit.

Whether on the city, county, or state level, the value of technology is recognized and encouraged. The world of real estate is right in the thick of the technological revolution, a trend that will likely continue.

referred to under a variety of names, such as "commissioner's deed" in some states and a "sheriff's deed" in other states. The important point about these deeds is that they do not, by themselves, give the successful bidder absolute rights to the property. There is even a question about whether the deed authorizes the eviction of the current residents. Why then would anyone bid at a tax auction? The simple answer is that a tax auction deed could qualify as "colorable claim of title" for adverse possession purposes. Under that rule, discussed in Chapter 4, a person can acquire title to property by open, notorious, hostile, or adverse possession of another's property under colorable claim of title. A tax auction deed could be exactly what a person needs in order to trigger the provisions of adverse possession. In some states, a tax auction deed can ripen into fee simple absolute after the passage of time and a court action by the successful bidder.

 ## ASSESSMENTS

While taxes are applied to all qualifying real property within the county, an assessment is an individual charge placed against a particular parcel. The most common example of a special assessment arises when the local government installs a feature that benefits only a particular area. Constructing a playground, installing a sidewalk or erecting streetlights are all examples of specific improvements that would justify an assessment. In this case, all parcels that benefit from this improvement can be assessed with a fee. This is not a tax that must be paid by everyone in the jurisdiction. Instead, the bill is only for specific parcels.

FIGURE 14-8

Sale at Public Auction (Florida)

(1) The lands advertised for sale to the highest bidder as a result of an application filed under s. 197.502 shall be sold at public auction by the clerk of the circuit court, or his or her deputy, of the county where the lands are located on the date, at the time, and at the location as set forth in the published notice, which shall be during the regular hours the clerk's office is open. At the time and place, the clerk shall read the notice of sale and shall offer the lands described in the notice for sale to the highest bidder for cash at public outcry. The amount required to redeem the tax certificate, plus the amounts paid by the holder to the clerk of the circuit court in charges for costs of sale, redemption of other tax certificates on the same lands, and all other costs to the applicant for tax deed, plus interest thereon at the rate of 1.5 percent per month for the period running from the month after the date of application for the deed through the month of sale and costs incurred for the service of notice provided for in s. 197.522(2), shall be considered the bid of the certificateholder for the property. However, if the land to be sold is assessed on the latest tax roll as homestead property, the bid of the certificateholder shall be increased to include an amount equal to one-half of the assessed value of the homestead property as required by s. 197.502. If there are no higher bids, the land shall be struck off and sold to the certificateholder, who shall forthwith pay to the clerk the documentary stamp tax and recording fees due, and a tax deed shall thereupon be issued and recorded by the clerk.[8]

FIGURE 14-9

Tax Auctions (Florida)

The tax collector shall require immediate payment of a reasonable deposit from any person who wishes to bid for a tax certificate. A person who fails or refuses to pay any bid made by, or on behalf of, him or her is not entitled to bid or have any other bid accepted or enforced by the tax collector until a new deposit of 100 percent of the amount of estimated purchases has been paid to the tax collector. When tax certificates are ready for issuance, the tax collector shall notify each person to whom a certificate was struck off that the certificate is ready for issuance and payment must be made within 48 hours from the mailing of such notice or the deposit shall be forfeited and the bid canceled. In any event, payment shall be made before delivery of the certificate by the tax collector.[9]

---

[8] Fla. Stat. Ann. (West's) § 197.542.
[9] Fla. Stat. Ann. (West's) § 197.432

COUNTY TAX RECORD — ANNOTATED DOCUMENT

RESIDENTIAL   123 MAPLE STREET   BARNES COUNTY, PLACID LRK 029727   REVALUATION DATE OF: JANUARY 1, 2003   PAGE 1

1330 SOUTHWEST BLVD   MAP# 044N   -01-001-A -0 Card   1 Of 1   Neighborhood ID: 108.00   Zoning:RES   Class:R   Pin Number: 3639-12-97-0129.0000

H. & M. SIMPSON
123 MAPLE ST.
SPRINGFIELD,   PL

ASSESSMENT INFORMATION:
Current Values:
Land Value   60,900
Use Value
Building   168,800
Total   229,700

Land Use Code: 011   Township # 9

LAND DATA AND COMPUTATION:

Type	Map Ftrg	Size	Rate	Value
HOME SITE		1.000	21,000	16,590
FRONTAGE		2.000	21,000	33,180
RESIDUAL		1.450	6,900	11,110

SHAPE/SIZE   VAL/LOC ADJ. -21
VAL/LOC ADJ. -21
VAL/LOC ADJ. 11

Calc Acres: 4.450   Total Land Value 60,900
Use Value:

Account No: 077123500
Tax District: 03   38
School District: 03
Fire District: 00   1
Building Code:
City Code: 08

Date   Type   Price   Source Validity
19850601 LAND + BLDG   117,000 BUYER

Deed Book:1405
Deed Page: 0333
Deed Date:19860101

NOTES:
148%X75%=+11%

Appraiser: JPT   229,700
Lister: JPT 20020125
PROPERTY FACTORS;
Topo: St/Rd:
ROLLING ALL PUBLIC PAVED

ADDITION DATA;
	Value
H	1000
I	19100
J	3400
K	6400
L	294000
M	700
N	1500

	Area
A	360
B	320
C	80
D	644
E	300
F	60
G	144

This presentation of information is considered a Restricted Appraisal Report used to appraise Fee Simple Interest of Real Property. The estimated Market Value is to be used for tax purposes only. This appraisal as required by General Statute 105-283 has been completed using Catawba County's 2003 Schedule of Values. Highest and Best Use for this property is RES . Market Value as defined by General Statute 105-283 has been determined by considering all three approaches to value: cost, market, and income. Additional information considered by the appraiser is in the work file of the appraiser. The COST VALUE approach has been used for this property.

BUILDING PERMIT RECORD:
Issue Date Number Amount Purpose

DWELLING DATA:

1st FL	2nd FL	3rd FL
LL		

OFP
1SMs
EFP
Cport
1SMs
FUt
Cnpy

1sFr

DWELLING COMPUTATIONS
Base Price: 150,400
Attic:
Plumbing Adjustment: 11,850
Heat/Cent A/c Adj: 7,860
Basement Adjustment: 5,290
Exterior Trim: -5,690
Finish Basement Living Area:
Bsmt Recreation Area:
Unfinished Area:
Well/Septic: 8,820
Fireplaces: 71,500
Additions: 250,135
Grade Factor (X)
C & D Factor (X)   337,510
Replacement Cost New: 0.50
Percent Good:
Market Adjustment: 168,800
RCNLD

Style: TWO STORY
Story Height: 2.00
Attic: PART FINISH
Basement: PART
Total Rooms: 9
Bedrooms: 4
Full Baths: 3
Half Baths/Fixtures:
Year Built: 1940
Year Remodeled: 1993
Exterior Walls: BRICK
Ground Floor Area: 1144
Total Living Area: 3494
Fin. Basement Living Area:
Basement Recreation Area:
Fireplace Stacks/Openings: 2 / 2
Metal Fireplace Stacks:
Heating System: CENTRAL A/C
Heat Type: HEAT PUMP
Fuel Type: ELECTRIC
Quality Grade: B+
Cond/Desirability/Utility: AV
Physical Condition: AVERAGE

Type	Qty	Year	Size	Area	Grd	Cond	Mod Code	MA	RCN	Mod Code	%Gd	Value

48.31

OUTBUILDING DATA:

OBY MISC VALUE
Total Oby Value

Last Update:20030215

 TAX DODGES

Every few years, there are anti-tax movements. In recent decades there have been groups that have claimed that the government does not have the power to assess taxes, or that specific provisions of the U.S. Constitution concerning income or property taxes were never properly enacted. As a legal professional, you may come into contact with individuals who have "foolproof" methods to avoid paying taxes. Always be cautious about any such scheme, and remember the old saying that in life there are only two certainties: death and taxes. Anyone who claims to be able to avoid either one is probably selling something that is at best a fantasy and, at worst, a criminal enterprise.

 METROPOLITAN GOV'T OF NASHVILLE AND DAVIDSON v. DELINQUENT TAXPAYERS

METROPOLITAN GOVERNMENT OF NASHVILLE AND DAVIDSON COUNTY v. DELINQUENT TAXPAYERS
2005 WL 737126 (Tenn. Ct. App. 2005)

DAVID R. FARMER, J.

This appeal arises from an action brought by the metropolitan government to collect delinquent property taxes. The taxpayer owned 37.25 acres of property that were zoned commercial but were granted "greenbelt" status. In 1999, the taxpayer leased 1.21 acres of his property to a retail pharmacy, but he did not inform the assessor's office of the change in use of the 1.21 acre portion of his land. In 2000, after the assessor's office learned of the change in use through a review of a building permit summary, the assessor changed the classification on the entire 37.25 acre parcel from "greenbelt" to commercial. As a result, a "rollback" was issued causing taxes to be due on the entire 37.25 acre parcel at a commercial rate for the three previous years. The assessor mailed the taxpayer a 1999 tax bill showing the amount owed due to the rollback. Although the assessor informed the taxpayer that the matter could no longer be corrected through the assessor's office, the taxpayer did not file an administrative appeal or bring a lawsuit to dispute the error in classification and assessment. Following a hearing on the delinquent tax lawsuit, the trial court found that the assessor's office erred in removing the taxpayer's entire parcel from "greenbelt" classification and subjecting the entire parcel to a tax "rollback." The court found that only the 1.21 acre portion of the parcel used for construction of the pharmacy should have lost "greenbelt" status. Additionally, the court found that, because the parties stipulated that no change in use of the property had occurred since the underlying action was initiated, its findings were dispositive not only for tax years 1999 and 2000, but also through the date of the final order, November 26, 2003. The metropolitan government appealed arguing that the taxpayer was barred by statute from contesting the validity of the assessment once the delinquent tax lawsuit was filed.

We reverse.

FACTUAL BACKGROUND AND PROCEDURAL HISTORY

John E. Cain, III ("Mr. Cain") is the owner of a parcel of land, consisting of 37.25 acres, located at 2788 Murfreesboro Pike in Antioch, Tennessee. In 1997, Mr. Cain's property consisted of 55.06 acres, all of which remained vacant and undeveloped. At that time, the property was "split-zoned," with some acreage being zoned for commercial use and the remaining portion being zoned residential. Additionally, Mr. Cain applied for and was granted "greenbelt"[1] classification for the property. In 1998, he subdivided the property and sold 17.81 acres, leaving him 37.25 acres that retained greenbelt status.

In March of 1999, Mr. Cain entered into a long-term commercial lease agreement with Hook-SupeRx, Inc., a retail pharmacy chain. Pursuant to their agreement, Mr. Cain began commercial development of a 1.21 acre portion of the 37.25 acre tract for use as a CVS pharmacy. On June 29, 1999, a notice of the lease agreement was recorded in the county registrar's office. The recorded notice of lease included a statement that the leased premises consisted of approximately 10,125 square feet, a copy of the lease agreement, and a site layout plan that provided a metes and bounds description of the 1.21 acres. On December 23, 1999, Mr. Cain reserved a book and page number in the registrar's office for the anticipated recording of a plat showing the separation of the 37.25 acre tract into three separate tracts, consisting of a 1.21 acre tract, a 15.19 acre tract, and a 20.85 acre tract. On February 9, 2000, the Metro Planning Commission approved Mr. Cain's proposed plat and the separation of the 37.25 acre property into three separate tracts.

During the course of the development of the CVS Pharmacy site and the simultaneous interaction with other branches of the county government, Mr. Cain never informed the office of the Assessor of Property (the "Assessor") about the proposed development. He did not inform the Assessor about the commercial development of the 1.21 acres, the recording of the notice of lease, the reservation of the book and page number, or the approval by the Metro Planning Commission of the plat separation.

In 2000, the Assessor became aware of the CVS Pharmacy development through an electronic summary of the building permit issued for the pharmacy, which was received through the county's computerized permit tracking system. The summary stated that the building permit was issued July 1, 1999, and the purpose for the permit was to "Construct 75' × 135', 10,125 Sq. Ft. Non Residence Building For 'CVS/Pharmacy' With 14.5' × 16' Drive Thru Canopy." According to the testimony of Jim Clary, who worked in the Assessor's office and reviewed the building permit summary, at the time the summary

---

[1] Pursuant to the Agricultural, Forest and Open Space Land Act of 1976, open land that exists near growing commercial and residential areas may be "threatened" by "urban sprawl" and the system of property taxation. *See* Tenn. Code Ann. § 67-5-1002(1) (2003). As a result, this type of open space real property, that might otherwise be classified as residential, commercial, or other higher density use and thereby be subject to higher property taxes, may be eligible for classification as "agricultural land," "forest land," or "open space land," resulting in a lesser tax burden. *See id.* § 67-5-1004 (2003). This act, although given a different title by the legislature, has come to be known generally as the "Greenbelt law." *See Marion County v. State Bd. of Equalization*, 70 S.W.2d 521, 522 (Tenn. Ct. App. 1986).

was brought to the attention of the Assessor, the parcel had not yet been separated into three separate tracts, but consisted of the entire 37.25 acres. However, Mr. Clary also testified that anyone in the Assessor's office could have followed up on the parcel and its status through the computerized permit tracking system, which would have indicated that only a 1.21 acre portion of the property was being used for a commercial purpose. Based solely upon the summary of the building permit, the Assessor changed the classification of the entire 37.25 acres of Mr. Cain's property from greenbelt classification to commercial use. Consequently, the change in classification resulted in a "rollback," causing taxes at the commercial rate to be due for the three previous years, 1999, 1998, and 1997.

On May 18, 2000, the Assessor mailed a "Notice of Appraised Value Classification and Assessment" showing the new classification for the entire 37.25 acres, along with a statement of the much higher, newly assessed value. Included in the appraisal notice was a statement that the document was an appraisal and "not a tax bill." In addition, the notice included an explanation regarding the taxpayer's right to appeal the appraisal, classification, and assessment with the Metropolitan Board of Equalization, along with an announcement that the board of equalization would hear appeals during the first week of June 2000. Mr. Cain was also later mailed a "1999 Real Property Tax Statement" showing the adjusted tax amount owed due to the rollback. The tax bill did not indicate the date on which it was sent, but it did show that the rollback adjustment was made on July 3, 2000 and that any penalty or interest charges would not be applied if the full amount was paid within thirty (30) days of the adjustment, i.e., August 3, 2000. During his testimony, however, Mr. Cain stated that the notice of appraisal and the tax bill were mailed to his title insurance company, and he did not receive these documents until some point after the date they were originally mailed.

Once Mr. Cain became aware of the reassessment and rollback adjustment, he enlisted the aid of Terry Hunter, a former member of the county board of equalization, to assist in handling this issue with the Assessor's office. Mr. Hunter spoke with Ed Fox, the head of the commercial department of the Assessor's office, who, according to Mr. Hunter's testimony, informed Mr. Hunter that, from the Assessor's perspective, the 1.21 acre tract had never been officially removed from the larger parcel. Thus, as Mr. Fox put it, the removal of greenbelt classification from the entire parcel had become a "legal issue," and the Assessor's office could no longer change the classification.

Despite the foregoing, Mr. Cain neither appealed the rollback adjustment with the Davidson County Board of Equalization or the State of Tennessee Board of Equalization, nor did he file a lawsuit to challenge the action of the Assessor's office. Rather, his first attempt to dispute the reclassification and rollback assessment occurred in the form of his answer to the present delinquent tax action.

On March 9, 2001, the Metropolitan Government of Nashville and Davidson County ("Metro") filed a complaint in this matter in Davidson County Chancery Court, originally for the purpose of collecting delinquent taxes owed for the year 1999. A default judgment, which was entered against Mr. Cain due to his failure to respond, was set aside, and Mr. Cain filed his answer on August 30, 2001. In his answer, Mr. Cain asserted that Metro's declassification of all of his property was contrary to section 67-5-1008(d) of the Tennessee Code.

The amount of tax savings calculated under this subdivision (d) shall be the rollback taxes due as the result of disqualification or withdrawal of the land from classification under this part. Rollback taxes shall be payable from the date written notice is provided by the assessor, but shall not be delinquent until March 1 of the following year. When the assessor determines there is liability for rollback taxes, the assessor shall give written notice to the tax collecting official identifying the basis of the rollback taxes and the person the assessor finds to be responsible for payment, and the assessor shall provide a copy of the notice to the responsible person. Rollback taxes shall be a first lien on the disqualified property in the same manner as other property taxes, and shall also be a personal responsibility of the current owner or seller of the land as provided in this part. The assessor may void the rollback assessment if it is determined that the assessment was imposed in error, except there shall be no refund of rollback taxes that have been collected at the request of a buyer or seller at the time of sale. Liability for rollback taxes, but not property values, may be appealed to the state board of equalization by March 1 of the year following the notice by the assessor. However, property values fixing the amount of rollback taxes may only be appealed as otherwise provided by law.

(4)(A) If, under the provisions of subdivision (d)(1), only a portion of a parcel is subject to rollback taxes, the tax assessor shall apportion the assessment of such parcel on the first tax roll prepared after such taxes become payable, and enter the apportioned amount attributable to such portion as a separately assessed parcel on the tax roll.

(B) Such apportionment shall be made for each of the years to which the rollback taxes apply. Tenn. Code Ann. § 67-5-1008(d) (2003).

Prior to trial, the parties submitted a joint stipulation. Originally, Metro brought two separate actions against Mr. Cain, one each for the tax years 1999 and 2000. By stipulation, however, the parties agreed that the trial court's findings regarding the 1999 tax delinquency lawsuit would be dispositive of the case brought for the year 2000. In the stipulation, the parties acknowledged that, from the time Mr. Cain obtained greenbelt status for the entire 37.25 acres of property, there had been no changes in the use of the property, except for the 1.21 acre portion leased to CVS pharmacy for commercial use. The parties further stipulated that, should the trial court find that the entire 37.25 acre tract lost greenbelt status, then the total adjusted 1999 real property tax amount owed would be $61,221.70. For the tax year 2000, the parties agreed that Mr. Cain would owe $48,256.29 should the court find that greenbelt status was properly removed from the entire parcel. The stipulation further provided that, if the trial court found that only the 1.21 acre portion lost greenbelt status, Mr. Cain would owe taxes for the remaining 36.04 acres of his property in the amount of $113.13 for both tax years 1999 and 2000. None of these amounts include penalties, interest or attorney fees, which the parties agreed would be assessed against Mr. Cain. Approximately two weeks prior to trial, Mr. Cain paid $10,000 into the court under protest.

After conducting a hearing on the merits, the trial court entered a final order ruling that there were no material facts in dispute, and that, as a matter of law, the Assessor erred in withdrawing Mr. Cain's entire parcel from greenbelt classification and subjecting it to rollback taxes. The trial court found that only the 1.21 acre portion leased to CVS should have lost greenbelt status and been subject to rollback taxes. In addition, the trial court ruled that its findings of fact and conclusions of law were dispositive for the year 1999 through the date of the final order, November 26, 2003, because there had been no changes in the use to the 36.04 acre portion of Mr. Cain's property, which retained its greenbelt classification.

On appeal from the trial court's final order, Metro presents, as we perceive them, the following issues for our review:

(1) Whether the trial court erred by allowing Mr. Cain to challenge the classification and resulting assessment of his property after the delinquent taxpayer lawsuit was filed by Metro, and

(2) Whether the trial court erred by holding that its findings of fact and conclusions of law in this case were dispositive of Mr. Cain's property tax classification for the years 2001, 2002, and 2003, when those matters were not before the court.

STANDARD OF REVIEW

In non-jury cases such as the one before us, the trial court's findings of fact are reviewed de novo upon the record, accompanied by a presumption of the correctness of those findings unless the evidence preponderates otherwise. Tenn. R. App. P. 13(d) (2004); Hawks v. City of Westmoreland, 960 S.W.2d 10, 15 (Tenn. 1997). We review questions of law, however, de novo without any presumption of correctness. Hawks, 960 S.W.2d at 15.

TAXPAYER'S CHALLENGE OF ASSESSMENT FOR TAX YEARS 1999 AND 2000

Turning to its first issue, Metro relies on various statutes for the proposition that, by the time Metro brought the delinquent tax lawsuit, Mr. Cain was barred from challenging the reclassification and resulting assessment. Although the record supports the trial court's finding that the Assessor erroneously withdrew Mr. Cain's entire parcel from greenbelt status, we conclude that the assessment, although erroneous, was conclusive because Mr. Cain failed to pursue in a timely fashion any of the means of appeal available to him.

Under the property tax laws of this state, taxpayers are provided several avenues for challenging the assessment and levy of property taxes. An objecting taxpayer may challenge an assessment administratively through an appeal to the county or state board of equalization. Tenn. Code Ann. § 67-5-1407 (2003). Under certain circumstances, a taxpayer may make payment of his or her taxes under formal protest and seek judicial review. In addition, when a taxpayer believes that the tax assessor has committed an obvious clerical error resulting in an erroneous assessment, he or she may proceed pursuant to section 67-5-509 of the Tennessee Code. From our review of these revenue statutes and the applicable case law, the procedures set forth above constitute the exclusive means by which a taxpayer may challenge an erroneous property tax assessment. Applying the aforementioned law to the facts of this case, we will address each of these means of appeal below.

In the event an aggrieved taxpayer seeks administrative review of an erroneous classification or assessment, the taxpayer may proceed by means of an appeal to the county board of equalization. Tenn. Code Ann. § 67-5-1407(a)(1)(A) (2003) ("Any owner of property or taxpayer . . . has the right . . . to make complaint before the county board of equalization . . . if the property under appeal or protest by the taxpayer has been erroneously classified or subclassified for purposes of taxation."). Additionally, the taxpayer may seek review directly with the state board of equalization. Id. § 67-5-1501(a) (2003) "("State board of equalization has jurisdiction over the valuation, classification, and assessment of all properties in the state."); see also Crown Enters., Inc. v. State Bd. of Equalization, 543 S.W.2d 583 (Tenn. 1976). However, section 67-5-1401 of the Tennessee Code provides that, ""if the taxpayer fails, neglects or refuses to appear before the county board of equalization prior to its final adjournment, the assessment as determined by the assessor shall be conclusive against the taxpayer, and such taxpayer shall be required to pay the taxes on such amount. . . ." Tenn. Code Ann. § 67-5-1401 (2003). It is clear from the record that Mr. Cain never appeared before either the county or state board of equalization. Therefore, under section 67-5-1401, the assessment would be deemed conclusive against Mr. Cain. Id.

However, besides pursuing an administrative appeal, the taxpayer may seek to have certain errors corrected directly through the Assessor's office, pursuant to section 67-5-509 of the Tennessee Code. Id. § 67-5-509. Section 67-5-509 provides, in pertinent part, as follows:

> (a) If the tax computed on an erroneous basis of valuation or assessment has been paid prior to certification of the corrected assessment by the assessor, the trustee or municipal collector shall, within sixty (60) days after receipt of such certification from the assessor, refund to the taxpayer that portion of such tax paid which resulted from the erroneous assessment, such refund to be made without the necessity of payment under protest or such other requirements as usually pertain to refunds of taxes unjustly or illegally collected.
>
> (f) Errors or omissions correctable under this section include only obvious clerical mistakes, involving no judgment of or discretion by the assessor, apparent from the face of the official tax and assessment records, such as the name or address of an owner, the location or physical description of property, misplacement of a decimal point or mathematical miscalculation, errors of classification, and duplicate assessment.

Under subsection (d), any ""correction of assessments pursuant to this section must be requested by the taxpayer, or initiated by the assessor, prior to March 1, no more than the second year following the tax year for which the correction is to be made." Id. § 67-5-509(d). If, within thirty (30) days of the taxpayer's request, the assessor fails or refuses to correct the alleged error, "any person aggrieved thereby may appeal directly to the state board of equalization. . . ." Id. § 67-5-509(e). However, the appeal to the state board of equalization under this section must be "filed within forty-five (45) days after the assessor's failure or refusal to correct the error." Id. Subsection (d) further provides that, ""once a suit has been filed for the collection of delinquent taxes pursuant to § 67-5-2405, the assessment and levy for all county, municipal and other property tax purposes are deemed to be valid and are not subject to correction under this section." Id. § 67-5-509(d).

In the Summer of 2000, Mr. Cain received the notice of assessment and tax bill for the year 1999. At Mr. Cain's request, Mr. Hunter went to the Assessor's office to seek an explanation and reach a resolution of this matter. During his discussion with Mr. Fox from the Assessor's office, Mr. Hunter was made aware that his attempt to have this matter resolved directly through the Assessor's office would be unsuccessful. By dispatching Mr. Hunter to the Assessor's office, Mr. Cain, although likely unintentionally, invoked the provisions of section 67-5-509. Although Mr. Cain brought his concerns to the attention of the Assessor, when he was made aware that the Assessor was either unable or not willing to correct his assessment, Mr. Cain failed to pursue the claim further.

In his brief, Mr. Cain asserts that section 67-5-509 does not apply in this case for two primary reasons. First, he argues that the statute was only designed to address errors in "assessment," not "classification." Mr. Cain contends that the parties here are only disputing the removal of greenbelt classification and that there was no dispute as to the amount of the appropriate assessment. Accordingly, Mr. Cain claims that such disputes over "classification" would not come under the ambit of section 67-5-509. We find this argument tenuous at best. Next, Mr. Cain argues that 67-5-509 only addresses obvious clerical mistakes. He claims that the Assessor's misjudgment of the classification in this situation was an error in discretion and, hence, a matter expressly not within the scope of 67-5-509, pursuant to subsection (f) of the statute. See Tenn. Code Ann. § 67-5-509(f). We tend to agree that the Assessor's mistake here was the result of an error in judgment and discretion, and not a product of a clerical blunder. See id. Although the mistake at issue was an "error of classification," we believe it is not one that would be "apparent from the face of the official tax and assessment records." See id. Clearly, when the Assessor made the decision to remove greenbelt status from the entire parcel, he was making a decision based upon information that, in his discretion, warranted such a reclassification. This type of action, we believe, does not fall under section 67-5-509 and is not comparable with the types of envisioned errors correctable under that section, such as an incorrect "name or address of an owner" or the "misplacement of a decimal point or mathematical miscalculation." See id. Thus, we conclude that section 67-5-509 does not serve as a bar to a potential appeal of an assessment by a taxpayer under the facts of this case. However, this conclusion does not end our analysis.

The final manner of appealing an error in assessment occurs where the claimed error raises purely legal issues. In that case, the taxpayer may bypass the administrative process altogether and proceed directly through the courts. If this course of procedure is chosen, however, the taxpayer is required, as a prerequisite to gaining access to the courts, to pay the disputed taxes under protest and sue for a refund.

In this case, Mr. Cain did not pay the disputed taxes and initiate an action for their recovery. Rather, he did not participate in this matter until after Metro filed the underlying delinquent taxpayer lawsuit and a default judgment was entered against him. After the default judgment was set aside, Mr. Cain raised the issue of an erroneous classification through his answer and an "affirmative defense." Less than two weeks prior to trial, Mr. Cain paid, under protest, $10,000 into the clerk and master's office.

Mr. Cain contends that he should be allowed to challenge the classification error as a defendant in the delinquent taxpayer action because the matter concerns a pure "legal issue." In support of his position, Mr. Cain relies on Castlewood, Inc. v. Anderson County, for the proposition that the Assessor's error in classification was a legal issue, and, therefore, the trial court correctly permitted Mr. Cain to challenge that error at the trial level. We believe, however, that Mr. Cain's reliance on Castlewood is misplaced. It is true that, where an erroneous assessment raises strictly legal issues, a taxpayer may proceed directly against the taxing authority through the courts. However, the distinguishing characteristic of Castlewood and every other case we have found, is that, in those cases, the taxpayer, not the government, initiated the lawsuit in a timely manner. In our research, we have found no case, and Mr. Cain has cited to none, which holds that a taxpayer may sit on his or her rights and challenge an erroneous assessment only after an action to collect delinquent taxes is brought against the taxpayer. Rather, we believe that the weight of authority is that, in order to raise a legal issue through judicial review regarding the actions of a taxing authority, a taxpayer has certain courses of procedure that he or she must follow. A taxpayer may proceed according to section 67-5-509; he or she may pursue administrative remedies through the boards of equalization; or, if the matter involves purely legal issues, the aggrieved taxpayer may file suit for the recovery of taxes unjustly assessed and paid. Here, Mr. Cain failed to pursue any of the available remedies. Therefore, we conclude that he is barred from challenging the assessments at this late stage in the proceedings. Accordingly, we reverse the trial court on this issue.

TRIAL COURT'S RULING REGARDING TAX YEARS 2001, 2002, AND 2003

Metro originally brought this delinquent tax lawsuit for the year 1999, and, by stipulation, the parties agreed that the trial court's judgment would also dispose of Metro's delinquency action brought for the year 2000. In the stipulation, the parties also agreed that, from the time Mr. Cain obtained greenbelt status for his 37.25 acre parcel, there had been no change in use of the property except for the 1.21 acre lot leased to CVS Pharmacy. Despite the fact that Metro brought this action only for tax years 1999 and 2000, the trial court ruled that its findings of fact and conclusions of law were to be "dispositive of these matters for the year 1999 through the date of the final order as there have been no changes in use of the 36.04 acres of Mr. Cain's property, which shall retain its Greenbelt classification." Metro argues that the trial court erred in making this finding because the taxes for years 2001, 2002, and 2003 were not before the court. Mr. Cain contends that, through the stipulation that the primary use of the property had not changed since green-belt status was obtained and the fact that Metro failed to object to the final order, this issue was tried by consent.

We agree with Metro that this action was filed in order to collect property taxes for tax years 1999 and 2000. There is nothing in the record to support the trial court's finding that any issues involving tax years 2001, 2002, and 2003 were tried by consent. Therefore, we conclude that the evidence preponderates against such a finding and reverse on this issue.

CONCLUSION

For the foregoing reasons, we reverse the judgment of the trial court and remand for further proceedings consistent with this opinion. Costs of this appeal are taxed to the Appellee, John E. Cain, III, for which execution may issue if necessary.

CASE QUESTIONS

1 Explain how the taxpayer in this case ended up facing a "rollback" on 37.25 acres.
2 How did the Assessor become aware of the change in Cain's property?
3 What action did the Assessor take once the building permit was discovered?

4   What action did Cain take when he became aware of the reclassification?
5   What did the court have to say about how Cain pursued his legal remedies, and what impact did this ultimately have on the case?

 SKILLS YOU NEED IN THE REAL WORLD

RESEARCHING TAX ISSUES

At some time or another all legal professionals who specialize in real property law will come into contact with tax issues. A client may wish to challenge an appraisal, or you may have to deal with the tax office on a particular issue. Keep in mind that tax issues in real estate are a world of their own. Case law on tax assessments and challenges involves terminology that may not be familiar from other real property issues. Taxes also involve issues on both federal and state levels. As a result, you must be able to research these issues on many different levels, from local tax ordinances to capital gains taxes on the federal level. Find a good reference on the issue of real estate taxes and hang on to it. You can annotate your copy as the tax rules change, and it will serve as a good backup whenever you are asked to research a particular complex tax issue.

CHAPTER SUMMARY

Governments are given the power to impose taxes by both federal and state constitutions. Most states base their real property taxes on an ad valorem system that taxes according to the value of the real estate. Tax assessors determine the value of all eligible properties in the jurisdiction and then the government assesses a tax based on that rate multiplied by the millage rate. Some properties are exempt from taxation. These include religious organizations, nonprofit organizations, and government properties. Governments have the right to enforce their tax regulations by imposing tax liens on property and by eventually auctioning off property at tax auctions.

Assessments are similar to taxes except that they are placed against particular parcels that receive the benefit of nearby improvements.

REVIEW QUESTIONS

1   What are ad valorem taxes?
2   How do governments enforce their tax rules and regulations?

3   Describe three types of property that are exempt from taxes.

4   What is a homestead exemption?

5   What are "enterprise zones"?

6   What is the difference between a property tax assessment and an appraisal?

7   What grounds can a taxpayer use to challenge a tax assessment?

8   What is the millage or tax rate?

9   What are some of the factors that tax assessors use to establish the value of property?

10   What is the difference between an assessment and a tax bill?

11   Why would a county only reassess its properties every few years?

12   What are the rules about lien priority when it comes to tax liens?

13   When are governments authorized to auction off property for back taxes?

14   What are some of the ethical concerns with "tax dodges"?

15   Why is it important to know how to research tax issues?

16   Why would someone challenge a tax bill?

17   What are the rules concerning when tax bills are due to be paid?

18   What is the procedure followed in a tax auction?

19   Explain the relationship between purchasing at a tax auction and adverse possession.

20   What is the significance of this chapter's case excerpt?

DISCUSSION QUESTIONS

Every few years there are new proposals to revamp or completely change the tax codes. One such proposal is to eliminate real property taxes entirely and charge a flat tax of 10 percent on all purchases. Part of these taxes would go to the federal, state, and local governments. Can you fashion an argument for and against such a proposal?

PRACTICAL APPLICATIONS

Contact your local tax office and find out how they determine their tax rate. What is the tax rate? What types of properties are exempt in your area? What would the real property taxes be for a nonexempt property that is valued at $100,000? When would these taxes be due?

WEB SITES

Real Property (Ad Valorem) Tax
http://public.findlaw.com/taxes/more-tax-topics/property-tax.html

Georgia Ad Valorem Taxes
https://etax.dor.ga.gov/ptd/county/index.aspx

Florida Millage Rates
http://www.pbcgov.com/papa/millage.htm

Michigan Millage Rates
http://www.michigan.gov/taxes/0,1607,7-238-43715-154015–F,00.html

TERMS AND PHRASES

Ad valorem taxes   Exemption   Millage rate

SIGNIFICANT CASES

Phelan v. Town of Ellicottville, 843 N.Y.S.2d 499 (N.Y. Sup., 2007)
Brown v. Archer, 929 So. 2d 172 (La. App. 4. Cir., 2006)
Pope v. Board of Com'rs of Fulton County, 622 S.E.2d 471 (Ga. App., 2005)
Illinois Health Maintenance Organization Guar. Ass'n v. Shapo, 826 N.E.2d 1135
   (Ill. App., 2005)
Zubke v. Melrose Tp., 731 N.W.2d 918 (S.D., 2007)
Tharp v. Vesta Holdings I, LLC, 625 S.E.2d 46 (Ga. App., 2005)

Glossary

Abandonment   Giving up or surrendering all legal rights.

Acknowledgment   Proof that the person who signed a document is who she claims to be.

Ad valorem taxes   Taxes assessed according to the value of the property.

Adverse possession   An action that can be brought by a person who possesses land owned by another, holds that land openly and against the claims of others, and continues in possession for a minimum period of time, such as 7 years.

Aesthetic zoning   The requirement that all commercial and residential structures in a specified area have the same general appearance.

Agency   A business relationship between a principal (who is the source of the authority for the transaction) and the agent (who has the power to carry it out).

Amortization   The gradual paying down and elimination of a debt through an application of payments toward both principal and interest.

Apartment   A leased residence containing more than five living units sharing a single roof or foundation.

Appurtenant easement   An easement created for an adjoining or servient estate.

Assessment   A payment made above and beyond normal taxes owed for real property.

Attestation   Signing a document.

Beneficiary   A person named in a will that the testator intends to receive an interest in property.

Binder   A preliminary agreement to issue an insurance policy.

Capacity   The requirement that all parties to agreements know and understand the consequences of entering a legally binding contract.

Chain of title   A complete listing of all owners of a particular parcel of real estate for a specified time period.

Closing   Also known as a settlement, the final phase of a real estate transaction at which all deeds are signed and funds are distributed to complete the sale of real property.

Collateral   Any type of asset that is used to secure a loan.

Conditional use permit   An exception to a zoning classification granted by a zoning board, usually to benefit area residents.

Condominium   A form of real property in which the owner has full title to the interior, but not the exterior of the structure.

Consideration   The contractual requirement that both parties incur some form of legal detriment in exchange for receiving something of value; consideration ensures that both parties are bound to the contract.

Constructive eviction   A legal doctrine that holds that leased premises that are unfit for human habitation effectively prevent the tenant from continuing to live there.

Contract   A legally recognized agreement that gives both parties the right to enforce the obligation through legal means.

Dedication   A grant of private land to the government.

Deed   The written instrument that conveys real property interests.

Deed of trust   A type of real estate financing in which a lender and a borrower authorize a third party, the trustee, to act on their behalf in the event of a loan default.

Default   Violation of a contractual duty.

Devise   Transfer property in a will.

Devisee   Another term for beneficiary.

Doctrine of laches   The legal principle that states that a person who fails to assert a legal right loses it

Dower and curtesy   A provision of common law that provided a set portion of the marital property would automatically vest in a surviving spouse; dower refers to the portion allotted to a surviving wife, while curtesy referred to the portion allotted to a surviving husband.

Easement   The right of a person other than the land-owner to use a portion of the owner's land, for example, a driveway or a right of way.

Equitable remedies   The power of a trial court to order a party to undertake specific actions, or to refrain from taking specific actions, such as injunctions and specific performance.

Equity   A person's value in property once he has subtracted the amount owed on the property from its current fair market value.

Escheat   Transfer of title to local government when a person dies without heirs.

Estate   A right to use or enjoy real property.

Estoppel certificate   The borrower's acknowledgment of the total amount borrowed in the mortgage.

Eviction   The legal process of removing a tenant from the leased premises.

Exemption   When an owner is not obligated to pay a specific tax.

Fee simple absolute   The real property estate in which an owner has the right to give, sell, mortgage, and lease the property, among other rights.

Fiduciary   A person who holds a special position of trust and confidence to another.

Fixture   Personal property that has become permanently attached to real property.

Forced share   The statutory claim that a surviving spouse has in the marital estate.

Foreclosure   The right of a lender (mortgagor) to initiate an action to auction off property for outstanding indebtedness in a mortgage or deed of trust.

Fraud   An intentional deception that causes injury to another person.

Grantee   One who receives a real property interest.

Granting clause   A deed clause that demonstrates the grantor's willingness to engage in the transaction.

Grantor   One who conveys a real property interest.

Grantor-grantee index   A listing of all property by the names of individuals who buy and sell it.

Habendum clause   A deed clause that conveys specified rights to the grantee.

Holographic will   A will written entirely in the testator's handwriting.

HUD-1 Settlement Form   A real estate settlement and disbursement form that has been widely adopted by U.S. lenders.

Improvements   Buildings, fences, barns, and other structures that add value to raw land.

In gross easement   An easement that allows someone to enter onto the land; there are no servient estates with in gross easements.

In rem jurisdiction   A court's power to render decisions based on the location of the land within the court's geographic boundaries.

Intestate   The term for a person who dies without a will.

Joint tenancy   A type of concurrent ownership in which two or more individuals own property together, with equal ownership rights and the right of survivorship.

Judicial foreclosure   Foreclosure based on state statutes.

Laches   The legal principle that states that a person who fails to assert a legal right loses it.

Latently ambiguous   A description that appears to be invalid, but refers to a document through which the property can be adequately described.

Landlord   The owner of the premises. The landlord retains all the rights normally associated with ownership except use, possession, and enjoyment.

Lease   The contractual arrangement between a landlord and tenant.

Leasehold estate   The body of rights conveyed to a tenant from the landlord.

Legality   The requirement that a contract must have a legal subject or action as its subject.

License   The right to the products of the land, but not the land itself. A licensee might have the right to enter the premises to harvest, but no right to any other use of the property.

Lien   A monetary claim against property brought by a creditor that may ripen into judgment.

Life estate   An estate granted to a specific person, allowing that person to use, possess, enjoy, and take profits from the real estate, but only as long as the person lives. On the possessor's death, title vests in a remainderman.

Loan package   A set of instructions from a lender about how financial documents should be prepared and distributed at the closing.

Material fact   An important or central fact in the contract or business negotiations that, if fully revealed, would change the outcome of the transaction.

Materialman   A creditor who has provided supplies for the benefit of real property.

Mechanic   A creditor who has provided a service for the benefit of real property.

Merger   The combination of two formerly separate tracts into a single unit.

Millage rate   A tax rate that equates to one dollar per thousand dollars in value.

Mistake A misunderstanding or confusion about a material fact in a contract that is shared by both parties.

Mortgage A contractual agreement in which a borrower transfers specific real property rights to a lender in exchange for the lender's pledge of funds to purchase the real estate.

Mutual assent "Meeting of the minds;" the requirement that the parties to the contract have the same understanding about the contract.

Negligent misrepresentation Liability for a statement that proved to be untrue when the person making the statement had no reasonable belief in its accuracy.

Nonconforming use A structure that violates a zoning classification, but predated the enactment of the zoning rule.

Nuisance A cause of action that is authorized when the defendant's behavior results in a loss of enjoyment or value in the plaintiff's property.

Nuncupative will An oral will, usually only permitted when the testator is in the last stages of life and is unable to draft a written will.

Option A contract between a seller and buyer, whereby the seller agrees not to sell the property to another person for a stated period of time.

Ordinary wear and tear The normal dents and scrapes that occur through daily use.

Parol evidence Oral testimony offered to explain or interpret the provisions of a written document, such as the property description in a deed.

Partition The right of co-tenants to divide up property according to their ownership interests.

Patently ambiguous A description that is invalid on its face.

Personal jurisdiction A court's power to render decisions based on an individual's personal connections and interactions within the court's geographic boundaries.

Policy The contract of insurance between the insurance company and the insured.

Power of Acceptance The legally recognized capacity of a party to accept an offer and create a binding, enforceable contract.

Power of sale foreclosure Foreclosure brought pursuant to a mortgage agreement.

Premium The periodic payment to keep an insurance policy in effect.

Principal The person for whom an agent works.

Private mortgage insurance An insurance policy that protects the lender and pays a specified amount in the event that the borrower defaults on the loan.

Profit 'a prendre (French) The right of a person to enter onto the land owned by another and remove an item or items previously agreed upon.

Promissory note A written document that binds the borrower to pay a specific amount at a specific time.

Proration The distribution of payments based on a person's liability for the debt.

Publication The announcement by a testator to witnesses that he or she has created a will and wishes to have it witnessed.

Pur autre vie (French) "For another's life"; a type of life estate.

Quiet enjoyment The right of a tenant to use the leased premises unmolested.

Remainderman A person with a future interest in property, but no present rights.

Restrictive covenant A condition or restriction on the way that land may be used that is imposed by private individuals.

Right of survivorship The right of a co-tenant to take fee simple title to property on the death of the other co-tenant.

Riparian rights The right to use and draw water for the benefit of real property.

Run with the land A right that transfers with the title to the property.

Seizin (French) Possession of real property.

Self-help eviction The landlord acts without legal process to evict a tenant and instead relies on physical force; no longer permitted in most states, at least for residential leases.

Specific performance A court's order compelling a party to abide by the terms of a contract to which that party was previously in agreement.

Spot zoning A practice that is often ruled unconstitutional where a particular parcel is singled out for special treatment that does not further any of the stated goals of zoning regulations.

Statute of Frauds Originally enacted in England and later adopted in all American states, it is a statute that requires certain types of contracts to be in writing before they can be enforced. Typical contracts covered by the Statute of Frauds include contracts to answer for the debt of another and transactions involving real estate.

Statutory share Synonymous with forced share.

Sublet One tenant rents the leased premises to another tenant.

Tacking The process of updating a previous title search.

Tenancy by entirety A joint tenancy available to married couples.

Tenancy in common   A type of concurrent ownership in which two or more people own property together without the right of survivorship.

Tenancy in partnership   A type of concurrent ownership among business partners, with the right of survivorship.

Tenant   The possessor of certain rights transferred away from the landlord; these rights include use, possession, and enjoyment.

Testate   A person who drafts a valid will before dying.

Title abstract   Forms that summarize important information about title to a particular piece of real estate.

Title examination   The process of reviewing public records to determine whether there are any outstanding claims that will affect the marketability of title to real property.

Title insurance   An insurance policy that protects against legal claims on title to real property.

Townhouse   A form of real property where the owner has title to both the interior and exterior of a structure that resembles an apartment instead of a traditional residence.

Trade fixture   A fixture that is necessary to the operation of a business.

Unimproved land   Raw land that contains no structures.

Variance   An exception to a zoning classification granted by a zoning board.

Warranty of habitability   A legal doctrine that imposes on landlords the implied duty to provide leased premises that are fit for human habitation.

Waste   An action by a life tenant that adversely affects the nature or quality of the remainderman's future interest in real property.

Zoning   The division of land in a local area into separate districts that are regulated by their use and development.

Appendix

COMMERCIAL LEASE

State of Placid

County of Springfield

Commercial Lease

This lease is made and entered into as on the 22nd day of May, 2005, between Smithers Property Management Inc. (hereinafter referred to as landlord) and Simpson Pharmaceuticals, Inc. (hereinafter referred to as tenants).

1. The premises. Landlord leases to tenant, and tenant accents from landlord, the premises (hereinafter referred to as "premises") located in Springfield County, State of placid, and described in the exhibit attached to this lease and marked "exhibit a", which exhibit is hereby incorporated by reference into this lease as if it were fully set out at a separate paragraph.

2. Use of premises. The premises may only be used for retail sales and shall not be used by anyone for any other purposes without the prior written consent of landlord.

3. Term of lease. The term of this lease shall be for a period of three years to commence on January 1, 2005 and to terminate on December 31, 2008. The parties may, at their option, agree, in writing, to an extension of the term and a revised rental during the extended time limit.

4. Amount of rent. Beginning on the commencement date, and set out in paragraph 3, and continuing on from that period of time, tenant shall pay to landlord in monthly rental installments, the amount of $1500. In the second year of the lease term, the base rental will be $1750. In the third year of the lease, the base rental installments shall be $2000. All such rental installments to be due and payable in advance on the first day of each calendar month for and during the term. If any rental is not paid to landlord within five days of the due date, in addition to all other remedies contained in this lease, landlord may assess and tenant shall be obligated to pay, a late charge equivalent to the Greater 5% to amount or $50, whichever is greater. All rental payments are to be mailed to Smithers property management Inc., 1000 Burns Street, Springfield.

5. Assignment or subletting. Tenant shall not have the right to assign the lease or to sublet the premises in whole or in part, without the prior written consent of the landlord.

6. Compliance with statutory law. Tenant shall comply with all legal requirements affecting the premises. Tenant shall neither create nor permit the creation of any nuisance upon, in or about the premises, and tenant shall cause all trash, refuse and garbage to be removed from the premises in a timely manner.

7. Insurance. Tenant shall obtain, at tenant's own costs, fire and other hazard insurance sufficient to cover all equipment, trade fixtures, and inventory. The cost of paying premiums for all tenants insurance shall fall on the tenants.

8. Utilities. Tenant shall pay for all electricity, gas, heat, water and other utilities consumed or use on the premises. Landlord shall not be in any way obligated or responsible for the failure to furnish utilities services, and the lack thereof shall not constitute constructive eviction.

9. Taxes and assessments. Landlord shall timely list the premises for taxes and pay all tax assessments all of whatever kind or nature assessed against the premises, splitting any tax assessed against leasehold improvements, sales taxes, inventory taxes, or other taxes related to the administration called a retail establishment.

10. Alterations, changes and/or improvements to premises. Tenant shall not make, and shall not have the right to make, any alterations, changes and/or improvements to the premises without the prior written consent of the landlord.

11. Repairs. Except as otherwise stated, landlord shall, at landlord's own expense, he and maintain, in a good and workmanlike manner, the entire premises in good maintenance, replacement and repair. Tenant shall allow no liens to attach to the premises or to tenant's interest therein. The roof, structural members and outside walls (not including in grants and eagerness doors, windows and our plate glass are the responsibility of the tenant) all the premises shall be performed within a reasonable time after notice from tenants in any such repairs are needed.

12. Safe and sanitary condition. Tenant shall not permit, allow our cause any act or deed to be performed in, or about the premises, which shall cause or be likely to cause injury to any person.

13. Fire or casualty. If the premises shall be partially or completely damaged or destroyed by fire or other casualty, landlord shall have the right to terminate this lease agreement. If said option to terminate is not exercised by landlord, landlord shall, as soon as reasonably possible, make all required repairs and reconstruction necessary to bring premises back to substantially the same condition as they were prior to the damage or destruction. No rental payments shall be two during this time.

14. Condemnation. If the entire premises are taken or condemned for a public use, then this lease shall terminate at the instant in which title to the premises shifts from the landlord to a governmental entity.

15. Inspection. Landlord shall have the right to inspect the premises at all reasonable times and to enter the premises in order to effect an inspection.

16. Condition of premises upon termination of lease. Upon the termination of this lease agreement, tenant shall return the premises to the landlord in substantially the same condition as received, except for ordinary wear and tear.

17. Security deposit. Tenant shall deliver to landlord is some of $1500 to serve as a further assurance of the tenant's performance under the provisions of this lease. As long as tenant complies with the terms of this lease, the security deposit will be returned to the tenant within 30 days of the termination of lease agreement. If the tenant reaches any condition of this lease, landlord is entitled to retain such deposit.

This the _____ day of _____ , 2005.

_____   _____

Smithers Property Mgt. Inc.   Simpson Pharmaceuticals, Inc.

AFFIDAVIT REGARDING LIENS

I hereby certify that as of the 22nd day of May, 2005, there are no outstanding or unpaid subcontractor bills, statements or remittances for work performed on the construction of a residential unit on 123 Maple Street, Anytown, County of Springfield, State of Placid.

_____

Carl Contractor, General Subcontractor
Moe's Contracting Service, Inc.

CERTIFICATION OF INSURANCE COVERAGE

Name of insured: _____

Insured address: _____

Hazard Insurance

Policy number: _____ policy period: (from)

_____ (to) _____

Insurance amount: $_____ premium: $_____

Insurance company: _____

Insurance agent: _____

Agent's address: _____

Insurance type: homeowners insurance

    Insurance cover full replacement cost? Yes.

Flood Insurance

Policy number: _____ policy period: (from)

_____ (to) _____

Insurance amount: $_____ premium: $_____

Insurance company: _____

Insurance agent: _____

Agent's address: _____

Closing Agent's Certification

    At the time of the settlement of the above-described premises, I/we have reviewed evidence showing that the mortgagors have obtained fire and extended hazard insurance coverage on the subject property as required by statute.

_____   _____

Signature   Date

ESCROW WITHHOLDING AGREEMENT

State of Placid

Springfield County

Escrow Withholding Agreement

We, the sellers of the property located at _____ , do hereby authorize attorney Clarence Arrow to escrow the judgment amount and interest to _____ , (deed book reference) through June 25, 2005.

We understand that we have 60 days from today to produce a cancellation of this judgment to attorney Clarence Arrow, at which time we will be reimbursed for any difference between the deposit and the difference in the escrow amount, or we can authorize attorney Clarence Arrow to disperse payment to First National Bank at any time within this 60 day time period. Attorney Clarence Arrow will return any portion exceeding the payoff amount to us.

In the event that said judgment has not been canceled, we hereby authorize attorney Clarence Arrow to disperse this escrow amount to First National Bank on July 25, 2005.

This the 22nd day of May, 2005.

_____

Seller

_____

Seller

GOOD FAITH ESTIMATE

The information provided below reflects estimates of the charges which you are likely to incur at the settlement of your loan. The fees listed are estimates – the actual charges may be more or less. Your transaction may not involve a fee for every item listed. The numbers listed beside the estimates generally correspond to the numbered lines contained in the HUD-1 or HUD-1A settlement statement which you will be receiving at settlement. The HUD-1 or HUD-1A settlement statement will show you the actual cost for items paid at settlement.

Items Payable In Connection with Loan				Amount or Range
	801.	Loan Origination Fee (%)		$
	802.	Loan Discount Fee (%)		$
	803.	Appraisal		$ 275.00
	804.	Credit Report		$ 25.00
	805.	Inspection Fee		$
	806.	Mortgage Insurance Application Fee		$
	807.	Mortgage Broker Fee		$
	808.	Flood Cert		$ 25.00
	809.			$
Items Required by Lender to be Paid in Advance	901.	Interest @ $ per day for days		$
	902.	Mortgage Insurance Premium		$
	903.	Hazard Insurance Premium		$
	904.			$
Reserves Deposited with Lender	1001.	Hazard Insurance (months coverage)		$
	1002.	Mortgage Insurance (months coverage)		$
	1003.	City Property Taxes		$
	1004.	County Property Taxes		$
	1005.	Annual Assessments		$
	1006.			$
Title Charges	1101.	Settlement or Closing Fee		$
	1102.	Abstract or Title Search Fee		$
	1103.	Title Examination Fee		$
	1104.	Title Insurance Binder Fee		$
	1105.	Document Preparation Fee		$
	1106.	Notary Fees		$
	1107.	Attorneys Fees		$ 500.00 – 700.0
	1108.	Title Insurance		$
	1111.			$
Government Recording and Transfer Charges	1201.	Recording Fees		$
	1202.	City/County Tax/Stamps		$
	1203.	State Tax/Stamps		$
	1204.			$
Additional Settlement Charges	1301.	Survey		$
	1302.	Pest Inspection		$
	1303.	Architectural/Engineering Services		$
	1304.	Building Permit		$
	1305.			$
	1400.	TOTAL AMOUNT/RANGE OF ESTIMATED CHARGES		$ 825.00 – 1025.

P.O.C. Paid Outside Closing

These estimates are provided pursuant to the Real Estate Settlement Procedures Act of 1974, as amended (RESPA). If you are using the loan proceeds to purchase a dwelling, additional information can be found in the HUD Special Information Booklet titled *Buying Your Home: Settlement Costs and Helpful Information*, which is to be provided to you by your mortgage broker or lender.

REQUIRED PROVIDER (If Applicable Check the Appropriate Box)

We will require you to use a particular provider for the settlement services marked above with an asterisk (•). The estimate of charges is based on the costs charged by these providers.

☐ The name, address and telephone number and a description of our business relationship with that provider, if any, is attached.

☐ We will require you to use a provider from a list we maintain. We will provide the name of the specific provider and the actual cost at closing.

X _____   X _____

APPLICANT SIGNATURE   DATE   CO-APPLICANT SIGNATURE   DATE

DATE SENT   AUTHORIZED OFFICIAL   EST775 6849LL

HUD SETTLEMENT STATEMENT

A. Settlement Statement

U.S. Department of Housing
and Urban Development

OMB Approval No. 2502-0265
(expires 9/30/2006)

B. Type of Loan

1. ☐ FHA	2. ☐ FmHA	3. ☐ Conv. Unins.
4. ☐ VA	5. ☐ Conv. Ins.	

6. File Number:	7. Loan Number:	8. Mortgage Insurance Case Number:

C. Note: This form is furnished to give you a statement of actual settlement costs. Amounts paid to and by the settlement agent are shown. Items marked "(p.o.c.)" were paid outside the closing; they are shown here for informational purposes and are not included in the totals.

D. Name & Address of Borrower:	E. Name & Address of Seller:	F. Name & Address of Lender:

G. Property Location:	H. Settlement Agent:
	Place of Settlement: I. Settlement Date:

J. Summary of Borrower's Transaction		K. Summary of Seller's Transaction	
100. Gross Amount Due From Borrower		**400. Gross Amount Due To Seller**	
101. Contract sales price		401. Contract sales price	
102. Personal property		402. Personal property	
103. Settlement charges to borrower (line 1400)		403.	
104.		404.	
105.		405.	
Adjustments for items paid by seller in advance		**Adjustments for items paid by seller in advance**	
106. City/town taxes to		406. City/town taxes to	
107. County taxes to		407. County taxes to	
108. Assessments to		408. Assessments to	
109.		409.	
110.		410.	
111.		411.	
112.		412.	
120. Gross Amount Due From Borrower		**420. Gross Amount Due To Seller**	
200. Amounts Paid By Or In Behalf Of Borrower		**500. Reductions In Amount Due To Seller**	
201. Deposit or earnest money		501. Excess deposit (see instructions)	
202. Principal amount of new loan(s)		502. Settlement charges to seller (line 1400)	
203. Existing loan(s) taken subject to		503. Existing loan(s) taken subject to	
204.		504. Payoff of first mortgage loan	
205.		505. Payoff of second mortgage loan	
206.		506.	
207.		507.	
208.		508.	
209.		509.	
Adjustments for items unpaid by seller		**Adjustments for items unpaid by seller**	
210. City/town taxes to		510. City/town taxes to	
211. County taxes to		511. County taxes to	
212. Assessments to		512. Assessments to	
213.		513.	
214.		514.	
215.		515.	
216.		516.	
217.		517.	
218.		518.	
219.		519.	
220. Total Paid By/For Borrower		**520. Total Reduction Amount Due Seller**	
300. Cash At Settlement From/To Borrower		**600. Cash At Settlement To/From Seller**	
301. Gross Amount due from borrower (line 120)		601. Gross amount due to seller (line 420)	
302. Less amounts paid by/for borrower (line 220)	(	602. Less reductions in amt. due seller (line 520)	( )
303. Cash ☐ From ☐ To Borrower		**603. Cash** ☐ To ☐ From Seller	

Section 5 of the Real Estate Settlement Procedures Act (RESPA) requires the following: • HUD must develop a Special Information Booklet to help persons borrowing money to finance the purchase of residential real estate to better understand the nature and costs of real estate settlement services; • Each lender must provide the booklet to all applicants from whom it receives or for whom it prepares a written application to borrow money to finance the purchase of residential real estate; • Lenders must prepare and distribute with the Booklet a Good Faith Estimate of the settlement costs that the borrower is likely to incur in connection with the settlement. These disclosures are mandatory.

Section 4(a) of RESPA mandates that HUD develop and prescribe this standard form to be used at the time of loan settlement to provide full disclosure of all charges imposed upon the borrower and seller. These are third party disclosures that are designed to provide the borrower with pertinent information during the settlement process in order to be a better shopper.

The Public Reporting Burden for this collection of information is estimated to average one hour per response, including the time for reviewing instructions, searching existing data sources, gathering and maintaining the data needed, and completing and reviewing the collection of information.

This agency may not collect this information, and you are not required to complete this form, unless it displays a currently valid OMB control number.

The information requested does not lend itself to confidentiality.

L. Settlement Charges

700. Total Sales/Broker's Commission based on price $ @ % =		Paid From Borrowers Funds at Settlement	Paid From Seller's Funds at Settlement
Division of Commission (line 700) as follows:			
701. $ to			
702. $ to			
703. Commission paid at Settlement			
704.			
800. Items Payable In Connection With Loan			
801. Loan Origination Fee %			
802. Loan Discount %			
803. Appraisal Fee to			
804. Credit Report to			
805. Lender's Inspection Fee			
806. Mortgage Insurance Application Fee to			
807. Assumption Fee			
808.			
809.			
810.			
811.			
900. Items Required By Lender To Be Paid In Advance			
901. Interest from to @$ /day			
902. Mortgage Insurance Premium for months to			
903. Hazard Insurance Premium for years to			
904. years to			
905.			
1000. Reserves Deposited With Lender			
1001. Hazard insurance months @ $ per month			
1002. Mortgage insurance months @ $ per month			
1003. City property taxes months @ $ per month			
1004. County property taxes months @ $ per month			
1005. Annual assessments months @ $ per month			
1006. months @ $ per month			
1007. months @ $ per month			
1008. months @ $ per month			
1100. Title Charges			
1101. Settlement or closing fee to			
1102. Abstract or title search to			
1103. Title examination to			
1104. Title insurance binder to			
1105. Document preparation to			
1106. Notary fees to			
1107. Attorney's fees to			
(includes above items numbers:)			
1108. Title insurance to			
(includes above items numbers:)			
1109. Lender's coverage $			
1110. Owner's coverage $			
1111.			
1112.			
1113.			
1200. Government Recording and Transfer Charges			
1201. Recording fees: Deed $; Mortgage $; Releases $			
1202. City/county tax/stamps: Deed $; Mortgage $			
1203. State tax/stamps: Deed $; Mortgage $			
1204.			
1205.			
1300. Additional Settlement Charges			
1301. Survey to			
1302. Pest inspection to			
1303.			
1304.			
1305.			
1400. Total Settlement Charges (enter on lines 103, Section J and 502, Section K)			

LOAN SPECIFIC CLOSING INSTRUCTIONS

First National Bank of Springfield

Mortgage Loan Department

To: Closing Attorney
Date: May 22, 2005
Address: 123 Main St., Anytown, USA 003300
Loan Specific Closing Instructions

These loan specific closing instructions are in addition to the enclosed Uniform General Closing Instructions. Under no circumstances should you close this loan without further authorization from the Springfield Mortgage Loan Department. You should not close this loan without authorization if restrictive covenants of record are violated, or there are other encumbrances, including easements or encroachments on the property, or liens of record.

You are instructed to close the loan and disburse our enclosed check only after you have secured and/or complied with all items on both the Uniform General and Loan Specific Closing Instructions, and are prepared to file your final certificate for title policy.

This is an escrow account and requires notification of such to the insurance company in addition to standard provisions outlined in the Uniform General Instructions.

We expect this loan to close on June 22, 2005. Please contact our office for new closing instructions and/or to correct data for forms completion if the loan does not disburse on this date.

Borrowers	Account number	Age
1. _____	_____	_____
Borrowers	Account number	Age
2. _____	_____	_____

Borrowers contact information:

_____

Home telephone

_____

Work telephone

If the borrower is married and the spouse is not named as an additional borrower, then, because of the marital interest in the subject property, the spouse's name and signature will be required on the security instrument, the writer to the Security Instrument and the Truth in Lending disclosure forms to protect our liens on the property. The spouse must also sign the Notice of Right to Cancel if the loan is subject to a rescission.

All borrowers' names must appear on the deed.

Title company to be used: Springfield Title Guaranty Company. Written approval must be obtained from the lender prior to changing title companies.

NOTICE CONCERNING PRIVATE
MORTGAGE INSURANCE

Notice concerning Private Mortgage Insurance — Initial
Disclosure — Fixed Rate Mortgages

Borrower names: _____   Lender: _____

Mortgage loan number: _____

Property address: _____

_____

_____

Date: May 22, 2005

You are obtaining a mortgage loan that requires Private mortgage insurance ("PMI"). PMI protects lenders and others against financial loss when borrowers default. Charges for the insurance are added to your loan payments. Under certain circumstances, federal law gives you the right to cancel PMI or requires that PMI automatically terminate. This disclosure describes wind cancellation and termination may occur. Please note that PMI is not the same as property/casualty insurance, such as homeowners' or flood insurance, which protects you against damage to your property. Cancellation or termination of PMI does not affect any obligation you may have to maintain other types of insurance under your mortgage agreement.

In this disclosure, "loan" means a mortgage loan you are obtaining. "You" means the original borrower, successors or assigns. "Property" means the property that is used to secure the mortgage loan.

Amortization Schedule

An amortization schedule showing the principal and interest due under the loan, along with the balance remaining after each scheduled payment is attached for your reference.

Borrower Request to Cancel PMI

You have the right to request that PMI be canceled on or after the following dates:

1. The date of the principal balance of your loan is first scheduled to reach 80% of the original value of the property. This date is January 10, 2015. For balloon months, if applicable, this date will not be reached before the loan matures.
2. The date the principal balance actually reaches 80% of the original value of the property.

"Original value" means the lesser of contract sales price of the property or the appraised value of the property at the time the loan was closed. PMI will only be canceled at all of the following conditions are met:

1. You submit a written request for cancellation;

2. You have a good payment history; and

3. We receive, if requested and at your expense, evidence satisfactory to the holder of your loan that the value of the property has not declined below its original value, and additional certification that there are no subordinate liens on your property.

"Good payment history" means no payments 60 or more days past due within two years and no payments 30 or more days past due within one year of the cancellation date.

Automatic Termination of PMI

If you are current on your loan payments, PMI will automatically terminate on the date the principal balance of your loan is first scheduled to reach 78% of the original value of the property. This date is November 30, 2014.

Exceptions to Cancellation and Automatic Termination

The cancellation and automatic termination requirements described may not apply to certain loans that may present a higher risk of default. Your loan, however, does not fall into this category. As a result, the cancellation and automatic termination provisions described above do apply to your loan.

I/we have received a copy of this disclosure.

_____   _____

Borrower   Date

NOTICE OF RIGHT TO CANCEL

You are entering into a transaction that will result in a lien on your home. You have a legal right under federal law to cancel this transaction, without cost, within **three business days** from which ever on the following events occurs last:

1. The date of the transaction, which is May 22, 2005; or
2. The date you received your Truth in Lending disclosures; or
3. The date you received this notice of the right to cancel.

If you cancel the transaction, the lien is also canceled. Within **20 calendar days** after we receive your notice, we must take the steps necessary to reflect the fact that the lien on your home has been canceled, and we must return to you any money or property given by you or anyone else in connection with this transaction.

You may keep any money or property we have given you until we have done the tasks mentioned above, but you must then offer to return the money or property. If it is impractical or unfair for you to return the property, you must offer its reasonable value instead. You may offer to return the property at your home or the location of the property. Money must be returned to the address below. If we do not take possession of the money or property within 20 calendar days of your offer, you may keep it without further obligation.

If you decide to cancel this transaction, you may do so by notifying us in writing at:

(Lender's address)

You may use any written statement that is signed and dated by you and state your intention to cancel and/or you may use this notice by dating and signing below. Keep one copy of this notice because it contains important information about your rights.

If you cancel by mail or telegram, you must send notice no later than midnight of _____ (or midnight of the **Third Business Day** following the latest of the three events listed above. If you send or deliver your written notice to cancel some other way, it must be delivered to the above address no later than that time period.

I Wish to Cancel

Signature   Date
_____   _____

The undersigned each acknowledges receipt of two copies of Notice of Right to Cancel and one copy of the Federal Truth in Lending disclosures statement, all given by lender in compliance with the Lending Simplification and Reform Act of 1980 (Public Law 96–221).

Each borrower in this transaction has the right to cancel. The exercise of this right by one borrower shall be effective to all borrowers.

_____   _____
Borrower   Date

_____   _____
Borrower   Date

_____   _____
Borrower   Date

PAYOFF TRANSMITTAL

To: _____

Date: May 22, 2005

From: Law offices of Clarence Arrow

Re: Payoff all existing mortgage, mortgage number 11- 2348.

Please find enclosed a check for $_____ , in full payment and complete satisfaction of the outstanding mortgage listed above. This payoff amount is based on information provided by you.

Please apply these funds to the outstanding mortgage and cancel or release this mortgage found in deed book 496, page 23 of the Barnes County Registry.

Thank you for your attention to this matter. If you should have any questions about this payoff, please do not hesitate to contact our firm.

Sincerely,

Clarence Arrow

COMMITMENT FOR TITLE INSURANCE

Issued by Springfield Title Guaranty Company

Springfield Title Guaranty Company, hereinafter referred to as "the Company," for valuable consideration, in hand received, hereby commits to issue its policy of title insurance, as identified in Schedule A, for the benefit of the insured identified in that schedule, as owner or mortgagee of the estate or interest hereby in the land described or referred to in Schedule A, upon payment of the required premium and other charges, all subject to the provisions contained in Schedules A and B and to the conditions and stipulations hereafter described.

This commitment shall become effective on the date identified in the attached policy and the amount of the policy commitment inserted in Schedule A by the Company, and supplemented by additional riders or subsequent endorsements.

This commitment is preliminary to the issuance of such policy of title insurance and all liabilities and obligations set out shall cease and terminate six months after the effective date hereof or when the policy or policies committed for shall issue, which ever occurs first, provided that the failure to issue such policy is not the fault of the Company.

Signed under seal for the Company, but this insurance policy shall not be valid or binding until it bears an authorized countersignature.

In witness whereof, Springfield Title Guaranty Company has caused its corporate name and seal to be affixed by its duly authorized officers on the date shown in Schedule A.

_____   _____

Chairman of the Board   Corporate president

Countersigned by:

_____

Authorized Signatory
Springfield title guaranty Company
City of Springfield, Placid

UNIFORM RESIDENTIAL APPRAISAL REPORT

The purpose of this summary appraisal report is to provide the lender/client with an accurate, and adequately supported, opinion of the market value of the subject property.

Property Address	City	State	Zip Code
Borrower	Owner of Public Record	County	
Legal Description			

Assessor's Parcel #	Tax Year	R.E. Taxes $
Neighborhood Name	Map Reference	Census Tract

Occupant ☐ Owner ☐ Tenant ☐ Vacant   Special Assessments $ ☐ PUD   HOA $ ☐ per year ☐ per month

Property Rights Appraised ☐ Fee Simple ☐ Leasehold ☐ Other (describe)

Assignment Type ☐ Purchase Transaction ☐ Refinance Transaction ☐ Other (describe)

Lender/Client   Address

Is the subject property currently offered for sale or has it been offered for sale in the twelve months prior to the effective date of this appraisal? ☐ Yes ☐ No

Report data source(s) used, offering price(s), and date(s).

I ☐ did ☐ did not analyze the contract for sale for the subject purchase transaction. Explain the results of the analysis of the contract for sale or why the analysis was not performed.

Contract Price $ Date of Contract   Is the property seller the owner of public record? ☐ Yes ☐ No Data Source(s)

Is there any financial assistance (loan charges, sale concessions, gift or downpayment assistance, etc.) to be paid by any party on behalf of the borrower? ☐ Yes ☐ No

If Yes, report the total dollar amount and describe the items to be paid.

Note: Race and the racial composition of the neighborhood are not appraisal factors.

Neighborhood Characteristics	One-Unit Housing Trends	One-Unit Housing	Present Land Use %
Location ☐ Urban ☐ Suburban ☐ Rural	Property Values ☐ Increasing ☐ Stable ☐ Declining	PRICE AGE	One-Unit %
Built-Up ☐ Over 75% ☐ 25-75% ☐ Under 25%	Demand/Supply ☐ Shortage ☐ In Balance ☐ Over Supply	$ (000) (yrs)	2-4 Unit %
Growth ☐ Rapid ☐ Stable ☐ Slow	Marketing Time ☐ Under 3 mths ☐ 3-6 mths ☐ Over 6 mths	Low	Multi-Family %
Neighborhood Boundaries		High	Commercial %
		Pred.	Other %

Neighborhood Description

Market Conditions (including support for the above conclusions)

Dimensions	Area	Shape	View

Specific Zoning Classification   Zoning Description

Zoning Compliance ☐ Legal ☐ Legal Nonconforming (Grandfathered Use) ☐ No Zoning ☐ Illegal (describe)

Is the highest and best use of the subject property as improved (or as proposed per plans and specifications) the present use? ☐ Yes ☐ No If No, describe

Utilities	Public	Other (describe)		Public	Other (describe)	Off-site Improvements—Type	Public	Private
Electricity	☐	☐	Water	☐	☐	Street	☐	☐
Gas	☐	☐	Sanitary Sewer	☐	☐	Alley	☐	☐

FEMA Special Flood Hazard Area ☐ Yes ☐ No FEMA Flood Zone   FEMA Map #   FEMA Map Date

Are the utilities and off-site improvements typical for the market area? ☐ Yes ☐ No If No, describe

Are there any adverse site conditions or external factors (easements, encroachments, environmental conditions, land uses, etc.)? ☐ Yes ☐ No If Yes, describe

General Description	Foundation	Exterior Description materials/condition	Interior materials/condition
Units ☐ One ☐ One with Accessory Unit	☐ Concrete Slab ☐ Crawl Space	Foundation Walls	Floors
# of Stories	☐ Full Basement ☐ Partial Basement	Exterior Walls	Walls
Type ☐ Det. ☐ Att. ☐ S-Det./End Unit	Basement Area sq. ft.	Roof Surface	Trim/Finish
☐ Existing ☐ Proposed ☐ Under Const.	Basement Finish %	Gutters & Downspouts	Bath Floor
Design (Style)	☐ Outside Entry/Exit ☐ Sump Pump	Window Type	Bath Wainscot
Year Built	Evidence of ☐ Infestation	Storm Sash/Insulated	Car Storage ☐ None
Effective Age (Yrs)	☐ Dampness ☐ Settlement	Screens	☐ Driveway # of Cars
Attic ☐ None	Heating ☐ FWA ☐ HWBB ☐ Radiant	Amenities ☐ Woodstove(s) #	Driveway Surface
☐ Drop Stair ☐ Stairs	☐ Other Fuel	☐ Fireplace(s) # ☐ Fence	☐ Garage # of Cars
☐ Floor ☐ Scuttle	Cooling ☐ Central Air Conditioning	☐ Patio/Deck ☐ Porch	☐ Carport # of Cars
☐ Finished ☐ Heated	☐ Individual ☐ Other	☐ Pool ☐ Other	☐ Att. ☐ Det. ☐ Built-in

Appliances ☐ Refrigerator ☐ Range/Oven ☐ Dishwasher ☐ Disposal ☐ Microwave ☐ Washer/Dryer ☐ Other (describe)

Finished area **above** grade contains: Rooms Bedrooms Bath(s) Square Feet of Gross Living Area Above Grade

Additional features (special energy efficient items, etc.)

Describe the condition of the property (including needed repairs, deterioration, renovations, remodeling, etc.)

Are there any physical deficiencies or adverse conditions that affect the livability, soundness, or structural integrity of the property? ☐ Yes ☐ No If Yes, describe

Does the property generally conform to the neighborhood (functional utility, style, condition, use, construction, etc.)? ☐ Yes ☐ No If No, describe

Uniform Residential Appraisal Report

File #

| There are | comparable properties currently offered for sale in the subject neighborhood ranging in price from $ | | to $ |
| There are | comparable sales in the subject neighborhood within the past twelve months ranging in sale price from $ | | to $ |

FEATURE	SUBJECT	COMPARABLE SALE # 1		COMPARABLE SALE # 2		COMPARABLE SALE # 3	
Address							
Proximity to Subject							
Sale Price	$		$		$		$
Sale Price/Gross Liv. Area	$ sq. ft.	$ sq. ft.		$ sq. ft.		$ sq. ft.	
Data Source(s)							
Verification Source(s)							
VALUE ADJUSTMENTS	DESCRIPTION	DESCRIPTION	+(-) $ Adjustment	DESCRIPTION	+(-) $ Adjustment	DESCRIPTION	+(-) $ Adjustment
Sale or Financing Concessions							
Date of Sale/Time							
Location							
Leasehold/Fee Simple							
Site							
View							
Design (Style)							
Quality of Construction							
Actual Age							
Condition							
Above Grade	Total Bdrms. Baths	Total Bdrms. Baths		Total Bdrms. Baths		Total Bdrms. Baths	
Room Count							
Gross Living Area	sq. ft.	sq. ft.		sq. ft.		sq. ft.	
Basement & Finished Rooms Below Grade							
Functional Utility							
Heating/Cooling							
Energy Efficient Items							
Garage/Carport							
Porch/Patio/Deck							
Net Adjustment (Total)		☐ + ☐ -	$	☐ + ☐ -	$	☐ + ☐ -	$
Adjusted Sale Price of Comparables		Net Adj. % Gross Adj. %	$	Net Adj. % Gross Adj. %	$	Net Adj. % Gross Adj. %	$

I ☐ did ☐ did not research the sale or transfer history of the subject property and comparable sales. If not, explain

My research ☐ did ☐ did not reveal any prior sales or transfers of the subject property for the three years prior to the effective date of this appraisal.

Data source(s)

My research ☐ did ☐ did not reveal any prior sales or transfers of the comparable sales for the year prior to the date of sale of the comparable sale.

Data source(s)

Report the results of the research and analysis of the prior sale or transfer history of the subject property and comparable sales (report additional prior sales on page 3).

ITEM	SUBJECT	COMPARABLE SALE # 1	COMPARABLE SALE # 2	COMPARABLE SALE # 3
Date of Prior Sale/Transfer				
Price of Prior Sale/Transfer				
Data Source(s)				
Effective Date of Data Source(s)				

Analysis of prior sale or transfer history of the subject property and comparable sales

Summary of Sales Comparison Approach

Indicated Value by Sales Comparison Approach $

Indicated Value by: Sales Comparison Approach $ Cost Approach (if developed) $ Income Approach (if developed) $

This appraisal is made ☐ "as is", ☐ subject to completion per plans and specifications on the basis of a hypothetical condition that the improvements have been completed, ☐ subject to the following repairs or alterations on the basis of a hypothetical condition that the repairs or alterations have been completed, or ☐ subject to the following required inspection based on the extraordinary assumption that the condition or deficiency does not require alteration or repair:

Based on a complete visual inspection of the interior and exterior areas of the subject property, defined scope of work, statement of assumptions and limiting conditions, and appraiser's certification, my (our) opinion of the market value, as defined, of the real property that is the subject of this report is $, as of   , which is the date of inspection and the effective date of this appraisal.

Uniform Residential Appraisal Report

File #

ADDITIONAL COMMENTS

COST APPROACH TO VALUE (not required by Fannie Mae)

Provide adequate information for the lender/client to replicate the below cost figures and calculations.

Support for the opinion of site value (summary of comparable land sales or other methods for estimating site value)

ESTIMATED ☐ REPRODUCTION OR ☐ REPLACEMENT COST NEW	OPINION OF SITE VALUE		= $
Source of cost data	Dwelling	Sq. Ft. @ $	=$
Quality rating from cost service Effective date of cost data		Sq. Ft. @ $	=$
Comments on Cost Approach (gross living area calculations, depreciation, etc.)			
	Garage/Carport	Sq. Ft. @ $	=$
	Total Estimate of Cost-New		= $
	Less Physical Functional External		
	Depreciation		=$( )
	Depreciated Cost of Improvements		=$
	"As-is" Value of Site Improvements		=$
Estimated Remaining Economic Life (HUD and VA only) Years	Indicated Value By Cost Approach		=$

INCOME APPROACH TO VALUE (not required by Fannie Mae)

Estimated Monthly Market Rent $ X Gross Rent Multiplier   = $ Indicated Value by Income Approach

Summary of Income Approach (including support for market rent and GRM)

PROJECT INFORMATION FOR PUDs (if applicable)

Is the developer/builder in control of the Homeowners' Association (HOA)? ☐ Yes ☐ No   Unit type(s) ☐ Detached ☐ Attached

Provide the following information for PUDs ONLY if the developer/builder is in control of the HOA and the subject property is an attached dwelling unit.

Legal name of project

Total number of phases   Total number of units   Total number of units sold

Total number of units rented   Total number of units for sale   Data source(s)

Was the project created by the conversion of an existing building(s) into a PUD? ☐ Yes ☐ No If Yes, date of conversion

Does the project contain any multi-dwelling units? ☐ Yes ☐ No Data source(s)

Are the units, common elements, and recreation facilities complete? ☐ Yes ☐ No If No, describe the status of completion.

Are the common elements leased to or by the Homeowners' Association? ☐ Yes ☐ No If Yes, describe the rental terms and options.

Describe common elements and recreational facilities

Uniform Residential Appraisal Report   File

This report form is designed to report an appraisal of a one-unit property or a one-unit property with an accessory unit; including a unit in a planned unit development (PUD). This report form is not designed to report an appraisal of a manufactured home or a unit in a condominium or cooperative project.

This appraisal report is subject to the following scope of work, intended use, intended user, definition of market value, statement of assumptions and limiting conditions, and certifications. Modifications, additions, or deletions to the intended use, intended user, definition of market value, or assumptions and limiting conditions are not permitted. The appraiser may expand the scope of work to include any additional research or analysis necessary based on the complexity of this appraisal assignment. Modifications or deletions to the certifications are also not permitted. However, additional certifications that do not constitute material alterations to this appraisal report, such as those required by law or those related to the appraiser's continuing education or membership in an appraisal organization, are permitted.

SCOPE OF WORK: The scope of work for this appraisal is defined by the complexity of this appraisal assignment and the reporting requirements of this appraisal report form, including the following definition of market value, statement of assumptions and limiting conditions, and certifications. The appraiser must, at a minimum: (1) perform a complete visual inspection of the interior and exterior areas of the subject property, (2) inspect the neighborhood, (3) inspect each of the comparable sales from at least the street, (4) research, verify, and analyze data from reliable public and/or private sources, and (5) report his or her analysis, opinions, and conclusions in this appraisal report.

INTENDED USE: The intended use of this appraisal report is for the lender/client to evaluate the property that is the subject of this appraisal for a mortgage finance transaction.

INTENDED USER: The intended user of this appraisal report is the lender/client.

DEFINITION OF MARKET VALUE: The most probable price which a property should bring in a competitive and open market under all conditions requisite to a fair sale, the buyer and seller, each acting prudently, knowledgeably and assuming the price is not affected by undue stimulus. Implicit in this definition is the consummation of a sale as of a specified date and the passing of title from seller to buyer under conditions whereby: (1) buyer and seller are typically motivated; (2) both parties are well informed or well advised, and each acting in what he or she considers his or her own best interest; (3) a reasonable time is allowed for exposure in the open market; (4) payment is made in terms of cash in U. S. dollars or in terms of financial arrangements comparable thereto; and (5) the price represents the normal consideration for the property sold unaffected by special or creative financing or sales concessions* granted by anyone associated with the sale.

*Adjustments to the comparables must be made for special or creative financing or sales concessions. No adjustments are necessary for those costs which are normally paid by sellers as a result of tradition or law in a market area; these costs are readily identifiable since the seller pays these costs in virtually all sales transactions. Special or creative financing adjustments can be made to the comparable property by comparisons to financing terms offered by a third party institutional lender that is not already involved in the property or transaction. Any adjustment should not be calculated on a mechanical dollar for dollar cost of the financing or concession but the dollar amount of any adjustment should approximate the market's reaction to the financing or concessions based on the appraiser's judgment.

STATEMENT OF ASSUMPTIONS AND LIMITING CONDITIONS: The appraiser's certification in this report is subject to the following assumptions and limiting conditions:

1. The appraiser will not be responsible for matters of a legal nature that affect either the property being appraised or the title to it, except for information that he or she became aware of during the research involved in performing this appraisal. The appraiser assumes that the title is good and marketable and will not render any opinions about the title.

2. The appraiser has provided a sketch in this appraisal report to show the approximate dimensions of the improvements. The sketch is included only to assist the reader in visualizing the property and understanding the appraiser's determination of its size.

3. The appraiser has examined the available flood maps that are provided by the Federal Emergency Management Agency (or other data sources) and has noted in this appraisal report whether any portion of the subject site is located in an identified Special Flood Hazard Area. Because the appraiser is not a surveyor, he or she makes no guarantees, express or implied, regarding this determination.

4. The appraiser will not give testimony or appear in court because he or she made an appraisal of the property in question, unless specific arrangements to do so have been made beforehand, or as otherwise required by law.

5. The appraiser has noted in this appraisal report any adverse conditions (such as needed repairs, deterioration, the presence of hazardous wastes, toxic substances, etc.) observed during the inspection of the subject property or that he or she became aware of during the research involved in performing this appraisal. Unless otherwise stated in this appraisal report, the appraiser has no knowledge of any hidden or unapparent physical deficiencies or adverse conditions of the property (such as, but not limited to, needed repairs, deterioration, the presence of hazardous wastes, toxic substances, adverse environmental conditions, etc.) that would make the property less valuable, and has assumed that there are no such conditions and makes no guarantees or warranties, express or implied. The appraiser will not be responsible for any such conditions that do exist or for any engineering or testing that might be required to discover whether such conditions exist. Because the appraiser is not an expert in the field of environmental hazards, this appraisal report must not be considered as an environmental assessment of the property.

6. The appraiser has based his or her appraisal report and valuation conclusion for an appraisal that is subject to satisfactory completion, repairs, or alterations on the assumption that the completion, repairs, or alterations of the subject property will be performed in a professional manner.

Uniform Residential Appraisal Report   File

APPRAISER'S CERTIFICATION: The Appraiser certifies and agrees that:

1. I have, at a minimum, developed and reported this appraisal in accordance with the scope of work requirements stated in this appraisal report.

2. I performed a complete visual inspection of the interior and exterior areas of the subject property. I reported the condition of the improvements in factual, specific terms. I identified and reported the physical deficiencies that could affect the livability, soundness, or structural integrity of the property.

3. I performed this appraisal in accordance with the requirements of the Uniform Standards of Professional Appraisal Practice that were adopted and promulgated by the Appraisal Standards Board of The Appraisal Foundation and that were in place at the time this appraisal report was prepared.

4. I developed my opinion of the market value of the real property that is the subject of this report based on the sales comparison approach to value. I have adequate comparable market data to develop a reliable sales comparison approach for this appraisal assignment. I further certify that I considered the cost and income approaches to value but did not develop them, unless otherwise indicated in this report.

5. I researched, verified, analyzed, and reported on any current agreement for sale for the subject property, any offering for sale of the subject property in the twelve months prior to the effective date of this appraisal, and the prior sales of the subject property for a minimum of three years prior to the effective date of this appraisal, unless otherwise indicated in this report.

6. I researched, verified, analyzed, and reported on the prior sales of the comparable sales for a minimum of one year prior to the date of sale of the comparable sale, unless otherwise indicated in this report.

7. I selected and used comparable sales that are locationally, physically, and functionally the most similar to the subject property.

8. I have not used comparable sales that were the result of combining a land sale with the contract purchase price of a home that has been built or will be built on the land.

9. I have reported adjustments to the comparable sales that reflect the market's reaction to the differences between the subject property and the comparable sales.

10. I verified, from a disinterested source, all information in this report that was provided by parties who have a financial interest in the sale or financing of the subject property.

11. I have knowledge and experience in appraising this type of property in this market area.

12. I am aware of, and have access to, the necessary and appropriate public and private data sources, such as multiple listing services, tax assessment records, public land records and other such data sources for the area in which the property is located.

13. I obtained the information, estimates, and opinions furnished by other parties and expressed in this appraisal report from reliable sources that I believe to be true and correct.

14. I have taken into consideration the factors that have an impact on value with respect to the subject neighborhood, subject property, and the proximity of the subject property to adverse influences in the development of my opinion of market value. I have noted in this appraisal report any adverse conditions (such as, but not limited to, needed repairs, deterioration, the presence of hazardous wastes, toxic substances, adverse environmental conditions, etc.) observed during the inspection of the subject property or that I became aware of during the research involved in performing this appraisal. I have considered these adverse conditions in my analysis of the property value, and have reported on the effect of the conditions on the value and marketability of the subject property.

15. I have not knowingly withheld any significant information from this appraisal report and, to the best of my knowledge, all statements and information in this appraisal report are true and correct.

16. I stated in this appraisal report my own personal, unbiased, and professional analysis, opinions, and conclusions, which are subject only to the assumptions and limiting conditions in this appraisal report.

17. I have no present or prospective interest in the property that is the subject of this report, and I have no present or prospective personal interest or bias with respect to the participants in the transaction. I did not base, either partially or completely, my analysis and/or opinion of market value in this appraisal report on the race, color, religion, sex, age, marital status, handicap, familial status, or national origin of either the prospective owners or occupants of the subject property or of the present owners or occupants of the properties in the vicinity of the subject property or on any other basis prohibited by law.

18. My employment and/or compensation for performing this appraisal or any future or anticipated appraisals was not conditioned on any agreement or understanding, written or otherwise, that I would report (or present analysis supporting) a predetermined specific value, a predetermined minimum value, a range or direction in value, a value that favors the cause of any party, or the attainment of a specific result or occurrence of a specific subsequent event (such as approval of a pending mortgage loan application).

19. I personally prepared all conclusions and opinions about the real estate that were set forth in this appraisal report. If I relied on significant real property appraisal assistance from any individual or individuals in the performance of this appraisal or the preparation of this appraisal report, I have named such individual(s) and disclosed the specific tasks performed in this appraisal report. I certify that any individual so named is qualified to perform the tasks. I have not authorized anyone to make a change to any item in this appraisal report; therefore, any change made to this appraisal is unauthorized and I will take no responsibility for it.

20. I identified the lender/client in this appraisal report who is the individual, organization, or agent for the organization that ordered and will receive this appraisal report.

Uniform Residential Appraisal Report File

21. The lender/client may disclose or distribute this appraisal report to: the borrower; another lender at the request of the borrower; the mortgagee or its successors and assigns; mortgage insurers; government sponsored enterprises; other secondary market participants; data collection or reporting services; professional appraisal organizations; any department, agency, or instrumentality of the United States; and any state, the District of Columbia, or other jurisdictions; without having to obtain the appraiser's or supervisory appraiser's (if applicable) consent. Such consent must be obtained before this appraisal report may be disclosed or distributed to any other party (including, but not limited to, the public through advertising, public relations, news, sales, or other media).

22. I am aware that any disclosure or distribution of this appraisal report by me or the lender/client may be subject to certain laws and regulations. Further, I am also subject to the provisions of the Uniform Standards of Professional Appraisal Practice that pertain to disclosure or distribution by me.

23. The borrower, another lender at the request of the borrower, the mortgagee or its successors and assigns, mortgage insurers, government sponsored enterprises, and other secondary market participants may rely on this appraisal report as part of any mortgage finance transaction that involves any one or more of these parties.

24. If this appraisal report was transmitted as an "electronic record" containing my "electronic signature," as those terms are defined in applicable federal and/or state laws (excluding audio and video recordings), or a facsimile transmission of this appraisal report containing a copy or representation of my signature, the appraisal report shall be as effective, enforceable and valid as if a paper version of this appraisal report were delivered containing my original hand written signature.

25. Any intentional or negligent misrepresentation(s) contained in this appraisal report may result in civil liability and/or criminal penalties including, but not limited to, fine or imprisonment or both under the provisions of Title 18, United States Code, Section 1001, et seq., or similar state laws.

SUPERVISORY APPRAISER'S CERTIFICATION: The Supervisory Appraiser certifies and agrees that:

1. I directly supervised the appraiser for this appraisal assignment, have read the appraisal report, and agree with the appraiser's analysis, opinions, statements, conclusions, and the appraiser's certification.

2. I accept full responsibility for the contents of this appraisal report including, but not limited to, the appraiser's analysis, opinions, statements, conclusions, and the appraiser's certification.

3. The appraiser identified in this appraisal report is either a sub-contractor or an employee of the supervisory appraiser (or the appraisal firm), is qualified to perform this appraisal, and is acceptable to perform this appraisal under the applicable state law.

4. This appraisal report complies with the Uniform Standards of Professional Appraisal Practice that were adopted and promulgated by the Appraisal Standards Board of The Appraisal Foundation and that were in place at the time this appraisal report was prepared.

5. If this appraisal report was transmitted as an "electronic record" containing my "electronic signature," as those terms are defined in applicable federal and/or state laws (excluding audio and video recordings), or a facsimile transmission of this appraisal report containing a copy or representation of my signature, the appraisal report shall be as effective, enforceable and valid as if a paper version of this appraisal report were delivered containing my original hand written signature.

APPRAISER

Signature_____
Name _____
Company Name _____
Company Address_____
_____
Telephone Number _____
Email Address_____
Date of Signature and Report_____
Effective Date of Appraisal _____
State Certification # _____
or State License # _____
or Other (describe) _____ State # _____
State _____
Expiration Date of Certification or License _____

ADDRESS OF PROPERTY APPRAISED

_____
_____
APPRAISED VALUE OF SUBJECT PROPERTY $ _____
LENDER/CLIENT
Name _____
Company Name _____
Company Address_____
_____
Email Address _____

SUPERVISORY APPRAISER (ONLY IF REQUIRED)

Signature_____
Name _____
Company Name _____
Company Address_____
_____
Telephone Number _____
Email Address_____
Date of Signature _____
State Certification # _____
or State License # _____
State _____
Expiration Date of Certification or License _____

SUBJECT PROPERTY

☐ Did not inspect subject property
☐ Did inspect exterior of subject property from street
   Date of Inspection _____
☐ Did inspect interior and exterior of subject property
   Date of Inspection _____

COMPARABLE SALES

☐ Did not inspect exterior of comparable sales from street
☐ Did inspect exterior of comparable sales from street
   Date of Inspection _____

OFFER TO PURCHASE AND CONTRACT OF SALE

PURCHASE OFFER NO:

OMB Approved No. 2900-0029
Respondent Burden: 21 Minutes

VA Department of Veterans Affairs   **OFFER TO PURCHASE AND CONTRACT OF SALE**

PRIVACY ACT STATEMENT: The information collected on this form will serve as an offer to purchase a VA-acquired property. The acquisition and sale of such property is authorized by law (38 U.S.C. 3720 (a) (5)). You are not required to furnish the information but urged to do so since it is vital to proper action by VA in processing your offer to purchase the subject property. Responses may be disclosed outside the VA only if the disclosure is authorized under the Privacy Act, including the routine uses identified in VA system of records, 55VA26, Loan Guaranty Home, Condominium and Manufactured Home Loan Applicant Records, Specially Adapted Housing Applicant Records, and Vendee Loan Applicant Records - VA, published in the Federal Register.

RESPONDENT BURDEN: VA may not conduct or sponsor, and respondent is not required to respond to this collection of information unless it displays a valid OMB Control Number. Public reporting burden for this collection of information is estimated to average 20 minutes per response, including the time for reviewing instructions, searching existing data sources, gathering and maintaining the data needed, and completing and reviewing the collection of information. If you have comments regarding this burden estimate or any other aspect of this collection of information, call 1-800-827-1000 for mailing information on where to send your comments.

INSTRUCTIONS TO BROKER - Send original and one copy with all attachments to the VA Regional Office listing the property. If a vendee loan (seller financing) is requested and there is a co-purchaser who is not the spouse of the purchaser, a separate credit statement is required.

1A. ADDRESS OF PROPERTY TO BE PURCHASED *(Include No., Street or rural route, City or P.O. Box, State and ZIP Code)* | 1B. PROPERTY IDENTIFIER

SECTION I - PURCHASER(S) INFORMATION

2A. NAME OF PURCHASER | 2B. ADDRESS OF PURCHASER *(Include No., Street or rural route, City or P.O. Box, State and ZIP Code)* | 2C. HOME PHONE ( ) | 2D. BUSINESS PHONE ( )

3A. NAME OF PURCHASER | 3B. ADDRESS OF PURCHASER *(Include No., Street or rural route, City or P.O. Box, State and ZIP Code) (If same as above write "SAME")* | 3C. HOME PHONE ( ) | 3D. BUSINESS PHONE ( )

4. STATE EXACT NAME(S) IN WHICH TITLE IS TO BE CONVEYED | 5. DO YOU PLAN TO OCCUPY THE PROPERTY? YES NO

5A. IS ANY PURCHASER A VETERAN? YES NO *(If "YES", complete Items 5B and 5C)* | 5B. SERVICE/SERIAL NUMBER | 5C. DATES OF LATEST SERVICE

6. IS THE PROPERTY BEING PURCHASED DIRECTLY OR INDIRECTLY BY OR FOR ANY OF THE FOLLOWING PERSONS OR THEIR CLOSE RELATIVE? *(If the answer(s) for Items 6A through 6D is/are "YES," give a detailed statement of circumstances on a separate sheet. The term "Close relative" as used means the spouse, parents, children, brother or sister, or any other relative who is a member of the purchaser's household.)*

A. ANY PERSON WHO AT ANY TIME OBTAINED OR ASSUMED THE PAYMENT OF ANY LOAN MADE OR HELD BY VA OR GUARANTEED OR INSURED BY VA UNDER CHAPTER 37, TITLE 38, U.S. CODE?   YES NO

B. ANY PERSON EMPLOYED BY VA OR RENDERING SERVICES TO VA ON A FEE OR COMMISSION BASIS; i.e., A VA AFFILIATE (SEE ITEM 12c1-5 ON THE REVERSE FOR A FULL DEFINITION OF "AFFILIATES"). *(If "YES," is checked please give relationship)* YES NO

C. ANY PERSON WHO AT ANY TIME WAS THE OWNER OF THE PROPERTY?

D. ANY PERSON WHO PREVIOUSLY PURCHASED A PROPERTY FROM VA?

SECTION II - TERMS OF PURCHASE, CERTIFICATIONS AND CONDITIONS OF TRANSMITTAL OF OFFER

7. CASH OFFER		8. TERM OFFER	
A. OFFERED PRICE	$	A. OFFERED PRICE	$ 0.00
DEDUCTIONS:		B. LESS (-) DOWNPAYMENT	$ 0.00
B. DISCOUNT POINTS	$	C. AMOUNT OF VENDEE LOAN REQUESTED *(Item A - Item B)*	$0.00
C. LOAN ORIGINATION FEE	$	D. TIMES (X) CASH EQUIVALENT FACTOR	95.00 %
D. CLOSING COSTS	$	E. CASH EQUIVALENT VALUE (CEV) OF LOAN AMOUNT *(Item C x Item D)*	$0.00
E. SALES COMMISSION	$	F. PLUS (+) FUNDING FEE *(2. 25% of Item C)*	$ 0.00
F. SALES BONUS	$	G. PLUS (+) DOWNPAYMENT *(Item B)*	$ 0.00
G. TOTAL DEDUCTIONS *(Item B through Item F)*	$ 0.00	H. ADDITIONS TO CEV OF LOAN AMOUNT *(Item F + Item G)*	$ 0.00
H. NET TO VA *(Item A - Item G)*	$0.00	I. CASH EQUIVALENT VALUE OF TOTAL OFFER *(Item E + Item H)*	$0.00
		J. LESS (-) SALES COMMISSION	$
		K. LESS (-) SALES BONUS	$
		L. TOTAL DEDUCTIONS *(Item J + Item K)*	$
I. PURCHASER(S) AGREE TO CLOSE WITHIN _____ DAYS AFTER OFFER IS ACCEPTED BY VA.		M. NET TO VA *(Item I - Item L)*	$0.00
		N. INTEREST RATE _____ %	O. NO. OF YEARS	P. MONTHLY P @ I PAYMENT $

9. AMOUNT OF EARNEST MONEY DEPOSIT ▶ $

VA WILL ACCEPT THE OFFER WHICH PROVIDES THE HIGHEST NET RETURN TO VA, BASED ON CORRECT CALCULATIONS. ERRORS IN THE COMPUTATION OF THE NET TO VA MAY RESULT IN THE OFFER BEING REJECTED AND ANOTHER OFFER ACCEPTED.

The "Conditions of Sale" on the reverse of this Offer to Purchase and Contract of Sale and any required Attachments and Addendums to it executed by the purchaser(s) are incorporated herein and are a part hereof. All parties hereto acknowledge they have read and understand the "Conditions of Sale" on the reverse of this Offer to Purchase and Contract of Sale (and any required Attachments and Addendums) as evidenced by their signature(s) herein below.

PENALTY - The law provides severe penalties which include fine or imprisonment, or both, for the willful submission of any statement or evidence of a material fact, knowing it to be false.

10A. SIGNATURE OF PURCHASER	10B. DATE SIGNED	11A. SIGNATURE OF SPOUSE OR CO-PURCHASER	11B. DATE SIGNED
12A. NAME AND ADDRESS OF REAL ESTATE FIRM		12B. NAME OF PRINCIPAL BROKER	
		12C. TAX ID OR SOCIAL SECURITY NUMBER	
		12D. NAME OF SALES PERSON	
		12E. TELEPHONE NUMBER ( )	
13A. SIGNATURE OF PRINCIPAL BROKER OR AUTHORIZED REPRESENTATIVE			13B. DATE SIGNED

SECTION III - ACCEPTANCE BY THE DEPARTMENT OF VETERANS

Acceptance of this offer is hereby evidenced by my signature below and by the return to the Purchaser or Sales Broker of a copy hereof, so signed. (If the offer is not accepted it will not be signed in Item 14A on behalf of VA and the prospective purchaser will be notified of the rejection.)

14A. THE SECRETARY OF VETERANS AFFAIRS	14B. DATE ACCEPTED
BY: TITLE:	

VA FORM OCT 1997 **26-6705**   SUPERSEDES VA FORM 26-6705, DEC 1993 AND VA FORM 26-6705C, FEB 1996 WHICH WILL NOT BE USED.   (Continued on Reverse)

SECTION IV - CONDITIONS OF SALE

1. This Contract of Sale contains the final and entire agreement between the parties hereto and they shall not be bound by any terms, conditions, statements, or representations, oral or written, not contained in this contract. This Contract of Sale is not assignable by the Purchaser(s).

2. Funding Fee Notice: Title 38, U.S. Code, Section 3729 requires that VA collect a funding fee from each person who obtains a vendee (VA/ Seller financed) loan to purchase a VA-acquired property. This fee must be paid in cash or certified funds at closing. The fee may not be collected from a veteran who is receiving compensation (or who, but for the receipt of retirement pay would be entitled to receive compensation) or from a surviving spouse as described in 38 U.S.C. 3701(b)(2).

3. Risk of loss or damage by fire or other causes is assumed by the Seller until the sales transaction is closed.

4. Seller may rescind this contract and return the Purchaser's earnest money deposit under any of the following conditions:

a. The property is damaged prior to the date of closing.

b. The Seller is unable to deliver the property vacant if so advertised.

c. The Seller is unable or unwilling to remove valid objections to title prior to closing.

d. The Seller has not, and is unable to timely acquire title to the property.

e. The property is subject to outstanding redemption rights and such rights are exercised. (In such cases the Seller shall be entitled to the redemption money and shall return to the Purchaser(s) all payments made by him/her to the Seller on account of this sale, without interest, less the fair rental value).

f. Vendee financing is requested and the Seller determines the Purchaser(s) is/are not (an) acceptable borrower(s).

5. The return of the earnest money deposited by the Purchaser(s) shall release the Seller from any and all claims arising from this transaction.

6. The seller may retain all or a portion of the earnest money deposited herewith as liquidated damages if the Purchaser(s) refuse(s), or otherwise fails to perform in accordance with this Contract of Sale. Purchaser's failure to obtain mortgage financing to complete the purchase will not be considered a failure to perform and the earnest money deposit will be returned if the Purchaser(s) can show he/she reasonably and diligently pursued such financing without undue extensions of time.

7. Purchasers who request, but do not qualify for a VA Vendee (VA/Seller) loan agree that the vendee loan processing fee, if required, will not be refunded, or if the loan application was processed by VA, a processing fee not to exceed $300 may be deducted from the earnest money deposit.

8. If Vendee financing is requested, the Purchaser(s) will inform the Seller of any changes in employment and/or financial position, including bankruptcy, judgments, pending litigation, income tax liens, garnishments, and other similar matters.

9. Closing shall be as soon as possible and within a reasonable time after indication by the Seller of readiness to close. Seller will indicate place of closing for Vendee financed loans. Purchaser(s) agree(s):

a. To pay sufficient money at closing, as determined by an escrow analysis as required by Title 24 CFR 3500, for Seller to properly establish escrow accounts to pay taxes, assessments, ground rents (if any), and hazard and flood insurance required by the Seller.

b. To pay monthly, in addition to the monthly installments of principal and interest shown for seller financed sales, 1/12 of the annual charges that the Seller reasonably anticipates paying from the escrow account for hazard insurance, ground rents (if any), and any and all taxes and assessments now or hereafter levied against the property, in order that the Seller may pay such charges when due.

c. To pay for any examination of title or continuation of policies as he/she may require, documentary stamps on the deed of conveyance by the Seller and on all other closing instruments, recording taxes, recording fees, and any other expenses incidental to the closing. Copies of any title evidence in the possession of the Seller will be made available to the Purchaser(s) for examination upon request. Said evidence will be delivered to Purchaser(s) when loan is paid in full.

d. That all assessments, rents (if any), ground rents (if any), and taxes shall be prorated as of the closing date, and the purchaser(s) will assume all taxes, assessments, and ground rents (if any), due on and after the closing date.

e. To furnish hazard insurance (and flood insurance if required) policies satisfactory to the Seller, with loss-payable clauses in favor of the Seller, successors or assigns. Policies will be effective as of the closing date and will be delivered to the Seller at closing along with receipts for the payment of the first year premium.

10. The Seller will prepare, on standard VA forms, the instruments required for closing the sale. At that time, the Seller, at the Seller's option, will either enter into an installment contract or will deliver the deed of conveyance. The deed will contain a covenant which warrants against the acts of the Seller and all claiming by, through, or under him or her conveying good title to said real estate subject to easements, restrictions, and agreements of record. In a sales transaction financed by VA, the deed will be delivered simultaneously with the execution and delivery by the Purchaser(s) to the Seller of a mortgage, or deed of trust, and note covering the balance of the purchase price. If the sale

is under an installment contract, said contract will provide for delivery of such deed and the necessary note or bond and security instruments at the time determined by the Seller. In a cash sales transaction, the deed will be delivered simultaneously with the balance of the purchase price.

11. This sale is subject to the rights of any parties in possession.

SALES BROKER CERTIFICATION

12. I, the undersigned sales broker, have received from the prospective purchaser(s) the deposit shown on the reverse which I am holding for the Department of Veterans Affairs. I certify and agree that:

a. I am acting as Trustee of these funds which will be placed in my Trust Escrow Account. If the purchase offer is not accepted by VA, the deposit shall be returned to the prospective purchaser(s), without interest.

b. The statements of the prospective purchaser(s) shown on the reverse and in the attached credit statement, if required, are believed to be true and correct. I do not know of any loans, gifts, or financial assistance being made to the prospective purchaser(s). I will disclose to VA any such information coming to my attention if seller financing is involved.

c. The sales commission shall not be deemed earned unless and until the sale is actually closed, and that the sales commission shall be payable in amount and time as established by VA. In addition, sales commissions may not be payable, if the purchaser(s) or co-purchaser(s) is/are a VA affiliate in one of the following categories:

(1) Loan Guaranty (LGY) employees at the listing station who are involved in the pricing of VA-acquired properties (including the LGY Officer, Assistant LGY Officer and the Chief of Property Management); (2) Any other VBA employees assigned to the field station listing the property; (3) The MB to whom the property has been assigned; (4) Spouses, parents, in-laws, children, stepchildren, brothers and sisters of, and persons who reside with any of the above; and, (5) The MB's partners, employees and sales associates.

d. I am duly licensed to sell real estate by the appropriate governmental agency in the area where this property is located.

e. Neither the broker nor any of his/her sales, management, or rental personnel, employees, or others authorized to act for the broker will, in violation of Title VIII of the Civil Rights Act of 1968 as amended (The Fair Housing Act), or Executive Order 11063, decline to show or will discriminate in the sale or rental of any property now or here after listed with him/her. It is further agreed that the undersigned will:

(1) Instruct the staff in the policies of nondiscrimination and applicable laws; (2) Prominently display the Fair Housing Poster in all offices in which sale or rental activity takes place; (3) Use the approved Equal Housing Opportunity logo, slogan, or statement in all advertising in conformance with Advertising guidelines for Fair Housing; (4) When advertising VA-acquired properties located in predominantly white areas, utilize any available minority media (solely or in addition to other media); and, (5) Maintain a nondiscriminatory hiring policy in affirmatively recruiting from both minority and majority groups for staff.

f. Non-compliance by the broker or any employee of his or her organization with the laws, executive orders, or regulations, against discrimination in the sale or rental of any property, or with this certification will be proper basis for barring the undersigned from participation in the program of selling, renting, or managing HUD or VA owned properties. I also understand that such determination of debarment by either HUD or VA shall be honored by both.

13. Prompt Payment Notice: In accordance with Chapter 39, Title 31, United States Code, payment under this contract will be due on the 15th calendar day after the receipt of a proper invoice or after acceptance of goods or services by VA, whichever is later. For the purpose of determining the payment due date, a technical acceptance inspection will be completed within 7 calendar days of delivery of the goods or services provided under the contract.

14. DRUG-FREE WORKPLACE NOTICE: The provisions of FAR 52.223-5, Certification Regarding a Drug-Free Workplace and FAR 52.223-6, Drug-Free Workplace, are incorporated by reference.

PURCHASER(S) CERTIFICATIONS

15. I offer to purchase the property herein described at the price and terms shown on the reverse, subject to all the applicable conditions of this Contract of Sale shown above and on the reverse which I have read and which constitute part of my offer. I understand this property is subject to prior sale, change of price or withdrawal from the market, and to approval and acceptance by the Department of Veterans Affairs. **I have examined this property and agree to accept same in its present "as is" condition, and further agree that VA makes no warranties, expressed or implied, with respect thereto.** It is understood and agreed that acceptance of this offer by VA can be evidenced only by the delivery to me/us or my/our sales broker of a copy hereof, executed by a duly authorized officer of VA.

16. Neither I, nor anyone authorized to act for me, will refuse to sell or rent, after the making of a bona fide offer, or refuse to negotiate for the sale or rental of, otherwise make unavailable or deny the dwelling or property covered by this offer to purchase to any person because of race, color, religion, sex, familial status or national origin. I recognize that any restrictive covenant on this property relating to race, color, religion, sex, familial status, or national origin is illegal and void and any such covenant is hereby specifically disclaimed. I understand that civil action for preventative relief may be brought by the Attorney General of the United States in any appropriate U.S. District Court against any person responsible for the violation of the applicable law.

DEED OF TRUST

Account Number: 4340-5802-0262-9343

RETURN TO: First Union National Bank
           Consumer Loan Operations
           P.O. Box 50010, VA0343
           Roanoke, VA 24022-0343

This instrument was prepared by:

G. REDMOND DILL, JR., Attorney,
(Name)

P.O. Box 332, Valdese, N.C. 28690
(Address)

DEED OF TRUST

THIS DEED OF TRUST is made this __20th__ day of April __1998__ , among the Grantor, __ROBERT H. JUSTICE__ and __wife, ODENE M. JUSTICE__ _____ (herein "Borrower"), and __TRSTE, INC.__ _____ (herein "Trustee") and the Beneficiary, First Union National Bank a national banking association whose address is __301 SOUTH TRYON STREET NC5432, CHARLOTTE, NC 28288-5432__ (herein "Lender").

WHEREAS, Borrower is indebted to Lender in the principal sum of U.S. $__37,000.00__ , which indebtedness is evidenced by Borrower's Prime Equity Line Agreement and Disclosure Statement which provides for changes in the interest rate and advances of all or part of the loan proceeds from time to time dated __April 20 1998__ and extensions and renewals thereof (said agreement referred to in this Deed of Trust as "Note"), providing for monthly installments of principal and interest, with the balance of indebtedness, if not sooner paid, due and payable on __April 20 2013__ ;

TO SECURE to Lender the repayment of the indebtedness evidenced by the Note, with interest thereon; the payment of all other sums, with interest thereon, advanced in accordance herewith to protect the security of this Deed of Trust; and the performance of the covenants and agreements of Borrower herein contained, Borrower does hereby grant and convey to Trustee the following described property located in the County of __BURKE , MORGANTON__ , State of North Carolina: _BOOK 898, Page 2293_
                                 TOWNSHIP

(SEE ATTACHED)

FILED
BURKE COUNTY NC
04/21/98 4:03 PM
ELIZABETH COOPER
Register Of Deeds
By _Brenda E. Thompson_ Deputy/Asst.

which has the address of __124 STEPHENS DR., MORGANTON, NC 28655__ (herein "Property Address");

This Deed of Trust secures a Prime Equity Line governed by the provisions of Article 9, Chapter 45 of the North Carolina General Statutes. The maximum principal amount which may be secured by this Deed of Trust at any one time is $__37,000.00__ .

TOGETHER with all the improvements now or hereafter erected on the property, and all easements, rights, appurtenances and rents all of which shall be deemed to be and remain a part of the property covered by this Deed of Trust; and all of the foregoing, together with said property (or the leasehold estate if this Deed of Trust is on a leasehold) are hereinafter referred to as the "Property."

Borrower covenants that Borrower is lawfully seised of the estate hereby conveyed and has the right to grant and convey the Property, and that the Property is unencumbered, except for encumbrances of record. Borrower covenants that Borrower warrants and will defend generally the title to the Property against all claims and demands, subject to encumbrances of record.

UNIFORM COVENANTS. Borrower and Lender covenant and agree as follows:

1. Payment of Principal and Interest. Borrower shall promptly pay when due the principal and interest indebtedness evidenced by the Note and late charges as provided in the Note. This Deed of Trust secures payment of said Note according to its terms, which are incorporated herein by reference.

2. Application of Payments. Unless applicable law provides otherwise, all payments received by Lender under the Note and paragraph 1 hereof shall be applied by Lender first to interest due on the Note, second to the principal due on the Note, and then to late charges due on the Note.

3. Prior Mortgages and Deed of Trust; Charges; Liens. Borrower shall perform all of Borrower's obligations, under any mortgage, deed of trust or other security agreement with a lien which has priority over this Deed of Trust, including Borrower's covenants to make payments when due. Borrower shall pay or cause to be paid all taxes, assessments and others charges, fines and impositions attributable to the Property which may attain a priority over this Deed of Trust, and leasehold payments or ground rents, if any.

4. Hazard Insurance. Borrower shall keep the improvements now existing or hereafter erected on the Property insured against loss by fire, hazards included within the term "extended coverage", and such other hazards as Lender may require and in such amounts and for such periods as Lender may require.
The insurance carrier providing the insurance shall be chosen by Borrower subject to approval by Lender; provided, that such approval shall not be unreasonably withheld. All insurance policies and renewals thereof shall be in a form acceptable to Lender and shall include a standard mortgagee clause in favor of and in a form acceptable to Lender. Lender shall have the right to hold the policies and renewals thereof, subject to the terms of any mortgage, deed of trust or other security agreement with a lien which has priority over this Deed of Trust.
In the event of loss, Borrower shall give prompt notice to the insurance carrier and Lender. Lender may make proof of loss if not made promptly by Borrower.

If the Property is abandoned by Borrower, or if Borrower fails to respond to Lender within 30 days from the date notice is mailed

5. Preservation and Maintenance of Property; Leaseholds; Condominiums; Planned Unit Developments. Borrower shall keep the Property in good repair and shall not commit waste or permit impairment or deterioration of the Property and shall comply with the provisions of any lease if this Deed of Trust is on a leasehold. If this Deed of Trust is on a unit in a condominium or a planned unit development, Borrower shall perform all of Borrower's obligations under the declaration or covenants creating or governing the condominium or planned unit development, the by-laws and regulations of the condominium or planned unit development, and constituent documents.

6. Protection of Lender's Security. If Borrower fails to perform the covenants and agreements contained in this Deed of Trust, or if any action or proceeding is commenced which materially affects Lender's interest in the Property, then Lender, at Lender's option, upon notice to Borrower, may make such appearances, disburse such sums, including reasonable attorneys' fees, and take such action as is necessary to protect Lender's interest.
Any amounts disbursed by Lender pursuant to this paragraph 6, with interest thereon, at the Note rate, shall become additional indebtedness of Borrower secured by this Deed of Trust. Unless Borrower and Lender agree to other terms of payment, such amounts shall be payable upon notice from Lender to Borrower requesting payment thereof. Nothing contained in this paragraph 6 shall require Lender to incur any expense or take any action hereunder.

7. Inspection. Lender may make or cause to be made reasonable entries upon and inspections of the Property, provided that Lender shall give Borrower notice prior to any such inspection specifying reasonable cause therefor related to Lender's interest in the Property.

8. Condemnation. The proceeds of any award or claim for damages, direct or consequential, in connection with any condemnation or other taking of the Property, or part thereof, or conveyance in lieu of condemnation, are hereby assigned and shall be paid to Lender, subject to the terms of any mortgage, deed of trust or other security agreement with a lien which has priority over this Deed of Trust.

9. Borrower Not Released; Forbearance By Lender Not a Waiver. The Borrower shall remain liable for full payment of the principal and interest on the Note (or any advancement or obligation) secured hereby, notwithstanding any of the following: (a) The sale of all or a part of the premises, (b) the assumption by another party of the Borrower's obligations hereunder, (c) the forbearance or extension of time for payment or performance of any obligation hereunder, whether granted to Borrower or a subsequent owner of the property, and (d) the release of all or any part of the premises securing said obligations or the release of any party who assumes payment of the same. None of the foregoing shall in any way affect the full force and effect of the lien of this Deed of Trust or impair Lender's right to a deficiency judgement (in the event of foreclosure) against Borrower or any party assuming the obligations hereunder.
Any forbearance by Lender in exercising any right or remedy hereunder, or otherwise afforded by applicable law, shall not be a waiver of or preclude the exercise of any such right or remedy.

10. Successors and Assigns Bound; Joint and Several Liability; Co-signers. The covenants and agreements herein contained shall bind, and the rights hereunder shall inure to, the respective successors and assigns of Lender and Borrower, subject to the provisions of paragraph 14 hereof. All covenants and agreements of Borrower shall be joint and several. Any Borrower who co-signs this Deed of Trust, but does not execute the Note, (a) is co-signing this Deed of Trust only to grant and convey that Borrower's interest in the Property to Lender under the terms of this Deed of Trust, (b) is not personally liable on the Note or under this Deed of Trust, and (c) agrees that Lender and any other Borrower hereunder may agree to extend, modify, forbear, or make any other accommodations with regard to the terms of this Deed of Trust or the Note without that Borrower's consent and without releasing that Borrower or modifying this Deed of Trust as to that Borrower's interest in the Property.

11. Notice. Except for any notice required under applicable law to be given in another manner, (a) any notice to Borrower provided for in this Deed of Trust shall be given by delivering it or by mailing such notice by first class mail addressed to Borrower or the current owner at the Property Address or at such other address as Borrower may designate by notice to Lender as provided herein, and any other person personally liable on this Note as these person's names and addresses appear in the Lender's records at the time of giving notice, and (b) any notice to Lender shall be given by first class mail to Lender's address stated herein or to such other address as Lender may designate by notice to Borrower as provided herein. Any notice provided for in this Deed of Trust shall be deemed to have been given to Borrower or Lender when given the manner designated herein.

12. Governing Law; Severability. The state and local laws applicable to this Deed of trust shall be the laws of the jurisdiction in which the Property is located. The foregoing sentence shall not limit the applicability of federal law to this Deed of Trust. In the event that any provision or clause of this Deed of Trust or the Note conflicts with applicable law, such conflict shall not affect other provisions of this Deed of Trust or the Note which can be given effect without the conflicting provision, and to this end the provisions of this Deed of Trust and the Note are declared to be severable. As used herein, "costs", "expenses", and "attorneys' fees" include all sums to the extent not prohibited by applicable law or limited herein.

13. Borrower's Copy. Borrower shall be furnished a conformed copy of the Note, this Deed of Trust and Rider(s), if any, at the time of execution or after recordation hereof.

14. Transfer of the Property or a Beneficial Interest in Borrower, Assumption. If all or any part of the Property or any interest in it is sold or transferred (or if a beneficial interest in Borrower is sold or transferred and Borrower is not a natural person) without Lender's prior written consent, Lender may, at its option, require immediate payment in full of all sums secured by this Security Instrument. However, this option shall not be exercised by Lender if exercise is prohibited by Federal law as of the date of this Security Instrument.
If Lender exercised this option, Lender shall give Borrower notice of acceleration. The notice shall provide a period of not less than 30 days from the date the notice is delivered or mailed within which Borrower must pay all sums secured by this Security Instrument. If Borrower fails to pay these sums prior to the expiration of this period, Lender may invoke any remedies permitted by this Security Instrument without further notice or demand on Borrower.
This Deed of Trust may not be assumed by a purchaser without the Lender's consent. If an assumption is allowed, the Lender may charge an assumption fee and require the person(s) assuming the loan to pay additional charges as authorized by law.

NON-UNIFORM COVENANTS. Borrower and Lender further covenant and agree as follows:

in such proceeding all expenses of foreclosure, including, but not limited to, reasonable attorneys' fees and costs of documentary evidence, abstracts and title reports.

In addition to the remedies provided on Borrower's breach of any covenant or agreement of the Borrower in this Deed of Trust, Lender may declare Borrower in default under this Deed of Trust if any of the following events occur:

(a)if Borrower fails to make the payments within 10 days of the due date; (b)if Borrower writes Drafts in excess of the available credit limit or the maximum credit limit; (c)if a petition is filed or other proceedings started under the Federal Bankruptcy code or any state insolvency statute or if a receiver is appointed or writ or order of attachment, levy or judgment is issued against Borrower or the Property, assets or income that affects the ability to repay this Agreement in accordance with the terms of this Agreement or that adversely affects Lender's security rights in the Property; (d)if Borrower permits any other lienholder to gain or appear to gain priority over Lender, except whatever first mortgage, deed of trust or deed to secure debt is outstanding on the Property, as Lender agrees, at the time of recording of Lender's Security Instrument to secure this Agreement; (e)if the Property is condemned or is totally or partially destroyed by fire or other hazards or any proceeding is commenced which materially affects Lender's interest in the Property; (f)if the secured note for any prior mortgage, deed of trust or deed to secure debt or lien on the real Property is in default by failure to pay principal, interest, charges, fees, escrow items or the commencement of a foreclosure proceeding or collection action that adversely affects Lender's security interest in the Property; (g)if Lender believes, in good faith, that Borrower has allowed the Property to deteriorate, committed waste or destructively used or failed to maintain the Property; (h)if Borrower commits fraud or misrepresent any information in the loan application, this Agreement or the Security Instrument at any time; (i)if Borrower fails to disclose any known environmental condition or hazard which adversely affects Lender's security interest in the Property; (j)if Borrower fails to maintain adequate insurance coverage on the Property naming Lender as insured; (k)if Borrower fails to pay taxes and assessments on the Property that results in a filing of a lien senior to Lender's lien that impairs Lender's security interest in the Property; or (l)if Borrower transfers any interest or title to the Property without Lender's consent as set forth in the terms of the Security Instrument or transfer of title occurs due to Borrower's death or by governmental action such as condemnation, however, Borrower understands Lender will not terminate this Agreement and accelerate payment if such action is prohibited by federal law as of the date of this Agreement.

In case of a conflict between the terms of the Note and this Security Instrument governing remedies on default or termination of advances, the priority of controlling terms shall be the Note and then this Security Instrument.

If Lender invokes the power of sale, Lender or Trustee shall give to Borrower (and the owner of the Property, if a different person) notice of sale in the manner prescribed by applicable law. Trustee shall give public notice by advertising, in accordance with applicable law, once a week for two successive weeks in a newspaper having general circulation in the county or city in which the Property or some portion thereof is located, and by such additional or different form of advertisement as the Trustee may deem advisable, if any. Trustee may sell the Property on the eighth day after the first advertisement, or any day thereafter, but not later than 30 days following the last advertisement. Trustee, without demand on Borrower, shall sell the Property at public auction to the highest bidder at the time and place and under the terms designated in the notice of sale in one or more parcels and in such order as Trustee may determine. Trustee may postpone sale of all or any parcel of the Property by advertising in accordance with applicable law. Lender or Lender's designee may purchase the Property at any sale.

Trustee shall deliver to the purchaser Trustee's deed conveying the Property so sold with special warranty of title. The recitals in Trustee's deed shall be prima facie evidence of the truth of the statements made therein. Trustee shall apply the proceeds of the sale in the following order: (a) to all reasonable costs and expenses of the sale, including, but not limited to, Trustee's fees of 5% of the gross sale price, reasonable attorney's fees and costs of title evidence; (b) to the discharge of all taxes, levies and assessments on the Property, if any, as provided by applicable law; (c) to all sums secured by this Deed of Trust; and (d) the excess, if any, to the person or persons legally entitled thereto. Trustee shall not be required to take possession of the Property prior to the sale thereof or to deliver possession of the Property to the purchaser at such sale.

16. Assignment of Rents; Appointment of Receiver. As additional security hereunder, Borrower hereby assigns to Lender the rents of the Property, provided that Borrower shall, prior to acceleration under paragraph 15 hereof or abandonment of the Property, have the right to collect and retain such rents as they become due and payable.

Upon acceleration under paragraph 15 hereof or abandonment of the Property, Lender shall be entitled to have a receiver appointed by a court to enter upon, take possession of and manage the Property and to collect the rents of the Property including those past due. All rents collected by the receiver shall be applied first to payment of the costs of management of the Property and collection of rents, including, but not limited to, receiver's fees, premiums on receiver's bonds and reasonable attorneys' fees, and then to the sums secured by this Deed of Trust. The receiver shall be liable to account only for those rents actually received.

17. Loan Charges. If the loan secured by this Deed of Trust is subject to a law which sets maximum loan charges, and that law is finally interpreted so that the interest or other loan charges collected or to be collected in connection with the loan exceed permitted limits, then: (1) any such loan charge shall be reduced by the amount necessary to reduce the charge to the permitted limit; and (2) any sums already collected from Borrower which exceed permitted limits will be refunded to Borrower. Lender may choose to make this refund by reducing the principal owed under the Note or by making a direct payment to Borrower. If a refund reduces principal, the reduction will be treated as a partial prepayment under the Note.

18. Legislation. If, after the date hereof, enactment or expiration of applicable laws have the effect either of rendering the provisions of the Note, the Deed of Trust or any Equity Line of Credit Rider, unenforceable according to their terms, or all or any part of the sums secured hereby uncollectible, as otherwise provided in the Deed of Trust or any Equity Line of Credit Rider; or of diminishing the value of Lender's security, then Lender, at Lender's option, may declare all sums secured by the Deed of Trust to be immediately due and payable.

19. Release. When the balance of all outstanding sums secured by the Security Instrument including outstanding Drafts, finance charges or other charge if any, is zero, the Lender shall upon request of the Borrower, release the Security Instrument without a charge to the Borrower, however Borrower will pay all cost of recordation, if any, of the satisfaction or release. Absent a request from the Borrower, the Security Instrument shall remain in full force and effect for the term set forth above. Lender, at Lender's option, may allow a partial release of the Property on terms acceptable to the Lender may charge a release fee.

20. Substitute Trustee. Lender may from time to time in Lender's discretion remove Trustee and appoint a successor trustee to any Trustee appointed hereunder. Without conveyance of the Property, the successor trustee shall succeed to all the title, power and duties conferred upon the Trustee herein and by applicable law.

21. Termination of Lender's obligation to Advance Funds. Borrower acknowledges that Lender may cancel its obligation to make any future credit extensions on further advances under the Note in accordance with the provisions of the Note. Borrower acknowledges that its obligation under the Note will continue until all sums owed by Borrower to Lender have been paid.

22. Additional Representations, Warranties and Covenants. Borrower further represents, warrants and agrees that:

(a) Borrower is the owner of the Property;

(b) All representations made by Borrower in the loan application are correct and there has not been any material adverse change in the financial condition of Borrower from the date of the application;

(c) Borrower has no knowledge of any environmental condition or hazard which adversely affects the Property;

(d) No work has been done on or materials furnished to or improvements made to the Property within the last 90 days, except such improvements, work and materials, if any, as have been paid in full;

(e) There are no lien rights, or possibility of lien rights, judgments, executions, suits or bankruptcies, which may be or have been asserted against the Property except for any lien or encumbrance listed below;

(f) Borrower will indemnify and save harmless Noteholder from loss or damage which it may suffer on account of any lien claims, valid or invalid, that may be asserted against the Property;

(g) The Property is used as Borrower's principal dwelling;

(h) The only liens or encumbrances on the Property in addition to the lien created by this Deed of Trust are as follows:

   N/A

(i) If the proceeds of this loan are being used to purchase the Property, the total purchase price of $_____ is being paid to _____ (Seller) and no credits of any type, including, but not limited to, rent credits or credits of any improvement to the Property, will reduce the purchase price; and

(j) If the Property is a condominium, this Deed of Trust is permitted under any condominium documents and if any approvals are required, such approvals have been obtained.

IN WITNESS WHEREOF, Borrower has executed this Deed of Trust and adopted as his seal the word "(SEAL)" appearing beside his name.

_____ (SEAL)
                                    -Borrower
ROBERT H. JUSTICE

_____ (SEAL)
                                    -Borrower
ODENE M. JUSTICE

_____ (SEAL)
                                    -Borrower

_____ (SEAL)
                                    -Borrower

ELIZABETH T. COOPER

STATE OF NORTH CAROLINA

COUNTY OF BURKE

I, KATHY J. KERNS , a Notary Public of the County of Burke , State of North Carolina, do hereby certify that ROBERT H. JUSTICE and personally appeared before me this day and acknowledged the due execution of the foregoing instrument.
wife, ODENE M. JUSTICE

WITNESS my hand and official seal this 20th day of April , 1998.

_____
KATHY J. KERNS

My Commission Expires: 8/10/02

EXHIBIT "A"

TO DEED OF TRUST DATED ___April 20, 1998___ FROM

___ROBERT H. JUSTICE and wife, ODENE M. JUSTICE___ , GRANTOR TO

___TRSTE, INC.___ ,TRUSTEE

FOR FIRST UNION NATIONAL BANK

BEGINNING on an iron stake at a point, South 40° East 300' from the intersection of Maple Street and Stephens Drive, Harrington's corner, and runs with Stephens Drive, North 40° West 80' to an iron stake, Moody's corner; thence with his line, South 50° West 125' to an iron stake; thence South 45° East 80.41' to an iron stake; thence with Harrington's line, South 50° East 125' to the BEGINNING.

DEED REFERENCES: Book 300, Page 576; Book 174, page 278; Book 166, Page 3; all of the Burke Registry.

EASEMENT

CALDWELL COUNTY NC

Book 1336
Pages 1700-1701

Utility Easement

STATE OF NORTH CAROLINA

COUNTY OF ___Caldwell___

FILED   2 PAGE(S)
01/25/2001 8:02 AM
LOIS GREENE
Register Of Deeds

KNOW ALL MEN BY THESE PRESENTS, that ___Paul A Burson and wife Lisa A Burson___

hereinafter called "Grantor" (whether one or more), in consideration of the sum of One Dollar ($1.00) and other good and valuable considerations, the receipt and sufficiency whereof are hereby acknowledged, does hereby grant unto BLUE RIDGE ELECTRIC MEMBERSHIP CORPORATION, its successors and assigns, hereinafter called "Grantee", the right, privilege and easement to go in and upon that certain land of Grantor (hereinafter "premises") situated in said County and State, ___Little River___ Township, and bounded by the property of: ___Paul A Burson and Lisa A Burson___ and over and across said premises with a right of way strip having a width of fifteen (15) feet on each side of a centerline determined by the centerline of the electrical facilities as installed, to (check applicable):

LAB PAB construct, maintain and operate with poles, crossarms, wires, guys, anchors, cable, transformers and other necessary apparatus and appliances, overhead lines for the purpose of transporting electricity and for the communications purposes of Grantee and regulated telephone utilities and other licensees of Grantee. The following rights are also granted to Grantee: to enter said premises to inspect said line, to perform necessary maintenance and repairs, and to make alterations and additions thereto; to remove from the right of way strip, now or at any time in the future, trees, structures, or other obstructions that may endanger the proper maintenance and operation of said lines and trees of any species that Grantee determines will grow at maturity to a height that will endanger the proper maintenance and operation of said lines; to trim or remove and to keep trimmed or removed dead, diseased, weak or leaning trees or limbs outside of the right of way strip which, in the opinion of Grantee, might interfere with or fall upon the electric or communication facilities within the right of way strip; and to install guy wires and anchors extending beyond the limits of the right of way strip when determined necessary by Grantee. This easement also includes the right to prohibit the construction of buildings or other facilities under any electric line or within such proximity to an above ground electric facility that would endanger the operation or prevent the maintenance of the line or system.

LAB PAB to place, construct by digging, trenching and by other reasonable means, maintain, operate, relocate and replace underground electric distribution facilities, lines and conduits with other necessary apparatus and appliances, either above ground or below ground, to include transformers and service connections, for the purpose of transporting electricity and for the communications purposes of Grantee and its licensees. The following rights are also granted to Grantee: to enter said premises to inspect said lines, to perform necessary maintenance and repairs, and to make alterations and additions thereto; and to clear the land within the right to way strip and to keep it clear of trees, structures or other obstructions; and to clear that land outside the right of way strip within ten feet of the service door or any transformer or cabinet located within the right of way strip and to keep the area within ten feet of said door clear of trees, structures or other obstructions; the right to prohibit and prevent the construction or placing of any building or other major structures upon, over or within (5) five lateral feet from said line. All underground facilities are to be installed in accordance with the provisions of Grantee's Underground Distribution Installment Agreement, receipt of a copy of which is acknowledged by Grantor.

This right of way is given to permit the construction of electrical facilities presently proposed. Facilities at other locations and future extensions of presently constructed facilities are not permitted by this agreement. The foregoing notwithstanding, Grantee may relocate its electrical facilities and right of way strip over the premises to conform to any future highway or street relocation, widening or improvement.

The rights granted to Grantee herein for ingress and egress shall extend over and across the other lands of the Grantor by means of existing roads and lanes thereon, adjacent thereto, or crossing said easement; otherwise by such route or routes as shall occasion the least practicable damage and inconvenience to the Grantor; provided, that such right of ingress and egress shall not extend to any portion of said lands which is separated from said easement by any public road or highway, now crossing or hereafter crossing said lands.

Grantor shall retain all other rights to easement not inconsistent with the rights and easements herein contained, but Grantor cannot interfere with or endanger the construction, operation, or maintenance of the Grantee's facilities.

Grantee shall repair any damage it shall do to Grantor's private lanes, roads, or crops and shall reimburse Grantor for any actual loss or damage which shall be caused by the exercise of said ingress and egress.

The failure of Grantee to exercise any of the rights herein acquired shall not be construed as a waiver or abandonment of the rights thereafter at any time and from time to time to exercise any or all of them.

The undersigned Grantor agrees that all poles, wires and other facilities, installed on the above described lands at Grantee's expense, shall remain the property of the Grantee, removable at the option of the Grantee.

O-66 6-15-89

1701

The Grantor covenants that he is the owner of the above described lands and that the said lands are free and clear or encumbrances and liens of whatsoever character except those held by the following persons:

Pfefferkorn Company Inc (Winston Salem)

It is further understood that, whenever necessary, words used in this instrument in the singular shall be construed to read in the plural and that words used in the masculine gender shall be construed to read in the feminine.

IN WITNESS WHEREOF, the Grantor has hereunto set his hand and seal, or if corporate, has caused this instrument to be signed in its corporate name by its duly authorized officers and its seal to be hereunto affixed by authority of its Board of Directors, this the ____7____ day of ____Dec____, ☒ _2000_.

Paul A. Burson _____ (Seal)

Lisa A. Burson _____ (Seal)

STATE OF NORTH CAROLINA
COUNTY OF _Caldwell_

I, a Notary Public, in and for the above referenced State and County, do hereby certify that

Paul A. Burson and Lisa A. Burson

personally appeared before me this day and acknowledged the due execution of the foregoing instrument.

This the ____7th____ day of ____December____, 19 _2000_.

Carole Kay Gunet
Notary Public

My Commission Expires: ___6-30-2002___

STATE OF NORTH CAROLINA
COUNTY OF ~~Caldwell~~

I, a Notary Public, in and for the above referenced State and County, do hereby certify that

Lisa A. B

Secretary of _____

and that by authority duly given and as the act of the corporation, the foregoing and annexed instrument was signed

in its name by its _____ President, sealed

with its corporate seal in its name by its _____ Secretary.

This the _____ day of _____, 19 _____.

_____
Notary Public

My Commission Expires: _____

* OFFICIAL SEAL *
Notary Public, North Carolina
County of Caldwell
Carole Kay Lumsden
My Commission Expires 6/30/2002

State of North Carolina
County of _____CALDWELL_____
The foregoing certificate(s) of _CAROLE KAY LUMSDEN A NIP_

is (are) certified to be correct. This instrument was presented for registration this day and
hour and duly recorded in the office of the Register of Deeds of _CALDWELL_
County, North Carolina in Book _1336_ Page _1700_
This _25_ day of _APRIL_ A.D., ☒ _2001_ at _8:02_ A.M.
LOIS GREENE   By: _____
Register of Deeds   Assistant/Deputy

EXECUTOR'S DEED

Prepared by: Fritz Austin, Attorney at Law, Austin & Dick, PLLC, 803-A North Main Street, High Point, North Carolina 27262

NORTH CAROLINA   )
)   EXECUTOR'S DEED
CALDWELL COUNTY   )

    THIS DEED, made this _28_ day of July, 1995, by Ann Sears Austin of Caldwell County, North Carolina, Executrix under the Will of **Doris I. Sears** of Route 1 Box 451, Granite Falls, North Carolina who deceased on December 24, 1993 (see 94-E-32 Caldwell County) party of the first part, to JAMES ROBERT SEARS of Route 1 Box 451, Caldwell County party of the second part;

W I T N E S S E T H :

    That the said party of the first part, in consideration of Ten Dollars ($10.00), to her paid by the said party of the second part, receipt of which is hereby acknowledged, has bargained and sold and by these presents does bargain, sell and convey to the said party of the second part, his heirs and assigns, that certain parcel or tract of land, situated in Little River Township, Caldwell County, North Carolina, described as follows:

    BEGINNING on an iron pin and large white oak tree pointer, a new and independent corner located on the West side of the spring, and runs a new line North 32 degrees 30" West 173 feet to a walnut tree, a new corner, thence still a new line North 60 degrees East 315 feet to an iron pin, a new corner; thence still a new line South 20 degrees East 300 feet to an iron pin, a new corner; thence a new line South 61 degrees West 220 feet to a poplar tree, a new corner; thence still a new line North 46 degrees West 125 feet to the point of beginning, containing 1.8 acres, more or less,. Being a part of the property conveyed to Eugene Sears by a deed from G.W. Wilkie, et. al., dated March 9th, 1940, Book 184 at page 459, Caldwell County Registry and BEING All of the property described in Tax Map 46 Block 2, Lot 35, containing 1.80 acres, more or less. See Deed Book 721 at page 932, Caldwell County Registry.

    TO HAVE AND TO HOLD the aforesaid parcel or tract of land and all privileges and appurtenances thereunto belonging to the said party of the second part, his heirs and assigns .

BK1140PG0844

AND THE SAID ANN SEARS AUSTIN as Executrix under the Will of Doris I. Sears, does hereby covenant that she has not placed or suffered to be placed any presently existing liens or encumbrances on said premises with the exception of the 1995 Ad valorem taxes and that she will warrant and defend the title to the same against the lawful claims of all persons claiming by, through, under or on account of Ann Austin, as Executrix under the Will of Doris I. Sears, insofar as it is her duty to do by virtue of her office as Executrix under the Will of DORIS I. SEARS, but no further.

IN TESTIMONY WHEREOF, said party of the first part, acting as Executrix as aforesaid has caused these presents to be signed by her.

No title search was done for the preparation of this instrument and no opinion of title is expressed or implied by the preparation of this instrument.

The property is subject to the easements, rights of way, and covenants of record, if any.

Ann Sears Austin (SEAL)
ANN SEARS AUSTIN, Executrix
under the will of DORIS I. SEARS

FILED
LOIS GREENE

'95 JUL 28 AM 36
REGISTER OF DEEDS
CALDWELL CO., N.C.

GIFT DEED

GIFT DEED

NORTH DAKOTA

CALDWELL COUNTY

THIS GIFT DEED, made this the 25ᵗʰ day of August, 1995, by JAMES ROBERT SEARS and wife. NANCY SEARS, parties of the first part of Caldwell County, North Dakota to PAUL BURSON and wife, ANNETTE BURSON, parties of the second part whose address is 2787 Babe Sears Lane, Granite Falls, North Dakota, 45612, Caldwell County

W I T N E S S E T H :

That the said parties of the first part and in consideration of the natural love and affection borne for them by the parties of the second part, their daughter and son in law, and for the further consideration of the sum of Ten Dollar ($10.00) to them paid, has given, granted, and conveyed and by these presents does give, grant, and convey unto the said party of the second part a certain lot or parcel of land lying and being in the Little River Township, Caldwell County, State of North Dakota more particularly described as follows:

BEGINNING on an iron pin and large white oak tree pointer, a new and independent corner located on the West side of the spring, and runs a new line North 32 degrees 30" West 173 feet to a Walnut Tree, a new corner, thence still a new line North 60 degrees East 315 feet to an iron pin, a new corner; thence still a new line South 20 degrees East 300 feet to an iron pin, a new corner; thence a new line South 61 degrees West 220 feet to a poplar tree, a new corner; thence still a new line North 46 degrees West 125 feet to the point of beginning, containing 1.8 acres, more or less. Being a part of the property conveyed to Eugene Sears by a deed from G.W. Wilkie, et. al., dated March 9, 1940, Book 184 at page 459, Caldwell County Registry and **Being** all of the property described in Tax Map 46 Block 2, Lot 35, containing 1.80 acres, more or less. See Deed Book 721 at page 932, Caldwell County Registry and Estate of Doris I. Sears, 94 E 32, Caldwell County Clerk of Court.

This conveyance is made subject to any and all easements, and restriction of record; if any. No title search was done for the preparation of this Deed. No opinion as to the title is expressed or implied by the preparation of this instrument.

TO HAVE AND TO HOLD the aforesaid lot or parcel of land together with all rights, privileges, and appurtenances thereunto

BK1142PG1282

belonging unto them, the said parties of the second part, theirs heirs and assigns, in fee simple.

IN TESTIMONY WHEREOF, the said party of the first parties have hereunto set their hands and seals the day and year first above written.

_____ (SEAL)
JAMES ROBERT SEARS

FILED
LOIS GREENE

_____ (SEAL)
NANCY SEARS

'95 AUG 25 P 4:07

REGISTER OF DEEDS
CALDWELL CO., N.C.

OPTION TO PURCHASE

STATE OF PLACID
COUNTY OF BARNES

This agreement, made the 15th day of May, 2005, by and between Alton McKesson (hereinafter referred to as optioner) and Carpe Diem, Inc., (hereinafter referred to as optionee):

That said Optioner in consideration of the sum of $1000, receipt of which is hereby acknowledged, gives and grants to optionee and to its successors, the option to purchase all of that said tract of land lying in the city of Anytown, Barnes County (more particularly described in Exhibit A.). This option may be exercised by giving notice to Optioner within the time set out in this agreement. This option may be exercised only if the land described herein is needed optionee for any of the following purposes: 1. Commercial development; 2. Residential development; 3. Combination of commercial and residential development. This option may be exercised with a 24 months of the date set out below. Optionee shall notify Optioner of its intention to act on this option by notifying Optioner in writing, return receipt requested, but its intention to purchase the property at its current appraised value. Valuation shall be prepared by an independent appraisal company, licensed under the laws of the state, and agreed to buy both Optioner and optionee. Purchase Price shall be set at fair market value as determined by that appraisal. In the event of any dispute between Optioner and optionee at the appraised value, each shall select its own appraiser. The two appraisers selected by Optioner and optionee shall, in turn, select a third appraiser whose final determination of the fair market value of the property shall be conclusive.

Within a reasonable time after the fair market value purchase price has been established by the procedures set out above, Optioner shall execute and deliver to optionee a good and sufficient General warranty deed conveying title to said property free and clear of all encumbrances except ad valorem taxes for the year in which the property is conveyed. The fair market value purchase price, less any deductions necessary to pay off any mortgages or other encumbrances on said property, shall be paid to Optioner upon delivery of the deed and the parties shall execute any and all documents or papers that may be necessary on or before the date of final settlement. Optioner shall vacate and optionee shall be given possession of said land on or about the date of final settlement.

In witness whereof, this instrument is executed on the date first above written.

_____

Alton McKesson–optioner

_____

Patsy Dellinger, President
Optionee

QUITCLAIM DEED

QUITCLAIM DEED

I, AUDLEY H. JONES,

of Fitchburg, Worcester County, Massachusetts,

for consideration paid of $1.00

grant to **AUDLEY H. JONES, TRUSTEE OF IOWA PRINCE REALTY TRUST,** under a Declaration of Trust dated April 6, 2001 recorded with Middlesex North District Registry of Deeds, herewith,

of P.O. Box 946, Fitchburg, Worcester County, Massachusetts,

A certain tract of land, with any buildings and improvements thereon, situated on the northerly side of Iowa Street in Lowell, Middlesex County, Massachusetts, being shown as Parcel "B" on a plan of land entitled "Plan of Land in Lowell, MA No. 30 –34 Iowa Street, Prepared For: Audley Jones, Scale: 1" = 10', Date: October 3, 2000, Bradford Engineering Co." recorded with Middlesex North District Registry of Deeds in Plan Book 204, Plan 89, and being more particularly bounded and described according to said plan as follows:

Beginning at the most southeasterly corner thereof on the northerly side of Iowa Street; thence N. 01° 43' 00" E. one hundred six and 72/100 (106.72) feet by land now or formerly of Joseph Michael Fortes to a point; thence N. 88° 57' 00" W. one hundred thirteen and 32/100 (113.32) feet by land now or formerly of Dutton Assoc. Ltd Partnership to a point; thence S. 01° 33' 00" W. sixty and 52/100 (60.52) feet by land now or formerly of John W. Fratus to a point; thence S. 88° 59" E. twenty eight and 00/100 (28.00) feet by Parcel "A" to a point; thence N. 0° 57' 01" E. nineteen and 40/100 (19.40) feet by Parcel "A" to a point; thence S. 88° 02' 59" E. sixty six and 92/100 (66.92) feet by Parcel "A" to a point; thence S. 01° 57' 01" W. sixty three and 95/100 (63.95) feet by Parcel "A" to a point; thence S. 88° 27' 00" E. by the the northerly sideline of Iowa Street to the point of beginning. Parcel "B" contains 6,470 square feet of land according to said plan.

Said premises are conveyed subject to and with the benefit of passing rights as described in a deed recorded with Middlesex North District Registry of Deeds in Book 3359, Page 144; and further subject to Grant of Rights to Lowell Electric Light dated June 19, 1930, recorded with said Registry of Deeds in Book 793, Page 436, and to Grant of Rights to Massachusetts Electric Company and New England Telephone and Telegraph Company dated February 5, 1970, recorded with said Registry of Deeds in Book 1915, Page 395

Property Address: 34 Iowa Street, Lowell, Massachusetts

RELEASE

Project: 8.2921901
Parcel No.: 161

STATE OF VIRGINIA

2697   RELEASE   BOOK 1110 PAGE 161

COUNTY OF ___Catawba___

THIS RELEASE, executed this __10th__ day of __August__ 19 76 ,

by __George L. Lyerly, Jr.__ , Trustee, and __First Savings & Loan Association__ ,

Cestui Que Trust under that Deed of Trust from __Adrian M. Sigmon__ ,

dated __November 3__ , 19 67 , and recorded in _____ Book __886__

Page __210__ , ___Catawba___ County Registry:

W I T N E S S E T H:

THAT for and in consideration of the sum of One Dollar ($1.00) and other

valuable considerations, receipt of which is hereby acknowledged, the under-

signed do hereby release and convey to the Board of Transportation, an agency

of the State of North Carolina, any right, title, estate, claim or interest

which they have or may have by virtue of said Deed of Trust recorded in

_____ Book __886__ Page __210__ , ___Catawba___ County

Registry, in and to so much of the lands described in said Deed of Trust

as are subject to that easement, in perpetuity, conveyed to the North Carolina

Board of Transportation by __Adrian M. Sigmon and wife, Edith S. Sigmon__

by Right of Way Agreement dated __July 27__ , 19 76 , recorded in

_____ Book _____ Page _____ , ___Catawba___ County

Registry:

AND the undersigned do hereby release $ __1,300.00__ of the total

consideration of $1,300.00 recited in said Right of Way Agreement to be paid

to Adrian M. Sigmon and wife, Edith S. Sigmon

WITNESS our hands and seals the day and year first above written.

FIRST SAVINGS & LOAN ASSOCIATION

By: _____ (SEAL)
      W. W. Seabock   President

_____ (SEAL)
George L. Lyerly, Jr.   Trustee

ATTEST:

_____
Betty B. Temple   Secretary

Revised July 1973

DECLARATION OF COVENANTS, CONDITIONS AND RESTRICTIONS

This declaration of covenants, conditions and restrictions (hereafter known as "declaration") is made this 14th day of September, 1990 by Crescent resources, Inc. a South Carolina corporation.

Statement of Purpose

Declarant is the owner of certain property located in Burke County, North Carolina, which is more particularly described as that certain map recorded in math book nine, pages 189 and 190 of the Burke County public registry. Declarant desires to create on the property shown on said Matt and exclusive residential community of single — family residences to be named East Shores (hereafter referred to as "the Development".

Declarant's desires to ensure the attractiveness of the development, to prevent any future impairment thereof, to prevent nuisances and enhance the value and amenities of all properties within the development, and to provide for the maintenance and upkeep of all common areas within the development. As part of such common areas, Declarant desires to construct and provide for the maintenance and upkeep of lighted entrance monuments to be located at the entrance to the development and other intersections within the development, which entrance monuments will be for the common use and benefit of all property owners in the development. In addition, as part of such common areas, Declarant desires to construct a pier, containing boat slips, over the waters of Lake James and adjoining a portion of the development, which pier and boat slips will be for the common use and benefit of property owners in the development whose property does not adjoining the waters of Lake James or is otherwise provided in this declaration, and to provide for the maintenance and upkeep of such pier, boat slips and the portion of the development adjoining them. Further, Declarant desires to construct a private road and entrance monuments serving a portion of the development, which private road and entrance monuments will be for the common use and benefit of property owners in the development whose property adjoins a private road, and to provide for the maintenance and upkeep of such private road. Finally, Declarant desires to provide for the maintenance and upkeep of the system of publicly dedicated rose in the development prior to their acceptance by governmental authorities for public maintenance, which system will be for the common use and benefit of all property owners in the development.

Declarant desires to provide a system whereby the owners of property in the development will pay for the maintenance and upkeep of the common areas; and, in accordance with an established budget, for the maintenance and upkeep of the public roads prior to their acceptance for public maintenance; provided, however, that maintenance and upkeep of the pier, boat slips and adjoining land will be paid for only by property owners in the development whose property does not adjoin the waters of Lake Wilson or as otherwise provided in this declaration, and maintenance and upkeep of the private road and the entrance monument for the private road shall be paid for only by property owners in the development whose property adjoins the private road. Property owners in the development whose property adjoins the waters of Lake Wilson will pay only for the cost and maintenance and upkeep of the entrance monuments but such property owners will not be entitled to the use and enjoyment of the pier, boat slips and adjoining land. Property owners in the development whose property adjoins a public road will not pay for the cost for maintenance and upkeep of the private road, but such property owners shall not be entitled to the east and enjoyment of the private road.

To these ends, declarant desires to subject real property described herein to the covenants, conditions, restrictions, easements, charges and means hereinafter set forth, each and all of which is and are for the benefit of said property and each owner thereof.

Declarant further desires to create an organization to which will be delegated and assigned the powers of owning, maintaining and administering the common areas, administering and enforcing the covenants and restrictions contained herein, and collecting and dispersing the assessments and charges herein after creating, in order to efficiently preserve, protect and enhance the values and amenities in the development, to ensure the residents enjoyment of the specific rights, privileges and easements in the common areas, and to provide for the maintenance and upkeep of the common areas and amenities.

To that end, the declarant has or will cause to be incorporated under North Carolina law, pursuant to the Articles of Incorporation attached hereto as Exhibit "A" and incorporated herein by reference, East Shores Owners Association, Inc., as a nonprofit corporation for the purpose of exercising and performing the aforesaid functions, said corporation to be governed by the bylaws attached hereto as Exhibit "B" and incorporated herein by reference.

RIGHT OF WAY AGREEMENT

5417   BOOK 1221 PAGE 667

RIGHT OF WAY AGREEMENT

STATE OF NORTH CAROLINA

COUNTY OF _Catawba_   _Lai-bee Drive_
                                       Local Name of Road
TOWNSHIP OF _Clines_

Blake Eugene Lail and wife Bette L. Lail, Sadie L. Berry (widow)
2501 North Main Newton

the undersigned owners of that certain property described in Deed Book _907_ at Page
_515_ in the Register of Deeds office of _Catawba_ County, and bounded by

recognizing the benefits to said property by reason of the Department of Transportation
assuming responsibility for the maintenance of the above-described road, hereby grants
to the Department of Transportation, the right of way for said proposed road and releases
the Department from all claims for damages by reason of said right of way across the
lands of the undersigned and the past and future use thereof by the Department, its
successors and assigns for all purposes for which the Department is authorized by law
to subject said right of way; said right of way being the width indicated and across
said property as follows:
     60 ft. in width measured 30 ft. on each side of the center line of said proposed
road, and such additional widths as might be necessary to provide for cut and fill slopes
and drainage of road.
          It is understood and agreed that the center line of the 60 ft. right of way
hereinabove referred to is along the center line of the existing road across property of
the undersigned. It is further agreed that the property owners will erect no fencing nor
engage in cultivation upon the right of way described herein.

     There are no conditions to this agreement not expressed herein. The under-
signed hereby covenant and warrant that they are the sole owners of said property; that
they solely have the right to grant this right of way, and that they will forever warrant
and defend the title to the same against the lawful claims of all persons whomsoever.

          IN WITNESS WHEREOF, we have hereunto set our hands and affixed our seals this
the _27_ day of _Oct_, 19_79_.

STATE OF NORTH CAROLINA, _Catawba_ County

The foregoing certificate(s) of _____

_____

is (are) certified to be correct.
This instrument was presented for registra-
tion this day and hour and duly recorded in
the office of the Register of Deeds of
_____ County, N.C., in Book _____ Page
_____. This _____ day of _____
A.D. 19___ at _____ o'clock ___.M.

_____
Register of Deeds
Recorded and verified:

Blake Eugene Lail (SEAL)
Blake Eugene Lail   (SEAL)
Bette L. Lail (SEAL)
Bette L. Lail   (SEAL)
Sadie L. Berry (SEAL)
Sudie L. Berry   (SEAL)
                                 (SEAL)
                                 (SEAL)

DRAWN FOR DEPARTMENT OF TRANSPORTATION

BY: _____

(For addition to system along existing center line)

Revised July 1977

ROAD MAINTENANCE AGREEMENT

BK1263PG0506

OHIO

COUNTY OF GREENE   ROAD MAINTENANCE AGREEMENT

THIS AGREEMENT, Made and entered into this 12 day of May, 1999, by and between Paul Burson and wife, Annette Burson, their heirs and assigns, all of the above County and State:

W I T N E S S E T H:

That whereas all the parties hereto reside in Little River Township, Greene County, Ohio; and

Whereas the parties hereto are all the owners of homes serviced by a certain road which fronts the properties of each of the parties hereto, said road running from said homes to State Road No. ____, and being approximately 200 feet in length; and

Whereas all the parties hereto desire that said road be maintained in good condition, being usable in all weather and all seasons;

NOW THEREFORE, It is agreed:

1. All the parties hereto shall share in the expense of maintaining the road described above in a usable condition for all weather and all seasons, said expense to be shared proportionately among the houses being served by said road.

2. The parties hereto shall meet from time to time and agree upon the service work to be performed. Such meetings may be called by any of the parties with notice to the others, and may be conducted by telephone or other convenient method.

IN TESTIMONY WHEREOF, the parties hereto have set their hands and seals this 12 day of May, 1999.

_____(SEAL)   _____ (SEAL)

POWER OF ATTORNEY

STATE OF WASHINGTON
COUNTY OF BURLE   DURABLE POWER OF ATTORNEY

KNOW ALL MEN BY THESE PRESENTS, that I, BRENDA. B. CANTRELL ,

the undersigned, of Morganton, North Carolina ,

hereby make, constitute and appoint   JOHN CANTRELL and/or ANNE C. DAY and/or ,

WILLIAM D. CANTRELL ,

of   Morganton, NC and Charlotte, NC and Sarasota, FL. ,

(herein "Attorney-In-Fact"), my true and lawful Attorney-In-Fact for me and in my name, place and stead, giving unto said Attorney-In-Fact full power to act in my name, place and stead in any way which I myself could do if I were personally present with respect to the following matters as each of them is defined in Chapter 32A of the North Carolina General Statutes to the extent I am permitted by law to act through an agent:

(1) real property transactions;
(2) personal property transactions;
(3) bond, share and commodity transactions;
(4) banking transactions;
(5) safe deposits;
(6) business operating transactions;
(7) insurance transactions;
(8) estate transactions;
(9) personal relationships and affairs;
(10) tax, social security and unemployment;
(11) benefits from military service.

FILED
ELIZABETH T. COOPER
BOOK 921, Page 1238
1999 MAR 22 P 3 26
Elizabeth T Cooper
REGISTER OF DEEDS
BURKE COUNTY

In addition to the foregoing matters, to the extent that I am permitted by law to act through an agent, my Attorney-In-Fact shall have full power to act in my name, place and stead, to take any action or perform any act deemed to be in my best interest in the discretion of my said Attorney-In-Fact, as fully and to the same extent as I can or could act on my own behalf.

My Attorney-In-Fact shall have full power of substitution and revocation. I hereby ratify and affirm that which my Attorney-In-Fact, or Substitute Attorney-In-Fact, shall lawfully do or cause to be done by said Attorney-In-Fact (or the Substitute Attorney-In-Fact lawfully designated) by virtue of the power herein conferred upon said Attorney-In-Fact.

My Attorney-In-Fact is relieved of any responsibilities in connection with the filing of any inventories and accounts with the Clerk of Superior Court, even though otherwise required by law, I hereby specifically waive any requirement that my Attorney-In-Fact must qualify or make any filing with the Clerk of Superior Court, or a corresponding governmental official of any other county or state. My Attorney-In-Fact shall file an inventory with the undersigned each year and with the undersigned's executor or representative of the undersigned's estate in the year of death of the undersigned. My Attorney-In-Fact shall receive and be paid such commissions as are customarily charged by the Attorney-In-Fact for like services at the time the services hereunder are rendered, or, in accordance with any regularly published schedule of charges for such services at the time the services are rendered by my said Attorney-In-Fact. If my Attorney-In-Fact does not regularly act in said capacity and has no established charges for acting under Powers of Attorney, then the charges of my Attorney-In-Fact shall be limited to five percent (5%) of receipts and disbursements, unless the Clerk of Superior Court, in his/her discretion, shall allow additional fees pursuant to the provisions of G.S. 32-50(c). Nothing herein shall require that my Attorney-In-Fact make any charges for acting in said capacity.

This Power of Attorney shall not be affected by my subsequent incapacity or mental incompetence.

In the event of my subsequent incapacity or mental incompetence, I hereby nominate my Attorney-In-Fact, or an Attorney-In-Fact substituted as herein provided, to be appointed as my conservator, guardian of my estate, or guardian of my person if protective proceedings for my personal estate are hereafter commenced. The nomination of my Attorney-In-Fact, or my Substitute Attorney-In-Fact, is made pursuant to the provisions of G.S. 32A-10(b).

Where the term "Attorney-In-Fact" is herein used, it shall include each Attorney-In-Fact herein designated, or Co-Attorneys-In-Fact, if so designated, and any substitute Attorneys-In-Fact hereinafter designated; the singular shall be deemed to include the plural, and vice versa, as the context may require.

All Powers of Attorney for any purpose heretofore filed or executed by me are hereby revoked.

This Power of Attorney is dated this 16 day of March, 1999.

Brenda B. Cantrell (SEAL)
Brenda B. Cantrell

SURVEY

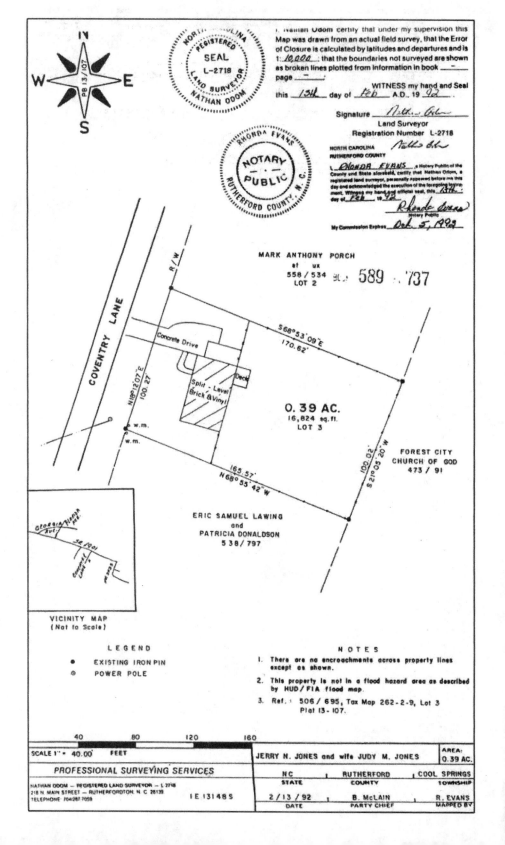

Index

A

Acceleration clause, mortgages, 232
Acceptance, 136
Acceptance, communicating, 137
   mailbox rule, 138
   power of, 136
Accretion, 62
Acknowledgment, deeds, 200
Ad valorem taxes, 392
Adjustable rate mortgages, 235-236
Adverse possession, 95-97
   color of title, 97
   doctrine of, 95
   elements of, 96-97
   time periods, 97
Advertising real estate, 304
Aesthetic zoning, 263
Agency law, real estate transactions,
   298-299
Agency, defined, 292
   law of, 292-298
Agent
   duty not to commit fraud, 295
   duty of accounting, 294
   duty of care, 293
   duty of honesty and fair dealing, 294
   duty of loyalty, 293
   duty of obedience, 293
   duty to avoid negligent
     misrepresentation, 296
   duty to third parties, 294-296
   material fact, 295
   sales tactics, 295-296
Agreement, listing, 143-144
Air rights, 120-121
Ambiguities, latent, 55
   patent, 54
Ambiguous property descriptions, deeds,
   196
Amortization, mortgages, 235
Apartments, 9
Appraisal, 240

Appraisers, 308-309
Appurtenant easements, 112
Assessments, 119-120, 399-400
Attestation, deeds, 200
Attorneys, real estate, 310
Auction, foreclosure, 90
Auctions, tax, 98
Avulsion, 62-63

B

Balloon mortgages, 237
Beneficiary, 84
Binder, defined, 325
Boards, planning, 269
Breach of contract, 149-150
Breach of duty, landlord-tenant
     relationship, 174-179
Building codes, 269

C

Capacity, 79, 139-140
Capacity, deeds, 196
Chain of title, defined, 332
Civil judgment, 94-95
Civil unions, 36-37
Clause, escrow, 149
   time is of the essence, 148-149
   title, 149
Clauses, contract, 148-149
Clerk of court, title search, 339
Closing
   attorney certificate, 359
   basic preparations, 356-361
   conducting the, 369-375
   defined, 356
   dispersing the funds, 372-375
   doctrine of relation back, 376
   documents exchanged, 362-369
   dual representation, 376-377
   escrow, 375-376
   filing and priority, 377
   hazard insurance, 362

   HUD-1 settlement statement, 364-365
   IRS forms, 364
   lien waiver affidavits, 364
   loan package, 362
   loan payoff, 360
   other issues, 375-377
   people present, 371-372
   private mortgage insurance, 366
   Pro ration, 374
   procedure, 361-369
   promissory note, 363
   software, 361
   subordination agreement, 363
   survey, 369
   termite and other inspections, 360-361
   termite inspection letter, 369
   title defects, 359
   trust disbursement records, 366
   truth in lending, 366-368
   USA Patriot Act, 365-366
Codes, building, 269
Collateral, mortgages, 231
Color of title, 97
Commercial leases, 165
Commercial property, 12-13
Commercial zoning, 264
Compensatory damages, tenant, 175
Concurrent ownership in real estate, 35-39
Condemnation, 93-94
   inverse, 94
Conditional fee simple estates, 29-32
Conditional use permit, zoning, 266
Condominiums, 9
Condominiums and townhouses, 9-10
Consideration, 78, 139
   deeds, 201
Constructive eviction, 176
Consumer reporting agencies, 239
Contract, clauses, 148-149
   acceptance, 136
   breach of, 149-150
   capacity, 139-140

consideration, 139
defined, 134
fraud, 142-143
legality, 139
mistake, 142
mutual assent, 139
offer, 134
offer of purchase, 144-148
Contractors, 312
Contracts, real estate, 143-148
Cooperatives, 10
Counter offer, 138
Covenants, restrictive, 272-277

D

Damage deposit, tenant, 174
Date, deeds, 202
Dedication, 86-87
Deed reservation, easements, 114
Deed, defined, 189
Deeds of trust, 204, 229
    foreclosure, 93
Deeds, acknowledgment, 200
    ambiguous property descriptions, 196
    attestation, 200
    capacity, 196
    consideration, 201
    date, 202
    delivery, 197-199
    delivery and escrow, 200
    elements of, 190-202
    exceptions and exclusions, 201
    general warranty, 202-203
    granting clause, 197
    habendum clause, 197
    history of, 189-190
    minimum requirements, 191-202
    quitclaim, 205
    Seals, 200-201
    special warranty, 203-204
    types of, 202-206
    witnesses, 202
Deposits, pet and security, 163
Devise, 84
Devisee, 84
Doctrine of relation back, closing, 376
Dower and curtesy, 33
Dual representation, closing, 376-377
Due on sale clause, mortgages, 232
Duty to repair, landlord, 169

E

Easements, 111-117
    abandonment, 117
    agreement, 113-114

appurtenant, 112
creating, 113-116
deed reservation, 114
eminent domain, 115-116
implication, 114
in gross, 112
merger, 116
necessity, 114-115
prescription, 115
run with the land, 113
terminating, 116-117
terminating by agreement, 116-117
Economic characteristics of land, 4-5
Electronic recording, 199
Eminent domain, 93-94
    easements, 115-116
Equitable relief, tenant, 174-175
Equity, 5
Equity lines of credit, 238
Erosion, 62
Escheat, 94
Escrow, 149
Escrow closing, 375-376
Escrow, deeds, 200
Estate, 28
    fee simple, 28
Estoppel certificate, mortgages, 232
Eviction, 177
    constructive, 176
    defined, 164
    procedure, 177-178
    retaliatory, 178-179
    self-help, 178
Eviction, wrongful, 176-177
Exceptions and exclusions, deeds, 201
Exclusive listing, 143
Exemption, defined, 393

F

Fair Credit Reporting Act, 240
Fannie Mae, 6, 222
Farm and rural property, 13
Federal Reserve Board, 223-224
Federal Truth in Lending, 225
Fee simple absolute, 28
Fee simple determinable, 31
Fee simple estate, 28
Fee simple estates, conditional, 29-31
Fee simple on a condition subsequent 31-32
Fee simple owners, rights of, 29
Fiduciary, 292
Fixed rate mortgages, 235
Fixed rent lease, 160

Fixture, damage, 110
    intent test, 109
    manner of attachment test, 109-110
    use test, 110
Fixtures, 108-111
    trade, 110-111
Forced share, 33
Foreclosing a tax lien, 398
Foreclosure, 87-93
    auction, 90, 247
    deeds of trust, 93
    default, 89
    judicial, 246
    mortgages, 93
    notice to borrower, 89
    power of sale, 247-248
    purchasing at auction, 92
    right of redemption, 91
    rising rates of, 247-248
    steps, 90
    terminating rights of creditors, 92
    types of, 246-248
Fraud, contract, 142-143
Freddie Mac, 223

G

General warranty deeds, 202-203
Gift, 86
Ginnie Mae, 223
Government-owned land, 14
Government survey system, 59
Grantee, defined, 190
Granting clause, deeds, 197
    mortgages, 231
Grantor–grantee index, defined, 329
Grantor, defined, 190
Ground lease, 161

H

Habendum clause, deeds, 197
Habitability, warranty of, 172
Heavy industry, 13
Historical districts, 269-270
Holographic wills, 83
Homestead exemption, tax, 393
Homesteading, 87
HUD, 223
HUD-1 settlement statement, closing, 364-365

I

Implication, easements, 114
Improvements, 8
In gross easements, 112

In rem jurisdiction, 4
Independent contractors, 298
Industrial parks, 13
Industrial property, 13
Industrial zoning, 264
Infants, 79
Inspection, conducting a, 313
Inspectors, 312
Internet lenders, mortgage, 245
Interstate Land Sales Full Disclosure
    Act, 271
Intestate, 86
Intestate succession, 86
Intoxicated persons, 79
IRS forms, closing, 364

J

Joint tenancy, 36-37
Judgment, civil, 94-95
Judgments, title search, 339

K

Kit homes, 10

L

Landlord, 157
Landlord–tenant relationship, classifying,
    179-181
   creating, 158-159
   duties created, 167-179
   modern changes, 158-159
Landlord, discriminatory practices, 170-171
   duty to third parties, 170
   remedies against tenant, 177-179
Landlord's rights, 168-171
   duty to repair, 169
   right to reenter premises, 169
Latent ambiguities, 55
Lease provisions, common, 162-164
Lease, commercial, 165
   defined, 159
   federal law requirements, 166
   fixed rent, 160
   ground, 161
   mineral, 161
   net, 160
   oil and gas, 162
   percentage, 160
   public policy concerns, 166
   rent to own, 160-161
   statute of frauds, 167
   subletting, 164
   timber, 161
   trade fixtures, 165-166
Leasehold estate, 157

Leases, 159-162
Legality, contract, 139
License, 162
   defined, 117
Licenses, 117
Lien waiver affidavits, closing, 364
Lien, defined, 118
   materialman's, 119
   mechanic's, 119
Liens, 118-119
Liens, title search, 337
Life estate, 32-35
Life estate pur autre vie, 35
Life estate, historical basis, 33
Light industry, 13
Listing agreement, 143-144
Listing, exclusive, 143
Listing, multiple, 144
Listing, open, 143
Loan officer, 308
Loan package, 362

M

Mailbox rule, acceptance, 138
Manufactured housing, 12
Material fact, defined, 295
Materialman's lien, 119
Mechanic's lien, 119
Mentally incompetent persons, 79
Merger, restrictive covenants, 277
Metes and bounds descriptions, 55-59
   drafting, 57-58
   technology, 59
Millage rate, defined, 396
Mineral lease, 161
Mineral rights, 122
Mistake, contract, 142
Mobile homes, 10
Mortgage market, primary, 219-220
Mortgage markets, 219-228
Mortgage, defined, 217
   discharging, 246
   Internet lenders, 245
   points, 240
   qualifying for, 239-245
   underwriting, 239
Mortgages, 204
   versus deeds of trust, 229-234
   acceleration clause, 232
   adjustable rate, 235-236
   balloon, 237
   collateral, 231
   due on sale clause, 232
   estoppel certificate, 232
   fixed rate, 235

   foreclosure, 93
   granting clause, 231
   power of sale provision, 232
   priority of, 233
   promissory note, 231
   purchase money, 237
   recording, 233
   second, 238
   subordination agreement, 233
   types of, 234-238
   wraparound, 237-238
Multiple listing, 144
Multiple listing service, real estate
   agent, 303
Mutual assent, 78, 139

N

Navigable waters, 63
Necessity, easements, 114-115
Negligent misrepresentation, 296
Net leases, 160
Non-navigable waters, 63-64
Nonconforming use, zoning, 266
Nuisance actions, 277-278
Nuisance, defined, 277
   private, 278
   public, 278
Nuncupative wills, 83

O

Offer, 134
Offer of purchase and contract, 144-148
Offer, rejecting, 136
Offers, communicating by e-mail, 135
   reasonable person standard, 136
Oil and gas lease, 162
Online title search, 335
Open listing, 143
Options, 148
Ordinary wear and tear, tenant, 173

P

Paralegals, real estate, 310
Parol evidence, 54
Partition, 39, 94
   right to, 39
Patent ambiguities, 54
Percentage leases, 160
Personal jurisdiction, 4
Pet and security deposits, 163
Pet deposit, tenant, 174
Physical characteristics of land, 4
Planning boards, 269
Plats, 60
Points, mortgage, 240

Policy, defined, 325
Power of acceptance, 136
Power of sale provision, mortgages, 232
Premium, defined, 326
Prescription, easements, 115
Primary mortgage market, 219-220
Principal, defined, 292
    duty not to injure agent's reputation,
        298
    duty to compensate agent, 296-297
    duty to cooperate, 297
Principal's duty to agent, 296-298
Priority of mortgages, 233
Private mortgage insurance, defined, 366
Pro ration, defined, 374
Probate records, title search, 339
Profit a prendere, 117-118
Promissory note, closing, 363
Promissory note, mortgages, 231
Property boundaries, litigating, 53-55
Property description, elements of, 51
    legal requirements, 51
    sale, 80
Property descriptions, history of, 50
Property managers, 312
Publication, 83
Public policy concerns, lease, 166
Punitive damages, tenant, 175-176
Pur autre vie, life estate, 35
Purchase money mortgages, 237

Q

Quiet enjoyment, 172
Quitclaim deeds, 205

R

Real estate agent, becoming, 301
    classifications, 300-301
    duty of care, 299
    duty to disclose, 299-300
    locating buyers, 303-304
    multiple listing service, 303
    regulations, 302-303
    services provided, 303
Real estate and taxation, 399
Real estate attorneys, 310
Real estate contracts, 143-148
Real Estate Investment Trusts, 307
Real estate investments, 305-308
Real estate market, 7-8
Real estate marketing technology, 58
Real estate paralegals, 310
Real Estate Settlement Procedures Act, 225
Real estate title searchers, 310-312
Real property versus personal property, 1-5
Recording mortgages, 233

Recording statutes, 206-207
Recreational property, 14
Redemption, right of in foreclosure, 91
Reliction, 63
Remaindermen, 33
Rent to own leases, 160-161
Residential property, 9
Residential zoning, 264
Restrictive covenants, 272-277
Restrictive covenants, merger, 277
Retail property, 12
Right of survivorship, 37
Right to partition, 39
Rights, air, 120-121
    landlord, 168-171
    mineral, 122
    tenant, 171-172
    water, 121-122
Riparian rights, 61
Robo–signing, 80

S

Sale of real estate, 76-80
Sale, capacity, 79
    consideration, 78
    infants, 79
    intoxicated persons, 79
    mentally incompetent persons, 79
    property description, 80
Seals, deeds, 200-201
Second mortgages, 238
Secondary mortgage market, 220-228
Share, forced, 33
Share, statutory, 33
Shopping centers, 13
Single-family homes, 9
Social media monitoring, 220
Special warranty deeds, 203-204
Spot zoning, 268
Statute of Frauds, 2, 140-141
    lease, 167
Statutory share, 33
Subdivision rules and regulations, 277
Sublet, defined, 164
Subletting, 164
Subordination agreement, closing, 363
    mortgages, 233
Survey, closing, 369
Surveyors, 310

T

Tacking, title search, 342-343
Tax auctions, 98
Taxes, assessments, 395-397
    enterprise zones, 394-395
    exemptions, 393

foreclosing a tax lien, 398
Homestead exemption, 393
liens, 397
millage rate, 396
the power to levy, 392
priorities, 398
regulations, 397
Tenancy at sufferance, 181
Tenancy at will, 180-181
Tenancy by entirety, 38-39
Tenancy for years, 179-180
Tenancy from year-to-year, 180
Tenancy in partnership, 39
Tenant, 157
    compensatory damages, 175
    damage deposit, 174
    equitable relief, 174-175
    ordinary wear and tear, 173
    pet deposit, 174
    punitive damages, 175-176
    remedies against landlord, 174
    responsibility for damages, 173
Tenant's duties to landlord, 172-174
Tenants in common, 35-36
Tenant's rights, 171-172
Termite inspection letter, closing, 369
Testate, 86
Testate succession, 86
Timber lease, 161
Time is of the essence, 148-149
Title abstract, defined, 340
Title certificates, final, 340
    preliminary, 340
Title clause, 149
Title examination, defined, 326
Title examinations, 326-331
Title insurance, 324-326
Title search, abstracts, 340
    clerk of court, 339
    common problems, 344
    creating chain of title, 332-335
    establishing out conveyances, 335-338
    judgments, 339
    liens, 337
    online, 335
    paralegal's role, 343
    probate records, 339
    steps in, 331-343
    tacking, 342-343
    UCC listings, 337
Title searchers, real estate, 310-312
Torrens registration, 60-61
Townhouses, 10
Tract indexing, 60
Trade fixtures, 110-111
    lease, 165-166

Troubled Asset Relief Program, 224-225
Trust disbursement records,
        closing, 366
Truth in Lending, closing, 366-368

U
UCC listings, title search, 337
Uniform Residential Landlord and
        Tenant Act, 167-168
Unimproved land, 8
Urban planning, 270-271
USA Patriot Act, closing, 365-366

V
Variance, zoning, 266-267
Virtual planning, 269

W
Warranty of habitability, 172
Waste, 34
Water and property boundaries,
        63-64
Water rights, 61-64, 121-122
Waters, navigable, 63
Waters, non-navigable,
        63-64
Wi-Fi, using to lure tenants, 159
Will, 82-86
    in writing, 82
    signed by testator, 83
    testator's state of mind, 84
    witnessed, 82-83
Wills versus sales, 85

Witnesses, deeds, 202
Wraparound mortgages, 237-238

Z
Zoning, 262-269
    aesthetic, 263
    commercial, 264
    conditional use permit, 266
    enforcing regulations, 263-264
    industrial, 264
    nonconforming use, 266
    residential, 264
    "spot", 268
    unconstitutional regulations,
        267-268
    variance, 266-267